FIFTY READINGS
IN PHILOSOPHY

THIRD EDITION

Donald C. Abel
St. Norbert College

Boston   Burr Ridge, IL   Dubuque, IA   New York
San Francisco   St. Louis   Bangkok   Bogotá   Caracas   Kuala Lumpur
Lisbon   London   Madrid   Mexico City   Milan   Montreal   New Delhi
Santiago   Seoul   Singapore   Sydney   Taipei   Toronto

The McGraw·Hill Companies

McGraw-Hill
Higher Education

Published by McGraw-Hill, an imprint of The McGraw-Hill Companies, Inc., 1221 Avenue of the Americas, New York, NY 10020. Copyright © 2008. All rights reserved. No part of this publication may be reproduced or distributed in any form or by any means, or stored in a database or retrieval system, without the prior written consent of The McGraw-Hill Companies, Inc., including, but not limited to, in any network or other electronic storage or transmission, or broadcast for distance learning.

This book is printed on acid-free paper.

3 4 5 6 7 8 9 0 DOC/DOC 0 9

ISBN: 978-0-07-353570-8
MHID: 0-07-353570-2

Editor in Chief: *Emily Barrosse*
Publisher: *Lisa Moore*
Sponsoring Editor: *Mark Georgiev*
Marketing Manager: *Pamela Cooper*
Director of Development: *Rhona Robbins*
Developmental Editor: *Marley Magaziner*
Production Editor: *Chanda Feldman*
Manuscript Editor: *Jan Fehler*
Art Director: *Jeanne Schreiber*
Design Manager: *Andrei Pasternak*
Cover Designer: *Asylum Studios*
Production Supervisor: *Tandra Jorgensen*
Composition: *10/12 Palatino by Laserwords Private Limited*
Printing: *45# New Era Matte, R. R. Donnelley & Sons*

Credits: The credits section for this book begins on page 525 and is considered an extension of the copyright page.

LIBRARY OF CONGRESS CATALOGING-IN-PUBLICATION DATA

Fifty readings in philosophy / [compiled by] Donald C. Abel.
   p. cm.
   Includes bibliographical references and index.
   ISBN: 978-0-07-353570-8 (alk. paper)
   1. Philosophy. I. Abel, Donald C., 1948-
B29.F5314 2008
100 – dc22

                                        2006053082

The Internet addresses listed in the text were accurate at the time of publication. The inclusion of a Web site does not indicate an endorsement by the authors or McGraw-Hill, and McGraw-Hill does not guarantee the accuracy of the information presented at these sites.

www.mhhe.com

About the Author

DONALD C. ABEL is Professor of Philosophy at St. Norbert College in De Pere, Wisconsin. He holds a B.A. in Philosophy from Gonzaga University, an M.A. in Philosophy from Tulane University, a Ph.L. in Philosophy from St. Michael's Institute, an M.Div. in Theology from Loyola University of Chicago, and a Ph.D. in Philosophy from Northwestern University. He is the author of *Freud on Instinct and Morality* (1989), *Theories of Human Nature: Classical and Contemporary Readings* (McGraw-Hill, 1992), and *Fifty Readings Plus: An Introduction to Philosophy* (McGraw-Hill, 2005). He is the editor of *Discourses*, an electronic database of philosophy readings that is part of Primis, McGraw-Hill's online resource for creating customized textbooks. Professor Abel has received two awards for excellence in teaching and an award for outstanding scholarship. He is a member of the American Philosophical Association, the American Catholic Philosophical Association, the Society for Ancient Greek Philosophy, and the Society for Philosophy and Psychology.

Contents

Preface   viii

1   What Is Philosophy?   1

1. Plato   *Euthyphro* (complete)   4
   Translated by G. M. A. Grube, revised by John M. Cooper
2. Bertrand Russell   *The Value of Philosophy* (complete)   19

2   Philosophy of Religion   24

A.   THE EXISTENCE OF GOD   27

3. Anselm   *Proslogion and Exchange with Gaunilo* (selection)   27
   Translated by Thomas Williams
4. Thomas Aquinas   *Treatise on God* (selection)   32
   Translated by William P. Baumgarth and Richard J. Regan
5. William Paley   *Natural Theology* (selection)   39
6. David Hume   *Dialogues Concerning Natural Religion* (selection)   47
7. Richard Dawkins   *The Blind Watchmaker* (selection)   56

B.   THE PROBLEM OF EVIL   67

8. Augustine   *On Free Choice of the Will*   67
   Translated by Thomas Williams
9. J. L. Mackie   *Evil and Omnipotence* (complete)   78
10. John Hick   *The Problem of Evil* (selection)   89

C.   FAITH AND REASON   100

11. Blaise Pascal   *Pensées* (selection)   100
    Translated by A. J. Krailsheimer
12. William James   *The Will to Believe* (selection)   106

3   Theories of Knowledge   115

13. Plato   *Republic* (selection)   118
    Translated by G. M. A. Grube, revised by C. D. C. Reeve

14. René Descartes *Meditations on First Philosophy* (selection)   128
       Translated by John Cottingham
15. John Locke *An Essay Concerning Human Understanding*
       (selection)   139
16. George Berkeley *Three Dialogues Between Hylas and Philonous*
       (selection)   150
17. David Hume *An Enquiry Concerning Human Understanding*
       (selection)   165
18. Immanuel Kant *Critique of Pure Reason* (selection)   175
       Translated by Paul Guyer and Allen W. Wood
19. Alison M. Jaggar *Love and Knowledge: Emotion in Feminist
       Epistemology* (selection)   188

4 Philosophy of Mind   199

A. THE MIND-BODY PROBLEM   201
20. René Descartes *Meditations on First Philosophy* (selection)   201
       Translated by John Cottingham
21. D. M. Armstrong *The Nature of Mind* (complete)   209

B. CONSCIOUSNESS   220
22. Thomas Nagel *What Is It Like to Be a Bat?* (complete)   220
23. David J. Chalmers *Facing Up to the Problem of Consciousness*
       (selection)   230

C. PERSONAL IDENTITY   244
24. Pali Canon *The Middle-Length Discourses of the Buddha* (selection) 244
       Translated by Nyanamoli Thera
25. David Hume *A Treatise of Human Nature* (selection)   259
26. Daniel C. Dennett *The Origins of Selves* (complete)   265

5 Free Will and Determinism   277

A. HARD DETERMINISM   280
27. Paul-Henri Thiry, Baron d'Holbach *Of the System of Man's
       Free Agency* (selection)   280
       Translated by H. D. Robinson
28. John Hospers *The Range of Human Freedom* (selection)   287

B. LIBERTARIANISM   295
29. William James *The Dilemma of Determinism* (selection)   295
30. Richard Taylor *Freedom and Determinism* (selection)   304

C. SOFT DETERMINISM   314
31. W. T. Stace *The Problem of Morals* (selection)   314
32. Nancy Holmstrom *Firming Up Soft Determinism* (complete)   322

6   Ethics   335

A. CLASSICAL ETHICAL THEORIES   338

   33. Aristotle   *Nicomachean Ethics* (selection)   338
       Translated by Christopher Rowe
   34. Thomas Aquinas   *Treatise on Law* (selection)   349
       Translated by Richard J. Regan
   35. Immanuel Kant   *Groundwork of the Metaphysics of Morals*
      (selection)   354
       Translated by Mary Gregor
   36. John Stuart Mill   *Utilitarianism* (selection)   365

B. CRITIQUES OF CLASSICAL THEORIES   374

   37. Søren Kierkegaard   *Is There a Teleological Suspension of the
      Ethical?* (complete)   374
       Translated by Howard V. Hong and Edna H. Hong
   38. Friedrich Nietzsche   *Beyond Good and Evil* (selection)   384
       Translated by Judith Norman
   39. Jean-Paul Sartre   *Existentialism Is a Humanism* (selection)   392
       Translated by Philip Mairet
   40. James Rachels   *The Challenge of Cultural Relativism* (selection)   402
       Revised by Stuart Rachels
   41. Rita C. Manning   *Just Caring* (selection)   415

7   Political and Social Philosophy   427

   42. Plato *Crito* (complete)
       Translated by G. M. A. Grube, revised by John M. Cooper   430
   43. Thomas Hobbes   *Leviathan* (selection)   441
   44. John Locke   *The Second Treatise of Government* (selection)   450
   45. Mary Wollstonecraft   *A Vindication of the Rights of Woman*
      (selection)   462
   46. Karl Marx and Friedrich Engels   *Manifesto of the Communist
      Party* (selection)   470
       Translated by Samuel Moore
   47. John Stuart Mill   *On Liberty* (selection)   481
   48. Martin Luther King, Jr.   *Letter from Birmingham Jail* (complete)   488
   49. John Rawls   *A Theory of Justice* (selection)   502
   50. Joseph Raz   *Multiculturalism* (complete)   512

Sources and Credits   525

Index   529

Preface

This edition of *Fifty Readings in Philosophy*, like the previous two, is designed for an introductory course in philosophy based on texts of classical Western philosophers and contemporary authors writing in that tradition. To enable students to see alternative philosophical approaches to specific topics, I have included a reading from the Buddhist Pali Canon on personal identity and feminist readings on epistemology, ethics, and social and political philosophy.

This third edition of *Fifty Readings in Philosophy* features five new readings, a revised reading, an expanded reading, and a reorganized chapter. Biographies of living authors have been updated and some new explanatory notes have been added.

The five new readings are:

Augustine, *On Free Choice of the Will* (selection)
David J. Chalmers, "Facing Up to the Problem of Consciousness" (selection)
Alison M. Jaggar, "Love and Knowledge: Emotion in Feminist Epistemology" (selection)
Søren Kierkegaard, "Is There a Teleological Suspension of the Ethical?" (*Fear and Trembling*, Problem 1, complete)
Joseph Raz, "Multiculturalism" (complete)

The revised reading is a new version of James Rachels's essay "The Challenge of Cultural Relativism," revised by Stuart Rachels. The reading from Thomas Aquinas's "Treatise on God" has been expanded to include the article "Can We Demonstrate the Existence of God?" The fourth chapter has been retitled "Philosophy of Mind" and now has these subtopics: "The Mind-Body Problem," "Consciousness," and "Personal Identity."

The readings in this book were selected on the basis of their cogency of thought, clarity of expression, historical significance, diversity of views, and accessibility. They are organized into seven thematic chapters: the nature of philosophy; philosophy of religion; theories of knowledge; philosophy of mind; free will and determinism; ethics; and political and social philosophy.

Since most beginning philosophy students need assistance in reading primary texts, *Fifty Readings in Philosophy* incorporates editorial features that enable students to read the works with greater understanding and benefit:

- *Chapter introductions:* Each of the seven chapters begins with an overview of the topic and states the basic position taken by each author in the chapter. The overview focuses on fundamental questions intended to generate the students' interest. The brief summaries of the authors' positions show students the diversity of views on these questions and, I hope, will encourage students to enter into the ongoing philosophical dialogue and to formulate their own views on the topic.

- *Length of readings:* Each reading is long enough to present a self-contained argument, but not so lengthy that students lose track of the author's main point.

- *Headnotes:* Each reading begins with a headnote that gives a biographical sketch of the author and a brief overview of the reading. The biography helps place the reading in a personal and historical context; the overview, which guides students through the main arguments but is not so detailed as to serve as a substitute for reading the text itself, enables students to approach the reading with greater confidence.

- *Explanatory notes:* Notes explain terms and references likely to be unfamiliar to beginning students. Some readings retained from the second edition have additional notes.

- *Retention of original headings:* To help students better understand the context and organization of each reading, all the original headings and subheadings of the book, chapter, or article are included. This format also makes it easier for students to locate excerpts in the original complete text from which the reading is taken.

- *Contemporary translations:* All the translations used in this anthology (except Robinson's translation of Holbach, which is the only one available) are by contemporary scholars whose work reflects the latest scholarship and the modern idiom.

- *Stylistic modernization of classical British authors:* To make the selections from Hobbes, Locke, Berkeley, Hume, Paley, and Wollstonecraft more accessible, I have revised archaic punctuation, capitalization, italicization, and spelling.

- *Self-contained chapters:* Each of the seven chapters is an independent unit; neither the chapter introduction nor the readings within the chapter presuppose familiarity with any prior section of the book. It is therefore possible to read the chapters in a different order or to omit some of them.

- *Self-contained readings:* Each reading, together with its headnote, is a self-contained unit. The headnote provides enough background for students to understand the selection even when the author builds on or criticizes a theory presented earlier in the chapter. This feature enables instructors to vary the order of the readings or to omit some of them.

I wish to thank Mark Georgiev, Editor for Philosophy and Religion at McGraw-Hill, for his invitation to prepare this third edition of *Fifty Readings in Philosophy* and for his support of the project. My thanks to Chanda Feldman,

Production Editor, Beth Ebenstein, former Development Editor, and Marley Magaziner, Editorial Assistant, for their help in producing the book. Authors D. M. Armstrong, David J. Chalmers, Richard Dawkins, John Hick, Nancy Holmstrom, John Hospers, the late James Rachels, Stuart Rachels, and the late Richard Taylor kindly provided me with biographical information for use in the headnotes. In addition, Penelope Mackie supplied information about her late father, J. L. Mackie.

I appreciate the thoughtful suggestions for revision given by Torin Alter, University of Alabama at Tuscaloosa; Theodore Benditt, University of Alabama at Birmingham; Jeff Broome, Colorado State University at Pueblo (Colorado); Bernard Comeau, Tacoma Community College (Washington); Darin Davis, Baylor University (Texas); Richard Greene, Weber State University (Utah); Christine James, Valdosta State University (Georgia); Anne Knop, Manor College (Pennsylvania); Susanne Langham, Bakersfield College (California); Diane Legomsky, specialist in Greek philosophy (Wisconsin); Chris McCord, Kirkwood Community College (Iowa); Jon Moran, Missouri State University; James Swindal, Duquesne University (Pennsylvania); and Robert Trundle, Northern Kentucky University.

The students in my introductory classes at St. Norbert College have contributed to this book by their helpful comments on various readings that I have tried out in the classroom over the years. Finally, I would like to thank the publishers (listed at the end of the book) who granted permission to reproduce copyrighted material.

Donald C. Abel

Fifty Readings in Philosophy

CHAPTER 1   What Is Philosophy?

The ancient Greek thinkers who explored fundamental questions about the world and about human existence called themselves *philosophoi,* "lovers of wisdom." They took time to stop and wonder about such things as the nature of the universe, the purpose of life, and the meaning of "good" and "bad." In their search for wisdom, they were not content to rely on answers provided by religious and cultural tradition; they used reason and evidence gained from their own experience to formulate new hypotheses. Although not all the Greek philosophers thought it possible to find the ultimate answers to their questions, they all believed that the very activity of seeking wisdom is highly worthwhile. The philosopher Socrates was so convinced of the importance of philosophizing that he declared: "The unexamined life is not worth living for a human being."

The Greek conception of philosophy as the "love of wisdom" is still valid today. Philosophy now, as then, begins with the realization that we know very little about the most important things in life. Philosophers continue to ponder basic questions about the universe and human existence. They are aware of the answers provided by common sense and by authority (religious or secular), but know that such answers can be partially or entirely mistaken. Philosophers are "skeptical" in the root sense of "taking a close look" (*skepesthai* in Greek) at an idea before accepting it. They seek answers based on reason and experience, realizing that any proposed answer (including their own) is tentative and subject to debate. In fact, practically every major philosophical question is still energetically disputed, even after centuries of debate. The lack of definitive answers in philosophy may seem frustrating until we come to see that the value of philosophizing lies not so much in the theories it produces as in the very activity of seeking wisdom. To engage in philosophy is to deepen our understanding of fundamental issues and thereby enrich our lives.

The readings in this book present the reflections of classical and contemporary philosophers on seven basic topics. The readings in Chapter 1 deal with the nature and value of philosophy. (Paradoxically, to ask what philosophy is, is itself a philosophical question, since to understand the nature and importance of the search for wisdom is itself a part of wisdom.) The balance of the book presents differing—and often opposing—views on six topics: the existence of God and the rationality of religious belief (Chapter 2), the nature and grounds of human knowledge (Chapter 3), the relation of the mind to the body and the nature of consciousness and personal identity (Chapter 4), the existence of free will (Chapter 5), the nature and requirements of morality (Chapter 6), and the nature and origin of political authority and of social justice (Chapter 7).

Chapter 1, "What Is Philosophy?," contains two readings, one from Plato and one from Bertrand Russell. In the *Euthyphro* Plato illustrates his and Socrates' method of philosophical inquiry. The work depicts a conversation between Socrates and a priest named Euthyphro on the subject of piety (holiness)—something that Plato believes is an essential element in living rightly and therefore a fitting topic for a philosophical dialogue. In the conversation Socrates uses a question-and-answer method to elicit and clarify Euthyphro's opinions about the nature of piety, to make Euthyphro aware of his implicit assumptions, to show him inconsistencies in his views, and to encourage him to think more deeply and coherently about piety. Socrates and Plato believe that this dialectical ("Socratic") method exemplified in the *Euthyphro*—whether used in conversation with another person or in an interior dialogue with oneself—is the surest path to wisdom. In the second reading, Russell presents his views on the value of philosophy. He argues that philosophizing enriches our mental lives. This enrichment comes not from attaining definitive answers to questions (since practically all philosophical questions remain undecided) but from teaching us to question our own beliefs and to see that there are alternative ways of viewing reality. Russell holds that philosophy helps us see the world more objectively by liberating us from our tendency to interpret everything in terms of how it affects us personally.

Plato and Russell would agree that philosophy is the love of wisdom, but—not surprisingly, given the controversial nature of philosophical questions—not all philosophers would. And even those who do agree would almost certainly have different views about what "wisdom" is and what it means to "love" wisdom. To illustrate the diversity of opinion among philosophers about the nature of philosophy, this introduction concludes with a series of brief quotations from a variety of well-known thinkers from Plato to the present. (Whether one considers these thinkers *philosophers* depends, of course, on how one defines philosophy!)

The feeling of wonder is the mark of the philosopher; philosophy has no other beginning than this.

—Plato

Philosophy is the cultivation of mental faculties.

—Marcus Tullius Cicero

The beginning of philosophy is the recognition of the conflict between opinions.

—Epictetus

Philosophy is the unusually stubborn attempt to think clearly.

—William James

Philosophy . . . has its origin and value in an attempt to give a reasonable account of our own personal attitude toward the more serious business of life.

—Josiah Royce

The proper method of philosophy consists in clearly conceiving insoluble problems in all their insolubility and then in simply contemplating them.

—Simone Weil

Philosophy is a battle against the bewitchment of our intelligence by means of language.

—Ludwig Wittgenstein

Philosophy [is] the endeavor to discover by systematic reflection the ultimate nature of things.

—Brand Blanshard

To philosophize is to act in such a way that one steps out of the workaday world.

—Josef Pieper

The main concern of philosophy is to question and understand very common ideas that all of us use every day without thinking about them.

—Thomas Nagel

Euthyphro

Plato

Plato was born in Athens in about 428 B.C.E. As a youth he associated with Socrates, a philosopher who constantly challenged fellow Athenians to think about virtue and to improve their souls. Plato's initial interest was in politics, but he soon became disillusioned, especially when, under the democracy that was restored after the rule of the "Thirty Tyrants," Socrates was arrested on false charges of impiety and the corruption of youth, convicted, and condemned to die. After the execution of Socrates, Plato moved to nearby Megara for a time and may have traveled to Egypt. In 388 he visited Italy and the city of Syracuse in Sicily. Returning to Athens, he founded the Academy, a school devoted both to philosophical inquiry and to the philosophically based education of politicians. Plato spent most of his life teaching at the Academy (Aristotle was his most famous student) and writing philosophical works. He made two more trips to Syracuse, in 368 and 361, apparently with the intention of turning the city's ruler, Dionysius the Younger, into a "philosopher-king." (If this was indeed his purpose, he failed.) Plato died in Athens in 347 at the age of eighty-one.

Most of Plato's works are written as conversations between Socrates and one or more interlocutors on some topic concerning morality. His best-known "dialogues" (the name by which his surviving works are known) are the *Euthyphro, Apology, Crito, Phaedo, Meno, Symposium,* and *Republic.*

Our reading here is the *Euthyphro,* a work that illustrates how the historical Socrates used the method of question-and-answer to show people that they know less than they think they do about some moral topic and to encourage them to think more deeply and more consistently about it. In this dialogue Socrates meets a priest named Euthyphro at the court of the magistrate in charge of cases involving the state religion. Socrates has come there to deal with preliminary matters concerning the charges of impiety and corruption of youth that a man named Meletus has filed against him; Euthyphro is at the court to charge his father with murder. Since it was generally considered highly impious to bring legal action against one's father, Socrates tells Euthyphro that he must be very knowledgeable about piety, or else he would never have initiated such an action. Euthyphro quickly agrees that he is "far advanced in wisdom." At Socrates' request, he agrees to explain the nature of piety. Socrates expresses his gratitude, since a knowledge of piety will enable him to defend himself in court against the charge of impiety.

Euthyphro first says that piety (holiness, godliness) is doing what he is doing: prosecuting the wrongdoer. Socrates points out that while prosecuting wrongdoers may be an *example* of piety, it is not a *definition* because it does not specify the form (characteristic) of piety—the element that is common to all instances of piety and makes them be instances of piety. Euthyphro proceeds to define piety as "what is dear to the gods." Socrates' questioning shows Euthyphro the inadequacy of this definition. Euthyphro then proposes other definitions, but each time Socrates points out inconsistencies in Euthyphro's thought. The dialogue ends with Euthyphro telling Socrates that he is in a hurry and has to go.

EUTHYPHRO: What's new, Socrates, to make you leave your usual haunts in the Lyceum[1] and spend your time here by the king-archon's[2] court? Surely you are not prosecuting anyone before the king-archon as I am?

SOCRATES: The Athenians do not call this a prosecution but an indictment, Euthyphro.

EUTHYPHRO: What is this you say? Someone must have indicted you, for you are not going to tell me that you have indicted someone else.

SOCRATES: No indeed.

EUTHYPHRO: But someone else has indicted you?

SOCRATES: Quite so.

EUTHYPHRO: Who is he?

SOCRATES: I do not really know him myself, Euthyphro. He is apparently young and unknown. They call him Meletus, I believe. He belongs to the Pitthean deme,[3] if you know anyone from that deme called Meletus, with long hair, not much of a beard, and a rather aquiline nose.

EUTHYPHRO: I don't know him, Socrates. What charge does he bring against you?

SOCRATES: What charge? A not ignoble one I think, for it is no small thing for a young man to have knowledge of such an important subject. He says he knows how our young men are corrupted and who corrupts them. He is likely to be wise, and when he sees my ignorance corrupting his contemporaries, he proceeds to accuse me to the city as to their mother. I think he is the only one of our public men to start out the right way, for it is right to care first that the young should be as good as possible, just as a good farmer is likely to take care of the young plants first, and of the others later. So, too, Meletus first gets rid of us who corrupt the young shoots, as he says, and then afterwards he will obviously take care of the older ones and become a source of great blessings for the city, as seems likely to happen to one who started out this way.

EUTHYPHRO: I could wish this were true, Socrates, but I fear the opposite may happen. He seems to me to start out by harming the very heart of the city by attempting to wrong you. Tell me, what does he say you do to corrupt the young?

SOCRATES: Strange things, to hear him tell it, for he says that I am a maker of gods, and on the ground that I create new gods while not believing in the old gods, he has indicted me for their sake, as he puts it.

EUTHYPHRO: I understand, Socrates. This is because you say that the divine sign[4] keeps coming to you. So he has written this indictment against you as one who makes innovations in religious matters, and he comes to court to slander you, knowing that such things are easily misrepresented to the crowd. The same is true in my case. Whenever I speak of divine matters in the assembly and foretell the future, they laugh me down as if I were crazy; and yet I have foretold nothing that did not happen. Nevertheless, they envy all of us who do this. One need not worry about them, but meet them head-on.

SOCRATES: My dear Euthyphro, to be laughed at does not matter perhaps, for the Athenians do not mind anyone they think clever, as long as he does not teach his own wisdom. But if they think that he makes others to be like himself they get angry, whether through envy, as you say, or for some other reason.

EUTHYPHRO: I have certainly no desire to test their feelings towards me in this matter.

SOCRATES: Perhaps you seem to make yourself but rarely available, and not be willing to teach your own wisdom, but I'm afraid that my liking for people makes them think that I pour out to anybody anything I have to say, not only without charging a fee but even glad to reward anyone who is willing to listen. If then they were intending to laugh at me, as you say they laugh at you, there would be nothing unpleasant in their spending their time in court laughing and jesting, but if they are going to be serious, the outcome is not clear except to you prophets.

EUTHYPHRO: Perhaps it will come to nothing, Socrates, and you will fight your case as you think best, as I think I will mine.

SOCRATES: What is your case, Euthyphro? Are you the defendant or the prosecutor?

EUTHYPHRO: The prosecutor.

SOCRATES: Whom do you prosecute?

EUTHYPHRO: One whom I am thought crazy to prosecute.

SOCRATES: Are you pursuing someone who will easily escape you?

EUTHYPHRO: Far from it, for he is quite old.

SOCRATES: Who is it?

EUTHYPHRO: My father.

SOCRATES: My dear sir! Your own father?

EUTHYPHRO: Certainly.

SOCRATES: What is the charge? What is the case about?

EUTHYPHRO: Murder, Socrates.

SOCRATES: Good heavens! Certainly, Euthyphro, most men would not know how they could do this and be right. It is not the part of anyone to do this, but of one who is far advanced in wisdom.

EUTHYPHRO: Yes, by Zeus, Socrates, that is so.

SOCRATES: Is then the man your father killed one of your relatives? Or is that obvious—for you would not prosecute your father for the murder of a stranger.

EUTHYPHRO: It is ridiculous, Socrates, for you to think that it makes any difference whether the victim is a stranger or a relative. One should only watch whether the killer acted justly or not; if he acted justly, let him go, but if not, one should prosecute, if, that is to say, the killer shares your hearth and table. The pollution is the same if you knowingly keep company with such a man and do not cleanse yourself and him by bringing him to justice. The victim was a dependent of mine, and when we were farming in Naxos[5] he was a servant of ours. He killed one of our household slaves in drunken anger, so my father bound him hand and foot and threw him in a ditch, then sent a man here to inquire from the priest what should be done. During that time he gave no thought or care to the bound man, as being a killer, and it was no matter if he died, which he did. Hunger and cold and his bonds caused his death before the messenger came back from the seer. Both my father and my other relatives are angry that I am prosecuting my father for murder on behalf of a murderer when he hadn't even killed him, they say, and even if he had, the dead man does not deserve a thought, since he was a killer. For, they say, it is impious for a son to prosecute his father for murder. But their ideas of the divine attitude to piety and impiety are wrong, Socrates.

SOCRATES: Whereas, by Zeus, Euthyphro, you think that your knowledge of the divine, and of piety and impiety, is so accurate that, when those things happened as you say, you have no fear of having acted impiously in bringing your father to trial?

EUTHYPHRO: I should be of no use, Socrates, and Euthyphro would not be superior to the majority of men, if I did not have accurate knowledge of all such things.

SOCRATES: It is indeed most important, my admirable Euthyphro, that I should become your pupil and, as regards this indictment, challenge Meletus about these very things and say to him that in the past too I considered knowledge about the divine to be most important, and that now that he says that I am guilty of improvising and innovating about the gods, I have become your pupil. I would say to him: "If, Meletus, you agree that Euthyphro is wise in these matters, consider me, too, to have the right beliefs and do not bring me to trial. If you do not think so, then prosecute that teacher of mine, not me, for corrupting the older men— me and his own father—by teaching me and by exhorting and punishing him." If he is not convinced, and does not discharge me or indict you instead of me, I shall repeat the same challenge in court.

EUTHYPHRO: Yes, by Zeus, Socrates, and, if he should try to indict me, I think I would find his weak spots and the talk in court would be about him rather than about me.

SOCRATES: It is because I realize this that I am eager to become your pupil, my dear friend. I know that other people as well as this Meletus do not even seem to notice you, whereas he sees me so sharply and clearly that he indicts me for ungodliness. So tell me now, by Zeus, what you just now maintained you clearly knew. What kind of thing do you say that godliness and ungodliness are, both as regards murder and other things? Or is the pious not the same and alike in every action, and the impious the opposite of all that is pious and like itself, and everything that is to be impious presents us with one form or appearance insofar as it is impious?

EUTHYPHRO: Most certainly, Socrates.

SOCRATES: Tell me then, what is the pious, and what the impious—what do you say?

EUTHYPHRO: I say that the pious is to do what I am doing now, to prosecute the wrongdoer, be it about murder or temple robbery or anything else, whether the wrongdoer is your father or your mother or anyone else; not to prosecute is impious. And observe, Socrates, that I can cite powerful evidence that the law is so. I have already said to others that such actions are right, not to favor the ungodly, whoever they are. These people themselves believe that Zeus is the best and most just of the gods, yet they agree that he bound his father because he unjustly swallowed his sons, and that he in turn castrated his father for similar reasons. But they are angry with me because I am prosecuting my father for his wrongdoing. They contradict themselves in what they say about the gods and about me.

SOCRATES: Indeed, Euthyphro, this is the reason why I am a defendant in the case, because I find it hard to accept things like that being said about the gods, and it is likely to be the reason why I shall be told I do wrong. Now, however, if you, who have full knowledge of such things, share their opinions, then we must agree with them, too, it would seem. For what are we to say, we who agree that we ourselves have no knowledge of them? Tell me, by the god of friendship, do you really believe these things are true?

EUTHYPHRO: Yes, Socrates, and so are even more surprising things, of which the majority has no knowledge.

SOCRATES: And do you believe that there really is war among the gods, and terrible enmities and battles, and other such things as are told by the poets, and other sacred stories such as are embroidered by good writers and by representations of which the robe of the goddess is adorned when it is carried up to the Acropolis?[6] Are we to say these things are true, Euthyphro?

EUTHYPHRO: Not only these, Socrates, but, as I was saying just now, I will, if you wish, relate many other things about the gods which I know will amaze you.

SOCRATES: I should not be surprised, but you will tell me these at leisure some other time. For now, try to tell me more clearly what I was asking just now; for, my friend, you did not teach me adequately when I asked you what the pious was, but you told me that what you are doing now, in prosecuting your father for murder, is pious.

EUTHYPHRO: And I told the truth, Socrates.

SOCRATES: Perhaps. You agree, however, that there are many other pious actions.

EUTHYPHRO: There are.

SOCRATES: Bear in mind then that I did not bid you tell me one or two of the many pious actions but that form itself that makes all pious actions pious, for you agreed that all impious actions are impious and all pious actions pious through one form, or don't you remember?

EUTHYPHRO: I do.

SOCRATES: Tell me then what this form itself is, so that I may look upon it, and using it as a model, say that any action of yours or another's that is of that kind is pious, and if it is not that it is not.

EUTHYPHRO: If that is how you want it, Socrates, that is how I will tell you.

SOCRATES: That is what I want.

EUTHYPHRO: Well then, what is dear to the gods is pious, what is not is impious.

SOCRATES: Splendid, Euthyphro! You have now answered in the way I wanted. Whether your answer is true I do not know yet, but you will obviously show me that what you say is true.

EUTHYPHRO: Certainly.

SOCRATES: Come then, let us examine what we mean. An action or a man dear to the gods is pious, but an action or a man hated by the gods is impious. They are not the same, but quite opposite, the pious and the impious. Is that not so?

EUTHYPHRO: It is indeed.

SOCRATES: And that seems to be a good statement?

EUTHYPHRO: I think so, Socrates.

SOCRATES: We have also stated that the gods are in a state of discord, that they are at odds with each other, Euthyphro, and that they are at enmity with each other. Has that, too, been said?

EUTHYPHRO: It has.

SOCRATES: What are the subjects of difference that cause hatred and anger? Let us look at it this way. If you and I were to differ about numbers as to which is the greater, would this difference make us enemies and angry with each other, or would we proceed to count and soon resolve our difference about this?

EUTHYPHRO: We would certainly do so.

SOCRATES: Again, if we differed about the larger and the smaller, we would turn to measurement and soon cease to differ.

EUTHYPHRO: That is so.

SOCRATES: And about the heavier and the lighter, we would resort to weighing and be reconciled.

EUTHYPHRO: Of course.

SOCRATES: What subject of difference would make us angry and hostile to each other if we were unable to come to a decision? Perhaps you do not have an answer ready, but examine as I tell you whether these subjects are the just and the unjust, the beautiful and the ugly, the good and the bad. Are these not the subjects of difference about which, when we are unable to come to a satisfactory decision, you and I and other men become hostile to each other whenever we do?

EUTHYPHRO: That is the difference, Socrates, about those subjects.

SOCRATES: What about the gods, Euthyphro? If indeed they have differences, will it not be about these same subjects?

EUTHYPHRO: It certainly must be so.

SOCRATES: Then according to your argument, my good Euthyphro, different gods consider different things to be just, beautiful, ugly, good, and bad, for they would not be at odds with one another unless they differed about these subjects, would they?

EUTHYPHRO: You are right.

SOCRATES: And they like what each of them considers beautiful, good, and just, and hate the opposites of these?

EUTHYPHRO: Certainly.

SOCRATES: But you say that the same things are considered just by some gods and unjust by others, and as they dispute about these things they are at odds and at war with each other. Is that not so?

EUTHYPHRO: It is.

SOCRATES: The same things then are loved by the gods and hated by the gods, and would be both god-loved and god-hated.

EUTHYPHRO: It seems likely.

SOCRATES: And the same things would be both pious and impious, according to this argument?

EUTHYPHRO: I'm afraid so.

SOCRATES: So you did not answer my question, you surprising man. I did not ask you what same thing is both pious and impious, and it appears that what is loved by the gods is also hated by them. So it is in no way surprising if your present action, namely punishing your father, may be pleasing to Zeus but displeasing to Cronus and Uranus, pleasing to Hephaestus but displeasing to Hera, and so with any other gods who differ from each other on this subject.

EUTHYPHRO: I think, Socrates, that on this subject no gods would differ from one another, that whoever has killed anyone unjustly should pay the penalty.

SOCRATES: Well now, Euthyphro, have you ever heard any man maintaining that one who has killed or done anything else unjustly should not pay the penalty?

EUTHYPHRO: They never cease to dispute on this subject, both elsewhere and in the courts, for when they have committed many wrongs they do and say anything to avoid the penalty.

SOCRATES: Do they agree they have done wrong, Euthyphro, and in spite of so agreeing do they nevertheless say they should not be punished?

EUTHYPHRO: No, they do not agree on that point.

SOCRATES: So they do not say or do just anything. For they do not venture to say this, or dispute that they must not pay the penalty if they have done wrong, but I think they deny doing wrong. Is that not so?

EUTHYPHRO: That is true.

SOCRATES: Then they do not dispute that the wrongdoer must be punished, but they may disagree as to who the wrongdoer is, what he did and when.

EUTHYPHRO: You are right.

SOCRATES: Do not the gods have the same experience, if indeed they are at odds with each other about the just and the unjust, as your argument maintains? Some assert that they wrong one another, while others deny it, but no one among gods or men ventures to say that the wrongdoer must not be punished.

EUTHYPHRO: Yes, that is true, Socrates, as to the main point.

SOCRATES: And those who disagree, whether men or gods, dispute about each action, if indeed the gods disagree. Some say it is done justly, others unjustly. Is that not so?

EUTHYPHRO: Yes, indeed.

SOCRATES: Come now, my dear Euthyphro, tell me, too, that I may become wiser, what proof you have that all the gods consider that man to have been killed unjustly who became a murderer while in your service, was bound by the master of his victim, and died in his bonds before the one who bound him found out from the seers what was to be done with him, and that it is right for a son to denounce and to prosecute his father on behalf of such a man. Come, try to show me a clear sign that all the gods definitely believe this action to be right. If you can give me adequate proof of this, I shall never cease to extol your wisdom.

EUTHYPHRO: This is perhaps no light task, Socrates, though I could show you very clearly.

SOCRATES: I understand that you think me more dull-witted than the jury, as you will obviously show them that these actions were unjust and that all the gods hate such actions.

EUTHYPHRO: I will show it to them clearly, Socrates, if only they will listen to me.

SOCRATES: They will listen if they think you show them well. But this thought came to me as you were speaking, and I am examining it, saying to myself: "If Euthyphro shows me conclusively that all the gods consider such a death unjust, to what greater extent have I learned from him the nature of piety and impiety? This action would then, it seems, be hated by the gods, but the pious and the impious were not thereby now defined, for what is hated by the gods has also been shown to be loved by them." So I will not insist on this point; let us assume, if you wish, that all the gods consider this unjust and that they all hate it. However, is this the correction we are making in our discussion, that what all the gods hate is impious, and what they all love is pious, and that what some gods love and others hate is neither or both? Is that how you now wish us to define piety and impiety?

EUTHYPHRO: What prevents us from doing so, Socrates?

SOCRATES: For my part nothing, Euthyphro. But you look whether on your part this proposal will enable you to teach me most easily what you promised.

EUTHYPHRO: I would certainly say that the pious is what all the gods love, and the opposite, what all the gods hate, is the impious.

SOCRATES: Then let us again examine whether that is a sound statement, or do we let it pass, and if one of us, or someone else, merely says that something is so, do we accept that it is so? Or should we examine what the speaker means?

EUTHYPHRO: We must examine it, but I certainly think that this is now a fine statement.

SOCRATES: We shall soon know better whether it is. Consider this: Is the pious being loved by the gods because it is pious, or is it pious because it is being loved by the gods?

EUTHYPHRO: I don't know what you mean, Socrates.

SOCRATES: I shall try to explain more clearly. We speak of something carried and something carrying, of something led and something leading, of something seen and something seeing, and you understand that these things are all different from one another and how they differ?

EUTHYPHRO: I think I do.

SOCRATES: So there is also something loved and—a different thing— something loving.

EUTHYPHRO: Of course.

SOCRATES: Tell me then whether the thing carried is a carried thing because it is being carried, or for some other reason?

EUTHYPHRO: No, that is the reason.

SOCRATES: And the thing led is so because it is being led, and the thing seen because it is being seen?

EUTHYPHRO: Certainly.

SOCRATES: It is not being seen because it is a thing seen, but on the contrary it is a thing seen because it is *being* seen;[7] nor is it because it is something led that it is being led, but because it is *being* led that it is something led; nor is something being carried because it is something carried, but it is something carried because it is *being* carried. Is what I want to say clear, Euthyphro? I want to say this, namely, that if anything is being changed or is being affected in any way, it is not being changed because it is something changed, but rather it is something changed because it is *being* changed; nor is it being affected because it is something affected, but it is something affected because it is *being* affected. Or do you not agree?

EUTHYPHRO: I do.

SOCRATES: Is something loved either something changed or something affected by something?

EUTHYPHRO: Certainly.

SOCRATES: So it is in the same case as the things just mentioned: It is not being loved by those who love it because it is something loved, but it is something loved because it is *being* loved by them.

EUTHYPHRO: Necessarily.

SOCRATES: What then do we say about the pious, Euthyphro? Surely that it is *being* loved by all the gods, according to what you say?

EUTHYPHRO: Yes.

SOCRATES: Is it being loved because it is pious, or for some other reason?

EUTHYPHRO: For no other reason.

SOCRATES: It is being loved then because it is pious, but it is not pious because it is being loved?

EUTHYPHRO: Apparently.

SOCRATES: And yet it is something loved and god-loved because it is being loved by the gods?

EUTHYPHRO: Of course.

SOCRATES: Then the god-loved is not the same as the pious, Euthyphro, nor the pious the same as the god-loved, as you say it is, but one differs from the other.

EUTHYPHRO: How so, Socrates?

SOCRATES: Because we agree that the pious is being loved for this reason, that it is pious, but it is not pious because it is being loved. Is that not so?

EUTHYPHRO: Yes.

SOCRATES: And that the god-loved, on the other hand, is so because it is being loved by the gods, by the very fact of being loved, but it is not being loved because it is god-loved.

EUTHYPHRO: True.

SOCRATES: But if the god-loved and the pious were the same, my dear
Euthyphro, then if the pious was being loved because it was pious,
the god-loved would also be being loved because it was god-loved; and
if the god-loved was god-loved because it was being loved by the gods,
then the pious would also be pious because it was being loved by the
gods. But now you see that they are in opposite cases as being altogether different from each other: The one is such as to be loved because
it is being loved, the other is being loved because it is such as to be loved.
I'm afraid, Euthyphro, that when you were asked what piety is, you did
not wish to make its nature clear to me, but you told me an affect or
quality of it, that the pious has the quality of being loved by all the gods,
but you have not yet told me what the pious is. Now, if you will, do not
hide things from me but tell me again from the beginning what piety is,
whether being loved by the gods or having some other quality—we
shall not quarrel about that—but be keen to tell me what the pious and
the impious are.

EUTHYPHRO: But Socrates, I have no way of telling you what I have in mind,
for whatever proposition we put forward goes around and refuses to
stay put where we establish it.

SOCRATES: Your statements, Euthyphro, seem to belong to my ancestor,
Daedalus.[8] If I were stating them and putting them forward, you would
perhaps be making fun of me and say that because of my kinship with
him my conclusions in discussion run away and will not stay where one
puts them. As these propositions are yours, however, we need some
other jest, for they will not stay put for you, as you say yourself.

EUTHYPHRO: I think the same jest will do for our discussion, Socrates, for I
am not the one who makes them go around and not remain in the same
place. It is you who are the Daedalus, for as far as I am concerned they
would remain as they were.

SOCRATES: It looks as if I was cleverer than Daedalus in using my skill, my
friend, insofar as he could only cause to move the things he made himself, but I can make other people's move as well as my own. And the
smartest part of my skill is that I am clever without wanting to be, for I
would rather have your statements to me remain unmoved than possess
the wealth of Tantalus[9] as well as the cleverness of Daedalus. But enough
of this. Since I think you are making unnecessary difficulties, I am as eager as you are to find a way to teach me about piety, and do not give up
before you do. See whether you think all that is pious is of necessity just.

EUTHYPHRO: I think so.

SOCRATES: And is then all that is just pious? Or is all that is pious just, but
not all that is just pious, but some of it is and some is not?

EUTHYPHRO: I do not follow what you are saying, Socrates.

SOCRATES: Yet you are younger than I by as much as you are wiser. As I say,
you are making difficulties because of your wealth of wisdom. Pull
yourself together, my dear sir; what I am saying is not difficult to grasp.
I am saying the opposite of what the poet said who wrote:

> You do not wish to name Zeus, who had done it, and who made
> All things grow, for where there is fear there is also shame.[10]

I disagree with the poet. Shall I tell you why?

EUTHYPHRO: Please do.

SOCRATES: I do not think that "where there is fear there is also shame," for I think that many people who fear disease and poverty and many other such things feel fear, but are not ashamed of the things they fear. Do you not think so?

EUTHYPHRO: I do indeed.

SOCRATES: But where there is shame there is also fear. For is there anyone who, in feeling shame and embarrassment at anything, does not also at the same time fear and dread a reputation for wickedness?

EUTHYPHRO: He is certainly afraid.

SOCRATES: It is then not right to say "where there is fear there is also shame," but that where there is shame there is also fear, for fear covers a larger area than shame. Shame is a part of fear just as odd is a part of number, with the result that it is not true that where there is number there is also oddness, but that where there is oddness there is also number. Do you follow me now?

EUTHYPHRO: Surely.

SOCRATES: This is the kind of thing I was asking before, whether where there is piety there is also justice, but where there is justice there is not always piety, for the pious is a part of justice. Shall we say that, or do you think. otherwise?

EUTHYPHRO: No, but like that, for what you say appears to be right.

SOCRATES: See what comes next: If the pious is a part of the just, we must, it seems, find out what part of the just it is. Now if you asked me something of what we mentioned just now, such as what part of number is the even, and what number that is, I would say it is the number that is divisible into two equal, not unequal, parts. Or do you not think so?

EUTHYPHRO: I do.

SOCRATES: Try in this way to tell me what part of the just the pious is, in order to tell Meletus not to wrong us any more and not to indict me for ungodliness, since I have learned from you sufficiently what is godly and pious and what is not.

EUTHYPHRO: I think, Socrates, that the godly and pious is the part of the just that is concerned with the care of the gods, while that concerned with the care of men is the remaining part of justice.

SOCRATES: You seem to me to put that very well, but I still need a bit of information. I do not know yet what you mean by care, for you do not mean the care of the gods in the same sense as the care of other things—as, for example, we say, don't we, that not everyone knows how to care for horses, but the horse breeder does.

EUTHYPHRO: Yes, I do mean it that way.

SOCRATES: So horse breeding is the care of horses.

EUTHYPHRO: Yes.

SOCRATES: Nor does everyone know how to care for dogs, but the hunter does.

EUTHYPHRO: That is so.

SOCRATES: So hunting is the care of dogs.

EUTHYPHRO: Yes.

SOCRATES: And cattle raising is the care of cattle.

EUTHYPHRO: Quite so.

SOCRATES: While piety and godliness is the care of the gods, Euthyphro. Is that what you mean?

EUTHYPHRO: It is.

SOCRATES: Now care in each case has the same effect; it aims at the good and the benefit of the object cared for, as you can see that horses cared for by horse breeders are benefited and become better. Or do you not think so?

EUTHYPHRO: I do.

SOCRATES: So dogs are benefited by dog breeding, cattle by cattle raising, and so with all the others. Or do you think that care aims to harm the object of its care?

EUTHYPHRO: By Zeus, no.

SOCRATES: It aims to benefit the object of its care?

EUTHYPHRO: Of course.

SOCRATES: Is piety then, which is the care of the gods, also to benefit the gods and make them better? Would you agree that when you do something pious you make some one of the gods better?

EUTHYPHRO: By Zeus, no.

SOCRATES: Nor do I think that this is what you mean—far from it—but that is why I asked you what you meant by the care of gods, because I did not believe you meant this kind of care.

EUTHYPHRO: Quite right, Socrates, that is not the kind of care I mean.

SOCRATES: Very well, but what kind of care of the gods would piety be?

EUTHYPHRO: The kind of care, Socrates, that slaves take of their masters.

SOCRATES: I understand. It is likely to be a kind of service of the gods.

EUTHYPHRO: Quite so.

SOCRATES: Could you tell me to the achievement of what goal service to doctors tends? Is it not, do you think, to achieving health?

EUTHYPHRO: I think so.

SOCRATES: What about service to shipbuilders? To what achievement is it directed?

EUTHYPHRO: Clearly, Socrates, to the building of a ship.

SOCRATES: And service to housebuilders to the building of a house?

EUTHYPHRO: Yes.

SOCRATES: Tell me then, my good sir, to the achievement of what aim does service to the gods tend? You obviously know since you say that you, of all men, have the best knowledge of the divine.

EUTHYPHRO: And I am telling the truth, Socrates.

SOCRATES: Tell me then, by Zeus, what is that excellent aim that the gods achieve, using us as their servants?

EUTHYPHRO: Many fine things, Socrates.

SOCRATES: So do generals, my friend. Nevertheless you could easily tell me their main concern, which is to achieve victory in war, is it not?

EUTHYPHRO: Of course.

SOCRATES: The farmers, too, I think, achieve many fine things, but the main point of their efforts is to produce food from the earth.

EUTHYPHRO: Quite so.

SOCRATES: Well then, how would you sum up the many fine things that the gods achieve?

EUTHYPHRO: I told you a short while ago, Socrates, that it is a considerable task to acquire any precise knowledge of these things, but, to put it simply, I say that if a man knows how to say and do what is pleasing to the gods at prayer and sacrifice, those are pious actions such as preserve both private houses and public affairs of state. The opposite of these pleasing actions are impious and overturn and destroy everything.

SOCRATES: You could tell me in far fewer words, if you were willing, the sum of what I asked, Euthyphro, but you are not keen to teach me, that is clear. You were on the point of doing so, but you turned away. If you had given that answer, I should now have acquired from you sufficient knowledge of the nature of piety. As it is, the lover of inquiry must follow his beloved wherever it may lead him. Once more then, what do you say that piety and the pious are? Are they a knowledge of how to sacrifice and pray?

EUTHYPHRO: They are.

SOCRATES: To sacrifice is to make a gift to the gods, whereas to pray is to beg from the gods?

EUTHYPHRO: Definitely, Socrates.

SOCRATES: It would follow from this statement that piety would be a knowledge of how to give to and beg from the gods.

EUTHYPHRO: You understood what I said very well, Socrates.

SOCRATES: That is because I am so desirous of your wisdom, and I concentrate my mind on it, so that no word of yours may fall to the ground. But tell me, what is this service to the gods? You say it is to beg from them and to give to them?

EUTHYPHRO: I do.

SOCRATES: And to beg correctly would be to ask from them things that we need?

EUTHYPHRO: What else?

SOCRATES: And to give correctly is to give them what they need from us, for it would not be skillful to bring gifts to anyone that are in no way needed.

EUTHYPHRO: True, Socrates.

SOCRATES: Piety would then be a sort of trading skill between gods and men?

EUTHYPHRO: Trading yes, if you prefer to call it that.

SOCRATES: I prefer nothing, unless it is true. But tell me, what benefit do the gods derive from the gifts they receive from us? What they give us is obvious to all. There is for us no good that we do not receive from them.

But how are they benefited by what they receive from us? Or do we have such an advantage over them in the trade that we receive all our blessings from them and they receive nothing from us?

EUTHYPHRO: Do you suppose, Socrates, that the gods are benefited by what they receive from us?

SOCRATES: What could those gifts from us to the gods be, Euthyphro?

EUTHYPHRO: What else, do you think, than honor, reverence, and what I mentioned just now, gratitude?

SOCRATES: The pious is then, Euthyphro, pleasing to the gods, but not beneficial or dear to them?

EUTHYPHRO: I think it is of all things most dear to them.

SOCRATES: So the pious is once again what is dear to the gods.

EUTHYPHRO: Most certainly.

SOCRATES: When you say this, will you be surprised if your arguments seem to move about instead of staying put? And will you accuse me of being Daedalus who makes them move, though you are yourself much more skillful than Daedalus and make them go around in a circle? Or do you not realize that our argument has moved around and come again to the same place? You surely remember that earlier the pious and the god-loved were shown not to be the same but different from each other. Or do you not remember?

EUTHYPHRO: I do.

SOCRATES: Do you then not realize now that you are saying that what is dear to the gods is the pious? Is this not the same as the god-loved? Or is it not?

EUTHYPHRO: It certainly is.

SOCRATES: Either we were wrong when we agreed before, or, if we were right then, we are wrong now.

EUTHYPHRO: That seems to be so.

SOCRATES: So we must investigate again from the beginning what piety is, as I shall not willingly give up before I learn this. Do not think me unworthy, but concentrate your attention and tell the truth. For you know it, if any man does, and I must not let you go, like Proteus,[11] before you tell me. If you had no clear knowledge of piety and impiety you would never have ventured to prosecute your old father for murder on behalf of a servant. For fear of the gods you would have been afraid to take the risk lest you should not be acting rightly, and would have been ashamed before men, but now I know well that you believe you have clear knowledge of piety and impiety. So tell me, my good Euthyphro, and do not hide what you think it is.

EUTHYPHRO: Some other time, Socrates, for I am in a hurry now, and it is time for me to go.

SOCRATES: What a thing to do, my friend! By going you have cast me down from a great hope I had, that I would learn from you the nature of the pious and the impious and so escape Meletus' indictment by showing him that I had acquired wisdom in divine matters from Euthyphro, and my ignorance would no longer cause me to be careless and inventive about such things, and that I would be better for the rest of my life.

NOTES

1. *Lyceum:* a public facility for gymnastic exercise, named for the god Apollo Lyceios. [D. C. ABEL]
2. *king-archon:* the magistrate with jurisdiction of cases involving the state religion. [D. C. ABEL]
3. *deme:* a unit of local government. [D. C. ABEL]
4. *divine sign:* In the defense speech he gave at his trial, Socrates explained that he hears a divine voice that sometimes turns him away from something he is about to do. [D. C. ABEL]
5. *Naxos:* a large island in the Aegean Sea, southeast of Athens. [G. M. A. GRUBE, TRANSLATOR]
6. *Acropolis:* the fortified section of Athens, where the Parthenon, a temple of Athena, the patron goddess of Athens, was located. The robe of Athena was carried to the Parthenon during certain religious festivals. [D. C. ABEL]
7. The reason that something is seen is because of its *"being* seen," that is, because of the act of the other entity that sees it; it is not seen because of its own state of being seen. [D. C. ABEL]
8. *Daedalus:* a legendary artist, inventor, and artisan. His statues were said to be so lifelike that they moved. [D. C. ABEL]
9. *Tantalus:* a legendary king of Lydia. [D. C. ABEL]
10. Author unknown. [G. M. A. GRUBE]
11. *Proteus:* a sea god able to assume different shapes. If held until he takes his true shape, he will answer questions. [D. C. ABEL]

The Value of Philosophy

Bertrand Russell

Bertrand Russell was born in Trelleck, Wales, in 1872. Both his parents died when he was young, and he and his older brother were raised by their paternal grandmother. Russell received his initial education from governesses and tutors. In 1890 he enrolled in Cambridge University, where he studied mathematics and then philosophy, receiving his degree in 1894. Russell was a fellow at Cambridge from 1895 to 1901 and a lecturer in philosophy from 1910 to 1916. In 1908 he became a member of the Royal Society. After his lectureship at Cambridge, Russell supported himself by writing and giving public lectures. On the death of his brother in 1931, he became Earl Russell. He moved to the United States in 1938, teaching first at the University of Chicago and then at the University of California at Los Angeles. He lectured at the Barnes Foundation in Philadelphia from 1941 to 1943. The following year he returned to England, having been invited to become a fellow again at Cambridge. In 1949 he became an honorary member of the British Academy and received the Order of Merit. The following year he was awarded the Nobel Prize for Literature. Russell died in 1970 near Penrhyndeudraeth, Wales, at the age of ninety-seven.

Russell's numerous works include *The Principles of Mathematics* (1903), *Principia Mathematica* (coauthored with Alfred North Whitehead; three volumes, 1910, 1912, 1913), *The Problems of Philosophy* (1912), *Our Knowledge of the External World* (1914), *The Conquest of Happiness* (1930), *An Inquiry into Meaning and Truth* (1940), and *A History of Western Philosophy* (1945).

Our reading is the final chapter of *The Problems of Philosophy*, "The Value of Philosophy." Russell argues that, although philosophy does not enhance our physical well-being, it greatly enriches our mental lives. This enrichment does not come from providing definitive answers to philosophical questions, for practically all philosophical questions remain undecided. For example, no one has ever proved—or is likely ever to prove—that the universe has or does not have a purpose. For Russell, the uncertainty in philosophy is an asset rather than a liability: By teaching us to inquire about the universe and to question our ordinary beliefs, philosophy liberates us from the prejudices of common sense, culture, and custom. Although philosophy does not provide definite answers about how things *are*, it broadens our mind by showing us many different ways that they *might be*.

A further value of philosophy, according to Russell, is its ability to free us from our instinctive tendency to interpret everything in terms of self. By attempting to see the universe as it is, rather than simply how it affects us, we enlarge our self by leaving behind (as much as is possible) our hopes and fears, our preconceptions and prejudices. And when we enlarge our self, we also enlarge the sphere of our actions and affections.

Having now come to the end of our brief and very incomplete review of the problems of philosophy, it will be well to consider, in conclusion, what is the value of philosophy and why it ought to be studied. It is the more necessary to consider this question, in view of the fact that many men, under the influence of science or of practical affairs, are inclined to doubt whether philosophy is anything better than innocent but useless trifling, hair-splitting distinctions, and controversies on matters concerning which knowledge is impossible.

This view of philosophy appears to result, partly from a wrong conception of the ends of life, partly from a wrong conception of the kind of goods which philosophy strives to achieve. Physical science, through the medium of inventions, is useful to innumerable people who are wholly ignorant of it; thus the study of physical science is to be recommended, not only, or primarily, because of the effect on the student, but rather because of the effect on mankind in general. This utility does not belong to philosophy. If the study of philosophy has any value at all for other than students of philosophy, it must be only indirectly, through its effects upon the lives of those who study it. It is in these effects, therefore, if anywhere, that the value of philosophy must be primarily sought.

But further, if we are not to fail in our endeavor to determine the value of philosophy, we must first free our minds from the prejudices of what are wrongly called "practical" men. The "practical" man, as this word is often used, is one who recognizes only material needs, who realizes that men must have food for the body, but is oblivious of the necessity of providing food for the mind. If all men were well off, if poverty and disease had been reduced to their lowest possible point, there would still remain much to be done to produce a valuable society; and even in the existing world the goods of the mind are at least as important as the goods of the body. It is exclusively among the goods of the mind that the value of philosophy is to be found; and only those who are not indifferent to these goods can be persuaded that the study of philosophy is not a waste of time.

Philosophy, like all other studies, aims primarily at knowledge. The knowledge it aims at is the kind of knowledge which gives unity and system to the body of the sciences, and the kind which results from a critical examination of the grounds of our convictions, prejudices, and beliefs. But it cannot be maintained that philosophy has had any very great measure of success in its attempts to provide definite answers to its questions. If you ask a mathematician, a mineralogist, a historian, or any other man of learning, what definite body of truths has been ascertained by his science, his answer will last as long as you are willing to listen. But if you put the same question to a philosopher, he will, if he is candid, have to confess that his study has not achieved positive results such as have been achieved by other sciences. It is true that this is partly accounted for by the fact that, as soon as definite knowledge concerning any subject becomes possible, this subject ceases to be called philosophy, and becomes a separate science. The whole study of the heavens, which now belongs to astronomy, was once included in philosophy; Newton's great work was called "the mathematical principles of natural philosophy."[1] Similarly, the study of the human mind, which was, until very lately, a part of philosophy, has now been separated from philosophy and has become the science of psychology. Thus, to a great extent, the uncertainty of philosophy is more apparent than real: Those questions which are already capable of definite answers are placed in the sciences, while those only to which, at present, no definite answer can be given, remain to form the residue which is called philosophy.

This is, however, only a part of the truth concerning the uncertainty of philosophy. There are many questions—and among them those that are of the profoundest interest to our spiritual life—which, so far as we can see, must remain

insoluble to the human intellect unless its powers become of quite a different order from what they are now. Has the universe any unity of plan or purpose, or
is it a fortuitous concourse of atoms? Is consciousness a permanent part of the
universe, giving hope of indefinite growth in wisdom, or is it a transitory accident on a small planet on which life must ultimately become impossible? Are
good and evil of importance to the universe or only to man? Such questions are
asked by philosophy, and variously answered by various philosophers. But it
would seem that, whether answers be otherwise discoverable or not, the answers suggested by philosophy are none of them demonstrably true. Yet, however slight may be the hope of discovering an answer, it is part of the business
of philosophy to continue the consideration of such questions, to make us aware
of their importance, to examine all the approaches to them, and to keep alive
that speculative interest in the universe which is apt to be killed by confining
ourselves to definitely ascertainable knowledge.

Many philosophers, it is true, have held that philosophy could establish the
truth of certain answers to such fundamental questions. They have supposed
that what is of most importance in religious beliefs could be proved by strict
demonstration to be true. In order to judge of such attempts, it is necessary to
take a survey of human knowledge, and to form an opinion as to its methods
and its limitations. On such a subject it would be unwise to pronounce dogmat-
ically; but if the investigations of our previous chapters have not led us astray,
we shall be compelled to renounce the hope of finding philosophical proofs of
religious beliefs. We cannot, therefore, include as part of the value of philosophy any definite set of answers to such questions. Hence, once more, the value
of philosophy must not depend upon any supposed body of definitely ascertainable knowledge to be acquired by those who study it.

The value of philosophy is, in fact, to be sought largely in its very uncertainty. The man who has no tincture of philosophy goes through life imprisoned
in the prejudices derived from common sense, from the habitual beliefs of his
age or his nation, and from convictions which have grown up in his mind without the cooperation or consent of his deliberate reason. To such a man the world
tends to become definite, finite, obvious; common objects rouse no questions,
and unfamiliar possibilities are contemptuously rejected. As soon as we begin
to philosophize, on the contrary, we find . . . that even the most everyday things
lead to problems to which only very incomplete answers can be given. Philosophy, though unable to tell us with certainty what is the true answer to the
doubts which it raises, is able to suggest many possibilities which enlarge our
thoughts and free them from the tyranny of custom. Thus, while diminishing
our feeling of certainty as to what things are, it greatly increases our knowledge
as to what they may be; it removes the somewhat arrogant dogmatism of those
who have never travelled into the region of liberating doubt, and it keeps alive
our sense of wonder by showing familiar things in an unfamiliar aspect.

Apart from its utility in showing unsuspected possibilities, philosophy has
a value—perhaps its chief value—through the greatness of the objects which it
contemplates, and the freedom from narrow and personal aims resulting from
this contemplation. The life of the instinctive man is shut up within the circle of
his private interests: Family and friends may be included, but the outer world is

not regarded except as it may help or hinder what comes within the circle of instinctive wishes. In such a life there is something feverish and confined, in comparison with which the philosophic life is calm and free. The private world of
instinctive interests is a small one, set in the midst of a great and powerful world
which must, sooner or later, lay our private world in ruins. Unless we can so enlarge our interests as to include the whole outer world, we remain like a garrison
in a beleaguered fortress, knowing that the enemy prevents escape and that ultimate surrender is inevitable. In such a life there is no peace, but a constant strife
between the insistence of desire and the powerlessness of will. In one way or another, if our life is to be great and free, we must escape this prison and this strife.

One way of escape is by philosophic contemplation. Philosophic contemplation does not, in its widest survey, divide the universe into two hostile
camps—friends and foes, helpful and hostile, good and bad—it views the
whole impartially. Philosophic contemplation, when it is unalloyed, does not
aim at proving that the rest of the universe is akin to man. All acquisition of
knowledge is an enlargement of the self, but this enlargement is best attained
when it is not directly sought. It is obtained when the desire for knowledge is
alone operative, by a study which does not wish in advance that its objects
should have this or that character, but adapts the self to the characters which it
finds in its objects. This enlargement of self is not obtained when, taking the self
as it is, we try to show that the world is so similar to this self that knowledge of
it is possible without any admission of what seems alien. The desire to prove
this is a form of self-assertion, and like all self-assertion, it is an obstacle to the
growth of self which it desires, and of which the self knows that it is capable.
Self-assertion, in philosophic speculation as elsewhere, views the world as a
means to its own ends; thus it makes the world of less account than self, and the
self sets bounds to the greatness of its goods. In contemplation, on the contrary,
we start from the not-self, and through its greatness the boundaries of self are
enlarged; through the infinity of the universe the mind which contemplates it
achieves some share in infinity.

For this reason greatness of soul is not fostered by those philosophies which
assimilate the universe to man. Knowledge is a form of union of self and not-self;
like all union, it is impaired by dominion, and therefore by any attempt to force
the universe into conformity with what we find in ourselves. There is a widespread philosophical tendency towards the view which tells us that man is the
measure of all things, that truth is man-made, that space and time and the world
of universals[2] are properties of the mind, and that, if there be anything not created by the mind, it is unknowable and of no account for us. This view . . . is untrue; but in addition to being untrue, it has the effect of robbing philosophic
contemplation of all that gives it value, since it fetters contemplation to self. What
it calls knowledge is not a union with the not-self, but a set of prejudices, habits,
and desires, making an impenetrable veil between us and the world beyond. The
man who finds pleasure in such a theory of knowledge is like the man who never
leaves the domestic circle for fear his word might not be law.

The true philosophic contemplation, on the contrary, finds its satisfaction
in every enlargement of the not-self, in everything that magnifies the objects

contemplated, and thereby the subject contemplating. Everything, in contemplation, that is personal or private, everything that depends upon habit, self-interest, or desire, distorts the object, and hence impairs the union which the intellect seeks. By thus making a barrier between subject and object, such personal and private things become a prison to the intellect. The free intellect will see as God might see, without a *here* and *now,* without hopes and fears, without the trammels of customary beliefs and traditional prejudices, calmly, dispassionately, in the sole and exclusive desire of knowledge—knowledge as impersonal, as purely contemplative, as it is possible for man to attain. Hence also the free intellect will value more the abstract and universal knowledge into which the accidents of private history do not enter, than the knowledge brought by the senses, and dependent, as such knowledge must be, upon an exclusive and personal point of view and a body whose sense-organs distort as much as they reveal.

The mind which has become accustomed to the freedom and impartiality of philosophic contemplation will preserve something of the same freedom and impartiality in the world of action and emotion. It will view its purposes and desires as parts of the whole, with the absence of insistence that results from seeing them as infinitesimal fragments in a world of which all the rest is unaffected by any one man's deeds. The impartiality which, in contemplation, is the unalloyed desire for truth, is the very same quality of mind which, in action, is justice, and in emotion is that universal love which can be given to all, and not only to those who are judged useful or admirable. Thus contemplation enlarges not only the objects of our thoughts, but also the objects of our actions and our affections; it makes us citizens of the universe, not only of one walled city at war with all the rest. In this citizenship of the universe consists man's true freedom, and his liberation from the thralldom of narrow hopes and fears.

Thus, to sum up our discussion of the value of philosophy: Philosophy is to be studied, not for the sake of any definite answers to its questions, since no definite answers can, as a rule, be known to be true, but rather for the sake of the questions themselves; because these questions enlarge our conception of what is possible, enrich our intellectual imagination, and diminish the dogmatic assurance which closes the mind against speculation; but above all because, through the greatness of the universe which philosophy contemplates, the mind also is rendered great, and becomes capable of that union with the universe which constitutes its highest good.

NOTES

1. Isaac Newton (1642–1727) was an English mathematician and physicist. His *Philosophiae Naturalis Principia Mathematica* ("The Mathematical Principles of Natural Philosophy") was published in 1687. [D. C. ABEL]
2. *universals:* realities corresponding to general concepts or terms. [D. C. ABEL]

Philosophy of Religion

Religion plays an important role in the lives of the vast majority of human beings. Adherents of religion are aptly called "believers" because their commitment to their doctrines is based on faith. But could one's faith be misplaced and mistaken? Is it reasonable to accept doctrines on faith? Can some religious beliefs, most of all the belief that God exists, be supported—or even *proved*—by strictly rational argumentation? These are some of the questions addressed by the branch of philosophy called the philosophy of religion.

Since the fundamental doctrine of practically every religion is that there is a God (there are exceptions, such as Theravada Buddhism), the central question of the philosophy of religion is whether God's existence can be proved. Relying on reason and experience rather than faith, can we show that there must be a Supreme Being? Can we show that this Supreme Being is (in some sense of the word) a *person?* A second major topic in the philosophy of religion is the "problem of evil." Let us suppose that there is a personal God (whether or not this can be proved) and that God is all-good and all-powerful. How then do we account for the existence of evil? If God is all-good, God would presumably want to eliminate all evils in the world, such as human and animal suffering. If God is all-powerful, God would presumably be able to eliminate all evils. Yet there is abundant evil in the world. This problem of evil has led some philosophers to claim that we can prove that God does *not* exist. A third major topic in the philosophy of religion is the connection of faith to reason. Is it reasonable to accept religious beliefs, or does faith lie wholly outside the realm of reason? Can there be legitimate *non*rational grounds for accepting claims that cannot be decided rationally?

Our readings present a diversity of views on each of these three topics. The first group of readings, "The Existence of God," includes arguments both for and against God's existence. Anselm presents what is now known as the "ontological argument" for the existence of God. He defines God as "something than which nothing greater can be thought" and claims that once we admit that such a being exists in our understanding, we must also admit that it exists in reality—for if it existed only in our understanding, it would *not* be something than which nothing greater can be thought because a being that also existed in reality would be greater. Thomas Aquinas rejects Anselm's ontological argument and formulates five succinct proofs of his own. He argues that there must be a first mover, a first cause of change, a necessary being that is its own source of necessity, a being that causes the perfections in all other beings, and a being that directs natural beings toward their goals—and he concludes that God is each of these five things. In the next reading, William Paley sets forth the "argument from design": Just as the existence of a watch indicates the existence of an intelligent artisan, so the existence of the infinitely more complex works of nature implies the existence of an intelligent Creator. In fictional dialogues that question the validity of traditional arguments for God's existence, David Hume has Philo raise objections to Cleanthes' argument from design and has Cleanthes reject Demea's argument that there must be a first cause. In the final reading in this section, Richard Dawkins argues that the scientific theory of cumulative natural selection can explain the origin of complex organisms without recourse to an intelligent designer.

The second section, "The Problem of Evil," contains three readings. Augustine contends that the evil that we suffer is God's just punishment for our evildoing, and that evildoing consists in our freely choosing to misuse our free will. J. L. Mackie argues that the various attempts made by theists to reconcile the existence of evil with the power and goodness of God are unsuccessful because they end up limiting either God's power or God's goodness. John Hick explains the answers to the problem of evil proposed by Augustine, Irenaeus, and contemporary "process theologians." Hick concludes that although each answer can be challenged (he refers to Mackie's objections, for example), many believers find one or more of these responses sufficient to preserve their belief in God.

The final section, "Faith and Reason," presents two views in support of religious belief. Blaise Pascal contends that since we are unable, in this life, to know whether God exists, we must make a "wager" and either believe or not believe—and that it is more reasonable to lay down our wager on the side of belief. William James argues that it is legitimate for our "passional nature" to accept or reject certain hypotheses that cannot be settled on rational grounds—and that "the religious hypothesis" is one such postulate.

A. The Existence of God

READING 3 ## Proslogion and Exchange with Gaunilo
Anselm

Anselm was born in Aosta, Italy, in about 1033. Despite objections from his father, who wanted him to pursue a career in politics, Anselm joined the Benedictine order, entering the monastery at Bec in Normandy, France, in 1060. He became prior of Bec in 1063 and abbot in 1078. As abbot he made several trips to England to inspect the lands that William the Conqueror had given to the monastery. Anselm made many friends in England and in 1093 was appointed Archbishop of Canterbury by William Rufus (son and successor of William the Conqueror). Anselm subsequently became involved in a series of controversies about the authority of secular rulers in ecclesiastical matters, strongly defending the autonomy of the Church. He died at Canterbury in 1109.

Anselm's major works are the *Monologion* ("Soliloquy," originally entitled "An Example of Meditation on the Meaning of Faith"), the *Proslogion* ("Discourse," originally entitled "Faith Seeking Understanding"), and *Cur Deus Homo* ("Why God Became a Human Being"). Our readings consist of (1) the section from the *Proslogion* in which Anselm presents his "ontological argument" for the existence of God, (2) an excerpt from a short work by Gaunilo (a monk contemporary with Anselm) that criticizes the ontological argument, and (3) a section from Anselm's reply to Gaunilo. (The term "ontological argument" is not Anselm's; it seems to have been coined in the eighteenth century by Immanuel Kant.)

Our reading from the *Proslogion* begins with Anselm's declaration that he believes that God is "something than which nothing greater can be thought." But does this God exist? Not everyone thinks so; the fool in the Book of Psalms, for example, says in his heart that there is no God. Anselm observes that the fool nonetheless understands what it is whose existence he or she is denying. And since whatever someone understands exists in the understanding, God exists in the fool's understanding. To exist in the understanding, of course, is different from existing in reality. Anselm then points out that to exist in reality is greater than to exist only in the understanding. But this means that it is self-contradictory to deny that God exists in reality: A person cannot consistently say that "something than which nothing greater can be thought" does not exist in reality, because if this being did *not* exist in reality, the person *could* conceive a greater being—namely, one that exists not only in the understanding but also in reality. And then the being which, by definition, is that than which nothing greater can be conceived, is one than which a greater *can* be conceived—an obvious contradiction.

Gaunilo, in his brief work "On Behalf of the Fool" (namely, the fool in the Book of Psalms who says that there is no God), contends that the ontological argument is invalid because this type of reasoning leads to obviously false conclusions. One could prove, for example, that a perfect island exists because it wouldn't be perfect if it existed only in our understanding. Anselm responds to Gaunilo's objection by denying that the ontological argument can be applied to an island or to any other finite being. For the only being whose nonexistence cannot be thought is the being than which nothing greater can be thought, and only God fits this description.

PROSLOGION

Chapter 2. That God Truly Exists

Lord, you who grant understanding to faith, grant that, insofar as you know it is useful for me, I may understand that you exist as we believe you exist, and that you are what we believe you to be. Now we believe that you are something than which nothing greater can be thought. So can it be that no such being exists, since "The fool has said in his heart, 'There is no God'"?[1] But when this same fool hears me say "something than which nothing greater can be thought," he surely understands what he hears; and what he understands exists in his understanding, even if he does not understand that it exists [in reality]. For it is one thing for an object to exist in the understanding and quite another to understand that the object exists [in reality]. When a painter, for example, thinks out in advance what he is going to paint, he has it in his understanding, but he does not yet understand that it exists, since he has not yet painted it. But once he has painted it, he both has it in his understanding and understands that it exists because he has now painted it. So even the fool must admit that something than which nothing greater can be thought exists at least in his understanding, since he understands this when he hears it, and whatever is understood exists in the understanding. And surely that than which a greater cannot be thought cannot exist only in the understanding. For if it exists only in the understanding, it can be thought to exist in reality as well, which is greater. So if that than which a greater cannot be thought exists only in the understanding, then that than which a greater *cannot* be thought is that than which a greater *can* be thought. But that is clearly impossible. Therefore, there is no doubt that something than which a greater cannot be thought exists both in the understanding and in reality.

Chapter 3. That He Cannot Be Thought Not to Exist

This [being] exists so truly that it cannot be thought not to exist. For it is possible to think that something exists that cannot be thought not to exist, and such a being is greater than one that can be thought not to exist. Therefore, if that than which a greater cannot be thought can be thought not to exist, then that than which a greater cannot be thought is *not* that than which a greater cannot be thought; and this is a contradiction. So that than which a greater cannot be thought exists so truly that it cannot be thought not to exist.

And this is you, O Lord our God. You exist so truly, O Lord my God, that you cannot be thought not to exist. And rightly so, for if some mind could think something better than you, a creature would rise above the Creator and sit in judgment upon him, which is completely absurd. Indeed, everything that exists, except for you alone, can be thought not to exist. So you alone among all things have existence most truly, and therefore most greatly. Whatever else exists has existence less truly, and therefore less greatly. So then why did "the fool say in his heart, 'There is no God,'" when it is so evident to the rational mind that you of all beings exist most greatly? Why indeed, except because he is stupid and a fool?

Chapter 4. How the Fool Said in His Heart What Cannot Be Thought

But how has he said in his heart what he could not think? Or how could he not think what he said in his heart, since to say in one's heart is the same as to think? But if he really—or rather, *since* he really—thought this, because he said it in his heart, and did not say it in his heart, because he could not think it, there must be more than one way in which something is "said in one's heart" or "thought." In one sense of the word, to think a thing is to think the word that signifies that thing. But in another sense, it is to understand what exactly the thing is. God can be thought not to exist in the first sense, but not at all in the second sense. No one who understands what God is can think that God does not exist, although he may say these words in his heart with no signification at all, or with some peculiar signification. For God is that than which a greater cannot be thought. Whoever understands this properly, understands that this being exists in such a way that he cannot, even in thought, fail to exist. So whoever understands that God exists in this way cannot think that he does not exist.

   Thanks be to you, my good Lord, thanks be to you. For what I once believed through your grace, I now understand through your illumination, so that even if I did not want to *believe* that you exist, I could not fail to *understand* that you exist.

Chapter 5. That God Is Whatever It Is Better to Be Than Not to Be; and That He Alone Exists Through Himself, and Makes All Other Things from Nothing

Then what are you, Lord God, than whom nothing greater can be thought? What are you, if not the greatest of all beings, who alone exists through himself and made all other things from nothing? For whatever is not this is less than the greatest than can be thought, but this cannot be thought of you. What good is missing from the highest good, through which every good thing exists? And so you are just, truthful, happy, and whatever it is better to be than not to be. For it is better to be just than unjust, and better to be happy than unhappy.

GAUNILO'S REPLY ON BEHALF OF THE FOOL

. . . I am offered the . . . argument that [something than which nothing greater can be thought] necessarily exists in reality, since if it did not, everything that exists in reality would be greater than it. And so this thing, which of course has been proved to exist in the understanding, would not be greater than everything else. To that argument I reply that if we are to say that something exists in the understanding that cannot even be thought on the basis of the true nature of any-thing whatever, then I shall not deny that even this thing exists in my under-standing. But since there is no way to derive from this the conclusion that this thing also exists in reality, there is simply no reason for me to concede to him that this thing exists in reality until it is proved to me by some unassailable argument.

And when he says that this thing exists because otherwise that which is greater than everything else would not be greater than everything else, he does not fully realize whom he is addressing. For I do not yet admit—indeed, I ac-tually deny, or at least doubt—that this greater being is greater than any real thing. Nor do I concede that it exists at all, except in the sense that something ex-ists (if you want to call it "existence") when my mind tries to imagine some com-pletely unknown thing solely on the basis of a word that it has heard. How, then, is the fact that this being has been proved to be greater than everything else sup-posed to show me that it exists in actual fact? For I continue to deny, or at least doubt, that this has been proved, so that I do not admit that this thing exists in my understanding or thought even in the way that many doubtful and uncer-tain things exist there. First I must become certain that this thing truly exists somewhere, and only then will the fact that it is greater than everything else show clearly that it also subsists in itself.

For example, there are those who say that somewhere in the ocean is an island that, because of the difficulty—or rather, impossibility—of finding what does not exist, some call "the Lost Island." This island (so the story goes) is more plentifully endowed than even the Isles of the Blessed with an indescribable abundance of all sorts of riches and delights. And because it has neither owner nor inhabitant, it is everywhere superior in its abundant riches to all the other lands that human be-ings inhabit. Suppose that someone tells me all this. The story is easily told and in-volves no difficulty, and so I understand it. But if this person went on to draw a conclusion, and say, "You cannot any longer doubt that this island, more excellent than all others on earth, truly exists somewhere in reality. For you do not doubt that this island exists in your understanding, and since it is more excellent to ex-ist not merely in the understanding, but also in reality, this island must also exist in reality. For if it did not, any land that exists in reality would be greater than it. And so this more excellent thing that you have understood would not in fact be more excellent."—If, I say, he should try to convince me by this argument that I should no longer doubt whether the island truly exists, either I would think he was joking, or I would not know whom I ought to think more foolish: myself, if I grant him his conclusion, or him, if he thinks he can establish the existence of that island with any degree of certainty, without first showing that its excellence exists in my understanding [precisely] as a thing that truly and undoubtedly exists, and not in any way like something false or uncertain.

ANSELM'S REPLY TO GAUNILO

. . . I said that if [something than which nothing greater can be thought] exists only in the understanding, it can be thought to exist in reality as well, which is greater. Therefore, if it exists only in the understanding, the very same thing is both that than which a greater *cannot* be thought and that than which a greater *can* be thought. Now I ask you, what could be more logical? For if it exists only in the understanding, can it not be thought to exist in reality as well? And if it can, does not the one who thinks it, think something greater than that thing is if it exists only in the understanding? So if that than which a greater *cannot* be thought exists only in the understanding, it is that than which a greater *can* be thought: What more logical conclusion could there be? But of course that than which a greater cannot be thought is not the same in anyone's understanding as that than which a greater can be thought. Does it not follow, therefore, that if that than which a greater cannot be thought exists in any understanding at all, it does not exist only in the understanding? For if it exists only in the understanding, it is that than which a greater can be thought, which is absurd.

But, you say, this is just the same as if someone were to claim that it cannot be doubted that a certain island in the ocean, surpassing all other lands in its fertility (which, from the difficulty—or rather, impossibility—of finding what does not exist, is called "the Lost Island"), exists in reality, because someone can easily understand it when it is described to him in words. I say quite confidently that if anyone can find for me something existing either in reality or only in thought to which he can apply this inference in my argument, besides that than which a greater cannot be thought, I will find and give to him that Lost Island, never to be lost again. In fact, however, it has already become quite clear that that than which a greater cannot be thought cannot be thought not to exist, since its existence is a matter of such certain truth. For otherwise it would not exist at all. Finally, if someone says that he thinks it does not exist, I say that when he thinks this, either he is thinking something than which a greater cannot be thought, or he is not. If he is not, then he is not thinking that it does not exist, since he is not thinking it at all. But if he is, he is surely thinking something that cannot be thought not to exist. For if it could be thought not to exist, it could be thought to have a beginning and an end, which is impossible. Therefore, someone who is thinking it, is thinking something that cannot be thought not to exist. And of course someone who is thinking this, does not think that that very thing does not exist. Otherwise he would be thinking something that cannot be thought. Therefore, that than which a greater cannot be thought cannot be thought not to exist.

NOTE

1. Psalms 15:1 (14:1 in some versions); Psalms 53:1 (51:1). [D. C. ABEL]

Treatise on God

Thomas Aquinas

Thomas Aquinas was born in Roccasecca, Italy, in about 1224. After receiving his initial education from the Benedictine monks at Monte Cassino, he studied at the University of Naples, where he encountered members of the Dominican order. Attracted to the Dominicans, he joined the order despite opposition from his family. He was trained in philosophy and theology in Paris and in Cologne, Germany, under the Dominican Albert (later known as Albert the Great). After being ordained a priest, Aquinas pursued advanced studies in theology at the University of Paris, receiving his degree in 1256. He taught for a few years at the University of Paris and was then assigned to teach at various Dominican schools in Italy. Aquinas returned to the University of Paris in 1268, but four years later he went back to Italy to establish a new Dominican house of study at the University of Naples. He died in 1274 at Fossanova, Italy, while traveling to Lyons to serve as a papal consultant at the Second Council of Lyons.

Aquinas's major works include *Summa Contra Gentiles* ("Comprehensive Treatise against the Gentiles"), *Summa Theologiae* ("Comprehensive Treatise on Theology"), *Disputed Questions* (summaries of debates he conducted on various topics as a professor of theology), and detailed commentaries on the principal works of Aristotle.

Our reading is from the section of Part One of the *Summa Theologiae* known as the "Treatise on God." More specifically, the reading is the second "question" (topic) of this section, "On the Existence of God." This question consists of three "articles" (subdivisions). The first article asks whether the existence of God is self-evident. (If God's existence is self-evident, there would seem to be no need to formulate a proof that God exists.) Aquinas contends that God's existence is self-evident *in itself* but not *to us*. A proposition is self-evident in itself if the subject implies the predicate. Since God *is* existence (as Aquinas argues elsewhere), the term "God" implies "existence" and God's existence is therefore self-evident in itself. But God's existence is not self-evident to us because our limited human minds are incapable of grasping the full meaning of the term "God."

Since God's existence is not self-evident to us, Aquinas proceeds to ask, in the second article, whether the existence of God can be demonstrated (proved). He explains that God's existence can be demonstrated by reasoning from effects that we experience, back to God as their cause. In the third article, Aquinas presents five proofs that God exists, based on five kinds of facts that we experience. (1) The fact that there are things in motion implies that there is a first mover that is not itself in motion—and this first mover is God. (2) The fact that there are series of efficient causes (agents that bring things into existence or impart change) implies that there is a first efficient cause—and this first cause is God. (3) The fact that there are possible beings (beings that can not-exist) implies that there must be a necessary being (a being that *cannot* not-exist) that is its own source of necessity—and this being is God. (4) The fact that there are beings with different degrees of various perfections (for example, of goodness) implies that there is a being that is the cause of all these perfections—and this being is God. (5) Finally, the fact that natural beings without intelligence act for goals (for example, plants act to grow and reproduce) implies that there is an intelligent being that directs natural beings toward their goals—and this being is God.

Note that Aquinas begins each article by formulating objections against his own view. Then, after setting forth his own position, he responds to the objections he raised.

QUESTION 2. ON THE EXISTENCE OF GOD

First Article. Is the Existence of God Self-Evident?

I proceed in this way to the first article: It seems that the existence of God is self-evident.

Objection 1. Things of which we possess knowledge by nature, are said to be self-evident to us, as is manifest in the case of first principles. But, as Damascene says in the beginning of his book, "All are by nature endowed with knowledge of God's existence."[1] Therefore, the existence of God is self-evident.

Objection 2. Things that we know as soon as we know terms, are said to be self-evident, and the Philosopher in the *Posterior Analytics* attributes this to the first principles of demonstration;[2] when one knows what a whole is, and what a part is, one immediately knows that every whole is greater than one of its parts. But when one understands what the term "God" means, one immediately grasps that God exists, for the term "God" means that than which nothing greater can be signified. What exists in fact as well as in the intellect, however, is greater than what exists in the intellect alone. And so, since God exists in the intellect as soon as we understand the term "God," it also follows that God exists in fact. Therefore, the existence of God is self-evident.[3]

Objection 3. The existence of truth is self-evident, because one who denies the existence of truth admits its existence: If there is indeed no truth, it is true that truth does not exist; if, on the other hand, something is true, it is necessary that truth exists. But God is truth itself, as John says: "I am the way, the truth, and the life."[4] Therefore, the existence of God is self-evident.

On the contrary, no one can think the opposite of what is self-evident, as the Philosopher makes clear in the *Metaphysics*[5] and the *Posterior Analytics*[6] concerning the first principles of demonstration. But one can think the opposite of the proposition that God exists, as the Psalm says: "The fool has said in his heart, 'God does not exist.'"[7] Therefore, the existence of God is not self-evident.

I answer that something may be self-evident in two ways: in one way, in itself but not to us; in the second way, in itself and to us. For a proposition is self-evident because its predicate is contained in its subject's essence, as in the proposition "Human beings are animals," for "animal" belongs to the nature of "human being." Therefore, if all know the proposition's predicate and its subject's essence, the proposition will be self-evident to all. This is evident, for example, in the case of the first principles of demonstration, whose terms are general notions that everyone knows: being and nonbeing, whole and part, and the like. If, however, some persons happen not to know the predicate and the subject's essence, the proposition will indeed be self-evident in itself but not to those who do not know the predicate and the subject. And so it happens, as Boethius says in his book *De Hebdomatibus*, that only the wise have certain general and self-evident notions, such as "Incorporeal things do not exist in a place."[8]

I say, therefore, that the proposition "God exists" is in itself self-evident, because its predicate is the same as its subject; God is indeed his existence. . . . But because we do not know what God is, the proposition is not self-evident to us but needs to be demonstrated by things more known to us and less known as regards their nature—namely, by effects.

Reply to Objection 1. We are by nature endowed with knowledge of God's existence in a general way, with a certain confusion—namely, insofar as God is the happiness of human beings, for human beings by nature desire happiness, and they by nature know what they by nature desire. But this is not to know unconditionally that God exists, just as to know that someone is approaching, is not to know Peter, although Peter is the one who is approaching. For many deem riches to be the perfect human good, which is happiness, but certain others deem sensual pleasures the perfect human good, while still others deem something else the perfect human good.

Reply to Objection 2. Perhaps someone who hears the term "God," does not understand that it means that than which nothing greater can be thought, since some believe that God is a material substance. Even supposing that someone understands that the term "God" means what we assert (namely, that than which nothing greater can be thought), yet it does not thereby follow that such a one would understand that what the term means, exists in the real world, but only that it exists in the intellect's apprehension. Nor can it be proved that God really exists unless one grants that there really exists something than which no greater can be thought, and this is not granted by those who hold that God does not exist.

Reply to Objection 3. The existence of truth in general is self-evident, but it is not self-evident to us that a First Truth exists.

Second Article. Can We Demonstrate the Existence of God?

I proceed in this way to the second article: It seems that we cannot demonstrate the existence of God.

Objection 1. The existence of God is an article of faith. But we cannot demonstrate what belongs to faith, since demonstration causes knowledge, while faith concerns things that are not evident, as the Apostle [Paul] makes clear in the Letter to the Hebrews.[9] Therefore, we cannot demonstrate the existence of God.

Objection 2. The means of a demonstration is something's essence. But we cannot know what God is, but only what he is not, as Damascene says.[10] Therefore, we cannot demonstrate that God exists.

Objection 3. If one were to demonstrate the existence of God, this would be only by his effects. But his effects are not proportioned to him, since he himself is infinite, and the effects are finite, while there is no proportion of the finite to the infinite. Therefore, since we cannot demonstrate a cause by an effect that is not proportioned to its cause, it seems that we cannot demonstrate the existence of God.

On the contrary, the Apostle says in the Letter to the Romans, "The invisible things of God are visible when understood through the things that have been made."[11] But this would only be the case if we could demonstrate the existence of God through what he has made, for the first thing that we need to understand about something, is whether or not it exists.

I answer that we demonstrate in two ways. One is by means of a cause, and we call this a "demonstration why" something is so, and it is by means of what is first without qualification. The other is by means of an effect, and we call this a "demonstration that" something is, and this demonstration is by what is first as to us, for we proceed to knowledge of a cause through its effect, because the effect is more manifest to us than its cause is. But we can demonstrate the existence of a particular cause from any of its effects—provided that the cause's effects are nonetheless more known in relation to us—because effects depend on their cause, and so a cause necessarily preexists whenever an effect is posited. Therefore, since God's existence is not self-evident in relation to us, we can demonstrate his existence by means of the effects known to us.

Reply to Objection 1. God's existence and other such matters that natural reason can know about God, as the Letter to the Romans says,[12] are not articles of faith but preambles to the articles, for faith in this way presupposes natural knowledge, as grace presupposes nature, and as perfecting presupposes something perfectible. Nothing, however, prevents someone who does not undertake a demonstration, from accepting as an object of faith something that in itself can be demonstrated and known.

Reply to Objection 2. When a cause is demonstrated by means of its effect, we need to use the effect instead of the cause's definition to prove that the cause exists, and this happens especially in the case of God. This is so because, in order to prove the existence of something, we need to take as the means of demonstration what the term means, not what the object is, since the question "What is it?" logically follows the question "Does it exist?" We posit names of God, however, from his effects. . . . Therefore, when we demonstrate the existence of God from effects, we can take as the means of demonstration what the name "God" means.

Reply to Objection 3. We cannot have perfect knowledge about a cause by means of effects unproportioned to their cause, but we can nonetheless clearly demonstrate the existence of such a cause by any one of the cause's effects, as I have said. And so we can demonstrate God's existence by means of his effects, although we cannot perfectly know him according to his essence by the effects.

Third Article. Does God Exist?

I proceed in this way to the third article: It seems that God does not exist.

Objection 1. It seems that God does not exist: If one of two contraries is infinite, the other would be completely destroyed. But we understand by the term "God" something infinite—namely, something good without limit. Therefore, if God were to exist, we would not find anything bad. But we do find bad things in the world. Therefore, God does not exist.

Objection 2. More sources do not accomplish what fewer sources can. But, supposing that God does not exist, other sources seem capable of accomplishing everything evident in the world, since we trace things of nature back to nature as their source, and we trace things of free choice back to human reason or will as their source. Therefore, we do not need to posit that God exists.

On the contrary, the Book of Exodus says in the person of God: "I am who am."[13]

I answer that we can prove in five ways that God exists.

The FIRST and more evident WAY, moreover, is the one we take from motion,[14] for it is sure and evident to the senses that some things in this world are moved. But everything moved is moved by something else. For an object is only moved insofar as it has potentiality for that to which it is moved, while something produces motion only insofar as it is actual. To move something, certainly, is only to bring it from potentiality to actuality, and only an actual being can bring something to actuality. For example, something actually hot, like fire, causes wood, which is potentially hot, to be actually hot, and thereby moves and changes the wood. The same object, however, cannot at the same time be actual and potential in the same respect but only in different respects; for example, something actually hot cannot at the same time be potentially hot, although it is at the same time potentially cold. Nothing, therefore, can produce and undergo motion, or move itself, in the same respect and in the same way. Everything that is moved, therefore, needs to be moved by something else. Therefore, if the cause of a motion is moved, the cause itself needs to be moved by another, and that other by another. But this regress ought not to be endless, because there would thus be no first cause of motion and so no other cause of motion, since second causes produce motion only because the first cause moves them. A stick, for example, only causes motion because a hand moves it. Therefore, we need to arrive at a first cause of motion, one that is moved by nothing else, and all understand this first cause of motion to be God.

The SECOND WAY is by considering efficient causes. For we find that there is an order of efficient causes in the case of those sensible[15] objects, and yet we do not find, nor can we, that anything is the efficient cause of its very self, because such a thing would thus pre-exist itself, and this is impossible. But we cannot regress endlessly in the matter of efficient causes. This is so because, in all ordered efficient causes, something first causes something intermediate, and something intermediate causes something last, whether the intermediate things be several or only one. But the effect is taken away if its cause is taken away. Therefore, there will be nothing intermediate or last if there be nothing first in the case of efficient causes. But if we should regress endlessly in the case of efficient causes, there will be no first efficient cause, and there will thus be neither a final effect nor intermediate efficient causes, and this is clearly false. Therefore, we need to posit a first efficient cause, and all call this cause God.

We take the THIRD WAY from the possible and the necessary, and the argument proceeds as follows. We certainly find in reality kinds of things that can exist and can not-exist, since we find that certain things come to be and pass away, and so can exist and can not-exist. But it is impossible that all such things always exist, because what can not-exist, at some point of time does not exist. Therefore, if everything can not-exist, there was a time when nothing really existed. But if this is so, nothing would also now exist, because something nonexistent begins to exist only through the agency of something that does exist. Therefore, if nothing existed, nothing could begin to exist, and so nothing would now exist, and this conclusion is obviously false. Therefore, not every being is something that can not-exist, but there needs to be something necessary in reality. But everything necessary either has or does not have the ground of its necessity from another source. There cannot, however, be an endless regress in the case of necessary things that have the ground of their necessity in another source, just as there cannot be an endless regress in the case of efficient causes, as I have shown. We need, therefore, to posit something that is intrinsically necessary, that does not have the ground of its necessity from another source, but which causes other things to be necessary, and all call this intrinsically necessary being God.

We take the FOURTH WAY from the gradations that we find in reality. For we find in reality things that are more good and less good, more true and less true, more excellent and less excellent, and similarly in the case of other such things. But we say "more" and "less" about different things as they in various ways approximate what is most; for example, an object is hotter if it more approximates what is hottest. Therefore, there is something that is most true and most good and most excellent, and so being in the highest degree, for things that are most true, are beings in the highest degree, as the *Metaphysics* says.[16] What we call most in a genus,[17] moreover, causes everything belonging to that genus; for example, fire, which is hottest, causes everything hot, as the same work says.[18] Therefore, there exists something that causes the existing and the goodness and whatever perfection of every being, and we call this cause God.

We take the FIFTH WAY from the governance of things. For we see that certain things that lack knowledge—namely, natural material substances—act for the sake of an end.[19] And this is evident because they always or more frequently act in the same way in order to achieve what is best, and hence it is evident that they reach their goal by striving, not by chance. But things that lack knowledge, do not strive for goals unless a being with knowledge and intelligence directs them, as, for example, an archer aims an arrow. Therefore, there is a being with intelligence who orders all the things of nature to their ends, and we call this being God.

Reply to Objection 1. As Augustine says in his *Enchiridion,* "Because God is the highest good, he would in no way allow anything bad to exist in his works were he not so all-powerful and good as to act well even with respect to what is bad."[20] It belongs to the infinite goodness of God, therefore, to permit bad things and to bring forth good things from them.

Reply to Objection 2. We also need to trace things produced by nature back to God as their first cause, because nature, by reason of its fixed end, acts at the direction of a higher efficient cause. Likewise, we need to trace even things done by free choice back to a higher cause that is not the reason and will of human beings, since things done by free choice can change and fall short. We indeed need to trace everything that can change and fall short, back to a first source that cannot change and is intrinsically necessary, as I have shown.

NOTES

1. John Damascene, *On the Orthodox Faith* (a Latin translation of *Pēgē Gnōseōs* ["The Fountain of Wisdom"]), Book I, Chapter 1, Section 3. Damascene (about 675–749) was a Greek theologian. [D. C. ABEL]
2. Aristotle, *Posterior Analytics,* Book 1, Chapter 3. Aquinas regularly refers to Aristotle as simply "the Philosopher." For a biography of Aristotle, see p. 338. [D. C. ABEL]
3. This argument, now known as the "ontological argument," was first formulated by Anselm in his *Proslogion.* Anselm (about 1033–1109) was an Italian theologian and philosopher. For a biography of Anselm and the text of his argument, see pp. 27–31. [D. C. ABEL]
4. John 14:6. [W. P. BAUMGARTH AND R. J. REGAN, TRANSLATORS]
5. Aristotle, *Metaphysics,* Book III, Chapter 3. [W. P. BAUMGARTH AND R. J. REGAN]
6. Aristotle, *Posterior Analytics,* Book I, Chapter 10. [W. P. BAUMGARTH AND R. J. REGAN]
7. Psalms 15:1 (14:1 in some versions); Psalms 53:1 (51:1). [D. C. ABEL]
8. Boethius, *De Hebdomatibus* ("On Groups of Seven," also known as *How Substances Can Be Good in Virtue of Their Existence without Being Absolute Goods*), Point 1. Boethius (about 480–524) was a Roman politician, philosopher, and theologian. [D. C. ABEL]
9. Hebrews 11:1. [W. P. BAUMGARTH AND R. J. REGAN]
10. John Damascene, *On the Orthodox Faith,* Book I, Chapter 4. [D. C. ABEL]
11. Romans 1:20. [W. P. BAUMGARTH AND R. J. REGAN]
12. Romans 1:19. [W. P. BAUMGARTH AND R. J. REGAN]
13. Exodus 3:14. [W. P. BAUMGARTH AND R. J. REGAN]
14. *motion:* a change from a state of *potentiality* to a state of *actuality.* A being has a *potentiality* for receiving a new quality if it can receive it but has not actually done so; it is brought from potentiality to *actuality* when it receives the new quality. In Aquinas's terminology, motion includes not only change in location (locomotion) but other kinds of change as well (such as a qualitative change from cold to hot, to use Aquinas's example). [D. C. ABEL]
15. *sensible:* able to be sensed. [D. C. ABEL]
16. Aristotle, *Metaphysics,* Book II, Chapter 1. [W. P. BAUMGARTH AND R. J. REGAN]
17. *genus:* category. [D. C. ABEL]
18. Aristotle, *Metaphysics,* Book II, Chapter 1. [W. P. BAUMGARTH AND R. J. REGAN]
19. *end:* goal. [D. C. ABEL]
20. Augustine, *Enchiridion,* Chapter 11. Augustine (354–430) was a North African theologian and philosopher; for a biography, see p. 67. [D. C. ABEL]

Natural Theology

William Paley

William Paley was born in 1743 in Peterborough, England. In 1759 he entered Cambridge University, where he studied mathematics. He graduated from Cambridge in 1763 and three years later was elected a fellow there. He was ordained to the Anglican priesthood in 1767 and became a tutor at Cambridge the following year. In 1776 Paley ended his teaching career to take an ecclesiastical position, the rectorship of Musgrave. He was subsequently appointed to various offices in the Church. He became Archdeacon of Carlisle in 1782, but despite his great ability, he rose no higher in the Church—apparently because he held liberal political views. In 1785 Paley published *The Principles of Moral and Political Philosophy,* based on his lectures at Cambridge. He strongly defended the rationality of Christian belief in his two most influential works, *A View of the Evidence of Christianity* (1794) and *Natural Theology; or, Evidences of the Existence and Attributes of the Deity, Collected from the Appearances of Nature* (1802). He died in Lincoln in 1805.

Our selection is from *Natural Theology.* As Paley's subtitle indicates, "natural theology" refers to truths about God that can be known by reflecting on nature. "Revealed theology," by contrast, denotes doctrines made known through divine revelation. Paley contends that the design evident in living organisms proves that God exists. He begins his treatise by asking us to imagine that, when crossing a heath, we find a watch lying on the ground. We notice that all its parts work together for the purpose of measuring time. We would hardly conclude that the watch came to exist by chance; rather, we would infer that it was made by an intelligent artisan "who formed it for the purpose which we find it actually to answer; who comprehended its construction, and designed its use." If we were to find that the watch, in addition to measuring time, could produce another watch like itself, we would admire the skill of the artisan even more; for even though the watch we encounter may have been produced by a previous watch, there must have been an intelligent agent who designed watches in such a way that they could reproduce.

The kind of design evident in artificial objects like watches, Paley argues, is also present in the works of nature, "with the difference, on the side of nature, of being greater and more, and that in a degree which exceeds all computation." For example, the design of the eye is much more complex than that of the telescope. Anticipating an objection, Paley argues that the presence of imperfections in nature no more disproves the existence of an intelligent Creator than defects in watches disprove the existence of intelligent watchmakers. Furthermore, we should judge the skill of artists by their best works, not by their least perfect ones. Imperfections in the works of accomplished artists should be attributed not to personal failings but rather to "some intractableness and imperfection in the materials, or . . . some invincible difficulty in the execution."

CHAPTER I. THE STATE OF THE ARGUMENT

In crossing a heath, suppose I pitched my foot against a stone and were asked how the stone came to be there. I might possibly answer that, for anything I knew to the contrary, it had lain there forever; nor would it perhaps be very easy to show the absurdity of this answer. But suppose I had found a *watch* upon the ground and it should be inquired how the watch happened to be in that place. I should hardly think of the answer which I had given before, that, for anything I knew, the watch might have always been there. Yet why should not this answer serve for the watch as well as for the stone? Why is it not as admissible in the second case, as in the first? For this reason, and for no other, namely, that when we come to inspect the watch, we perceive (what we could not discover in the stone) that its several parts are framed and put together for a purpose—for example, that they are so formed and adjusted as to produce motion, and that motion so regulated as to point out the hour of the day; that, if the different parts had been differently shaped from what they are, of a different size from what they are, or placed after any other manner or in any other order than that in which they are placed, either no motion at all would have been carried on in the machine, or none which would have answered the use that is now served by it. To reckon up a few of the plainest of these parts and of their offices,[1] all tending to one result: We see a cylindrical box containing a coiled elastic spring which, by its endeavor to relax itself, turns round the box. We next observe a flexible chain (artificially wrought for the sake of flexure) communicating the action of the spring from the box to the fusee.[2] We then find a series of wheels, the teeth of which catch in and apply to each other, conducting the motion from the fusee to the balance, and from the balance to the pointer; and at the same time, by the size and shape of those wheels, so regulating that motion as to terminate in causing an index,[3] by an equable and measured progression, to pass over a given space in a given time. We take notice that the wheels are made of brass in order to keep them from rust; the springs of steel, no other metal being so elastic; that over the face of the watch there is placed a glass, a material employed in no other part of the work, but in the room[4] of which, if there had been any other than a transparent substance, the hour could not be seen without opening the case. This mechanism being observed (it requires indeed an examination of the instrument, and perhaps some previous knowledge of the subject, to perceive and understand it; but being once, as we have said, observed and understood), the inference, we think, is inevitable—that the watch must have had a maker, that there must have existed, at some time and at some place or other, an artificer or artificers who formed it for the purpose which we find it actually to answer, who comprehended its construction and designed its use.

1. Nor would it, I apprehend, weaken the conclusion, that we had never seen a watch made; that we had never known an artist capable of making one; that we were altogether incapable of executing such a piece of workmanship ourselves or of understanding in what manner it was performed—all this being no more than what is true of some exquisite remains of ancient art, of some lost arts, and, to the generality of mankind, of the more curious productions of modern manufacture. Does one man in a million know how oval frames are turned? Ignorance of this kind exalts our opinion of the unseen and unknown artist's skill, if he be unseen and unknown, but raises no doubt in our minds of the existence and agency of such an artist at some former time and in some place or other. Nor can I perceive that it varies at all the inference, whether the question arise concerning a human agent, or concerning an agent of a different species, or an agent possessing, in some respects, a different nature.

2. Neither, secondly, would it invalidate our conclusion, that the watch sometimes went wrong or that it seldom went exactly right. The purpose of the machinery, the design, and the designer might be evident, and in the case supposed would be evident, in whatever way we accounted for the irregularity of the movement, or whether we could account for it or not. It is not necessary that a machine be perfect in order to show with what design it was made. Still less necessary, where the only question is whether it were made with any design at all.

3. Nor, thirdly, would it bring any uncertainty into the argument if there were a few parts of the watch concerning which we could not discover, or had not yet discovered, in what manner they conduced to the general effect; or even some parts concerning which we could not ascertain whether they conduced to that effect in any manner whatever. For, as to the first branch of the case: If by the loss or disorder or decay of the parts in question, the movement of the watch were found in fact to be stopped or disturbed or retarded, no doubt would remain in our minds as to the utility or intention of these parts, although we should be unable to investigate the manner according to which, or the connection by which, the ultimate effect depended upon their action or assistance. And the more complex is the machine, the more likely is this obscurity to arise. Then, as to the second thing supposed, namely, that there were parts which might be spared without prejudice[5] to the movement of the watch, and that we had proved this by experiment: These superfluous parts, even if we were completely assured that they were such, would not vacate[6] the reasoning which we had instituted concerning other parts. The indication of contrivance remained, with respect to them, nearly as it was before.

4. Nor, fourthly, would any man in his senses think the existence of the watch, with its various machinery, accounted for, by being told that it was one out of possible combinations of material forms; that whatever he had found in the place where he found the watch, must have contained some internal configuration or other; and that this configuration might be the structure now exhibited, namely, of the works of a watch, as well as a different structure.

5. Nor, fifthly, would it yield his inquiry more satisfaction to be answered that there existed in things a principle of order which had disposed the parts of the watch into their present form and situation. He never knew a watch made by the principle of order nor can he even form to himself an idea of what is meant by a principle of order distinct from the intelligence of the watchmaker.

6. Sixthly, he would be surprised to hear that the mechanism of the watch was no proof of contrivance, only a motive to induce the mind to think so—

7. And not less surprised to be informed that the watch in his hand was nothing more than the result of the laws of metallic nature. It is a perversion of language to assign any law as the efficient, operative cause[7] of any thing. A law presupposes an agent, for it is only the mode according to which an agent proceeds. It implies a power, for it is the order according to which that power acts. Without this agent, without this power, which are both distinct from itself, the law does nothing, is nothing. The expression, "the law of metallic nature," may sound strange and harsh to a philosophic ear; but it seems quite as justifiable as some others which are more familiar to him, such as "the law of vegetable nature,"

"the law of animal nature," or indeed as "the law of nature" in general, when assigned as the cause of phenomena in exclusion of agency and power, or when it is substituted into the place of these.

8. Neither, lastly, would our observer be driven out of his conclusion or from his confidence in its truth by being told that he knew nothing at all about the matter. He knows enough for his argument: He knows the utility of the end;[8] he knows the subserviency and adaptation of the means to the end. These points being known, his ignorance of other points, his doubts concerning other points, affect not the certainty of his reasoning. The consciousness of knowing little need not beget a distrust of that which he does know.

CHAPTER II. THE STATE OF THE ARGUMENT CONTINUED

Suppose, in the next place, that the person who found the watch should, after some time, discover that in addition to all the properties which he had hitherto observed in it, it possessed the unexpected property of producing, in the course of its movement, another watch like itself (the thing is conceivable); that it contained within it a mechanism, a system of parts—a mold for instance, or a complex adjustment of lathes, files, and other tools—evidently and separately calculated for this purpose. Let us inquire what effect ought such a discovery to have upon his former conclusion.

1. The first effect would be to increase his admiration of the contrivance and his conviction of the consummate skill of the contriver. Whether he regarded the object of the contrivance, the distinct apparatus, the intricate yet in many parts intelligible mechanism by which it was carried on, he would perceive in this new observation nothing but an additional reason for doing what he had already done—for referring the construction of the watch to design and to supreme art. If that construction *without* this property, or which is the same thing, before this property had been noticed, proved intention and art to have been employed about it; still more strong would the proof appear, when he came to the knowledge of this further property, the crown and perfection of all the rest.

2. He would reflect that though the watch before him were *in some sense* the maker of the watch which was fabricated in the course of its movements, yet it was in a very different sense from that in which a carpenter, for instance, is the maker of a chair ([that is,] the author of its contrivance, the cause of the relation of its parts to their use). With respect to these, the first watch was no cause at all to the second: In no such sense as this was it the author of the constitution and order either of the parts which the new watch contained, or of the parts by the aid and instrumentality of which it was produced. We might possibly say, but with great latitude of expression, that a stream of water ground corn. But no latitude of expression would allow us to say, no stretch of conjecture could lead us to think, that the stream of water built the mill, though it were too ancient for us to know who the builder was. What the stream of water does in the affair, is neither more nor less than this: By the application of an unintelligent impulse to a mechanism previously arranged, arranged independently of it and arranged by

intelligence, an effect is produced—namely, the corn is ground. But the effect results from the arrangement. The force of the stream cannot be said to be the cause or author of the effect, still less of the arrangement. Understanding and plan in the formation of the mill were not the less necessary, for any share which the water has in grinding the corn. Yet is this share the same as that which the watch would have contributed to the production of the new watch, upon the supposition assumed in the last section. Therefore,

   3. Though it be now no longer probable that the individual watch which our observer had found was made immediately by the hand of an artificer, yet . . . this alteration [does not] in any wise affect the inference that an artificer had been originally employed and concerned in the production. The argument from design remains as it was. Marks of design and contrivance are no more accounted for now than they were before. In the same thing, we may ask for the cause of different properties. We may ask for the cause of the color of a body, of its hardness, of its head; and these causes may be all different. We are now asking for the cause of that subserviency to a use, that relation to an end, which we have remarked in the watch before us. No answer is given to this question by telling us that a preceding watch produced it. There cannot be design without a designer; contrivance without a contriver; order without choice; arrangement without anything capable of arranging; subserviency and relation to a purpose, without that which could intend a purpose; means suitable to an end and executing their office in accomplishing that end, without the end ever having been contemplated or the means accommodated to it. Arrangement, disposition of parts, subserviency of means to an end, relation of instruments to a use, imply the presence of intelligence and mind. No one therefore can rationally believe that the insensible,[9] inanimate watch from which the watch before us issued was the proper cause of the mechanism we so much admire in it—could be truly said to have constructed the instrument, disposed its parts, assigned their office, determined their order, action, and mutual dependency, combined their several motions into one result, and that also a result connected with the utilities of other beings. All these properties, therefore, are as much unaccounted for as they were before.

   4. Nor is anything gained by running the difficulty farther back, that is, by supposing the watch before us to have been produced from another watch, that from a former, and so on indefinitely. Our going back ever so far, brings us no nearer to the least degree of satisfaction upon the subject. Contrivance is still unaccounted for. We still want a contriver. A designing mind is neither supplied by this supposition nor dispensed with. If the difficulty were diminished the further we went back, by going back indefinitely we might exhaust it. And this is the only case to which this sort of reasoning applies. Where there is a tendency or, as we increase the number of terms, a continual approach towards a limit, *there*, by supposing the number of terms to be what is called infinite, we may conceive the limit to be attained. But where there is no such tendency or approach, nothing is effected by lengthening the series. There is no difference as to the point in question (whatever there may be as to many points) between one series and another, between a series which is finite and a series which is infinite. A chain composed of an infinite number of links can no more support itself than

a chain composed of a finite number of links. And of this we are assured (though we never can have tried the experiment) because, by increasing the number of links, from ten for instance to a hundred, from a hundred to a thousand, and so on, we make not the smallest approach, we observe not the smallest tendency, towards self-support. There is no difference in this respect (yet there may be a great difference in several respects) between a chain of a greater or less length, between one chain and another, between one that is finite and one that is infinite. This very much resembles the case before us. The machine which we are inspecting demonstrates, by its construction, contrivance and design. Contrivance must have had a contriver; design, a designer—whether the machine immediately proceeded from another machine or not. That circumstance alters not the case. That other machine may, in like manner, have proceeded from a former machine—nor does that alter the case; contrivance must have had a contriver. That former one from one preceding it—no alteration still, a contriver is still necessary. No tendency is perceived, no approach towards a diminution of this necessity. It is the same with any and every succession of these machines; a succession of ten, of a hundred, of a thousand; with one series, as with another; a series which is finite, as with a series which is infinite. In whatever other respects they may differ, in this they do not. In all equally, contrivance and design are unaccounted for. . . .

CHAPTER III. APPLICATION OF THE ARGUMENT

. . . Every indication of contrivance, every manifestation of design which existed in the watch, exists in the works of nature—with the difference, on the side of nature, of being greater and more, and that in a degree which exceeds all computation. I mean that the contrivances of nature surpass the contrivances of art in the complexity, subtlety, and curiosity of the mechanism; and still more, if possible, do they go beyond them in number and variety; yet, in a multitude of cases, are not less evidently mechanical, not less evidently contrivances, not less evidently accommodated to their end or suited to their office, than are the most perfect productions of human ingenuity.

I know no better method of introducing so large a subject, than that of comparing a single thing with a single thing—an eye, for example, with a telescope. As far as the examination of the instrument goes, there is precisely the same proof that the eye was made for vision, as there is that the telescope was made for assisting it. They are made upon the same principles, both being adjusted to the laws by which the transmission and refraction of rays of light are regulated. I speak not of the origin of the laws themselves; but, such laws being fixed, the construction in both cases is adapted to them. For instance, these laws require, in order to produce the same effect, that the rays of light, in passing from water into the eye, should be refracted by a more convex surface than when it passes out of air into the eye. Accordingly we find that the eye of a fish, in that part of it called the crystalline lens, is much rounder than the eye of terrestrial animals. What plainer manifestation of design can there be than this difference? What could a mathematical instrument maker have done more, to show his knowledge of his principle, his application of that knowledge, his suiting of his means to his end? I will not say to display the compass or excellence of his skill and art, for in these all comparison is indecorous, but to testify counsel, choice, consideration, purpose. . . .

CHAPTER V. APPLICATION OF THE ARGUMENT CONTINUED

. . . When we are inquiring simply after the *existence* of an intelligent Creator, imperfection, inaccuracy, liability to disorder, occasional irregularities, may subsist in a considerable degree without inducing any doubt into the question—just as a watch may frequently go wrong, seldom perhaps exactly right, may be faulty in some parts, defective in some, without the smallest ground of suspicion from thence arising that it was not a watch, not made, or not made for the purpose ascribed to it. When faults are pointed out and when a question is started concerning the skill of the artist or dexterity with which the work is executed, then indeed, in order to defend these qualities from accusation, we must be able either to expose some intractableness and imperfection in the materials or point out some invincible difficulty in the execution, into which imperfection and difficulty the matter of complaint may be resolved; or if we cannot do this, we must adduce such specimens of consummate art and contrivance, proceeding from the same hand, as may convince the inquirer of the existence, in the case before him, of impediments like those which we have mentioned, although, what from the nature of the case is very likely to happen, they be unknown and unperceived by him. This we must do in order to vindicate the artist's skill, or at least the perfection of it—as we must also judge of his intention, and of the provisions employed in fulfilling that intention, not from an instance in which they fail, but from the great plurality of instances in which they succeed. But after all, these are different questions from the question of the artist's existence, or (which is the same) whether the thing before us be a work of art or not. And the questions ought always to be kept separate in the mind. So likewise it is in the works of nature. Irregularities and imperfections are of little or no weight in the consideration, when that consideration relates simply to the existence of a Creator. When the argument respects his attributes, they are of weight; but are then to be taken in conjunction (the attention is not to rest upon them, but they are to be taken in conjunction) with the unexceptionable evidences which we possess of skill, power, and benevolence displayed in other instances—which evidences may, in strength, number, and variety, be such, and may so overpower apparent blemishes, as to induce us, upon the most reasonable ground, to believe that these last ought to be referred to some cause, though we be ignorant of it, other than defect of knowledge or of benevolence in the author.

NOTES

1. *offices:* functions. [D. C. ABEL]
2. *fusee:* the cone-shaped pulley in a mechanical watch. [D. C. ABEL]
3. *index:* indicator. [D. C. ABEL]

4. *room:* place. [D. C. ABEL]
5. *prejudice:* injury. [D. C. ABEL]
6. *vacate:* annul. [D. C. ABEL]
7. *efficient, operative cause:* the agent that brings something into being or imparts change. [D. C. ABEL]
8. *end:* purpose, goal. [D. C. ABEL]
9. *insensible:* having no sensation. [D. C. ABEL]

Dialogues Concerning Natural Religion

David Hume

David Hume was born in 1711 in Edinburgh, Scotland. His family wanted him to become a lawyer, but he found himself more interested in liberal arts than law. After three years at the University of Edinburgh (1723–1725), Hume withdrew to study literature, history, and philosophy privately at home. His intensive study took its toll on his health, and in 1729 he nearly had a nervous breakdown. In 1734 Hume went to Bristol, England, to take a job as a clerk for a sugar company. But he disliked the life of commerce and soon resigned his job. Hume then lived in France for three years, studying philosophy. In 1744 he applied for a position in moral philosophy at the University of Edinburgh. Not chosen for the post, he spent the next several years in various occupations in England and abroad. Hume lived in Edinburgh from 1751 to 1763 and then went to Paris, where he served as secretary to the British Embassy for three years. Upon his return, he first lived in London but then moved back to Edinburgh, where he died in 1776.

Hume's major works are *A Treatise of Human Nature* (three volumes, 1739–1740), *An Enquiry Concerning Human Understanding* (1748; originally entitled *Philosophical Essays Concerning Human Understanding,* but renamed in the 1758 edition), *An Enquiry Concerning the Principles of Morals* (1751), *History of England* (six volumes, 1754–1762), and *Dialogues Concerning Natural Religion* (published posthumously, 1779).

Our reading is from the *Dialogues Concerning Natural Religion.* "Natural religion" refers to truths about God that can be known by reflecting on the phenomena in nature; it is contrasted with "revealed religion," which derives its doctrines from divine revelation. The three participants in Hume's fictional discussion about natural religion are Cleanthes, Demea, and Philo.

Our selection begins with Cleanthes defending natural religion. He argues that the world is an intricate machine, composed of many lesser machines, and that just as artificial machines are produced by intelligent agents (human beings), so the natural world must be the product of an intelligent being (God). Demea rejects this argument because it is a posteriori (based on experience); he thinks that only an a priori argument (one in which the conclusion is deduced from abstract principles and does not depend on experience) can indubitably establish God's existence. Philo proceeds to give his reason for rejecting Cleanthes' argument: The argument is based on the questionable analogy between the world and an artifact. Conscious design plays a role in human production, but it is rash to conclude that the universe as a whole is the product of conscious design. Knowledge comes from experience, and while we have seen the manufacture of artifacts, no one has witnessed the origin of the world.

Demea then presents an a priori argument for God's existence. He asserts that whatever exists must have either a cause or a reason for its existence. But since no series of *causes* can extend back infinitely, there must exist a being that has its *reason* for existence in itself. This being, which necessarily exists, is God. Our selection concludes with Cleanthes' objections to Demea's argument.

PART II

. . . [Cleanthes:] Look round the world; contemplate the whole and every part of it. You will find it to be nothing but one great machine subdivided into an infinite number of lesser machines, which again admit of subdivisions, to a degree beyond what human senses and faculties can trace and explain. All these various machines, and even their most minute parts, are adjusted to each other with an accuracy which ravishes into admiration all men who have ever contemplated them. The curious adapting of means to ends, throughout all nature, resembles exactly, though it much exceeds, the productions of human contrivance, of human designs, thought, wisdom, and intelligence. Since therefore the effects resemble each other, we are led to infer by all the rules of analogy that the causes also resemble; and that the Author of Nature is somewhat similar to the mind of man, though possessed of much larger faculties, proportioned to the grandeur of the work which he has executed. By this argument a posteriori,[1] and by this argument alone, do we prove at once the existence of a Deity and his similarity to human mind and intelligence.

I shall be so free, Cleanthes, said Demea, as to tell you that from the beginning I could not approve of your conclusion concerning the similarity of the Deity to men. Still less can I approve of the mediums by which you endeavor to establish it. What! No demonstration of the Being of a God? No abstract arguments? No proofs a priori?[2] Are these, which have hitherto been so much insisted on by philosophers, all fallacy, all sophism? Can we reach no farther in this subject than experience and probability? I will not say that this is betraying the cause of a Deity. But surely, by this affected candor, you give advantage to atheists which they never could obtain by the mere dint of argument and reasoning.

What I chiefly scruple in this subject, said Philo, is not so much that all religious arguments are by Cleanthes reduced to experience, as that they appear not to be even the most certain and irrefragable[3] of that inferior kind. That a stone will fall, that fire will burn, that the earth has solidity, we have observed a thousand and a thousand times; and when any new instance of this nature is presented, we draw without hesitation the accustomed inference. The exact similarity of the cases gives us a perfect assurance of a similar event and a stronger evidence is never desired nor sought after. But wherever you depart, in the least, from the similarity of the cases, you diminish proportionably the evidence; and may at last bring it to a very weak analogy, which is confessedly liable to error and uncertainty. After having experienced the circulation of the blood in human creatures, we make no doubt that it takes place in Titius and Maevius. But from its circulation in frogs and fishes, it is only a presumption, though a strong one, from analogy, that it takes place in men and other animals. The analogical reasoning is much weaker when we infer the circulation of the sap in vegetables from our experience that the blood circulates in animals; and those who hastily followed that imperfect analogy are found, by more accurate experiments,[4] to have been mistaken.

If we see a house, Cleanthes, we conclude with the greatest certainty that it had an architect or builder, because this is precisely that species of effect which we have experienced to proceed from that species of cause. But surely you will not affirm that the universe bears such a resemblance to a house, that we can with the same certainty infer a similar cause, or that the analogy is here entire and perfect. The dissimilitude is so striking that the utmost you can here pretend to is a guess, a conjecture, a presumption concerning a similar cause. And how that pretension will be received in the world, I leave you to consider.

It would surely be very ill received, replied Cleanthes, and I should be deservedly blamed and detested, did I allow that the proofs of a Deity amounted to no more than a guess or conjecture. But is the whole adjustment of means to ends in a house and in the universe so slight a resemblance? The economy of final causes?[5] The order, proportion, and arrangement of every part? Steps of a stair are plainly contrived that human legs may use them in mounting: and this inference is certain and infallible. Human legs are also contrived for walking and mounting; and this inference, I allow, is not altogether so certain, because of the dissimilarity which you remark. But does it, therefore, deserve the name only of presumption or conjecture?

Good God! cried Demea, interrupting him; where are we? Zealous defenders of religion allow that the proofs of a Deity fall short of perfect evidence! And you, Philo . . . do you assent to all these extravagant opinions of Cleanthes? For what other name can I give them? . . .

You seem not to apprehend, replied Philo, that I argue with Cleanthes in his own way; and by showing him the dangerous consequences of his tenets, hope at last to reduce him to our opinion. But what sticks most with you, I observe, is the representation which Cleanthes has made of the argument a posteriori; and finding that that argument is likely to escape your hold and vanish into air, you think it so disguised that you can scarcely believe it to be set in its true light. Now, however much I may dissent in other respects from the dangerous principles of Cleanthes, I must allow that he has fairly represented that argument; and I shall endeavor so to state the matter to you, that you will entertain no farther scruples with regard to it.

Were a man to abstract from everything which he knows or has seen, he would be altogether incapable, merely from his own ideas, to determine what kind of scene the universe must be, or to give the preference to one state or situation of things above another. For as nothing which he clearly conceives could be esteemed[6] impossible or implying a contradiction, every chimera[7] of his fancy would be upon an equal footing; nor could he assign any just reason why he adheres to one idea or system and rejects the others, which are equally possible.

Again, after he opens his eyes and contemplates the world as it really is, it would be impossible for him, at first, to assign the cause of any one event— much less of the whole of things or of the universe. He might set his fancy arambling, and [it] might bring him in an infinite variety of reports and representations. These would all be possible; but being all equally possible, he would never, of himself, give a satisfactory account for his preferring one of them to the rest. Experience alone can point out to him the true cause of any phenomenon.

Now according to this method of reasoning, Demea, it follows (and is, indeed, tacitly allowed by Cleanthes himself) that order, arrangement, or the adjustment of final causes is not, of itself, any proof of design—but only so far as it has been experienced to proceed from that principle. For aught we can know a priori, matter may contain the source or spring of order originally, within itself, as well as mind does; and there is no more difficulty in conceiving that the several elements, from an internal unknown cause, may fall into the most exquisite arrangement, than to conceive that their ideas, in the great universal mind, from a like internal, unknown cause, fall into that arrangement. The equal possibility of both these suppositions is allowed. But by experience we find (according to Cleanthes) that there is a difference between them. Throw several pieces of steel together, without shape or form; they will never arrange themselves so as to compose a watch. Stone and mortar and wood, without an architect, never erect a house. But the ideas in a human mind, we see, by an unknown, inexplicable economy, arrange themselves so as to form the plan of a watch or house. Experience, therefore, proves that there is an original principle of order in mind, not in matter. From similar effects we infer similar causes. The adjustment of means to ends is alike in the universe, as in a machine of human contrivance. The causes therefore must be resembling.

I was from the beginning scandalized, I must own,[8] with this resemblance which is asserted between the Deity and human creatures, and must conceive it to imply such a degradation of the Supreme Being as no sound theist could endure. With your assistance therefore, Demea, I shall endeavor to defend what you justly called the adorable mysteriousness of the divine nature and shall refute this reasoning of Cleanthes, provided he allows that I have made a fair representation of it.

When Cleanthes had assented, Philo, after a short pause, proceeded in the following manner.

That all inferences, Cleanthes, concerning fact are founded on experience, and that all experimental[9] reasonings are founded on the supposition that similar causes prove similar effects, and similar effects similar causes; I shall not, at present, much dispute with you. But observe, I entreat you, with what extreme caution all just reasoners proceed in the transferring of experiments to similar cases. Unless the cases be exactly similar, they repose no perfect confidence in applying their past observation to any particular phenomenon. Every alteration of circumstances occasions a doubt concerning the event, and it requires new experiments to prove certainly that the new circumstances are of no moment or importance. A change in bulk, situation, arrangement, age, disposition of the air, or surrounding bodies—any of these particulars may be attended with the most unexpected consequences. And unless the objects be quite familiar to us, it is the highest temerity to expect with assurance, after any of these changes, an event similar to that which before fell under our observation. The slow and deliberate steps of philosophers, here if anywhere, are distinguished from the precipitate march of the vulgar, who, hurried on by the smallest similitudes, are incapable of all discernment or consideration.

But can you think, Cleanthes, that your usual phlegm[10] and philosophy have been preserved in so wide a step as you have taken, when you compared to the universe houses, ships, furniture, machines; and from their similarity in some circumstances inferred a similarity in their causes? Thought, design, intelligence, such as we discover in men and other animals, is no more than one of the springs and principles of the universe, as well as heat or cold, attraction or repulsion, and a hundred others which fall under daily observation. It is an active cause, by which some particular parts of nature, we find, produce alterations on other parts. But can a conclusion with any propriety be transferred from parts to the whole? Does not the great disproportion bar all comparison and inference? From observing the growth of a hair, can we learn anything concerning the generation of a man? Would the manner of a leaf's blowing, even though perfectly known, afford us any instruction concerning the vegetation of a tree?

But allowing that we were to take the operations of one part of nature upon another for the foundation of our judgment concerning the origin of the whole (which never can be admitted), yet why select so minute, so weak, so bounded a principle as the reason and design of animals is found to be upon this planet? What peculiar privilege has this little agitation of the brain which we call *thought*, that we must thus make it the model of the whole universe? Our partiality in our own favor does indeed present it on all occasions, but sound philosophy ought carefully to guard against so natural an illusion.

So far from admitting, continued Philo, that the operations of a part can afford us any just conclusion concerning the origin of the whole, I will not allow any one part to form a rule for another part, if the latter be very remote from the former. Is there any reasonable ground to conclude that the inhabitants of other planets possess thought, intelligence, reason, or anything similar to these faculties in men? When Nature has so extremely diversified her manner of operation in this small globe, can we imagine that she incessantly copies herself throughout so immense a universe? And if thought, as we may well suppose, be confined merely to this narrow corner, and has even there so limited a sphere of action, with what propriety can we assign it for the original cause of all things? The narrow views of a peasant, who makes his domestic economy the rule for the government of kingdoms, is in comparison a pardonable sophism.

But were we ever so much assured that a thought and reason, resembling the human, were to be found throughout the whole universe, and were its activity elsewhere vastly greater and more commanding than it appears in this globe; yet I cannot see why the operations of a world constituted, arranged, adjusted, can with any propriety be extended to a world which is in its embryo-state and is advancing towards that constitution and arrangement. By observation we know somewhat of the economy, action, and nourishment of a finished animal. But we must transfer with great caution that observation to the growth of a fetus in the womb, and still more, in the formation of an animalcule[11] in the loins of its male parent. Nature, we find, even from our limited experience, possesses an infinite number of springs and principles, which incessantly discover themselves on every change of her position and situation. And what new and unknown principles would actuate her in so new and unknown a situation as that of the formation of a universe, we cannot, without the utmost temerity, pretend to determine.

A very small part of this great system, during a very short time, is very imperfectly discovered to us. And do we then pronounce decisively concerning the origin of the whole?

Admirable conclusion! Stone, wood, brick, iron, brass, have not, at this time, in this minute globe of earth, an order or arrangement without human art and contrivance. Therefore the universe could not originally attain its order and arrangement without something similar to human art. But is a part of nature a rule for another part very wide of the former? Is it a rule for the whole? Is a very small part a rule for the universe? Is nature in one situation, a certain rule for nature in another situation, vastly different from the former?

And can you blame me, Cleanthes, if I here imitate the prudent reserve of Simonides[12] who, according to the noted story, being asked by Hiero[13] what God was, desired a day to think of it, and then two days more; and after that manner continually prolonged the term, without ever bringing in his definition or description? Could you even blame me, if I had answered at first that I did not know and was sensible[14] that this subject lay vastly beyond the reach of my faculties? You might cry out *skeptic* and *rallier* as much as you pleased; but having found in so many other subjects, much more familiar, the imperfections and even contradictions of human reason, I never should expect any success from its feeble conjectures in a subject so sublime and so remote from the sphere of our observation. When two species of objects have always been observed to be conjoined together, I can *infer*, by custom, the existence of one wherever I see the existence of the other; and this I call an argument from experience. But how this argument can have place where the objects, as in the present case, are single, individual, without parallel or specific resemblance, may be difficult to explain. And will any man tell me with a serious countenance that an orderly universe must arise from some thought and art like the human, because we have experience of it? To ascertain this reasoning, it were requisite that we had experience of the origin of worlds; and it is not sufficient, surely, that we have seen ships and cities arise from human art and contrivance. . . .

PART IX

But if so many difficulties attend the argument a posteriori, said Demea, had we not better adhere to that simple and sublime argument a priori, which, by offering to us infallible demonstration, cuts off at once all doubt and difficulty? By this argument, too, we may prove the *infinity* of the divine attributes, which, I am afraid, can never be ascertained with certainty from any other topic. For how can an effect, which either is finite or, for aught we know, may be so—how can such an effect, I say, prove an infinite cause? The unity too of the divine nature it is very difficult, if not absolutely impossible, to deduce merely from contemplating the works of nature. Nor will the uniformity alone of the plan, even were it allowed, give us any assurance of that attribute. Whereas the argument a priori . . . [15]

You seem to reason, Demea, interposed Cleanthes, as if those advantages and conveniencies in the abstract argument were full proofs of its solidity. But it is first proper, in my opinion, to determine what argument of this nature you choose to insist on; and we shall afterwards, from itself, better than from its useful consequences, endeavor to determine what value we ought to put upon it.

The argument, replied Demea, which I would insist on is the common one. Whatever exists must have a cause or reason of its existence, it being absolutely impossible for anything to produce itself, or be the cause of its own existence. In mounting up, therefore, from effects to causes, we must either go on in tracing an infinite succession, without any ultimate cause at all; or must at last have recourse to some ultimate cause that is *necessarily* existent. Now, that the first supposition is absurd may be thus proved. In the infinite chain or succession of causes and effects, each single effect is determined to exist by the power and efficacy of that cause which immediately preceded. But the whole eternal chain or succession, taken together, is not determined or caused by anything; and yet it is evident that it requires a cause or reason, as much as any particular object which begins to exist in time. The question is still reasonable, why this particular succession of causes existed from eternity, and not any other succession, or no succession at all. If there be no necessarily-existent being, any supposition which can be formed is equally possible; nor is there any more absurdity in Nothing's having existed from eternity, than there is in that succession of causes which constitutes the universe. What was it, then, which determined something to exist rather than nothing, and bestowed being on a particular possibility, exclusive of the rest? External causes, there are supposed to be none. *Chance* is a word without a meaning. Was it Nothing? But that can never produce anything. We must, therefore, have recourse to a necessarily-existent Being, who carries the *reason* of his existence in himself and who cannot be supposed not to exist without an express contradiction. There is consequently such a Being—that is, there is a Deity.

I shall not leave it to Philo, said Cleanthes (though I know that starting objections is his chief delight) to point out the weakness of this metaphysical[16] reasoning. It seems to me so obviously ill-grounded and at the same time of so little consequence to the cause of true piety and religion, that I shall myself venture to show the fallacy of it.

I shall begin with observing that there is an evident absurdity in pretending to demonstrate a matter of fact or to prove it by any arguments a priori. Nothing is demonstrable unless the contrary implies a contradiction. Nothing that is distinctly conceivable implies a contradiction. Whatever we conceive as existent, we can also conceive as nonexistent. There is no being, therefore, whose nonexistence implies a contradiction. Consequently there is no being whose existence is demonstrable. I propose this argument as entirely decisive and am willing to rest the whole controversy upon it.

It is pretended[17] that the Deity is a necessarily-existent being; and this necessity of his existence is attempted to be explained by asserting that, if we knew his whole essence or nature, we should perceive it to be as impossible for him not to exist as for twice two not to be four. But it is evident that this can never happen while our faculties remain the same as at present. It will still be possible for us, at any time, to conceive the nonexistence of what we formerly conceived to exist; nor can the mind ever lie under a necessity of supposing any object to remain always in being, in the same manner as we lie under a necessity of always conceiving twice two to be four. The words, therefore, *necessary existence* have no meaning; or, which is the same thing, none that is consistent.

But farther: Why may not the material universe be the necessarily-existent Being, according to this pretended explication of necessity? We dare not affirm that we know all the qualities of matter; and for aught we can determine, it may contain some qualities which, were they known, would make its nonexistence appear as great a contradiction as that twice two is five. I find only one argument employed to prove that the material world is not the necessarily-existent Being and this argument is derived from the contingency[18] both of the matter and the form of the world. "Any particle of matter," it is said, "may be *conceived* to be annihilated, and any form may be *conceived* to be altered. Such an annihilation or alteration, therefore, is not impossible."[19] But it seems a great partiality not to perceive that the same argument extends equally to the Deity, so far as we have any conception of him; and that the mind can at least imagine him to be nonexistent, or his attributes to be altered. It must be some unknown, inconceivable qualities which can make his nonexistence appear impossible or his attributes unalterable. And no reason can be assigned why these qualities may not belong to matter. As they are altogether unknown and inconceivable, they can never be proved incompatible with it.

Add to this, that in tracing an eternal succession of objects, it seems absurd to inquire for a general cause or first author. How can anything that exists from eternity have a cause, since that relation implies a priority in time and a beginning of existence?

In such a chain too, or succession of objects, each part is caused by that which preceded it and causes that which succeeds it. Where then is the difficulty? But the *whole,* you say, wants a cause. I answer that the uniting of these parts into a whole, like the uniting of several distinct counties into one kingdom, or several distinct members into one body, is performed merely by an arbitrary act of the mind and has no influence on the nature of things. Did I show you the particular causes of each individual in a collection of twenty particles of matter, I should think it very unreasonable, should you afterwards ask me, what was the cause of the whole twenty. This is sufficiently explained in explaining the cause of the parts.

NOTES

1. *argument a posteriori:* an argument based on experience (literally, in Latin, "from what comes later"). [D. C. ABEL]
2. *proofs a priori:* arguments in which the conclusion is deduced from abstract principles (literally, in Latin, "from what comes earlier"); contrasted with a posteriori proofs (see note 1). [D. C. ABEL]
3. *irrefragable:* irrefutable. [D. C. ABEL]
4. *experiments:* experiences. [D. C. ABEL]
5. *final causes:* the purposes of things, as reasons for their existence. [D. C. ABEL]
6. *esteemed:* regarded. [D. C. ABEL]
7. *chimera:* mental fabrication. [D. C. ABEL]
8. *own:* admit. [D. C. ABEL]
9. *experimental:* based on experience. [D. C. ABEL]

10. *phlegm:* calm self-possession. [D. C. ABEL]
11. *animalcule:* a minute organism. [D. C. ABEL]
12. *Simonides:* a Greek poet who lived from about 556 to about 468 B.C.E. [D. C. ABEL]
13. *Hiero:* a ruler of Syracuse, Sicily, who died about 467 B.C.E. [D. C. ABEL]
14. *sensible:* aware. [D. C. ABEL]
15. This ellipsis is Hume's; no text has been deleted. [D. C. ABEL]
16. *metaphysical:* relating to *metaphysics,* the study of the nature and kinds of reality. [D. C. ABEL]
17. *Pretended:* claimed. [D. C. Abel]
18. *contingency:* the condition of being able to exist or not to exist; contrasted with *necessary* existence. [D. C. ABEL]
19. This quotation is from the English philosopher Samuel Clarke (1675–1729). [D. C. ABEL]

The Blind Watchmaker

Richard Dawkins

Richard Dawkins was born in 1941 in Nairobi, Kenya, where his father worked for the British Colonial Service. In 1949 his family returned to England, where he was educated at boarding schools and then at Oxford University. He chose to study zoology mainly as a way to explore the philosophical implications of evolution and the negative impact of evolution theory on religion. He pursued graduate studies in zoology at Oxford under Nobel Prize–winning ethologist Niko Tinbergen and received his doctorate in 1966. Dawkins then accepted a position at the University of California at Berkeley, where he taught from 1967 to 1969. The following year he returned to Oxford to become a lecturer in zoology and a fellow of New College. He was appointed a reader in zoology at Oxford in 1991, and Charles Simonyi Professor of Public Understanding of Science in 1995. Among his awards are the Royal Society of Literature Award (1987), the Los Angeles Times Literary Prize (1987), the Zoological Society of London Silver Medal (1989), the Royal Society of London's Michael Faraday Award (1990), and appointment to the Royal Society of Literature (1997).

Dawkins's books include *The Selfish Gene* (1976, translated into fifteen languages), *The Extended Phenotype: The Gene as the Unit of Selection* (1982), *The Blind Watchmaker: Why the Evidence of Evolution Reveals a Universe without Design* (1986, translated into thirteen languages); *River out of Eden: A Darwinian View of Life* (1995), *Unweaving the Rainbow: Science, Delusion, and the Appetite for Wonder* (1998), *The Ancestor's Tale: A Pilgrimage to the Dawn of Evolution* (2004), and *The God Delusion* (2006).

Our selection is from *The Blind Watchmaker*. As Dawkins explains, the title alludes to a famous argument advanced by William Paley in his book *Natural Theology* (1802). Paley asks us to imagine walking across a field and finding a watch lying on the ground. The fact that all its parts work together for the purpose of measuring time would lead us to conclude that it was made by an intelligent artisan. Since living organisms are much more complex than any artificial objects, the natural world must be the product of a supremely intelligent designer— namely, God. (Paley's argument appears on pp. 39–46 of this book.) Dawkins agrees with Paley that organisms are entirely too complex to have arisen all at once by some chance occurrence, but he believes that the complexity can be fully explained by the theory of evolution. He argues that although Paley's argument was plausible in his own day, the discoveries of modern biological science have made an appeal to a conscious designer unnecessary.

Dawkins explains that the theory of evolution does not contend that any organism arose through some single chance event; each organism is the end product of a long sequence of minor transformations, each one of which was small enough to have happened by chance. Species of organisms evolve through a gradual process of "natural selection"— if an organism acquires a trait that enables it to adapt to its environment, it will survive and transmit this trait to its offspring. Natural selection is *cumulative* selection; the new traits that randomly occur in organisms are slight variations on traits already possessed by the previous generation. Cumulative selection differs from single-step selection, which does *not* build on previous variations. If natural selection were single-step selection, it admittedly would be unable to account for the complexity of organisms. Dawkins argues that the cumulative nature of natural selection adequately explains the origin of species: The "designer" of species is natural selection, and natural selection is blind.

CHAPTER 1. EXPLAINING THE VERY IMPROBABLE

We animals are the most complicated things in the known universe. The universe that we know, of course, is a tiny fragment of the actual universe. There may be yet more complicated objects than us on other planets, and some of them may already know about us. But this doesn't alter the point that I want to make. Complicated things, everywhere, deserve a very special kind of explanation. We want to know how they came into existence and why they are so complicated. . . .

The process by which an airliner came into existence is not fundamentally mysterious to us, because humans built it. The systematic putting together of parts to a purposeful design is something we know and understand, for we have experienced it at first hand, even if only with our childhood Meccano or Erector set.

What about our own bodies? Each one of us is a machine, like an airliner only much more complicated. Were we designed on a drawing board too, and were our parts assembled by a skilled engineer? The answer is no. It is a surprising answer, and we have known and understood it for only a century or so. When Charles Darwin[1] first explained the matter, many people either wouldn't or couldn't grasp it. I myself flatly refused to believe Darwin's theory when I first heard about it as a child. Almost everybody throughout history, up to the second half of the nineteenth century, has firmly believed in the opposite—the conscious designer theory. Many people still do, perhaps because the true, Darwinian explanation of our own existence is still, remarkably, not a routine part of the curriculum of a general education. It is certainly very widely misunderstood.

The watchmaker of my title is borrowed from a famous treatise by the eighteenth-century theologian William Paley. His *Natural Theology; or, Evidences of the Existence and Attributes of the Deity, Collected from the Appearances of Nature*, published in 1802, is the best-known exposition of the "Argument from Design," always the most influential of the arguments for the existence of a God. It is a book that I greatly admire, for in his own time its author succeeded in doing what I am struggling to do now. He had a point to make, he passionately believed in it, and he spared no effort to ram it home clearly. He had a proper reverence for the complexity of the living world, and he saw that it demands a very special kind of explanation. The only thing he got wrong—admittedly quite a big thing!—was the explanation itself. He gave the traditional religious answer to the riddle, but he articulated it more clearly and convincingly than anybody had before. The true explanation is utterly different, and it had to wait for one of the most revolutionary thinkers of all time, Charles Darwin.

Paley begins *Natural Theology* with a famous passage:

> In crossing a heath, suppose I pitched my foot against a stone and were asked how the stone came to be there. I might possibly answer, that, for anything I knew to the contrary, it had lain there forever; nor would it perhaps be very easy to show the absurdity of this answer. But suppose I had found a *watch* upon the ground and it should be inquired how the watch happened to be in that place. I should hardly think of the answer which I had given before, that, for anything I knew, the watch might have always been there.[2]

Paley here appreciates the difference between natural physical objects like stones, and designed and manufactured objects like watches. He goes on to expound the precision with which the cogs and springs of a watch are fashioned, and the intricacy with which they are put together. If we found an object such as a watch upon a heath, even if we didn't know how it had come into existence, its own precision and intricacy of design would force us to conclude:

> that the watch must have had a maker that there must have existed, at some time and at some place or other, an artificer or artificers who formed it for the purpose which we find it actually to answer, who comprehended its construction and designed its use.

Nobody could reasonably dissent from this conclusion, Paley insists, yet that is just what the atheist, in effect, does when he contemplates the works of nature, for:

> every indication of contrivance, every manifestation of design, which existed in the watch, exists in the works of nature—with the difference, on the side of nature, of being greater and more, and that in a degree which exceeds all computation.

Paley drives his point home with beautiful and reverent descriptions of the dissected machinery of life, beginning with the human eye, a favorite example which Darwin was later to use. . . . Paley compares the eye with a designed instrument such as a telescope, and concludes that "there is precisely the same proof that the eye was made for vision, as there is that the telescope was made for assisting it." The eye must have had a designer, just as the telescope had.

Paley's argument is made with passionate sincerity and is informed by the best biological scholarship of his day, but it is wrong, gloriously and utterly wrong. The analogy between telescope and eye, between watch and living organism, is false. All appearances to the contrary, the only watchmaker in nature is the blind forces of physics, albeit deployed in a very special way. A true watchmaker has foresight: He designs his cogs and springs, and plans their interconnections, with a future purpose in his mind's eye. Natural selection, the blind, unconscious, automatic process which Darwin discovered, and which we now know is the explanation for the existence and apparently purposeful form of all life, has no purpose in mind. It has no mind and no mind's eye. It does not plan for the future. It has no vision, no foresight, no sight at all. If it can be said to play the role of watchmaker in nature, it is the *blind* watchmaker.

I shall explain all this, and much else besides. But one thing I shall not do is belittle the wonder of the living "watches" that so inspired Paley. On the contrary, I shall try to illustrate my feeling that here Paley could have gone even further. When it comes to feeling awe over living "watches" I yield to nobody. I feel more in common with the Reverend William Paley than I do with the distinguished modern philosopher, a well-known atheist, with whom I once discussed the matter at dinner. I said that I could not imagine being an atheist at any time before 1859, when Darwin's *Origin of Species* was published. "What about Hume?"[3] replied the philosopher. "How did Hume explain the organized complexity of the living world?" I asked. "He didn't," said the philosopher. "Why does it need any special explanation?"

Paley knew that it needed a special explanation; Darwin knew it, and I suspect that in his heart of hearts my philosopher companion knew it too. In any case it will be my business to show it here. As for David Hume himself, it is sometimes said that that great Scottish philosopher disposed of the argument from design a century before Darwin. But what Hume did was criticize the logic of using apparent design in nature as *positive* evidence for the existence of a God. He did not offer any *alternative* explanation for apparent design, but left the question open. An atheist before Darwin could have said, following Hume: "I have no explanation for complex biological design. All I know is that God isn't a good explanation, so we must wait and hope that somebody comes up with a better one." I can't help feeling that such a position, though logically sound, would have left one feeling pretty unsatisfied, and that although atheism might have been *logically* tenable before Darwin, Darwin made it possible to be an intellectually fulfilled atheist. I like to think that Hume would agree, but some of his writings suggest that he underestimated the complexity and beauty of biological design. The boy naturalist Charles Darwin could have shown him a thing or two about that, but Hume had been dead 40 years when Darwin enrolled in Hume's University of Edinburgh. . . .

CHAPTER 3. ACCUMULATING SMALL CHANGE

. . . Living things are too improbable and too beautifully "designed" to have come into existence by chance. How, then, did they come into existence? The answer, Darwin's answer, is by gradual, step-by-step transformations from simple beginnings, from primordial entities sufficiently simple to have come into existence by chance. Each successive change in the gradual evolutionary process was simple enough, *relative to its predecessor*, to have arisen by chance. But the whole sequence of cumulative steps constitutes anything but a chance process, when you consider the complexity of the final end-product relative to the original starting point. The cumulative process is directed by nonrandom survival. The purpose of this chapter is to demonstrate the power of this *cumulative selection* as a fundamentally nonrandom process.

If you walk up and down a pebbly beach, you will notice that the pebbles are not arranged at random. The smaller pebbles typically tend to be found in segregated zones running along the length of the beach, the larger ones in different zones or stripes. The pebbles have been sorted, arranged, selected. A tribe living near the shore might wonder at this evidence of sorting or arrangement in the world, and might develop a myth to account for it, perhaps attributing it to a Great Spirit in the sky with a tidy mind and a sense of order. We might give a superior smile at such a superstitious notion, and explain that the arranging was really done by the blind forces of physics, in this case the action of waves. The waves have no purposes and no intentions, no tidy mind, no mind at all. They just energetically throw the pebbles around, and big pebbles and small pebbles respond differently to this treatment so they end up at different levels of the beach. A small amount of order has come out of disorder, and no mind planned it.

The waves and the pebbles together constitute a simple example of a system that automatically generates nonrandomness. The world is full of such systems. The simplest example I can think of is a hole. Only objects smaller than the hole can pass through it. This means that if you start with a random collection of objects above the hole, and some force shakes and jostles them about at random, after a while the objects above and below the hole will come to be nonrandomly sorted. The space below the hole will tend to contain objects smaller than the hole, and the space above will tend to contain objects larger than the hole. Mankind has, of course, long exploited this simple principle for generating nonrandomness, in the useful device known as the sieve.

The solar system is a stable arrangement of planets, comets, and debris orbiting the sun, and it is presumably one of many such orbiting systems in the universe. The nearer a satellite is to its sun, the faster it has to travel if it is to counter the sun's gravity and remain in stable orbit. For any given orbit, there is only one speed at which a satellite can travel and remain in that orbit. If it were travelling at any other velocity, it would either move out into deep space, or crash into the sun, or move into another orbit. And if we look at the planets of our solar system, lo and behold, every single one of them is travelling at exactly the right velocity to keep it in its stable orbit around the sun. A blessed miracle of provident design? No, just another natural "sieve." Obviously all the planets that we see orbiting the sun must be travelling at exactly the right speed to keep them in their orbits, or we wouldn't see them there because they wouldn't be there! But equally obviously this is not evidence for conscious design. It is just another kind of sieve.

Sieving of this order of simplicity is not, on its own, enough to account for the massive amounts of nonrandom order that we see in living things. Nowhere near enough. . . . The kind of nonrandomness that can be generated by simple sieving is roughly equivalent to opening a combination lock with only one dial: It is easy to it by sheer luck. The kind of nonrandomness that we see in living systems, on the other hand, is equivalent to a gigantic combination lock with an almost uncountable number of dials. To generate a biological molecule like hemoglobin, the red pigment in blood, by simple sieving would be equivalent to taking all the amino-acid building blocks of hemoglobin, jumbling them up at random, and hoping that the hemoglobin molecule would reconstitute itself by sheer luck. The amount of luck that would be required for this feat is unthinkable, and has been used as a telling mind-boggler by Isaac Asimov[4] and others.

A hemoglobin molecule consists of four chains of amino acids twisted together. Let us think about just one of these four chains. It consists of 146 amino acids. There are 20 different kinds of amino acids commonly found in living things. The number of possible ways of arranging 20 kinds of thing in chains 146 links long is an inconceivably large number, which Asimov calls the "hemoglobin number." It is easy to calculate, but impossible to visualize the answer. The first link in the 146-long chain could be any one of the 20, so the number of possible 2-link chains is 20×20, or 400. The number of possible 3-link chains is $20 \times 20 \times 20$, or 8000. The number of possible 146-link chains is 20 times itself 146 times. This is a staggeringly large number. A million is a 1 with 6 naughts after it. A billion (1000 million) is a 1 with 9 naughts after it. The number we seek, the "hemoglobin number," is (near enough) a 1 with 190 naughts after it! This is the chance against happening to hit upon hemoglobin by luck. And a hemoglobin molecule has only a minute fraction of the complexity of a living body. Simple sieving, on its own, is obviously nowhere near capable of generating the amount of order in a living thing. Sieving is an essential ingredient in the generation of living order, but it is very far from being the whole story. Something else is needed. To explain the point, I shall need to make a distinction between "single-step" selection and "cumulative" selection. The simple sieves we have been considering so far in this chapter are all examples of single-step selection. Living organization is the product of cumulative selection.

The essential difference between single-step selection and cumulative selection is this. In single-step selection the entities selected or sorted, pebbles or whatever they are, are sorted once and for all. In cumulative selection, on the other hand, they "reproduce"; or in some other way the results of one sieving process are fed into a subsequent sieving, which is fed into . . . , and so on. The entities are subjected to selection or sorting over many "generations" in succession. The end-product of one generation of selection is the starting point for the next generation of selection, and so on for many generations. It is natural to borrow such words as "reproduce" and "generation," which have associations with living things, because living things are the main examples we know of things that participate in cumulative selection. They may in practice be the only things that do. But for the moment I don't want to beg that question by saying so outright.

Sometimes clouds, through the random kneading and carving of the winds, come to look like familiar objects. There is a much published photograph, taken by the pilot of a small airplane, of what looks a bit like the face of Jesus, staring out of the sky. We have all seen clouds that reminded us of something—a sea horse, say, or a smiling face. These resemblances come about by single-step selection, that is to say by a single coincidence. They are, consequently, not very impressive. The resemblance of the signs of the zodiac to the animals after which they are named, Scorpio, Leo, and so on, is as unimpressive as the predictions of astrologers. We don't feel overwhelmed by the resemblance, as we are by biological adaptations—the products of cumulative selection. We describe as weird, uncanny or spectacular, the resemblance of, say, a leaf insect to a leaf or a praying mantis to a cluster of pink flowers. The resemblance of a cloud to a weasel is only mildly diverting, barely worth calling to the attention of our companion. Moreover, we are quite likely to change our mind about exactly what the cloud most resembles.

Hamlet.	Do you see yonder cloud that's almost in shape of a camel?
Polonius.	By the mass, and 'tis like a camel, indeed.
Hamlet.	Methinks it is like a weasel.
Polonius.	It is backed like a weasel.
Hamlet.	Or like a whale?
Polonius.	Very like a whale.[5]

I don't know who it was first pointed out that, given enough time, a monkey bashing away at random on a typewriter could produce all the works of

Shakespeare. The operative phrase is, of course, given enough time. Let us limit the task facing our monkey somewhat. Suppose that he has to produce, not the complete works of Shakespeare but just the short sentence "Methinks it is like a weasel," and we shall make it relatively easy by giving him a typewriter with a restricted keyboard, one with just the 26 (capital) letters and a space bar. How long will he take to write this one little sentence?

The sentence has 28 characters in it, so let us assume that the monkey has a series of discrete "tries," each consisting of 28 bashes at the keyboard. If he types the phrase correctly, that is the end of the experiment. If not, we allow him another "try" of 28 characters. I don't know any monkeys, but fortunately my 11-month-old daughter is an experienced randomizing device, and she proved only too eager to step into the role of monkey typist. Here is what she typed on the computer:

UMMK JK CDZZ F ZD DSDSKSM
S SS FMCV PU I DDRGLKDXRRDO
RDTE QDWFDVIOY UDSKZWDCCVYT
H CHVY NMGNBAYTDFCCVD D
RCDFYYYRM N DFSKD LD K WDWK
JJKAUIZMZI UXDKIDISFUMDKUDXI

She has other important calls on her time, so I was obliged to program the computer to simulate a randomly typing baby or monkey:

WDLDMNLT DTJBKWIRZREZLMQCO P
Y YVMQKZPGJXWVHGLAWFVCHQYOPY
MWR SWTNUXMLCDLEUBXTQHNZVJQF
FU OVAODVYKDGXDEKYVMOGGS VT
HZQZDSFZIHIVPHZPETPWVOVPMZGF
GEWRGZRPBCTPGQMCKHFDBGW ZCCF

And so on and on. It isn't difficult to calculate how long we should reasonably expect to wait for the random computer (or baby or monkey) to type METHINKS IT IS LIKE A WEASEL. Think about the total number of *possible* phrases of the right length that the monkey or baby or random computer *could* type. It is the same kind of calculation as we did for hemoglobin, and it produces a similarly large result. There are 27 possible letters (counting "space" as one letter) in the first position. The chance of the monkey happening to get the first letter—M—right is therefore 1 in 27. The chance of it getting the first two letters—ME—right is the chance of it getting the second letter—E—right (1 in 27) *given that* it has also got the first letter—M—right, therefore $1/27 \times 1/27$, which equals $1/729$. The chance of it getting the first word—METHINKS—right is $1/27$ for each of the 8 letters, therefore $(1/27) \times (1/27) \times (1/27) \times (1/27) \dots$, and so on, 8 times, or $(1/27)$ to the power 8. The chance of it getting the entire phrase of 28 characters right is $(1/27)$ to the power 28—that is, $(1/27)$ multiplied by itself 28 times. These are very small odds, about 1 in 10,000 million million million million million million. To put it mildly, the phrase we seek would be a long time coming, to say nothing of the complete works of Shakespeare.

So much for single-step selection of random variation. What about cumulative selection; how much more effective should this be? Very very much more effective, perhaps more so than we at first realize, although it is almost obvious when we reflect further. We again use our computer monkey, but with a crucial difference in its program. It again begins by choosing a random sequence of 28 letters, just as before:

WDLMNLT DTJBKWIRZREZLMQCO P

It now "breeds from" this random phrase. It duplicates it repeatedly, but with a certain chance of random error—"mutation"—in the copying. The computer examines the mutant nonsense phrases, the "progeny" of the original phrase, and chooses the one which, *however slightly,* most resembles the target phrase, METHINKS IT IS LIKE A WEASEL. In this instance the winning phrase of the next "generation" happened to be:

WDLTMNLT DTJBSWIRZREZLMQCO P

Not an obvious improvement! But the procedure is repeated, again mutant "progeny" are "bred from" the phrase, and a new "winner" is chosen. This goes on, generation after generation. After 10 generations, the phrase chosen for "breeding" was:

MDLDMNLS ITJISWHRZREZ MECS P

After 20 generations it was:

MELDINLS IT ISWPRKE Z WECSEL

By now, the eye of faith fancies that it can see a resemblance to the target phrase. By 30 generations there can be no doubt:

METHINGS IT ISWLIKE B WECSEL

Generation 40 takes us to within one letter of the target:

METHINKS IT IS LIKE I WEASEL

And the target was finally reached in generation 43. A second run of the computer began with the phrase:

Y YVMQKZPFJXWVHGLAWFVCHQXYOPY,

passed through (again reporting only every tenth generation):

Y YVMQKSPFTXWSHLIKEFV HQYSPY
YETHINKSPITXISHLIKEFA WQYSEY
METHINKS IT ISSLIKE A WEFSEY
METHINKS IT ISBLIKE A WEASES
METHINKS IT ISJLIKE A WEASEO
METHINKS IT IS LIKE A WEASEP

and reached the target phrase in generation 64. In a third run the computer started with:

GEWRGZRPBCTPGQMCKHFDBGW ZCCF

and reached METHINKS IT IS LIKE A WEASEL in 41 generations of selective "breeding."

The exact time taken by the computer to reach the target doesn't matter. If you want to know, it completed the whole exercise for me, the first time, while I was out to lunch. It took about half an hour. (Computer enthusiasts may think this unduly slow. The reason is that the program was written in BASIC, a sort of computer baby-talk. When I rewrote it in Pascal, it took 11 seconds.) Computers are a bit faster at this kind of thing than monkeys, but the difference really isn't significant. What matters is the difference between the time taken by *cumulative* selection, and the time which the same computer, working flat out at the same rate, would take to reach the target phrase if it were forced to use the other procedure of *single-step selection:* about a million million million million million years. This is more than a million million million times as long as the universe has so far existed. Actually it would be fairer just to say that, in comparison with the time it would take either a monkey or a randomly programmed computer to type our target phrase, the total age of the universe so far is a negligibly small quantity, so small as to be well within the margin of error for this sort of back-of-an-envelope calculation. Whereas the time taken for a computer working randomly but with the constraint of *cumulative selection* to perform the same task is of the same order as humans ordinarily can understand, between 11 seconds and the time it takes to have lunch.

There is a big difference, then, between cumulative selection (in which each improvement, however slight, is used as a basis for future building) and single-step selection (in which each new "try" is a fresh one). If evolutionary progress had had to rely on single-step selection, it would never have got anywhere. If, however, there was any way in which the necessary conditions for *cumulative* selection could have been set up by the blind forces of nature, strange and wonderful might have been the consequences. As a matter of fact that is exactly what happened on this planet, and we ourselves are among the most recent, if not the strangest and most wonderful, of those consequences.

It is amazing that you can still read calculations like my hemoglobin calculation, used as though they constituted arguments *against* Darwin's theory. The people who do this, often expert in their own field, astronomy or whatever it may be, seem sincerely to believe that Darwinism explains living organization in terms of chance—"single-step selection"—alone. This belief, that Darwinian evolution is "random," is not merely false. It is the exact opposite of the truth. Chance is a minor ingredient in the Darwinian recipe, but the most important ingredient is cumulative selection which is quintessentially *non*random. . . .

CHAPTER 11. DOOMED RIVALS

. . . We have dealt with all the alleged alternatives to the theory of natural selection except the oldest one. This is the theory that life was created, or its evolution master-minded, by a conscious designer. It would obviously be unfairly easy to demolish some particular version of this theory such as the one (or it may be two) spelled out in Genesis. Nearly all peoples have developed their own creation myth, and the Genesis story is just the one that happened to have been adopted by one particular tribe of Middle Eastern herders. It has no more special status than the belief of a particular West African tribe that the world was created from the excrement of ants. All these myths have in common that they depend upon the deliberate intentions of some kind of supernatural being.

At first sight there is an important distinction to be made between what might be called "instantaneous creation" and "guided evolution." Modern theologians of any sophistication have given up believing in instantaneous creation. The evidence for some sort of evolution has become too overwhelming. But many theologians who call themselves evolutionists . . . smuggle God in by the back door: They allow him some sort of supervisory role over the course that evolution has taken, either influencing key moments in evolutionary history (especially, of course, *human* evolutionary history), or even meddling more comprehensively in the day-to-day events that add up to evolutionary change.

We cannot disprove beliefs like these, especially if it is assumed that God took care that his interventions always closely mimicked what would be expected from evolution by natural selection. All that we can say about such beliefs is, firstly, that they are superfluous and, secondly, that they *assume* the existence of the main thing we want to *explain,* namely organized complexity. The one thing that makes evolution such a neat theory is that it explains how organized complexity can arise out of primeval simplicity.

If we want to postulate a deity capable of engineering all the organized complexity in the world, either instantaneously or by guiding evolution, that deity must already have been vastly complex in the first place. The creationist, whether a naive Bible-thumper or an educated bishop, simply *postulates* an already existing being of prodigious intelligence and complexity. If we are going to allow ourselves the luxury of postulating organized complexity without offering an explanation, we might as well make a job of it and simply postulate the existence of life as we know it! . . . The theory of evolution by cumulative natural selection is the only theory we know of that is in principle *capable* of explaining the existence of organized complexity. Even if the evidence did not favor it, it would *still* be the best theory available! In fact the evidence does favor it. But that is another story.

Let us hear the conclusion of the whole matter. The essence of life is statistical improbability on a colossal scale. Whatever is the explanation for life, therefore, it cannot be chance. The true explanation for the existence of life must embody the very antithesis of chance. The antithesis of chance is nonrandom survival, properly understood. Nonrandom survival, improperly understood, is not the antithesis of chance, it is chance itself. There is a continuum connecting these two extremes, and it is the continuum from single-step selection to cumulative selection. Single-step selection is just another way of saying pure chance. This is what I mean by nonrandom survival improperly understood. *Cumulative selection,* by slow and gradual degrees, is the explanation, the only workable explanation that has ever been proposed, for the existence of life's complex design.

The whole book has been dominated by the idea of chance, by the astronomically long odds against the spontaneous arising of order, complexity and apparent design. We have sought a way of taming chance, of drawing its fangs. "Untamed chance," pure, naked chance, means ordered design springing into existence from nothing, in a single leap. It would be untamed chance if once there was no eye, and then, suddenly, in the twinkling of a generation, an eye appeared, fully fashioned, perfect and whole. This is possible, but the odds against it will keep us busy writing naughts till the end of time. The same applies to the odds against the spontaneous existence of any fully fashioned, perfect and whole beings, including—I see no way of avoiding the conclusion—deities.

To "tame" chance means to break down the very improbable into less improbable small components arranged in series. No matter how improbable it is that an X could have arisen from a Y in a single step, it is always possible to conceive of a series of infinitesimally graded intermediates between them. However improbable a large-scale change may be, smaller changes are less improbable. And provided we postulate a sufficiently large series of sufficiently finely graded intermediates, we shall be able to derive anything from anything else, without invoking astronomical improbabilities. We are allowed to do this only if there has been sufficient time to fit all the intermediates in. And also only if there is a mechanism for guiding each step in some particular direction—otherwise the sequence of steps will career off in an endless random walk.

It is the contention of the Darwinian world-view that both these provisos are met, and that slow, gradual, cumulative natural selection is the ultimate explanation for our existence. If there are versions of the evolution theory that deny slow gradualism, and deny the central role of natural selection, they may be true in particular cases. But they cannot be the whole truth, for they deny the very heart of the evolution theory, which gives it the power to dissolve astronomical improbabilities and explain prodigies of apparent miracle.

NOTES

1. Darwin (1809–1892) was an English naturalist. He formulated the theory of natural selection, which states that if an organism develops traits that enable it to adapt to its environment, it will survive and transmit these traits to its offspring, and that if the organism *fails* to develop adaptive traits, it will perish. [D. C. ABEL]
2. This passage appears on pp. 39–40 of this book; a biography of Paley appears on p. 39. [D. C. ABEL]
3. David Hume (1711–1776) was a Scottish philosopher and historian; for a biography, see p. 47. [D. C. ABEL]
4. Asimov (1920–1992) was an American biochemist and author, known mainly for his science fiction novels. [D. C. ABEL]
5. William Shakespeare, *Hamlet,* act III, scene ii, lines 384–390. [D. C. ABEL]

B. The Problem of Evil

READING 8 On Free Choice of the Will

Augustine

Augustine was born in 354 in the town of Tagaste in northern Africa (now Souk-Ahras, Algeria). As a youth he received instruction in Christianity but was not baptized. At seventeen, he went to Carthage to study rhetoric, which he later taught at Tagaste, Carthage, Rome, and Milan. In 373 Augustine became a member of the Manichaean religion, which held that the equally powerful forces of Light (goodness) and Darkness (evil) govern the universe. Ten years later he abandoned Manichaeism and became attracted to skepticism, the view that it is impossible to attain truth. Augustine then became deeply influenced by the works of Plotinus, an Egyptian-born Roman philosopher who saw himself carrying forward the theories of Plato. When teaching in Milan, Augustine went to hear the sermons of the Catholic bishop Ambrose to study their rhetorical style, but he ended up paying attention to their content. After a dramatic conversion experience, he was baptized by Ambrose in 387. Augustine returned to Tagaste, where he and some friends set up a sort of monastery. In 391 he was ordained a priest at Hippo (now Annaba, Algeria) and four years later became bishop. He remained bishop until his death in 430. Augustine's works include *On Free Choice of the Will* (begun in 388, finished in 395), the *Confessions* (his autobiography, written between 397 and 401), *On the Trinity* (399–419), and *The City of God* (413–426).

Our reading is from Book I of *On Free Choice of the Will,* a work cast as a dialogue between Augustine and his friend Evodius. The topic of the conversation is stated by Evodius in the opening line: "Please tell me: Isn't God the cause of evil?" Augustine begins his answer to Evodius's question by distinguishing the evil that people *suffer* from the evil that they *do.* He argues that God causes the former kind of evil as just punishment for people's sins, but that God does not cause the latter kind. Evildoers themselves are the cause of the evil they commit because they choose evil by their own free will (hence the title of the dialogue). Augustine holds that the essence of all evildoing is inordinate desire, and that inordinate desire consists in pursuing temporal and changeable things, which can be lost against our will, at the expense of eternal and unchangeable things, which cannot be lost against our will. Since the mind is stronger than desire, if we yield to temptation and choose the temporal and changeable over the eternal and unchangeable, we do so through our own free choice. And since our evildoing is voluntary, it is just for God to punish us for it.

BOOK ONE

Chapter 1

EVODIUS: Please tell me: Isn't God the cause of evil?

AUGUSTINE: I will tell you once you have made clear what kind of evil you are asking about. For we use the word "evil" in two senses: first, when we say that someone has *done* evil; and second, when we say that someone has *suffered* evil.

EVODIUS: I want to know about both.

AUGUSTINE: But if you know or believe that God is good—and it is not right to believe otherwise—then he does no evil. On the other hand, if we acknowledge that God is just—and it is impious to deny it—then he rewards the good and punishes the wicked. Those punishments are certainly evils for those who suffer them. Therefore, if no one is punished unjustly—and we must believe this, since we believe that this universe is governed by divine providence—it follows that God is a cause of the second kind of evil, but in no way causes the first kind.

EVODIUS: Then is there some other cause of the evil that God does not cause?

AUGUSTINE: There certainly is. Such evil could not occur unless someone caused it. But if you ask who that someone is, it is impossible to say. For there is no single cause of evil; rather, everyone who does evil is the cause of his own evildoing. If you doubt this, recall what I said earlier: Evil deeds are punished by the justice of God. They would not be punished unjustly if they had not been performed voluntarily.

EVODIUS: It seems that no one could sin unless he had first learned how to sin. And if that is the case, I must ask this: From whom did we learn to sin?

AUGUSTINE: Do you think learning is a good thing?

EVODIUS: Who would dare to say that learning is a bad thing?

AUGUSTINE: What if it is neither good nor bad?

EVODIUS: I think it is good.

AUGUSTINE: Indeed it is, since knowledge is given or awakened through learning, and no one comes to know anything except through learning. Don't you agree?

EVODIUS: I think that we come to know only good things through learning.

AUGUSTINE: Then we do not come to know evil things; for the word "learning" is correctly applied only when we come to know something.

EVODIUS: But if we do not come to know evil things, how is it that human beings perform evil acts?

AUGUSTINE: Perhaps because they turn away from learning and become strangers to it. But whether that is the correct explanation or not, one thing is certainly clear: Since learning is good, and the word "learning" is correctly applied only when we come to know something, we simply cannot come to know evil things. If we could, then they would be part of learning, and so learning would not be a good thing. But it *is* a good thing, as you said yourself. Therefore, we do not come to know evil things, and there is no point in your asking from whom we learn to do evil things. Or else we do come to know them, but only as things to be avoided, not as things to be done. It follows that doing evil is nothing but running away from learning.

EVODIUS: I rather think that there are two sorts of learning: one by means of which we learn to do right, and another by means of which we learn to do evil. But when you asked whether learning was good, the love of good itself caught my attention, and I saw only the sort of learning by which we learn to do right. That is why I answered that it is good. But now I remember that there is another sort of learning. I have no doubt that it is evil, and I would like to know its cause.

AUGUSTINE: Do you at least consider understanding good?

EVODIUS: Certainly. I consider it so good that I cannot see how any human trait could be better. And I would in no way say that any understanding can be bad.

AUGUSTINE: When someone is being taught but does not understand, would you think that he has learned?

EVODIUS: Of course not.

AUGUSTINE: Well then, if all understanding is good, and no one who does not understand learns, then everyone who learns is doing good. For everyone who learns, understands; and everyone who understands is doing good. So someone who wants to know the cause of our learning something really wants to know the cause of our doing good. So let's have no more of your wanting to hunt down this mysterious evil teacher. If he is evil, he is no teacher; and if he is a teacher, he is not evil.

Chapter 2

EVODIUS: Now that you have convinced me that we do not learn to do evil, please explain to me what *is* the source of our evildoing.

AUGUSTINE: You have hit upon the very question that worried me greatly when I was still young, a question that wore me out, drove me into the company of heretics,[1] and knocked me flat on my face. I was so hurt by this fall, buried under a mountain of silly fairy tales, that if my love of finding the truth had not secured divine help, I would not have been able to get out from under them to breathe freely and begin to seek the truth. And since such pains were taken to free me from this difficulty, I will lead you on the same path that I followed in making my escape. God will be with us, and he will make us understand what we have believed. For we are well aware that we are at the stage described by the prophet, who says, "Unless you believe, you will not understand."[2] We believe that everything that exists comes from the one God, and yet we believe that God is not the cause of sins. What is troubling is that if you admit that sins come from the souls that God created, and those souls come from God, pretty soon you'll be tracing those sins back to God.

EVODIUS: You have stated plainly what bothers me in thinking about this question. That is the problem that has compelled me and drawn me into this inquiry.

AUGUSTINE: Be courageous and go on believing what you believe. There is no better belief, even if you do not yet see the explanation for why it is true. The truest beginning of piety is to think as highly of God as possible; and doing so means that one must believe that he is omnipotent, and not changeable in the smallest respect; that he is the creator of all good things, but is himself more excellent than all of them; that he is the supremely just ruler of everything that he created; and that he was not aided in creating by any other being, as if he were not sufficiently powerful by himself. It follows that he created all things from nothing. He did not create from himself, but generated one who is equal to himself, whom we call the only Son of God. In trying to describe the Son more clearly we call him "the power of God and the wisdom of God,"[3] through whom God made all the things that were made from nothing. On that basis let us try, with God's help, to achieve an understanding of the problem you have raised.

Chapter 3

AUGUSTINE: You want to know the source of our evildoing. So we must first discuss what evildoing *is*. State your view on the matter. If you cannot explain the whole thing at once in a few words, you can at least show me your view by naming particular evil deeds.

EVODIUS: Adultery, murder, and sacrilege, not to mention others that time and memory do not permit me to enumerate. Who could fail to recognize these as evil deeds?

AUGUSTINE: Tell me first, why do you think adultery is evil? Because the law forbids it?

EVODIUS: On the contrary. Clearly, it is not evil because the law forbids it; rather, the law forbids it because it is evil.

AUGUSTINE: But suppose someone were to make things difficult for us by extolling the pleasures of adultery and asking why we think adultery evil and deserving of condemnation. Surely you do not think that people who want to understand, and not merely to believe, would have to take refuge in an appeal to the authority of the law? Now like you I do believe, and believe most firmly, and cry out that all peoples and nations should believe, that adultery is evil. But now we are attempting to know and hold firmly by understanding what we have already accepted by faith. So think this over as carefully as you can, and tell me what reason you have by which you know that adultery is evil.

EVODIUS: I know that it is evil because I would not tolerate it if someone tried to commit adultery with my own wife. Anyone who does to another what he does not want done to himself does evil.

AUGUSTINE: What if someone's lust is so great that he offers his wife to another and willingly allows him to commit adultery with her, and is eager to enjoy the same freedom with the other man's wife? Do you think that this man has done nothing evil?

EVODIUS: Far from it!

AUGUSTINE: But by your rule he does not sin, since he is not doing anything that he is unwilling to have done to himself. You must therefore look for some other argument to show that adultery is evil.

EVODIUS: The reason that I think it is evil is that I have often seen people condemned for this crime.

AUGUSTINE: But haven't people often been condemned for good deeds? Not to refer you to any other books, recall the story that is superior to all others by virtue of its divine authority. There you will find that we must think very poorly of the apostles and martyrs if we intend to make condemnation a sure sign of wrongdoing. All of them were judged worthy of condemnation because of their confession of faith. It follows that if everything that is condemned is evil, it was evil in those days to believe in Christ and to confess that faith. But if not everything that is condemned is evil, find some other way to show why adultery is evil.

EVODIUS: I can't think how to respond.

AUGUSTINE: Then perhaps what makes adultery evil is inordinate desire, whereas so long as you look for the evil in the external, visible act, you are bound to encounter difficulties. In order to understand that inordinate desire is what makes adultery evil, consider this: If a man is unable to sleep with someone else's wife, but it is somehow clear that he would like to, and would do so if he had the chance, he is no less guilty than if he were caught in the act.

EVODIUS: Nothing could be clearer. Now I see that there is no need for a long discussion to persuade me that this is the case with murder and sacrilege and every sin whatsoever. For it is clear now that inordinate desire is what drives every kind of evildoing.

Chapter 4

AUGUSTINE: Do you know that inordinate desire is also called "cupidity"?

EVODIUS: Yes.

AUGUSTINE: Do you think there is any difference between cupidity and fear? Or are they quite the same?

EVODIUS: Indeed, I think there is a huge difference between the two.

AUGUSTINE: I suppose you think so because cupidity desires its object, and fear flees from it.

EVODIUS: You're quite right.

AUGUSTINE: Then suppose a man kills someone, not out of cupidity for something that he desires to gain, but because he fears that some harm will come to himself. Would he be a murderer?

EVODIUS: Yes, he would. But even in this deed, cupidity is the driving force—for a man who kills someone out of fear surely desires to live without fear.

AUGUSTINE: Do you think that living without fear is a small good?

EVODIUS: It is a great good, but that murderer cannot achieve it by his action.

AUGUSTINE: I am not asking what he can achieve, but what he desires. Someone who desires a life free from fear certainly desires a good thing, so his desire is not blameworthy; otherwise we will have to blame everyone who loves the good. Consequently, we will have to say that there is an instance of murder in which cupidity is not the driving force; and it will be false that inordinate desire is what drives all sins, to the extent that they are evil. Either that, or there will be an instance of murder that is not sinful.

EVODIUS: If murder is just killing a human being, then there can be murder that is not sinful. When a soldier kills the enemy, when a judge or his representative puts a criminal to death, or when a weapon accidentally slips out of someone's hand without his willing or noticing it—these people do not seem to me to be sinning when they kill someone.

AUGUSTINE: I agree, but such people are not usually called murderers. So consider someone who kills his master because he fears severe torture. Do you think that he should be classed among those who kill a human being but do not deserve to be called murderers?

EVODIUS: I think this case is entirely different. In the earlier examples, those men are acting in accordance with the law, or at least not contrary to the law; but no law approves of the deed in your example.

AUGUSTINE: Again you refer me to authority. You must remember that we took up this discussion in order to understand what we believe. We believe the laws, and so we must try to understand, if we can, whether the law that punishes this deed does so unjustly.

EVODIUS: It is in no way unjust to punish someone who knowingly and willingly kills his master. None of the men in my earlier examples did that.

AUGUSTINE: But do you not remember that a little while ago you said that inordinate desire is what drives every evil deed, and that this is the very reason why the deed is evil?

EVODIUS: Of course I remember.

AUGUSTINE: And did you not also grant that someone who desires to live without fear does not have an evil desire?

EVODIUS: I remember that too.

AUGUSTINE: It follows that, since the master is killed by the slave as a result of this desire, he is not killed as a result of a blameworthy desire. And so we have not yet figured out why this deed is evil. For we are agreed that all wrongdoing is evil only because it results from inordinate desire, that is, from blameworthy cupidity.

EVODIUS: At this point it seems to me that the slave is unjustly condemned, which I would not dream of saying if I could think of some other response.

AUGUSTINE: You have let yourself be persuaded that this great crime should go unpunished, without considering whether the slave wanted to be free of the fear of his master in order to satisfy his own inordinate desires. All wicked people, just like good people, desire to live without fear. The difference is that the good, in desiring this, turn their love away from things that cannot be possessed without the fear of losing them. The wicked, on the other hand, try to get rid of anything that prevents them from enjoying such things securely. Thus they lead a wicked and criminal life, which would better be called death.

EVODIUS: Now I've come to my senses. I am glad that I understand so clearly the nature of that blameworthy cupidity that is called inordinate desire. Obviously it is the love of those things that one can lose against one's will. . . .

Chapter 10

. . . AUGUSTINE: Do you think that inordinate desire is more powerful than the mind, which we know is granted control over inordinate desires by the eternal law? I do not think so at all, for it would violate perfect order if the weaker controlled the stronger. Therefore, I think the mind must be more powerful than cupidity, precisely because it is right and just for the mind to rule over cupidity.

EVODIUS: I think so too.

AUGUSTINE: And surely we do not doubt that every virtue is superior to every vice, so that the better and more sublime the virtue, the stronger and more invincible it is.

EVODIUS: Who could doubt that?

AUGUSTINE: Then no vicious spirit defeats a spirit armed with virtue.

EVODIUS: Quite correct.

AUGUSTINE: And I don't think you will deny that any sort of spirit is better and more powerful than any material object.

EVODIUS: No one will deny it who sees (as is easy to do) that a living substance is better than a nonliving one, and one that gives life is better than one that receives life.

AUGUSTINE: Much less, then, can a material object of any sort overpower a spirit endowed with virtue.

EVODIUS: That is quite obvious.

AUGUSTINE: Can a just spirit (a mind that is preserving its proper right and authority) take another mind that is ruling with the same equity and virtue, drive it from its stronghold, and subject it to inordinate desire?

EVODIUS: Not at all, for two reasons. First, each mind possesses the same degree of excellence. And second, any mind that would attempt such a thing must have already fallen from justice and become vicious, and therefore weaker.

AUGUSTINE: Very sharp. It remains for you to say, if you can, whether you think anything is superior to a rational and wise mind.

EVODIUS: Nothing but God, I think.

AUGUSTINE: That is my view as well. But it is a difficult matter, and this is not the time to attempt to come to understand it, although we hold it most firmly by faith. We must complete our careful and deliberate investigation of the question at hand.

Chapter 11

AUGUSTINE: In the present case we can be sure that whatever nature is by right superior to a mind empowered by virtue, it cannot be an unjust one. Therefore, even if it has the power to do so, it will not force the mind to be a slave to inordinate desire.

EVODIUS: Thus far there is nothing that anyone would have the smallest hesitation about accepting.

AUGUSTINE: The conclusions that we have reached thus far indicate that a mind that is in control (one that possesses virtue) cannot be made a slave to inordinate desire by anything equal or superior to it, because such a thing would be just, or by anything inferior to it, because such a thing would be too weak. Just one possibility remains: Only its own will and free choice can make the mind a companion of cupidity.

EVODIUS: I can't see any other alternative.

AUGUSTINE: Then you must also think that the mind justly suffers punishment for so great a sin.

EVODIUS: I cannot deny it.

AUGUSTINE: Surely the very fact that inordinate desire rules the mind is itself no small punishment. Stripped by opposing forces of the splendid wealth of virtue, the mind is dragged by inordinate desire into ruin and poverty; now taking false things for true, and even defending those falsehoods repeatedly; now repudiating what it had once believed and nonetheless rushing headlong into still other falsehoods; now withholding assent and often shying away from clear arguments; now despairing completely of finding the truth and lingering in the shadows of folly; now trying to enter the light of understanding but reeling back in exhaustion.

In the meantime cupidity carries out a reign of terror, buffeting the whole human soul and life with storms coming from every direction. Fear attacks from one side and desire from the other; from one side, anxiety; from the other, an empty and deceptive happiness; from one side, the agony of losing what one loved; from the other, the passion to acquire what one did not have; from one side, the pain of an injury received; from the other, the burning desire to avenge it. Wherever you turn, avarice can pinch, extravagance squander, ambition destroy, pride swell, envy torment, apathy crush, obstinacy incite, oppression chafe, and countless other evils crowd the realm of inordinate desire and run riot. In short, can we consider this punishment trivial—a punishment that, as you realize, all who do not cleave to wisdom must suffer? . . .

Chapter 12

. . . AUGUSTINE: . . . Tell me this: Do we have a will?

EVODIUS: I don't know.

AUGUSTINE: Do you want to know?

EVODIUS: I don't know that either.

AUGUSTINE: Then don't ask me any more questions.

EVODIUS: Why not?

AUGUSTINE: First, because there's no reason for me to answer your questions unless you want to know the answer. Second, because I should not discuss these sorts of things with you unless you want to attain wisdom. And finally, because you can't be my friend unless you want things to go well for me. But surely you have already seen whether you will your own happiness.

EVODIUS: You're right; it can't be denied that we have a will. Do go on—let's see what you deduce from that fact.

AUGUSTINE: I shall. But first tell me whether you think you have a *good* will.

EVODIUS: What is a good will?

AUGUSTINE: It is a will by which we desire to live upright and honorable lives and to attain the highest wisdom. So just ask yourself: Do you desire an upright and honorable life and fervently will to be wise? And is it indisputable that when we will these things, we have a good will?

EVODIUS: My answer to both questions is yes. I now admit that I have not just a will, but a good will.

AUGUSTINE: How highly do you value this will? You surely do not think it should be compared with wealth or honors or physical pleasures, or even all of these together.

EVODIUS: God forbid such wicked madness!

AUGUSTINE: Then should we not rejoice a little that we have something in our souls—this very thing that I call a good will—in comparison with which those things we mentioned are utterly worthless, things that a great many human beings will spare no effort and shirk no danger to obtain?

EVODIUS: Indeed, we should rejoice greatly.

AUGUSTINE: Then do you think that those who do not attain such joy suffer a small loss by missing so great a good?

EVODIUS: It is a great loss.

AUGUSTINE: Then I believe you realize that it is up to our will whether we enjoy or lack such a great and true good. For what is so much in the power of the will as the will itself? To have a good will is to have something far more valuable than all earthly kingdoms and pleasures; to lack it is to lack something that only the will itself can give, something that is better than all the goods that are not in our power. Some people consider themselves utterly miserable if they do not achieve a splendid reputation, great wealth, and various goods of the body. But don't you consider them utterly miserable, even if they have all these things, when they cleave to things that they can quite easily lose, things that they do not have simply in virtue of willing them, while they lack a good will, which is incomparably better than those things and yet, even though it is such a great good, can be theirs if only they will to have it?

EVODIUS: I certainly do.

AUGUSTINE: Then fools, even if they were never wise (which is a doubtful and obscure issue), are justly and deservedly afflicted with such misery.

EVODIUS: I agree. . . .

Chapter 14

AUGUSTINE: . . . Do you think that there is anyone who does not in every way will and desire a happy life?

EVODIUS: Clearly, every human being wills that.

AUGUSTINE: Then why doesn't everyone attain it? We have found that it is by the will that human beings deserve—and therefore receive—either a happy or an unhappy life. There's a sort of contradiction here; unless we take great care to examine it, it will undermine our careful and persuasive argument. How can anyone suffer an unhappy life by the will, when absolutely no one wills to be unhappy? Or to put it another way, how can we claim that it is by the will that human beings achieve a happy life, when so many are unhappy despite the fact that everyone wills to be happy?

Perhaps it is because it is one thing to will rightly or wrongly, and quite another to deserve something because of a good or bad will. Those who are happy, who must also be good, are not happy simply because they will to be happy—even the wicked will that—but because they will it in the right way, whereas the wicked do not. So it's no surprise that unhappy human beings do not attain the happy life that they will. For they do not likewise will the one thing that goes along with the happy life, without which no one attains it or is worthy to attain it—and that is, to live rightly. For the eternal law (to which it is time for us to return) has established with unshakable firmness that the will is rewarded with happiness or punished with unhappiness depending on its merit. And so when we say that it is by the will that human beings are unhappy, we don't mean that they will to be unhappy, but that their will is in such a state that unhappiness must follow whether they will it or not. So it does not contradict our earlier argument to say that everyone wills to be happy but not everyone can be; for not everyone has the will to live rightly, which must accompany the will to live happily. Or do you have some objection to make?

EVODIUS: None at all. . . .

Chapter 16

AUGUSTINE: . . . We have clearly and carefully distinguished between two sorts of things, eternal and temporal; and in turn between two sorts of human beings, those who pursue and love eternal things and those who pursue and love temporal things. We have determined that the choice to follow and embrace one or the other lies with the will, and that only the will can depose the mind from its stronghold of power and deprive it of right order. And it has become clear that we should not blame anything when someone uses the will wrongly; we should blame the one who uses it wrongly. Given all of that, why don't we return to the question we posed at the beginning of this discussion and see whether it has been answered.

We set out to discover what evildoing is. This whole discussion was aimed at answering that question. So we are now in a position to ask whether evildoing is anything other than neglecting eternal things (which the mind perceives and enjoys by means of itself and which it cannot lose if it loves them) and instead pursuing temporal things (which are perceived by means of the body, the least valuable part of a human being, and which can never be certain) as if they were great and marvelous things. It seems to me that all evil deeds—that is, all sins— fall into this one category. But I want to know what you think about this.

EVODIUS: I agree; all sins come about when someone turns away from divine things that truly persist and toward changeable and uncertain things. These things do have their proper place, and they have a certain beauty of their own; but when a perverse and disordered soul pursues them it becomes enslaved to the very things that divine order and law command it to rule over.

And I think that we have answered another question. After we asked what evildoing is, we set out to discover the source of our evildoing. Now unless I am mistaken, our argument showed that we do evil by free choice of the will.

NOTES

1. Augustine refers to the Manichaeans, who held that the source of evil is the principle of Darkness, which is in eternal combat with the principle of Light (goodness). [D. C. ABEL]
2. Isaiah 7:9. The text of the Hebrew Scriptures that Augustine used was a Latin translation of the Greek Septuagint version. Sometimes, as here, the Septuagint rendering of the original Hebrew is inaccurate. The Hebrew of Isaiah 7:9 means "Have faith, or you will not stand firm" (New English Bible). [D. C. ABEL]
3. 1 Corinthians 1:24. [T. WILLIAMS, TRANSLATOR]

Evil and Omnipotence

J. L. Mackie

J. L. Mackie was born in 1917 in Sydney, Australia. He entered the University of Sydney in 1935 and received his bachelor's degree in 1938. He then went to England to study at Oxford University, where he won the Cromer Greek Essay Prize in 1941 for an essay on Heraclitus. During World War II Mackie served in the British armed forces in the Middle East and Italy, attaining the rank of captain. After the war, in 1946, he accepted a position in philosophy at the University of Sydney. He taught there until 1963, except for his four years as a faculty member at the University of Otago in New Zealand (1955–1959). In 1963 he returned to England, where he became the first holder of the Chair of Philosophy at the University of York. In 1967 he became a fellow and tutor in philosophy at Oxford University. Mackie was elected a Fellow of the British Academy in 1974. He died in Oxford in 1981.

Mackie's books include *Truth, Probability, and Paradox: Studies in Philosophical Logic* (1973), *The Cement of the Universe: A Study of Causation* (1974), *Problems from Locke* (1976), *Ethics: Inventing Right and Wrong* (1977), *Hume's Moral Theory* (1980), and *The Miracle of Theism: Arguments For and Against the Existence of God* (published posthumously, 1982).

Our reading here is "Evil and Omnipotence," an article that Mackie published in 1955. Mackie discusses the "problem of evil," the problem of how a theist can consistently hold all three of the following propositions: God is all-powerful, God is all-good, and evil exists. On the face of it, it seems that if there were an omnipotent and completely benevolent God, this God would not permit evil to exist.

Mackie distinguishes logically adequate and logically fallacious solutions to the problem of evil. A theist solves the problem of evil in a logically adequate way if he or she denies one or more of the initial propositions: God has limited power (and therefore cannot prevent all evil), God has limited goodness (and therefore does not want to prevent all evil), or evil does not exist (it is merely an illusion). Although these solutions are logically adequate, they require abandoning the traditional concept of God as an all-good and all-powerful being or maintaining the highly implausible view that there really is no evil.

The fallacious solutions to the problem of evil say that all three of the initial propositions are true, but in the process of explaining how they are compatible, these theories end up implicitly rejecting one or more of them. In other words, these theories *appear* to defend all three propositions but in fact do not. Mackie examines in detail four such arguments. The first two arguments are that good cannot exist without evil and that evil is a necessary means to good. Both arguments end up denying God's omnipotence. The third solution, that the universe as a whole is better with some evil in it than it would be with no evil, compromises God's benevolence. The final solution states that the possibility of evil is a necessary result of God's endowing human beings with free will, which is a good. Mackie argues that this solution denies the omnipotence and benevolence of God, since God could have made human beings in such a way that they always freely choose the good.

The traditional arguments for the existence of God have been fairly thoroughly criticized by philosophers. But the theologian can, if he wishes, accept this criticism. He can admit that no rational proof of God's existence is possible. And he can still retain all that is essential to his position, by holding that God's existence is known in some other, nonrational way. I think, however, that a more telling criticism can be made by way of the traditional problem of evil. Here it can be shown, not that religious beliefs lack rational support, but that they are positively irrational, that the several parts of the essential theological doctrine are inconsistent with one another, so that the theologian can maintain his position as a whole only by a much more extreme rejection of reason than in the former case. He must now be prepared to believe, not merely what cannot be proved, but what can be *disproved* from other beliefs that he also holds.

The problem of evil, in the sense in which I shall be using the phrase, is a problem only for someone who believes that there is a God who is both omnipotent and wholly good. And it is a logical problem, the problem of clarifying and reconciling a number of beliefs: It is not a scientific problem that might be solved by further observations, or a practical problem that might be solved by a decision or an action. These points are obvious; I mention them only because they are sometimes ignored by theologians, who sometimes parry a statement of the problem with such remarks as "Well, can you solve the problem yourself?" or "This is a mystery which may be revealed to us later" or "Evil is something to be faced and overcome, not to be merely discussed."

In its simplest form the problem is this: God is omnipotent; God is wholly good; and yet evil exists. There seems to be some contradiction between these three propositions, so that if any two of them were true the third would be false. But at the same time all three are essential parts of most theological positions: The theologian, it seems, at once *must* adhere and *cannot consistently* adhere to all three. (The problem does not arise only for theists, but I shall discuss it in the form in which it presents itself for ordinary theism.)

However, the contradiction does not arise immediately; to show it we need some additional premises, or perhaps some quasi-logical rules connecting the terms "good," "evil," and "omnipotent." These additional principles are that good is opposed to evil, in such a way that a good thing always eliminates evil as far as it can, and that there are no limits to what an omnipotent thing can do. From these it follows that a good omnipotent thing eliminates evil completely, and then the propositions that a good omnipotent thing exists, and that evil exists, are incompatible.

A. ADEQUATE SOLUTIONS

Now once the problem is fully stated it is clear that it can be solved, in the sense that the problem will not arise if one gives up at least one of the propositions that constitute it. If you are prepared to say that God is not wholly good, or not quite omnipotent, or that evil does not exist, or that good is not opposed to the kind of evil that exists, or that there are limits to what an omnipotent thing can do, then the problem of evil will not arise for you.

There are, then, quite a number of adequate solutions of the problem of evil, and some of these have been adopted, or almost adopted, by various thinkers. For example, a few have been prepared to deny God's omnipotence, and rather more have been prepared to keep the term "omnipotence" but severely to restrict its meaning, recording quite a number of things that an omnipotent being cannot do. Some have said that evil is an illusion, perhaps because they held that the whole world of temporal, changing things is an illusion, and that what we call evil belongs only to this world, or perhaps because they held that although temporal things *are* much as we see them, those that we call evil are not really evil. Some have said that what we call evil is merely the privation of good, that evil in a positive sense, evil that would really be opposed to good, does not exist. Many have agreed with Pope that discord is harmony not understood, and that partial evil is universal good.[1] Whether any of these views is *true* is, of course, another question. But each of them gives an adequate solution of the problem of evil in the sense that if you accept it this problem does not arise for you, though you may, of course, have *other* problems to face.

But often enough these adequate solutions are only *almost* adopted. The thinkers who restrict God's power, but keep the term "omnipotence," may reasonably be suspected of thinking, in other contexts, that his power is really unlimited. Those who say that evil is an illusion may also be thinking, inconsistently, that this illusion is itself an evil. Those who say that "evil" is merely privation of good may also be thinking, inconsistently, that privation of good is an evil. (The fallacy here is akin to some forms of the "naturalistic fallacy"[2] in ethics, where some think, for example, that "good" is just what contributes to evolutionary progress, and that evolutionary progress is itself good.) If Pope meant what he said in the first line of his couplet, that "discord" is only harmony not understood, the "partial evil" of the second line must, for consistency, mean "that which, taken in isolation, falsely appears to be evil," but it would more naturally mean "that which, in isolation, really is evil." The second line, in fact, hesitates between two views, that "partial evil" isn't really evil, since only the universal quality is real, and that "partial evil" is really an evil, but only a little one.

In addition, therefore, to adequate solutions, we must recognize unsatisfactory inconsistent solutions, in which there is only a half-hearted or temporary rejection of one of the propositions which together constitute the problem. In these, one of the constituent propositions is explicitly rejected, but it is covertly reasserted or assumed elsewhere in the system.

B. FALLACIOUS SOLUTIONS

Besides these half-hearted solutions, which explicitly reject but implicitly assert one of the constituent propositions, there are definitely fallacious solutions which explicitly maintain all the constituent propositions, but implicitly reject at least one of them in the course of the argument that explains away the problem of evil.

There are, in fact, many so-called solutions which purport to remove the contradiction without abandoning any of its constituent propositions. These must be fallacious, as we can see from the very statement of the problem, but it is not so easy to see in each case precisely where the fallacy lies. I suggest that in all cases the fallacy has the general form suggested above: In order to solve the problem one (or perhaps more) of its constituent propositions is given up, but in such a way that it appears to have been retained, and can therefore be asserted without qualification in other contexts. Sometimes there is a further complication: The supposed solution moves to and fro between, say, two of the constituent propositions, at one point asserting the first of these but covertly abandoning the second, at another point asserting the second but covertly abandoning the first. These fallacious solutions often turn upon some equivocation[3] with the words "good" and "evil," or upon some vagueness about the way in which good and evil are opposed to one another, or about how much is meant by "omnipotence." I propose to examine some of these so-called solutions, and to exhibit their fallacies in detail. Incidentally, I shall also be considering whether an adequate solution could be reached by a minor modification of one or more of the constituent propositions, which would, however, still satisfy all the essential requirements of ordinary theism.

1. "Good cannot exist without evil" or "Evil is necessary as a counterpart to good."

It is sometimes suggested that evil is necessary as a counterpart to good, that if there were no evil there could be no good either, and that this solves the problem of evil. It is true that it points to an answer to the question "Why should there be evil?" But it does so only by qualifying some of the propositions that constitute the problem.

First, it sets a limit to what God can do, saying that God *cannot* create good without simultaneously creating evil, and this means either that God is not omnipotent or that there are *some* limits to what an omnipotent thing can do. It may be replied that these limits are always presupposed, that omnipotence has never meant the power to do what is logically impossible, and on the present view the existence of good without evil would be a logical impossibility. This interpretation of omnipotence may, indeed, be accepted as a modification of our original account which does not reject anything that is essential to theism, and I shall in general assume it in the subsequent discussion. It is, perhaps, the most common theistic view, but I think that some theists at least have maintained that God can do what is logically impossible. Many theists, at any rate, have held that logic itself is created or laid down by God, that logic is the way in which God arbitrarily chooses to think. (This is, of course, parallel to the ethical view that morally right actions are those which God arbitrarily chooses to command, and the two views encounter similar difficulties.) And *this* account of logic is clearly inconsistent with the view that God is bound by logical necessities—unless it is possible for an omnipotent being to bind himself, an issue which we shall consider later, when we come to the paradox of omnipotence. This solution of the problem of evil cannot, therefore, be consistently adopted along with the view that logic is itself created by God.

But, secondly, this solution denies that evil is opposed to good in our original sense. If good and evil are counterparts, a good thing will not "eliminate evil as far as it can." Indeed, this view suggests that good and evil are not strictly qualities of things at all. Perhaps the suggestion is that good and evil are related in much the same way as great and small. Certainly, when the term "great" is used relatively as a condensation of "greater than so-and-so," and "small" is used correspondingly, greatness and smallness are counterparts and cannot exist without each other. But in this sense greatness is not a quality, not an intrinsic feature of anything; and it would be absurd to think of a movement in favor of greatness and against smallness in this sense. Such a movement would be self-defeating, since relative greatness can be promoted only by a simultaneous promotion of relative smallness. I feel sure that no theists would be content to regard God's goodness as analogous to this—as if what he supports were not the *good* but the *better,* and as if he had the paradoxical aim that all things should be better than other things.

This point is obscured by the fact that "great" and "small" seem to have an absolute as well as a relative sense. I cannot discuss here whether there is absolute magnitude or not, but if there is, there could be an absolute sense for "great," it could mean of at least a certain size, and it would make sense to speak of all things getting bigger, of a universe that was expanding all over, and therefore it would make sense to speak of promoting greatness. But in *this* sense great and small are not logically necessary counterparts: Either quality could exist without the other. There would be no logical impossibility in everything's being small or in everything's being great.

Neither in the absolute nor in the relative sense, then, of "great" and "small" do these terms provide an analogy of the sort that would be needed to support this solution of the problem of evil. In neither case are greatness and smallness *both* necessary counterparts *and* mutually opposed forces or possible objects for support and attack.

It may be replied that good and evil are necessary counterparts in the same way as any quality and its logical opposite: Redness can occur, it is suggested, only if nonredness also occurs. But unless evil is merely the privation of good, they are not logical opposites, and some further argument would be needed to show that they are counterparts in the same way as genuine logical opposites. Let us assume that this could be given. There is still doubt of the correctness of the metaphysical[4] principle that a quality must have a real opposite: I suggest that it is not really impossible that everything should be, say, red, that the truth is merely that if everything were red we should not notice redness, and so we should have no word "red"; we observe and give names to qualities only if they have real opposites. If so, the principle that a term must have an opposite would belong only to our language or to our thought, and would not be an ontological[5] principle, and, correspondingly, the rule that good cannot exist without evil would not state a logical necessity of a sort that God would just have to put up with. God might have made everything good, though *we* should not have noticed it if he had.

But, finally, even if we concede that this *is* an ontological principle, it will provide a solution for the problem of evil only if one is prepared to say, "Evil exists, but only just enough evil to serve as the counterpart of good." I doubt whether any theist will accept this. After all, the *ontological* requirement that nonredness should occur would be satisfied even if all the universe, except for a minute speck, were red, and, if there were a corresponding requirement for evil as a counterpart to good, a minute dose of evil would presumably do. But theists are not usually willing to say, in all contexts, that all the evil that occurs is a minute and necessary dose.

2. "Evil is necessary as a means to good."

It is sometimes suggested that evil is necessary for good not as a counterpart but as a means. In its simple form this has little plausibility as a solution of the problem of evil, since it obviously implies a severe restriction of God's power. It would be a *causal* law that you cannot have a certain end without a certain means, so that if God has to introduce evil as a means to good, he must be subject to at least some causal laws. This certainly conflicts with what a theist normally means by omnipotence. This view of God as limited by causal laws also conflicts with the view that causal laws are themselves made by God, which is more widely held than the corresponding view about the laws of logic. This conflict would, indeed, be resolved if it were possible for an omnipotent being to bind himself, and this possibility has still to be considered. Unless a favorable answer can be given to this question, the suggestion that evil is necessary as a means to good solves the problem of evil only by denying one of its constituent propositions, either that God is omnipotent or that "omnipotent" means what it says.

   3. "The universe is better with some evil in it than it could be if there were no evil."

   Much more important is a solution which at first seems to be a mere variant of the previous one, that evil may contribute to the goodness of a whole in which it is found, so that the universe as a whole is better as it is, with some evil in it, than it would be if there were no evil. This solution may be developed in either of two ways. It may be supported by an aesthetic analogy, by the fact that contrasts heighten beauty, that in a musical work, for example, there may occur discords which somehow add to the beauty of the work as a whole. Alternatively, it may be worked out in connection with the notion of progress, that the best possible organization of the universe will not be static, but progressive, that the gradual overcoming of evil by good is really a finer thing than would be the eternal unchallenged supremacy of good.

   In either case, this solution usually starts from the assumption that the evil whose existence gives rise to the problem of evil is primarily what is called physical evil, that is to say, pain. In Hume's[6] rather half-hearted presentation of the problem of evil, the evils that he stresses are pain and disease, and those who reply to him argue that the existence of pain and disease makes possible the existence of sympathy, benevolence, heroism, and the gradually successful struggle of doctors and reformers to overcome these evils. In fact, theists often seize the opportunity to accuse those who stress the problem of evil of taking a low, materialistic view of good and evil, equating these with pleasure and pain, and of ignoring the more spiritual goods which can arise in the struggle against evils.

   But let us see exactly what is being done here. Let us call pain and misery "first order evil" or "evil (1)." What contrasts with this, namely pleasure and happiness, will be called "first order good" or "good (1)." Distinct from this is "second order good" or "good (2)," which somehow emerges in a complex situation in which evil (1) is a necessary component—logically, not merely causally, necessary. (Exactly *how* it emerges does not matter: In the crudest version of this solution, good (2) is simply the heightening of happiness by the contrast with misery; in other versions it includes sympathy with suffering, heroism in facing danger, and the gradual decrease of first order evil and increase of first order good.) It is also being assumed that second order good is more important than first order good or evil, in particular that it more than outweighs the first order evil it involves.

Now this is a particularly subtle attempt to solve the problem of evil. It defends God's goodness and omnipotence on the ground that (on a sufficiently long view) this is the best of all logically possible worlds, because it includes the important second order goods, and yet it admits that real evils—namely first order evils—exist. But does it still hold that good and evil are opposed? Not, clearly, in the sense that we set out originally: Good does not tend to eliminate evil in general. Instead, we have a modified, a more complex pattern. First order good (for example, happiness) *contrasts with* first order evil (for example, misery): These two are opposed in a fairly mechanical way; some second order goods (for example, benevolence) try to maximize first order good and minimize first order evil; but God's goodness is not this, it is rather the will to maximize *second* order good. We might, therefore, call God's goodness an example of a third order goodness, or good (3). While this account is different from our original one, it might well be held to be an improvement on it, to give a more accurate description of the way in which good is opposed to evil, and to be consistent with the essential theist position.

There might, however, be several objections to this solution.

First, some might argue that such qualities as benevolence—and a fortiori[7] the third order goodness which promotes benevolence—have a merely derivative value, that they are not higher sorts of good, but merely means to good (1), that is, to happiness, so that it would be absurd for God to keep misery in existence in order to make possible the virtues of benevolence, heroism, and so on. The theist who adopts the present solution must, of course, deny this, but he can do so with some plausibility, so I should not press this objection.

Secondly, it follows from this solution that God is not in our sense benevolent or sympathetic: He is not concerned to minimize evil (1), but only to promote good (2); and this might be a disturbing conclusion for some theists.

But, thirdly, the fatal objection is this. Our analysis shows clearly the possibility of the existence of a *second* order evil, an evil (2) contrasting with good (2) as evil (1) contrasts with good (1). This would include malevolence, cruelty, callousness, cowardice, and states in which good (1) is decreasing and evil (1) increasing. And just as good (2) is held to be the important kind of good, the kind that God is concerned to promote, so evil (2) will, by analogy, be the important kind of evil, the kind which God, if he were wholly good and omnipotent, would eliminate. And yet evil (2) plainly exists, and indeed most theists (in other contexts) stress its existence more than that of evil (1). We should, therefore, state the problem of evil in terms of second order evil, and against this form of the problem the present solution is useless.

An attempt might be made to use this solution again, at a higher level, to explain the occurrence of evil (2). Indeed, the next main solution that we shall examine does just this, with the help of some new notions. Without any fresh notions, such a solution would have little plausibility. For example, we could hardly say that the really important good was a good (3), such as the increase of benevolence in proportion to cruelty, which logically required for its occurrence the occurrence of some second order evil. But even if evil (2) could be explained in this way, it is fairly clear that there would be third order evils contrasting with this third order good—and we should be well on the way to an infinite regress, where the solution of a problem of evil, stated in terms of evil (n), indicated the existence of an evil ($n + 1$), and a further problem to be solved.

4. "Evil is due to human free will."

Perhaps the most important proposed solution of the problem of evil is that evil is not to be ascribed to God at all, but to the independent actions of human beings, supposed to have been endowed by God with freedom of the will. This solution may be combined with the preceding one: First order evil (for example, pain) may be justified as a logically necessary component in second order good (for example, sympathy) while second order evil (for example, cruelty) is not *justified*, but is so ascribed to human beings that God cannot be held responsible for it. This combination evades my third criticism of the preceding solution.

The free will solution also involves the preceding solution at a higher level. To explain why a wholly good God gave men free will although it would lead to some important evils, it must be argued that it is better on the whole that men should act freely, and sometimes err, than that they should be innocent automata, acting rightly in a wholly determined way. Freedom, that is to say, is now treated as a third order good, and as being more valuable than second order goods (such as sympathy and heroism) would be if they were deterministically[8] produced, and it is being assumed that second order evils, such as cruelty, are logically necessary accompaniments of freedom, just as pain is a logically necessary precondition of sympathy.

I think that this solution is unsatisfactory primarily because of the incoherence of the notion of freedom of the will. But I cannot discuss this topic adequately here, although some of my criticisms will touch upon it.

First, I should query the assumption that second order evils are logically necessary accompaniments of freedom. I should ask this: If God has made men such that in their free choices they sometimes prefer what is good and sometimes what is evil, why could he not have made men such that they always freely choose the good? If there is no logical impossibility in a man's freely choosing the good on one, or on several occasions, there cannot be a logical impossibility in his freely choosing the good on every occasion. God was not, then, faced with a choice between making innocent automata and making beings who, in acting freely, would sometimes go wrong; there was open to him the obviously better possibility of making beings who would act freely but always go right. Clearly, his failure to avail himself of this possibility is inconsistent with his being both omnipotent and wholly good.

If it is replied that this objection is absurd, that the making of some wrong choices is logically necessary for freedom, it would seem that "freedom" must here mean complete randomness or indeterminacy, including randomness with regard to the alternatives good and evil—in other words, that men's choices and consequent actions can be "free" only if they are not determined by their characters. Only on this assumption can God escape the responsibility for men's actions; for if he made them as they are, but did not determine their wrong choices, this can only be because the wrong choices are not determined by men as they are. But then if freedom is randomness, how can it be a characteristic of *will*? And, still more, how can it be the most important good? What value or merit would there be in free choices if these were random actions which were not determined by the nature of the agent?

I conclude that to make this solution plausible two different senses of "freedom" must be confused, one sense which will justify the view that freedom is a third order good, more valuable than other goods would be without it, and another sense, sheer randomness, to prevent us from ascribing to God a decision to make men such that they sometimes go wrong when he might have made them such that they would always freely go right.

This criticism is sufficient to dispose of this solution. But besides this there is a fundamental difficulty in the notion of an omnipotent God creating men with free will, for if men's wills are really free this must mean that even God cannot control them—that is, that God is no longer omnipotent. It may be objected that God's gift of freedom to men does not mean that he *cannot* control their wills, but that he always *refrains* from controlling their wills. But why, we may ask, should God refrain from controlling evil wills? Why should he not leave men free to will rightly, but intervene when he sees them beginning to will wrongly? If God could do this, but does not, and if he is wholly good, the only explanation could be that even a wrong free act of will is not really evil, that its freedom is a value which outweighs its wrongness, so that there would be a loss of value if God took away the wrongness and the freedom together. But this is utterly opposed to what theists say about sin in other contexts. The present solution of the problem of evil, then, can be maintained only in the form that God has made men so free that he *cannot* control their wills.

This leads us to what I call the paradox of omnipotence: Can an omnipotent being make things which he cannot subsequently control? Or, what is practically equivalent to this, can an omnipotent being make rules which then bind himself? (These are practically equivalent because any such rules could be regarded as setting certain things beyond his control, and vice versa.) The second of these formulations is relevant to the suggestions that we have already met, that an omnipotent God creates the rules of logic or causal laws, and is then bound by them.

It is clear that this is a paradox: The questions cannot be answered satisfactorily either in the affirmative or in the negative. If we answer "Yes," it follows that if God actually makes things which he cannot control, or makes rules which bind himself, he is not omnipotent once he has made them; there are *then* things which he cannot do. But if we answer "No," we are immediately asserting that there are things which he cannot do—that is to say, that he is already not omnipotent.

It cannot be replied that the question which sets this paradox is not a proper question. It would make perfectly good sense to say that a human mechanic has made a machine which he cannot control. If there is any difficulty about the question, it lies in the notion of omnipotence itself.

This, incidentally, shows that although we have approached this paradox from the free will theory, it is equally a problem for a theological determinist.

No one thinks that machines have free will, yet they may well be beyond the control of their makers. The determinist might reply that anyone who makes anything determines its ways of acting, and so determines its subsequent behavior. Even the human mechanic does this by his *choice* of materials and structure for his machine, though he may not foresee his machine's actions. And since God is omniscient, and since his creation of things is total, he both determines and foresees the ways in which his creatures will act. We may grant this, but it is beside the point. The question is not whether God *originally* determined the future actions of his creatures, but whether he can *subsequently* control their actions, or whether he was able in his original creation to put things beyond his subsequent control. Even on determinist principles the answers "Yes" and "No" are equally irreconcilable with God's omnipotence.

Before suggesting a solution of this paradox, I would point out that there is a parallel paradox of sovereignty. Can a legal sovereign make a law restricting its own future legislative power? For example, could the British parliament make a law forbidding any future parliament to socialize banking, and also forbidding the future repeal of this law itself? Or could the British parliament, which was legally sovereign in Australia in, say, 1899, pass a valid law, or series of laws, which made it no longer sovereign in 1933? Again, neither the affirmative nor the negative answer is really satisfactory. If we were to answer "Yes," we should be admitting the validity of a law which, if it were actually made, would mean that parliament was no longer sovereign. If we were to answer "No," we should be admitting that there is a law, not logically absurd, which parliament cannot validly make—that is, that parliament is not now a legal sovereign. This paradox can be solved in the following way. We should distinguish between first order laws, that is, laws governing the actions of individuals and bodies other than the legislature; and second order laws, that is, laws about laws, laws governing the actions of the legislature itself. Correspondingly, we should distinguish two orders of sovereignty, first order sovereignty (sovereignty (1)), which is unlimited authority to make first order laws; and second order sovereignty (sovereignty (2)), which is unlimited authority to make second order laws. If we say that parliament is sovereign we might mean that any parliament at any time has sovereignty (1), or we might mean that parliament has both sovereignty (1) and sovereignty (2) at present, but we cannot without contradiction mean both that the present parliament has sovereignty (2) and that every parliament at every time has sovereignty (1), for if the present parliament has sovereignty (2) it may use it to take away the sovereignty (1) of later parliaments. What the paradox shows is that we cannot ascribe to any continuing institution legal sovereignty in an inclusive sense.

The analogy between omnipotence and sovereignty shows that the paradox of omnipotence can be solved in a similar way. We must distinguish between first order omnipotence (omnipotence (1)), that is, unlimited power to act; and second order omnipotence (omnipotence (2)), that is, unlimited power to determine what powers to act things shall have. Then we could consistently say that God all the time has omnipotence (1), but if so no beings at any time have powers to act independently of God. Or we could say that God at once time had omnipotence (2), and used it to assign independent powers to act to certain things, so that God thereafter did not have omnipotence (1). But what the paradox shows is that we cannot consistently ascribe to any continuing being omnipotence in an inclusive sense.

An alternative solution of this paradox would be simply to deny that God is a continuing being, that any times can be assigned to his actions at all. But on this assumption (which also has difficulties of its own) no meaning can be given to the assertion that God made men with wills so free that he could not control them. The paradox of omnipotence can be avoided by putting God outside time, but the free will solution of the problem of evil cannot be saved in this way, and equally it remains impossible to hold that an omnipotent God *binds himself* by causal or logical laws.

CONCLUSION

Of the proposed solutions of the problem of evil which we have examined, none has stood up to criticism. There may be other solutions which require examination, but this study strongly suggests that there is no valid solution of the problem which does not modify at least one of the constituent propositions in a way which would seriously affect the essential core of the theistic position.

Quite apart from the problem of evil, the paradox of omnipotence has shown that God's omnipotence must in any case be restricted in one way or another, that unqualified omnipotence cannot be ascribed to any being that continues through time. And if God and his actions are not in time, can omnipotence, or power of any sort, be meaningfully ascribed to him?

NOTES

1. Alexander Pope (1688–1744), an English poet, writes in *An Essay on Man* (Epistle 1, lines 290–91): "All Discord, Harmony, not understood; / All partial Evil, universal Good." [D. C. ABEL]
2. *"naturalistic fallacy"*: the alleged mistake of identifying ethical goodness with a "natural" object. [D. C. ABEL]
3. *equivocation:* the use of a word or phrase in different senses, which makes an apparently correct argument actually incorrect. [D. C. ABEL]
4. *metaphysical:* relating to *metaphysics*, the study of the nature and kinds of reality. [D. C. ABEL]
5. *ontological:* relating to *ontology,* a synonym for *metaphysics* (see note 4). [D. C. ABEL]
6. David Hume (1711–1776) was a Scottish philosopher and historian; for a biography, see p. 47. [D. C. ABEL]
7. *a fortiori*: with greater reason (Latin for "from the stronger [argument]"). [D. C. ABEL]
8. *deterministically:* in accordance with *determinism,* the doctrine that all events are determined by preceding causes and that we can never act otherwise than we do. [D. C. ABEL]

The Problem of Evil

John Hick

John Hick was born in 1922 in Scarborough, England. He received his master's degree from the University of Edinburgh in Scotland in 1948 and his doctorate from Oxford University in 1950. He spent the next three years studying theology at Westminster Theological College in Cambridge, England. Hick then served as a Presbyterian minister in Northumberland, England. In 1956 he came to the United States, where he taught at Cornell University for three years and at Princeton Theological Seminary for five years. Returning to England in 1964, he taught at Cambridge University for three years and then was named H. G. Wood Professor of Theology at the University of Birmingham. From 1982 until his retirement in 1992, Hick was Danforth Professor of the Philosophy of Religion and director of the Blaisdell Programs in World Religions and Cultures at the Claremont Graduate School in California. He currently lives in Birmingham, England, where he is a Fellow of the Institute for Advanced Research in the Humanities at the University of Birmingham.

Hick's publications include *Faith and Knowledge: A Modern Introduction to the Problem of Religious Knowledge* (1957; 2d ed., 1966), *Philosophy of Religion* (1963; 4th ed., 1990), *Evil and the God of Love* (1966; 2d ed., 1977), *Arguments for the Existence of God* (1971), *An Interpretation of Religion: Human Responses to the Transcendent* (1989; 2d ed., 2004), *The Metaphor of God Incarnate* (1993; 2d ed., 2006), and *The Fifth Dimension: An Exploration of the Spiritual Realm* (1999).

Our selection is from Chapter 4 of *Philosophy of Religion,* "The Problem of Evil." The existence of evil is a problem for those who believe in God, since an *all-loving* God would presumably want to abolish evil, and an *all-powerful* God would be able to do so. Believers have given various answers to the problem of evil, and in our reading Hick explains the three main theories proposed by Christian theologians: those of Augustine (354 – 430), Irenaeus (about 130 – 202), and contemporary "process theologians." Hick points out that although each theory can be challenged, many believers find one or more of these theories sufficient to preserve their faith despite the hard fact of evil in the world.

Augustine holds that God created all things and that since God is good, all things are good. There is evil, but evil is not a "thing"—it is a *malfunctioning* of a thing. This malfunctioning is not caused by God but by creatures who possess free will (namely, angels and human beings) and use it wrongly. The misuse of free will is sin, and sin is a spiritual evil. This spiritual evil, according to Augustine, is ultimately responsible for the *physical* evils in the world, such as diseases and earthquakes.

Irenaeus focuses not on the sinfulness of human beings but on their capacity for spiritual growth. Building on Irenaeus's theology, some Christians argue that God permits evil because evil provides human beings with the opportunity to respond in a way that promotes personal growth. God intends the world as a place for "soul making," not as a hedonistic paradise.

Process theologians base their work on that of English philosopher and mathematician Alfred North Whitehead (1861–1947). Rejecting the traditional theological view that God created the universe, they hold that the universe is uncreated and that God is one part of it.

From *Philosophy of Religion,* 4/e, by Hick, John H., © 1990. Reprinted by permission of Pearson Education, Inc., Upper Saddle River, N.J.

Like all other beings, God has power; also like other beings, God has *limited* power. God tries to "lure" creatures toward the good but is unable to control their actions. Hence, evil happens despite the fact that God desires that it not happen. Moreover, process theology sees evil as an inherent part of the creative process.

. . . As a challenge to theism, the problem of evil has traditionally been posed in the form of a dilemma: If God is perfectly loving, God must wish to abolish all evil; and if God is all-powerful, God must be able to abolish all evil. But evil exists; therefore God cannot be both omnipotent and perfectly loving.

One possible solution (offered, for example, by contemporary Christian Science) can be ruled out immediately so far as the traditional Judaic-Christian faith is concerned. To say that evil is an illusion of the human mind is impossible within a religion based upon the stark realism of the Bible. Its pages faithfully reflect the characteristic mixture of good and evil in human experience. They record every kind of sorrow and suffering, every mode of "man's inhumanity to man"[1] and of our painfully insecure existence in the world. There is no attempt to regard evil as anything but dark, menacingly ugly, heartrending, and crushing. There can be no doubt, then, that for biblical faith evil is entirely real and in no sense an illusion.

There are three main Christian responses to the problem of evil: the Augustinian response, hinging upon the concept of the fall of man from an original state of righteousness; the Irenaean response, hinging upon the idea of the gradual creation of a perfected humanity through life in a highly imperfect world; and the response of modern process theology, hinging upon the idea of a God who is not all-powerful and not in fact able to prevent the evils arising either in human beings or in the processes of nature.

Before examining each of these three responses, or theodicies,[2] we will discuss a position that is common to all of them.

The common ground is some form of what has come to be called the free-will defense, at least so far as the moral evil of human wickedness is concerned, for Christian thought has always seen moral evil as related to human freedom and responsibility. To be a person is to be a finite center of freedom, a (relatively) self-directing agent responsible for one's own decisions. This involves being free to act wrongly as well as rightly. There can therefore be no certainty in advance that a genuinely free moral agent will never choose amiss. Consequently, according to the strong form of free-will defense, the possibility of wrongdoing is logically inseparable from the creation of finite persons, and to say that God should not have created beings who might sin amounts to saying that God should not have created people.

This thesis has been challenged by those who claim that no contradiction is involved in saying that God might have made people who would be genuinely free but who could at the same time be guaranteed always to act rightly. To quote from one of these:

> If there is no logical impossibility in a man's freely choosing the good on one, or on several occasions, there cannot be a logical impossibility in his freely choosing the good on every occasion. God was not, then, faced with a choice between making innocent automata and making beings who, in acting freely, would sometimes go wrong; there was open to him the obviously better possibility of making beings

who would act freely but always go right. Clearly, his failure to avail himself of this possibility is inconsistent with his being both omnipotent and wholly good.[3]

This argument has considerable power. A modified form of free-will defense has, however, been suggested in response to it. If by free actions we mean actions that are not externally compelled, but flow from the nature of agents as they react to the circumstances in which they find themselves, then there is indeed no contradiction between our being free and our actions' being "caused" (by our own God-given nature) and thus being in principle predictable. However, it is suggested, there is a contradiction in saying that *God* is the cause of our acting as we do *and* that we are free beings specifically in relation to God. The contradiction is between holding that God has so made us that we shall of necessity act in a certain way, and that we are genuinely independent persons *in relation to God.* If all our thoughts and actions are divinely predestined, then however free and responsible we may seem to ourselves to be, we are not free and responsible in the sight of God but must instead be God's puppets. Such "freedom" would be comparable to that of patients acting out a series of posthypnotic suggestions: They appear to themselves to be free, but their volitions have actually been predetermined by the will of the hypnotist, in relation to whom the patients are therefore not genuinely free agents. Thus, it is suggested, while God *could* have created such beings, there would have been no point in doing so—at least not if God is seeking to create sons and daughters rather than human puppets.

THE AUGUSTINIAN THEODICY

The main traditional Christian response to the problem of evil was formulated by St. Augustine (354–430 A.D.) and has constituted the majority report of the Christian mind through the centuries, although it has been much criticized in recent times. It includes both philosophical and theological strands. The main philosophical position is the idea of the negative or privative nature of evil. Augustine holds firmly to the Hebrew-Christian conviction that the universe is *good*—that is to say, it is the creation of a good God for a good purpose. There are, according to Augustine, higher and lower, greater and lesser goods in immense abundance and variety; however, everything that has being is good in its own way and degree, except insofar as it has become spoiled or corrupted. Evil—whether it be an evil will, an instance of pain, or some disorder or decay in nature—has therefore not been set there by God but represents the going wrong of something that is inherently good. Augustine points to blindness as an example. Blindness is not a "thing." The only thing involved is the eye, which is in itself good; the evil of blindness consists of the lack of a proper functioning of the eye. Generalizing the principle, Augustine holds that evil always consists of the malfunctioning of something that is in itself good.

As it originally came forth from the hand of God, then, the universe was a perfect harmony expressing the creative divine intention. It was a graded hierarchy of higher and lower forms of being, each good in its own place. How, then, did evil come about? It came about initially in those levels of the universe that involve free will: the free will of the angels and of human beings. Some of the angels turned from the supreme Good, which is God, to lesser goods, thereby rebelling against their creator; they in turn tempted the first man and woman to fall. This fall of angelic and human beings was the origin of moral evil or sin. The natural evils of disease, of "nature red in tooth and claw,"[4] and of earthquake, storm, and so on are the penal consequences of sin, for humanity was intended to be guardian of the earth, and this human defection has set all nature awry. Thus Augustine could say, "All evil is either sin or the punishment for sin."[5]

The Augustinian theodicy adds that at the end of history there will come the judgment, when many will enter into eternal life and many others (who in their freedom have rejected God's offer of salvation) into eternal torment. For Augustine, "since there is happiness for those who do not sin, the universe is perfect; and it is no less perfect because there is misery for sinners. . . . The penalty of sin corrects the dishonor of sin."[6] He is invoking here a principle of moral balance according to which sin that is justly punished is thereby cancelled out and no longer regarded as marring the perfection of God's universe.

The Augustinian theodicy fulfills the intention lying behind it, which is to clear the creator of any responsibility for the existence of evil by loading that responsibility without remainder upon the creature. Evil stems from the culpable misuse of creaturely freedom in a tragic act, of cosmic significance, in the pre-history of the human race—an act that was prefigured in the heavenly realms by the incomprehensible fall of some of the angels, the chief of whom is now Satan, God's Enemy.

This theodicy has been criticized in the modern period, the first major critic being the great German Protestant theologian Friedrich Schleiermacher (1768–1834).[7]

The basic criticism is directed at the idea that a universe which God has created with absolute power, so as to be exactly as God wishes it to be, containing no evil of any kind, has nevertheless gone wrong. It is true that the free creatures who are part of it are free to fall. However, since they are finitely perfect, without any taint or trace of evil in them, and since they dwell in a finitely perfect environment, they will never in fact fall into sin. Thus, it is said, the very idea of a perfect creation's going wrong spontaneously and without cause is a self-contradiction. It amounts to the self-creation of evil out of nothing! It is significant that Augustine himself, when he asks why it is that some of the angels fell while others remained steadfast, has to conclude that "these angels, therefore, either received less of the grace of the divine love than those who persevered in the same; or if both were created equally good, then, while the one fell by their evil will, the others were more abundantly assisted, and attained to the pitch of blessedness at which they have become certain that they should never fall from it."[8]

The basic criticism, then, is that a flawless creation would never go wrong and that if the creation does in fact go wrong the ultimate responsibility for this must be with its creator, for "This is where the buck stops!"

This criticism agrees with Mackie's contention . . . that it was logically possible for God to have created free beings who would never in fact fall. As we shall see in the next section, the alternative Irenaean theodicy takes up the further thought that although God *could* have created beings who were from the beginning finitely perfect, God has not in fact done so because such beings would never be able to become free and responsible sons and daughters of God. . . .

THE IRENAEAN THEODICY

Even from before the time of Augustine another response to the problem of evil had already been present within the developing Christian tradition. This has its basis in the thought of the early Greek-speaking Fathers of the Church, perhaps the most important of whom was St. Irenaeus (circa 130–circa 202 A.D.). He distinguished two stages of the creation of the human race.[9] In the first stage human beings were brought into existence as intelligent animals endowed with the capacity for immense moral and spiritual development. They were not the perfect pre-fallen Adam and Eve of the Augustinian tradition, but immature creatures, at the beginning of a long process of growth. In the second stage of their creation, which is now taking place, they are gradually being transformed through their own free responses from human animals into "children of God." (Irenaeus himself described the two stages as humanity being made first in the "image" and then into the "likeness" of God—referring to Genesis 1:26).

If, going beyond Irenaeus himself, we ask why humans should have been initially created as immature and imperfect beings rather than as a race of perfect creatures, the answer centers upon the positive value of human freedom. Two mutually supporting considerations are suggested. One depends upon the intuitive judgment that a human goodness that has come about through the making of free and responsible moral choices, in situations of real difficulty and temptation, is intrinsically more valuable—perhaps even limitlessly more valuable—than a goodness that has been created ready-made, without the free participation of the human agent. This intuition points to the creation of the human race, not in a state of perfection, but in a state of imperfection from which it is nevertheless possible to move through moral struggle toward eventual completed humanization.

The other consideration is that if men and women had been initially created in the direct presence of God (who is infinite in life, power, goodness, and knowledge), they would have no genuine freedom in relation to their Maker. In order to be fully personal and therefore morally free beings, they have accordingly (it is suggested) been created at a distance from God—not a spatial but an epistemic distance, a distance in the dimension of knowledge. They are formed within and as part of an autonomous universe within which God is not overwhelmingly evident but in which God may become known by the free interpretative response of faith. Thus the human situation is one of tension between the natural selfishness arising from our instinct for survival, and the calls of both morality and religion to transcend our self-centeredness. Whereas the Augustinian theology sees our perfection as lying in the distant past, in an original state long since forfeited by the primordial calamity of the fall, the Irenaean type of theology sees our perfection as lying before us in the future, at the end of a lengthy and arduous process of further creation through time.

Thus the answer of the Irenaean theodicy to the question of the origin of moral evil is that it is a necessary condition of the creation of humanity at an epistemic distance from God, in a state in which one has a genuine freedom in relation to one's Maker and can freely develop, in response to God's noncoercive presence, toward one's own fulfillment as a child of God.

We may now turn to the problem of pain and suffering. Even though the bulk of actual human pain is traceable, as a sole or part cause, to misused human freedom, there remain other sources of pain that are entirely independent of the human will—for example, bacteria, earthquake, hurricane, storm, flood, drought, and blight. In practice it is often impossible to trace a boundary between the suffering that results from human wickedness and folly and that which befalls humanity from without; both are inextricably mingled in our experience. For our present purpose, however, it is important to note that the latter category does exist and that it seems to be built into the very structure of our world. In response to it, theodicy, if it is wisely conducted, follows a negative path. It is not possible to show positively that each item of human pain serves God's purpose of good; on the other hand, it does seem possible to show that the divine purpose, as it is understood in the Irenaean theology, could not be forwarded in a world that was designed as a permanent hedonistic paradise.

An essential premise of this argument concerns the nature of the divine purpose in creating the world. The skeptic's normal assumption is that humanity is to be viewed as a completed creation and that God's purpose in making the world was to provide a suitable dwelling place for this fully formed creature. Since God is good and loving, the environment that God creates for human life will naturally be as pleasant and as comfortable as possible. The problem is essentially similar to that of someone who builds a cage for a pet animal. Since our world in fact contains sources of pain, hardship, and danger of innumerable kinds, the conclusion follows that this world cannot have been created by a perfectly benevolent and all-powerful deity.

According to the Irenaean theodicy, however, God's purpose was not to construct a paradise whose inhabitants would experience a maximum of pleasure and a minimum of pain. The world is seen, instead, as a place of "soul making"[10] or person making in which free beings, grappling with the tasks and challenges of their existence in a common environment, may become "children of God" and "heirs of eternal life." Our world, with all its rough edges, is the sphere in which this second and harder stage of the creative process is taking place.

This conception of the world (whether or not set in Irenaeus's theological framework) can be supported by the method of "counterfactual hypothesis." Suppose that, contrary to fact, this world were a paradise from which all possibility of pain and suffering were excluded. The consequences would be very far-reaching. For example, no one could ever injure anyone else: The murderer's knife would turn to paper or the bullets to thin air; the bank safe, robbed of a million dollars, would miraculously become filled with another million dollars; fraud, deceit, conspiracy, and treason would somehow leave the fabric of society undamaged. No one would ever be injured by accident: The mountain climber, steeplejack, or playing child falling from a height would float unharmed to the ground; the reckless driver would never meet with disaster. There would be no need to work, since no harm could result from avoiding work; there would be no call to be concerned for others in time of need or danger, for in such a world there could be no real needs or dangers.

To make possible this continual series of individual adjustments, nature would have to work by "special providences" instead of running according to general laws that we must learn to respect on penalty of pain or death. The laws of nature would have to be extremely flexible: Sometimes gravity would operate, sometimes not; sometimes an object would be hard, sometimes soft. There could be no sciences, for there would be no enduring world structure to investigate. In eliminating the problems and hardships of an objective environment with its own laws, life would become like a dream in which, delightfully but aimlessly, we would float and drift at ease.

One can at least begin to imagine such a world—and it is evident that in it our present ethical concepts would have no meaning. If, for example, the notion of harming someone is an essential element in the concept of a wrong action, in a hedonistic paradise there could be no wrong actions—nor therefore any right actions in distinction from wrong. Courage and fortitude would have no point in an environment in which there is, by definition, no danger or difficulty. Generosity, kindness, the *agapē*[11] aspect of love, prudence, unselfishness, and other ethical notions that presuppose life in an objective environment could not even be formed. Consequently, such a world, however well it might promote pleasure, would be very ill adapted for the development of the moral qualities of human personality. In relation to this purpose it might well be the worst of all possible worlds!

It would seem, then, that an environment intended to make possible the growth in free beings of the finest characteristics of personal life must have a good deal in common with our present world. It must operate according to general and dependable laws, and it must present real dangers, difficulties, problems, obstacles, and possibilities of pain, failure, sorrow, frustration, and defeat. If it did not contain the particular trials and perils that—subtracting the considerable human contribution—our world contains, it would have to contain others instead.

To realize this fact is not by any means to be in possession of a detailed theodicy. However, it is to understand that this world, with all its "heartaches and the thousand natural shocks that flesh is heir to,"[12] an environment so manifestly not designed for the maximization of human pleasure and the minimization of human pain, may nevertheless be rather well adapted to the quite different purpose of "soul making."[13]

And so the Irenaean answer to the question, Why natural evil?, is that only a world that has this general character could constitute an effective environment for the second stage (or the beginning of the second stage) of God's creative work, whereby human animals are being gradually transformed through their own free responses into "children of God." . . .

Philosophical critics have argued that, while it shows with some plausibility that a person-making world cannot be a paradise, it does not thereby justify the *actual extent* of human suffering, including such gigantic evils as the Jewish Holocaust. Others, however, claim that this theodicy does succeed in showing why God's world, as a sphere involving contingency and freedom, is such that even these things must, alas, be possible—even though human history would have been much better without these conspicuous crimes and horrors. There is also unresolvable disagreement as to whether so painful a creative process, even though leading to an infinite good, can be said to be the expression of divine goodness.

PROCESS THEODICY

Process theology is a modern development in which a number of Christian theologians have adopted as their metaphysical[14] framework the philosophy of A. N. Whitehead (1861–1947). For a number of reasons, including the fact of evil in the world, process theology holds that God cannot be unlimited in power but interacts with a universe which God has not created but is nevertheless able to influence. Although different process theologians have offered hints toward a theodicy, it is only with the publication of David Griffin's *God, Power, and Evil: A Process Theodicy*[15] that a systematic version has become available. An item of contrast with the more traditional Augustinian and Irenaean theodicies will provide an apt point of departure for an account of Griffin's position. According to the main Christian tradition, God is the creator and sustainer of the entire universe *ex nihilo* (out of nothing), and God's ultimate power over the creation is accordingly unlimited. However, in order to allow for the existence and growth of free human beings, God withholds the exercise of unlimited divine power, thereby forming an autonomous creaturely realm within which God acts noncoercively, seeking the creatures' free responses. Process theology likewise holds that God acts noncoercively, by "persuasion" and "lure," but in contrast to the notion of divine self-limitation, holds that God's exercise of persuasive rather than controlling power is necessitated by the ultimate metaphysical structure of reality. God is subject to the limitations imposed by the basic laws of the universe, for God has not created the universe *ex nihilo*, thereby establishing its structure, but rather the universe is an uncreated process which includes the deity. . . . Accordingly, as Griffin says, "God does not refrain from controlling the creatures simply because it is better for God to use persuasion, but because it is necessarily the case that God cannot completely control the creatures."[16]

One should add at this point a second difference from traditional Christian thought, which becomes important in relation to the final outcome of the creative process. This is that for the former, in its Irenaean form, the creatures whom God is seeking to make perfect through their own freedom, were initially created by God and thus are formed with a Godward bias to their nature. For process thought, on the other hand, their very creation came about in struggle with the primordial chaos, so that the divine purpose is only imperfectly written into their nature.

The ultimate reality, according to process theology, is creativity continually producing new unities of experience out of the manifold of the previous moment. Creativity is not, however, something additional to actuality—that is, to what actually exists at a given instant—but is the creative power within all actuality. Every actuality, or "actual entity," or "actual occasion," is a momentary event, charged with creativity. As such it exerts some degree of power. It exerts power first in the way in which it receives and organizes the data of the preceding moment. . . . An actual occasion is never completely determined by the past. It is partly so determined but partly a determiner of the future, as the present occasion is itself prehended[17] by succeeding occasions. As part determiner of the future it is again exercising power. This dual efficacy is inseparable from being actual, and so every actual occasion, as a moment of creativity, necessarily exerts some degree of power.

However, finite actualities do not exercise power because God has delegated it to them, but because to be a part of the universe *is* to exercise creativity and hence power. Indeed because to be actual is to be creative, thereby exercising some degree of power, it is impossible for even God to hold a monopoly of power. Every actual occasion is, by its very nature, partially self-creative as well as partially created by previous actual occasions which were themselves partially self-created. Thus God's power over each occasion, and in directing the stream of occasions as a whole, is necessarily limited, and the reality of evil in the world is the measure of the extent to which God's will is in fact thwarted. God continually offers the best possibility to each occasion as it creates itself, but the successive occasions are free not to conform to the divine plan. And, as Whitehead says, "So far as the conformation is incomplete, there is evil in the world."[18]

Evil is, according to process theology, of two kinds, contrasting with two kinds of good. The criteria are ultimately aesthetic rather than moral. An actual occasion is a moment of experience, and the values that experience can embody are harmony and intensity. The concrescence of a multiplicity into a new complex unity, a fresh moment of experience, may be more or less richly harmonious and more or less vivid and intense. Insofar as it fails to attain harmony it exhibits the evil of discord. This discord, says Whitehead, "is the feeling of evil in the most general sense, namely physical pain or merital evil, such as sorrow, horror, dislike."[19] Insofar as a moment of experience fails to attain the highest appropriate intensity, it exhibits the other form of evil, which is needless triviality. To some extent harmony and intensity are in conflict with one another, for a higher level of intensity is made possible by increased complexity, thus endangering harmony. So one form of evil or the other, either discord or needless triviality, is virtually inevitable within the creative process. Even more important perhaps, greater complexity, making possible greater richness of experience, also makes possible new dimensions of suffering. Thus human beings can have qualities of enjoyment beyond the capacity of lower forms of life, but they are also subject to moral and spiritual anguishes which far exceed those of the lower animals and which can even drive humans to suicide. For this reason also evil is an inherent part of the creative process.

The evolution of the universe as a whole, and of life on this planet, is due to the continual divine impetus to maximize harmony and intensity in each present occasion, at the same time creating new possibilities for yet greater harmony and intensity in the future; and this divine impetus is justified on the ground that the good that has been produced, and is yet to be produced, outweighs and renders worthwhile the evil that has been produced and that will yet be produced. For God could have left the primal chaos undisturbed instead of forming it into an ordered universe evolving ever higher forms of actuality. God is therefore responsible for having initiated and continued the development of the finite realm from disordered chaos toward ever greater possibilities of both good and evil.

Thus this particular conception of a limited deity still requires a theodicy, a justifying of God's goodness in face of the fact of evil. As Griffin says, "God is responsible in the sense of having urged the creation forward to those states in which discordant feelings could be felt with great intensity."[20] The theodicy proposed is that the good created in the course of the world process could not have come about without the possibility and, as it has turned out, the actuality of all the evil that has been inextricably intertwined with it. God's goodness is vindicated in that the risk-taking venture in the evolution of the universe was calculated to produce, and has produced, a sufficient quality and quantity of good to outweigh all the evil that has in fact been involved or that might have been involved. For the alternative to the risk of creation was not sheer nothingness but the evil of needless triviality in the primordial chaos. . . .

The process doctrine (as presented by Griffin) is . . . that the possibility of creating the degree of human good that has in fact come about involved the possibility of creating also the degree of human evil that has in fact come about. According to this theodicy, the good that has occurred renders worthwhile all the wickedness that has been committed and all the suffering that has been endured.

Clearly, it can be questioned whether such a God is to be equated with the God of the New Testament, understood as the Creator who values all human creatures with a universal and impartial love. Clearly, again, this is far from being the God of contemporary liberation theology, who is the God of the poor and the oppressed, the enslaved, and all against whom the structures of human society discriminate. These individuals are deprived of the opportunity of developing the moral and spiritual, intellectual and aesthetic potentialities of their nature. The God of the process theodicy is—according to this line of criticism—the God of the elite, of the great and successful among humankind. God is apparently the God of saints rather than of sinners; of geniuses rather than of the dull, retarded, and mentally defective; of the cream of humanity rather than of the anonymous millions who have been driven to self-seeking, violence, greed, and deceit in a desperate struggle to survive. This is not the God of those millions who have been crippled by malnutrition and have suffered and died under oppression and exploitation, plague and famine, flood and earthquake, or again of those—perhaps numbering about half the sum of human births—who have perished in infancy. . . .

Returning now to the problem of evil as a challenge to theistic belief, we can see that there are various ways in which the challenge has been sought to be met. One or other of these ways has seemed sufficient to many religious believers—sufficient, that is, to show that intellectually there is no need to abandon belief in God, even though of course no amount of intellectual justification can hope to assuage the actual pains and sorrows and sufferings of the human heart.

NOTES

1. Robert Burns, "Man Was Made to Mourn: A Dirge," line 55. Burns (1759–1796) was a Scottish poet. [D. C. ABEL]

2. *theodicies:* attempts to reconcile the existence of evil with the existence of God. The word was formed by the German philosopher Gottfried Wilhelm Leibniz (1646–1716) from the Greek words *theos* (God) and *dikē* (law, right). [D. C. ABEL, AFTER J. HICK]

3. J. L. Mackie, "Evil and Omnipotence," *Mind* 64 (April 1955), p. 209. [J. HICK] The passage appears on p. 85 of this book. [D. C. ABEL]

4. Alfred Lord Tennyson, *In Memoriam,* Section 65, stanza 4, line 3. [D. C. ABEL]

5. Augustine, *The Literal Meaning of Genesis,* Book I, Chapter 3. [J. HICK] For a biography of Augustine, see p. 67. [D. C. ABEL]

6. Augustine, *On Free Choice of the Will,* Book III, Chapter 9, Section 25. [J. HICK]

7. Friedrich Schleiermacher, *The Christian Faith,* Second Part, "Explication of the Consciousness of Sin." [J. HICK]

8. Augustine, *The City of God,* Book XII, Chapter 9. [J. HICK]

9. Irenaeus, *Against Heresies,* Book IV, Chapters 37–38. [J. HICK]

10. English poet John Keats (1795–1821), in a letter to his brother George and his sister Georgiana, dated February 14, 1819, described this world as "the vale of Soul-making." [D. C. ABEL]

11. *agapē:* the Christian notion of love (the word for "love" used most frequently in the Greek New Testament). [D. C. ABEL]

12. William Shakespeare, *Hamlet,* act III, scene 1, lines 62–63. [D. C. ABEL]

13. This discussion has been confined to the problem of human suffering. The large and intractable problem of animal pain is not taken up here. [J. HICK]

14. *metaphysical:* relating to *metaphysics,* the study of the nature and kinds of reality. [D. C. ABEL]

15. David Griffin, *God, Power, and Evil: A Process Theodicy* (Philadelphia: Westminster, 1976). [J. HICK]

16. Ibid., p. 276. [J. HICK]

17 *prehended:* absorbed and made part of (an actual occasion's) experience. [D. C. ABEL]

18. Alfred North Whitehead, *Religion in the Making* (Cambridge, England: Cambridge University Press, 1930), p. 51. [J. HICK]

19. Alfred North Whitehead, *Adventures of Ideas* (Cambridge, England: Cambridge University Press, 1933), p. 330. [J. HICK]

20. Griffin, *God, Power, and Evil,* p. 300. [J. HICK]

C. Faith and Reason

READING 11   # Pensées

Blaise Pascal

Blaise Pascal was born in 1623 in Clermont (now Clermont-Ferrand), France. His mother died when he was three, and in 1631 his father moved the family to Paris. Pascal had no formal schooling; he was educated by his father. He proved to be a precocious mathematician, publishing a paper on conic sections at the age of sixteen and inventing a calculating machine when he was nineteen. Pascal then turned his attention to physics. He made important discoveries—and published his findings—on such topics as atmospheric pressure, the equilibrium of fluids, and the problem of the vacuum. His later work on the mathematics of chance laid the foundations of modern probability theory. In 1646 Pascal's entire family converted to Jansenism (a highly rigorous form of Roman Catholicism, later condemned as heretical). One night in November 1654 Pascal had a powerful religious experience, and from that time on he devoted his intellectual energies primarily to religious matters. He defended Jansenism in a series of satirical letters known as the *Provincial Letters,* written in 1656 and 1657 under an assumed name. In 1659 he began (but never finished) a general defense of Christianity entitled *Apologie de la religion chrétienne* ("Apology for the Christian Religion"). Pascal died in Paris in 1662, at the age of thirty-nine, apparently from meningitis following a stomach ulcer.

In 1670 Pascal's fragmentary notes for the *Apologie* were published in a rearranged and abridged form. The editor called the work *Pensées sur la religion* ("Thoughts on Religion"), and they have been known by the shortened French title *Pensées* ever since. Our reading is from sections of the *Pensées* in which Pascal presents an argument (now known as "Pascal's wager") for believing in God and discusses the immortality of the soul.

Pascal explains that, in this life, we will never be able to know whether God exists, since our minds are finite and God (if God exists) is infinite and "infinitely beyond our comprehension." Despite our inability to know whether God exists, we must make a "wager" and either believe or not believe in God—there is no way to avoid the choice. If we bet that God exists and are right (assuming that we live morally and that there is an afterlife), we gain an eternity of happiness; if we are wrong, we lose nothing except the finite benefits we might have gained from immoral behavior. We may either win or lose our bet, but since we stand to make an infinite gain from a finite amount wagered, we would be foolish not to believe in God. Those who find themselves unable to believe despite their acceptance of the logic of this argument must learn to control their passions and love of pleasure, and begin to behave as if they did believe. Pascal goes on to stress the importance of trying to find out whether the soul is immortal and whether anything lies beyond the unhappiness of this life, and he castigates those who ignore these vital questions.

387

Order. I should be much more afraid of being mistaken and then finding out that Christianity is true, than of being mistaken in believing it to be true. . . .

418

Infinity—nothing. . . . If there is a God, he is infinitely beyond our comprehension, since, being indivisible and without limits, he bears no relation to us. We are therefore incapable of knowing either *what* he is or *whether* he is. That being so, who would dare to attempt an answer to the question? Certainly not we, who bear no relation to him.

Who then will condemn Christians for being unable to give rational grounds for their belief, professing as they do a religion for which they cannot give rational grounds? They declare that it is a folly, *stultitia*,[1] in expounding it to the world, and then you complain that they do not prove it. If they did prove it they would not be keeping their word. It is by being without proof that they show they are not without sense. "Yes, but although that excuses those who offer their religion as such, and absolves them from the criticism of producing it without rational grounds, it does not absolve those who accept it." Let us then examine this point, and let us say: "Either God is or he is not." But to which view shall we be inclined? Reason cannot decide this question. Infinite chaos separates us. At the far end of this infinite distance a coin is being spun which will come down heads or tails. How will you wager? Reason cannot make you choose either; reason cannot prove either wrong.

Do not then condemn as wrong those who have made a choice, for you know nothing about it. "No, but I will condemn them not for having made this particular choice, but any choice, for, although the one who calls heads and the other one are equally at fault, the fact is that they are both at fault: The right thing is not to wager at all."

Yes, but you must wager. There is no choice, you are already committed. Which will you choose then? Let us see: Since a choice must be made, let us see which offers you the least interest. You have two things to lose: the true and the good; and two things to stake: your reason and your will (your knowledge and your happiness). And your nature has two things to avoid: error and wretchedness. Since you must necessarily choose, your reason is no more affronted by choosing one rather than the other. That is one point cleared up. But your happiness? Let us weigh up the gain and the loss involved in calling heads that God exists. Let us assess the two cases: If you win you win everything, if you lose you lose nothing. Do not hesitate then; wager that he does exist. "That is wonderful. Yes, I must wager, but perhaps I am wagering too much." Let us see: Since there is an equal chance of gain and loss, if you stood to win only two lives for one you could still wager, but supposing you stood to win three?

You would have to play (since you must necessarily play) and it would be unwise of you, once you are obliged to play, not to risk your life in order to win three lives at a game in which there is an equal chance of losing and winning. But there is an eternity of life and happiness. That being so, even though there were an infinite number of chances, of which only one were in your favor, you would still be right to wager one in order to win two; and you would be acting wrongly, being obliged to play, in refusing to stake one life against three in a game where out of an infinite number of chances there is one in your favor, if there were an infinity of infinitely happy life to be won. But here there is an infinity of infinitely happy life to be won, one chance of winning against a finite number of chances of losing, and what you are staking is finite. That leaves no choice; wherever there is infinity, and where there are not infinite chances of losing against that of winning, there is no room for hesitation—you must give everything. And thus, since you are obliged to play, you must be renouncing reason if you hoard your life rather than risk it for an infinite gain, just as likely to occur as a loss amounting to nothing.

For it is no good saying that it is uncertain whether you will win, that it is certain that you are taking a risk, and that the infinite distance between the certainty of what you are risking and the uncertainty of what you may gain makes the finite good you are certainly risking equal to the infinite good that you are not certain to gain. This is not the case. Every gambler takes a certain risk for an uncertain gain, and yet he is taking a certain finite risk for an uncertain finite gain without sinning against reason. Here there is no infinite distance between the certain risk and the uncertain gain—that is not true. There is, indeed, an infinite distance between the certainty of winning and the certainty of losing, but the proportion between the uncertainty of winning and the certainty of what is being risked is in proportion to the chances of winning or losing. And hence, if there are as many chances on one side as on the other, you are playing for even odds. And in that case the certainty of what you are risking is equal to the uncertainty of what you may win; it is by no means infinitely distant from it. Thus our argument carries infinite weight, when the stakes are finite in a game where there are even chances of winning and losing and an infinite prize to be won.

This is conclusive; and if men are capable of any truth, this is it.

"I confess, I admit it, but is there really no way of seeing what the cards are?"—"Yes. Scripture and the rest, and so on."—"Yes, but my hands are tied and my lips are sealed; I am being forced to wager and I am not free; I am being held fast and I am so made that I cannot believe. What do you want me to do then?"—"That is true, but at least get it into your head that, if you are unable to believe, it is because of your passions, since reason impels you to believe and yet you cannot do so. Concentrate then not on convincing yourself by multiplying proofs of God's existence but by diminishing your passions. You want to find faith and you do not know the road. You want to be cured of unbelief and you ask for the remedy. Learn from those who were once bound like you and who now wager all they have. These are people who know the road you wish to follow, who have been cured of the affliction of which you wish to be cured: Follow the way by which they began. They behaved just as if they did believe, taking holy water, having Masses said, and so on. That will make you believe quite naturally, and will make you more docile."—"But that is what I am afraid of."—"But why? What have you to lose? But to show you that this is the way, the fact is that this diminishes the passions, which are your great obstacles. . . . "

End of this address. "Now what harm will come to you from choosing this course? You will be faithful, honest, humble, grateful, full of good works, a sincere, true friend. . . . It is true you will not enjoy noxious pleasures, glory, and good living; but will you not have others? I tell you that you will gain even in this life, and that at every step you take along this road you will see that your gain is so certain and your risk so negligible that in the end you will realize that you have wagered on something certain and infinite for which you have paid nothing."

"How these words fill me with rapture and delight!"

"If my words please you and seem cogent, you must know that they come from a man who went down upon his knees before and after to pray this infinite and indivisible being, to whom he submits his own, that he might bring your being also to submit to him for your own good and for his glory, and that strength might thus be reconciled with lowliness." . . .

427

. . . The immortality of the soul is something of such vital importance to us, affecting us so deeply, that one must have lost all feeling not to care about knowing the facts of the matter. All our actions and thoughts must follow such different paths, according to whether there is hope of eternal blessings or not, that the only possible way of acting with sense and judgment is to decide our course in the light of this point, which ought to be our ultimate objective.

Thus our chief interest and chief duty is to seek enlightenment on this subject, on which all our conduct depends. And that is why, amongst those who are not convinced, I make an absolute distinction between those who strive with all their might to learn and those who live without troubling themselves or thinking about it.

I can feel nothing but compassion for those who sincerely lament their doubt, who regard it as the ultimate misfortune, and who, sparing no effort to escape from it, make their search their principal and most serious business.

But as for those who spend their lives without a thought for this final end of life and who, solely because they do not find within themselves the light of conviction, neglect to look elsewhere and to examine thoroughly whether this opinion is one of those which people accept out of credulous simplicity or one of those which, though obscure in themselves, nonetheless have a most solid and unshakeable foundation—as for them, I view them very differently.

This negligence in a matter where they themselves, their eternity, their all are at stake, fills me more with irritation than pity; it astounds and appalls me; it seems quite monstrous to me. I do not say this prompted by the pious zeal of spiritual devotion. I mean on the contrary that we ought to have this feeling from principles of human interest and self-esteem. For that we need only see what the least enlightened see.

One needs no great sublimity of soul to realize that in this life there is no true and solid satisfaction, that all our pleasures are mere vanity, that our afflictions are infinite, and finally that death which threatens us at every moment must in a few years infallibly face us with the inescapable and appalling alternative of being annihilated or wretched throughout eternity.

Nothing could be more real or more dreadful than that. Let us put on as bold a face as we like—that is the end awaiting the world's most illustrious life. Let us ponder these things, and then say whether it is not beyond doubt that the only good thing in this life is the hope of another life, that we become happy only as we come nearer to it, and that, just as no more unhappiness awaits those who have been quite certain of eternity, so there is no happiness for those who have no inkling of it.

It is therefore quite certainly a great evil to have such doubts, but it is at least an indispensable obligation to seek when one does thus doubt; so the doubter who does not seek is at the same time very unhappy and very wrong. If in addition he feels a calm satisfaction which he openly professes, and even regards as a reason for joy and vanity, I can find no terms to describe so extravagant a creature. . . .

428

. . . It is indubitable that this life is but an instant of time, that the state of death is eternal, whatever its nature may be, and thus that all our actions and thoughts must follow such different paths according to the state of this eternity, that the only possible way of acting with sense and judgment is to decide our course in the light of this point, which ought to be our ultimate objective.

There is nothing more obvious than this, and it follows, according to rational principles, that men are behaving quite reasonably if they do not choose another path. Let us then judge on that score those who live without a thought for the final end of life, drifting wherever their inclinations and pleasures may take them, without reflection or anxiety, as if they could annihilate eternity by keeping their minds off it, concerned solely with attaining instant happiness.

However, eternity exists, and death, which must begin it and which threatens at every moment, must infallibly face them with the inescapable and appalling alternative of being either eternally annihilated or wretched, without their knowing which of these two forms of eternity stands ready to meet them forever.

The consequences are undeniably terrible. They risk an eternity of wretchedness; whereupon, as if the matter were not worth their trouble, they omit to consider whether this is one of those opinions which are accepted by the people with too ready credulity or one of those which, though obscure in themselves, have a very solid, though concealed, foundation. Thus they do not know whether the fact is true or false, nor whether the proofs are strong or weak. The proofs lie before their eyes, but they refuse to look, and in this state of ignorance they choose to do everything necessary to fall into this calamity, if it exists, to wait for death before testing the proofs, while yet remaining highly satisfied in that state, professing it openly, and indeed with pride. Can we seriously think how important this matter is without being horrified at such extravagant behavior?

To settle down in such ignorance is a monstrous thing, and those who spend their lives thus must be made to feel how extravagant and stupid it is by having it pointed out to them so that they are confounded by the sight of their own folly. For this is how men argue when they choose to live without knowing what they are and without seeking enlightenment. "I do not know," they say. . . .

577

If we must never take any chances, we ought not to do anything for religion, for it is not certain. But how many chances we do take—sea voyages, battles. Therefore, I say, we should have to do nothing at all, for nothing is certain. And there is more certainty in religion than that we shall live to see tomorrow.

For it is not certain that we shall see tomorrow, but it is certainly possible that we shall not. We cannot say the same of religion. It is not certain that it is true, but who would dare to say that it is certainly possible that it is not?

Now when we work for tomorrow and take chances we are behaving reasonably, for we ought to take chances, according to the rule of probability already demonstrated. . . .

748

Objection. Those who hope for salvation are happy in that respect, but this is counterbalanced by their fear of hell.

Reply. Who has more cause to fear hell, someone who does not know whether there is a hell, but is certain to be damned if there is, or someone who is completely convinced that there is a hell, and hopes to be saved if there is?

816

"I would soon have given up a life of pleasure," they say, "if I had faith." But I tell you: "You would soon have faith if you gave up a life of pleasure. Now it is up to you to begin. If I could give you faith, I would. But I cannot, nor can I test the truth of what you say, but you can easily give up your pleasure and test whether I am telling the truth."

NOTE

1. *stultitia:* the Latin equivalent of the Greek noun *mōria* ("folly"), a term Paul uses in 1 Corinthians 1:18 and 21. [D. C. ABEL]

The Will to Believe

William James

William James was born in New York City in 1842. As a youth he attended schools in England, France, Switzerland, and Germany. He also learned a great deal from his father (an energetic and unconventional scholar) and from extensive reading. He was interested in both science and art and decided to become a painter. When he was eighteen, he began to study painting, but soon realized that he did not have the talent to become a great artist. The following year he enrolled in the Lawrence Scientific School at Harvard University. In 1864 James transferred to the medical school. He took time out from his studies to accompany naturalist Louis Agassiz on a trip to the Amazon River. He later spent time studying experimental physiology in Germany. James received his medical degree from Harvard in 1869. He had long been in poor health, and he spent the next few years as a semi-invalid at his father's house. In 1873 he began teaching physiology at Harvard. Two years later he began teaching psychology, and four years after that he started teaching philosophy. Except for a two-year period spent recovering from serious illness, he continued teaching at Harvard until his retirement in 1907. James died in 1910 in Chocorua, New Hampshire.

James's principal works are *Principles of Psychology* (1890), *The Will to Believe and Other Essays in Popular Philosophy* (1897), *The Varieties of Religious Experience* (1902), *Pragmatism: A New Name for Old Ways of Thinking* (1907), and *A Pluralistic Universe* (1909).

Our selection is from "The Will to Believe," a lecture James gave in 1896 to the philosophy clubs of Yale and Brown Universities. James's lecture is a response to an essay by the English mathematician and philosopher William Kingdon Clifford. In "The Ethics of Belief" (published in 1877), Clifford argued that it is always morally wrong to believe something on insufficient evidence. In "The Will to Believe," James contends that, in some cases, we are justified in believing something on nonrational grounds. He begins by defining some basic terms. A *hypothesis* is something proposed to our belief. A hypothesis is *live* if there is a possibility that we will accept it; it is *dead* if there is no such possibility. A decision between two hypotheses is an *option*. An option is *living* if both hypotheses are live; it is *forced* if we cannot avoid choosing one of the hypotheses; it is *momentous* if something important is at stake, the opportunity is unique, and the outcome is irreversible. If an option is living, forced, and momentous, it is a *genuine* option.

According to James, when we are faced with a genuine option that cannot be decided on rational grounds, our "passional nature" is justified in accepting either of the two hypotheses. James argues that the decision whether to adopt or reject religious belief fulfills these conditions: There is insufficient evidence to settle the question on intellectual grounds, and—assuming that religious doctrine is a live hypothesis for us—the option is genuine. James concludes that the acceptance of religious belief (as well as its rejection) is justifiable on passional grounds.

I

Let us give the name of *hypothesis* to anything that may be proposed to our belief; and just as the electricians speak of live and dead wires, let us speak of any hypothesis as either *live* or *dead*. A live hypothesis is one that appeals as a real possibility to him to whom it is proposed. If I ask you to believe in the Mahdi,[1] the notion makes no electric connection with your nature; it refuses to scintillate with any credibility at all. As a hypothesis it is completely dead. To an Arab, however (even if he be not one of the Mahdi's followers), the hypothesis is among the mind's possibilities; it is alive. This shows that deadness and liveness in a hypothesis are not intrinsic properties, but relations to the individual thinker. They are measured by his willingness to act. The maximum of liveness in a hypothesis means willingness to act irrevocably. Practically that means belief, but there is some believing tendency wherever there is willingness to act at all.

Next, let us call the decision between two hypotheses an *option*. Options may be of several kinds. They may be (a) *living* or *dead;* (b) *forced* or *avoidable;* (c) *momentous* or *trivial;* and for our purposes we may call an option a *genuine* option when it is of the forced, living and momentous kind.

(a) A living option is one in which both hypotheses are live ones. If I say to you: "Be a theosophist[2] or a Mohammedan," it is probably a dead option, because for you neither hypothesis is likely to be alive. But if I say: "Be an agnostic[3] or a Christian," it is otherwise: Trained as you are, each hypothesis makes some appeal, however small, to your belief.

(b) Next, if I say to you: "Choose between going out with your umbrella or without it," I do not offer you a genuine option, for it is not forced. You can easily avoid it by not going out at all. Similarly, if I say, "Either love me or hate me," "Either call my theory true or call it false," your option is avoidable. You may remain indifferent to me, neither loving or hating, and you may decline to offer any judgment as to my theory. But if I say, "Either accept this truth or go without it," I put on you a forced option, for there is no standing place outside of the alternative. Every logical dilemma, with no possibility of not choosing, is an option of this forced kind.

(c) Finally, if I were Dr. Nansen[4] and proposed to you to join my North Pole expedition, your option would be momentous, for this would probably be your only similar opportunity, and your choice now would either exclude you from the North Pole sort of immortality altogether or put at least the chance of it in your hands. He who refuses to embrace a unique opportunity loses the prize as surely as if he tried and failed. Per contra,[5] the option is trivial when the opportunity is not unique, when the stake is insignificant, or when the decision is reversible if it later prove unwise. Such trivial options abound in the scientific life. A chemist finds an hypothesis live enough to spend a year in its verification: He believes in it to that extent. But if his experiments prove inconclusive either way, he is quit for[6] his loss of time, no vital harm being done. It will facilitate our discussion if we keep these distinctions well in mind. . . .

IV

. . . The thesis I defend is, briefly stated, this: *Our passional nature must, and lawfully may, decide an option between propositions, whenever it is a genuine option that cannot by its nature be decided on intellectual grounds; for to say, under such circum-stances, "Do not decide but leave the question open," is itself a passional decision, just like deciding "yes" or "no," and is attended with the same risk of losing the truth.* The thesis thus abstractly expressed will, I trust, soon become quite clear. But I must first indulge in a bit more of preliminary work.

VII

. . . There are two ways of looking at our duty in the matter of opinion, ways entirely different, and yet ways about whose difference the theory of knowl-edge seems hitherto to have shown very little concern. *We must know the truth;* and *we must avoid error*—these are our first and great commandments as would-be knowers. But they are not two ways of stating an identical com-mandment; they are two separable laws. Although it may indeed happen that, when we believe a truth A, we escape as an incidental consequence from be-lieving the falsehood B, it hardly ever happens that by merely disbelieving the falsehood B, we incidentally must needs[7] believe the truth A. We may, in es-caping B, fall into believing other falsehoods, C or D, just as bad as B; or we may escape B by not believing anything at all, not even A. "Believe truth!" "Shun error!"—these, we see, are two materially[8] different laws; and by choos-ing between them we may color differently our whole intellectual life. We may regard the chase for truth as paramount, and the avoidance of error as sec-ondary; or we may, on the other hand, treat the avoidance of error as more im-perative, and let truth take its chance. Clifford[9] . . . tells us, keep your mind in suspense forever, rather than by closing it on insufficient evidence incur the awful risk of believing lies. You, on the other hand, may think that the risk of being in error is a very small matter when compared with the blessings of real knowledge, and be ready to be duped many times in your investigation rather than postpone indefinitely the chance of guessing true. I myself find it impos-sible to go with Clifford. We must remember that these feelings of our duty about either truth or error are in any case only expressions of our passional life. Biologically considered, our minds are as ready to grind out falsehood as veracity, and he who says, "Better go without belief forever than believe a lie!" merely shows his own preponderant private horror of becoming a dupe. He may be critical of many of his desires and fears, but this fear he slavishly obeys. He cannot detach himself from it even hypothetically or imagine any-one questioning its binding force. For my own part, I have also a horror of be-ing duped. But I can believe that worse things than being duped may happen to a man in this world, so Clifford's exhortation has to my ears a thoroughly fantastic sound. It is like a general informing his soldiers that it is better to keep out of battle forever than to risk a single wound. Not so are victories ei-ther over enemies or over nature gained. Our errors are surely not such aw-fully solemn things. In a world where we are so certain to incur them in spite of all our caution, a certain lightness of heart seems healthier than this exces-sive nervousness on their behalf. At any rate it seems the fittest thing for the empiricist[10] philosopher.

VIII

And now, after all this introduction, let us go straight at our question. I have said, and now repeat it, that not only as a matter of fact do we find our passional nature influencing us in our opinions, but that there are some options between opinions in which this influence must be regarded both as an inevitable and as a lawful determinant of our choice.

I fear here that some of you my hearers will begin to scent danger and lend an inhospitable ear. Two first steps of passion you have indeed had to admit as necessary—we must think so as to avoid dupery, and we must think so as to gain truth—but the surest path to those ideal consummations, you will probably consider, is from now onwards to take no farther passional step. Well, of course, I agree as far as the facts will allow. Wherever the option between losing truth and gaining it is not momentous, we can throw the chance of *gaining truth* away, and at any rate save ourselves from any chance of *believing falsehood*, by not making up our minds at all till objective evidence has come. In scientific questions, this is almost always the case. And in human affairs in general, even, the need of acting is seldom so urgent that a false belief to act on is better than no belief at all. Law courts, indeed, have to decide on the best evidence attainable for the moment, because a judge's duty is to make law as well as to ascertain it, and (as a learned judge once said to me) few cases are worth spending much time over—the great thing is to have them decided on *any* acceptable principle, and got out of the way. But in our dealings with objective nature we obviously are mere recorders, not makers of the truth; and decisions for the mere sake of deciding promptly and getting on to the next business would be wholly out of place. Throughout the breadth of physical nature facts are what they are quite independently of us, and seldom is there any such hurry about them that the risks of being duped by believing a premature theory need be faced. The questions here are always trivial options, the hypotheses are hardly living (at any rate not living for us spectators), the choice between believing truth or falsehood is seldom forced. The attitude of skeptical balance is therefore the absolutely wise one if we wish to escape mistakes. What difference, indeed, does it make to most of us whether we have or have not a theory of the Roentgen rays, whether we believe or not in mind-stuff, or have a definitive conviction about the causality of conscious states? It makes no difference. Such options are not forced on us. On every account it is better not to make them, but still keep weighing reasons *pro et contra*[11] with an indifferent hand. I speak, of course, here of the purely judging mind. For purposes of discovery such indifference is to be less highly recommended, and science would be far less advanced than she is if the passionate desires of individuals to get their own faiths confirmed had been kept out of the game. In fact, if you want an absolute duffer in an investigation, you must, after all, take the man who has no interest whatever in its results. He is the warranted incapable, the positive fool. The most useful investigator, because the most sensitive observer, is always he whose eager interest in one side of the question is balanced by an equally keen nervousness lest he become deceived. Science has organized this nervousness into a regular *technique,* her so-called method of verification, and she has fallen so deeply in love with the method that one may even say she has ceased to care for truth by itself at all. It is only truth as technically verified that interests her. The truth of truths might come in merely oracular or affirmative form, and she would decline to look at it. Such truth as that, she might [say], . . . would be stolen in defiance of her duty to mankind. Human passions, however, are stronger than technical rules. *"Le coeur a ses raisons,"* as Pascal says, *"que la raison ne connaît pas"*;[12] and however indifferent to all but the bare rules of the game the umpire, the abstract intellect, may be, the concrete players who furnish him the materials to judge of, are usually, each one of them, in love with some pet "live hypothesis" of his own.

Let us agree, however, that wherever there is no forced option, the dispassionately judicial intellect, with no pet hypothesis, saving us at any rate from dupery, ought to be our ideal. The question next arises: Are there not *somewhere* forced options in our speculative questions, and can we (as men who may be interested at least as much in positively gaining truth as in merely escaping dupery) always wait with impunity till the coercive evidence shall have arrived? It seems a priori[13] improbable that the truth should be so nicely adjusted to our needs and powers as that. In the great boarding-house of nature, the cakes and the butter and the syrup seldom come out so even and leave the plates so clean. Indeed we should view them with scientific suspicion if they did.

IX

Moral questions immediately present themselves as questions whose solution cannot wait for sensible[14] proof. A moral question is a question not of what sensibly exists, but of what is good, or would be good if it did exist. Science can tell us what exists, but to compare the *worths*, both of what exists and of what does not exist, we must consult not science but what Pascal calls our heart. . . .

Turn now from these wide questions of good to a certain class of questions of fact, questions concerning personal relations, states of mind between one man and another—*Do you like me or not?* for example. Whether you do or not depends, in countless instances, on whether I meet you half-way, am willing to assume that you *must* like me, and show you trust and expectation. The previous faith on my part in your liking's existence is what makes your liking come. If I stand aloof and refuse to budge an inch until I have objective evidence, until you have done something apt, as the absolutists say, *ad extorquendum assensum meum*,[15] ten to one your liking never comes. How many women's hearts are vanquished by the mere sanguine insistence of some man that they *must* love him; he will not consent to the hypothesis that they cannot! The desire for a certain kind of truth here brings about that special truth's existence, and so it is in innumerable cases of other sorts. Who gains promotions, boons, appointments, but the man in whose life they are seen to play the part of live hypotheses, who discounts them, sacrifices other things for their sake before they have come, and takes risks for them in advance? His faith acts on the powers above him as a claim and creates its own verification.

Where faith in a fact, based on need of the fact, can create the fact, that would be an insane logic which should say that faith based on inner need, and running ahead of scientific evidence, is the "lowest kind of immorality" into which a thinking being can fall. Yet such is the logic by which our scientific absolutists pretend to regulate our lives!

X

In truths dependent on our personal action, then, faith based on desire is certainly a lawful, and possibly an indispensable thing. But now, it will be said, these are all childish human cases, and have nothing to do with great cosmical matters, like the question of religious faith. Let us then pass on to that! Religions differ so much in their accidents[16] that in discussing the religious question we must make it very generic and broad. What then do we now mean by the religious hypothesis? Science says things *are;* morality says some things are *better than* other things; and religion says essentially two things:

First, she says that the best things are the more eternal things, the overlapping things, the things in the universe that throw the last stone, so to speak, and say the final word. "Perfection is eternal"—this phrase of Charles Secrétan[17] seems a good way of putting this first affirmation of religion, an affirmation that obviously cannot yet be verified scientifically at all.

And the second affirmation of religion is that we are better off even now *if we believe* that first religious truth.

Now let us consider what the logical elements of this situation are *in case the religious hypothesis in both its branches be really true.* (Of course we must admit that possibility at the outset. If we are to discuss the question at all, it must involve a living option. If for any of you religion be a hypothesis that cannot, by any living possibility be true, then you need go no further. I speak to the "saving remnant" alone.) So proceeding, we see, first, that religion offers itself as a *momentous* option. We are supposed to gain, even now, by our belief, and to lose by our nonbelief, a certain vital good. Secondly, religion is a *forced* option, so far as that good goes. We cannot escape the issue by remaining skeptical and waiting for more light, because, although we do avoid error in that way *if religion be untrue,* we lose the good *if it be true,* just as certainly as if we positively chose to disbelieve. It is as if a man should hesitate indefinitely to ask a certain woman to marry him because he was not sure whether she would prove an angel or a devil after he brought her home. Would he not cut himself off from that particular angel-possibility as decisively as if he went and married someone else? Skepticism, then, is not avoidance of option; it is option of a certain particular kind of risk. *Better risk loss of truth than chance of error*—that is your faith-vetoer's exact position. He is actively playing his stake as much as the believer is; he is backing the field against the religious hypothesis, just as the believer is backing the religious hypothesis against the field. To preach skepticism to us as a duty until "sufficient evidence" for religion be found, is tantamount therefore to telling us when in presence of the religious hypothesis, that to yield to our fear of its being error is wiser and better than to yield to our hope that it may be true.

It is not intellect against all passions, then; it is only intellect with one passion laying down its law. And by what, forsooth, is the supreme wisdom of this passion warranted? And dupery for dupery, what proof is there that dupery through hope is so much worse a kind of dupery than dupery through fear? I, for one, can see no proof. And I simply refuse obedience to the scientist's command to imitate his kind of option, in a case where my own stake is important enough to give me the right to choose my own form of risk. If religion be true and the evidence for it be still insufficient, I do not wish, by putting your extinguisher upon my nature (which feels to me as if it had some business in this matter), to forfeit my sole chance in life of getting upon the winning side—that chance depending, of course, on my willingness to run the risk of acting as if my passional need of taking the world religiously might be prophetic and right.

All this is on the supposition that it really *may* be prophetic and right; that, even to us who are discussing the matter, religion is a live hypothesis. Now to most of us religion comes in a still farther way that makes a veto on our active faith even more illogical. The more perfect and more eternal aspect of the universe is represented in our religions as having personal form. The universe is no longer a mere *It* to us, but a *Thou*, if we are religious; and any relation that may be possible from person to person might be possible here. For instance, although in one sense we are passive portions of the universe, in another we show a curious autonomy, as if we were small active centers on our own account. We feel, too, as if the appeal of religion to us were made to our own active good will, as if evidence might be forever withheld from us unless we met the hypothesis half-way. To take a trivial illustration, just as a man who, in a company of gentlemen, made no advances, asked a warrant for every concession, and believed no one's word without proof, would cut himself off by such churlishness from all the social rewards that a more trusting spirit would earn; so here, one who should shut himself up in snarling logicality and try to make the gods extort his recognition willy-nilly, or not get it at all, might cut himself off forever from his only opportunity of making the gods' acquaintance. This feeling, forced on us we know not whence, that by obstinately believing that there *are* gods (although not to do so would be so easy both for our logic and our life) we are doing the universe the deepest service we can, seems part of the living essence of the religious hypothesis. If the hypothesis *were* true in all its parts, including this one, then pure intellectualism, with its veto on our making willing advances, would be an absurdity; and some participation of our sympathetic nature would be logically required. I, therefore, for one, cannot see my way to accepting the agnostic rules for truth seeking, or willfully agree to keep my willing nature out of the game. I cannot do so for this plain reason, that *a code that would absolutely prevent me from acknowledging certain kinds of truth if those kinds of truth were really there, would be an irrational code*. This for me is the long and short of the formal logic of the situation, no matter what the kinds of truth might materially be.

I confess I do not see how this logic can be escaped. But sad experience makes me fear that some of you may still shrink from radically saying with me *in abstracto*[18] that we have the right to believe at our own risk any hypothesis that is live enough to tempt our will. I suspect, if this is so, however, that it is because you have got away from the abstract logical point of view altogether, and are thinking (perhaps without realizing it) of some particular religious hypothesis which for you is dead. The freedom to "believe what we will" you apply to the case of some patent superstition, and the faith you think of is the faith defined by the schoolboy when he said, "Faith is when you believe something that you know ain't true." I can only repeat that this is misapprehension. *In concreto*[19] the freedom to believe can only cover living options which the intellect cannot by itself resolve; and living options never seem absurdities to him who has them to consider. When I look at the religious question, as it really puts itself to concrete men, when I think of all the possibilities which it theoretically involves, then this command that we shall put a stopper on our heart, instincts and courage, and wait—*acting* of course meanwhile more or less as if religion were *not* true—till doomsday, or till such time as our intellect and senses working together may have raked in evidence enough—this command, I say, seems to me the queer-est idol ever manufactured in the philosophic cave. Were we scholastic[20] abso-lutists, there might be more excuse. If we had an infallible intellect with its objective certitudes, we might feel ourselves disloyal to such an organ of knowledge in not trusting to it exclusively, in not waiting for its solving word. But if we are empiricists, if we believe that no bell in us tolls to let us know for certain when truth is in our grasp, then it seems a piece of idle fantasticality to preach so solemnly our duty of waiting for the bell. Indeed we may wait if we will; but we do so at our peril, as much as if we believed. In *either* case we *act,* taking our life in our hands. No one of us ought to issue vetoes to the other, nor should we bandy words of abuse. We ought, on the contrary, delicately and profoundly to respect each other's mental freedom—then only shall we bring about the intellectual republic; then only shall we have that spirit of inner tol-erance without which all our outer tolerance is soulless, and which is empiri-cism's glory; then only shall we live and let live, in speculative as well as in practical things.

NOTES

1. the *Mahdi:* the expected messiah of the Muslims. [D. C. ABEL]
2. *theosophist:* an adherent of *theosophy,* a doctrine that emphasizes mystical in-sight and whose tenets include pantheism and reincarnation. [D. C. ABEL]
3. *agnostic:* someone who claims that God's existence is unknown, and perhaps unknowable. [D. C. ABEL]
4. Fridtjof Nansen (1861–1930) was a Norwegian explorer and politician. [D. C. ABEL]
5. *per contra:* (Latin) "on the contrary." [D. C. ABEL]
6. *is quit for:* has lost nothing more than. [D. C. ABEL]
7. *needs:* necessarily. [D. C. ABEL]
8. *materially:* relating to the content (material), rather than to the form. [D. C. ABEL]

9. James refers to an essay by William Kingdon Clifford entitled "The Ethics of Belief," published in The *Contemporary Review* (January 1877). Clifford (1845–1879) was an English mathematician and philosopher. [D. C. ABEL]

10. *empiricist:* relating to *empiricism,* the doctrine that knowledge is attained primarily through sense experience. [D. C. ABEL]

11. *pro et contra:* (Latin) "for and against." [D. C. ABEL]

12. "The heart has its reasons, which reason does not know" (*Pensées,* no. 423 [277 in older editions]). Blaise Pascal (1623–1662) was a French philosopher and mathematician; for a biography, see p. 100. [D. C. ABEL]

13. *a priori:* based on prior, reasonable assumptions (literally, in Latin, "from what comes earlier"). [D. C. ABEL]

14. *sensible:* able to be perceived by the senses. [D. C. ABEL]

15. *ad extorquendum assensum meum:* (Latin) "to force my assent." [D. C. ABEL]

16. *accidents:* qualities of a thing that are not essential to its nature. [D. C. ABEL]

17. Charles Secrétan, *Discours laiques* (Paris, France: Sandoz & Fischbacher, 1877), p. 5. Secrétan (1815–1895) was a Swiss philosopher. [D. C. ABEL]

18. *in abstracto:* (Latin) "abstractly." [D. C. ABEL]

19. *in concreto:* (Latin) "concretely"; contrasted with *in abstracto* (see note 18). [D. C. ABEL]

20. *scholastic:* relating to *scholasticism,* a medieval approach to philosophy that emphasized commentaries on classic texts. [D. C. ABEL]

CHAPTER 3 Theories of Knowledge

None of us would be so presumptuous as to claim that we know everything, but we all are quite sure that we know *some* things. But what do we mean when we say that we know something? Does knowing something imply that we have verified it for ourselves? If we have not verified it, do we have *belief* rather than knowledge? If I have never been to India, can I legitimately say that I *know* India exists? Is it more accurate to say that I *believe* that it exists because I trust publishers who sell atlases that label a certain region "India," newspapers that print stories about India, teachers who lecture about India, and friends who tell me about their travels there and show me photographs? Perhaps one kind of verification is *sight:* If I see it, I know it is true. If so, do I know that the print on this page is black because I am looking at it and it appears black? Is it possible that even though the print *appears* black, it is really some other color? But how can print have any color *at all* if it is made up of colorless atoms? Is it more accurate to say that the print causes me to *experience* a color, but that the print itself is colorless? To carry this questioning even further, how can I even be sure that I am looking at a printed page right now? Could I really be home sleeping and simply *dreaming* that I am reading a book? Can I be absolutely certain of anything at all? Is absolute certainty necessary for knowledge? Assuming that I can attain knowledge, is the ultimate source of my knowledge sensation, reason, intuition, or some combination of these and/or other factors?

These are some of the questions addressed by *epistemology,* the study of the nature and grounds of knowledge. This section presents eight readings that address these and related epistemological issues.

115

Plato in the *Republic* contrasts knowledge and opinion. The objects of knowledge are the forms—immaterial and unchanging realities, such as the beautiful itself. The objects of opinion are the Many—material and changing things, such as beautiful trees and horses. The forms are fully real and grasped by the mind, whereas the Many are partly real and partly unreal and are grasped by the senses.

René Descartes argues that genuine knowledge requires absolute certainty. Trying to achieve certainty by using a "method of doubt," he refuses to accept as true anything about which he could possibly be deceived. Descartes discovers that he can be sure that he exists, because he could not even be deceived if he did not exist. This discovery leads him to claim that anything that he perceives very clearly and very distinctly is true. He also holds that the mind contains innate ideas, including the idea of God.

Descartes's theory of knowledge is considered a form of *rationalism* (derived from *ratio,* Latin for "reason") because it emphasizes knowledge attained through the mind (innate ideas, intuition, relations among ideas, logical inference, and so on). The next three theories, by contrast, are forms of *empiricism* (derived from *empeiria,* Greek for "experience") because they emphasize knowledge attained through sense experience.

John Locke rejects Descartes's rationalist doctrine that the mind is furnished with innate ideas. Locke claims that the mind is originally blank, like a sheet of white paper; all our ideas come either from experiencing external objects or from experiencing the operations of our mind. He distinguishes two kinds of qualities that objects cause us to experience: *primary qualities,* which really exist in things (three-dimensionality and shape, for example), and *secondary qualities,* which do not exist in things but are only in our mind (color and taste, for example). The next empiricist theory is that of George Berkeley. Berkeley has Philonous ("lover of the mind" in Greek) argue that *neither* primary nor secondary qualities exist in things; both exist only in the mind. From this Philonous concludes that material things themselves exist only in the mind. But since material things affect us independently of our will, their existence depends not on *our* mind but on an infinite, divine mind. Our third empiricist philosopher, David Hume, holds that all knowledge begins with "impressions" (direct sense experiences) and that impressions give rise to "ideas" (copies of impressions). When we attempt to extend our knowledge beyond that provided by impressions and ideas, we rely on the notion of cause and effect. But we cannot *know* that causality exists because we have no impression of a "cause" linking two events: All we experience is the temporal succession of the two events.

Immanuel Kant proposes a theory of knowledge that combines elements of rationalism and empiricism. He accepts the empiricist claim that our knowledge begins with experience, but also accepts the rationalist contention that part of the content of knowledge comes from our mind. Both points are correct, Kant argues, because our mind is constructed in such a way that we necessarily experience objects in certain ways (for example, as being caused and as existing in space and time). Therefore, although we know that objects will invariably *appear to us* to possess certain attributes, we do not experience objects as they are *in themselves*. It would be an error, for example, to say that things themselves are caused, spatial, or temporal.

Our final reading is from Alison M. Jaggar, who points out that most theories of knowledge exalt dispassionate reason as the sole path to knowledge and see emotion as subverting the knowing process. Jaggar argues that emotion in fact plays a helpful and necessary role in attaining knowledge. She contends that an important avenue to knowledge is the exploration of the emotional responses of members of subordinate groups in society.

Republic

Plato

A biography of Plato appears on p. 4.

This reading from Plato is from the *Republic,* a work cast as a report by Socrates of a conversation he had the previous day with several people, including Glaucon and Adeimantus (Plato's older brothers). In the dialogue Socrates presents his views on a number of topics, but scholars agree these views are Plato's own, not those of the historical Socrates. Our readings are taken from exchanges between Socrates and Glaucon in Books V, VI, and VII.

In Book V Glaucon asks Socrates who the true philosophers are. Socrates, alluding to the etymology of the word ("lovers of wisdom"), says that they are "those who love the sight of truth." Expanding on this notion, Socrates explains that philosophers are those who love the One rather than the Many. For example, a philosopher goes beyond the love of individual beautiful things to love the beautiful itself (absolute beauty, the *form* of beauty). The forms are fully real and are the objects of genuine knowledge, whereas the Many lie between being and not-being and are the objects of mere opinion.

In Book VI Socrates explains that the Many belong to the visible world, which is seen by the eye, while the forms reside in the intelligible world, which is grasped by the mind. He illustrates the two worlds by describing a line divided into two main parts, with each of these parts subdivided into two parts. Each of the resulting four segments of the line represents a type of object of cognition. Corresponding to each of the four types of object of cognition is a distinct condition of the soul. (See the diagram of the divided line on p. 121.)

Socrates further illustrates this theory of knowledge in Book VII through the famous allegory of the cave. We are like prisoners who live their entire lives inside a cave. Just as such prisoners would think that shadows on the cave wall were real and would be unaware of the real world outside the cave, so we think that the visible world of the Many is real, ignorant of the intelligible world of forms. (See the diagram of the cave on p. 124.)

BOOK V

. . . [Glaucon asked:] Who are the true philosophers?

[I, Socrates, replied:] Those who love the sight of truth.

That's right, but what exactly do you mean by it?

It would not be easy to explain to someone else, but I think that you will agree to this.

To what?

Since the beautiful is the opposite of the ugly, they are two.

Of course.

And since they are two, each is one?

I grant that also.

And the same account is true of the just and the unjust, the good and the bad, and all the forms. Each of them is itself one, but because they manifest themselves everywhere in association with actions, bodies, and one another, each of them appears to be many.

That's right.

So, I draw this distinction: On one side are those you just now called lovers of sights, lovers of crafts, and practical people; on the other side are those we are arguing about and whom one would alone call philosophers.

How do you mean?

The lovers of sights and sounds like beautiful sounds, colors, shapes, and everything fashioned out of them, but their thought is unable to see and embrace the nature of the beautiful itself.

That's for sure.

In fact, there are very few people who would be able to reach the beautiful itself and see it by itself. Isn't that so?

Certainly.

What about someone who believes in beautiful things, but doesn't believe in the beautiful itself and isn't able to follow anyone who could lead him to the knowledge of it? Don't you think he is living in a dream rather than a wakened state? Isn't this dreaming—whether asleep or awake, to think that a likeness is not a likeness but rather the thing itself that it is like?

I certainly think that someone who does that is dreaming.

But someone who, to take the opposite case, believes in the beautiful itself, can see both it and the things that participate in it and doesn't believe that the participants are it or that it itself is the participants—is he living in a dream or is he awake?

He's very much awake.

So we'd be right to call his thought knowledge, since he knows, but we should call the other person's thought opinion, since he opines?

Right. . . .

I want to address a question to our friend who doesn't believe in the beautiful itself or any form of the beautiful itself that remains always the same in all respects but who does believe in the many beautiful things—the lover of sights who wouldn't allow anyone to say that the beautiful itself is one or that the just is one or any of the rest: "My dear fellow," we'll say, "of all the many beautiful things, is there one that will not also appear ugly? Or is there one of those just things that will not also appear unjust? Or one of those pious things that will not also appear impious?"

There isn't one, for it is necessary that they appear to be beautiful in a way and also to be ugly in a way, and the same with the other things you asked about.

What about the many doubles? Do they appear any the less halves than doubles?

Not one.

So, with the many bigs and smalls and lights and heavies, is any one of them any more the thing someone says it is than its opposite?

No, each of them always participates in both opposites.

Is any one of the manys what someone says it is, then, any more than it is not what he says it is?

No, they are like the ambiguities one is entertained with at dinner parties or like the children's riddle about the eunuch who threw something at a bat—the one about what he threw at it and what it was in[1]—for they are ambiguous, and one cannot understand them as fixedly being or fixedly not being, or as both or as neither.

Then do you know how to deal with them? Or can you find a more appropriate place to put them than intermediate between being and not being? For they can't be darker than what is not, in the sense of having less being than that, nor clearer than what is, in the sense of having more being.

Very true.

We've now discovered, it seems, that according to the many conventions of the majority of people about beauty and the others, [the many participants in beauty and in the other forms] are rolling around as intermediates between what is not and what purely is.

We have.

And we agreed earlier that anything of that kind would have to be called the opinable, not the knowable—the wandering intermediate grasped by the intermediate power.

We did.

As for those who study the many beautiful things but do not see the beautiful itself and are incapable of following another who leads them to it, who see many just things but not the just itself, and so with everything—these people, we shall say, opine everything but have no knowledge of anything they opine.

Necessarily.

What about the ones who in each case study the things themselves that are always the same in every respect? Won't we say that they know and don't opine?

That's necessary too.

Shall we say, then, that these people love and embrace the things that knowledge is set over, as the others do the things that opinion is set over? Remember we said that the latter saw and loved beautiful sounds and colors and the like but wouldn't allow the beautiful itself to be anything?

We remember, all right.

We won't be in error, then, if we call such people lovers of opinion rather than philosophers or lovers of wisdom and knowledge. Will they be angry with us if we call them that?

Not if they take my advice, for it isn't right to be angry with those who speak the truth.

As for those who in each case embrace the thing itself, we must call them philosophers, not lovers of opinion.

Most definitely.

BOOK VI

. . . We say that there are many beautiful things and many good things, and so on for each kind, and in this way we distinguish them in words.

We do.

And what is the main thing, we speak of beauty itself and good itself; and so, in the case of all the things that we then set down as many, we turn about and set down a single form of each, believing that there is but one, and call it "the being"[2] of each.

That's true.

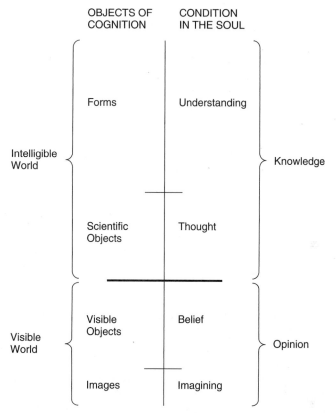

The Divided Line

And we say that the many beautiful things and the rest are visible but not intelligible, while the forms are intelligible but not visible.

That's completely true. . . .

You have two kinds of thing, visible and intelligible.

Right.

It is like a line divided into two unequal sections. Then divide each section— namely, that of the visible and that of the intelligible—in the same ratio as the line. In terms now of relative clarity and opacity, one subsection of the visible consists of images. And by images I mean, first, shadows, then reflections in water and in all close-packed, smooth, and shiny materials, and everything of that sort, if you understand.

I do.

In the other subsection of the visible, put the originals of these images— namely, the animals around us, all the plants, and the whole class of manufactured things.

Consider them put.

Would you be willing to say that, as regards truth and untruth, the division is in this proportion: As the opinable is to the knowable, so the likeness is to the thing that it is like?

Certainly.

Consider now how the section of the intelligible is to be divided.

How?

As follows: In one subsection, the soul, using as images the things that were imitated before, is forced to investigate from hypotheses, proceeding not to a first principle but to a conclusion. In the other subsection, however, it makes its way to a first principle that is *not* a hypothesis, proceeding from a hypothesis but without the images used in the previous subsection, using forms themselves and making its investigation through them.

I don't yet fully understand what you mean.

Let's try again. You'll understand it more easily after the following preamble. I think you know that students of geometry, calculation, and the like hypothesize the odd and the even, the various figures, the three kinds of angles, and other things akin to these in each of their investigations, as if they knew them. They make these their hypotheses and don't think it necessary to give any account of them, either to themselves or to others, as if they were clear to everyone. And going from these first principles through the remaining steps, they arrive in full agreement.

I certainly know that much.

Then you also know that, although they use visible figures and make claims about them, their thought isn't directed to them but to those other things that they are like. They make their claims for the sake of the square itself and the diagonal itself, not the diagonal they draw, and similarly with the others. These figures that they make and draw, of which shadows and reflections in water are images, they now in turn use as images, in seeking to see those others themselves that one cannot see except by means of thought.

That's true.

This, then, is the kind of thing that, on the one hand, I said is intelligible, and, on the other, is such that the soul is forced to use hypotheses in the investigation of it, not travelling up to a first principle, since it cannot reach beyond its hypotheses, but using as images those very things of which images were made in the section below, and which, by comparison to their images, were thought to be clear and valued as such.

I understand that you mean what happens in geometry and related sciences.

Then also understand that, by the other subsection of the intelligible, I mean that which reason itself grasps by the power of dialectic.[3] It does not consider these hypotheses as first principles but truly as hypotheses—stepping stones to take off from, enabling it to reach the unhypothetical first principle of everything. Having grasped this principle, it reverses itself and, keeping hold of what follows from it, comes down to a conclusion without making use of anything visible at all, but only of forms themselves, moving on from forms to forms, and ending in forms.

I understand, if not yet adequately (for in my opinion you're speaking of an enormous task), that you want to distinguish the intelligible part of that which is, the part studied by the science of dialectic, as clearer than the part studied by the so-called sciences, for which their hypotheses are first principles. And although those who study the objects of these sciences are forced to do so by means of thought rather than sense perception, still, because they do not go back to a genuine first principle, but proceed from hypotheses, you don't think that they understand them, even though, given such a principle, they are intelligible. And you seem to me to call the state of the geometers thought but not understanding, thought being intermediate between opinion and understanding.

Your exposition is most adequate. Thus there are four such conditions in the soul, corresponding to the four subsections of our line: Understanding for the highest, thought for the second, belief for the third, and imaging for the last. Arrange them in a ratio, and consider that each shares in clarity to the degree that the subsection it is set over shares in truth.

I understand, agree, and arrange them as you say.

BOOK VII

Next, I said, compare the effect of education and of the lack of it on our nature to an experience like this: Imagine human beings living in an underground, cavelike dwelling, with an entrance a long way up, which is both open to the light and as wide as the cave itself. They've been there since childhood, fixed in the same place, with their necks and legs fettered, able to see only in front of them, because their bonds prevent them from turning their heads around. Light is provided by a fire burning far above and behind them. Also behind them, but on higher ground, there is a path stretching between them and the fire. Imagine that along this path a low wall has been built, like the screen in front of puppeteers above which they show their puppets.

I'm imagining it.

Then also imagine that there are people along the wall, carrying all kinds of artifacts that project above it—statues of people and other animals, made out of stone, wood, and every material. And, as you'd expect, some of the carriers are talking, and some are silent.

It's a strange image you're describing, and strange prisoners.

They're like us. Do you suppose, first of all, that these prisoners see anything of themselves and one another besides the shadows that the fire casts on the wall in front of them?

How could they, if they have to keep their heads motionless throughout life?

What about the things being carried along the wall? Isn't the same true of them?

Of course.

And if they could talk to one another, don't you think they'd suppose that the names they use apply to the things they see passing before them?

They'd have to.

And what if their prison also had an echo from the wall facing them? Don't you think they'd believe that the shadows passing in front of them were talking whenever one of the carriers passing along the wall was doing so?

I certainly do.

Then the prisoners would in every way believe that the truth is nothing other than the shadows of those artifacts.

The Cave

They must surely believe that.

Consider, then, what being released from their bonds and cured of their ignorance would naturally be like if something like this came to pass. When one
of them was freed and suddenly compelled to stand up, turn his head, walk, and
look up toward the light, he'd be pained and dazzled and unable to see the
things whose shadows he'd seen before. What do you think he'd say, if we told
him that what he'd seen before was inconsequential, but that now—because he
is a bit closer to the things that are and is turned towards things that are more—
he sees more correctly? Or, to put it another way, if we pointed to each of the
things passing by, asked him what each of them is, and compelled him to answer, don't you think he'd be at a loss and that he'd believe that the things he
saw earlier were truer than the ones he was now being shown?

Much truer.

And if someone compelled him to look at the light itself, wouldn't his eyes
hurt, and wouldn't he turn around and flee towards the things he's able to see,
believing that they're really clearer than the ones he's being shown?

He would.

And if someone dragged him away from there by force, up the rough, steep
path, and didn't let him go until he had dragged him into the sunlight, wouldn't
he be pained and irritated at being treated that way? And when he came into the
light, with the sun filling his eyes, wouldn't he be unable to see a single one of the
things now said to be true?

He would be unable to see them, at least at first.

I suppose, then, that he'd need time to get adjusted before he could see
things in the world above. At first he'd see shadows most easily, then images of
men and other things in water, then the things themselves. Of these, he'd be able
to study the things in the sky and the sky itself more easily at night, looking at

the light of the stars and the moon, than during the day, looking at the sun and the light of the sun.

Of course.

Finally, I suppose, he'd be able to see the sun—not images of it in water or some alien place, but the sun itself, in its own place—and be able to study it.

Necessarily so.

And at this point he would infer and conclude that the sun provides the seasons and the years, governs everything in the visible world, and is in some way the cause of all the things that he used to see.

It's clear that would be his next step.

What about when he reminds himself of his first dwelling place, his fellow prisoners, and what passed for wisdom there? Don't you think that he'd count himself happy for the change and pity the others?

Certainly.

And if there had been any honors, praises, or prizes among them for the one who was sharpest at identifying the shadows as they passed by and who best remembered which usually came earlier, which later, and which simultaneously, and who could thus best divine the future, do you think that our man would desire these rewards or envy those among the prisoners who were honored and held power? Instead, wouldn't he feel, with Homer, that he'd much prefer to "work the earth as a serf to another, one without possessions,"[4] and go through any sufferings, rather than share their opinions and live as they do?

I suppose he would rather suffer anything than live like that.

Consider this too. If this man went down into the cave again and sat down in his same seat, wouldn't his eyes—coming suddenly out of the sun like that—be filled with darkness?

They certainly would.

And before his eyes had recovered—and the adjustment would not be quick—while his vision was still dim, if he had to compete again with the perpetual prisoners in recognizing the shadows, wouldn't he invite ridicule? Wouldn't it be said of him that he'd returned from his upward journey with his eyesight ruined and that it isn't worthwhile even to try to travel upward? And, as for anyone who tried to free them and lead them upward, if they could somehow get their hands on him, wouldn't they kill him?[5]

They certainly would.

This whole image, Glaucon, must be fitted together with what we said before. The visible realm should be likened to the prison dwelling, and the light of the fire inside it to the power of the sun. And if you interpret the upward journey and the study of things above as the upward journey of the soul to the intelligible realm, you'll grasp what I hope to convey, since that is what you wanted to hear about. Whether it's true or not, only the god knows. But this is how I see it: In the knowable realm, the form of the good is the last thing to be seen, and it is reached only with difficulty. Once one has seen it, however, one must conclude that it is the cause of all that is correct and beautiful in anything, that it produces both light and its source in the visible realm, and that in the intelligible realm it controls and provides truth and understanding, so that anyone who is to act sensibly in private or public must see it.

I have the same thought, at least as far as I'm able.

Come, then, share with me this thought also: It isn't surprising that the ones who get to this point are unwilling to occupy themselves with human affairs and that their souls are always pressing upwards, eager to spend their time above—for, after all, this is surely what we'd expect, if indeed things fit the image I described before.

It is.

What about what happens when someone turns from divine study to the evils of human life? Do you think it's surprising, since his sight is still dim, and he hasn't yet become accustomed to the darkness around him, that he behaves awkwardly and appears completely ridiculous if he's compelled, either in the courts or elsewhere, to contend about the shadows of justice or the statues of which they are the shadows and to dispute about the way these things are understood by people who have never seen justice itself?

That's not surprising at all.

No, it isn't. But anyone with any understanding would remember that the eyes may be confused in two ways and from two causes, namely, when they've come from the light into the darkness *and* when they've come from the darkness into the light. Realizing that the same applies to the soul, when someone sees a soul disturbed and unable to see something, he won't laugh mindlessly, but he'll take into consideration whether it has come from a brighter life and is dimmed through not having yet become accustomed to the dark or whether it has come from greater ignorance into greater light and is dazzled by the increased brilliance. Then he'll declare the first soul happy in its experience and life, and he'll pity the latter—but even if he chose to make fun of it, at least he'd be less ridiculous than if he laughed at a soul that has come from the light above.

What you say is very reasonable.

If that's true, then here's what we must think about these matters: Education isn't what some people declare it to be, namely, putting knowledge into souls that lack it, like putting sight into blind eyes.

They do say that.

But our present discussion, on the other hand, shows that the power to learn is present in everyone's soul and that the instrument with which each learns is like an eye that cannot be turned around from darkness to light without turning the whole body. This instrument cannot be turned around from that which is coming into being without turning the whole soul until it is able to study that which is and the brightest thing that is—namely, the one we call the good. Isn't that right?

Yes.

NOTES

1. The children's riddle illustrates Socrates' point about the same thing having opposite qualities: A eunuch is a man and not a man, a bat is a bird and not a bird, the pumice stone thrown by the eunuch is a stone and not a stone, and the tree that the poor-sighted eunuch thought the bat was in is not a tree but a piece of timber. [D. C. ABEL]
2. *"the being"*: the "what it is" of a thing; its essence. [D. C. ABEL]
3. *dialectic:* a process of question-and-answer in which one person, by asking a series of probing questions on a topic, stimulates the other person to reflect more deeply on the topic and understand it more fully. [D. C. ABEL]
4. Homer, *Odyssey,* Book XI, lines 489–90. The words are spoken by the ghost of Achilles, the greatest Greek warrior of the Trojan War. Homer (eighth century B.C.E.) was a Greek epic poet. [D. C. ABEL]
5. Plato alludes to the fate of Socrates, whom the Athenians convicted of corrupting the youth and executed. [D. C. ABEL]

Meditations on First Philosophy

René Descartes

René Descartes was born in La Haye (now called Descartes), France, in 1596. As a youth he was educated by the Jesuits at their college in La Flèche. In about 1614 he began studying at the University of Poitiers, receiving his law degree in 1616. Deciding to travel rather than practice law, he went to Holland in 1618 to serve in the army of the Dutch Prince Maurice of Nassau as a gentleman volunteer. One day in November 1619, while on a military tour of Germany, Descartes sat alone in a room reflecting on a new philosophical system that would unify all branches of knowledge and give them the certainty of mathematics. That night he had three dreams, which he interpreted as a divine commission to construct this new system of knowledge. He left the army shortly afterwards and traveled for several years. In 1628 he settled in Holland, where he lived for more than twenty years. There he did research in science and in mathematics (laying the foundations for analytic geometry) and developed his philosophy. In 1649, after much hesitation, Descartes acceded to the request of Queen Christina of Sweden to come to Stockholm to tutor her in philosophy. The harsh winter and the rigorous schedule imposed on him by the queen (philosophy lessons at five o'clock in the morning, for example) took their toll on his health: He died of pneumonia in 1650.

Descartes's major works are *Rules for the Direction of the Mind* (written in 1628, published posthumously), *Discourse on Method* (1637), *Meditations on First Philosophy* (1641), *Principles of Philosophy* (1644), and *The Passions of the Soul* (1649).

Our reading is from *Meditations on First Philosophy*. (By "first philosophy" Descartes means truths about the basic topics of philosophy, which for him are God, the soul [mind], and the external world.) In the First Meditation, Descartes explains his "method of doubt": He will not accept as true anything of which he cannot be absolutely certain. But practically everything seems open to doubt; Descartes reflects that he might even be deceived in his belief that there is an external world. For how can he be sure that there is not some powerful "malicious demon" who tricks him into thinking there is an external world by placing images directly in his mind?

In the Second Meditation, Descartes realizes that he can be absolutely certain of at least one thing—that he exists. For even if he is deceived about the existence of the external world, he could not be deceived unless he existed. As he formulates this argument elsewhere, "I think, therefore I am." This "I" that exists is "a thing that thinks." Descartes goes on to argue that if there are material things, their essential nature would be extension (three-dimensionality), and that extension is grasped by the mind, not by the senses.

In our selection from the Third Meditation, Descartes reflects on the certitude of his own existence and formulates a general criterion for truth: "All things which I perceive very clearly and very distinctly are true." He then presents a proof for the existence of God. He finds that his mind contains an idea of an infinite being, and reasons that he himself—who is merely a *finite* being—could not have invented such an idea. Descartes concludes that the idea of an infinite being must have been placed in his mind by the infinite being itself. Therefore this infinite being (God) exists.

FIRST MEDITATION. WHAT CAN BE CALLED INTO DOUBT

Some years ago I was struck by the large number of falsehoods that I had accepted as true in my childhood, and by the highly doubtful nature of the whole edifice that I had subsequently based on them. I realized that it was necessary, once in the course of my life, to demolish everything completely and start again right from the foundations if I wanted to establish anything at all in the sciences that was stable and likely to last. But the task looked an enormous one, and I began to wait until I should reach a mature enough age to ensure that no subsequent time of life would be more suitable for tackling such inquiries. This led me to put the project off for so long that I would now be to blame if by pondering over it any further I wasted the time still left for carrying it out. So today I have expressly rid my mind of all worries and arranged for myself a clear stretch of free time. I am here quite alone, and at last I will devote myself sincerely and without reservation to the general demolition of my opinions.

But to accomplish this, it will not be necessary for me to show that all my opinions are false, which is something I could perhaps never manage. Reason now leads me to think that I should hold back my assent from opinions which are not completely certain and indubitable just as carefully as I do from those which are patently false. So, for the purpose of rejecting all my opinions, it will be enough if I find in each of them at least some reason for doubt. And to do this I will not need to run through them all individually, which would be an endless task. Once the foundations of a building are undermined, anything built on them collapses of its own accord; so I will go straight for the basic principles on which all my former beliefs rested.

Whatever I have up till now accepted as most true I have acquired either from the senses or through the senses. But from time to time I have found that the senses deceive, and it is prudent never to trust completely those who have deceived us even once.

Yet although the senses occasionally deceive us with respect to objects which are very small or in the distance, there are many other beliefs about which doubt is quite impossible, even though they are derived from the senses—for example, that I am here, sitting by the fire, wearing a winter dressing-gown, holding this piece of paper in my hands, and so on. Again, how could it be denied that these hands or this whole body are mine? Unless perhaps I were to liken myself to madmen, whose brains are so damaged by the persistent vapors of melancholia that they firmly maintain they are kings when they are paupers, or say they are dressed in purple when they are naked, or that their heads are made of earthenware, or that they are pumpkins, or made of glass. But such people are insane, and I would be thought equally mad if I took anything from them as a model for myself.

A brilliant piece of reasoning! As if I were not a man who sleeps at night, and regularly has all the same experiences while asleep as madmen do when awake—indeed sometimes even more improbable ones. How often, asleep at night, am I convinced of just such familiar events—that I am here in my dressing-gown, sitting by the fire—when in fact I am lying undressed in bed! Yet at the moment my eyes are certainly wide awake when I look at this piece of paper; I shake my head and it is not asleep; as I stretch out and feel my hand I do so deliberately, and I know what I am doing. All this would not happen with such distinctness to someone asleep. Indeed! As if I did not remember other occasions when I have been tricked by exactly similar thoughts while asleep! As I think about this more carefully, I see plainly that there are never any sure signs by means of which being awake can be distinguished from being asleep. The result is that I begin to feel dazed, and this very feeling only reinforces the notion that I may be asleep.

Suppose then that I am dreaming, and that these particulars—that my eyes are open, that I am moving my head and stretching out my hands—are not true. Perhaps, indeed, I do not even have such hands or such a body at all. Nonetheless, it must surely be admitted that the visions which come in sleep are like paintings, which must have been fashioned in the likeness of things that are real, and hence that at least these general kinds of things—eyes, head, hands, and the body as a whole—are things which are not imaginary but are real and exist. For even when painters try to create sirens and satyrs[1] with the most extraordinary bodies, they cannot give them natures which are new in all respects; they simply jumble up the limbs of different animals. Or if perhaps they manage to think up something so new that nothing remotely similar has ever been seen before—something which is therefore completely fictitious and unreal—at least the colors used in the composition must be real. By similar reasoning, although these general kinds of things—eyes, head, hands, and so on—could be imaginary, it must at least be admitted that certain other even simpler and more universal things are real. These are as it were the real colors from which we form all the images of things, whether true or false, that occur in our thought.

This class appears to include corporeal nature in general, and its extension; the shape of extended things; the quantity, or size and number of these things; the place in which they may exist, the time through which they may endure, and so on.

So a reasonable conclusion from this might be that physics, astronomy, medicine, and all other disciplines which depend on the study of composite things, are doubtful; while arithmetic, geometry, and other subjects of this kind, which deal only with the simplest and most general things, regardless of whether they really exist in nature or not, contain something certain and indubitable. For whether I am awake or asleep, two and three added together are five, and a square has no more than four sides. It seems impossible that such transparent truths should incur any suspicion of being false.

And yet firmly rooted in my mind is the long-standing opinion that there is an omnipotent God who made me the kind of creature that I am. How do I know that he has not brought it about that there is no earth, no sky, no extended thing, no shape, no size, no place, while at the same time ensuring that all these things appear to me to exist just as they do now? What is more, just as I consider that others sometimes go astray in cases where they think they have the most perfect knowledge, how do I know that God has not brought it about that I too go wrong every time I add two and three or count the sides of a square, or in some even simpler matter, if that is imaginable? But perhaps God would not have allowed me to be deceived in this way, since he is said to be supremely good. But if it were inconsistent with his goodness to have created me such that I am deceived all the time, it would seem equally foreign to his goodness to allow me to be deceived even occasionally; yet this last assertion cannot be made.

Perhaps there may be some who would prefer to deny the existence of so powerful a God rather than believe that everything else is uncertain. Let us not argue with them, but grant them that everything said about God is a fiction. According to their supposition, then, I have arrived at my present state by fate or chance or a continuous chain of events, or by some other means; yet since deception and error seem to be imperfections, the less powerful they make my original cause, the more likely it is that I am so imperfect as to be deceived all the time. I have no answer to these arguments, but am finally compelled to admit that there is not one of my former beliefs about which a doubt may not properly be raised; and this is not a flippant or ill-considered conclusion, but is based on powerful and well thought-out reasons. So in the future I must withhold my assent from these former beliefs just as carefully as I would from obvious falsehoods, if I want to discover any certainty.

But it is not enough merely to have noticed this; I must make an effort to remember it. My habitual opinions keep coming back, and, despite my wishes, they capture my belief, which is as it were bound over to them as a result of long occupation and the law of custom. I shall never get out of the habit of confidently assenting to these opinions, so long as I suppose them to be what in fact they are, namely highly probable opinions—opinions which, despite the fact that they are in a sense doubtful, as has just been shown, it is still much more reasonable to believe than to deny. In view of this, I think it will be a good plan to turn my will in completely the opposite direction and deceive myself, by pretending for a time that these former opinions are utterly false and imaginary. I shall do this until the weight of preconceived opinion is counterbalanced and the distorting influence of habit no longer prevents my judgment from perceiving things correctly. In the meantime, I know that no danger or error will result from my plan, and that I cannot possibly go too far in my distrustful attitude. This is because the task now in hand does not involve action but merely the acquisition of knowledge.

I will suppose therefore that not God, who is supremely good and the source of truth, but rather some malicious demon of the utmost power and cunning has employed all his energies in order to deceive me. I shall think that the sky, the air, the earth, colors, shapes, sounds, and all external things are merely the delusions of dreams which he has devised to ensnare my judgment. I shall consider myself as not having hands or eyes, or flesh, or blood or senses, but as falsely believing that I have all these things. I shall stubbornly and firmly persist in this meditation; and, even if it is not in my power to know any truth, I shall at least do what is in my power, that is, resolutely guard against assenting to any falsehoods, so that the deceiver, however powerful and cunning he may be, will be unable to impose on me in the slightest degree. But this is an arduous undertaking, and a kind of laziness brings me back to normal life. I am like a prisoner who is enjoying an imaginary freedom while asleep; as he begins to suspect that he is asleep, he dreads being woken up, and goes along with the pleasant illusion as long as he can. In the same way, I happily slide back into my old opinions and dread being shaken out of them, for fear that my peaceful sleep may be followed by hard labor when I wake, and that I shall have to toil not in the light, but amid the inextricable darkness of the problems I have now raised.

SECOND MEDITATION. THE NATURE OF THE HUMAN MIND, AND HOW IT IS BETTER KNOWN THAN THE BODY

So serious are the doubts into which I have been thrown as a result of yesterday's meditation that I can neither put them out of my mind nor see any way of resolving them. It feels as if I have fallen unexpectedly into a deep whirlpool which tumbles me around so that I can neither stand on the bottom nor swim up to the top. Nevertheless I will make an effort and once more attempt the same path which I started on yesterday. Anything which admits of the slightest doubt I will set aside just as if I had found it to be wholly false; and I will proceed in this way until I recognize something certain, or, if nothing else, until I at least recognize for certain that there is no certainty. Archimedes[2] used to demand just one firm and immovable point in order to shift the entire earth; so I too can hope for great things if I manage to find just one thing, however slight, that is certain and unshakable.

I will suppose then, that everything I see is spurious. I will believe that my memory tells me lies, and that none of the things that it reports ever happened. I have no senses. Body, shape, extension, movement, and place are chimeras.[3] So what remains true? Perhaps just the one fact that nothing is certain.

Yet apart from everything I have just listed, how do I know that there is not something else which does not allow even the slightest occasion for doubt? Is there not a God, or whatever I may call him, who puts into me the thoughts I am now having? But why do I think this, since I myself may perhaps be the author of these thoughts? In that case am not I, at least, something? But I have just said that I have no senses and no body. This is the sticking point: What follows from this? Am I not so bound up with a body and with senses that I cannot exist without them? But I have convinced myself that there is absolutely nothing in the world, no sky, no earth, no minds, no bodies. Does it now follow that I too do not exist? No: If I convinced myself of something, then I certainly existed. But there is a deceiver of supreme power and cunning who is deliberately and constantly deceiving me. In that case I too undoubtedly exist, if he is deceiving me; and let him deceive me as much as he can, he will never bring it about that I am nothing so long as I think that I am something. So after considering everything very thoroughly, I must finally conclude that this proposition "I am, I exist" is necessarily true whenever it is put forward by me or conceived in my mind.

But I do not yet have a sufficient understanding of what this "I" is, that now necessarily exists. So I must be on my guard against carelessly taking something else to be this "I," and so making a mistake in the very item of knowledge that I maintain is the most certain and evident of all. I will therefore go back and meditate on what I originally believed myself to be, before I embarked on this present train of thought. I will then subtract anything capable of being weakened, even minimally, by the arguments now introduced, so that what is left at the end may be exactly and only what is certain and unshakable.

What then did I formerly think I was? A man. But what is a man? Shall I say "a rational animal"? No; for then I should have to inquire what an animal is, what rationality is, and in this way one question would lead me down the slope to other harder ones, and I do not now have the time to waste on subtleties of this kind. Instead I propose to concentrate on what came into my thoughts spontaneously and quite naturally whenever I used to consider what I was. Well, the first thought to come to mind was that I had a face, hands, arms, and the whole mechanical structure of limbs which can be seen in a corpse, and which I called the body. The next thought was that I was nourished, that I moved about, and that I engaged in sense-perception and thinking; and these actions I attributed to the soul. But as to the nature of this soul, either I did not think about this or else I imagined it to be something tenuous, like a wind or fire or ether, which permeated my more solid parts. As to the body, however, I had no doubts about it, but thought I knew its nature distinctly. If I had tried to describe the mental conception I had of it, I would have expressed it as follows: By a body I understand whatever has a determinable shape and a definable location and can occupy a space in such a way as to exclude any other body; it can be perceived by touch, sight, hearing, taste, or smell, and can be moved in various ways, not by itself but by whatever else comes into contact with it. For, according to my judgment, the power of self-movement, like the power of sensation or of thought, was quite foreign to the nature of a body; indeed, it was a source of wonder to me that certain bodies were found to contain faculties of this kind.

But what shall I now say that I am, when I am supposing that there is some supremely powerful and, if it is permissible to say so, malicious deceiver, who is deliberately trying to trick me in every way he can? Can I now assert that I possess even the most insignificant of all the attributes which I have just said belong to the nature of a body? I scrutinize them, think about them, go over them again, but nothing suggests itself; it is tiresome and pointless to go through the list once more. But what about the attributes I assigned to the soul? Nutrition or movement? Since now I do not have a body, these are mere fabrications. Sense-perception? This surely does not occur without a body, and besides, when asleep I have appeared to perceive through the senses many things which I afterwards realized I did not perceive through the senses at all. Thinking? At last I have discovered it: thought—this alone is inseparable from me. I am, I exist—that is certain. But for how long? For as long as I am thinking. For it could be that were I totally to cease from thinking, I should totally cease to exist. At present I am not admitting anything except what is necessarily true. I am, then, in the strict sense, only a thing that thinks; that is, I am a mind, or intelligence, or intellect, or reason—words whose meaning I have been ignorant of until now. But for all that, I am a thing which is real and which truly exists. But what kind of a thing? As I have just said—a thinking thing.

What else am I? I will use my imagination. I am not that structure of limbs which is called a human body. I am not even some thin vapor which permeates the limbs—a wind, fire, air, breath, or whatever I depict in my imagination; for these are things which I have supposed to be nothing. Let this supposition stand; for all that, I am still something. And yet may it not perhaps be the case that these very things which I am supposing to be nothing, because they are unknown to me, are in reality identical with the "I" of which I am aware? I do not know, and for the moment I shall not argue the point, since I can make judgments only about things which are known to me. I know that I exist; the question is, what is this "I" that I know? If the "I" is understood strictly as we have been taking it, then it is quite certain that knowledge of it does not depend on things of whose existence I am as yet unaware; so it cannot depend on any of the things which I invent in my imagination. And this very word "invent" shows me my mistake. It would indeed be a case of fictitious invention if I used my imagination to establish that I was something or other; for imagining is simply contemplating the shape or image of a corporeal thing. Yet now I know for certain both that I exist and at the same time that all such images and, in general, everything relating to the nature of body, could be mere dreams <and chimeras>.[4] Once this point has been grasped, to say "I will use my imagination to get to know more distinctly what I am" would seem to be as silly as saying "I am now awake, and see some truth; but since my vision is not yet clear enough, I will deliberately fall asleep so that my dreams may provide a truer and clearer representation." I thus realize that none of the things that the imagination enables me to grasp is at all relevant to this knowledge of myself which I possess, and that the mind must therefore be most carefully diverted from such things if it is to perceive its own nature as distinctly as possible.

But what then am I? A thing that thinks. What is that? A thing that doubts, understands, affirms, denies, is willing, is unwilling, and also imagines and has sensory perceptions. . . .

Let us consider the things which people commonly think they understand most distinctly of all; that is, the bodies which we touch and see. I do not mean bodies in general—for general perceptions are apt to be somewhat more confused—but one particular body. Let us take, for example, this piece of wax. It has just been taken from the honeycomb; it has not yet quite lost the taste of the honey; it retains some of the scent of the flowers from which it was gathered; its color, shape, and size are plain to see; it is hard, cold, and can be handled without difficulty; if you rap it with your knuckles it makes a sound. In short, it has everything which appears necessary to enable a body to be known as distinctly as possible. But even as I speak, I put the wax by the fire, and look: The residual taste is eliminated, the smell goes away, the color changes, the shape is lost, the size increases; it becomes liquid and hot; you can hardly touch it, and if you strike it, it no longer makes a sound. But does the same wax remain? It must be admitted that it does; no one denies it, no one thinks otherwise. So what was it in the wax that I understood with such distinctness? Evidently none of the features which I arrived at by means of the senses; for whatever came under taste, smell, sight, touch, or hearing has now altered—yet the wax remains.

Perhaps the answer lies in the thought which now comes to my mind—namely, the wax was not after all the sweetness of the honey, or the fragrance of the flowers, or the whiteness, or the shape, or the sound, but was rather a body which presented itself to me in these various forms a little while ago, but which now exhibits different ones. But what exactly is it that I am now imagining? Let us concentrate, take away everything which does not belong to the wax, and see what is left: merely something extended, flexible, and changeable. But what is meant here by "flexible" and "changeable"? Is it what I picture in my imagination: that this piece of wax is capable of changing from a round shape to a square shape, or from a square shape to a triangular shape? Not at all; for I can grasp that the wax is capable of countless changes of this kind, yet I am unable to run through this immeasurable number of changes in my imagination, from which it follows that it is not the faculty of imagination that gives me my grasp of the wax as flexible and changeable. And what is meant by "extended"? Is the extension of the wax also unknown? For it increases if the wax melts, increases again if it boils, and is greater still if the heat is increased. I would not be making a correct judgment about the nature of wax unless I believed it capable of being extended in many more different ways than I will ever encompass in my imagination. I must therefore admit that the nature of this piece of wax is in no way revealed by my imagination, but is perceived by the mind alone. (I am speaking of this particular piece of wax; the point is even clearer with regard to wax in general.) But what is this wax which is perceived by the mind alone? It is of course the same wax which I see, which I touch, which I picture in my imagination, in short the same wax which I thought it to be from the start. And yet, and here is the point, the perception I have of it is a case not of vision or touch or imagination—nor has it ever been, despite previous appearances—but of purely mental scrutiny; and this can be imperfect and confused, as it was before, or clear and distinct as it is now, depending on how carefully I concentrate on what the wax consists in.

But as I reach this conclusion I am amazed at how <weak and> prone to error my mind is. For although I am thinking about these matters within myself, silently and without speaking, nonetheless the actual words bring me up short, and I am almost tricked by ordinary ways of talking. We say that we see the wax itself, if it is there before us, not that we judge it to be there from its color or shape; and this might lead me to conclude without more ado that knowledge of the wax comes from what the eye sees, and not from the scrutiny of the mind alone. But then if I look out of the window and see men crossing the square, as I just happen to have done, I normally say that I see the men themselves, just as I say that I see the wax. Yet do I see any more than hats and coats which could conceal automatons? I *judge* that they are men. And so something which I thought I was seeing with my eyes is in fact grasped solely by the faculty of judgment which is in my mind. . . .

THIRD MEDITATION. THE EXISTENCE OF GOD

I will now shut my eyes, stop my ears, and withdraw all my senses. I will eliminate from my thoughts all images of bodily things, or rather, since this is hardly possible, I will regard all such images as vacuous, false, and worthless. I will converse with myself and scrutinize myself more deeply; and in this way I will attempt to achieve, little by little, a more intimate knowledge of myself. I am a thing that thinks—that is, a thing that doubts, affirms, denies, understands a few things, is ignorant of many things, is willing, is unwilling, and also that imagines and has sensory perceptions. For, as I have noted before, even though the objects of my sensory experience and imagination may have no existence outside me, nonetheless the modes of thinking which I refer to as cases of sensory perception and imagination, insofar as they are simply modes of thinking, do exist within me—of that I am certain.

In this brief list I have gone through everything I truly know, or at least everything I have so far discovered that I know. Now I will cast around more carefully to see whether there may be other things within me which I have not yet noticed. I am certain that I am a thinking thing. Do I not therefore also know what is required for my being certain about anything? In this first item of knowledge there is simply a clear and distinct perception of what I am asserting; this would not be enough to make me certain of the truth of the matter if it could ever turn out that something which I perceived with such clarity and distinctness was false. So I now seem to be able to lay it down as a general rule that whatever I perceive very clearly and distinctly is true. . . .

Among my ideas, some appear to be innate, some to be adventitious,[5] and others to have been invented by me. My understanding of what a thing is, what truth is, and what thought is, seems to derive simply from my own nature. But my hearing a noise, as I do now, or seeing the sun or feeling the fire, comes from things which are located outside me, or so I have hitherto judged. Lastly, sirens, hippogriffs,[6] and the like are my own invention. But perhaps all my ideas may be thought of as adventitious, or they may all be innate, or all made up; for as yet I have not clearly perceived their true origin.

But the chief question at this point concerns the ideas which I take to be derived from things existing outside me: What is my reason for thinking that they resemble these things? Nature has apparently taught me to think this. But in addition I know by experience that these ideas do not depend on my will, and hence that they do not depend simply on me. Frequently I notice them even when I do not want to. Now, for example, I feel the heat whether I want to or not, and this is why I think that this sensation or idea of heat comes to me from something other than myself, namely the heat of the fire by which I am sitting. And the most obvious judgment for me to make is that the thing in question transmits to me its own likeness rather than something else.

I will now see if these arguments are strong enough. When I say "Nature taught me to think this," all I mean is that a spontaneous impulse leads me to believe it, not that its truth has been revealed to me by some natural light. There is a big difference here. Whatever is revealed to me by the natural light—for example that from the fact that I am doubting it follows that I exist, and so on—cannot in any way be open to doubt. This is because there cannot be another faculty both as trustworthy as the natural light and also capable of showing me that such things are not true. But as for my natural impulses, I have often judged in the past that they were pushing me in the wrong direction when it was a question of choosing the good, and I do not see why I should place any greater confidence in them in other matters.

Then again, although these ideas do not depend on my will, it does not follow that they must come from things located outside me. Just as the impulses which I was speaking of a moment ago seem opposed to my will even though they are within me, so there may be some other faculty not yet fully known to me, which produces these ideas without any assistance from external things; this is, after all, just how I have always thought ideas are produced in me when I am dreaming.

And finally, even if these ideas did come from things other than myself, it would not follow that they must resemble those things. Indeed, I think I have often discovered a great disparity <between an object and its idea> in many cases. For example, there are two different ideas of the sun which I find within me. One of them, which is acquired as it were from the senses and which is a prime example of an idea which I reckon to come from an external source, makes the sun appear very small. The other idea is based on astronomical reasoning, that is, it is derived from certain notions which are innate in me (or else it is constructed by me in some other way), and this idea shows the sun to be several times larger than the earth. Obviously both these ideas cannot resemble the sun which exists outside me; and reason persuades me that the idea which seems to have emanated most directly from the sun itself has in fact no resemblance to it at all.

All these considerations are enough to establish that it is not reliable judgment but merely some blind impulse that has made me believe up till now that there exist things distinct from myself which transmit to me ideas or images of themselves through the sense organs or in some other way. . . .

Among my ideas, apart from the idea which gives me a representation of myself, which cannot present any difficulty in this context, there are ideas which variously represent God, corporeal and inanimate things, angels, animals, and finally other men like myself.

As far as concerns the ideas which represent other men, or animals, or angels, I have no difficulty in understanding that they could be put together from the ideas I have of myself, of corporeal things and of God, even if the world contained no men besides me, no animals and no angels.

As to my ideas of corporeal things, I can see nothing in them which is so great <or excellent> as to make it seem impossible that it originated in myself. . . .

So there remains only the idea of God; and I must consider whether there is anything in the idea which could not have originated in myself. By the word "God" I understand a substance that is infinite, <eternal, immutable,> independent, supremely intelligent, supremely powerful, and which created both myself and everything else (if anything else there be) that exists. All these attributes are such that, the more carefully I concentrate on them, the less possible it seems that they could have originated from me alone. So from what has been said it must be concluded that God necessarily exists.

It is true that I have the idea of substance in me in virtue of the fact that I am a substance. But this would not account for my having the idea of an infinite substance, when I am finite, unless this idea proceeded from some substance which really was infinite.

And I must not think that, just as my conceptions of rest and darkness are arrived at by negating movement and light, so my perception of the infinite is arrived at not by means of a true idea but merely by negating the finite. On the contrary, I clearly understand that there is more reality in an infinite substance than in a finite one, and hence that my perception of the infinite—that is, God—is in some way prior to my perception of the finite—that is, myself. For how could I understand that I doubted or desired (that is, lacked something) and that I was not wholly perfect, unless there were in me some idea of a more perfect being which enabled me to recognize my own defects by comparison? . . .

It only remains for me to examine how I received this idea from God. For I did not acquire it from the senses; it has never come to me unexpectedly, as usually happens with the ideas of things that are perceivable by the senses, when these things present themselves to the external sense organs—or seem to do so. And it was not invented by me either; for I am plainly unable either to take away anything from it or to add anything to it. The only remaining alternative is that it is innate in me, just as the idea of myself is innate in me.[7]

NOTES

1. In Greek mythology, *sirens* are female and partly human creatures who lure sailors to their destruction with their beautiful singing; *satyrs* are woodland creatures with features of both a horse and a goat, fond of unrestrained revelry. [D. C. ABEL]
2. Archimedes (about 287–212 B.C.E.) was a Greek mathematician and inventor. [D. C. ABEL]
3. *chimera*: mental fabrication. [D. C. ABEL]
4. Words placed in angle brackets appear in the French version of *Meditations on First Philosophy* but not in the original Latin version. Louis-Charles d'Albert, Duc de Luyens (1620–1690), published a French translation that included some alterations from the original text. Descartes approved the translation, but scholars do not consider it as authoritative as the original Latin text. [D. C. ABEL]
5. *adventitious*: coming from an external source. [D. C. ABEL]
6. *hippogriffs*: mythical animals that are part horse and part griffin (a griffin itself is a mythological animal that is part eagle and part lion). [D. C. ABEL]
7. In his Fifth Meditation, Descartes gives an additional proof for the existence of God. The argument appears on p. 206 of this book. [D. C. ABEL]

An Essay Concerning Human Understanding

John Locke

John Locke was born in Wrington, England, in 1632. After attending Westminster School, he enrolled in Oxford University, receiving his bachelor's degree in 1656 and his master's degree two years later. He then taught Latin and Greek at Oxford. In 1661 he began the study of medicine. He was appointed censor of moral philosophy in 1664, but two years later he left Oxford to become the personal physician of influential politician Anthony Ashley Cooper, Earl of Shaftesbury. He completed his medical degree in 1674. Locke then spent four years in France (1675–1679), where he explored the philosophical ideas of René Descartes, Pierre Gassendi, and others. The England to which Locke returned was in political turmoil, and Shaftesbury fled to Holland in 1682. The next year, Locke, who was under suspicion because of his close association with Shaftesbury, also fled to Holland. He returned to England in 1689, and the next year published two major philosophical works that were the fruit of many years of thought: *An Essay Concerning Human Understanding* and *Two Treatises of Government.* Locke continued to write and publish, his final project (published posthumously) being a series of commentaries on the epistles of Paul. He died in Oates in 1704 at the age of seventy-two.

Locke's main works, in addition to the *Essay* and the *Two Treatises,* are *A Letter Concerning Toleration* (1689), *Some Thoughts Concerning Education* (1693), and *The Reasonableness of Christianity* (1695).

Our selection is from the *Essay Concerning Human Understanding.* Locke begins by rejecting the view, popular in his day, that the mind is endowed with innate principles— the view that the mind by its very nature, prior to any experience, knows such truths as "it is impossible for the same thing to be and not to be." He argues that such principles cannot be innate because some people ("children and idiots") have no knowledge of them. Locke then proceeds to present his own theory of how ideas enter the mind. The mind is originally blank, like a sheet of white paper; ideas are imprinted through experience. All ideas arise either through sensation (experience of external objects) or reflection (experience of the operations of our mind). According to Locke, "we have nothing in our minds which did not come about in one of these two ways." After experience has furnished the mind with simple ideas, the mind can go on to combine them into complex ideas that are not the direct objects of experience.

Locke then explains how ideas are related to qualities. By "quality" he means the power of an object to produce an idea in our mind. For example, to say that a snowball has the qualities of being round and white means that it can create these ideas in us. Locke proceeds to distinguish two kinds of qualities. *Primary qualities* (which Locke also calls *original qualities*) are those that produce ideas that resemble the object and really exist in it; examples of these qualities are figure, extension, and motion or rest. Secondary qualities, by contrast, produce ideas that do *not* resemble the object and do *not* exist in it; examples of such qualities are color, sound, and taste. So although we experience a snowball as both round and white, it really is round but really is not white. Locke goes on to explain *how* qualities produce ideas in us.

BOOK I. NEITHER PRINCIPLES NOR IDEAS ARE INNATE

Chapter I. No Innate Speculative Principles

1. It is an established opinion among some men that there are in the understanding certain innate principles—some primary notions, *koinai ennoiai*,[1] characters, as it were, stamped upon the mind of man, which the soul receives in its very first being and brings into the world with it. It would be sufficient to convince unprejudiced readers of the falseness of this supposition, if I should only show (as I hope I shall in the following parts of this discourse) how men, barely[2] by the use of their natural faculties, may attain to all the knowledge they have without the help of any innate impressions, and may arrive at certainty without any such original notions or principles. For I imagine anyone will easily grant that it would be impertinent to suppose the ideas of colors innate in a creature to whom God has given sight and a power to receive them by the eyes from external objects. And no less unreasonable would it be to attribute several truths to the impressions of nature and innate characters, when we may observe in ourselves faculties fit to attain as easy and certain knowledge of them as if they were originally imprinted on the mind.

But because a man is not permitted without censure to follow his own thoughts in the search of truth when they lead him ever so little out of the common road, I shall set down the reasons that made me doubt of the truth of that opinion, as an excuse for my mistake, if I be in one—which I leave to be considered by those who, with me, dispose themselves to embrace truth wherever they find it.

2. There is nothing more commonly taken for granted than that there are certain principles, both speculative and practical (for they speak of both), universally agreed upon by all mankind; which therefore, they argue, must needs[3] be the constant impressions which the souls of men receive in their first beings, and which they bring into the world with them, as necessarily and really as they do any of their inherent faculties.

3. This argument, drawn from universal consent, has this misfortune in it, that if it were true in matter of fact, that there were certain truths wherein all mankind agreed, it would not prove them innate, if there can be any other way shown how men may come to that universal agreement in the things they do consent in, which I presume may be done.

4. But, which is worse, this argument of universal consent, which is made use of to prove innate principles, seems to me a demonstration that there are none such, because there are none to which all mankind give an universal assent. I shall begin with the speculative, and instance in those magnified principles of demonstration, "Whatsoever is, is" and "It is impossible for the same thing to be and not to be"—which, of all others, I think have the most allowed title to innate. These have so settled a reputation of maxims universally received that it will no doubt be thought strange if anyone should seem to question it. But yet I take liberty to say that these propositions are so far from having an universal assent, that there are a great part of mankind to whom they are not so much as known.

5. For first it is evident that all children and idiots have not the least apprehension or thought of them. And the want of that is enough to destroy that universal assent which must needs be the necessary concomitant of all innate truths—it seeming to me near a contradiction to say that there are truths imprinted on the soul, which it perceives or understands not; imprinting, if it signify anything, being nothing else but the making certain truths to be perceived. For to imprint anything on the mind without the mind's perceiving it seems to me hardly intelligible. If therefore children and idiots have souls, have minds, with those impressions upon them, they must unavoidably perceive them and necessarily know and assent to these truths; which since they do not, it is evident that there are no such impressions. For if they are not notions naturally imprinted, how can they be innate? And if they are notions imprinted, how can they be unknown? To say a notion is imprinted on the mind, and yet at the same time to say that the mind is ignorant of it and never yet took notice of it, is to make this impression nothing. No proposition can be said to be in the mind which it never yet knew, which it was never yet conscious of. For if any *one* [proposition] may, then, by the same reason, *all* propositions that are true and the mind is capable ever of assenting to, may be said to be in the mind, and to be imprinted: Since, if any one can be said to be in the mind, which it never yet knew, it must be only because it is capable of knowing it; and so the mind is of all truths it ever shall know. Nay, thus truths may be imprinted on the mind which it never did nor ever shall know; for a man may live long, and die at last in ignorance of many truths which his mind was capable of knowing, and that with certainty. So that if the capacity of knowing be the natural impression contended for, all the truths a man ever comes to know will, by this account, be every one of them innate; and this great point will amount to no more, but only to a very improper way of speaking—which, while it pretends to assert the contrary, says nothing different from those who deny innate principles. For nobody, I think, ever denied that the mind was capable of knowing several truths. The capacity, they say, is innate; the knowledge acquired. But then to what end such contest for certain innate maxims? If truths can be imprinted on the understanding without being perceived, I can see no difference there can be between any truths the mind is capable of knowing in respect of their original:[4] They must all be innate or all adventitious;[5] in vain shall a man go about to distinguish them. He therefore that talks of innate notions in the understanding cannot (if he intend thereby any distinct sort of truths) mean such truths to be in the understanding as it never perceived, and is yet wholly ignorant of. For if these words "to be in the understanding" have any propriety, they signify to be understood. So that to be in the understanding and not to be understood, to be in the mind and never to be perceived, is all one as to say anything is and is not in the mind or understanding. If therefore these two propositions, "Whatsoever is, is" and "It is impossible for the same thing to be and not to be," are by nature imprinted, children cannot be ignorant of them: Infants and all that have souls must necessarily have them in their understandings, know the truth of them, and assent to [them]. . . .

BOOK II. OF IDEAS

Chapter I. Of Ideas in General, and Their Original

1. Every man being conscious to himself that he thinks, and that which his mind is applied about while thinking being the ideas that are there, it is past doubt that men have in their minds several ideas—such as are those expressed by the words whiteness, hardness, sweetness, thinking, motion, man, elephant, army, drunkenness, and others. It is in the first place then to be inquired, how he comes by them.

I know it is a received doctrine that men have native ideas and original characters stamped upon their minds in their very first being. This opinion I have at large examined already; and I suppose what I have said in the foregoing Book will be much more easily admitted when I have shown whence the understanding may get all the ideas it has, and by what ways and degrees they may come into the mind—for which I shall appeal to everyone's own observation and experience.

2. Let us then suppose the mind to be, as we say, white paper, void of all characters, without any ideas. How comes it to be furnished? Whence comes it by that vast store which the busy and boundless fancy of man has painted on it with an almost endless variety? Whence has it all the materials of reason and knowledge? To this I answer, in one word, from *experience*. In that all our knowledge is founded; and from that it ultimately derives itself. Our observation, employed either about external sensible[6] objects or about the internal operations of our minds perceived and reflected on by ourselves, is that which supplies our understandings with all the materials of thinking. These two are the fountains of knowledge from whence all the ideas we have, or can naturally have, do spring.

3. First, our senses, conversant about particular sensible objects, do convey into the mind several distinct perceptions of things, according to those various ways wherein those objects do affect them. And thus we come by those ideas we have of yellow, white, heat, cold, soft, hard, bitter, sweet, and all those which we call sensible qualities; which when I say the senses convey into the mind, I mean, they from external objects convey into the mind what produces there those perceptions. This great source of most of the ideas we have, depending wholly upon our senses, and derived by them to the understanding, I call *sensation*.

4. Secondly, the other fountain from which experience furnishes the understanding with ideas is the perception of the operations of our own mind within us, as it is employed about the ideas it has got—which operations, when the soul comes to reflect on and consider, do furnish the understanding with another set of ideas, which could not be had from things without. And such are perception, thinking, doubting, believing, reasoning, knowing, willing, and all the different actings of our own minds—which we being conscious of, and observing in ourselves, do from these receive into our understandings as distinct ideas as we do from bodies affecting our senses. This source of ideas every man has wholly in himself; and though it be not

sense, as having nothing to do with external objects, yet it is very like it, and might properly enough be called *internal sense.* But as I call the other sensation, so I call this *reflection,* the ideas it affords being such only as the mind gets by reflecting on its own operations within itself. By reflection, then, in the following part of this discourse, I would be understood to mean, that notice which the mind takes of its own operations, and the manner of them, by reason whereof there come to be ideas of these operations in the understanding. These two, I say—namely, external material things, as the objects of *sensation,* and the operations of our own minds within, as the objects of *reflection*—are to me the only originals from whence all our ideas take their beginnings. The term *operations* here I use in a large sense, as comprehending not barely the actions of the mind about its ideas, but some sort of passions[7] arising sometimes from them, such as is the satisfaction or uneasiness arising from any thought.

5. The understanding seems to me not to have the least glimmering of any ideas which it does not receive from one of these two. External objects furnish the mind with the ideas of sensible qualities, which are all those different perceptions they produce in us; and the mind furnishes the understanding with ideas of its own operations.

These, when we have taken a full survey of them and their several modes, combinations, and relations, we shall find to contain all our whole stock of ideas; and that we have nothing in our minds which did not come in one of these two ways. Let anyone examine his own thoughts and thoroughly search into his understanding; and then let him tell me, whether all the original ideas he has there, are any other than of the objects of his senses, or of the operations of his mind, considered as objects of his reflection. And how great a mass of knowledge soever he imagines to be lodged there, he will, upon taking a strict view, see that he has not any idea in his mind but what one of these two have imprinted—though perhaps, with infinite variety compounded and enlarged by the understanding, as we shall see hereafter.

6. He that attentively considers the state of a child at his first coming into the world, will have little reason to think him stored with plenty of ideas that are to be the matter of his future knowledge. It is by degrees he comes to be furnished with them. And though the ideas of obvious and familiar qualities imprint themselves before the memory begins to keep a register of time or order, yet it is often so late before some unusual qualities come in the way, that there are few men that cannot recollect the beginning of their acquaintance with them. And if it were worthwhile, no doubt a child might be so ordered as to have but a very few, even of the ordinary ideas, till he were grown up to a man. But all that are born into the world, being surrounded with bodies that perpetually and diversely affect them—[a] variety of ideas, whether care be taken of it or not, are imprinted on the minds of children. Light and colors are busy at hand everywhere, when the eye is but open; sounds and some tangible qualities fail not to solicit their proper senses and force an entrance to the mind—but yet, I think, it will be granted easily that if a child were kept in a place where he never saw any other but black and white till he were a man, he would have no more ideas of scarlet or green,

than he that from his childhood never tasted an oyster or a pineapple has of those particular relishes.

7. Men then come to be furnished with fewer or more simple ideas from without, according as the objects they converse with afford greater or less variety; and from the operations of their minds within, according as they more or less reflect on them. For, though he that contemplates the operations of his mind cannot but have plain and clear ideas of them, yet, unless he turn his thoughts that way and considers them attentively, he will no more have clear and distinct ideas of all the operations of his mind and all that may be observed therein, than he will have all the particular ideas of any landscape, or of the parts and motions of a clock, who will not turn his eyes to it and with attention heed all the parts of it. The picture or clock may be so placed that they may come in his way every day, but yet he will have but a confused idea of all the parts they are made up of, till he applies himself with attention to consider them each in particular.

8. And hence we see the reason why it is pretty late before most children get ideas of the operations of their own minds, and [why] some have not any very clear or perfect ideas of the greatest part of them all their lives. Because, though they pass there continually, yet, like floating visions, they make not deep impressions enough to leave in their mind clear, distinct, lasting ideas, till the understanding turns inward upon itself, reflects on its own operations, and makes them the objects of its own contemplation. Children, when they come first into it, are surrounded with a world of new things which, by a constant solicitation of their senses, draw the mind constantly to them, forward to take notice of new—and [they are] apt to be delighted with the variety of changing objects. Thus the first years are usually employed and diverted in looking abroad. Men's business in them is to acquaint themselves with what is to be found without, and so, growing up in a constant attention to outward sensations, seldom make any considerable reflection on what passes within them, till they come to be of riper years—and some scarce ever at all. . . .

Chapter II. Of Simple Ideas

1. The better to understand the nature, manner, and extent of our knowledge, one thing is carefully to be observed concerning the ideas we have; and that is, that some of them are *simple* and some *complex*.

Though the qualities that affect our senses are, in the things themselves, so united and blended that there is no separation, no distance between them; yet it is plain, the ideas they produce in the mind enter by the senses simple and unmixed. For, though the sight and touch often take in from the same object, at the same time, different ideas—as a man sees at once motion and color, the hand feels softness and warmth in the same piece of wax—yet the simple ideas thus united in the same subject are as perfectly distinct as those that come in by different senses. The coldness and hardness which a man feels in a piece of ice [are] as distinct ideas in the mind as the smell and whiteness of a lily, or as the taste of sugar and smell of a rose. And there is nothing can be plainer to a man than the clear and distinct perception he has of those simple ideas; which, being each in itself uncompounded, contains in it nothing but one uniform appearance, or conception in the mind, and is not distinguishable into different ideas.

2. These simple ideas, the materials of all our knowledge, are suggested and furnished to the mind only by those two ways above mentioned, namely sensation and reflection. When the understanding is once stored with these simple ideas, it has the power to repeat, compare, and unite them, even to an almost infinite variety, and so can make at pleasure new complex ideas. But it is not in the power of the most exalted wit or enlarged understanding, by any quickness or variety of thought, to invent or frame one new simple idea in the mind, not taken in by the ways before mentioned; nor can any force of the understanding destroy those that are there. The dominion of man in this little world of his own understanding [is] much the same as it is in the great world of visible things; wherein his power, however managed by art and skill, reaches no farther than to compound and divide the materials that are made to his hand, but can do nothing towards the making the least particle of new matter or destroying one atom of what is already in being. The same inability will everyone find in himself, who shall go about to fashion in his understanding one simple idea not received in by his senses from external objects or by reflection from the operations of his own mind about them. I would have anyone try to fancy any taste which had never affected his palate, or frame the idea of a scent he had never smelled, and when he can do this, I will also conclude that a blind man has ideas of colors, and a deaf man true distinct notions of sounds. . . .

Chapter VIII. Some Further Considerations Concerning Our Simple Ideas of Sensation

1. Concerning the simple ideas of sensation, it is to be considered that whatsoever is so constituted in nature as to be able, by affecting our senses, to cause any perception in the mind, does thereby produce in the understanding a simple idea; which, whatever be the external cause of it, when it comes to be taken notice of by our discerning faculty, it is by the mind looked on and considered there to be a real positive idea in the understanding, as much as any other whatsoever; though, perhaps, the cause of it be but a privation of the subject.

2. Thus the ideas of heat and cold, light and darkness, white and black, motion and rest, are equally clear and positive ideas in the mind; though, perhaps, some of the causes which produce them are barely privations in those subjects from whence our senses derive those ideas. These the understanding, in its view of them, considers all as distinct positive ideas, without taking notice of the causes that produce them—which is an inquiry not belonging to the idea, as it is in the understanding, but to the nature of the things existing without us. These are two very different things and carefully to be distinguished, it being one thing to perceive and know the idea of white or black, and quite another to

examine what kind of particles they must be, and how ranged in the superficies,[8] to make any object appear white or black. . . .

7. To discover the nature of our ideas the better, and to discourse of them intelligibly, it will be convenient to distinguish them as they are ideas or perceptions in our minds, and as they are modifications of matter in the bodies that cause such perceptions in us, that so we may not think (as perhaps usually is done) that they are exactly the images and resemblances of something inherent in the subject—most of those of sensation being in the mind no more the likeness of something existing without us, than the names that stand for them are the likeness of our ideas, which yet upon hearing they are apt to excite in us.

8. Whatsoever the mind perceives in itself, or is the immediate object of perception, thought, or understanding, that I call *idea;* and the power to produce any idea in our mind, I call *quality* of the subject wherein that power is. Thus a snowball having the power to produce in us the ideas of white, cold, and round, the power to produce those ideas in us as they are in the snowball, I call qualities; and as they are sensations or perceptions in our understandings, I call them ideas; which ideas, if I speak of sometimes as in the things themselves, I would be understood to mean those qualities in the objects which produce them in us.

9. Qualities thus considered in bodies are:
First, such as are utterly inseparable from the body, in what state soever it be; and such as in all the alterations and changes it suffers, all the force can be used upon it, it constantly keeps; and such as sense constantly finds in every particle of matter which has bulk enough to be perceived; and the mind finds inseparable from every particle of matter, though less than to make itself singly be perceived by our senses. For example, take a grain of wheat, divide it into two parts. Each part has still solidity, extension, figure, and mobility. Divide it again, and it retains still the same qualities; and so divide it on, till the parts become insensible;[9] they must retain still each of them all those qualities. For division (which is all that a mill, or pestle, or any other body, does upon another, in reducing it to insensible parts) can never take away either solidity, extension, figure, or mobility from any body, but only makes two or more distinct separate masses of matter, of that which was but one before; all which distinct masses, reckoned as so many distinct bodies, after division, make a certain number.

These I call *original* or *primary qualities* of body, which I think we may observe to produce simple ideas in us, namely solidity, extension, figure, motion or rest, and number.

10. Secondly, such qualities which in truth are nothing in the objects themselves but powers to produce various sensations in us by their primary qualities, that is, by the bulk, figure, texture, and motion of their insensible parts, as colors, sounds, tastes, and so on. These I call *secondary qualities.* To these might be added a *third* sort, which are allowed to be barely powers; though they are as much real qualities in the subject as those which I, to comply with the common way of speaking, call qualities—but for distinction [call] *secondary* qualities. For the power in fire to produce a new color or consistency

in wax or clay by its primary qualities, is as much a quality in fire as the power it has to produce *in me* a new idea or sensation of warmth or burning which I felt not before, by the same primary qualities (namely the bulk, texture, and motion of its insensible parts).

11. The next thing to be considered is how bodies produce ideas in us; and that is manifestly by impulse, the only way which we can conceive bodies to operate in.

12. If then external objects be not united to our minds when they produce ideas therein; and yet we perceive these original qualities in such of them as singly fall under our senses, it is evident that some motion must be thence continued by our nerves or animal spirits, by some parts of our bodies, to the brains or the seat of sensation, there to produce in our minds the particular ideas we have of them. And since the extension, figure, number, and motion of bodies of an observable bigness may be perceived at a distance by the sight, it is evident some singly imperceptible bodies must come from them to the eyes, and thereby convey to the brain some motion; which produces these ideas which we have of them in us.

13. After the same manner that the ideas of these original qualities are produced in us, we may conceive that the ideas of secondary qualities are also produced, namely by the operation of insensible particles on our senses. For, it being manifest that there are bodies and good store of bodies, each [of which] are so small that we cannot by any of our senses discover either their bulk, figure, or motion—as is evident in the particles of the air and water, and others extremely smaller than those; perhaps as much smaller than the particles of air and water, as the particles of air and water are smaller than peas or hailstones—let us suppose at present that the different motions and figures, bulk and number, of such particles, affecting the several organs of our senses, produce in us those different sensations which we have from the colors and smells of bodies; for example, that a violet, by the impulse of such insensible particles of matter, of peculiar figures and bulks, and in different degrees and modifications of their motions, causes the ideas of the blue color and sweet scent of that flower to be produced in our minds. It [is] no more impossible to conceive that God should annex such ideas to such motions, with which they have no similitude, than that he should annex the idea of pain to the motion of a piece of steel dividing our flesh, with which that idea has no resemblance.

14. What I have said concerning colors and smells may be understood also of tastes and sounds, and other the like sensible qualities; which, whatever reality we by mistake attribute to them, are in truth nothing in the objects themselves, but powers to produce various sensations in us; and depend on those primary qualities, namely bulk, figure, texture, and motion of parts, as I have said.

15. From whence I think it easy to draw this observation—that the ideas of primary qualities of bodies are resemblances of them, and their patterns do really exist in the bodies themselves, but the ideas produced in us by these secondary qualities have no resemblance of them at all. There is nothing like our

ideas, existing in the bodies themselves. They are, in the bodies we denominate from them, only a power to produce those sensations in us; and what is sweet, blue, or warm in idea, is but the certain bulk, figure, and motion of the insensible parts in the bodies themselves, which we call so.

16. Flame is denominated hot and light; snow, white and cold; and manna, white and sweet, from the ideas they produce in us—which qualities are commonly thought to be the same in those bodies [as] those ideas are in us, the one the perfect resemblance of the other, as they are in a mirror, and it would by most men be judged very extravagant if one should say otherwise. And yet he that will consider that the same fire that at one distance produces in us the sensation of warmth, does, at a nearer approach, produce in us the far different sensation of pain, ought to bethink himself what reason he has to say that this idea of warmth, which was produced in him by the fire, is *actually in the fire;* and his idea of pain, which the same fire produced in him the same way, is *not* in the fire. Why are whiteness and coldness in snow, and pain not, when it produces the one and the other idea in us; and can do neither, but by the bulk, figure, number, and motion of its solid parts?

17. The particular bulk, number, figure, and motion of the parts of fire or snow are really in them—whether anyone's senses perceive them or no. And therefore they may be called *real* qualities, because they really exist in those bodies. But light, heat, whiteness, or coldness are no more really in them than sickness or pain is in manna. Take away the sensation of them; let not the eyes see light or colors, nor the ears hear sounds; let the palate not taste, nor the nose smell—and [then] all colors, tastes, odors, and sounds, as they are such particular ideas, vanish and cease and are reduced to their causes, that is, bulk, figure, and motion of parts. . . .

26. To conclude: Beside those before-mentioned primary qualities in bodies—namely bulk, figure, extension, number, and motion of their solid parts—all the rest, whereby we take notice of bodies and distinguish them one from another, are nothing else but several powers in them, depending on those primary qualities; whereby they are fitted, either by immediately operating on our bodies to produce several different ideas in us; or else, by operating on other bodies, so to change their primary qualities as to render them capable of producing ideas in us different from what before they did. The former of these, I think, may be called secondary qualities *immediately perceivable;* the latter, secondary qualities *mediately perceivable.*

NOTES

1. *koinai ennoiai:* (Greek) "common conceptions." [D. C. Abel]
2. *barely:* merely. [D. C. Abel]
3. *needs:* necessarily. [D. C. Abel]
4. *original:* origin. [D. C. Abel]
5. *adventitious:* coming from an external source. [D. C. Abel]

6. *sensible:* able to be sensed. [D. C. ABEL]
7. *passions:* states of being acted upon (being "passive"); contrasted with *actions*. [D. C. ABEL]
8. *superficies:* surface. [D. C. ABEL]
9. *insensible:* not able to be sensed. [D. C. ABEL]

Three Dialogues Between Hylas and Philonous

George Berkeley

George Berkeley was born near Thomastown in County Kilkenny, Ireland, in 1685. After studying at Kilkenny College, he entered Trinity College in Dublin, receiving his bachelor's degree in 1704. Three years later he became a fellow at Trinity; three years after that he was ordained to the Anglican priesthood. He went to London in 1713 and later made two extended trips to the Continent (1713–1714 and 1716–1720). In 1724 he was appointed ecclesiastical dean of Derry. Berkeley became increasingly interested in the New World and decided to establish a college in Bermuda to train colonists, Native Americans, and blacks for the ministry. Funding from the British government appeared likely, and in 1728 Berkeley went to Newport, Rhode Island, to set up farms to supply food for the college. In 1731, when it became clear that funding would be not be granted, Berkeley returned to London. Three years later he was consecrated Bishop of Cloyne, Ireland. In 1752, after serving as bishop for nineteen years, he retired to Oxford. He died there the following year.

Berkeley's major works are *An Essay towards a New Theory of Vision* (1709), *A Treatise Concerning the Principles of Human Knowledge* (1710), *Three Dialogues Between Hylas and Philonous* (1713), and *Alciphron* (1732).

Our selection is taken from the *Dialogues,* which are conversations between the fictional characters Hylas (whose name derives from the Greek word for matter) and Philonous ("lover of the mind"). The first dialogue opens with Hylas expressing amazement at Philonous's (Berkeley's) view that there is no such thing as matter. A material thing is something perceived by the senses, and what the senses perceive are qualities such as color and heat. Philonous argues that these qualities do not exist in objects, but only in the perceiving mind. Just as the sensations of pleasure and pain exist only in a perceiving subject, so do the sensations of color and heat. Using a distinction made by John Locke and others, Hylas agrees that "secondary qualities" like color and heat exist only in the mind, but maintains that "primary qualities" like extension (three-dimensionality) and figure really exist in objects. Philonous then convinces Hylas that primary qualities, like secondary ones, exist only as ideas in the mind. Hylas then argues that matter, although devoid of primary and secondary qualities, must exist as a sort of substratum that causes our sensations. But when questioned about this supposed substratum, Hylas admits that he has no idea what it is. Hylas agrees with Philonous that it is contradictory to conceive of a material object not conceived by a mind.

In the second dialogue, Philonous uses his theory about the mind-dependent nature of material objects to show that God exists. The fact that material things affect us independently of our will shows that their existence does not depend on *our* mind. But since material things are mind-dependent, there must be an infinite mind in which they all exist. And this infinite mind is God.

THE FIRST DIALOGUE

PHILONOUS: Good morrow,[1] Hylas. I did not expect to find you abroad so early.

HYLAS: It is indeed something unusual. But my thoughts were so taken up with a subject I was discoursing of last night that, finding I could not sleep, I resolved to rise and take a turn in the garden. . . . You were represented in last night's conversation as one who maintained the most extravagant opinion that ever entered into the mind of man, to wit, that there is no such thing as material substance in the world.

PHILONOUS: That there is no such thing as what philosophers call material substance, I am seriously persuaded. But, if I were made to see anything absurd or skeptical[2] in this, I should then have the same reason to renounce this, that I imagine I have now to reject the contrary opinion.

HYLAS: What! Can anything be more fantastical, more repugnant to common sense, or a more manifest piece of skepticism, than to believe there is no such thing as matter?

PHILONOUS: Softly, good Hylas. What if it should prove that you, who hold there is, are by virtue of that opinion a greater skeptic, and maintain more paradoxes and repugnances to common sense, than I who believe no such thing?

HYLAS: You may as soon persuade me, the part is greater than the whole, as that, in order to avoid absurdity and skepticism, I should ever be obliged to give up my opinion in this point. . . .

PHILONOUS: What mean you by *sensible things?*

HYLAS: Those things which are perceived by the senses. Can you imagine that I mean anything else?

PHILONOUS: Pardon me, Hylas, if I am desirous clearly to apprehend your notions, since this may much shorten our inquiry. Suffer me then to ask you this farther question. Are those things only perceived by the senses which are perceived immediately? Or may those things properly be said to be sensible which are perceived mediately, or not without the intervention of others?

HYLAS: I do not sufficiently understand you.

PHILONOUS: In reading a book, what I immediately perceive are the letters; but mediately, or by means of these, are suggested to my mind the notions of God, virtue, truth, and so on. Now, that the letters are truly sensible things, or perceived by sense, there is no doubt. But I would know whether you take the things suggested by them to be so too.

HYLAS: No, certainly: It were absurd to think *God* or *virtue* sensible things, though they be signified and suggested to the mind by sensible marks, with which they have an arbitrary connection.

PHILONOUS: It seems then, that by *sensible things* you mean those only which can be perceived *immediately* by sense?

HYLAS: Right.

PHILONOUS: Does it not follow from this, that though I see one part of the sky red, and another blue, and that my reason does thence evidently conclude there must be some cause of that diversity of colors, yet that cause cannot be said to be a sensible thing, or perceived by the sense of seeing?

HYLAS: It does.

PHILONOUS: In like manner, though I hear variety of sounds, yet I cannot be said to hear the causes of those sounds?

HYLAS: You cannot.

PHILONOUS: And when by my touch I perceive a thing to be hot and heavy, I cannot say, with any truth or propriety, that I feel the cause of its heat or weight?

HYLAS: To prevent any more questions of this kind, I tell you once for all, that by *sensible things* I mean those only which are perceived by sense; and that in truth the senses perceive nothing which they do not perceive *immediately*, for they make no inferences. The deducing therefore of causes or occasions from effects and appearances, which alone are perceived by sense, entirely relates to reason.

PHILONOUS: This point then is agreed between us—that *sensible things are those only which are immediately perceived by sense*. You will farther inform me whether we immediately perceive by sight anything beside light and colors and figures; or by hearing, anything but sounds; by the palate, anything beside tastes; by the smell, beside odors; or by the touch, more than tangible qualities.

HYLAS: We do not.

PHILONOUS: It seems, therefore, that if you take away all sensible qualities, there remains nothing sensible?

HYLAS: I grant it.

PHILONOUS: Sensible things therefore are nothing else but so many sensible qualities, or combinations of sensible qualities?

HYLAS: Nothing else.

PHILONOUS: *Heat* then is a sensible thing?

HYLAS: Certainly.

PHILONOUS: Does the reality of sensible things consist in being perceived? Or is it something distinct from their being perceived, and that bears no relation to the mind?

HYLAS: To *exist* is one thing, and to be *perceived* is another.

PHILONOUS: I speak with regard to sensible things only. And of these I ask whether by their real existence you mean a subsistence exterior to the mind and distinct from their being perceived?

HYLAS: I mean a real absolute being, distinct from, and without any relation to, their being perceived.

PHILONOUS: Heat therefore, if it be allowed a real being, must exist without[3] the mind?

HYLAS: It must.

PHILONOUS: Tell me, Hylas, is this real existence equally compatible to all degrees of heat which we perceive, or is there any reason why we should attribute it to some and deny it to others? And if there be, pray let me know that reason.

HYLAS: Whatever degree of heat we perceive by sense, we may be sure the same exists in the object that occasions it.

PHILONOUS: What! The greatest as well as the least?

HYLAS: I tell you, the reason is plainly the same in respect of both. They are both perceived by sense; nay, the greater degree of heat is more sensibly perceived; and consequently, if there is any difference, we are more certain of its real existence than we can be of the reality of a lesser degree.

PHILONOUS: But is not the most vehement and intense degree of heat a very great pain?

HYLAS: No one can deny it.

PHILONOUS: And is any unperceiving thing capable of pain or pleasure?

HYLAS: No, certainly.

PHILONOUS: Is your material substance a senseless being, or a being endowed with sense and perception?

HYLAS: It is senseless without doubt.

PHILONOUS: It cannot therefore be the subject of pain?

HYLAS: By no means.

PHILONOUS: Nor consequently of the greatest heat perceived by sense, since you acknowledge this to be no small pain?

HYLAS: I grant it.

PHILONOUS: What shall we say then of your external object—is it a material substance, or no?

HYLAS: It is a material substance with the sensible qualities inhering in it.

PHILONOUS: How then can a great heat exist in it, since you own[4] it cannot [exist] in a material substance? I desire you would clear this point.

HYLAS: Hold, Philonous, I fear I was out[5] in yielding intense heat to be a pain. It should seem rather, that pain is something distinct from heat, and the consequence or effect of it.

PHILONOUS: Upon putting your hand near the fire, do you perceive one simple uniform sensation, or two distinct sensations?

HYLAS: But one simple sensation.

PHILONOUS: Is not the heat immediately perceived?

HYLAS: It is.

PHILONOUS: And the pain?

HYLAS: True.

PHILONOUS: Seeing therefore they are both immediately perceived at the same time, and the fire affects you only with one simple or uncompounded idea, it follows that this same simple idea is both the intense heat immediately perceived, and the pain; and, consequently, that the intense heat immediately perceived is nothing distinct from a particular sort of pain.

HYLAS: It seems so.

PHILONOUS: Again, try in your thoughts, Hylas, if you can conceive a vehement sensation to be without pain or pleasure.

HYLAS: I cannot.

PHILONOUS: Or can you frame to yourself an idea of sensible pain or pleasure in general, abstracted from every particular idea of heat, cold, tastes, smells, and so on?

HYLAS: I do not find that I can.

PHILONOUS: Does it not therefore follow that sensible pain is nothing distinct from those sensations or ideas, in an intense degree?

HYLAS: It is undeniable. And to speak the truth, I begin to suspect a very great heat cannot exist but in a mind perceiving it.

PHILONOUS: What! Are you then in that skeptical state of suspense, between affirming and denying?

HYLAS: I think I may be positive in the point. A very violent and painful heat cannot exist without the mind.

PHILONOUS: It has not therefore, according to you, any *real* being?

HYLAS: I own it.

PHILONOUS: Is it therefore certain that there is no body in nature really hot?

HYLAS: I have not denied there is any real heat in bodies. I only say there is no such thing as an intense real heat.

PHILONOUS: But did you not say before that all degrees of heat were equally real; or, if there was any difference, that the greater were more undoubtedly real than the lesser?

HYLAS: True, but it was because I did not then consider the ground there is for distinguishing between them, which I now plainly see. And it is this: Because intense heat is nothing else but a particular kind of painful sensation, and pain cannot exist but in a perceiving being, it follows that no intense heat can really exist in an unperceiving corporeal substance. But this is no reason why we should deny heat in an inferior degree to exist in such a substance.

PHILONOUS: But how shall we be able to discern those degrees of heat which exist only in the mind from those which exist without it?

HYLAS: That is no difficult matter. You know the least pain cannot exist unperceived; whatever, therefore, degree of heat is a pain exists only in the mind. But as for all other degrees of heat, nothing obliges us to think the same of them.

PHILONOUS: I think you granted before that no unperceiving being was capable of pleasure, any more than of pain.

HYLAS: I did.

PHILONOUS: And is not warmth, or a more gentle degree of heat than what causes uneasiness, a pleasure?

HYLAS: What then?

PHILONOUS: Consequently, it cannot exist without the mind in an unperceiving substance, or body.

HYLAS: So it seems.

PHILONOUS: Since, therefore, as well those degrees of heat that are not painful, as those that are, can exist only in a thinking substance, may we not conclude that external bodies are absolutely incapable of any degree of heat whatsoever?

HYLAS: On second thoughts, I do not think it so evident that warmth is a pleasure as that a great degree of heat is a pain.

PHILONOUS: I do not pretend that warmth is as great a pleasure as heat is a pain. But, if you grant it to be even a small pleasure, it serves to make good my conclusion.

HYLAS: I could rather call it an *indolence*. It seems to be nothing more than a privation of both pain and pleasure. And that such a quality or state as this may agree to an unthinking substance, I hope you will not deny.

PHILONOUS: If you are resolved to maintain that warmth, or a gentle degree of heat, is no pleasure, I know not how to convince you otherwise than by appealing to your own sense. But what think you of cold?

HYLAS: The same that I do of heat. An intense degree of cold is a pain; for to feel a very great cold, is to perceive a great uneasiness. It cannot therefore exist without the mind, but a lesser degree of cold may, as well as a lesser degree of heat.

PHILONOUS: Those bodies, therefore, upon whose application to our own, we perceive a moderate degree of heat, must be concluded to have a moderate degree of heat or warmth in them; and those, upon whose application we feel a like degree of cold, must be thought to have cold in them.

HYLAS: They must.

PHILONOUS: Can any doctrine be true that necessarily leads a man into an absurdity?

HYLAS: Without doubt it cannot.

PHILONOUS: Is it not an absurdity to think that the same thing should be at the same time both cold and warm?

HYLAS: It is.

PHILONOUS: Suppose now one of your hands hot, and the other cold, and that they are both at once put into the same vessel of water, in an intermediate state. Will not the water seem cold to one hand, and warm to the other?

HYLAS: It will.

PHILONOUS: Ought we not therefore, by your principles, to conclude it is really both cold and warm at the same time—that is, according to your own concession, to believe an absurdity?

HYLAS: I confess it seems so.

PHILONOUS: Consequently, the principles themselves are false, since you have granted that no true principle leads to an absurdity.

HYLAS: But after all, can anything be more absurd than to say *there is no heat in the fire?*

PHILONOUS: To make the point still clearer, tell me whether, in two cases exactly alike, we ought not to make the same judgment?

HYLAS: We ought.

PHILONOUS: When a pin pricks your finger, does it not rend and divide the fibers of your flesh?

HYLAS: It does.

PHILONOUS: And when a coal burns your finger, does it any more?

HYLAS: It does not.

PHILONOUS: Since, therefore, you neither judge the sensation itself occasioned by the pin, nor anything like it to be in the pin; you should not, conformably to what you have now granted, judge the sensation occasioned by the fire, or anything like it, to be in the fire.

HYLAS: Well, since it must be so, I am content to yield this point and acknowledge that heat and cold are only sensations existing in our minds. But there still remain qualities enough to secure the reality of external things.

PHILONOUS: But what will you say, Hylas, if it shall appear that the case is the same with regard to all other sensible qualities, and that they can no more be supposed to exist without the mind, than heat and cold?

HYLAS: Then indeed you will have done something to the purpose, but that is what I despair of seeing proved.

PHILONOUS: Let us examine them in order. What think you of *tastes*—do they exist without the mind, or no?

HYLAS: Can any man in his senses doubt whether sugar is sweet, or wormwood bitter?

PHILONOUS: Inform me, Hylas. Is a sweet taste a particular kind of pleasure or pleasant sensation, or is it not?

HYLAS: It is.

PHILONOUS: And is not bitterness some kind of uneasiness or pain?

HYLAS: I grant it.

PHILONOUS: If therefore sugar and wormwood are unthinking corporeal substances existing without the mind, how can sweetness and bitterness, that is, pleasure and pain, agree to them?

HYLAS: Hold, Philonous, I now see what it was [that] deluded me all this time. You asked whether heat and cold, sweetness and bitterness, were not particular sorts of pleasure and pain; to which I answered simply, that they were. Whereas I should have thus distinguished: Those qualities, as perceived by us, are pleasures or pains; but not as existing in the external objects. We must not therefore conclude absolutely that there is no heat in the fire or sweetness in the sugar, but only that heat or sweetness, as perceived by us, are not in the fire or sugar. What say you to this?

PHILONOUS: I say it is nothing to the purpose. Our discourse proceeded altogether concerning sensible things, which you defined to be *the things we immediately perceive by our senses*. Whatever other qualities, therefore, you speak of, as distinct from these, I know nothing of them, neither do they at all belong to the point in dispute. You may, indeed, pretend to have discovered certain qualities which you do not perceive, and assert those insensible qualities exist in fire and sugar. But what use can be made of this to your present purpose, I am at a loss to conceive. Tell me then once more, do you acknowledge that heat and cold, sweetness and bitterness (meaning those qualities which are perceived by the senses), do not exist without the mind?

HYLAS: I see it is to no purpose to hold out, so I give up the cause as to those mentioned qualities. Though I profess it sounds oddly to say that sugar is not sweet.

PHILONOUS: But, for your farther satisfaction, take this along with you: That which at other times seems sweet, shall, to a distempered palate, appear bitter. And nothing can be plainer than that divers[6] persons perceive different tastes in the same food, since that which one man delights in, another abhors. And how could this be, if the taste was something really inherent in the food?

HYLAS: I acknowledge I know not how. . . .

PHILONOUS: And I hope you will make no difficulty to acknowledge the same of colors.

HYLAS: Pardon me; the case of colors is very different. Can anything be plainer than that we see them on the objects?

PHILONOUS: The objects you speak of are, I suppose, corporeal substances existing without the mind?

HYLAS: They are.

PHILONOUS: And have true and real colors inhering in them?

HYLAS: Each visible object has that color which we see in it. . . .

PHILONOUS: What! Are then the beautiful red and purple we see on yonder clouds really in them? Or do you imagine they have in themselves any other form than that of a dark mist or vapor?

HYLAS: I must own, Philonous, those colors are not really in the clouds as they seem to be at this distance. They are only apparent colors.

PHILONOUS: *Apparent* call you them? How shall we distinguish these apparent colors from real?

HYLAS: Very easily. Those are to be thought apparent which, appearing only at a distance, vanish upon a nearer approach.

PHILONOUS: And those, I suppose, are to be thought real which are discovered by the most near and exact survey.

HYLAS: Right.

PHILONOUS: Is the nearest and exactest survey made by the help of a microscope, or by the naked eye?

HYLAS: By a microscope, doubtless.

PHILONOUS: But a microscope often discovers colors in an object different from those perceived by the unassisted sight. And in case we had microscopes magnifying to any assigned degree, it is certain that no object whatsoever, viewed through them, would appear in the same color which it exhibits to the naked eye.

HYLAS: And what will you conclude from all this? You cannot argue that there are really and naturally no colors on objects, because by artificial managements they may be altered or made to vanish.

PHILONOUS: I think it may evidently be concluded from your own concessions, that all the colors we see with our naked eyes are only apparent as those on the clouds, since they vanish upon a more close and accurate inspection, which is afforded us by a microscope. Then, as to what you say by way of prevention: I ask you whether the real and natural state of an object is better discovered by a very sharp and piercing sight, or by one which is less sharp?

HYLAS: By the former without doubt.

PHILONOUS: Is it not plain from dioptrics[7] that microscopes make the sight more penetrating and represent objects as they would appear to the eye in case it were naturally endowed with a most exquisite sharpness?

HYLAS: It is.

PHILONOUS: Consequently the microscopical representation is to be thought that which best sets forth the real nature of the thing, or what it is in itself. The colors, therefore, by it perceived are more genuine and real than those perceived otherwise.

HYLAS: I confess there is something in what you say. . . .

PHILONOUS: . . . I would fain[8] know farther from you, what certain distance and position of the object, what peculiar texture and formation of the eye, what degree or kind of light is necessary for ascertaining that true color, and distinguishing it from apparent ones.

HYLAS: I own myself entirely satisfied that they are all equally apparent and that there is no such thing as color really inhering in external bodies, but that it is altogether in the light. And what confirms me in this opinion is that in proportion to the light colors are still more or less vivid; and if there be no light, then are there no colors perceived. Besides, allowing there are colors on external objects, yet, how is it possible for us to perceive them? For no external body affects the mind unless it acts first on our organs of sense. But the only action of bodies is motion, and motion cannot be communicated otherwise than by impulse. A distant object therefore cannot act on the eye, nor consequently make itself or its properties perceivable to the soul. Whence it plainly follows that it is immediately some contiguous substance which, operating on the eye, occasions a perception of colors—and such is light.

PHILONOUS: How? Is light then a substance?

HYLAS: I tell you, Philonous, external light is nothing but a thin fluid substance whose minute particles being agitated with a brisk motion, and in various manners reflected from the different surfaces of outward objects to the eyes, communicate different motions to the optic nerves; which, being propagated to the brain, cause therein various impressions; and these are attended with the sensations of red, blue, yellow, and so on.

PHILONOUS: It seems then the light does no more than shake the optic nerves.

HYLAS: Nothing else.

PHILONOUS: And consequent to each particular motion of the nerves, the mind is affected with a sensation which is some particular color.

HYLAS: Right.

PHILONOUS: And these sensations have no existence without the mind.

HYLAS: They have not.

PHILONOUS: How then do you affirm that colors are in the light, since by *light* you understand a corporeal substance external to the mind?

HYLAS: Light and colors, as immediately perceived by us, I grant cannot exist without the mind. But in themselves they are only the motions and configurations of certain insensible particles of matter.

PHILONOUS: Colors then, in the vulgar sense, or taken for the immediate objects of sight, cannot agree to any but a perceiving substance.

HYLAS: That is what I say.

PHILONOUS: Well then, since you give up the point as to those sensible qualities which are alone thought colors by all mankind beside, you may hold what you please with regard to those invisible ones of the philosophers. . . .

HYLAS: I frankly own, Philonous, that it is in vain to stand out any longer. Colors, sounds, tastes, in a word all those termed *secondary qualities*, have certainly no existence without the mind. But by this acknowledgment I must not be supposed to derogate anything from the reality of matter or external objects, seeing it is no more than several philosophers maintain, who nevertheless are the farthest imaginable from denying matter. For the clearer understanding of this, you must know sensible qualities are by philosophers divided into *primary* and *secondary*.[9] The former are extension, figure, solidity, gravity, motion, and rest; and these they hold exist really in bodies. The latter are those above enumerated—or, briefly, *all sensible qualities beside the primary*—which they assert are only so many sensations or ideas existing nowhere but in the mind. But all this, I doubt not, you are apprised of. For my part, I have been a long time sensible[10] there was such an opinion current among philosophers, but was never thoroughly convinced of its truth until now.

PHILONOUS: You are still then of opinion that *extension* and *figures* are inherent in external unthinking substances?

HYLAS: I am.

PHILONOUS: But what if the same arguments which are brought against secondary qualities will hold good against these also?

HYLAS: Why then I shall be obliged to think, they too exist only in the mind.

PHILONOUS: Is it your opinion the very figure and extension which you perceive by sense exist in the outward object or material substance?

HYLAS: It is.

PHILONOUS: Have all other animals as good grounds to think the same of the figure and extension which they see and feel?

HYLAS: Without doubt, if they have any thought at all.

PHILONOUS: Answer me, Hylas. Think you the senses were bestowed upon all animals for their preservation and well-being in life, or were they given to men alone for this end?

HYLAS: I make no question but they have the same use in all other animals.

PHILONOUS: If so, is it not necessary they should be enabled by them to perceive their own limbs and those bodies which are capable of harming them?

HYLAS: Certainly.

PHILONOUS: A mite therefore must be supposed to see his own foot, and things equal or even less than it, as bodies of some considerable dimension; though at the same time they appear to you scarce discernible, or at best as so many visible points?

HYLAS: I cannot deny it.

PHILONOUS: And to creatures less than the mite they will seem yet larger?

HYLAS: They will.

PHILONOUS: Insomuch that what you can hardly discern will to another extremely minute animal appear as some huge mountain?

HYLAS: All this I grant.

PHILONOUS: Can one and the same thing be at the same time in itself of different dimensions?

HYLAS: That were absurd to imagine.

PHILONOUS: But from what you have laid down it follows that both the extension by you perceived, and that perceived by the mite itself, as likewise all those perceived by lesser animals, are each of them the true extension of the mite's foot; that is to say, by your own principles you are led into an absurdity.

HYLAS: There seems to be some difficulty in the point.

PHILONOUS: Again, have you not acknowledged that no real inherent property of any object can be changed without some change in the thing itself?

HYLAS: I have.

PHILONOUS: But as we approach to or recede from an object, the visible extension varies, being at one distance ten or a hundred times greater than at another. Does it not therefore follow from hence likewise that it is not really inherent in the object?

HYLAS: I own I am at a loss what to think.

PHILONOUS: Your judgment will soon be determined, if you will venture to think as freely concerning this quality as you have done concerning the rest. Was it not admitted as a good argument, that neither heat nor cold was in the water, because it seemed warm to one hand and cold to the other?

HYLAS: It was.

PHILONOUS: Is it not the very same reasoning to conclude, there is no extension or figure in an object, because to one eye it shall seem little, smooth, and round, when at the same time it appears to the other, great, uneven, and angular?

HYLAS: The very same. But does this latter fact ever happen?

PHILONOUS: You may at any time make the experiment, by looking with one eye bare, and with the other through a microscope.

HYLAS: I know not how to maintain it, and yet I am loath to give up extension— I see so many odd consequences following upon such a concession.

PHILONOUS: Odd, say you? After the concessions already made, I hope you will stick at nothing for its oddness. . . .

HYLAS: I acknowledge, Philonous, that, upon a fair observation of what passes in my mind, I can discover nothing else but that I am a thinking being, affected with a variety of sensations; neither is it possible to conceive how a sensation should exist in an unperceiving substance. But then, on the other hand, when I look on sensible things in a different view, considering them as so many modes and qualities, I find it necessary to suppose a material substratum, without which they cannot be conceived to exist.

PHILONOUS: *Material substratum* call you it? Pray, by which of your senses came you acquainted with that being?

HYLAS: It is not itself sensible, its modes and qualities only being perceived by the senses.

PHILONOUS: I presume then it was by reflection and reason you obtained the idea of it?

HYLAS: I do not pretend to any proper positive idea of it. However, I conclude it exists, because qualities cannot be conceived to exist without a support.

PHILONOUS: It seems then you have only a relative *notion* of it, or that you conceive it not otherwise than by conceiving the relation it bears to sensible qualities.

HYLAS: Right.

PHILONOUS: Be pleased therefore to let me know wherein that relation consists.

HYLAS: Is it not sufficiently expressed in the term *substratum,* or *substance?*

PHILONOUS: If so, the word *substratum* should import that it is spread under the sensible qualities or accidents?[11]

HYLAS: True.

PHILONOUS: And consequently under extension?

HYLAS: I own it.

PHILONOUS: It is therefore somewhat[12] in its own nature entirely distinct from extension?

HYLAS: I tell you, extension is only a mode, and matter is something that supports modes. And is it not evident the thing supported is different from the thing supporting?

PHILONOUS: So that something distinct from, and exclusive of, extension is supposed to be the substratum of extension?

HYLAS: Just so.

PHILONOUS: Answer me, Hylas. Can a thing be spread without extension? Or is not the idea of extension necessarily included in spreading?

HYLAS: It is.

PHILONOUS: Whatsoever therefore you suppose spread under anything must have in itself an extension distinct from the extension of that thing under which it is spread?

HYLAS: It must.

PHILONOUS: Consequently, every corporeal substance, being the substratum of extension, must have in itself another extension, by which it is qualified to be a substratum—and so on to infinity? And I ask whether this be not absurd in itself, and repugnant to what you granted just now, to wit, that the substratum was something distinct from and exclusive of extension?

HYLAS: Aye but, Philonous, you take me wrong. I do not mean that matter is spread in a gross literal sense under extension. The word *substratum* is used only to express in general the same thing with *substance.*

PHILONOUS: Well then, let us examine the relation implied in the term *substance.* Is it not that it stands under accidents?[13]

HYLAS: The very same.

PHILONOUS: But, that one thing may stand under or support another, must it not be extended?

HYLAS: It must.

PHILONOUS: Is not therefore this supposition liable to the same absurdity with the former?

HYLAS: You still take things in a strict literal sense. That is not fair, Philonous.

PHILONOUS: I am not for imposing any sense on your words; you are at liberty to explain them as you please. Only, I beseech you, make me understand something by them. You tell me matter supports or stands under accidents. How? Is it as your legs support your body?

HYLAS: No; that is the literal sense.

PHILONOUS: Pray let me know any sense, literal or not literal, that you understand it in. How long must I wait for an answer, Hylas?

HYLAS: I declare I know not what to say. I once thought I understood well enough what was meant by matter's supporting accidents. But now, the more I think on it the less can I comprehend it. In short, I find that I know nothing of it.

PHILONOUS: It seems then you have no idea at all, neither relative nor positive, of matter. You know neither what it is in itself, nor what relation it bears to accidents?

HYLAS: I acknowledge it.

PHILONOUS: And yet you asserted that you could not conceive how qualities or accidents should really exist, without conceiving at the same time a material support of them?

HYLAS: I did.

PHILONOUS: That is to say, when you conceive the real existence of qualities, you do withal[14] conceive something which you cannot conceive?

HYLAS: It was wrong, I own. . . .

PHILONOUS: . . . But (to pass by all that has been hitherto said and reckon it for nothing, if you will have it so) I am content to put the whole upon this issue. If you can conceive it possible for . . . any sensible object whatever to exist without the mind, then I will grant it actually to be so.

HYLAS: If it comes to that, the point will soon be decided. What more easy than to conceive a tree or house existing by itself, independent of and unperceived by any mind whatsoever? I do at this present time conceive them existing after that manner.

PHILONOUS: How say you, Hylas, can you see a thing which is at the same time unseen?

HYLAS: No, that were a contradiction.

PHILONOUS: Is it not as great a contradiction to talk of *conceiving* a thing which is *unconceived*?

HYLAS: It is.

PHILONOUS: The tree or house therefore which you think of is conceived by you?

HYLAS: How should it be otherwise?

PHILONOUS: And what is conceived is surely in the mind?

HYLAS: Without question, that which is conceived is in the mind. . . .

PHILONOUS: You acknowledge then that you cannot possibly conceive how any one corporeal sensible thing should exist otherwise than in a mind?

HYLAS: I do. . . .

THE SECOND DIALOGUE

PHILONOUS: . . . To me it is evident, for the reasons you allow of, that sensible things cannot exist otherwise than in a mind or spirit. Whence I conclude, not that they have no real existence, but that, seeing they depend not on my thought and have an existence distinct from being perceived by me, *there must be some other Mind wherein they exist.* As sure, therefore, as the sensible world really exists, so sure is there an infinite omnipresent Spirit who contains and supports it.

HYLAS: What! This is no more than I and all Christians hold—nay, and all others too who believe there is a God and that He knows and comprehends all things.

PHILONOUS: Aye, but here lies the difference. Men commonly believe that all things are known or perceived by God, because they believe the being of a God; whereas I, on the other side, immediately and necessarily conclude the being of a God, because all sensible things must be perceived by Him.

HYLAS: But, so long as we all believe the same thing, what matter is it how we come by that belief?

PHILONOUS: But neither do we agree in the same opinion. For philosophers, though they acknowledge all corporeal beings to be perceived by God, yet they attribute to them an absolute subsistence distinct from their being perceived by any mind whatever; which I do not. Besides, is there no difference between saying "There is a God, therefore He perceives all things" and saying "Sensible things do really exist; and, if they really exist, they are necessarily perceived by an infinite Mind: Therefore there is an infinite Mind, or God"? This furnishes you with a direct and immediate demonstration, from a most evident principle, of the being of a God. Divines and philosophers had proved beyond all controversy, from the beauty and usefulness of the several parts of the creation, that it was the workmanship of God. But that—setting aside all help of astronomy and natural philosophy,[15] all contemplation of the contrivance, order, and adjustment of things—an infinite Mind should be necessarily inferred from the bare existence of the sensible world, is an advantage to them only who have made this easy reflection—that the sensible world is that which we perceive by our several senses, and that nothing is perceived by the senses beside ideas, and that no idea or archetype of an idea can exist otherwise than in a mind. You may now, without any laborious search into the sciences, without any subtlety of reason or tedious length of discourse, oppose and baffle the most strenuous advocate for atheism. . . . It is evident that the things I perceive are my own ideas, and that no idea can exist unless it be in a mind. Nor is it less plain that these ideas or things by me perceived, either themselves or their archetypes, exist independently of *my* mind, since I know myself not to be their author, it being out of my power to determine at pleasure what particular ideas I shall be affected with upon opening my eyes or ears.

They must therefore exist in some other Mind, whose will it is they should be exhibited to me. The things, I say, immediately perceived are ideas or sensations, call them which you will. But how can any idea or sensation exist in or be produced by anything but a mind or spirit? This indeed is inconceivable. And to assert that which is inconceivable is to talk nonsense, is it not?

HYLAS: Without doubt.

PHILONOUS: But on the other hand, it is very conceivable that they should exist in and be produced by a Spirit, since this is no more than I daily experience in myself, inasmuch as I perceive numberless ideas and, by an act of my will, can form a great variety of them and raise them up in my imagination—though, it must be confessed, these creatures of the fancy are not altogether so distinct, so strong, vivid, and permanent, as those perceived by my senses, which latter are called *real things*. From all which I conclude there is a Mind which affects me every moment with all the sensible impressions I perceive. And from the variety, order, and manner of these. I conclude the Author of them to be wise, powerful, and good, beyond comprehension.

NOTES

1. *morrow:* morning. [D. C. ABEL]
2. *skeptical:* relating to *skepticism,* the doctrine that we cannot attain certainty in knowledge. [D. C. ABEL]
3. *without:* outside. [D. C. ABEL]
4. *own:* admit. [D. C. ABEL]
5. *out:* mistaken. [D. C. ABEL]
6. *divers:* various, several. [D. C. ABEL]
7. *dioptrics:* the study of the refraction of light. [D. C. ABEL]
8. *fain:* gladly. [D. C. ABEL]
9. Berkeley refers here primarily to the English philosopher John Locke (1632–1704). For Locke's discussion of primary and secondary qualities, see pp. 146–148 in this book; for a biography of Locke, see p. 139. [D. C. ABEL]
10. *sensible:* aware. [D. C. ABEL]
11. *Substratum* in Latin means, literally, "spread under"; an *accident* is a property that inheres in a substrate or substance. [D. C. ABEL]
12. *somewhat:* something. [D. C. ABEL]
13. "Substance" derives from the Latin words meaning "to stand" (*stare*) and "under" (*sub*). [D. C. ABEL]
14. *withal:* with that. [D. C. ABEL]
15. *natural philosophy:* the philosophy of nature; natural science. [D. C. ABEL]

An Enquiry Concerning Human Understanding

David Hume

A biography of David Hume appears on p. 47.

This reading is from Hume's *Enquiry Concerning Human Understanding*. Hume begins by distinguishing two kinds of perceptions of the mind: impressions and ideas. *Impressions* consist of direct sense experiences of things outside us (sensations) or inside us (passions and emotions); *ideas* are copies of such impressions. Impressions are distinguished from ideas by their greater "force and vivacity"; hearing a sound is an impression, whereas recalling the sound is an idea. Some ideas (for example, a gold mountain) are not direct copies of a particular impression, but modifications or combinations of impressions (gold and a mountain). To clarify an idea, we need simply go back to the impression(s) from which it derives.

Hume next inquires about our knowledge of "matters of fact" (things that could be otherwise than they are). He observes that we rely on the notion of cause and effect when we go beyond the matters of fact provided by impressions and memories of impressions. But how do we *know* that one thing is caused by another? Judgments of causality are based on experience; when we see that event A is followed regularly by event B, we infer that A causes B and that if A occurs in the future, it will be followed by B. But what justifies this inference? It is not based on impressions—for while we do have impressions of A and B as successive events, we have no impression of a third entity, a "cause," that links A and B. Consequently, we can *never know* that there is such a thing as causality. Hume argues that our belief in causality results not from a reasoning process, but from the unavoidable human tendency to believe that two events we experience as constantly conjoined are related as cause and effect.

SECTION II. OF THE ORIGIN OF IDEAS

Everyone will readily allow that there is a considerable difference between the perceptions of the mind when a man feels the pain of excessive heat or the pleasure of moderate warmth, and when he afterwards recalls to his memory this sensation or anticipates it by his imagination. These faculties may mimic or copy the perceptions of the senses, but they never can entirely reach the force and vivacity of the original sentiment.[1] The utmost we say of them, even when they operate with greatest vigor, is that they represent their object in so lively a manner that we could *almost* say we feel or see it. But, except the mind be disordered by disease or madness, they never can arrive at such a pitch of vivacity as to render these perceptions altogether undistinguishable. All the colors of poetry, however splendid, can never paint natural objects in such a manner as to make the description be taken for a real landscape. The most lively thought is still inferior to the dullest sensation.

We may observe a like distinction to run through all the other perceptions of the mind. A man in a fit of anger is actuated in a very different manner from one who only thinks of that emotion. If you tell me that any person is in love, I easily understand your meaning and form a just conception of his situation, but never can mistake that conception for the real disorders and agitations of the passion. When we reflect on our past sentiments and affections, our thought is a faithful mirror and copies its objects truly, but the colors which it employs are faint and dull in comparison of those in which our original perceptions were clothed. It requires no nice discernment or metaphysical[2] head to mark the distinction between them.

Here therefore we may divide all the perceptions of the mind into two classes or species, which are distinguished by their different degrees of force and vivacity. The less forcible and lively are commonly denominated *thoughts* or *ideas*. The other species want a name in our language, and in most others—I suppose because it was not requisite for any but philosophical purposes to rank them under a general term or appellation. Let us, therefore, use a little freedom and call them *impressions,* employing that word in a sense somewhat different from the usual. By the term *impression,* then, I mean all our more lively perceptions, when we hear or see or feel or love or hate or desire or will. And impressions are distinguished from ideas, which are the less lively perceptions, of which we are conscious when we reflect on any of those sensations or movements above mentioned.

Nothing at first view may seem more unbounded than the thought of man, which not only escapes all human power and authority, but is not even restrained within the limits of nature and reality. To form monsters and join incongruous shapes and appearances costs the imagination no more trouble than to conceive the most natural and familiar objects. And while the body is confined to one planet, along which it creeps with pain and difficulty, the thought can in an instant transport us into the most distant regions of the universe—or even beyond the universe into the unbounded chaos, where nature is supposed to lie in total confusion. What never was seen or heard of may yet be conceived; nor is anything beyond the power of thought, except what implies an absolute contradiction.

But though our thought seems to possess this unbounded liberty, we shall find, upon a nearer examination, that it is really confined within very narrow limits and that all this creative power of the mind amounts to no more than the faculty of compounding, transposing, augmenting, or diminishing the materials afforded us by the senses and experience. When we think of a golden mountain, we only join two consistent ideas, *gold* and *mountain,* with which we were formerly acquainted. A virtuous horse we can conceive because, from our own feeling, we can conceive virtue; and this we may unite to the figure and shape of a horse, which is an animal familiar to us. In short, all the materials of thinking are derived either from our outward or inward sentiment: The mixture and composition of these belongs alone to the mind and will. Or, to express myself in philosophical language, all our ideas or more feeble perceptions are copies of our impressions or more lively ones.

To prove this, the two following arguments will, I hope, be sufficient. First, when we analyze our thoughts or ideas, however compounded or sublime, we always find that they resolve themselves into such simple ideas as were copied from a precedent[3] feeling or sentiment. Even those ideas which at first view seem the most wide of this origin are found, upon a nearer scrutiny, to be derived from it. The idea of God, as meaning an infinitely intelligent, wise, and good Being, arises from reflecting on the operations of our own mind and augmenting, without limit, those qualities of goodness and wisdom. We may prosecute[4] this inquiry to what length we please, where we shall always find that every idea which we examine is copied from a similar impression. Those who would assert that this position is not universally true nor without exception have only one, and that an easy method of refuting it—by producing that idea which, in their opinion, is not derived from this source. It will then be incumbent on us, if we would maintain our doctrine, to produce the impression, or lively perception, which corresponds to it.

Secondly, if it happen from a defect of the organ that a man is not susceptible of any species of sensation, we always find that he is as little susceptible of the correspondent ideas. A blind man can form no notion of colors; a deaf man of sounds. Restore either of them that sense in which he is deficient. By opening this new inlet for his sensations, you also open an inlet for the ideas, and he finds no difficulty in conceiving these objects. . . .

When we entertain, therefore, any suspicion that a philosophical term is employed without any meaning or idea (as is but too frequent), we need but inquire, *from what impression is that supposed idea derived?* And if it be impossible to assign any, this will serve to confirm our suspicion. By bringing ideas into so clear a light we may reasonably hope to remove all dispute which may arise concerning their nature and reality. . . .

SECTION IV. SKEPTICAL[5] DOUBTS CONCERNING THE OPERATIONS OF THE UNDERSTANDING

Part I

All the objects of human reason or inquiry may naturally be divided into two kinds, to wit, *relations of ideas* and *matters of fact*. Of the first kind are the sciences of geometry, algebra, and arithmetic; and in short, every affirmation which is either intuitively or demonstratively certain. *That the square of the hypotenuse is equal to the square of the two sides* is a proposition which expresses a relation between these figures. *That three times five is equal to the half of thirty* expresses a relation between these numbers. Propositions of this kind are discoverable by the mere operation of thought, without dependence on what is anywhere existent in the universe. Though there never were a circle or triangle in nature, the truths demonstrated by Euclid[6] would forever retain their certainty and evidence.

Matters of fact, which are the second objects of human reason, are not ascertained in the same manner; nor is our evidence of their truth, however great, of a like nature with the foregoing. The contrary of every matter of fact is still possible because it can never imply a contradiction and is conceived by the mind with the same facility and distinctness, as if ever so conformable to reality. *That the sun will not rise tomorrow* is no less intelligible a proposition and implies no more contradiction than the affirmation *that it will rise.* We should in vain, therefore, attempt to demonstrate its falsehood. Were it demonstratively false, it would imply a contradiction and could never be distinctly conceived by the mind.

It may, therefore, be a subject worthy of curiosity to inquire what is the nature of that evidence which assures us of any real existence and matter of fact, beyond the present testimony of our senses or the records of our memory. This part of philosophy, it is observable, has been little cultivated either by the ancients or moderns, and therefore our doubts and errors in the prosecution of so important an inquiry may be the more excusable, while we march through such difficult paths without any guide or direction. They may even prove useful, by exciting curiosity and destroying that implicit faith and security which is the bane of all reasoning and free inquiry. The discovery of defects in the common philosophy, if any such there be, will not, I presume, be a discouragement but rather an incitement, as is usual, to attempt something more full and satisfactory than has yet been proposed to the public.

All reasonings concerning matter of fact seem to be founded on the relation of *cause and effect*. By means of that relation alone we can go beyond the evidence of our memory and senses. If you were to ask a man why he believes any matter of fact which is absent—for instance, that his friend is in the country, or in France—he would give you a reason; and this reason would be some other fact, as a letter received from him or the knowledge of his former resolutions and promises. A man finding a watch or any other machine in a desert[7] island would conclude that there had once been men in that island. All our reasonings concerning fact are of the same nature. And here it is constantly supposed that there is a connection between the present fact and that which is inferred from it. Were there nothing to bind them together, the inference would be entirely precarious. The hearing of an articulate voice and rational discourse in the dark assures us of the presence of some person. Why? Because these are the effects of the human make and fabric, and closely connected with it. If we anatomize all the other reasonings of this nature, we shall find that they are founded on the relation of cause and effect, and that this relation is either near or remote, direct or collateral. Heat and light are collateral effects of fire, and the one effect may justly be inferred from the other.

If we would satisfy ourselves, therefore, concerning the nature of that evidence which assures us of matters of fact, we must inquire how we arrive at the knowledge of cause and effect.

I shall venture to affirm, as a general proposition which admits of no exception, that the knowledge of this relation is not, in any instance, attained by reasonings a priori[8] but arises entirely from experience, when we find that any particular objects are constantly conjoined with each other. Let an object be presented to a man of ever so strong natural reason and abilities; if that object be entirely new to him, he will not be able, by the most accurate examination of its sensible[9] qualities, to discover any of its causes or effects. Adam, though his rational faculties be supposed, at the very first, entirely perfect, could not have inferred from the fluidity and transparency of water that it would suffocate him, or from the light and warmth of fire that it would consume him. No object ever discovers, by the qualities which appear to the senses, either the causes which produced it or the effects which will arise from it; nor can our reason, unassisted by experience, ever draw any inference concerning real existence and matter of fact.

This proposition *that causes and effects are discoverable, not by reason but by experience* will readily be admitted with regard to such objects as we remember to have once been altogether unknown to us, since we must be conscious of the utter inability, which we then lay under, of foretelling what would arise from them. Present two smooth pieces of marble to a man who has no tincture of natural philosophy[10]—he will never discover that they will adhere together in such a manner as to require great force to separate them in a direct line, while they make so small a resistance to a lateral pressure. Such events as bear little analogy to the common course of nature are also readily confessed to be known only by experience; nor does any man imagine that the explosion of gunpowder or the attraction of a loadstone could ever be discovered by arguments a priori. In like manner, when an effect is supposed to depend upon an intricate machinery or secret[11] structure of parts, we make no difficulty in attributing all our knowledge of it to experience. Who will assert that he can give the ultimate reason why milk or bread is proper nourishment for a man, not for a lion or a tiger?

But the same truth may not appear, at first sight, to have the same evidence with regard to events which have become familiar to us from our first appearance in the world, which bear a close analogy to the whole course of nature and which are supposed to depend on the simple qualities of objects, without any secret structure of parts. We are apt to imagine that we could discover these effects by the mere operation of our reason, without experience. We fancy that were we brought on a sudden into this world, we could at first have inferred that one billiard ball would communicate motion to another upon impulse, and that we needed not to have waited for the event in order to pronounce with certainty concerning it. Such is the influence of custom, that, where it is strongest, it not only covers our natural ignorance but even conceals itself and seems not to take place, merely because it is found in the highest degree.

But to convince us that all the laws of nature and all the operations of bodies, without exception, are known only by experience, the following reflections may perhaps suffice. Were any object presented to us and were we required to pronounce concerning the effect which will result from it, without consulting past observation; after what manner, I beseech you, must the mind proceed in this operation? It must invent or imagine some event which it ascribes to the object as its effect, and it is plain that this invention must be entirely arbitrary. The mind can never possibly find the effect in the supposed cause by the most accurate scrutiny and examination. For the effect is totally different from the cause and consequently can never be discovered in it. Motion in the second billiard ball is a quite distinct event from motion in the first; nor is there anything in the one to suggest the smallest hint of the other. A stone or piece of metal raised into the air and left without any support immediately falls. But to consider the matter a priori, is there anything we discover in this situation which can beget the idea of a downward, rather than an upward or any other motion in the stone or metal?

And as the first imagination or invention of a particular effect in all natural operations is arbitrary, where we consult not experience; so must we also esteem[12] the supposed tie or connection between the cause and effect, which binds them together and renders it impossible that any other effect could result from the operation of that cause. When I see, for instance, a billiard ball moving in a straight line towards another; even suppose motion in the second ball should by accident be suggested to me, as the result of their contact or impulse; may I not conceive that a hundred different events might as well follow from that cause? May not both these balls remain at absolute rest? May not the first ball return in a straight line or leap off from the second in any line or direction? All these suppositions are consistent and conceivable. Why then should we give the preference to one, which is no more consistent or conceivable than the rest? All our reasonings a priori will never be able to show us any foundation for this preference.

In a word, then, every effect is a distinct event from its cause. It could not, therefore, be discovered in the cause, and the first invention or conception of it a priori must be entirely arbitrary. And even after it is suggested, the conjunction of it with the cause must appear equally arbitrary, since there are always many other effects which to reason must seem fully as consistent and natural. In vain, therefore, should we pretend[13] to determine any single event, or infer any cause or effect, without the assistance of observation and experience. . . .

Part II

But we have not yet attained any tolerable satisfaction with regard to the question first proposed. Each solution still gives rise to a new question as difficult as the foregoing and leads us on to farther inquiries. When it is asked, "What is the nature of all our reasonings concerning matter of fact?," the proper answer seems to be that they are founded on the relation of cause and effect. When again it is asked, "What is the foundation of all our reasonings and conclusions concerning that relation?," it may be replied in one word, experience. But if we still carry on our sifting humor[14] and ask, "What is the foundation of all conclusions from experience?," this implies a new question, which may be of more difficult solution and explication. Philosophers that give themselves airs of superior wisdom and sufficiency have a hard task when they encounter persons of inquisitive dispositions who push them from every corner to which they retreat, and who are sure at last to bring them to some dangerous dilemma. The best expedient to prevent this confusion is to be modest in our pretensions and even to discover the difficulty ourselves before it is objected to us. By this means, we may make a kind of merit of our very ignorance.

I shall content myself, in this section, with an easy task and shall pretend only to give a negative answer to the question here proposed. I say then, that even after we have experience of the operations of cause and effect, our conclusions from that experience are *not* founded on reasoning or any process of the understanding. This answer we must endeavor both to explain and to defend.

It must certainly be allowed that nature has kept us at a great distance from all her secrets and has afforded us only the knowledge of a few superficial qualities of objects, while she conceals from us those powers and principles on which the influence of those objects entirely depends. . . . If a body of like color and consistence with that bread which we have formerly eaten be presented to us, we make no scruple of repeating the experiment and foresee, with certainty, like nourishment and support. Now this is a process of the mind or thought, of which I would willingly know the foundation. It is allowed on all hands that there is no known connection between the sensible qualities and the secret powers, and consequently that the mind is not led to form such a conclusion concerning their constant and regular conjunction, by anything which it knows of their nature. As to past *experience*, it can be allowed to give *direct* and *certain* information of those precise objects only, and that precise period of time, which fell under its cognizance. But why this experience should be extended to future times and to other objects which, for aught we know, may be only in appearance similar—this is the main question on which I would insist. The bread which I formerly ate nourished me; that is, a body of such sensible qualities was, at that time, endued with such secret powers. But does it follow that other bread must also nourish me at another time, and that like sensible qualities must always be attended with like secret powers? The consequence seems nowise necessary. At least it must be acknowledged that there is here a consequence drawn by the mind; that there is a certain step taken—a process of thought and an inference which wants to be explained. These two propositions are far from being the same: "I have found that such an object has always been attended with such an effect" and "I foresee that other objects which are in appearance similar will be attended with similar effects." I shall allow, if you please, that the one proposition may justly be inferred from the other; I know, in fact, that it always is inferred. But if you insist that the inference is made by a chain of reasoning, I desire you to produce that reasoning. The connection between these propositions is not intuitive. There is required a medium[15] which may enable the mind to draw such an inference, if indeed it be drawn by reasoning and argument. What that medium is, I must confess, passes my comprehension—and it is incumbent on those to produce it, who assert that it really exists and is the origin of all our conclusions concerning matter of fact. . . .

When a new object endowed with similar sensible qualities is produced, we expect similar powers and forces and look for a like effect. From a body of like color and consistence with bread we expect like nourishment and support. But this surely is a step or progress of the mind, which wants to be explained. When a man says, "I have found, in all past instances, such sensible qualities conjoined with such secret powers," and when he says, "Similar sensible qualities will always be conjoined with similar secret powers," he is not guilty of a tautology, nor are these propositions in any respect the same. You say that the one proposition is an inference from the other. But you must confess that the inference is not intuitive; neither is it demonstrative. Of what nature is it, then? To say it is experimental[16] is begging the question. For all inferences from experience suppose, as their foundation, that the future will resemble the past and that similar powers will be conjoined with similar sensible qualities. If there be any suspicion that the course of nature may change and that the past may be no rule for the future, all experience becomes useless and can give rise to no inference or conclusion. It is impossible, therefore, that any arguments from experience can prove this resemblance of the past to the future, since all these arguments are founded on the supposition of that resemblance. Let the course of things be allowed hitherto ever so regular—that alone, without some new argument or inference, proves not that, for the future, it will continue so. In vain do you pretend to have learned the nature of bodies from your past experience. Their secret nature, and consequently all their effects and influence, may change without any change in their sensible qualities. This happens sometimes and with regard to some objects—why may it not happen always and with regard to all objects? What logic, what process of argument secures you against this supposition? My practice, you say, refutes my doubts. But you mistake the purport of my question. As an agent, I am quite satisfied in the point; but as a philosopher who has some share of curiosity (I will not say skepticism), I want to learn the foundation of this inference. No reading, no inquiry has yet been able to remove my difficulty or give me satisfaction in a matter of such importance. Can I do better than propose the difficulty to the public, even though, perhaps, I have small hopes of obtaining a solution? We shall at least, by this means, be sensible[17] of our ignorance, if we do not augment our knowledge. . . .

SECTION V. SKEPTICAL SOLUTION OF THESE DOUBTS

Part I

. . . Suppose a person, though endowed with the strongest faculties of reason and reflection, to be brought on a sudden into this world. He would, indeed, immediately observe a continual succession of objects, and one event following another; but he would not be able to discover anything farther. He would not at first, by any reasoning, be able to reach the idea of cause and effect, since the particular powers by which all natural operations are performed never appear to the senses. Nor is it reasonable to conclude, merely because one event, in one instance, precedes another, that therefore the one is the cause, the other the effect. Their conjunction may be arbitrary and casual. There may be no reason to infer the existence of one from the appearance of the other. And in a word, such a person, without more experience, could never employ his conjecture or reasoning concerning any matter of fact, or be assured of anything beyond what was immediately present to his memory and senses.

Suppose, again, that he has acquired more experience and has lived so long in the world as to have observed familiar objects or events to be constantly conjoined together. What is the consequence of this experience? He immediately infers the existence of one object from the appearance of the other. Yet he has not, by all his experience, acquired any idea or knowledge of the secret power by which the one object produces the other; nor is it by any process of reasoning [that] he is engaged to draw this inference. But still he finds himself determined to draw it. And though he should be convinced that his understanding has no part in the operation, he would nevertheless continue in the same course of thinking. There is some other principle which determines him to form such a conclusion.

This principle is custom or habit. For wherever the repetition of any particular act or operation produces a propensity to renew the same act or operation, without being impelled by any reasoning or process of the understanding, we always say that this propensity is the effect of *custom*. By employing that word, we pretend not to have given the ultimate reason of such a propensity. We only point out a principle of human nature which is universally acknowledged and which is well known by its effects. Perhaps we can push our inquiries no farther or pretend to give the cause of this cause, but must rest contented with it as the ultimate principle which we can assign of all our conclusions from experience. It is sufficient satisfaction that we can go so far, without repining at the narrowness of our faculties because they will carry us no farther. And it is certain we here advance a very intelligible proposition at least, if not a true one, when we assert that after the constant conjunction of two objects—heat and flame, for instance, weight and solidity—we are determined by custom alone to expect the one from the appearance of the other. This hypothesis seems even the only one which explains the difficulty why we draw from a thousand instances an inference which we are not able to draw from one instance that is in no respect different from them. Reason is incapable of any such variation. The conclusions which it draws from considering one circle are the same which it would form upon surveying all the circles in the universe. But no man, having seen only one body move after being impelled by another, could infer that every other body will move after a like impulse. All inferences from experience, therefore, are effects of custom, not of reasoning.

Custom, then, is the great guide of human life. It is that principle alone which renders our experience useful to us and makes us expect for the future a similar train of events with those which have appeared in the past. Without the influence of custom, we should be entirely ignorant of every matter of fact beyond what is immediately present to the memory and senses. We should never know how to adjust means to ends, or to employ our natural powers in the production of any effect. There would be an end at once of all action as well as of the chief part of speculation.

But here it may be proper to remark that though our conclusions from experience carry us beyond our memory and senses and assure us of matters of fact which happened in the most distant places and most remote ages, yet some fact must always be present to the senses or memory, from which we may first proceed in drawing these conclusions. A man who should find in a desert country the remains of pompous[18] buildings would conclude that the country had, in ancient times, been cultivated by civilized inhabitants. But did nothing of this nature occur to him, he could never form such an inference. We learn the events of former ages from history; but then we must peruse the volumes in which this instruction is contained, and thence carry up our inferences from one testimony to another till we arrive at the eyewitnesses and spectators of these distant events. In a word, if we proceed not upon some fact present to the memory or senses, our reasonings would be merely hypothetical; and however the particular links might be connected with each other, the whole chain of inferences would have nothing to support it, nor could we ever by its means arrive at the knowledge of any real existence. If I ask why you believe any particular matter of fact which you relate, you must tell me some reason; and this reason will be some other fact connected with it. But as you cannot proceed after this manner *in infinitum*,[19] you must at last terminate in some fact which is present to your memory or senses, or must allow that your belief is entirely without foundation.

What, then, is the conclusion of the whole matter? A simple one—though, it must be confessed, pretty remote from the common theories of philosophy. All belief of matter of fact or real existence is derived merely from some object present to the memory or senses and a customary conjunction between that and some other object. Or in other words, having found in many instances that any two kinds of objects—flame and heat, snow and cold—have always been conjoined together; if flame or snow be presented anew to the senses, the mind is carried by custom to expect heat or cold and to *believe* that such a quality does exist and will discover itself upon a nearer approach. This belief is the necessary result of placing the mind in such circumstances. It is an operation of the soul when we are so situated, as unavoidable as to feel the passion of love when we receive benefits, or hatred when we meet with injuries. All these operations are a species of natural instincts, which no reasoning or process of the thought and understanding is able either to produce or to prevent.

NOTES

1. *sentiment:* perception. [D. C. ABEL]
2. *metaphysical:* relating to *metaphysics,* the study of the nature and kinds of reality. [D. C. ABEL]
3. *precedent:* prior. [D. C. ABEL]
4. *prosecute:* pursue. [D. C. ABEL]
5. *skeptical:* relating to *skepticism,* the doctrine that we cannot attain certainty in knowledge. [D. C. ABEL]
6. Euclid (flourished around 300 B.C.E.) was a Greek geometer. [D. C. ABEL]
7. *desert:* desolate. [D. C. ABEL]
8. *a priori:* based on abstract reasoning, independent of experience (literally, in Latin, "from what comes earlier"). [D. C. ABEL]
9. *sensible:* able to be sensed. [D. C. ABEL]
10. *natural philosophy:* the philosophy of nature; natural science. [D. C. ABEL]
11. *secret:* unseen. [D. C. ABEL]
12. *esteem:* regard. [D. C. ABEL]
13. *pretend:* undertake. [D. C. ABEL]
14. *sifting humor:* questioning frame of mind. [D. C. ABEL]
15. *medium:* basis for an inference. [D. C. ABEL]
16. *experimental:* based on experience. [D. C. ABEL]
17. *sensible:* aware. [D. C. ABEL]
18. *pompous:* magnificent. [D. C. ABEL]
19. *in infinitum:* (Latin) "to infinity." [D. C. ABEL]

Critique of Pure Reason

Immanuel Kant

Immanuel Kant was born in 1724 in Königsberg, Prussia, where he spent his entire life. As a boy he attended the Collegium Fridericanum, a school run by the Pietists (the Lutheran sect to which his family belonged). In 1740 he enrolled in the University of Königsberg, where he studied a wide variety of subjects, including theology, philosophy, mathematics, physics, and medicine. He withdrew from the university in 1747 to support himself by working as a private tutor for various families in eastern Prussia. He resumed his studies in 1754 and completed his degree the following year. He then became a lecturer at the University of Königsberg, teaching such diverse subjects as mathematics, geography, mineralogy, and philosophy. Fifteen years later he was appointed professor of logic and metaphysics. His writings—especially his monumental *Critique of Pure Reason* (1781)—brought him increasing fame, and students came from afar to hear him lecture. In 1797 he stopped lecturing, but he continued to write. He died in Königsberg in 1804 at the age of seventy-nine.

Kant's principal works, in addition to *Critique of Pure Reason,* are *Prolegomena to Any Future Metaphysics* (1783), *Groundwork of the Metaphysics of Morals* (1785), *Critique of Practical Reason* (1788), and *Critique of Judgment* (1790).

Our reading is taken from Kant's second edition of *Critique of Pure Reason,* published in 1787. Kant's project in this book is to investigate how much we can know by "pure reason" (reason itself, apart from any experience). In his preface, Kant observes that we typically assume that our knowledge (cognition) must conform to objects—that when we know something, our mind must match the way the objects are. If this assumption is correct, it would be impossible to have any knowledge of objects a priori (prior to our experience of them). Kant rejects this assumption; he holds the converse, that *objects* must conform to our *knowledge*—that when we know something, objects must match the way our minds are. Objects conform to our way of receiving sense experience (intuition) and to our way of intellectually synthesizing this sense experience (thought). That is to say, our minds are constructed in such a way that we necessarily *sense* objects through the forms of "sensibility" (namely, space and time) and we necessarily *think* objects through certain "categories" (also called "concepts") of the understanding, such as causality and unity. This means that we can know certain things about objects a priori. For example, we know that we will experience them as existing in space and as being caused. But according to Kant, even though we know that objects will invariably *appear to us* in certain ways, we can never know how things are *in themselves.*

In his introduction, Kant explains that a priori knowledge is characterized by necessity and universality. He then explains that some of our judgments (those in mathematics and metaphysics, for example) are not only a priori but synthetic. (A *synthetic* proposition adds something to a concept; an *analytic* one does not.) Kant's doctrine about the structure of the mind is designed to explain how such synthetic a priori judgments are possible.

In the final two sections of our reading, Kant gives arguments to show that space and time (the forms of sensibility) are a priori, and explains that there are twelve categories of the understanding, corresponding to the twelve kinds of judgment.

PREFACE TO THE SECOND EDITION

Whether or not the treatment of the cognitions belonging to the concern of reason travels the secure course of a science is something which can soon be judged by its success. If after many preliminaries and preparations are made, a science gets stuck as soon as it approaches its end, or if in order to reach this end it must often go back and set out on a new path; or likewise if it proves impossible for the different coworkers to achieve unanimity as to the way in which they should pursue their common aim; then we may be sure that such a study is merely groping about, that it is still far from having entered upon the secure course of a science. And it is already a service to reason if we can possibly find that path for it, even if we have to give up as futile much of what was included in the end previously formed without deliberation. . . .

Up to now it has been assumed that all our cognition must conform to the objects; but all attempts to find out something about them a priori[1] through concepts that would extend our cognition have, on this presupposition, come to nothing. Hence let us once try whether we do not get farther with the problems of metaphysics[2] by assuming that the objects must conform to our cognition, which would agree better with the requested possibility of an a priori cognition of them, which is to establish something about objects before they are given to us. This would be just like the first thoughts of Copernicus,[3] who, when he did not make good progress in the explanation of the celestial motions if he assumed that the entire celestial host revolves around the observer, tried to see if he might not have greater success if he made the observer revolve and left the stars at rest. Now in metaphysics we can try in a similar way regarding the *intuition*[4] of objects. If intuition has to conform to the constitution of the objects, then I do not see how we can know anything of them a priori; but if the object (as an object of the senses) conforms to the constitution of our faculty of intuition, then I can very well represent this possibility to myself. Yet because I cannot stop with these intuitions, if they are to become cognitions, but must refer them as representations to something as their object and determine this object through them, I can assume *either* that the concepts through which I bring about this determination also conform to the objects, and then I am once again in the same difficulty about how I could know anything about them a priori, *or else* I assume that the objects, or what is the same thing, the *experience* in which alone they can be cognized (as given objects), conforms to those concepts—in which case I immediately see an easier way out of the difficulty, since experience itself is a kind of cognition requiring the understanding, whose rule I have to presuppose in myself before any object is given to me, hence a priori, which rule is expressed in concepts a priori, to which all objects of experience must therefore necessarily conform, and with which they must agree. . . .

INTRODUCTION TO THE SECOND EDITION

I. On the Difference Between Pure and Empirical Cognition

There is no doubt whatever that all our cognition begins with experience; for how else should the cognitive faculty be awakened into exercise if not through objects that stimulate our senses and in part themselves produce representations, in part bring the activity of our understanding into motion to compare these, to connect or separate them, and thus to work up the raw material of sensible impressions into a cognition of objects that is called experience? *As far as time is concerned*, then, no cognition in us precedes experience, and with experience every cognition begins.

But although all our cognition commences *with* experience, yet it does not on that account all arise *from* experience. For it could well be that even our experiential cognition is a composite of that which we receive through impressions and that which our own cognitive faculty (merely prompted by sensible impressions) provides out of itself, which addition we cannot distinguish from that fundamental material until long practice has made us attentive to it and skilled in separating it out.

It is therefore at least a question requiring closer investigation, and one not to be dismissed at first glance, whether there is any such cognition independent of all experience and even of all impressions of the senses. One calls such cognitions a priori, and distinguishes them from *empirical* ones, which have their sources a posteriori, namely in experience.

The former expression is nevertheless not yet sufficiently determinate to designate the whole sense of the question before us. For it is customary to say of many a cognition derived from experiential sources that we are capable of it or partake in it a priori, because we do not derive it immediately from experience, but rather from a general rule that we have nevertheless itself borrowed from experience. So one says of someone who undermined the foundation of his house that he could have known a priori that it would collapse—he need not have waited for the experience of it actually collapsing. Yet he could not have known this entirely a priori. For that bodies are heavy and hence fall if their support is taken away must first have become known to him through experience.

In the sequel therefore we will understand by a priori cognitions not those that occur independently of this or that experience, but rather those that occur *absolutely* independently of all experience. Opposed to them are empirical cognitions, or those that are possible only a posteriori, that is, through experience. Among a priori cognitions, however, those are called *pure* with which nothing empirical is intermixed. Thus, for example, the proposition "Every alteration has its cause" is an a priori proposition, only not pure, since alteration is a concept that can be drawn only from experience.

II. We Are in Possession of Certain A Priori Cognitions, and Even the Common Understanding Is Never Without Them

At issue here is a mark by means of which we can securely distinguish a pure cognition from an empirical one. Experience teaches us, to be sure, that something is constituted thus and so, but not that it could not be otherwise. *First*, then, if a proposition is thought along with its *necessity*, it is an a priori judgment. If it is, moreover, also not derived from any proposition except one that in turn is valid as a necessary proposition, then it is absolutely a priori. *Second*, experience never gives its judgments true or strict but only assumed and comparative *universality* (through induction), so properly it must be said: As far as we have yet perceived, there is no exception to this or that rule. Thus if a judgment is thought in strict universality—that is, in such a way that no exception at all is allowed to be possible—then it is not derived from experience, but is rather valid absolutely a priori. Empirical universality is therefore only an arbitrary increase in validity from that which holds in *most* cases to that which holds in *all* (as in, for example, the proposition "All bodies are heavy"), whereas strict universality belongs to a judgment essentially; this points to a special source of cognition for it, namely a faculty of a priori cognition. Necessity and strict universality are therefore secure indications of an a priori cognition, and also belong together inseparably. But since in their use it is sometimes easier to show the empirical limitation in judgments than the contingency[5] in them, or is often more plausible to show the unrestricted universality that we ascribe to a judgment than its necessity, it is advisable to employ separately these two criteria, each of which is in itself infallible.

Now it is easy to show that in human cognition there actually are such necessary and in the strictest sense universal, thus pure a priori judgments. If one wants an example from the sciences, one need only look at all the propositions of mathematics; if one would have one from the commonest use of the understanding, the proposition that every alteration must have a cause will do; indeed in the latter the very concept of a cause so obviously contains the concept of a necessity of connection with an effect and a strict universality of rule that it would be entirely lost if one sought, as Hume[6] did, to derive it from a frequent association of that which happens with that which precedes and a habit (thus a merely subjective necessity) of connecting representations arising from that association. Even without requiring such examples for the proof of the reality of pure a priori principles in our cognition, one could establish their indispensability for the possibility of experience itself, thus establish it a priori. For where would experience itself get its certainty if all rules in accordance with which it proceeds were themselves in turn always empirical, thus contingent? Hence one could hardly allow these to count as first principles. Yet here we can content ourselves with having displayed the pure use of our cognitive faculty as a fact together with its indication. Not merely in judgments, however, but even in concepts is an origin of some of them revealed a priori. Gradually remove from your experiential concept of a *body* everything that is empirical in it—the color, the hardness or softness, the weight, even the impenetrability—there still remains the *space* that was occupied by the body (which has now entirely disappeared), and you cannot leave that out. Likewise, if you remove from your empirical concept of every object, whether corporeal or incorporeal, all those properties of which experience teaches you, you could still not take from it that by means of which you think of it as a *substance* or as *dependent* on a substance (even though this concept contains more determination than that of an object in general). Thus, convinced by the necessity with which this concept presses itself on you, you must concede that it has its seat in your faculty of cognition a priori. . . .

IV. On the Difference Between Analytic and Synthetic Judgments

In all judgments in which the relation of a subject to the predicate is thought (if I consider only affirmative judgments, since the application to negative ones is easy), this relation is possible in two different ways. Either the predicate B belongs to the subject A as something that is (covertly) contained in this concept A; or B lies entirely outside the concept A, though to be sure it stands in connection with it. In the first case I call the judgment *analytic*, in the second *synthetic*. Analytic judgments (affirmative ones) are thus those in which the connection of the predicate is thought through identity, but those in which this connection is thought without identity are to be called synthetic judgments. One could also call the former *judgments of clarification*, and the latter *judgments of amplification*, since through the predicate the former do not add anything to the concept of the subject, but only break it up by means of analysis into its component concepts, which were already thought in it (though confusedly); while the latter, on the contrary, add to the concept of the subject a predicate that was not thought in it at all, and could not have been extracted from it through any analysis. For example, if I say "All bodies are extended," then this is an analytic judgment. For I do not need to go beyond the concept that I combine with the body in order to find that extension is connected with it, but rather I need only to analyze that concept—that is, become conscious of the manifold that I always think in it—in order to encounter this predicate therein. It is therefore an analytic judgment. On the contrary, if I say "All bodies are heavy," then the predicate is something entirely different from that which I think in the mere concept of a body in general. The addition of such a predicate thus yields a synthetic judgment.

Judgments of experience, as such, are all synthetic. For it would be absurd to ground an analytic judgment on experience, since I do not need to go beyond my concept at all in order to formulate the judgment, and therefore need no testimony from experience for that. That a body is extended is a proposition that is established a priori, and is not a judgment of experience. For before I go to experience, I already have all the conditions for my judgment in the concept, from which I merely draw out the predicate in accordance with the principle of contradiction, and can thereby at the same time become conscious of the necessity of the judgment, which experience could never teach me. On the contrary, although I do not at all include the predicate of weight in the concept of a body in general, the concept nevertheless designates an object of experience through a part of it, to which I can therefore add still other parts of the same experience as belonging with the former. I can first cognize the concept of body analytically through the marks of extension, of impenetrability, of shape, and so on, which are all thought in this concept. But now I amplify my cognition and, looking back to the experience from which I had extracted this concept of body, I find that weight is also always connected with the previous marks, and I therefore add this synthetically as predicate to that concept. It is thus experience on which the possibility of the synthesis of the predicate of weight with the concept of body is grounded, since both concepts, though the one is not contained in the other, nevertheless belong together, though only contingently, as parts of a whole, namely experience, which is itself a synthetic combination of intuitions.

But in synthetic a priori judgments this means of help is entirely lacking. If I am to go beyond the concept *A* in order to cognize another *B* as combined with it, what is it on which I depend and by means of which the synthesis becomes possible, since I here do not have the advantage of looking around for it in the field of experience? Take the proposition "Everything that happens has its cause." In the concept of something that happens, I think, to be sure, of an existence that was preceded by a time, and so on, and from that analytic judgments can be drawn. But the concept of a cause lies entirely outside that concept, and indicates something different from the concept of what happens in general, and is therefore not contained in the latter representation at all. How then do I come to say something quite different about that which happens in general, and to cognize the concept of cause as belonging to it, indeed necessarily, even though not contained in it? What is the unknown = *X* here on which the understanding depends when it believes itself to discover beyond the concept of *A* a predicate that is foreign to it yet which it nevertheless believes to be connected with it? It cannot be experience, for the principle that has been adduced adds the latter representations to the former not only with greater generality than experience can provide, but also with the expression of necessity, hence entirely a priori and from mere concepts. Now the entire final aim of our speculative a priori cognition rests on such synthetic, that is, ampliative principles; for the analytic ones are, to be sure, most important and necessary, but only for attaining that distinctness of concepts which is requisite for a secure and extended synthesis as a really new acquisition.

V. Synthetic A Priori Judgments Are Contained as Principles in All Theoretical Sciences of Reason

1. *Mathematical judgments are all synthetic.* This proposition seems to have escaped the notice of the analysts of human reason until now, indeed to be diametrically opposed to all of their conjectures, although it is incontrovertibly certain and is very important in the sequel. For since one found that the inferences of the mathematicians all proceed in accordance with the principle of contradiction (which is required by the nature of any apodictic[7] certainty), one was persuaded that the principles could also be cognized from the principle of contradiction, in which, however, they erred; for a synthetic proposition can of course be comprehended in accordance with the principle of contradiction, but only insofar as another synthetic proposition is presupposed from which it can be deduced, never in itself.

It must first be remarked that properly mathematical propositions are always a priori judgments and are never empirical, because they carry necessity with them, which cannot be derived from experience. But if one does not want to concede this, well then, I will restrict my proposition to *pure mathematics,* the concept of which already implies that it does not contain empirical but merely pure a priori cognition.

To be sure, one might initially think that the proposition "7 + 5 = 12" is a merely analytic proposition that follows from the concept of a sum of seven and five in accordance with the principle of contradiction. Yet if one considers it more closely, one finds that the concept of the sum of 7 and 5 contains nothing more than the unification of both numbers in a single one, through which it is not at all thought what this single number is which comprehends the two of them. The concept of twelve is by no means already thought merely by my thinking of that unification of seven and five, and no matter how long I analyze my concept of such a possible sum I will still not find twelve in it. One must go beyond these concepts, seeking assistance in the intuition that corresponds to one of the two, one's five fingers, say, or (as in Segner's arithmetic)[8] five points, and one after another add the units of the five given in the intuition to the concept of seven. For I take first the number 7, and, as I take the fingers of my hand as an intuition for assistance with the concept of 5, to that image of mine I now add the units that I have previously taken together in order to constitute the number 5 one after another to the number 7, and thus see the number 12 arise. That 7 *should* be added to 5 I have, to be sure, thought in the concept of a sum = 7 + 5, but not that this sum is equal to the number 12. The arithmetical proposition is therefore always synthetic; one becomes all the more distinctly aware of that if one takes somewhat larger numbers, for it is then clear that, twist and turn our concepts as we will, without getting help from intuition we could never find the sum by means of the mere analysis of our concepts.

Just as little is any principle of pure geometry analytic. That the straight line between two points is the shortest is a synthetic proposition. For my concept of *the straight* contains nothing of quantity, but only a quality. The concept of the shortest is therefore entirely additional to it, and cannot be extracted out of the concept of the straight line by any analysis. Help must here be gotten from intuition, by means of which alone the synthesis is possible. . . .

2. *Natural science* (physica)[9] *contains within itself synthetic a priori judgments as principles.* I will adduce only a couple of propositions as examples, such as the proposition that in all alterations of the corporeal world the quantity of matter remains unaltered; or that in all communication of motion, effect and counter-effect must always be equal. In both of these not only the necessity, thus their a priori origin, but also that they are synthetic propositions is clear. For in the concept of matter I do not think persistence, but only its presence in space through the filling of space. Thus I actually go beyond the concept of matter in order to add something to it a priori that I did not think *in it*. The proposition is thus not analytic, but synthetic, and nevertheless thought a priori, and likewise with the other propositions of the pure part of natural science.

3. *In metaphysics,* even if one regards it as a science that has thus far merely been sought but is nevertheless indispensable because of the nature of human reason, synthetic a priori cognitions are supposed to be contained, and it is not concerned merely with analyzing concepts that we make of things a priori and thereby clarifying them analytically, but we want to amplify our cognition a priori. To this end we must make use of such principles that add something to the given concepts that was not contained in them, and through synthetic a priori judgments go so far beyond that experience itself cannot follow us that far— for example, in the proposition "The world must have a first beginning" and others besides—and thus metaphysics, at least as far as *its end is concerned,* consists of purely synthetic a priori propositions.

VI. The General Problem of Pure Reason

One has already gained a great deal if one can bring a multitude of investigations under the formula of a single problem. For one thereby not only lightens one's own task, by determining it precisely, but also the judgment of anyone else who wants to examine whether we have satisfied our plan or not. The real problem of pure reason is now contained in the question: *How are synthetic judgments a priori possible?*

That metaphysics has until now remained in such a vacillating state of uncertainty and contradictions is to be ascribed solely to the cause that no one has previously thought of this problem and perhaps even of the distinction between analytic and synthetic judgments. On the solution of this problem, or on a satisfactory proof that the possibility that it demands to have explained does not in fact exist at all, metaphysics now stands or falls. David Hume, who among all philosophers came closest to this problem, still did not conceive of it anywhere near determinately enough and in its universality, but rather stopped with the synthetic proposition of the connection of the effect with its cause (*principium causalitatis*),[10] believing himself to have brought out that such an a priori proposition is entirely impossible. And according to his inferences everything that we call metaphysics would come down to a mere delusion of an alleged insight of reason into that which has in fact merely been borrowed from experience and from habit has taken on the appearance of necessity—an assertion, destructive of all pure philosophy, on which he would never have fallen if he had had our problem in its generality before his eyes, since then he would have comprehended that according to his argument there could also be no pure mathematics, since this certainly contains synthetic a priori propositions, an assertion from which his sound understanding would surely have protected him.

In the solution of the above problem there is at the same time contained the possibility of the pure use of reason in the grounding and execution of all sciences that contain a theoretical a priori cognition of objects—that is, the answer to the questions:

How is pure mathematics possible?
How is pure natural science possible?

About these sciences, since they are actually given, it can appropriately be asked *how* they are possible; for that they must be possible is proved through their actuality. As far as *metaphysics* is concerned, however, its poor progress up to now, and the fact that of no metaphysics thus far expounded can it even be said that, as far as its essential end is concerned, it even really exists, leaves everyone with ground to doubt its possibility.

But now this kind of cognition is in a certain sense also to be regarded as given, and metaphysics is actual, if not as a science yet as a natural predisposition (*metaphysica naturalis*).[11] For human reason, without being moved by the mere vanity of knowing it all, inexorably pushes on, driven by its own need, to such questions that cannot be answered by any experiential use of reason and of principles borrowed from such a use; and thus a certain sort of metaphysics has actually been present in all human beings as soon as reason has extended itself to speculation in them, and it will also always remain there. And now about this too the question is *How is metaphysics as a natural predisposition possible?*—that is, how do the questions that pure reason raises, and which it is driven by its own need to answer as well as it can, arise from the nature of universal human reason?

But since unavoidable contradictions have always been found in all previous attempts to answer these natural questions—for example, whether the world has a beginning or exists from eternity, and so on—one cannot leave it up to the mere natural predisposition to metaphysics, that is, to the pure faculty of reason itself, from which, to be sure, some sort of metaphysics (whatever it might be) always grows, but it must be possible to bring it to certainty regarding either the knowledge or ignorance of objects, that is, to come to a decision either about the objects of its questions or about the capacity and incapacity of reason for judging something about them, thus either reliably to extend our pure reason or else to set determinate and secure limits for it. This last question, which flows from the general problem above, would rightly be this: *How is metaphysics possible as science?*

The critique of reason thus finally leads necessarily to science; the dogmatic use of it without critique, on the contrary, leads to groundless assertions, to which one can oppose equally plausible ones, and thus leads to skepticism.

Further, this science cannot be terribly extensive, for it does not deal with objects of reason, whose multiplicity is infinite, but merely with itself, with problems that spring entirely from its own womb, and that are not set before it by the nature of things that are distinct from it but through its own nature; so that, once it has become completely familiar with its own capacity in regard to the objects that may come before it in experience, then it must become easy to determine, completely and securely, the domain and the bounds of its attempted use beyond all bounds of experience. . . .

THE TRANSCENDENTAL DOCTRINE OF ELEMENTS.[12] FIRST PART: THE TRANSCENDENTAL AESTHETIC[13]

In whatever way and through whatever means a cognition may relate to objects, that through which it relates immediately to them, and at which all thought as a means is directed as an end, is *intuition*. This, however, takes place only insofar as the object is given to us; but this in turn, <at least for us humans,>[14] is possible only if it affects the mind in a certain way. The capacity (receptivity) to acquire representations through the way in which we are affected by objects is called *sensibility*. Objects are therefore *given* to us by means of sensibility, and it alone affords us *intuitions;* but they are *thought* through the understanding, and from it arise *concepts.* But all thought, whether straightaway (*directe*) or through a detour (*indirecte*),[15] must, <by means of certain marks,> ultimately be related to intuitions, thus, in our case, to sensibility, since there is no other way in which objects can be given to us. . . .

    I call a science of all principles of a priori sensibility the *transcendental aesthetic.* There must therefore be such a science, which constitutes the first part of the transcendental doctrine of elements, in opposition to that which contains the principles of pure thinking, and which is named *transcendental logic.*

First Section. On Space

By means of outer sense (a property of our mind) we represent to ourselves objects as outside us, and all as in space. In space their shape, magnitude, and relation to one another is determined, or determinable. Inner sense, by means of which the mind intuits itself, or its inner state, gives, to be sure, no intuition of the soul itself, as an object; yet it is still a determinate form, under which the intuition of its inner state is alone possible, so that everything that belongs to the inner determinations is represented in relations of time. Time can no more be intuited externally than space can be intuited as something in us. Now what are space and time? Are they actual entities? Are they only determinations or relations of things, yet ones that would pertain to them even if they were not intuited, or are they relations that only attach to the form of intuition alone, and thus to the subjective constitution of our mind, without which these predicates could not be ascribed to any thing at all? In order to instruct ourselves about this, we will <expound the concept of space> first. . . .

    1. Space is not an empirical concept that has been drawn from outer experiences. For in order for certain sensations to be related to something outside me (that is, to something in another place in space from that in which I find myself), thus in order for me to represent them as outside <and next to> one another, thus not merely as different but as in different places, the representation of space must already be their ground. Thus the representation of space cannot be obtained from the relations of outer appearance through experience, but this outer experience is itself first possible only through this representation.

    2. Space is a necessary representation, a priori, that is the ground of all outer intuitions. One can never represent that there is no space, though one can very well think that there are no objects to be encountered in it. It is therefore to be regarded as the condition of the possibility of appearances, not as a determination dependent on them, and is an a priori representation that necessarily grounds outer appearances. . . .

Second Section: On Time

1. Time is not an empirical concept that is somehow drawn from an experience. For simultaneity or succession would not themselves come into perception if the representation of time did not ground them a priori. Only under its presupposition can one represent that several things exist at one and the same time (simultaneously) or in different times (successively).

2. Time is a necessary representation that grounds all intuitions. In regard to appearances in general one cannot remove time, though one can very well take the appearances away from time. Time is therefore given a priori. In it alone is all actuality of appearances possible. The latter could all disappear, but time itself (as the universal condition of their possibility) cannot be removed. . . .

THE ANALYTIC OF CONCEPTS.[16] FIRST CHAPTER: ON THE CLUE TO THE DISCOVERY OF ALL PURE CONCEPTS OF UNDERSTANDING

Second Section. On the Logical Function of Understanding in Judgments

If we abstract from all content of a judgment in general, and attend only to the mere form of the understanding in it, we find that the function of thinking in that can be brought under four titles, each of which contains under itself three moments. They can suitably be represented in the following table.

1.
Quantity of Judgments
Universal
Particular
Singular

2.		3.
Quality		*Relation*
Affirmative		Categorical
Negative		Hypothetical
Infinite		Disjunctive

4.
Modality
Problematic
Assertoric
Apodictic . . .

Third Section. On the Pure Concepts of the Understanding, or Categories

. . . There arise exactly as many pure concepts of the understanding, which apply to objects of intuition in general a priori, as there were logical functions of all possible judgments in the [above] table; for the understanding is completely exhausted and its capacity entirely measured by these functions. Following Aristotle we will call these concepts *categories,*[17] for our aim is basically identical with his although very distant from it in execution.

TABLE OF CATEGORIES

1.
Of Quantity
Unity
Plurality
Totality

2.
Of Quality
Reality
Negation
Limitation

3.
Of Relation
Of Inherence and Subsistence
(substantia et accidens)[18]
Of Causality and Dependence
(cause and effect)
Of Community (reciprocity
between agent and patient)[19]

4.
Of Modality
Possibility — Impossibility
Existence — Nonexistence
Necessity — Contingency

Now this is the listing of all original pure concepts of synthesis that the understanding contains in itself a priori, and on account of which it is only a pure understanding; for by these concepts alone can it understand something in the manifold of intuition—that is, think an object for it. This division is systematically generated from a common principle, namely the faculty for judging (which is the same as the faculty for thinking), and has not arisen rhapsodically from a haphazard search for pure concepts, of the completeness of which one could never be certain, since one would only infer it through induction, without reflecting that in this way one would never see why just these and not other concepts should inhabit the pure understanding.

NOTES

1. *a priori:* independent of experience (literally, in Latin, "from what comes earlier"); contrasted with a *posteriori,* dependent on experience ("from what comes later"). [D. C. ABEL]

2. *metaphysics:* the study of the nature and kinds of reality. [D. C. ABEL]
3. Nicolaus Copernicus (1473–1543) was a Polish astronomer. [D. C. ABEL]
4. *intuition:* sense experience. [D. C. ABEL]
5. *contingency:* the state of being able to be or not to be; contrasted with *necessity.* [D. C. ABEL]
6. David Hume (1711–1776) was a Scottish philosopher and historian; for a biography, see p. 47. [D. C. ABEL]
7. *apodictic:* absolute. [D. C. ABEL]
8. Johann Andreas von Segner, *Anfangsgründe der Arithmetic, Geometrie and der Geometrischen Berechnungen* ("Elements of Arithmetic, Geometry, and Geometric Calculations"), published in 1756. Segner (1704–1777) was a German mathematician and naturalist. [D. C. ABEL]
9. *physica:* the Greek term for (the study of) "natural things," rendered in English as "physics." [D. C. ABEL]
10. *principium causalitatis:* (Latin) "the principle of causality." [D. C. ABEL]
11. *metaphysica naturalis:* (Latin) "natural metaphysics." [D. C. ABEL]
12. *transcendental doctrine of elements: Elements* are the forms that our minds impose on objects; the doctrine Kant proposes is *transcendental* because the forms that our minds impose are a priori and thus transcend the objects themselves. [D. C. ABEL]
13. *aesthetic:* something pertaining to sensation (*aisthēsis* in Greek). [D. C. ABEL]
14. Words placed in angle brackets were added by Kant to the second edition of his book. [D. C. ABEL]
15. *Directe* and *indirecte* are Latin terms meaning, respectively, "directly" and "indirectly." [D. C. ABEL]
16. *analytic of concepts:* the study of the a priori forms of understanding (categories of the understanding), which synthesize what we perceive through sensation. The analytic of concepts is a part of *transcendental logic,* the study of the principles of pure thinking. [D. C. ABEL]
17. Aristotle wrote a treatise called *Categories* (*Katēgoriai,* "predicates"), which postulates ten ways in which we think about things and in which things exist. For a biography of Aristotle, see p. 338. [D. C. ABEL]
18. *substantia et accidens:* (Latin) "substance [what subsists in itself] and accident [what inheres in a substance]." [D. C. ABEL]
19. *agent and patient:* that which acts and that which is acted upon. [D. C. ABEL]

Love and Knowledge: Emotion in Feminist Epistemology

Alison M. Jaggar

Alison M. Jaggar was born in Sheffield, England, in 1942. She received her bachelor's degree in philosophy from the University of London in 1964 and her master's degree from the University of Edinburgh in Scotland three years later. She then came to the United States to pursue doctoral studies in philosophy at the State University of New York at Buffalo. Upon completing her doctorate in 1970, Jaggar began teaching at Miami University in Ohio. Two years later she went to the University of Cincinnati, where she later was appointed Obed J. Wilson Professor of Ethics. In 1990 Jaggar accepted her current position, Professor of Philosophy and Women's Studies at the University of Colorado at Boulder. She has also held visiting professorships at the University of Illinois at Chicago, the University of California at Los Angeles, and Rutgers University (where she was the first occupant of the Laurie New Jersey Chair in Women's Studies), Victoria University of Wellington, New Zealand, and the University of Oslo, Norway. Jaggar was a founding member of the Society for Women in Philosophy and has received fellowships from the American Association of University Women (1976), the National Endowment for the Humanities (1980, 1998), and the Rockefeller Foundation (1990).

Jaggar's books include *Feminist Frameworks: Alternative Theoretical Accounts of the Relations between Women and Men* (coeditor with Paula S. Rothenberg, 1978; 3d ed., 1993), *Feminist Politics and Human Nature* (1983), *Gender/Body/Knowledge: Feminist Reconstructions of Being and Knowing* (coeditor with Susan R. Bordo, 1989), *A Companion to Feminist Philosophy* (coeditor with Iris M. Young, 1998), and *Just Methodologies: An Interdisciplinary Feminist Reader* (editor, 2006).

Our selection is taken from Jaggar's 1989 article "Love and Knowledge: Emotion in Feminist Epistemology." Jaggar rejects the traditional Western philosophical doctrines that reason and emotion are completely separate faculties, that reason is the sole path to knowledge, and that emotion subverts knowledge. She argues that reason and emotion must be seen as interrelated and interdependent and that feelings play an essential role in attaining knowledge. Modern science has created the "myth of dispassionate investigation"—the notion that scientific inquiry is completely severed from values and feelings. Jaggar contends that this notion is false and that it is in fact an ideology that helps preserve the political power of the dominant group in a society. It does this by exalting reason and associating it with the dominant group, while devaluing emotion and associating it with subordinate groups. This ideology gives more credibility to the observations of members of the dominant group (in our society, mainly white males) than to the observations of members of subordinate groups (mainly people of color and women), thereby justifying the dominant group's claim to political authority.

The ideologies of a society greatly influence the emotional responses of all the members of the society; certain kinds of responses to certain kinds of situations become conventional and expected. But significant numbers of people in subordinate groups may not experience these expected emotions. For example, people on welfare may feel resentment rather than gratitude for what they receive. Jaggar calls these unconventional

188

feelings of subordinate groups "outlaw emotions" and contends that by exploring them we can often come to see things differently and more accurately than we presently do. The reason is that outlaw emotions of people in subordinate groups (especially of women) are usually more appropriate to the situation than conventional emotions. Jaggar concludes that since outlaw emotions are more appropriate responses, they are more reliable guides to the way things are, and therefore important elements in an adequate theory of knowledge.

INTRODUCTION

Within the Western philosophical tradition, emotions have usually been considered potentially or actually subversive of knowledge. From Plato until the present, with a few notable exceptions, reason rather than emotion has been regarded as the indispensable faculty for acquiring knowledge.

Typically, although again not invariably, the rational has been contrasted with the emotional, and this contrasted pair then often linked with other dichotomies. Not only has reason been contrasted with emotion, but it has also been associated with the mental, the cultural, the universal, the public, and the male, whereas emotion has been associated with the irrational, the physical, the natural, the particular, the private, and, of course, the female.

Although Western epistemology[1] has tended to give pride of place to reason rather than emotion, it has not always excluded emotion completely from the realm of reason. In the *Phaedrus,* Plato portrayed emotions, such as anger or curiosity, as irrational urges (horses) that must always be controlled by reason (the charioteer). On this model, the emotions were not seen as needing to be totally suppressed, but rather as needing direction by reason. For example, in a genuinely threatening situation, it was thought not only irrational but foolhardy not to be afraid. The split between reason and emotion was not absolute, therefore, for the Greeks. Instead, the emotions were thought of as providing indispensable motive power that needed to be channeled appropriately. Without horses, after all, the skill of the charioteer would be worthless.

The contrast between reason and emotion was sharpened in the seventeenth century by redefining reason as a purely instrumental faculty. For both the Greeks and the medieval philosophers, reason had been linked with value insofar as reason provided access to the objective structure or order of reality, seen as simultaneously natural and morally justified. With the rise of modern science, however, the realms of nature and value were separated: Nature was stripped of value and reconceptualized as an inanimate mechanism of no intrinsic worth. Values were relocated in human beings, rooted in their preferences and emotional responses. The separation of supposedly natural fact from human value meant that reason, if it were to provide trustworthy insight into reality, had to be uncontaminated by or abstracted from value. Increasingly, therefore, though never universally, reason was reconceptualized as the ability to make valid inferences from premises established elsewhere, the ability to calculate means but not to determine ends. The validity of logical inferences was thought independent of human attitudes and preferences; this was now the sense in which reason was taken to be objective and universal.

The modern redefinition of rationality required a corresponding reconceptualization of emotion. This was achieved by portraying emotions as nonrational and often irrational urges that regularly swept the body, rather as a storm sweeps over the land. The common way of referring to the emotions as the "passions" emphasized that emotions happened to or were imposed upon an individual, something she suffered rather than something she did.[2]

The epistemology associated with this new ontology[3] rehabilitated sensory perception that, like emotion, typically had been suspected or even discounted by the Western tradition as a reliable source of knowledge. British empiricism,[4] succeeded in the nineteenth century by positivism,[5] took its epistemological task to be the formulation of rules of inference that would guarantee the derivation of certain knowledge from the "raw data" supposedly given directly to the senses. Empirical testability became accepted as the hallmark of natural science; this, in turn, was viewed as the paradigm of genuine knowledge. Often epistemology was equated with the philosophy of science, and the dominant methodology of positivism prescribed that truly scientific knowledge must be capable of intersubjective verification. Because values and emotions had been defined as variable and idiosyncratic, positivism stipulated that trustworthy knowledge could be established only by methods that neutralized the values and emotions of individual scientists.

Recent approaches to epistemology have challenged some fundamental assumptions of the positivist epistemological model. . . . However, few challenges have been raised thus far to the purported gap between emotion and knowledge. In this paper, I wish to begin bridging this gap through the suggestion that emotions may be helpful and even necessary rather than inimical to the construction of knowledge. . . .

THE MYTH OF DISPASSIONATE INVESTIGATION

. . . [The] derogatory Western attitude toward emotion, like the earlier Western contempt for sensory observation, fails to recognize that emotion, like sensory perception, is necessary to human survival. Emotions prompt us to act appropriately, to approach some people and situations and to avoid others, to caress or cuddle, fight or flee. Without emotion, human life would be unthinkable. Moreover, emotions have an intrinsic as well as an instrumental value. Although not all emotions are enjoyable or even justifiable, as we shall see, life without any emotion would be life without any meaning.

Within the context of Western culture, however, people have often been encouraged to control or even suppress their emotions. Consequently, it is not unusual for people to be unaware of their emotional state or to deny it to themselves and others. This lack of awareness, especially combined with a neopositivist[6] understanding of emotion that construes it as just a feeling of which one is aware, lends plausibility to the myth of dispassionate investigation. But lack of awareness of emotions certainly does not mean that emotions are not present subconsciously or unconsciously, or that subterranean emotions do not exert a continuing influence on people's articulated values and observations, thoughts, and actions.

Within the positivist tradition, the influence of emotion is usually seen only as distorting or impeding observation or knowledge. Certainly it is true that contempt, disgust, shame, revulsion, or fear may inhibit investigation of certain situations or phenomena. Furiously angry or extremely sad people often seem quite unaware of their surroundings or even of their own conditions; they may fail to hear or may systematically misinterpret what other people say. People in love are notoriously oblivious to many aspects of the situation around them.

In spite of these examples, however, positivist epistemology recognizes that the role of emotion in the construction of knowledge is not invariably deleterious and that emotions may make a valuable contribution to knowledge. But the positivist tradition will allow emotion to play only the role of suggesting hypotheses for investigation. Emotions are allowed this because the so-called logic of discovery sets no limits on the idiosyncratic methods that investigators may use for generating hypotheses.

When hypotheses are to be tested, however, positivist epistemology imposes the much stricter logic of justification. The core of this logic is replicability, a criterion believed capable of eliminating or canceling out what are conceptualized as emotional as well as evaluative biases on the part of individual investigators. The conclusions of Western science thus are presumed "objective," precisely in the sense that they are uncontaminated by the supposedly "subjective" values and emotions that might bias individual investigators.

But if . . . the positivist distinction between discovery and justification is not viable, then such a distinction is incapable of filtering out values in science. For example, although such a split, when built into the Western scientific method, is generally successful in neutralizing the idiosyncratic or unconventional values of individual investigators, it has been argued that it does not, indeed, cannot, eliminate generally accepted social values. These values are implicit in the identification of the problems that are considered worthy of investigation, in the selection of the hypotheses that are considered worthy of testing, and in the solutions to the problems that are considered worthy of acceptance. The science of past centuries provides ample evidence of the influence of prevailing social values, whether seventeenth-century atomistic physics or nineteenth-century competitive interpretations of natural selection. . . .

Positivism views values and emotions as alien invaders that must be repelled by a stricter application of the scientific method. If the foregoing claims are correct, however, the scientific method and even its positivist construals themselves incorporate values and emotions. Moreover, such an incorporation seems a necessary feature of all knowledge and conceptions of knowledge. Therefore, rather than repressing emotion in epistemology it is necessary to rethink the relation between knowledge and emotion and construct conceptual models that demonstrate the mutually constitutive rather than oppositional relation between reason and emotion. Far from precluding the possibility of reliable knowledge, emotion as well as value must be shown as necessary to such knowledge. Despite its classical antecedents and as in the ideal of disinterested inquiry, the ideal of dispassionate inquiry is an impossible dream, but a dream nonetheless or perhaps a myth that has exerted enormous influence on Western epistemology. Like all myths, it is a form of ideology that fulfills certain social and political functions.

THE IDEOLOGICAL FUNCTION OF THE MYTH

So far, I have spoken very generally of people and their emotions, as though everyone experienced similar emotions and dealt with them in similar ways. It is an axiom of feminist theory, however, that all generalizations about "people" are suspect. The divisions in our society are so deep, particularly the divisions of race, class, and gender, that many feminist theorists would claim that talk about people in general is ideologically dangerous because such talk obscures the fact that no one is simply a person but instead is constituted fundamentally by race, class, and gender. Race, class, and gender shape every aspect of our lives, and our emotional constitution is not excluded. Recognizing this helps us to see more clearly the political functions of the myth of the dispassionate investigator.

Feminist theorists have pointed out that the Western tradition has not seen everyone as equally emotional. Instead, reason has been associated with members of dominant political, social, and cultural groups and emotion with members of subordinate groups. Prominent among those subordinate groups in our society are people of color, except for supposedly "inscrutable Orientals," and women.

Although the emotionality of women is a familiar cultural stereotype, its grounding is quite shaky. Women appear to be more emotional than men because they, along with some groups of people of color, are permitted and even required to express emotion more openly. In contemporary Western culture, emotionally inexpressive women are suspect as not being real women, whereas men who express their emotions freely are suspected of being homosexual or in some other way deviant from the masculine ideal. Modern Western men, in contrast with Shakespeare's heroes, for instance, are required to present a facade of coolness, lack of excitement, even boredom, to express emotion only rarely and then for relatively trivial events, such as sporting occasions, where the emotions expressed are acknowledged to be dramatized and so are not taken entirely seriously. Thus, women in our society form the main group allowed or even expected to express emotion. A woman may cry in the face of disaster, and a man of color may gesticulate, but a white man merely sets his jaw.

White men's control of their emotional expression may go to the extremes of repressing their emotions, failing to develop emotionally, or even losing the capacity to experience many emotions. Not uncommonly, these men are unable to identify what they are feeling, and even they may be surprised, on occasion, by their own apparent lack of emotional response to a situation, such as a death, where emotional reaction is perceived to be appropriate. . . . Paradoxically, men's lacking awareness of their own emotional responses frequently results in their being more influenced by emotion rather than less.

Although there is no reason to suppose that the thoughts and actions of women are any more influenced by emotion than the thoughts and actions of men, the stereotypes of cool men and emotional women continue to flourish because they are confirmed by an uncritical daily experience. In these circumstances, where there is a differential assignment of reason and emotion, it is easy to see the ideological function of the myth of the dispassionate investigator. It functions, obviously, to bolster the epistemic[7] authority of the currently dominant groups, composed largely of white men, and to discredit the observations and claims of the currently subordinate groups including, of course, the observations and claims of many people of color and women. The more forcefully and vehemently the latter groups express their observations and claims, the more emotional they appear and so the more easily they are discredited. The alleged epistemic authority of the dominant groups then justifies their political authority.

The previous section of this paper argued that dispassionate inquiry was a myth. This section has shown that the myth promotes a conception of epistemological justification vindicating the silencing of those, especially women, who are defined culturally as the bearers of emotion and so are perceived as more "subjective," biased, and irrational. In our present social context, therefore, the ideal of the dispassionate investigator is a classist, racist, and especially masculinist myth.

EMOTIONAL HEGEMONY AND EMOTIONAL SUBVERSION

. . . Within a hierarchical society, the norms and values that predominate tend to serve the interests of the dominant groups. Within a capitalist, white supremacist, and male-dominant society, the predominant values will tend to be those that serve the interests of rich white men. Consequently, we are all likely to develop an emotional constitution that is quite inappropriate for feminism. Whatever our color, we are likely to feel what Irving Thalberg[8] has called "visceral racism"; whatever our sexual orientation, we are likely to be homophobic; whatever our class, we are likely to be at least somewhat ambitious and competitive; whatever our sex, we are likely to feel contempt for women. Such emotional responses may be rooted in us so deeply that they are relatively impervious to intellectual argument and may recur even when we pay lip service to changed intellectual convictions.

By forming our emotional constitution in particular ways, our society helps to ensure its own perpetuation. The dominant values are implicit in responses taken to be precultural or acultural, our so-called gut responses. Not only do these conservative responses hamper and disrupt our attempts to live in or prefigure alternative social forms but also, and insofar as we take them to be natural responses, they blinker us theoretically. For instance, they limit our capacity for outrage; they either prevent us from despising or encourage us to despise; they lend plausibility to the belief that greed and domination are inevitable human motivations; in sum, they blind us to the possibility of alternative ways of living.

This picture may seem at first to support the positivist claim that the intrusion of emotion only disrupts the process of seeking knowledge and distorts the results of that process. The picture, however, is not complete; it ignores the fact that people do not always experience the conventionally acceptable emotions. They may feel satisfaction rather than embarrassment when their leaders make fools of themselves. They may feel resentment rather than gratitude for welfare payments and hand-me-downs. They may be attracted to forbidden modes of sexual expression. They may feel revulsion for socially sanctioned ways of treating children or animals. In other words, the hegemony that our society exercises over people's emotional constitution is not total.

People who experience conventionally unacceptable, or what I call "outlaw" emotions often are subordinated individuals who pay a disproportionately high price for maintaining the status quo. The social situation of such people makes them unable to experience the conventionally prescribed emotions. For instance, people of color are more likely to experience anger than amusement when a racist joke is recounted, and women subjected to male sexual banter are less likely to be flattered than uncomfortable or even afraid.

When unconventional emotional responses are experienced by isolated individuals, those concerned may be confused, unable to name their experience; they may even doubt their own sanity. Women may come to believe that they are "emotionally disturbed" and that the embarrassment or fear aroused in them by male sexual innuendo is prudery or paranoia. When certain emotions are shared or validated by others, however, the basis exists for forming a subculture defined by perceptions, norms, and values that systematically oppose the prevailing perceptions, norms, and values. By constituting the basis for such a subculture, outlaw emotions may be politically (because epistemologically) subversive.

Outlaw emotions are distinguished by their incompatibility with the dominant perceptions and values; and some, though certainly not all, of these outlaw emotions are potentially or actually feminist emotions. Emotions become feminist when they incorporate feminist perceptions and values, just as emotions are sexist or racist when they incorporate sexist or racist perceptions and values. For example, anger becomes feminist anger when it involves the perception that the persistent importuning endured by one woman is a single instance of a widespread pattern of sexual harassment, and pride becomes feminist pride when it is evoked by realizing that a certain person's achievement was possible only because that individual overcame specifically gendered obstacles to success. . . .

OUTLAW EMOTIONS AND FEMINIST THEORY

. . . Outlaw emotions may . . . enable us to perceive the world differently from its portrayal in conventional descriptions. They may provide the first indications that something is wrong with the way alleged facts have been constructed, with accepted understandings of how things are. Conventionally unexpected or inappropriate emotions may precede our conscious recognition that accepted descriptions and justifications often conceal as much as reveal the prevailing state of affairs. Only when we reflect on our initially puzzling irritability, revulsion, anger, or fear may we bring to consciousness our "gut-level" awareness that we are in a situation of coercion, cruelty, injustice, or danger. Thus, conventionally inexplicable emotions, particularly though not exclusively those experienced by women, may lead us to make subversive observations that challenge dominant conceptions of the status quo. They may help us to realize that what are taken generally to be facts have been constructed in a way that obscures the reality of subordinated people, especially women's reality.

But why should we trust the emotional responses of women and other subordinated groups? How can we determine which outlaw emotions are to be endorsed or encouraged and which rejected? In what sense can we say that some emotional responses are more appropriate than others? What reason is there for supposing that certain alternative perceptions of the world, perceptions informed by outlaw emotions, are to be preferred to perceptions informed by conventional emotions? Here I can indicate only the general direction of an answer, whose full elaboration must await another occasion.

I suggest that emotions are appropriate if they are characteristic of a society in which all humans (and perhaps some nonhuman life too) thrive, or if they are conducive to establishing such a society. For instance, it is appropriate to feel joy when we are developing or exercising our creative powers, and it is appropriate to feel anger and perhaps disgust in those situations where humans are denied their full creativity or freedom. Similarly, it is appropriate to feel fear if those capacities are threatened in us.

This suggestion, obviously, is extremely vague and may even verge on the tautologous. How can we apply it in situations where there is disagreement over what is or is not disgusting or exhilarating or unjust? Here I appeal to a claim for which I have argued elsewhere: The perspective on reality that is available from the standpoint of the subordinated, which in part at least is the standpoint of women, is a perspective that offers a less partial and distorted and therefore more reliable view.[9] Subordinated people have a kind of epistemological privilege insofar as they have easier access to this standpoint and therefore a better chance of ascertaining the possible beginnings of a society in which all could thrive. For this reason, I would claim that the emotional responses of subordinated people in general, and often of women in particular, are more likely to be appropriate than the emotional responses of the dominant class. That is, they are more likely to incorporate reliable appraisals of situations.

Even in contemporary science, where the ideology of dispassionate inquiry is almost overwhelming, it is possible to discover a few examples that seem to support the claim that certain emotions are more appropriate than others in both a moral and epistemological sense. For instance, Hilary Rose claims that women's practice of caring, even though warped by its containment in the alienated context of a coercive sexual division of labor, has nevertheless generated more accurate and less oppressive understandings of women's bodily functions, such as menstruation.[10] Certain emotions may be both morally appropriate and epistemologically advantageous in approaching the nonhuman and even the inanimate world. Jane Goodall's scientific contribution to our understanding of chimpanzee behavior seems to have been made possible only by her amazing empathy with or even love for these animals.[11] In her study of Barbara McClintock, Evelyn Fox Keller describes McClintock's relation to the objects of her research—grains of maize and their genetic properties—as a relation of affection, empathy, and "the highest form of love: love that allows for intimacy without the annihilation of difference." She notes that McClintock's "vocabulary is consistently a vocabulary of affection, of kinship, of empathy."[12] Examples like these prompt Hilary Rose to assert that a feminist science of nature needs to draw on heart as well as hand and brain.

SOME IMPLICATIONS OF RECOGNIZING THE EPISTEMIC POTENTIAL OF EMOTION

Accepting that appropriate emotions are indispensable to reliable knowledge does not mean, of course, that uncritical feeling may be substituted for supposedly dispassionate investigation. Nor does it mean that the emotional responses of women and other members of the underclass are to be trusted without question. Although our emotions are epistemologically indispensable, they are not epistemologically indisputable. Like all our faculties, they may be misleading, and their data, like all data, are always subject to reinterpretation and revision. Because emotions are not presocial, physiological responses to unequivocal situations, they are open to challenge on various grounds. They may be dishonest or self-deceptive, they may incorporate inaccurate or partial perceptions, or they may be constituted by oppressive values. Accepting the indispensability of appropriate emotions to knowledge means no more (and no less) than that discordant emotions should be attended to seriously and respectfully rather than condemned, ignored, discounted, or suppressed.

Just as appropriate emotions may contribute to the development of knowledge, so the growth of knowledge may contribute to the development of appropriate emotions. For instance, the powerful insights of feminist theory often stimulate new emotional responses to past and present situations. Inevitably, our emotions are affected by the knowledge that the women on our faculty are paid systematically less than the men, that one girl in four is subjected to sexual abuse from heterosexual men in her own family, and that few women reach orgasm in heterosexual intercourse. We are likely to feel different emotions toward older women or people of color as we reevaluate our standards of sexual attractiveness or acknowledge that black is beautiful. The new emotions evoked by feminist insights are likely in turn to stimulate further feminist observations and insights, and these may generate new directions in both theory and political practice. There is a continuous feedback loop between our emotional constitution and our theorizing such that each continually modifies the other and is in principle inseparable from it.

The ease and speed with which we can reeducate our emotions is unfortunately not great. Emotions are only partially within our control as individuals. Although affected by new information, they are habitual responses not quickly unlearned. Even when we come to believe consciously that our fear or shame or revulsion is unwarranted, we may still continue to experience emotions inconsistent with our conscious politics. We may still continue to be anxious for male approval, competitive with our comrades and sisters, and possessive with our lovers. These unwelcome, because apparently inappropriate emotions, should not be suppressed or denied; instead, they should be acknowledged and subjected to critical scrutiny. The persistence of such recalcitrant emotions probably demonstrates how fundamentally we have been constituted by the dominant world view, but it may also indicate superficiality or other inadequacy in our emerging theory and politics. We can only start from where we are—beings who have been created in a cruelly racist, capitalist, and male-dominated society that has shaped our bodies and our minds, our perceptions, our values and our emotions, our language, and our systems of knowledge.

The alternative epistemological models that I suggest would display the continuous interaction between how we understand the world and who we are as people. They would show how our emotional responses to the world change as we conceptualize it differently and how our changing emotional responses then stimulate us to new insights. They would demonstrate the need for theory to be self-reflexive, to focus not only on the outer world but also on ourselves and our relation to that world, to examine critically our social location, our actions, our values, our perceptions, and our emotions. The models would also show how feminist and other critical social theories are indispensable psychotherapeutic tools because they provide some insights necessary to a full understanding of our emotional constitution. Thus, the models would explain how the reconstruction of knowledge is inseparable from the reconstruction of ourselves. . . .

We can now see that women's subversive insights owe much to women's outlaw emotions, themselves appropriate responses to the situations of women's subordination. In addition to their propensity to experience outlaw emotions, at least on some level, women are relatively adept at identifying such emotions, in themselves and others, in part because of their social responsibility for caretaking, including emotional nurturance. It is true that women, like all subordinated peoples, especially those who must live in close proximity with their masters, often engage in emotional deception and even self-deception as the price of their survival. Even so, women may be less likely than other subordinated groups to engage in denial or suppression of outlaw emotions. Women's work of emotional nurturance has required them to develop a special acuity in recognizing hidden emotions and in understanding the genesis of those emotions. This emotional acumen can now be recognized as a skill in political analysis and validated as giving women a special advantage both in understanding the mechanisms of domination and in envisioning freer ways to live.

CONCLUSION

The claim that emotion is vital to systematic knowledge is only the most obvious contrast between the conception of theoretical investigation that I have sketched here and the conception provided by positivism. For instance, the alternative approach emphasizes that what we identify as emotion is a conceptual abstraction from a complex process of human activity that also involves acting, sensing, and evaluating. This proposed account of theoretical construction demonstrates the simultaneous necessity for and interdependence of faculties that our culture has abstracted and separated from each other: emotion and reason, evaluation and perception, observation and action. The model of knowing suggested here is nonhierarchical and antifoundationalist;[13] instead, it is appropriately symbolized by the radical feminist metaphor of the upward spiral.[14] Emotions are neither more basic than observation, reason, or action in building theory, nor secondary to them. Each of these human faculties reflects an aspect of human knowing inseparable from the other aspects. Thus, to borrow a famous phrase from a Marxian context,[15] the development of each of these faculties is a necessary condition for the development of all.

In conclusion, it is interesting to note that acknowledging the importance of emotion for knowledge is not an entirely novel suggestion within the Western epistemological tradition. That archrationalist, Plato himself, came to accept in the end that knowledge required a (very purified form of) love. It may be no accident that in the *Symposium* Socrates learns this lesson from Diotima, the wise woman!

NOTES

1. *epistemology:* the study of the nature and grounds of knowledge. [D. C. ABEL]
2. The noun "passion" derives from the Latin verb *pati,* "to undergo, to be acted upon." The adjective "passive" also derives from *pati.* [D. C. ABEL]
3. *ontology:* the study of the nature and kinds of reality. [D. C. ABEL]
4. *empiricism:* the doctrine that knowledge is attained primarily through sense experience. [D. C. ABEL]
5. *positivism:* the doctrine that the only source of genuine knowledge is empirical science. [D. C. ABEL]
6. *neopositivist:* relating to a revised, twentieth-century version of positivism (see note 5). [D. C. ABEL]
7. *epistemic:* relating to knowledge. [D. C. ABEL]
8. Thalberg (1899–1936) was an American movie producer. [D. C. ABEL]
9. Alison M. Jaggar, *Feminist Politics and Human Nature* (Totowa, N.J.: Rowman & Allanheld, 1983), Chapter 11. [A. M. JAGGAR]
10. Hilary Rose, "Hand, Brain, and Heart: A Feminist Epistemology for the Natural Sciences," *Signs: Journal of Women in Culture and Society* 9 (Autumn 1983): 73–70. [A. M. JAGGAR]
11. Jane Goodall, *The Chimpanzees of Gombe: Patterns of Behaviour* (Cambridge, Mass: Harvard University Press, 1986). [A. M. JAGGAR]
12. Evelyn Fox Keller, *Gender and Science* (New Haven, Conn.: Yale University Press, 1984), p. 184. [A. M. JAGGAR]
13. *antifoundationalist:* opposed to "foundationalist" theories of knowledge, which claim that all knowledge is founded ultimately on one basic class of things known. [D. C. ABEL]
14. The metaphor of knowledge as an upward spiral emphasizes the interaction among the various human faculties involved in the knowing process; it is intended as an alternative to the linear conception of knowledge implied by foundationalism. [D. C. ABEL]
15. The reference is to the statement by Karl Marx and Friedrich Engels that in a communist society, "the free development of each is the condition for the free development of all" (*Manifesto of the Communist Party,* end of Section II). The passage appears on p. 479 of this book; biographies of Marx and Engels are on p. 470. [D. C. ABEL]

CHAPTER 4

Philosophy of Mind

The mind is perhaps the most elusive aspect of human nature. While it is clear that we have a mind (how could we inquire about the mind if we didn't have one?), it is not at all clear what the mind is. Is it something located inside my brain? Is it *identical* with the brain, or perhaps an *activity* of the brain? Or is the mind a nonphysical entity, not located in space? How can the mind be conscious of things—conscious even of itself? Is the mind what accounts for me being the same person throughout my life? These kinds of questions constitute the branch of philosophy known as the philosophy of mind.

The readings in this chapter are divided into three sections. The first section is entitled "The Mind-Body Problem." The mind-body problem asks how the mind and body (or, more specifically, the mind and brain) are related. Is the mind a nonphysical entity, distinct from the body? If so, how does it interact with the body, which is physical? For example, if we assume that fear is a state of a nonphysical mind, how can it *cause* my heart to beat faster? And if pleasure is a nonphysical state, how can it *be caused* by the eating of ice cream? Our readings on the mind-body problem are by René Descartes and D. M. Armstrong. Descartes holds that the mind is a nonphysical substance (thing), but that the mind is somehow connected to the body. The mind is a *nonextended* (non-three-dimensional) and *thinking* substance, where as the body is an *extended* and *nonthinking* substance. Descartes finds it difficult to explain how these two different substances are joined together and how they can interact. Armstrong rejects Descartes's *dualism* (two-substance

199

theory of human nature). He argues that human beings are entirely physical creatures, and that mental states are simply brain states apt to produce certain ranges of behavior.

The second section, "Consciousness," consists of articles by Thomas Nagel and David J. Chalmers. Nagel claims that theorists like Armstrong, who hold that the mental states are physical states, have not been able to explain consciousness in physical terms. Nagel asks how it could be possible to provide an *objective* account of conscious experience, which by its very nature is *subjective*. How could objective, scientific analysis, which strives not to depend on any particular point of view, give an account of consciousness, which by its nature involves the subject's point of view? Chalmers argues that conscious experience cannot be explained in purely physical terms. We must expand our view of what is real by positing consciousness as a nonphysical, fundamental component of reality; only then can we begin to construct a plausible *theory* of consciousness.

The final section, "Personal Identity," addresses the question of what, if anything, makes us the same person throughout our life. The first reading comprises excerpts from classical Buddhist dialogues that present the Buddha's doctrine that there is no permanent self, no entity that persists throughout one's life and confers personal identity. According to the Buddha, what we call the self is simply a combination of things that are themselves constantly changing. In the second reading, David Hume, like the Buddha, argues that personal identity is a fiction: When Hume looks inside what he calls "himself," he finds no permanent reality but only a series of rapidly changing perceptions. In the last reading, Daniel C. Dennett holds that there *is* a self, and that we can understand its nature by seeing how selves arose in the course of evolution. He contends that selves originated when organisms began to distinguish themselves from their environment, and that the distinctively *human* self, which produces personal identity, results from the narrative that one creates about oneself.

A. The Mind-Body Problem

Meditations on First Philosophy
René Descartes

A biography of René Descartes appears on p. 128.

This selection is from Descartes's *Meditations on First Philosophy*. (By "first philosophy" Descartes means truths about the basic topics of philosophy, which for him are God, the soul [mind], and the external world.) Our reading begins with the Second Meditation, in which Descartes tries to find something of which he can be absolutely certain—something about which not even a powerful "malicious demon" (a term he used in the First Meditation, p. 129 of this book) could deceive him. Descartes points out that he might be deceived even about such seemingly obvious things as the existence of the external world. But there is one thing he can be certain of—that he exists. For it would not even be possible for him to be deceived, if he did not exist. As he formulates this argument elsewhere, "I think, therefore I am." But what is this "I" that exists? Descartes argues that since he could be deceived about having a body, he is simply "a thing that thinks." He goes on to point out that if material things do exist, their essential nature would be extension (three-dimensionality).

In the Fifth Meditation, Descartes presents a proof for God's existence. Descartes has an idea of a supremely perfect being, and since existence is a necessary attribute of such a being, his idea would be self-contradictory if God did not exist. In the Sixth Meditation, Descartes uses his knowledge that God exists to prove that the external world exists: Since God is good and not a deceiver, it would be contrary to God's nature to give someone the inclination to believe that material things (including one's body) exist, if they didn't actually exist. Descartes has a body, then, but how is he (a thinking, nonextended thing) related to it (an extended, nonthinking thing)? Descartes states (with little further explanation) that he is "very closely joined and, as it were, intermingled with it."

SECOND MEDITATION. THE NATURE OF THE HUMAN MIND, AND HOW IT IS BETTER KNOWN THAN THE BODY

. . . Anything which admits of the slightest doubt I will set aside just as if I had found it to be wholly false; and I will proceed in this way until I recognize something certain, or, if nothing else, until I at least recognize for certain that there is no certainty. Archimedes[1] used to demand just one firm and immovable point in order to shift the entire earth; so I too can hope for great things if I manage to find just one thing, however slight, that is certain and unshakable.

I will suppose then, that everything I see is spurious. I will believe that my memory tells me lies, and that none of the things that it reports ever happened. I have no senses. Body, shape, extension, movement, and place are chimeras.[2] So what remains true? Perhaps just the one fact that nothing is certain.

201

Yet apart from everything I have just listed, how do I know that there is not something else which does not allow even the slightest occasion for doubt? Is there not a God, or whatever I may call him, who puts into me the thoughts I am now having? But why do I think this, since I myself may perhaps be the author of these thoughts? In that case am not I, at least, something? But I have just said that I have no senses and no body. This is the sticking point: What follows from this? Am I not so bound up with a body and with senses that I cannot exist without them? But I have convinced myself that there is absolutely nothing in the world, no sky, no earth, no minds, no bodies. Does it now follow that I too do not exist? No: If I convinced myself of something, then I certainly existed. But there is a deceiver of supreme power and cunning who is deliberately and constantly deceiving me. In that case I too undoubtedly exist, if he is deceiving me; and let him deceive me as much as he can, he will never bring it about that I am nothing so long as I think that I am something. So after considering everything very thoroughly, I must finally conclude that this proposition, "I am, I exist" is necessarily true whenever it is put forward by me or conceived in my mind.

But I do not yet have a sufficient understanding of what this "I" is, that now necessarily exists. So I must be on my guard against carelessly taking something else to be this "I," and so making a mistake in the very item of knowledge that I maintain is the most certain and evident of all. I will therefore go back and meditate on what I originally believed myself to be, before I embarked on this present train of thought. I will then subtract anything capable of being weakened, even minimally, by the arguments now introduced, so that what is left at the end may be exactly and only what is certain and unshakable.

What then did I formerly think I was? A man. But what is a man? Shall I say "a rational animal"? No; for then I should have to inquire what an animal is, what rationality is, and in this way one question would lead me down the slope to other harder ones, and I do not now have the time to waste on subtleties of this kind. Instead I propose to concentrate on what came into my thoughts spontaneously and quite naturally whenever I used to consider what I was. Well, the first thought to come to mind was that I had a face, hands, arms, and the whole mechanical structure of limbs which can be seen in a corpse, and which I called the body. The next thought was that I was nourished, that I moved about, and that I engaged in sense-perception and thinking; and these actions I attributed to the soul. But as to the nature of this soul, either I did not think about this or else I imagined it to be something tenuous, like a wind or fire or ether, which permeated my more solid parts. As to the body, however, I had no doubts about it, but thought I knew its nature distinctly. If I had tried to describe the mental conception I had of it, I would have expressed it as follows: By a body I understand whatever has a determinable shape and a definable location and can occupy a space in such a way as to exclude any other body; it can be perceived by touch, sight, hearing, taste, or smell, and can be moved in various ways, not by itself but by whatever else comes into contact with it. For, according to my judgment, the power of self-movement, like the power of sensation or of thought, was quite foreign to the nature of a body; indeed, it was a source of wonder to me that certain bodies were found to contain faculties of this kind.

But what shall I now say that I am, when I am supposing that there is some supremely powerful and, if it is permissible to say so, malicious deceiver, who is deliberately trying to trick me in every way he can? Can I now assert that I possess even the most insignificant of all the attributes which I have just said belong to the nature of a body? I scrutinize them, think about them, go over them again, but nothing suggests itself; it is tiresome and pointless to go through the list once more. But what about the attributes I assigned to the soul? Nutrition or movement? Since now I do not have a body, these are mere fabrications. Sense-perception? This surely does not occur without a body, and besides, when asleep I have appeared to perceive through the senses many things which I afterwards realized I did not perceive through the senses at all. Thinking? At last I have discovered it: thought—this alone is inseparable from me. I am, I exist—that is certain. But for how long? For as long as I am thinking. For it could be that were I totally to cease from thinking, I should totally cease to exist. At present I am not admitting anything except what is necessarily true. I am, then, in the strict sense, only a thing that thinks; that is, I am a mind, or intelligence, or intellect, or reason—words whose meaning I have been ignorant of until now. But for all that, I am a thing which is real and which truly exists. But what kind of a thing? As I have just said—a thinking thing.

What else am I? I will use my imagination. I am not that structure of limbs which is called a human body. I am not even some thin vapor which permeates the limbs—a wind, fire, air, breath, or whatever I depict in my imagination; for these are things which I have supposed to be nothing. Let this supposition stand; for all that, I am still something. And yet may it not perhaps be the case that these very things which I am supposing to be nothing, because they are unknown to me, are in reality identical with the "I" of which I am aware? I do not know, and for the moment I shall not argue the point, since I can make judgments only about things which are known to me. I know that I exist; the question is, what is this "I" that I know? If the "I" is understood strictly as we have been taking it, then it is quite certain that knowledge of it does not depend on things of whose existence I am as yet unaware; so it cannot depend on any of the things which I invent in my imagination. And this very word "invent" shows me my mistake. It would indeed be a case of fictitious invention if I used my imagination to establish that I was something or other; for imagining is simply contemplating the shape or image of a corporeal thing. Yet now I know for certain both that I exist and at the same time that all such images and, in general, everything relating to the nature of body, could be mere dreams <and chimeras>.[3] Once this point has been grasped, to say "I will use my imagination to get to know more distinctly what I am" would seem to be as silly as saying "I am now awake, and see some truth; but since my vision is not yet clear enough, I will deliberately fall asleep so that my dreams may provide a truer and clearer representation." I thus realize that none of the things that the imagination enables me to grasp is at all relevant to this knowledge of myself which I possess, and that the mind must therefore be most carefully diverted from such things if it is to perceive its own nature as distinctly as possible.

But what then am I? A thing that thinks. What is that? A thing that doubts, understands, affirms, denies, is willing, is unwilling, and also imagines and has sensory perceptions.

This is a considerable list, if everything on it belongs to me. But does it? Is it not one and the same "I" who is now doubting almost everything, who nonetheless understands some things, who affirms that this one thing is true, denies everything else, desires to know more, is unwilling to be deceived, imagines many things even involuntarily, and is aware of many things which apparently come from the senses? Are not all these things just as true as the fact that I exist, even if I am asleep all the time, and even if he who created me is doing all he can to deceive me? Which of all these activities is distinct from my thinking? Which of them can be said to be separate from myself? The fact that it is I who am doubting and understanding and willing is so evident that I see no way of making it any clearer. But it is also the case that the "I" who imagines is the same "I." For even if, as I have supposed, none of the objects of imagination are real, the power of imagination is something which really exists and is part of my thinking. Lastly, it is also the same "I" who has sensory perceptions, or is aware of bodily things as it were through the senses. For example, I am now seeing light, hearing a noise, feeling heat. But I am asleep, so all this is false. Yet I certainly *seem* to see, to hear, and to be warmed. This cannot be false; what is called "having a sensory perception" is strictly just this, and in this restricted sense of the term it is simply thinking.

From all this I am beginning to have a rather better understanding of what I am. But it still appears—and I cannot stop thinking this—that the corporeal things of which images are formed in my thought, and which the senses investigate, are known with much more distinctness than this puzzling "I" which cannot be pictured in the imagination. And yet it is surely surprising that I should have a more distinct grasp of things which I realize are doubtful, unknown, and foreign to me, than I have of that which is true and known—my own self. But I see what it is: My mind enjoys wandering off and will not yet submit to being restrained within the bounds of truth. Very well then; just this once let us give it a completely free rein, so that after a while, when it is time to tighten the reins, it may more readily submit to being curbed.

Let us consider the things which people commonly think they understand most distinctly of all; that is, the bodies which we touch and see. I do not mean bodies in general—for general perceptions are apt to be somewhat more confused—but one particular body. Let us take, for example, this piece of wax. It has just been taken from the honeycomb; it has not yet quite lost the taste of the honey; it retains some of the scent of the flowers from which it was gathered; its color, shape, and size are plain to see; it is hard, cold, and can be handled without difficulty; if you rap it with your knuckles it makes a sound. In short, it has everything which appears necessary to enable a body to be known as distinctly as possible. But even as I speak, I put the wax by the fire, and look: The residual taste is eliminated, the smell goes away, the color changes, the shape is lost, the size increases; it becomes liquid and hot; you can hardly touch it, and if you strike it, it no longer makes a sound. But does the same wax remain? It must be admitted that it does; no one denies it, no one thinks otherwise. So what was it in the wax that I understood with such distinctness? Evidently none of the features which I arrived at by means of the senses; for whatever came under taste, smell, sight, touch, or hearing has now altered—yet the wax remains.

Perhaps the answer lies in the thought which now comes to my mind—namely, the wax was not after all the sweetness of the honey, or the fragrance of the flowers, or the whiteness, or the shape, or the sound, but was rather a body which presented itself to me in these various forms a little while ago, but which now exhibits different ones. But what exactly is it that I am now imagining? Let us concentrate, take away everything which does not belong to the wax, and see what is left: merely something extended, flexible and changeable. But what is meant here by "flexible" and "changeable"? Is it what I picture in my imagination: that this piece of wax is capable of changing from a round shape to a square shape, or from a square shape to a triangular shape? Not at all; for I can grasp that the wax is capable of countless changes of this kind, yet I am unable to run through this immeasurable number of changes in my imagination, from which it follows that it is not the faculty of imagination that gives me my grasp of the wax as flexible and changeable. And what is meant by "extended"? Is the extension of the wax also unknown? For it increases if the wax melts, increases again if it boils, and is greater still if the heat is increased. I would not be making a correct judgment about the nature of wax unless I believed it capable of being extended in many more different ways than I will ever encompass in my imagination. I must therefore admit that the nature of this piece of wax is in no way revealed by my imagination, but is perceived by the mind alone. (I am speaking of this particular piece of wax; the point is even clearer with regard to wax in general.) But what is this wax which is perceived by the mind alone? It is of course the same wax which I see, which I touch, which I picture in my imagination, in short the same wax which I thought it to be from the start. And yet, and here is the point, the perception I have of it is a case not of vision or touch or imagination—nor has it ever been, despite previous appearances—but of purely mental scrutiny; and this can be imperfect and confused, as it was before, or clear and distinct as it is now, depending on how carefully I concentrate on what the wax consists in. . . .

But what am I to say about this mind, or about myself? (So far, remember, I am not admitting that there is anything else in me except a mind.) What, I ask, is this "I" which seems to perceive the wax so distinctly? Surely my awareness of my own self is not merely much truer and more certain than my awareness of the wax, but also much more distinct and evident. For if I judge that the wax exists from the fact that I see it, clearly this same fact entails much more evidently that I myself also exist. It is possible that what I see is not really the wax; it is possible that I do not even have eyes with which to see anything. But when I see, or think I see (I am not here distinguishing the two), it is simply not possible that I who am now thinking am not something. By the same token, if I judge that the wax exists from the fact that I touch it, the same result follows, namely that I exist. If I judge that it exists from the fact that I imagine it, or for any other reason, exactly the same thing follows. And the result that I have grasped in the case of the wax may be applied to everything else located outside me. Moreover, if my perception of the wax seemed more distinct after it was established not just by sight or touch but by many other considerations, it must be admitted that I now know myself even more distinctly. This is because every consideration whatsoever which contributes to my perception of the wax, or of any other body, cannot but establish even more effectively the nature of my own mind. . . .

FIFTH MEDITATION. THE ESSENCE OF MATERIAL THINGS, AND THE EXISTENCE OF GOD CONSIDERED A SECOND TIME

. . . The idea of God, or a supremely perfect being, is one which I find within me just as surely as the idea of any shape or number. And my understanding that it belongs to his nature that he always exists is no less clear and distinct than is the case when I prove of any shape or number that some property belongs to its nature. Hence, even if it turned out that not everything on which I have meditated in these past days is true, I ought still to regard the existence of God as having at least the same level of certainty as I have hitherto attributed to the truths of mathematics.

At first sight, however, this is not transparently clear, but has some appearance of being a sophism.[4] Since I have been accustomed to distinguish between existence and essence in everything else, I find it easy to persuade myself that existence can also be separated from the essence of God, and hence that God can be thought of as not existing. But when I concentrate more carefully, it is quite evident that existence can no more be separated from the essence of God than the fact that its three angles equal two right angles can be separated from the essence of a triangle, or than the idea of a mountain can be separated from the idea of a valley. Hence it is just as much of a contradiction to think of God (that is, a supremely perfect being) lacking existence (that is, lacking a perfection), as it is to think of a mountain without a valley.

However, even granted that I cannot think of God except as existing, just as I cannot think of a mountain without a valley, it certainly does not follow from the fact that I think of a mountain with a valley that there is any mountain in the world; and similarly, it does not seem to follow from the fact that I think of God as existing that he does exist. For my thought does not impose any necessity on things; and just as I may imagine a winged horse even though no horse has wings, so I may be able to attach existence to God even though no God exists.

But there is a sophism concealed here. From the fact that I cannot think of a mountain without a valley, it does not follow that a mountain and valley exist anywhere, but simply that a mountain and a valley, whether they exist or not, are mutually inseparable. But from the fact that I cannot think of God except as existing, it follows that existence is inseparable from God, and hence that he really exists. It is not that my thought makes it so, or imposes any necessity on any thing; on the contrary, it is the necessity of the thing itself, namely the existence of God, which determines my thinking in this respect. For I am not free to think of God without existence (that is, a supremely perfect being without a supreme perfection) as I am free to imagine a horse with or without wings. . . .[5]

SIXTH MEDITATION. THE EXISTENCE OF MATERIAL THINGS, AND THE REAL DISTINCTION BETWEEN MIND AND BODY

. . . Now, when I am beginning to achieve a better knowledge of myself and the author of my being, although I do not think I should heedlessly accept everything I seem to have acquired from the senses, neither do I think that everything should be called into doubt.

First, I know that everything which I clearly and distinctly understand is capable of being created by God so as to correspond exactly with my understanding of it. Hence the fact that I can clearly and distinctly understand one thing apart from another is enough to make me certain that the two things are distinct, since they are capable of being separated, at least by God. The question of what kind of power is required to bring about such a separation does not affect the judgment that the two things are distinct. Thus, simply by knowing that I exist and seeing at the same time that absolutely nothing else belongs to my nature or essence except that I am a thinking thing, I can infer correctly that my essence consists solely in the fact that I am a thinking thing. It is true that I may have (or, to anticipate, that I certainly have) a body that is very closely joined to me. But nevertheless, on the one hand I have a clear and distinct idea of myself, insofar as I am simply a thinking, nonextended thing; and on the other hand I have a distinct idea of body, insofar as this is simply an extended, nonthinking thing. And accordingly, it is certain that I am really distinct from my body and can exist without it.

Besides this, I find in myself faculties for certain special modes of thinking, namely imagination and sensory perception. Now I can clearly and distinctly understand myself as a whole without these faculties; but I cannot, conversely, understand these faculties without me, that is, without an intellectual substance to inhere in. This is because there is an intellectual act included in their essential definition; and hence I perceive that the distinction between them and myself corresponds to the distinction between the modes of a thing and the thing itself. Of course I also recognize that there are other faculties (like those of changing position, of taking on various shapes, and so on) which, like sensory perception and imagination, cannot be understood apart from some substance for them to inhere in, and hence cannot exist without it. But it is clear that these other faculties, if they exist, must be in a corporeal or extended substance and not an intellectual one; for the clear and distinct conception of them includes extension, but does not include any intellectual act whatsoever. Now there is in me a passive faculty of sensory perception, that is, a faculty for receiving and recognizing the ideas of sensible[6] objects; but I could not make use of it unless there was also an active faculty, either in me or in something else, which produced or brought about these ideas. But this faculty cannot be in me, since clearly it presupposes no intellectual act on my part, and the ideas in question are produced without my cooperation and often even against my will. So the only alternative is that it is in another substance distinct from me—a substance which contains either formally or eminently[7] all the reality which exists objectively in the ideas[8] produced by this faculty. . . . This substance is either a body, that is, a corporeal nature, in which case it will contain formally <and in fact> everything which is to be found objectively <or representatively> in the ideas; or else it is God, or some creature more noble than a body, in which case it will contain eminently whatever is to be found in the ideas. But since God is not a deceiver, it is quite clear that he does not transmit the ideas to me either directly from himself, or indirectly via some creature which contains the objective reality of the ideas not formally but only eminently. For God has given me no faculty at all for recognizing any such source for these ideas; on the contrary, he has given me a great propensity to believe that they are produced by corporeal things. So I do not see how God could be understood to be anything but a deceiver if the ideas were transmitted from a source other than corporeal things. It follows that corporeal things exist. They may not all exist in a way that exactly corresponds with my sensory grasp of them, for in many cases the grasp of the senses is very obscure and confused. But at least they possess all the properties which I clearly and distinctly understand—that is, all those which, viewed in general terms, are comprised within the subject matter of pure mathematics. . . .

There is nothing that my own nature teaches me more vividly than that I have a body, and that when I feel pain there is something wrong with the body, and that when I am hungry or thirsty the body needs food and drink, and so on. So I should not doubt that there is some truth in this.

Nature also teaches me, by these sensations of pain, hunger, thirst, and so on, that I am not merely present in my body as a sailor is present in a ship, but that I am very closely joined and, as it were, intermingled with it, so that I and the body form a unit. If this were not so, I, who am nothing but a thinking thing, would not feel pain when the body was hurt, but would perceive the damage purely by the intellect, just as a sailor perceives by sight if anything in his ship is broken. Similarly, when the body needed food or drink, I should have an explicit understanding of the fact, instead of having confused sensations of hunger and thirst. For these sensations of hunger, thirst, pain, and so on are nothing but confused modes of thinking which arise from the union and, as it were, intermingling of the mind with the body.

NOTES

1. Archimedes (about 287–212 B.C.E.) was a Greek mathematician and inventor. [D. C. ABEL]
2. *chimeras:* mental fabrications. [D. C. ABEL]
3. Words placed in angle brackets appear in the French version of *Meditations on First Philosophy* but not in the original Latin version. Louis-Charles d'Albert, Duc de Luyens (1620–1690), published a French translation that included some alterations from the original text. Descartes approved the translation, but scholars do not consider it as authoritative as the original Latin text. [D. C. ABEL]
4. *sophism:* a plausible but incorrect argument, intended to deceive. [D. C. ABEL]
5. Earlier, in his Third Meditation, Descartes gave an additional proof for the existence of God (alluded to in the title of this Fifth Mediation). The argument appears on pp. 135–138 of this book. [D. C. ABEL]
6. *sensible*: able to be sensed. [D. C. ABEL]
7. A substance contains something *formally* if it possesses that thing in the *same form* as in the effect it produces; it contains something *eminently* if it possesses that thing in a form *higher* than the one it produces in the effect. For example, a tree as a cause of another tree contains "treeness" formally, but God as the cause of a tree contains "treeness" eminently. [D. C. ABEL]
8. *objectively in the ideas:* in the ideas as representing the object (subject matter) of the ideas. [D. C. ABEL]

The Nature of Mind

D. M. Armstrong

D. M. Armstrong was born in 1926 in Melbourne, Australia. He earned a bachelor of arts degree in philosophy at the University of Sydney in 1950, and then went to England to attend Oxford University, where he received his bachelor of philosophy degree in 1954. Armstrong then returned to Australia, accepting a teaching position at the University of Melbourne. While teaching at Melbourne, he did additional graduate study and was awarded his doctorate in philosophy in 1959. In 1964 Armstrong was appointed Challis Professor of Philosophy at the University of Sydney, a position he held until his retirement in 1991. He has held visiting professorships at a number of institutions, including Yale University, Stanford University, the University of Texas at Austin, the University of California at Irvine, and the University of Notre Dame. He was named a Fellow of the Australian Academy of the Humanities in 1969, an Officer of the Order of Australia in 1993, and a Corresponding Fellow of the British Academy in 1998.

Armstrong's publications include *Perception and the Physical World* (1961), *A Materialist Theory of the Mind* (1968), *Belief, Truth and Knowledge* (1973), *Universals and Scientific Realism* (1978), *The Nature of Mind and Other Essays* (1980), *A World of States of Affairs* (1997), *The Mind-Body Problem: An Opinionated Introduction* (1999), and *Truth and Truthmakers* (2004).

Our reading is Armstrong's article "The Nature of Mind" (the revised version, which appears in *The Nature of Mind and Other Essays;* the original version was published in 1970). Working from the assumption that the remarkable progress of natural science in recent decades indicates that human nature can be explained entirely in physical and chemical terms, he proposes a purely materialist account of the mind. (If a materialist theory of the mind could be established, the long-standing "mind-body problem"—how a nonphysical mind can interact with the body, which is physical—would be solved.) After briefly discussing the authority of science, Armstrong examines an earlier materialist theory of mind—the one proposed by behaviorism. Behaviorism's initial identification of the mind with behavior met with the obvious objection that a mental process can occur without producing any behavior. To address this difficulty, behaviorists introduced the notion of a *disposition to behave:* Just as glass can have the disposition to break without actually breaking, so a human being can have a disposition to act without actually acting. But this revised behaviorist theory also proved untenable, because when a mental event occurs in a person and produces no behavior, this mental event is more than a disposition. "Something is currently going on, in the strongest and most literal sense of 'going on,' and this something is my thought."

Although he sees no possibility of salvaging a behaviorist theory of mind, Armstrong accepts behaviorism's claim that mental states are *logically tied* to behavior. He proceeds to sketch his own materialist theory of mind, arguing that a mental state is "a state of the person apt for producing certain ranges of behavior." He then discusses how a materialist theory might explain the phenomenon of consciousness.

Men have minds, that is to say, they perceive, they have sensations, emotions, beliefs, thoughts, purposes, and desires. What is it to have a mind? What is it to perceive, to feel emotion, to hold a belief, or to have a purpose? Many contemporary philosophers think that the best clue we have to the nature of mind is furnished by the discoveries and hypotheses of modern science concerning the nature of man.

What does modern science have to say about the nature of man? There are, of course, all sorts of disagreements and divergencies in the views of individual scientists. But I think it is true to say that one view is steadily gaining ground, so that it bids fair to become established scientific doctrine. This is the view that we can give a complete account of man *in purely physicochemical terms.* This view has received a tremendous impetus in recent decades from the new subject of molecular biology, a subject that promises to unravel the physical and chemical mechanisms that lie at the basis of life. Before that time, it received great encouragement from pioneering work in neurophysiology pointing to the likelihood of a purely electrochemical account of the working of the brain. I think it is fair to say that those scientists who still reject the physicochemical account of man do so primarily for philosophical, or moral, or religious reasons, and only secondarily, and half-heartedly, for reasons of scientific detail. This is not to say that in the future new evidence and new problems may not come to light that will force science to reconsider the physicochemical view of man. But at present the drift of scientific thought is clearly set towards the physicochemical hypothesis. And we have nothing better to go on than the present.

For me, then, and for many philosophers who think like me, the moral is clear. We must try to work out an account of the nature of mind which is compatible with the view that man is nothing but a physicochemical mechanism.

And in this paper, I shall be concerned to do just this: to sketch (in barest outline) what may be called a materialist, or physicalist, account of the mind.

THE AUTHORITY OF SCIENCE

But before doing this, I should like to go back and consider a criticism of my position that must inevitably occur to some. What reason have I, it may be asked, for taking my stand on science? Even granting that I am right about what is the currently dominant scientific view of man, why should we concede science a special authority to decide questions about the nature of man? What of the authority of philosophy, of religion, of morality, or even of literature and art? Why do I set the authority of science above all these? Why this "scientism"?

It seems to me that the answer to this question is very simple. If we consider the search for truth, in all its fields, we find that it is only in science that men versed in their subject can, after investigation that is more or less prolonged, and which may in some cases extend beyond a single human lifetime, reach substantial agreement about what is the case. It is only as a result of scientific investigation that we ever seem to reach an intellectual consensus about controversial matters.

In the Epistle Dedicatory to *De Corpore,* Hobbes wrote of William Harvey, the discoverer of the circulation of the blood, that he was "the only man I know that, conquering envy, hath established a new doctrine in his lifetime."[1] Before Copernicus, Galileo, and Harvey, Hobbes remarks, "there was nothing certain in natural philosophy."[2] And, we might add, with the exception of mathematics there was nothing certain in any other learned discipline.

These remarks of Hobbes are incredibly revealing. They show us what a watershed in the intellectual history of the human race the seventeenth century was. Before that time, inquiry proceeded, as it were, in the dark. Men could not hope to see their doctrine *established*, that is to say, accepted by the vast majority of those properly versed in the subject under discussion. There was no intellectual consensus. Since that time, it has become a commonplace to see new doctrines, sometimes of the most far-reaching kind, established to the satisfaction of the learned, often within the lifetime of their first proponents. Science has provided us with a method of deciding disputed questions. This is not to say, of course, that the consensus of those who are learned and competent in a subject cannot be mistaken. Of course such a consensus can be mistaken. Sometimes it *has* been mistaken. But, granting fallibility, what better authority have we than such a consensus?

Now this is of the utmost importance. For in philosophy, in religion, in such disciplines as literary criticism, in moral questions in so far as they are thought to be matters of truth and falsity, there has been a notable failure to achieve an intellectual consensus about disputed questions among the learned. Must we not then attach a peculiar authority to the discipline that can achieve a consensus? And if it presents us with a certain vision of the nature of man, is this not a powerful reason for accepting that vision?

I will not take up here the deeper question *why* it is that the methods of science have enabled us to achieve an intellectual consensus about so many disputed matters. That question, I think, could receive no brief or uncontroversial answer. I am resting my argument on the simple fact that, as a result of scientific investigation, such a consensus has been achieved.

It may be replied—it often *is* replied—that while science is all very well in its own sphere (the sphere of the physical, perhaps), there are matters of fact on which it is not competent to pronounce. And among such matters, it may be claimed, is the question: What is the whole nature of man? But I cannot see that this reply has much force. Science has provided us with an island of truths, or, perhaps one should say, a raft of truths, to bear us up on the sea of our disputatious ignorance. There may have to be revisions and refinements; new results may set old findings in a new perspective—but what science has given us will not be altogether superseded. Must we not therefore appeal to these relative certainties for guidance when we come to consider uncertainties elsewhere? Perhaps science cannot help us to decide whether or not there is a God, whether or not human beings have immortal souls, or whether or not the will is free. But if science cannot assist us, what can? I conclude that it is the scientific vision of man, and not the philosophical or religious or artistic or moral vision of man, that is the best clue we have to the nature of man. And it is rational to argue from the best evidence we have.

DEFINING THE MENTAL

Having in this way attempted to justify my procedure, I turn back to my subject: the attempt to work out an account of mind, or, if you prefer, of mental process, within the framework of the physicochemical, or, as we may call it, the materialist view of man.

Now there is one account of mental process that is at once attractive to any philosopher sympathetic to a materialist view of man: This is behaviorism. Formulated originally by a psychologist, J. B. Watson,[3] it attracted widespread interest and considerable support from scientifically oriented philosophers. Traditional philosophy had tended to think of the mind as a rather mysterious inward arena that lay behind, and was responsible for, the outward or physical behavior of our bodies. Descartes[4] thought of this inner arena as a *spiritual substance,* and it was this conception of the mind as spiritual object that Gilbert Ryle attacked, apparently in the interest of behaviorism, in his important book *The Concept of Mind.* He ridiculed the Cartesian view as the dogma of "the ghost in the machine."[5] The mind was not something behind the behavior of the body, it was simply part of that physical behavior. My anger with you is not some modification of a spiritual substance that somehow brings about aggressive behavior; rather it is the aggressive behavior itself—my addressing strong words to you, striking you, turning my back on you, and so on. Thought is not an inner process that lies behind, and brings about, the words I speak and write; it *is* my speaking and writing. The mind is not an inner arena; it is outward act.

It is clear that such a view of mind fits in very well with a completely materialistic, or physicalist, view of man. If there is no need to draw a distinction between mental processes and their expression in physical behavior, but if instead the mental processes are identified with their so-called "expressions," then the existence of mind stands in no conflict with the view that man is nothing but a physicochemical mechanism.

However, the version of behaviorism that I have just sketched is a very crude version, and its crudity lays it open to obvious objections. One obvious difficulty is that it is our common experience that there can be mental processes going on although there is no behavior occurring that could possibly be treated as expressions of those processes. A man may be angry, but give no bodily sign; he may think, but say or do nothing at all.

In my view, the most plausible attempt to refine behaviorism with a view to meeting this objection was made by introducing the notion of a *disposition to behave.* (Dispositions to behave play a particularly important part in Ryle's account of the mind.) Let us consider the general notion of disposition first. Brittleness is a disposition, a disposition possessed by materials like glass. Brittle materials are those that, when subjected to relatively small forces, break or shatter easily. But breaking and shattering easily is not brittleness, rather it is the *manifestation* of brittleness. Brittleness itself is the tendency or liability of the material to break or shatter easily. A piece of glass may never shatter or break throughout its whole history, but it is still the case that it is brittle: It is liable to shatter or break if dropped quite a small way or hit quite lightly. Now a disposition to *behave* is simply a tendency or liability of a person to behave in a certain way under certain circumstances. The brittleness of glass is a disposition that the glass retains throughout its history, but clearly there also could be dispositions that come and go. The dispositions to behave that are of interest to the behaviorist are, for the most part, of this temporary character.

Now how did Ryle and others use the notion of a disposition to behave to meet the obvious objection to behaviorism that there can be mental process going on although the subject is engaging in no relevant behavior? Their strategy was to argue that in such cases, although the subject was not behaving in any relevant way, he or she was *disposed* to behave in some relevant way. The glass does not shatter, but it is still brittle. The man does not behave, but he does have a disposition to behave. We can say he thinks although he does not speak or act because at that time he was disposed to speak or act in a certain way. *If* he had been asked, perhaps, he would have spoken or acted. We can say he is angry although he does not behave angrily, because he is disposed so to behave. *If* only one more word had been addressed to him, he would have burst out. And so on. In this way it was hoped that behaviorism could be squared with the obvious facts.

It is very important to see just how these thinkers conceived of dispositions. I quote from Ryle:

> To possess a dispositional property *is not to be in a particular state, or to undergo a particular change;* it is to be bound or liable to be in a particular state, or to undergo a particular change, when a particular condition is realized.[6]

So to explain the breaking of a lightly struck glass on a particular occasion by saying it was brittle is, on this view of dispositions, simply to say that the glass broke because it is the sort of thing that regularly breaks when quite lightly struck. The breaking was the normal behavior, or not abnormal behavior, of such a thing. The brittleness is not to be conceived of as a *cause* for the breakage, or even, more vaguely, a *factor* in bringing about the breaking. Brittleness is just the fact that things of that sort break easily.

But although in this way the behaviorists did something to deal with the objection that mental processes can occur in the absence of behavior, it seems clear, now that the shouting and the dust have died, that they did not do enough. When I think, but my thoughts do not issue in any action, it seems as obvious as anything is obvious that there is something actually going on in me that constitutes my thought. It is not simply that I would speak or act if some conditions that are unfulfilled were to be fulfilled. Something is currently going on, in the strongest and most literal sense of "going on," and this something is my thought. Rylean behaviorism denies this, and so it is unsatisfactory as a theory of mind. Yet I know of no version of behaviorism that is more satisfactory. The moral for those of us who wish to take a purely physicalistic view of man is that we must look for some other account of the nature of mind and of mental processes.

But perhaps we need not grieve too deeply about the failure of behaviorism to produce a satisfactory theory of mind. Behaviorism is a profoundly unnatural account of mental processes. If somebody speaks and acts in certain ways, it is natural to speak of this speech and action as the *expression* of his thought. It is not at all natural to speak of his speech and action as identical with his thought. We naturally think of the thought as something quite distinct from the speech and action that, under suitable circumstances, brings the speech and action about. Thoughts are not to be identified with behavior, we think; they lie behind behavior. A man's behavior constitutes the *reason* we have for attributing certain mental processes to him, but the behavior cannot be *identified with* the mental processes.

This suggests a very interesting line of thought about the mind. Behaviorism is certainly wrong, but perhaps it is not altogether wrong. Perhaps the behaviorists are wrong in identifying the mind and mental occurrences with behavior, but perhaps they are right in thinking that our notion of a mind and of individual mental states is *logically tied to behavior*. For perhaps what we mean by a mental state is some state of the person that, under suitable circumstances, *brings about* a certain range of behavior. Perhaps mind can be defined not as behavior, but rather as the inner *cause* of certain behavior. Thought is not speech under suitable circumstances, rather it is something within the person that, in suitable circumstances, brings about speech. And, in fact, I believe that this is the true account, or, at any rate, a true first account, of what we mean by a mental state.

How does this line of thought link up with a purely physicalist view of man? The position is that while it does not make such a physicalist view inevitable, it does make it *possible*. It does not entail, but it is compatible with, a purely physicalist view of man. For if our notion of the mind and of mental states is nothing but that of a cause within the person of certain ranges of behavior, then it becomes a scientific question, and not a question of logical analysis, what in fact the intrinsic nature of that cause is. The cause might be, as Descartes thought it was, a spiritual substance working through the pineal gland to produce the complex bodily behavior of which men are capable. It might be breath, or specially smooth and mobile atoms dispersed throughout the body; it might be many other things. But in fact the verdict of modern science seems to be that the sole cause of mind-betokening behavior in man and the higher animals is the physicochemical workings of the central nervous system. And so, assuming we have correctly characterized our concept of a mental state as nothing but the cause of certain sorts of behavior, then we can identify these mental states with purely physical states of the central nervous system.

At this point we may stop and go back to the behaviorist's dispositions. We saw that, according to him, the brittleness of glass or, to take another example, the elasticity of rubber, is not a state of the glass or the rubber, but is simply the fact that things of that sort behave in the way they do. But now let us consider how a scientist would think about brittleness or elasticity. Faced with the phenomenon of breakage under relatively small impacts, or the phenomenon of stretching when a force is applied followed by contraction when the force is removed, he will assume that there is some current *state* of the glass or the rubber that is responsible for the characteristic behavior of samples of these two materials. At the beginning, he will not know what this state is, but he will endeavor to find out, and he may succeed in finding out. And when he has found out, he will very likely make remarks of this sort: "We have discovered that the brittleness of glass is in fact a certain sort of pattern in the molecules of the glass." That is to say, he will *identify* brittleness with the state of the glass that is responsible for the liability of the glass to break. For him, a disposition of an object is a state of the object. What makes the state a state of brittleness is the fact that it gives rise to the characteristic manifestations of brittleness. But the disposition itself is distinct from its manifestations: It is the state of the glass that gives rise to these manifestations in suitable circumstances.

This way of looking at dispositions is very different from that of Ryle and the behaviorists. The great difference is this: If we treat dispositions as actual states, as I have suggested that scientists do, even if states the intrinsic nature of which may yet have to be discovered, then we can say that dispositions are actual *causes*, or causal factors, which, in suitable circumstances, actually bring about those happenings that are the manifestations of the disposition. A certain molecular constitution of glass that constitutes its brittleness is actually *responsible* for the fact that, when the glass is struck, it breaks.

Now I cannot argue the matter here, because the detail of the argument is technical and difficult, but I believe that the view of dispositions as states, which is the view that is natural to science, is the correct one.[7] I believe it can be shown quite strictly that, to the extent that we admit the notion of dispositions at all, we are committed to the view that they are actual *states* of the object that has the disposition. I may add that I think that the same holds for the closely connected notions of capacities and powers. Here I will simply have to assume this step in my argument.

But perhaps it will be seen that the rejection of the idea that mind is simply a certain range of man's behavior in favor of the view that mind is rather the inner *cause* of that range of man's behavior, is bound up with the rejection of the Rylean view of dispositions in favor of one that treats dispositions as states of objects and so as having actual causal power. The behaviorists were wrong to identify the mind with behavior. They were not so far off the mark when they tried to deal with cases where mental happenings occur in the absence of behavior by saying that these are dispositions to behave. But in order to reach a correct view, I am suggesting, they would have to conceive of these dispositions as actual *states* of the person who has the disposition, states that have actual causal power to bring about behavior in suitable circumstances. But to do this is to abandon the central inspiration of behaviorism: that in talking about the mind we do not have to go behind outward behavior to inner states.

And so two separate but interlocking lines of thought have pushed me in the same direction. The first line of thought is that it goes profoundly against the grain to think of the mind as behavior. The mind is, rather, that which stands behind and brings about our complex behavior. The second line of thought is that the behaviorist's dispositions, properly conceived, are really states that underlie behavior and, under suitable circumstances, bring about behavior. Putting these two together, we reach the conception of a mental state as *a state of the person apt for producing certain ranges of behavior.* This formula—a mental state is a state of the person apt for producing certain ranges of behavior—I believe to be a very illuminating way of looking at the concept of a mental state. I have found it fruitful in the search for detailed logical analyses of the individual mental concepts.

I do not think that Hegel's dialectic[8] has much to tell us about the nature of reality. But I think that human thought often moves in a dialectical way, from thesis to antithesis and then to the synthesis. Perhaps thought about the mind is a case in point. I have already said that classical philosophy has tended to think of the mind as an inner arena of some sort. This we may call the thesis. Behaviorism moves to the opposite extreme: The mind is seen as outward behavior. This is the antithesis. My proposed synthesis is that the mind is properly conceived as an inner principle, but a principle that is identified in terms of the outward behavior it is apt for bringing about. This way of looking at the mind and mental states does not itself entail a materialist, or physicalist, view of man, for nothing is said in this analysis about the intrinsic nature of these mental states. But if we have, as I have argued that we do have, general scientific grounds for thinking that man is nothing but a physical mechanism, we can go on to argue that the mental states are in fact nothing but physical states of the central nervous system.

THE PROBLEM OF CONSCIOUSNESS

Along these lines, then, I would look for an account of the mind that is compatible with a purely materialist theory of man. There are, as may be imagined, all sorts of powerful objections that can be made to my view. But in the rest of this paper, I propose to do only one thing: I will develop one very important objection to my view of the mind—an objection felt by many philosophers—and then try to show how the objection should be met.

The view that our notion of mind is nothing but that of an inner principle apt for bringing about certain sorts of behavior may be thought to share a certain weakness with behaviorism. Modern philosophers have put the point about behaviorism by saying that, although behaviorism may be a satisfactory account of the mind from *an other-person point of view*, it will not do as a *first-person account*. To explain: In my encounters with other people, all I ever observe is their behavior—their actions, their speech, and so on. And so, if we simply consider other people, behaviorism might seem to do full justice to the facts. But the trouble about behaviorism is that it seems so unsatisfactory as applied to our *own* case. In our own case, we seem to be aware of so much more than mere behavior.

Suppose that now we conceive of the mind as an inner principle apt for bringing about certain sorts of behavior. This again fits the other-person cases very well. Bodily behavior of a very sophisticated sort is observed, quite different from the behavior that ordinary physical objects display. It is inferred that this behavior must spring from a very special sort of inner cause in the object that exhibits this behavior. This inner cause is christened "the mind," and those who take a physicalist view of man argue that it is simply the central nervous system of the body observed. Compare this with the case of glass. Certain characteristic behavior is observed: the breaking and shattering of the material when acted upon by relatively small forces. A special inner state of the glass is postulated to explain this behavior. Those who take a purely physicalist view of glass then argue that this state is a *material* state of the glass. It is, perhaps, an arrangement of its molecules and not, say, the peculiarly malevolent disposition of the demons that dwell in glass.

But when we turn to our own case, the position may seem less plausible. We are conscious, we have experiences. Now can we say that to be conscious, to have experiences, is simply for something to go on within us apt for the causing of certain sorts of behavior? Such an account does not seem to do any justice to the phenomena. And so it seems that our account of the mind, like behaviorism, will fail to do justice to the first-person case.

In order to understand the objection better, it may be helpful to consider a particular case. If you have driven for a very long distance without a break, you may have had experience of a curious state of automatism that can occur in these conditions. One can suddenly "come to" and realize that one has driven for long distances without being aware of what one was doing, or, indeed, without being aware of anything. One has kept the car on the road, used the brake and the clutch perhaps, yet all without any awareness of what one was doing.

Now if we consider this case, it is obvious that *in some sense* mental processes are still going on when one is in such an automatic state. Unless one's will was still operating in some way, and unless one was still perceiving in some way, the car would not still be on the road. Yet, of course, *something* mental is lacking. Now I think, when it is alleged that an account of mind as an inner principle apt for the production of certain sorts of behavior leaves out consciousness or experience, what is alleged to have been left out is just whatever is missing in the automatic driving case. It is conceded that an account of mental processes as states of the person apt for the production of certain sorts of behavior very possibly may be adequate to deal with such cases as that of automatic driving. It may be adequate to deal with most of the mental processes of animals, which perhaps spend most of their lives in this state of automatism. But, it is contended, it cannot deal with the consciousness that we normally enjoy.

I will now try to sketch an answer to this important and powerful objection. Let us begin in an apparently unlikely place and consider the way that an account of mental processes of the sort I am giving would deal with *sense-perception*.

Now psychologists, in particular, have long realized that there is a very close logical tie between sense-perception and *selective behavior*. Suppose we want to decide whether an animal can perceive the difference between red and green. We might give the animal a choice between two pathways, over one of which a red light shines and over the other of which a green light shines. If the animal happens by chance to choose the green pathway, we reward it; if it happens to choose the other pathway, we do not reward it. If, after some trials, the animal systematically takes the green-lighted pathway, and if we become assured that the only relevant differences in the two pathways are the differences in the color of the lights, we are entitled to say that the animal can see this color difference. Using its eyes, it selects between red-lighted and green-lighted pathways. So we say it can see the difference between red and green.

Now a behaviorist would be tempted to say that the animal's regular selection of the green-lighted pathway *was* its perception of the color difference. But this is unsatisfactory, because we all want to say that perception is something that goes on within the person or animal—within its mind—although, of course, this mental event is normally *caused* by the operation of the environment upon the organism. Suppose, however, that we speak instead of *capacities* for selective behavior towards the current environment, and suppose we think of these capacities, like dispositions, as actual inner states of the organism. We can then think of the animal's perception as a state within the animal apt, if the animal is so impelled, for selective behavior between the red- and green-lighted pathways.

In general, we can think of perceptions as inner states or events apt for the production of certain sorts of selective behavior towards our environment. To perceive is like acquiring a key to a door. You do not have to use the key: You can put it in your pocket and never bother about the door. But if you do want to open the door, the key may be essential. The blind man is a man who does not acquire certain keys and, as a result, is not able to operate in his environment in the way that somebody who has his sight can operate. It seems, then, a very promising view to take of perceptions that they are inner states defined by the sorts of selective behavior that they enable the perceiver to exhibit, if so impelled.

Now how is this discussion of perception related to the question of consciousness or experience, the sort of thing that the driver who is in a state of automatism has not got, but which we normally do have? Simply this. My proposal is that consciousness, in this sense of the word, is nothing but *perception or awareness of the state of our own mind*. The driver in a state of automatism perceives, or is aware of, the road. If he did not, the car would be in a ditch. But he is not currently aware of his awareness of the road. He perceives the road, but he does not perceive his perceiving, or anything else that is going on in his mind. He is not, as we normally are, conscious of what is going on in his mind.

And so I conceive of consciousness or experience, in this sense of the words, in the way that Locke and Kant[9] conceived it, as like perception. Kant, in a striking phrase, spoke of "inner sense." We cannot directly observe the minds of others, but each of us has the power to observe directly our own minds, and "perceive" what is going on there. The driver in the automatic state is one whose "inner eye" is shut, who is not currently aware of what is going on in his own mind.

Now if this account is along the right lines, why should we not give an account of this inner observation along the same lines as we have already given of perception? Why should we not conceive of it as an inner state, a state in this case directed towards other inner states and not to the environment, which enables us, if we are so impelled, to behave in a selective way *towards our own states of mind?* One who is aware, or conscious, of his thoughts or his emotions is one who has the capacity to make discriminations between his different mental states. His capacity might be exhibited in words. He might say that he was in an angry state of mind, when, and only when, he *was* in an angry state of mind. But such verbal behavior would be the mere *expression or result* of the awareness. The awareness itself would be an inner state—the sort of inner state that gave the man a capacity for such behavioral expressions.

So I have argued that consciousness of our own mental state may be assimilated to *perception* of our own mental state, and that, like other perceptions, it may then be conceived of as an inner state or event giving a capacity for selective behavior, in this case selective behavior towards our own mental state. All this is meant to be simply a logical analysis of consciousness, and none of it entails, although it does not rule out, a purely physicalist account of what these inner states are. But if we are convinced, on general scientific grounds, that a purely physical account of man is likely to be the true one, then there seems to be no bar to our identifying these inner states with purely physical states of the central nervous system. And so consciousness of our own mental state becomes simply the scanning of one part of our central nervous system by another. Consciousness is a self-scanning mechanism in the central nervous system.

As I have emphasized before, I have done no more than sketch a program for a philosophy of mind. There are all sorts of expansions and elucidations to be made, and all sorts of doubts and difficulties to be stated and overcome. But I hope I have done enough to show that a purely physicalist theory of the mind is an exciting and plausible intellectual option.

NOTES

1. Thomas Hobbes, "The Author's Epistle Dedicatory to the Most Honorable, My Most Honored Lord, William, Earl of Devonshire," in *The English Works of Thomas Hobbes of Malmesbury*, ed. William Molesworth, vol. 1 (London, England: John Bohn, 1839), p. viii. Hobbes (1588–1679) was an English philosopher; for a biography, see p. 441. Harvey (1578–1657) was an English physician and anatomist. [D. C. ABEL]
2. Ibid. *Natural philosophy* is the philosophy of nature—that is, natural science. Nicolaus Copernicus (1473–1543) was a Polish astronomer; Galileo Galilei (1564–1642) was an Italian astronomer and physicist. [D. C. ABEL]
3. Watson (1878–1958) was an American psychologist. [D. C. ABEL]
4. René Descartes (1596–1650) was a French philosopher and mathematician; for a biography, see p. 128. [D. C. ABEL]
5. Gilbert Ryle, *The Concept of Mind* (London, England: Hutchinson, 1949), pp. 15–18. [D. C. ABEL]
6. Ibid., p. 43; emphasis added. [D. M. ARMSTRONG]
7. I develop the argument in *Belief, Truth and Knowledge* (London, England: Cambridge University Press, 1973), Chapter 2, Section 2. [D. M. ARMSTRONG]
8. *Hegelian dialectic:* a process of development, postulated by the German philosopher Georg Wilhelm Friedrich Hegel (1770–1831), that begins when something (the thesis) gives rise to its opposite (the antithesis). Then the two opposites combine into a new, higher reality (the synthesis). [D. C. ABEL]
9. John Locke (1632–1704) was an English philosopher; for a biography, see p. 139. Immanuel Kant (1724–1804) was a German philosopher; for a biography, see p. 175. [D. C. ABEL]

B. Consciousness

What Is It Like to Be a Bat?

Thomas Nagel

Thomas Nagel was born in Belgrade, Yugoslavia, in 1937. He came to the United States in 1939 and became a naturalized citizen five years later. After completing his undergraduate degree from Cornell University in 1958, he studied at Oxford University, where he earned a bachelor of philosophy degree in 1960. Nagel then enrolled in the graduate program in philosophy at Harvard University, receiving his doctorate in 1963. He taught at the University of California at Berkeley until 1966 and at Princeton University for the next fourteen years. In 1980 he accepted an appointment as Professor of Philosophy at New York University. He was named Professor of Philosophy and Law in 1986, Fiorello LaGuardia Professor of Law in 2001, and University Professor in 2002. Nagel has held visiting appointments at Rockefeller University, the University of Pittsburgh, the University of Mexico, the University of Witwatersrand (Republic of South Africa), the University of California at Los Angeles, and All Souls College at Oxford University. He is a Fellow of the American Academy of Arts and Sciences, a Corresponding Fellow of the British Academy, and an Honorary Fellow of Corpus Christi College at Oxford University.

Nagel's publications include *The Possibility of Altruism* (1970), *Mortal Questions* (1979; translated into ten languages), *The View from Nowhere* (1986), *What Does It All Mean? A Very Short Introduction to Philosophy* (1987; translated into twenty languages), *Equality and Partiality* (1991), *The Last Word* (1997), and *Concealment and Exposure and Other Essays* (2002).

Our reading is Nagel's 1974 article, "What Is It Like to Be a Bat?" Nagel examines the *reductionist* theory that some contemporary philosophers propose as a solution to the problem of how the mind and body are related. Reductionism is the view that one kind of thing can be "reduced to" (explained fully in terms of) another kind of thing. In the philosophy of mind, reductionism holds that the mind and mental phenomena can be reduced to physical phenomena, such as neurological activity of the brain (hence the doctrine is known as *physicalism* or *materialism*). Nagel contends that the major difficulty facing reductionist, physicalist theories of mind is the phenomenon of consciousness. Although there may be some way to reduce consciousness to physical states, we are far from knowing how this might be done.

Nagel explains that the fact that an organism (human or nonhuman) has consciousness means that "there is something it is like to *be* that organism—something it is like *for* that organism." Consciousness is by nature a subjective phenomenon, and as such seems impossible to analyze exhaustively in terms of objective, physical phenomena. Subjectivity implies a single point of view, whereas objectivity requires a more universal point of view. Taking the example of a bat as a creature very different from us, Nagel argues that it seems impossible for us to capture in objective analysis the subjective experience of a bat. I might imagine what it would be like *for me* to behave as a bat behaves (hanging upside down by my feet, for example), but I seem unable to know what it is like *for the bat* to be a bat. Even

220

if I had complete knowledge of the working of the bat's neurological system, how could the subjective experience of the bat be reduced to this kind of objective analysis? Nagel points out that he does not claim to have disproved the physicalist claim that mental states are states of the body; he simply claims that the two terms of this alleged equation are so different that we have no idea what it means to say that a mental state "is" a physical state.

Consciousness is what makes the mind-body problem really intractable. Perhaps that is why current discussions of the problem give it little attention or get it obviously wrong. The recent wave of reductionist euphoria has produced several analyses of mental phenomena and mental concepts designed to explain the possibility of some variety of materialism, psychophysical identification,[1] or reduction. But the problems dealt with are those common to this type of reduction and other types, and what makes the mind-body problem unique, and unlike the water-H_2O problem or the Turing machine-IBM machine problem or the lightning-electrical discharge problem or the gene-DNA problem or the oak tree-hydrocarbon problem,[2] is ignored.

Every reductionist has his favorite analogy from modern science. It is most unlikely that any of these unrelated examples of successful reduction will shed light on the relation of mind to brain. But philosophers share the general human weakness for explanations of what is incomprehensible in terms suited for what is familiar and well understood, though entirely different. This has led to the acceptance of implausible accounts of the mental largely because they would permit familiar kinds of reduction. I shall try to explain why the usual examples do not help us to understand the relation between mind and body—why, indeed, we have at present no conception of what an explanation of the physical nature of a mental phenomenon would be. Without consciousness the mind-body problem would be much less interesting. With consciousness it seems hopeless. The most important and characteristic feature of conscious mental phenomena is very poorly understood. Most reductionist theories do not even try to explain it. And careful examination will show that no currently available concept of reduction is applicable to it. Perhaps a new theoretical form can be devised for the purpose, but such a solution, if it exists, lies in the distant intellectual future.

Conscious experience is a widespread phenomenon. It occurs at many levels of animal life, though we cannot be sure of its presence in the simpler organisms, and it is very difficult to say in general what provides evidence of it. (Some extremists have been prepared to deny it even of mammals other than man.) No doubt it occurs in countless forms totally unimaginable to us, on other planets in other solar systems throughout the universe. But no matter how the form may vary, the fact that an organism has conscious experience *at all* means, basically, that there is something it is like to *be* that organism. There may be further implications about the form of the experience; there may even (though I doubt it) be implications about the behavior of the organism. But fundamentally an organism has conscious mental states if and only if there is something that it is like to *be* that organism—something it is like *for* the organism.

We may call this the subjective character of experience. It is not captured by any of the familiar, recently devised reductive analyses of the mental, for all of them are

logically compatible with its absence. It is not analyzable in terms of any explanatory system of functional states, or intentional states,[3] since these could be ascribed
to robots or automata that behaved like people though they experienced nothing. It
is not analyzable in terms of the causal role of experiences in relation to typical human behavior—for similar reasons. I do not deny that conscious mental states and
events cause behavior, nor that they may be given functional characterizations. I
deny only that this kind of thing exhausts their analysis. Any reductionist program
has to be based on an analysis of what is to be reduced. If the analysis leaves something out, the problem will be falsely posed. It is useless to base the defense of
materialism on any analysis of mental phenomena that fails to deal explicitly with
their subjective character. For there is no reason to suppose that a reduction which
seems plausible when no attempt is made to account for consciousness, can be extended
to include consciousness. Without some idea, therefore, of what the subjective character of experience is, we cannot know what is required of a physicalist theory.

While an account of the physical basis of mind must explain many things, this
appears to be the most difficult. It is impossible to exclude the phenomenological[4]
features of experience from a reduction in the same way that one excludes the phenomenal[5] features of an ordinary substance from a physical or chemical reduction
of it—namely, by explaining them as effects on the minds of human observers. If
physicalism is to be defended, the phenomenological features must themselves be
given a physical account. But when we examine their subjective character it seems
that such a result is impossible. The reason is that every subjective phenomenon is
essentially connected with a single point of view, and it seems inevitable that an
objective, physical theory will abandon that point of view.

Let me first try to state the issue somewhat more fully than by referring to the
relation between the subjective and the objective, or between the *pour soi* and the
en soi.[6] This is far from easy. Facts about what it is like to be an X are very peculiar,
so peculiar that some may be inclined to doubt their reality, or the significance of
claims about them. To illustrate the connection between subjectivity and a point
of view, and to make evident the importance of subjective features, it will help to
explore the matter in relation to an example that brings out clearly the divergence
between the two types of conception, subjective and objective.

I assume we all believe that bats have experience. After all, they are mammals, and there is no more doubt that they have experience than that mice or pi-
geons or whales have experience. I have chosen bats instead of wasps or
flounders because if one travels too far down the phylogenetic tree, people
gradually shed their faith that there is experience there at all. Bats, although
more closely related to us than those other species, nevertheless present a range
of activity and a sensory apparatus so different from ours that the problem I
want to pose is exceptionally vivid (though it certainly could be raised with
other species). Even without the benefit of philosophical reflection, anyone who
has spent some time in an enclosed space with an excited bat knows what it is
to encounter a fundamentally *alien* form of life.

I have said that the essence of the belief that bats have experience is that there
is something that it is like to be a bat. Now we know that most bats (the mi-
crochiroptera, to be precise) perceive the external world primarily by sonar, or
echolocation, detecting the reflections, from objects within range, of their own

rapid, subtly modulated, high-frequency shrieks. Their brains are designed to correlate the outgoing impulses with the subsequent echoes, and the information thus acquired enables bats to make precise discriminations of distance, size, shape, motion, and texture comparable to those we make by vision. But bat sonar, though clearly a form of perception, is not similar in its operation to any sense that we possess, and there is no reason to suppose that it is subjectively like anything we can experience or imagine. This appears to create difficulties for the notion of what it is like to be a bat. We must consider whether any method will permit us to extrapolate to the inner life of the bat from our own case, and if not, what alternative methods there may be for understanding the notion.

Our own experience provides the basic material for our imagination, whose range is therefore limited. It will not help to try to imagine that one has webbing on one's arms, which enables one to fly around at dusk and dawn catching insects in one's mouth; that one has very poor vision, and perceives the surrounding world by a system of reflected high-frequency sound signals; and that one spends the day hanging upside down by one's feet in an attic. Insofar as I can imagine this (which is not very far), it tells me only what it would be like for *me* to behave as a bat behaves. But that is not the question. I want to know what it is like for a *bat* to be a bat. Yet if I try to imagine this, I am restricted to the resources of my own mind, and those resources are inadequate to the task. I cannot perform it either by imagining additions to my present experience, or by imagining segments gradually subtracted from it, or by imagining some combination of additions, subtractions, and modifications.

To the extent that I could look and behave like a wasp or a bat without changing my fundamental structure, my experiences would not be anything like the experiences of those animals. On the other hand, it is doubtful that any meaning can be attached to the supposition that I should possess the internal neurophysiological constitution of a bat. Even if I could by gradual degrees be transformed into a bat, nothing in my present constitution enables me to imagine what the experiences of such a future stage of myself thus metamorphosed would be like. The best evidence would come from the experiences of bats, if we only knew what they were like.

So if extrapolation from our own case is involved in the idea of what it is like to be a bat, the extrapolation must be incompletable. We cannot form more than a schematic conception of what it *is* like. For example, we may ascribe general *types* of experience on the basis of the animal's structure and behavior. Thus we describe bat sonar as a form of three-dimensional forward perception; we believe that bats feel some versions of pain, fear, hunger, and lust, and that they have other, more familiar types of perception besides sonar. But we believe that these experiences also have in each case a specific subjective character, which it is beyond our ability to conceive. And if there is conscious life elsewhere in the universe, it is likely that some of it will not be describable even in the most general experiential terms available to us. (The problem is not confined to exotic cases, however, for it exists between one person and another. The subjective character of the experience of a person deaf and blind from birth is not accessible to me, for example, nor presumably is mine to him. This does not prevent us each from believing that the other's experience has such a subjective character.)

If anyone is inclined to deny that we can believe in the existence of facts like this whose exact nature we cannot possibly conceive, he should reflect that in contemplating the bats we are in much the same position that intelligent bats or Martians would occupy if they tried to form a conception of what it was like to be us. The structure of their own minds might make it impossible for them to succeed, but we know they would be wrong to conclude that there is not anything precise that it is like to be us: that only certain general types of mental state could be ascribed to us (perhaps perception and appetite would be concepts common to us both; perhaps not). We know they would be wrong to draw such a skeptical conclusion because we know what it is like to be us. And we know that while it includes an enormous amount of variation and complexity, and while we do not possess the vocabulary to describe it adequately, its subjective character is highly specific, and in some respects describable in terms that can be understood only by creatures like us. The fact that we cannot expect ever to accommodate in our language a detailed description of Martian or bat phenomenology should not lead us to dismiss as meaningless the claim that bats and Martians have experiences fully comparable in richness of detail to our own. It would be fine if someone were to develop concepts and a theory that enabled us to think about those things; but such an understanding may be permanently denied to us by the limits of our nature. And to deny the reality or logical significance of what we can never describe or understand is the crudest form of cognitive dissonance.

This brings us to the edge of a topic that requires much more discussion than I can give it here—namely, the relation between facts on the one hand and conceptual schemes or systems of representation on the other. My realism[7] about the subjective domain in all its forms implies a belief in the existence of facts beyond the reach of human concepts. Certainly it is possible for a human being to believe that there are facts which humans never *will* possess the requisite concepts to represent or comprehend. Indeed, it would be foolish to doubt this, given the finiteness of humanity's expectations. After all, there would have been transfinite numbers even if everyone had been wiped out by the Black Death before Cantor[8] discovered them. But one might also believe that there are facts which *could* not ever be represented or comprehended by human beings, even if the species lasted forever—simply because our structure does not permit us to operate with concepts of the requisite type. This impossibility might even be observed by other beings, but it is not clear that the existence of such beings, or the possibility of their existence, is a precondition of the significance of the hypothesis that there are humanly inaccessible facts. (After all, the nature of beings with access to humanly inaccessible facts is presumably itself a humanly inaccessible fact.) Reflection on what it is like to be a bat seems to lead us, therefore, to the conclusion that there are facts that do not consist in the truth of propositions expressible in a human language. We can be compelled to recognize the existence of such facts without being able to state or comprehend them.

I shall not pursue this subject, however. Its bearing on the topic before us (namely, the mind-body problem) is that it enables us to make a general observation about the subjective character of experience. Whatever may be the status of facts about what it is like to be a human being, or a bat, or a Martian, these appear to be facts that embody a particular point of view.

I am not adverting here to the alleged privacy of experience to its possessor. The point of view in question is not one accessible only to a single individual. Rather it is a *type*. It is often possible to take up a point of view other than one's own, so the comprehension of such facts is not limited to one's own case. There is a sense in which phenomenological facts are perfectly objective: One person can know or say of another what the quality of the other's experience is. They are subjective, however, in the sense that even this objective ascription of experience is possible only for someone sufficiently similar to the object of ascription to be able to adopt his point of view—to understand the ascription in the first person as well as in the third, so to speak. The more different from oneself the other experiencer is, the less success one can expect with this enterprise. In our own case we occupy the relevant point of view, but we will have as much difficulty understanding our own experience properly if we approach it from another point of view as we would if we tried to understand the experience of another species without taking up *its* point of view.

This bears directly on the mind-body problem. For if the facts of experience—facts about what it is like *for* the experiencing organism—are accessible only from one point of view, then it is a mystery how the true character of experiences could be revealed in the physical operation of that organism. The latter is a domain of objective facts par excellence—the kind that can be observed and understood from many points of view and by individuals with differing perceptual systems. There are no comparable imaginative obstacles to the acquisition of knowledge about bat neurophysiology by human scientists, and intelligent bats or Martians might learn more about the human brain than we ever will.

This is not by itself an argument against reduction. A Martian scientist with no understanding of visual perception could understand the rainbow, or lightning, or clouds as physical phenomena, though he would never be able to understand the human concepts of rainbow, lightning, or cloud, or the place these things occupy in our phenomenal world. The objective nature of the things picked out by these concepts could be apprehended by him because, although the concepts themselves are connected with a particular point of view and a particular visual phenomenology, the things apprehended from that point of view are not: They are observable from the point of view but external to it; hence they can be comprehended from other points of view also, either by the same organisms or by others. Lightning has an objective character that is not exhausted by its visual appearance, and this can be investigated by a Martian without vision. To be precise, it has a *more* objective character than is revealed in its visual appearance. In speaking of the move from subjective to objective characterization, I wish to remain noncommittal about the existence of an end point, the completely objective intrinsic nature of the thing, which one might or might not be able to reach. It may be more accurate to think of objectivity as a direction in which the understanding can travel. And in understanding a phenomenon like lightning, it is legitimate to go as far away as one can from a strictly human viewpoint.

In the case of experience, on the other hand, the connection with a particular point of view seems much closer. It is difficult to understand what could be meant by the *objective* character of an experience, apart from the particular point of view from which its subject apprehends it. After all, what would be left of what it was like to be a bat if one removed the viewpoint of the bat? But if experience does not have, in addition to its subjective character, an objective nature that can be apprehended from many different points of view, then how can it be supposed that a Martian investigating my brain might be observing physical processes which were my mental processes (as he might observe physical processes which were bolts of lightning), only from a different point of view? How, for that matter, could a human physiologist observe them from another point of view?

We appear to be faced with a general difficulty about psychophysical reduction. In other areas the process of reduction is a move in the direction of greater objectivity, toward a more accurate view of the real nature of things. This is accomplished by reducing our dependence on individual or species-specific points of view toward the objective of investigation. We describe it not in terms of the impressions it makes on our senses, but in terms of its more general effects and of properties detectable by means other than the human senses. The less it depends on a specifically human viewpoint, the more objective is our description. It is possible to follow this path because although the concepts and ideas we employ in thinking about the external world are initially applied from a point of view that involves our perceptual apparatus, they are used by us to refer to things beyond themselves—toward which we *have* the phenomenal point of view. Therefore we can abandon it in favor of another, and still be thinking about the same things.

Experience itself, however, does not seem to fit the pattern. The idea of moving from appearance to reality seems to make no sense here. What is the analogue in this case to pursuing a more objective understanding of the same phenomena by abandoning the initial subjective viewpoint toward them in favor of another that is more objective but concerns the same thing? Certainly it *appears* unlikely that we will get closer to the real nature of human experience by leaving behind the particularity of our human point of view and striving for a description in terms accessible to beings that could not imagine what it was like to be us. If the subjective character of experience is fully comprehensible only from one point of view, then any shift to greater objectivity—that is, less attachment to a specific viewpoint—does not take us nearer to the real nature of the phenomenon; it takes us farther away from it.

In a sense, the seeds of this objection to the reducibility of experience are already detectable in successful cases of reduction; for in discovering sound to be, in reality, a wave phenomenon in air or other media, we leave behind one viewpoint to take up another, and the auditory, human or animal viewpoint that we leave behind remains unreduced. Members of radically different species may both understand the same physical events in objective terms, and this does not require that they understand the phenomenal forms in which those events appear to the senses of members of the other species. Thus it is a condition of their referring to a common reality that their more particular viewpoints are not part of the common reality that they both apprehend. The reduction can succeed only if the species-specific viewpoint is omitted from what is to be reduced.

But while we are right to leave this point of view aside in seeking a fuller understanding of the external world, we cannot ignore it permanently, since it is the essence of the internal world, and not merely a point of view on it. Most of the neobehaviorism[9] of recent philosophical psychology results from the effort to substitute an objective concept of mind for the real thing, in order to have nothing left over which cannot be reduced. If we acknowledge that a physical theory of mind must account for the subjective character of experience, we must admit that no presently available conception gives us a clue how this could be done. The problem is unique. If mental processes are indeed physical processes, then there is something it is like, intrinsically, to undergo certain physical processes. What it is for such a thing to be the case remains a mystery.

What moral should be drawn from these reflections, and what should be done next? It would be a mistake to conclude that physicalism must be false. Nothing is proved by the inadequacy of physicalist hypotheses that assume a faulty objective analysis of mind. It would be truer to say that physicalism is a position we cannot understand because we do not at present have any conception of how it might be true. Perhaps it will be thought unreasonable to require such a conception as a condition of understanding. After all, it might be said, the meaning of physicalism is clear enough: Mental states are states of the body; mental events are physical events. We do not know *which* physical states and events they are, but that should not prevent us from understanding the hypothesis. What could be clearer than the words "is" and "are"?

But I believe it is precisely this apparent clarity of the word "is" that is deceptive. Usually, when we are told that *X* is *Y* we know *how* it is supposed to be true, but that depends on a conceptual or theoretical background and is not conveyed by the "is" alone. We know how both "*X*" and "*Y*" refer, and the kinds of things to which they refer, and we have a rough idea how the two referential paths might converge on a single thing, be it an object, a person, a process, an event, or whatever. But when the two terms of the identification are very disparate it may not be so clear how it could be true. We may not have even a rough idea of how the two referential paths could converge, or what kind of things they might converge on, and a theoretical framework may have to be supplied to enable us to understand this. Without the framework, an air of mysticism surrounds the identification.

This explains the magical flavor of popular presentations of fundamental scientific discoveries, given out as propositions to which one must subscribe without really understanding them. For example, people are now told at an early age that all matter is really energy. But despite the fact that they know what "is" means, most of them never form a conception of what makes this claim true, because they lack the theoretical background.

At the present time the status of physicalism is similar to that which the hypothesis that matter is energy would have had if uttered by a pre-Socratic philosopher. We do not have the beginnings of a conception of how it might be true. In order to understand the hypothesis that a mental event is a physical event, we require more than an understanding of the word "is." The idea of how a mental and a physical term might refer to the same thing is lacking, and the usual analogies with theoretical identification in other fields fail to supply it. They fail because if we construe the reference of mental terms to physical events on the usual model, we either get a reappearance of separate subjective events as the effects through which mental reference to physical events is secured, or else we get a false account of how mental terms refer (for example, a causal behaviorist one).

Strangely enough, we may have evidence for the truth of something we cannot really understand. Suppose a caterpillar is locked in a sterile safe by someone unfamiliar with insect metamorphosis, and weeks later the safe is reopened, revealing a butterfly. If the person knows that the safe has been shut the whole time, he has reason to believe that the butterfly is or was once the caterpillar, without having any idea in what sense this might be so. (One possibility is that the caterpillar contained a tiny winged parasite that devoured it and grew into the butterfly.)

It is conceivable that we are in such a position with regard to physicalism. Donald Davidson has argued that if mental events have physical causes and effects, they must have physical descriptions. He holds that we have reason to believe this even though we do not—and in fact *could* not—have a general psychophysical theory.[10] His argument applies to intentional mental events, but I think we also have some reason to believe that sensations are physical processes, without being in a position to understand how. Davidson's position is that certain physical events have irreducibly mental properties, and perhaps some view describable in this way is correct. But nothing of which we can now form a conception corresponds to it; nor have we any idea what a theory would be like that enabled us to conceive of it.

Very little work has been done on the basic question (from which mention of the brain can be entirely omitted) whether any sense can be made of experiences having an objective character at all. Does it make sense, in other words, to ask what my experiences are *really* like, as opposed to how they appear to me? We cannot genuinely understand the hypothesis that their nature is captured in a physical description unless we understand the more fundamental idea that they *have* an objective nature (or that objective processes can have a subjective nature).

I should like to close with a speculative proposal. It may be possible to approach the gap between subjective and objective from another direction. Setting aside temporarily the relation between the mind and the brain, we can pursue a more objective understanding of the mental in its own right. At present we are completely unequipped to think about the subjective character of experience without relying on the imagination—without taking up the point of view of the experiential subject. This should be regarded as a challenge to form new concepts and devise a new method—an objective phenomenology not dependent on empathy or the imagination. Though presumably it would not capture everything, its goal would be to describe, at least in part, the subjective character of experiences in a form comprehensible to beings incapable of having those experiences.

We would have to develop such a phenomenology to describe the sonar experiences of bats; but it would also be possible to begin with humans. One might try, for example, to develop concepts that could be used to explain to a person blind from birth what it was like to see. One would reach a blank wall eventually, but it should be possible to devise a method of expressing in objective terms much more than we can at present, and with much greater precision. The loose intermodal analogies—for example, "Red is like the sound of a trumpet"—which crop up in discussions of this subject are of little use. That should be clear to anyone who has both heard a trumpet and seen red. But structural features of perception might be more accessible to objective description, even though something would be left out. And concepts alternative to those we learn in the first person may enable us to arrive at a kind of understanding even of our own experience which is denied us by the very ease of description and lack of distance that subjective concepts afford.

Apart from its own interest, a phenomenology that is in this sense objective may permit questions about the physical basis of experience to assume a more intelligible form. Aspects of subjective experience that admitted this kind of objective description might be better candidates for objective explanations of a more familiar sort. But whether or not this guess is correct, it seems unlikely that any physical theory of mind can be contemplated until more thought has been given to the general problem of subjective and objective. Otherwise we cannot even pose the mind-body problem without sidestepping it.

NOTES

1. *psychophysical identification:* the equating of the mind (psyche) with the body. [D. C. ABEL]
2. Nagel here gives examples of reductionism: water reduced to hydrogen and oxygen, intelligence reduced to computing ability (a *Turing machine* is a kind of computer imagined by the British mathematician Alan Turing [1912–1954]), lightning reduced to the discharge of electricity, genes reduced to DNA, and oak trees reduced to hydrocarbons. [D. C. ABEL]
3. To analyze conscious experience in terms of *functional states* is to define it in terms of the function it performs; to analyze it in terms of *intentional states* is to define it in terms of its property of referring to objects, of being *about* objects. [D. C. ABEL]
4. *phenomenological:* relating to *phenomenology,* the study of how things appear to and are experienced by a subject. [D. C. ABEL]
5. *phenomenal:* relating to phenomena. [D. C. ABEL]
6. the *pour soi* and the *en soi:* the "for itself" and the "in itself" (French). These terms are used by the French philosopher Jean-Paul Sartre to designate, respectively, mere things and consciousness. For a biography of Sartre, see p. 392. [D. C. ABEL]
7. *realism:* the view that a kind of entity (here, subjective states) really exists. [D. C. ABEL]
8. Georg Cantor (1845–1918) was a German mathematician. [D. C. ABEL]
9. *neobehaviorism:* the view that statements about the mind should be reformulated entirely in terms of physical, observable behavior. [D. C. ABEL]
10. Donald Davidson, "Mental Events," in *Experience and Theory,* ed. Lawrence Foster and J. W. Swanson (Amherst, Mass.: University of Massachusetts Press, 1970), pp. 79–101. [T. NAGEL]

Facing Up to the Problem of Consciousness

David J. Chalmers

David J. Chalmers was born in 1966 in Sydney, Australia. After completing his bachelor of science degree in mathematics in 1986 at the University of Adelaide in Australia, he enrolled in the graduate program in mathematics at Oxford University. After a year at Oxford, his interests shifted to philosophy and he entered the doctoral program in philosophy and cognitive science at Indiana University, where he completed his degree in 1993. For the next two years Chalmers was a McConnell Fellow in Philosophy, Neuroscience, and Psychology at Washington University in St. Louis. In 1995 he accepted an appointment as Assistant Professor in the Department of Philosophy at the University of California, Santa Cruz. He was promoted to Associate Professor in 1997 and to Professor the following year. In 1999 he transferred to the University of Arizona, where he was named Professor of Philosophy and Associate Director of the Center for Consciousness Studies. He was appointed Director for the Center of Consciousness Studies in 2002 and became Regents Professor in 2004. Since 2004 Chalmers has been at the Australian National University, serving as an Australian Research Council Federation Fellow, Professor of Philosophy, and Director of the Centre for Consciousness. He is a member of the Board of Directors of the Association for the Scientific Study of Consciousness and an associate editor of *Psyche: An Interdisciplinary Journal of Research on Consciousness.* He serves on over a dozen editorial boards and has organized numerous conferences on the topic of consciousness.

Chalmers's publications include *The Conscious Mind: In Search of a Fundamental Theory* (1996), *Toward a Science of Consciousness III: The Third Tucson Discussions and Debates* (coeditor with Stuart R. Hameroff and Alfred W. Kaszniak, 1999), and *Philosophy of Mind: Classical and Contemporary Readings* (editor, 2002). The book *Explaining Consciousness: The "Hard Problem,"* edited by Jonathan Shear (1997), is a collection of critical essays on Chalmers's views on consciousness, with a detailed response by Chalmers to each of his critics.

Our reading is from Chalmers's 1996 article, "Facing Up to the Problem of Consciousness." Chalmers distinguishes the "easy problems" of consciousness from the "hard problem." The (relatively) easy problems are those that can be explained in terms of the computational or neural mechanisms of the brain—for example, the problem of how we integrate information. The hard problem is the phenomenon of experience, the subjective feel of "what it is like" to be in a conscious state. The easy problems are easy because they can be solved by explaining cognitive functions. The hard problem is hard because experience is something that occurs *in addition* to functional activity, and no explanation of a function will itself explain why the performance of the function is accompanied by experience. Consciousness cannot be *reduced to* (explained entirely in terms of) physical processes because reductive explanations do not account for the experience that accompanies these processes.

Chalmers contends that consciousness can be explained only by a *nonreductive* theory—one that posits a nonphysical element. We must expand our ontology (our view of what is real) by positing consciousness as a nonphysical, fundamental component of reality. Once we posit consciousness as a nonphysical element of our ontology, we can begin constructing a *theory* of consciousness that explains how consciousness is related to the physical world. Chalmers's theory of consciousness contains three principles: structural coherence (the structure of any conscious experience has the same structure as its physical underpinnings), organizational invariance (any two systems with the same functional organization will have qualitatively identical conscious experiences), and the double-aspect theory of information (some information—and perhaps *all* information— has two basic aspects, physical and experiential). Chalmers's book *The Conscious Mind* presents this theory in much greater detail.

I. INTRODUCTION

Consciousness poses the most baffling problems in the science of the mind. There is nothing that we know more intimately than conscious experience, but there is nothing that is harder to explain. All sorts of mental phenomena have yielded to scientific investigation in recent years, but consciousness has stubbornly resisted. Many have tried to explain it, but the explanations always seem to fall short of the target. Some have been led to suppose that the problem is intractable, and that no good explanation can be given.

To make progress on the problem of consciousness, we have to confront it directly. In this paper, I first isolate the truly hard part of the problem, separating it from more tractable parts and giving an account of why it is so difficult to explain. . . . In the second half of the paper, I argue that if we move to a new kind of nonreductive explanation, a naturalistic[1] account of consciousness can be given. I put forward my own candidate for such an account: a nonreductive theory based on principles of structural coherence and organizational invariance, and a double-aspect theory of information.

II. THE EASY PROBLEMS AND THE HARD PROBLEM

There is not just one problem of consciousness. "Consciousness" is an ambiguous term, referring to many different phenomena. Each of these phenomena needs to be explained, but some are easier to explain than others. At the start, it is useful to divide the associated problems of consciousness into "hard" and "easy" problems. The easy problems of consciousness are those that seem directly susceptible to the standard methods of cognitive science, whereby a phenomenon is explained in terms of computational or neural mechanisms. The hard problems are those that seem to resist those methods.

The easy problems of consciousness include those of explaining the following phenomena:

- the ability to discriminate, categorize, and react to environmental stimuli;
- the integration of information by a cognitive system;
- the reportability of mental states;
- the ability of a system to access its own internal states;

- the focus of attention;
- the deliberate control of behavior;
- the difference between wakefulness and sleep.

All of these phenomena are associated with the notion of consciousness. For example, one sometimes says that a mental state is conscious when it is verbally reportable, or when it is internally accessible. Sometimes a system is said to be conscious of some information when it has the ability to react on the basis of that information, or, more strongly, when it attends to that information, or when it can integrate that information and exploit it in the sophisticated control of behavior. We sometimes say that an action is conscious precisely when it is deliberate. Often, we say that an organism is conscious as another way of saying that it is awake.

There is no real issue about whether *these* phenomena can be explained scientifically. All of them are straightforwardly vulnerable to explanation in terms of computational or neural mechanisms. To explain access and reportability, for example, we need only specify the mechanism by which information about internal states is retrieved and made available for verbal report. To explain the integration of information, we need only exhibit mechanisms by which information is brought together and exploited by later processes. For an account of sleep and wakefulness, an appropriate neurophysiological account of the processes responsible for organisms' contrasting behavior in those states will suffice. In each case, an appropriate cognitive or neurophysiological model can clearly do the explanatory work.

If these phenomena were all there were to consciousness, then consciousness would not be much of a problem. Although we do not yet have anything close to a complete explanation of these phenomena, we have a clear idea of how we might go about explaining them. This is why I call these problems the easy problems. Of course, "easy" is a relative term. Getting the details right will probably take a century or two of difficult empirical work. Still, there is every reason to believe that the methods of cognitive science and neuroscience will succeed.

The really hard problem of consciousness is the problem of *experience*. When we think and perceive, there is a whir of information-processing, but there is also a subjective aspect. As Nagel has put it, there is *something it is like* to be a conscious organism.[2] This subjective aspect is experience. When we see, for example, we *experience* visual sensations: the felt quality of redness, the experience of dark and light, the quality of depth in a visual field. Other experiences go along with perception in different modalities: the sound of a clarinet, the smell of mothballs. Then there are bodily sensations, from pains to orgasms; mental images that are conjured up internally; the felt quality of emotion; and the experience of a stream of conscious thought. What unites all of these states is that there is something it is like to be in them. All of them are states of experience.

It is undeniable that some organisms are subjects of experience. But the question of how it is that these systems are subjects of experience is perplexing. Why is it that when our cognitive systems engage in visual and auditory information-processing, we have visual or auditory experience: the quality of deep blue, the sensation of middle C? How can we explain why there is something it is like to entertain a mental image, or to experience an emotion? It is widely agreed that experience arises from a physical basis, but we have no good explanation of why and how it so arises. Why should physical processing give rise to a rich inner life at all? It seems objectively unreasonable that it should, and yet it does.

If any problem qualifies as *the* problem of consciousness, it is this one. In this central sense of "consciousness," an organism is conscious if there is something it is like to be that organism, and a mental state is conscious if there is something it is like to be in that state. Sometimes terms such as "phenomenal[3] consciousness" and "qualia"[4] are also used here, but I find it more natural to speak of "conscious experience" or simply "experience." Another useful way to avoid confusion is to reserve the term "consciousness" for the phenomena of experience, using the less loaded term "awareness" for the more straightforward phenomena described earlier. If such a convention were widely adopted, communication would be much easier; as things stand, those who talk about "consciousness" are frequently talking past each other.

The ambiguity of the term "consciousness" is often exploited by both philosophers and scientists writing on the subject. It is common to see a paper on consciousness begin with an invocation of the mystery of consciousness, noting the strange intangibility and ineffability of subjectivity, and worrying that so far we have no theory of the phenomenon. Here, the topic is clearly the hard problem—the problem of experience. In the second half of the paper, the tone becomes more optimistic, and the author's own theory of consciousness is outlined. Upon examination, this theory turns out to be a theory of one of the more straightforward phenomena—of reportability, of introspective access, or whatever. At the close, the author declares that consciousness has turned out to be tractable after all, but the reader is left feeling like the victim of a bait-and-switch. The hard problem remains untouched.

III. FUNCTIONAL EXPLANATION

Why are the easy problems easy, and why is the hard problem hard? The easy problems are easy precisely because they concern the explanation of cognitive *abilities* and *functions*. To explain a cognitive function, we need only specify a mechanism that can perform the function. The methods of cognitive science are well-suited for this sort of explanation, and so are well-suited to the easy problems of consciousness. By contrast, the hard problem is hard precisely because it is not a problem about the performance of functions. The problem persists even when the performance of all the relevant functions is explained.[5]

To explain reportability, for instance, is just to explain how a system could perform the function of producing reports on internal states. To explain internal access, we need to explain how a system could be appropriately affected by its internal states and use information about those states in directing later processes. To explain integration and control, we need to explain how a system's central processes can bring information contents together and use them in the facilitation of various behaviors. These are all problems about the explanation of functions.

How do we explain the performance of a function? By specifying a *mechanism* that performs the function. Here, neurophysiological and cognitive modeling are perfect for the task. If we want a detailed low-level explanation, we can specify the neural mechanism that is responsible for the function. If we want a more abstract explanation, we can specify a mechanism in computational terms. Either way, a full and satisfying explanation will result. Once we have specified the neural or computational mechanism that performs the function of verbal report, for example, the bulk of our work in explaining reportability is over. . . .

Throughout the higher-level sciences, reductive explanation works in just this way. To explain the gene, for instance, we needed to specify the mechanism that stores and transmits hereditary information from one generation to the next. It turns out that DNA performs this function; once we explain how the function is performed, we have explained the gene. To explain life, we ultimately need to explain how a system can reproduce, adapt to its environment, metabolize, and so on. All of these are questions about the performance of functions, and so are well-suited to reductive explanation. The same holds for most problems in cognitive science. To explain learning, we need to explain the way in which a system's behavioral capacities are modified in light of environmental information, and the way in which new information can be brought to bear in adapting a system's actions to its environment. If we show how a neural or computational mechanism does the job, we have explained learning. We can say the same for other cognitive phenomena, such as perception, memory, and language. Sometimes the relevant functions need to be characterized quite subtly, but it is clear that insofar as cognitive science explains these phenomena at all, it does so by explaining the performance of functions.

When it comes to conscious experience, this sort of explanation fails. What makes the hard problem hard and almost unique is that it goes *beyond* problems about the performance of functions. To see this, note that even when we have explained the performance of all the cognitive and behavioral functions in the vicinity of experience—perceptual discrimination, categorization, internal access, verbal report—there may still remain a further unanswered question: *Why is the performance of these functions accompanied by experience?* A simple explanation of the functions leaves this question open.

There is no analogous further question in the explanation of genes, or of life, or of learning. If someone says "I can see that you have explained how DNA stores and transmits hereditary information from one generation to the next, but you have not explained how it is a *gene*," then he or she is making a conceptual mistake. All it means to be a gene is to be an entity that performs the relevant storage and transmission function. But if someone says "I can see that you have explained how information is discriminated, integrated, and reported, but you have not explained how it is *experienced*," he or she is not making a conceptual mistake. This is a nontrivial further question.

This further question is the key question in the problem of consciousness. Why doesn't all this information-processing go on "in the dark," free of any inner feel? Why is it that when electromagnetic waveforms impinge on a retina and are discriminated and categorized by a visual system, this discrimination and categorization is experienced as a sensation of vivid red? We know that conscious experience *does* arise when these functions are performed, but the very fact that it arises is the central mystery. There is an explanatory gap[6] between the functions and experience, and we need an explanatory bridge to cross it. A mere account of the functions stays on one side of the gap, so the materials for the bridge must be found elsewhere. . . .

V. THE EXTRA INGREDIENT

. . . Purely physical explanation is well-suited to the explanation of physical *structures*, explaining macroscopic structures in terms of detailed microstructural constituents; and it provides a satisfying explanation of the performance of *functions*, accounting for these functions in terms of the physical mechanisms that perform them. This is because a physical account can *entail* the facts about structures and functions: Once the internal details of the physical account are given, the structural and functional properties fall out as an automatic consequence. But the structure and dynamics of physical processes yield only more structure and dynamics, so structures and functions are all we can expect these processes to explain. The facts about experience cannot be an automatic consequence of any physical account, as it is conceptually coherent that any given process could exist without experience. Experience may *arise* from the physical, but it is not *entailed* by the physical.

The moral of all this is that *you can't explain conscious experience on the cheap.* It is a remarkable fact that reductive methods—methods that explain a high-level phenomenon wholly in terms of more basic physical processes—work well in so many domains. In a sense, one *can* explain most biological and cognitive phenomena on the cheap, in that these phenomena are seen as automatic consequences of more fundamental processes. It would be wonderful if reductive methods could explain experience, too (I hoped for a long time that they might). Unfortunately, there are systematic reasons why these methods must fail. Reductive methods are successful in most domains because what needs explaining in those domains are structures and functions, and these are the kind of thing that a physical account can entail. When it comes to a problem over and above the explanation of structures and functions, these methods are impotent. . . .

It is tempting to note that all sorts of puzzling phenomena have eventually turned out to be explainable in physical terms. But each of these were problems about the observable behavior of physical objects, coming down to problems in the explanation of structures and functions. Because of this, these phenomena have always been the kind of thing that a physical account *might* explain, even if at some points there have been good reasons to suspect that no such explanation would be forthcoming. The tempting induction[7] from these cases fails in the case of consciousness, which is not a problem about physical structures and functions. The problem of consciousness is puzzling in an entirely different way. An analysis of the problem shows us that conscious experience is just not the kind of thing that a wholly reductive account could succeed in explaining.

VI. NONREDUCTIVE EXPLANATION

At this point some are tempted to give up, holding that we will never have a theory of conscious experience. McGinn, for example, argues that the problem is too hard for our limited minds; we are "cognitively closed" with respect to the phenomenon.[8] Others have argued that conscious experience lies outside the domain of scientific theory altogether.

I think this pessimism is premature. This is not the place to give up; it is the place where things get interesting. When simple methods of explanation are ruled out, we need to investigate the alternatives. Given that reductive explanation fails, *nonreductive* explanation is the natural choice.

Although a remarkable number of phenomena have turned out to be explicable wholly in terms of entities simpler than themselves, this is not universal. In physics, it occasionally happens that an entity has to be taken as *fundamental*. Fundamental entities are not explained in terms of anything simpler. Instead, one takes them as basic, and gives a theory of how they relate to everything else in the world. For example, in the nineteenth century it turned out that electromagnetic processes could not be explained in terms of the wholly mechanical processes that previous physical theories appealed to, so Maxwell[9] and others introduced electromagnetic charge and electromagnetic forces as new fundamental components of a physical theory. To explain electromagnetism, the ontology[10] of physics had to be expanded. New basic properties and basic laws were needed to give a satisfactory account of the phenomena.

Other features that physical theory takes as fundamental include mass and space-time. No attempt is made to explain these features in terms of anything simpler. But this does not rule out the possibility of a theory of mass or of space-time. There is an intricate theory of how these features interrelate, and of the basic laws they enter into. These basic principles are used to explain many familiar phenomena concerning mass, space, and time at a higher level.

I suggest that a theory of consciousness should take experience as fundamental. We know that a theory of consciousness requires the addition of *something* fundamental to our ontology, as everything in physical theory is compatible with the absence of consciousness. We might add some entirely new nonphysical feature, from which experience can be derived, but it is hard to see what such a feature would be like. More likely, we will take experience itself as a fundamental feature of the world, alongside mass, charge, and space-time. If we take experience as fundamental, then we can go about the business of constructing a theory of experience.

Where there is a fundamental property, there are fundamental laws. A nonreductive theory of experience will add new principles to the furniture of the basic laws of nature. These basic principles will ultimately carry the explanatory burden in a theory of consciousness. Just as we explain familiar high-level phenomena involving mass in terms of more basic principles involving mass and other entities, we might explain familiar phenomena involving experience in terms of more basic principles involving experience and other entities.

In particular, a nonreductive theory of experience will specify basic principles telling us how experience depends on physical features of the world. These *psychophysical* principles will not interfere with physical laws, as it seems that physical laws already form a closed system. Rather, they will be a supplement to a physical theory. A physical theory gives a theory of physical processes, and a psychophysical theory tells us how those processes give rise to experience. We know that experience depends on physical processes, but we also know that this dependence cannot be derived from physical laws alone. The new basic principles postulated by a nonreductive theory give us the extra ingredient that we need to build an explanatory bridge. . . .

VII. TOWARD A THEORY OF CONSCIOUSNESS

It is not too soon to begin work on a theory. We are already in a position to understand certain key facts about the relationship between physical processes and experience, and about the regularities that connect them. Once reductive explanation is set aside, we can lay those facts on the table so that they can play their proper role as the initial pieces in a nonreductive theory of consciousness, and as constraints on the basic laws that constitute an ultimate theory.

There is an obvious problem that plagues the development of a theory of consciousness, and that is the paucity of objective data. Conscious experience is not directly observable in an experimental context, so we cannot generate data about the relationship between physical processes and experience at will. Nevertheless, we all have access to a rich source of data in our own case. Many important regularities between experience and processing can be inferred from considerations about one's own experience. There are also good indirect sources of data from observable cases, as when one relies on the verbal report of a subject as an indication of experience. These methods have their limitations, but we have more than enough data to get a theory off the ground.

Philosophical analysis is also useful in getting value for money out of the data we have. This sort of analysis can yield a number of principles relating consciousness and cognition, thereby strongly constraining the shape of an ultimate theory. The method of thought-experimentation can also yield significant rewards, as we will see. Finally, the fact that we are searching for a *fundamental* theory means that we can appeal to such nonempirical constraints as simplicity, homogeneity, and the like in developing a theory. We must seek to systematize the information we have, to extend it as far as possible by careful analysis, and then make the inference to the simplest possible theory that explains the data while remaining a plausible candidate to be part of the fundamental furniture of the world.

Such theories will always retain an element of speculation that is not present in other scientific theories, because of the impossibility of conclusive intersubjective experimental tests. Still, we can certainly construct theories that are compatible with the data that we have, and evaluate them in comparison to each other. Even in the absence of intersubjective observation, there are numerous criteria available for the evaluation of such theories: simplicity, internal coherence, coherence with theories in other domains, the ability to reproduce the properties of experience that are familiar from our own case, and even an overall fit with the dictates of common sense. Perhaps there will be significant indeterminacies remaining even when all these constraints are applied, but we can at least develop plausible candidates. Only when candidate theories have been developed will we be able to evaluate them.

A nonreductive theory of consciousness will consist in a number of *psychophysical principles,* principles connecting the properties of physical processes to the properties of experience. We can think of these principles as encapsulating the way in which experience arises from the physical. Ultimately, these principles should tell us what sort of physical systems will have associated experiences, and for the systems that do, they should tell us what sort of physical properties are relevant to the emergence of experience, and just what sort of experience we should expect any given physical system to yield. This is a tall order, but there is no reason why we should not get started.

In what follows, I present my own candidates for the psychophysical principles that might go into a theory of consciousness. The first two of these are *nonbasic principles*—systematic connections between processing and experience at a relatively high level. These principles can play a significant role in developing and constraining a theory of consciousness, but they are not cast at a sufficiently fundamental level to qualify as truly basic laws. The final principle is my candidate for a *basic principle* that might form the cornerstone of a fundamental theory of consciousness. This final principle is particularly speculative, but it is the kind of speculation that is required if we are ever to have a satisfying theory of consciousness. I can present these principles only briefly here; I argue for them at much greater length in *The Conscious Mind.*[11]

1. The Principle of Structural Coherence

This is a principle of coherence between the *structure of consciousness* and the *structure of awareness.* Recall that "awareness" was used earlier to refer to the various functional phenomena that are associated with consciousness. I am now using it to refer to a somewhat more specific process in the cognitive underpinnings of experience. In particular, the contents of awareness are to be understood as those information contents that are accessible to central systems, and brought to bear in a widespread way in the control of behavior. Briefly put, we can think of awareness as *direct availability for global*[12] *control.* To a first approximation, the contents of awareness are the contents that are directly accessible and potentially reportable, at least in a language-using system.

Awareness is a purely functional notion, but it is nevertheless intimately linked to conscious experience. In familiar cases, wherever we find consciousness, we find awareness. Wherever there is conscious experience, there is some corresponding information in the cognitive system that is available in the control of behavior, and available for verbal report. Conversely, it seems that whenever information is available for report and for global control, there is a corresponding conscious experience. Thus, there is a direct correspondence between consciousness and awareness.

The correspondence can be taken further. It is a central fact about experience that it has a complex structure. The visual field has a complex geometry, for instance. There are also relations of similarity and difference between experiences, and relations in such things as relative intensity. Every subject's experience can be at least partly characterized and decomposed in terms of these structural properties: similarity and difference relations, perceived location, relative intensity, geometric structure, and so on. It is also a central fact that to each of these structural features, there is a corresponding feature in the information-processing structure of awareness.

Take color sensations as an example. For every distinction between color experiences, there is a corresponding distinction in processing. The different phenomenal colors that we experience form a complex three-dimensional space, varying in hue, saturation, and intensity. The properties of this space can be recovered from information-processing considerations: Examination of the visual systems shows that waveforms of light are discriminated and analyzed along three different axes, and it is this three-dimensional information that is relevant to later processing. The three-dimensional structure of phenomenal color space therefore corresponds directly to the three-dimensional structure of visual awareness. This is precisely what we would expect. After all, every color distinction corresponds to some reportable information, and therefore to a distinction that is represented in the structure of processing.

In a more straightforward way, the geometric structure of the visual field is directly reflected in a structure that can be recovered from visual processing. Every geometric relation corresponds to something that can be reported and is therefore cognitively represented. If we were given only the story about information-processing in an agent's visual and cognitive system, we could not *directly* observe that agent's visual experiences, but we could nevertheless infer those experiences' structural properties.

In general, any information that is consciously experienced will also be cognitively represented. The fine-grained structure of the visual field will correspond to some fine-grained structure in visual processing. The same goes for experiences in other modalities, and even for nonsensory experiences. Internal mental images have geometric properties that are represented in processing. Even emotions have structural properties, such as relative intensity, that correspond directly to a structural property of processing; where there is greater intensity, we find a greater effect on later processes. In general, precisely because the structural properties of experience are accessible and reportable, those properties will be directly represented in the structure of awareness.

It is this isomorphism[13] between the structures of consciousness and awareness that constitutes the principle of structural coherence. This principle reflects the central fact that even though cognitive processes do not conceptually entail facts about conscious experience, consciousness and cognition do not float free of one another but cohere in an intimate way.

This principle has its limits. It allows us to recover structural properties of experience from information-processing properties, but not all properties of experience are structural properties. There are properties of experience, such as the intrinsic nature of a sensation of red, that cannot be fully captured in a structural description. The very intelligibility of inverted spectrum scenarios, where experiences of red and green are inverted but all structural properties remain the same, shows that structural properties constrain experience without exhausting it. Nevertheless, the very fact that we feel compelled to leave structural properties unaltered when we imagine experiences inverted between functionally identical systems shows how central the principle of structural coherence is to our conception of our mental lives. It is not a *logically* necessary principle, as after all we can imagine all the information processing occurring without any experience at all, but it is nevertheless a strong and familiar constraint on the psychophysical connection. . . .

2. The Principle of Organizational Invariance

This principle states that any two systems with the same fine-grained *functional organization* will have qualitatively identical experiences. If the causal patterns of neural organization were duplicated in silicon, for example, with a silicon chip for every neuron and the same patterns of interaction, then the same experiences would arise. According to this principle, what matters for the emergence of experience is not the specific physical makeup of a system, but the abstract pattern of causal interaction between its components. This principle is controversial, of course. Some have thought that consciousness is tied to a specific biology,[14] so that a silicon isomorph[15] of a human need not be conscious. I believe that the principle can be given significant support by the analysis of thought-experiments, however.

Very briefly: Suppose (for the purposes of a reductio ad absurdum)[16] that the principle is false, and that there could be two functionally isomorphic systems with different experiences. Perhaps only one of the systems is conscious, or perhaps both are conscious but they have different experiences. For the purposes of illustration, let us say that one system is made of neurons and the other of silicon, and that one experiences red where the other experiences blue. The two systems have the same organization, so we can imagine gradually transforming one into the other, perhaps replacing neurons one at a time by silicon chips with the same local function. We thus gain a spectrum of intermediate cases, each with the same organization, but with slightly different physical makeup and slightly different experiences. Along this spectrum, there must be two systems A and B between which we replace less than one tenth of the system, but whose experiences differ. These two systems are physically identical, except that a small neural circuit in A has been replaced by a silicon circuit in B.

The key step in the thought-experiment is to take the relevant neural circuit in A, and install alongside it a causally isomorphic silicon circuit, with a switch between the two. What happens when we flip the switch? By hypothesis, the system's conscious experiences will change; from red to blue, say, for the purposes of illustration. This follows from the fact that the system after the change is essentially a version of B, whereas before the change it is just A.

But given the assumptions, there is no way for the system to *notice* the changes! Its causal organization stays constant, so that all of its functional states and behavioral dispositions stay fixed. As far as the system is concerned, nothing unusual has happened. There is no room for the thought, "Hmm! Something strange just happened!" In general, the structure of any such thought must be reflected in processing, but the structure of processing remains constant here. If there were to be such a thought, it must float entirely free of the system and would be utterly impotent to affect later processing. (If it affected later processing, the systems would be functionally distinct, contrary to hypothesis.) We might even flip the switch a number of times, so that experiences of red and blue dance back and forth before the system's "inner eye." According to the hypothesis, the system can never notice these "dancing qualia."

This I take to be a reductio [ad absurdum] of the original assumption. It is a central fact about experience, very familiar from our own case, that whenever experiences change significantly and we are paying attention, we can notice the change; if this were not to be the case, we would be led to the skeptical possibility that our experiences are dancing before our eyes all the time. This hypothesis has the same status as the possibility that the world was created five minutes ago: Perhaps it is logically coherent, but it is not plausible. Given the extremely plausible assumption that changes in experience correspond to changes in processing, we are led to the conclusion that the original hypothesis is impossible, and that any two functionally isomorphic systems must have the same sort of experiences. . . .

3. The Double-Aspect Theory of Information

The two preceding principles have been *nonbasic* principles. They involve high-level notions such as "awareness" and "organization," and therefore lie at the wrong level to constitute the fundamental laws in a theory of consciousness. Nevertheless, they act as strong constraints. What is further needed are *basic* principles that fit these constraints and that might ultimately explain them.

The basic principle that I suggest centrally involves the notion of *information*. I understand information in more or less the sense of Shannon.[17] Where there is information, there are *information states* embedded in an *information space*. An information space has a basic structure of *difference* relations between its elements, characterizing the ways in which different elements in a space are similar or different, possibly in complex ways. An information space is an abstract object, but following Shannon we can see information as *physically embodied* when there is a space of distinct physical states, the differences between which can be transmitted down some causal pathway. The states that are transmitted can be seen as themselves constituting an information space. To borrow a phrase from Bateson, physical information is a "difference that makes a difference."[18]

The double-aspect principle stems from the observation that there is a direct isomorphism between certain physically embodied information spaces and certain phenomenal (or experiential) information spaces. From the same sort of observations that went into the principle of structural coherence, we can note that the differences between phenomenal states have a structure that corresponds directly to the differences embedded in physical processes; in particular, to those differences that make a difference down certain causal pathways implicated in global availability and control. That is, we can find the *same* abstract information space embedded in physical processing and in conscious experience.

This leads to a natural hypothesis: that information (or at least some information) has two basic aspects, a physical aspect and a phenomenal aspect. This has the status of a basic principle that might underlie and explain the emergence of experience from the physical. Experience arises by virtue of its status of one aspect of information, when the other aspect is found embodied in physical processing. . . .

The double-aspect principle is extremely speculative and is also underdetermined,[19] leaving a number of key questions unanswered. An obvious question is whether *all* information has a phenomenal aspect. One possibility is that we need a further constraint on the fundamental theory, indicating just what *sort* of information has a phenomenal aspect. The other possibility is that there is no such constraint. If not, then experience is much more widespread than we might have believed, as information is everywhere. This is counterintuitive at first, but on reflection I think the position gains a certain plausibility and elegance. Where there is simple information processing, there is simple experience, and where there is complex information processing, there is complex experience. A mouse has a simpler information-processing structure than a human, and has correspondingly simpler experience; perhaps a thermostat, a maximally simple information-processing structure, might have maximally simple experience? Indeed, if experience is truly a fundamental property, it would be surprising for it to arise only every now and then; most fundamental properties are more evenly spread. In any case, this is very much an open question, but I believe that the position is not as implausible as it is often thought to be. . . .

VIII. CONCLUSION

The theory I have presented is speculative, but it is a candidate theory. I suspect that the principles of structural coherence and organizational invariance will be planks in any satisfactory theory of consciousness; the status of the double-aspect theory of information is less certain. Indeed, right now it is more of an idea than a theory. To have any hope of eventual explanatory success, it will have to be specified more fully and fleshed out into a more powerful form. Still, reflection on just what is plausible and implausible about it, on where it works and where it fails, can only lead to a better theory.

Most existing theories of consciousness either deny the phenomenon, explain something else, or elevate the problem to an eternal mystery. I hope to have shown that it is possible to make progress on the problem even while taking it seriously. To make further progress, we will need further investigation, more refined theories, and more careful analysis. The hard problem is a hard problem, but there is no reason to believe that it will remain permanently unsolved.

NOTES

1. *naturalistic:* relating to *naturalism,* the view that nature is all that exists, and that nothing supernatural exists. [D. C. ABEL]
2. Thomas Nagel, "What Is It Like to Be a Bat?," *Philosophical Review* 83 (October 1974): 435–50. [D. J. CHALMERS]
3. *phenomenal:* relating to experienced phenomena. [D. C. ABEL]
4. *qualia* (singular *quale*): (Latin, "things of such a kind") qualitative properties of conscious experience. [D. C. ABEL]
5. Here "function" is not used in the narrow teleological sense [that is, referring to goals or purposes] of something that a system is designed to do, but in the broader sense of any causal role in the production of behavior that a system might perform. [D. J. CHALMERS]
6. *explanatory gap:* a term due to Joseph Levine, "Materialism and Qualia: The Explanatory Gap," *Pacific Philosophical Quarterly* 64 (October 1983): 354–61. [D. J. CHALMERS]
7. *induction:* the inference of a general conclusion from particular cases. [D. C. ABEL]
8. Colin McGinn, "Can We Solve the Mind-Body Problem?," *Mind,* new series 98 (1989): 349–66. [D. J. CHALMERS]
9. James Clerk Maxwell (1831–1879), a Scottish physicist. [D. C. ABEL]
10. *ontology:* the study of the nature and kinds of reality. [D. C. ABEL]
11. David J. Chalmers, *Conscious Mind: In Search of a Fundamental Theory* (New York: Oxford University Press, 1996). [D. J. CHALMERS]
12. *global:* relating to the whole (organism). [D. C. ABEL]
13. *isomorphism:* the quality of having the same form or structure. [D. C. ABEL]
14. For example, John R. Searle in "Minds, Brains and Programs," *The Behavioral and Brain Sciences* 3 (1980): 417–57. [D. J. CHALMERS]
15. *isomorph:* one of a set of isomorphic items (see note 13). [D. C. ABEL]
16. *reductio ad absurdum:* refutation of a position by showing that it leads to an absurd conclusion (literally, in Latin, "a bringing back to the absurd"). [D. C. ABEL]
17. C. E. Shannon, "A Mathematical Theory of Communication," *The Bell System Technical Journal* 27 (July, October 1948): 397–423, 623–56. [D. J. CHALMERS] Reprinted in Claude E. Shannon and Warren Weaver, *The Mathematical Theory of Communication* (Urbana: University of Illinois Press, 1949). [D. C. ABEL]
18. Gregory Bateson, *Steps to an Ecology of Mind* (San Francisco: Chandler, 1972). [D. J. CHALMERS]
19. A principle or theory is *underdetermined* if it is possible that some other principle or theory could account for the evidence. [D. C. ABEL]

C. Personal Identity

READING 24 ## The Middle-Length Discourses of the Buddha

Pali Canon

The Buddha (literally, "the awakened one" or "the enlightened one") is a title that was given to Siddhatta Gotama (this is the Pali form of his name; the Sanskrit form is Siddhartha Gautama) after he achieved supreme spiritual enlightenment. Gotama was born in about 563 B.C.E. among the Sakya people, who lived in the lowlands of what is now Nepal. The son of the king and queen, he was probably born in the Sakyas' capital city of Kapilavatthu (now Lumbini). He spent his early years in pleasure and luxury, but he later renounced his princely life and became a wandering ascetic. According to legend, when he was twenty-nine he became suddenly aware of the suffering that pervades human life and abruptly left his home in the middle of the night (while his wife and infant son were still sleeping) to begin his quest for the solution to human suffering. Gotama wandered among the forests and cities and along the Ganges River, learning the doctrines and following the practices—including the self-infliction of severe bodily austerities—of several noted spiritual masters. Finding no solution to the problem of suffering, he resolved to find his own answer. Tradition states that one night, at the age of thirty-five, while seated in deep meditation under a fig tree (the species now known as the bodhi ["enlightenment"] or bo tree), he achieved supreme spiritual awakening. The Buddha then gathered disciples and formed communities of monks and nuns. In about 483, after forty-five years of teaching his doctrine and training disciples, the Buddha died in the village of Kusinara (now Kasia).

The Buddha did not write down his teachings, but after his death they were recorded by his disciples. The Buddhist scriptures are written in several languages and fill many volumes. Much of the Buddha's doctrine was written down in Pali, and the authoritative collection of these ancient works is called the Pali Canon. Our readings are taken from the section of the Pali Canon known as *The Middle-Length Discourses of the Buddha*. These writings are cast as dialogues between the Buddha (or one of his trusted followers) and his disciples (or opponents).

The "Shorter Discourse to Saccaka" begins with a clever and arrogant debater named Saccaka asking Assaji (a disciple of the Buddha) how the Buddha trains his followers. Assaji explains that the Blessed One teaches them that there is no permanent self, no entity that establishes personal identity. What we call the self is simply the combination of "bundles" (*khandhas* in Pali; *skandhas* in Sanskrit) of five kinds of force or energy: form (our material shape, our body), feelings, perceptions (sensations), formations (acts of will), and consciousness. Each bundle is simply a conjunction of ever-changing forces; there is nothing permanent in any one bundle and therefore nothing capable of constituting a self. Saccaka declares the "no self" doctrine false and engages the Buddha himself in debate, arguing that each of the five bundles is a self, because each one is a basis for a person gaining merit and demerit. The Buddha responds that if there were a self, it would be able to

244

control the bundles, but in fact we cannot control the bundles. Saccaka accepts the Buddha's doctrine and becomes a disciple.

In "Advice from Nandaka," the Buddha asks his follower Nandaka to instruct a group of five hundred nuns. Nandaka explains to the nuns that consciousness cannot be a permanent self because consciousness is impermanent: For each kind of the six kinds of consciousness (correlated to the five senses and the mind), the internal base (the particular sense or the mind) is impermanent, the external base (the object of the particular sense or the mind) is impermanent, and therefore the resulting form of consciousness (which occurs when the internal base encounters the external base) is impermanent. What is impermanent is painful. If there were a permanent self, it would not be painful.

In "Longer Discourse on the Destruction of Craving," the Buddha explains how the doctrine of dependent arising shows a way to attain liberation from suffering. There is a twelve-step causal sequence that begins with ignorance, leads to craving, and ends with suffering. The later steps depend for their arising on the earlier ones, and if we eliminate the first step in the series—namely ignorance—we eliminate craving and thereby eliminate suffering.

DISCOURSE 35. SHORTER DISCOURSE TO SACCAKA

Thus I heard:[1]

On one occasion the Blessed One[2] was living at Vesali in the Great Wood in the Hall with the Peaked Roof.

Now on that occasion Saccaka, the Nigantha's[3] son, was staying at Vesali. He was a debater and a clever speaker, regarded by many as a saint. He spoke these words before an assembly in Vesali: "I see no monk or [member of the priestly class], the head of a sangha,[4] head of a sect, teacher of a sect, even if he claims to be an arahant[5] and fully enlightened, who would not shake and shiver and tremble and sweat under the armpits on being engaged in argument with me. Even if I engaged a senseless post in argument, it would shake and shiver and tremble on being engaged in argument with me, so what shall I say of a human being?"

Then, it being morning, the venerable Assaji dressed, and taking his bowl and [outer] robe, he went into Vesali for alms. As Saccaka, the Nigantha's son, was walking and wandering for exercise in Vesali, he saw the venerable Assaji coming in the distance. When he saw him, he went up to him and exchanged greetings with him, and when the courteous and amiable talk was finished, he stood at one side. Then Saccaka, the Nigantha's son, said: "How does the monk Gotama discipline[6] disciples, Master Assaji; and in what way is the monk Gotama's instruction usually presented among disciples?"

"This is how the Blessed One disciplines disciples, Aggivessana;[7] and in this way the Blessed One's instruction is usually presented among disciples: 'Bhikkhus,[8] form is impermanent, feeling is impermanent, perception is impermanent, formations are impermanent, consciousness is impermanent. Bhikkhus, form is not self, feeling is not self, perception is not self, formations are not self, consciousness is not self. [Conditioned things] are all impermanent, dhammas[9] are all not self.' That is the way the Blessed One disciplines disciples, and that is the way in which the Blessed One's instruction is usually presented among disciples."

[Saccaka, the Nigantha's son, replied:] "If this is what the monk Gotama asserts, we hear indeed what is ill hearing. Now suppose, sometime or other, we were to meet Master Gotama, and suppose we had some conversation with him. Suppose we were to detach him from that evil view."

Now at that time five hundred Licchavis[10] had met together in an assembly hall for some business or other. Then Saccaka, the Nigantha's son, went to them and said: "Come forth, Licchavis, sirs, come forth. There will be conversation today between me and the monk Gotama. If the monk Gotama maintains to me what was maintained to me by one of his famous pupils, the bhikkhu called Assaji, then with argument I will drag the monk Gotama to, drag him fro, and drag him round about, just as a strong man might seize a long-haired ram by the hair and drag him to, drag him fro, and drag him round about. With argument I will drag the monk Gotama to, drag him fro, and drag him round about, just as a strong brewer's workman might throw a big brewer's sieve into a deep water tank and, taking it by the corners, drag it to, drag it fro, and drag it round about. With argument I will shake the monk Gotama down and shake him up and thump him, just as a strong brewer's mixer might take a strainer by the corners and shake it down and shake it up and thump it about. And just as a sixty-year-old elephant might go down into a pond and have great sport in the game of hemp-washing, so too I shall have great sport, I fancy, in the game of hemp-washing the monk Gotama. Come forth, Licchavis, sirs, come forth. There will be conversation today between me and the monk Gotama."

Thereupon some Licchavis said: "Will the monk Gotama refute Saccaka's, the Nigantha son's, assertions; or will Saccaka, the Nigantha's son, refute the monk Gotama's assertions?" And some Licchavis said: "How will Saccaka, the Nigantha's son, refute the Blessed One's assertions? On the contrary, the Blessed One will refute Saccaka's, the Nigantha son's, assertions."

Then Saccaka, the Nigantha's son, went with the five hundred Licchavis to the Hall with the Peaked Roof in the Great Wood.

Now on that occasion a number of bhikkhus were walking up and down[11] in the open. Then Saccaka, the Nigantha's son, went up to them and asked: "Where is Master Gotama living now, sirs? We want to see Master Gotama."

"The Blessed One has gone into the Great Wood, Aggivessana, and is sitting at the root of a tree for the day's abiding."[12]

Then Saccaka, the Nigantha's son, went together with a large following of Licchavis into the Great Wood to where the Blessed One was and exchanged greetings with him, and after the courteous and amiable talk was finished, he sat down at one side. And some of the Licchavis paid homage to the Blessed One and sat down at one side, and some exchanged greetings with him. And when this courteous and amiable talk was finished, they sat down at one side; some raised their hands palms together in salutation and sat down at one side. Some pronounced their name and clan in the Blessed One's presence and sat down at one side; some kept silence and sat down at one side.

When Saccaka, the Nigantha's son, had sat down, he said to the Blessed One: "I would question Master Gotama on a certain point, if Master Gotama would grant me the favor of an answer to the question."

"Ask what you like, Aggivessana."

"How does Master Gotama discipline his disciples, and in what way is Master Gotama's instruction usually presented among the disciples?"

"This is how I discipline disciples, Aggivessana, and this is the way my instruction is usually presented among disciples: Form is impermanent, feeling is impermanent, perception is impermanent, formations are impermanent, consciousness is impermanent. Form is not self, feeling is not self, perception is not self, formations are not self, consciousness is not self. [Conditioned things] are all impermanent, dhammas are all not self. That is the way I discipline disciples; and that is the way in which my instruction is usually presented among disciples."

"A simile occurs to me, Master Gotama."

"Let it occur to you, Aggivessana," the Blessed One said.

"Just as when seeds and plants, whatever their kind, reach growth, all do so in dependence on earth, based upon earth; and just as when the kinds of work to be done by the strong are done, all are done in dependence on earth, based upon earth—so too, Master Gotama, a man has form as self, he produces merit or demerit based on form. He has feeling as self, he produces merit or demerit based on feeling. He has perception as self, he produces merit or demerit based on perception. He has formations as self, he produces merit or demerit based on formations. He has consciousness as self, he produces merit or demerit based on consciousness."

"Aggivessana, are you not asserting thus: Form is my self, feeling is my self, perception is my self, formations are my self, consciousness is my self?"

"I assert thus, Master Gotama: Form is my self, feeling is my self, perception is my self, formations are my self, consciousness is my self. And so does this great multitude."

"What has this great multitude to do with you, Aggivessana? Please confine yourself to your own assertion alone."

"Then, Master Gotama, I assert thus: Form is my self, feeling is my self, perception is my self, formations are my self, consciousness is my self."

"In that case, Aggivessana, I shall ask you a question in return. Answer it as you like. How do you conceive this, Aggivessana: Would a head-anointed warrior-noble king have the power in his own realm to execute those who should be executed, to fine those who should be fined, to banish those who should be banished—for example, King Pasenadi of Kosala or King Ajatasattu Vedehiputta of Magadha?"

"Master Gotama, a head-anointed warrior-noble king would have the power in his own realm to execute those who should be executed, to fine those who should be fined, to banish those who should be banished—for example, King Pasenadi of Kosala or King Ajatasattu Vedehiputta of Magadha. For even these [oligarchic] communities and societies such as the Vajjians and the Mallians have the power in their own realm to execute those who should be executed, to fine those who should be fined, to banish those who should be banished, so all the more so would an anointed warrior king such as King Pasenadi of Kosala or King Ajatasattu Vedehiputta of Magadha. He would have it, Master Gotama, and he would be worthy to have it."

"How do you conceive this, Aggivessana: When you say 'Form is my self,' have you any such power over that form as 'Let my form be thus; let my form be not thus'?"

When this was said, Saccaka, the Nigantha's son, was silent.

A second time the Blessed One said to him: "How do you conceive this, Aggivessana: When you say 'Form is my self,' have you any such power over that form as 'Let my form be thus; let my form be not thus'?"

A second time Saccaka, the Nigantha's son, was silent.

Then the Blessed One said to him: "Aggivessana, answer now. Now is not the time to be silent. If anyone did not answer when asked a question according with Dhamma[13] up to the third time by the Tathagata,[14] his head would split into seven pieces there and then."

Now on that occasion a thunderbolt-wielding spirit with an iron bolt in his head, burning, blazing, glowing, appeared in the air above Saccaka, the Nigantha's son, [thinking]: "If this Saccaka, the Nigantha's son, does not answer when asked a question according with Dhamma up to the third time, I shall split his head into seven pieces here and now."

The Blessed One saw the thunderbolt-wielding spirit and so did Saccaka, the Nigantha's son. Then Saccaka, the Nigantha's son, was frightened and terrified and his hair stood on end. And seeking to make the Blessed One his shelter, his asylum and refuge, he said: "Ask me, Master Gotama; I will answer."

"How do you conceive this, Aggivessana: When you say 'Form is my self,' have you any such power over that form as 'Let my form be thus; let my form be not thus'?"

"No, Master Gotama."

"Pay attention, Aggivessana, pay attention how you reply. What you said before does not agree with what you said after, or what you said after with what you said before. How do you conceive this, Aggivessana: When you say 'Feeling is my self,' have you any such power over that feeling as 'Let my feeling be thus; let my feeling be not thus'?"

"No, Master Gotama."

"Pay attention, Aggivessana, pay attention how you reply. What you said before does not agree with what you said after, or what you said after with what you said before. How do you conceive this, Aggivessana: When you say 'Perception is my self,' have you any such power over that perception as 'Let my perception be thus; let my perception be not thus'?"

"No, Master Gotama."

"Pay attention, Aggivessana, pay attention how you reply. What you said before does not agree with what you said after, or what you said after with what you said before. How do you conceive this, Aggivessana: When you say 'Formations are my self,' have you any such power over those formations as 'Let my formations be thus; let my formations be not thus'?"

"No, Master Gotama."

"Pay attention, Aggivessana, pay attention how you reply. What you said before does not agree with what you said after, or what you said after with what you said before. How do you conceive this, Aggivessana: When you say 'Consciousness is my self,' have you any such power over that consciousness as 'Let my consciousness be thus; let my consciousness be not thus'?"

"No, Master Gotama."

"Pay attention, Aggivessana, pay attention how you reply. What you said before does not agree with what you said after, or what you said after with what you said before. How do you conceive this, Aggivessana: Is form permanent or impermanent?"

"Impermanent, Master Gotama."

"Now is what is impermanent, unpleasant or pleasant?"

"Unpleasant, Master Gotama."

"Now is what is impermanent, unpleasant, and subject to change fit to be regarded as: 'This is mine, this is I, this is my self'?"

"No, Master Gotama."

"How do you conceive this, Aggivessana: Is feeling permanent or impermanent?" . . . [15]

"How do you conceive this, Aggivessana: Is perception permanent or impermanent?" . . .

"How do you conceive this, Aggivessana: Are formations permanent or impermanent?" . . .

"How do you conceive this, Aggivessana: Is consciousness permanent or impermanent?" . . .

"Impermanent, Master Gotama."

"Now is what is impermanent, unpleasant or pleasant?"

"Unpleasant, Master Gotama."

"Now is what is impermanent, unpleasant, and subject to change fit to be regarded as: 'This is mine, this is I, this is my self'?"

"No, Master Gotama."

"How do you conceive this, Aggivessana: When a man adheres to suffering, resorts to suffering, accepts suffering, always views suffering as 'This is mine, this is I, this is my self,' would he himself ever fully understand suffering or abide with suffering quite exhausted?"

"Why should he, Master Gotama? No, Master Gotama."

"It is as though a man needing heartwood, seeking heartwood, and wandering in search of heartwood, took a sharp axe and went to the wood. There he saw a large plantain trunk, straight, young, with no fruit-bud core. Then he cut off the root and cut off the crown, and having cut off the crown he unrolled the leaf-sheaths. But as he went on unrolling the leaf-sheaths he would never come even to any sapwood, let alone heartwood. So too, Aggivessana, when you are pressed and questioned and cross-questioned by me about your own assertion, you are empty, vacant, and in the wrong. But these words of yours were spoken before this assembly: 'I see no monk or [member of the priestly class], the head of a sangha, head of a sect, teacher of a sect, even if he claims to be an arahant and fully enlightened, who would not shake and shiver and tremble and sweat under the armpits on being engaged in argument with me. Even if I engaged a senseless post in argument, it would shake and shiver and tremble, so what shall I say of a human being?' Now there are drops of sweat on your forehead and they have soaked through your upper robe and fallen to the ground. But there is no sweat on my body now."

And the Blessed One uncovered his golden-colored body before the assembly. When this was said, Saccaka, the Nigantha's son, sat silent, dismayed, with shoulders drooping and head down, glum and with nothing to say.

Then Dummukkha, the son of a Licchavi, seeing Saccaka, the Nigantha's son, thus, said to the Blessed One: "A simile occurs to me, Master Gotama."

"Let it occur to you, Dummukkha."

"Suppose, venerable sir, not far from a village or town there were a pond with a crab in it. And then a party of boys and girls went out from the town or village to the pond, and they went into the water and pulled the crab out of the water and put it on dry land. And whenever the crab extended a leg, they cut it off, broke it and smashed it with sticks and stones, so that the crab with all its legs cut off, broken, and smashed, would be unable to get back to the pond as before. So too, all Saccaka's, the Nigantha's son's, distortions, paradoxes, and travesties have been cut off, broken, and smashed by the Blessed One, and now he cannot get near the Blessed One as was the purpose of his words."

When this was said, Saccaka, the Nigantha's son, told him: "Wait, Dummukkha, wait. We are not dealing with you, here we are dealing with Master Gotama."

[Then Saccaka, addressing the Blessed One, said:] "Let that talk of mine be, Master Gotama; like that of many monks and many [members of the priestly class], it was just so many words, I fancy. But how does a disciple of the monk Gotama carry out the message, respond to advice, cross beyond uncertainty, lose his doubts, gain intrepidity, and become independent of others in the Teacher's message?"

"Here, Aggivessana, [with regard to] any kind of form whatever, whether past or future or present, in oneself or external, gross or subtle, inferior or superior, far or near—a disciple of mine sees with right understanding all form as it actually is, thus: 'This is not mine, this not I, this is not my self.' [With regard to] any kind of feeling whatever . . . [With regard to] any kind of perception whatever . . . [With regard to] any kind of formation whatever . . . [With regard to] any kind of consciousness whatever, whether past or future or present, in oneself or external, gross or subtle, inferior or superior, far or near—a disciple of mine sees with right understanding all consciousness as it actually is, thus: 'This is not mine, this is not I, this is not my self.' This is how a disciple of mine carries out the message, responds to advice, crosses beyond uncertainty, loses his doubts, gains intrepidity, and becomes independent of others in the Teacher's message."

"Master Gotama, how does a bhikkhu become an arahant, with the taints exhausted, who has lived the life, done what was to be done, laid down the burden, reached the highest goal, destroyed the fetters of being, and through right final knowledge is liberated?"

"Here, Aggivessana, [with regard to] any kind of form whatever, whether past or future or present, in oneself or external, gross or subtle, inferior or superior, far or near—a bhikkhu sees with right understanding all form as it actually is, thus: 'This is not mine, this is not I, this is not my self,' and through not clinging he is liberated. [With regard to] any kind of feeling whatever . . . [With regard to] any kind of perception whatever . . . [With regard to] any kind of formation whatever . . . [With regard to] any kind of consciousness, what ever, whether past or future or present, in oneself or external, gross or subtle, inferior or superior, far or near—a bhikkhu sees with right understanding all consciousness as it actually is, thus: 'This is not mine, this is not I, this is not my self,' and through not clinging he is liberated. That is how a bhikkhu becomes an arahant, with the taints exhausted, who has lived the life, done what was to be done, laid down the burden, reached the highest goal, destroyed the fetters of being, and through right final knowledge is liberated. When a bhikkhu's mind is thus liberated, he possesses three unsurpassabilities: unsurpassability in vision, unsurpassability in practice of the way, and unsurpassability in deliverance. When a bhikkhu is thus liberated, he honors, respects, reveres, and venerates only the Tathagata: The Blessed One is enlightened and teaches the Dhamma[16] by enlightenment. The Blessed One is controlled and he teaches the Dhamma by control. The Blessed One is serene and he teaches the Dhamma by serenity. The Blessed One has crossed over and he teaches the Dhamma by having crossed over. The Blessed One has attained nirvana[17] and he teaches the Dhamma by having attained nirvana."

When this was said, Saccaka, the Nigantha's son, replied: "Master Gotama, I was bold and forward in conceiving Master Gotama to be attackable by argument. A man might be such that he could with impunity attack a mad elephant, yet he could not attack Master Gotama with impunity. A man might be such that he could with impunity attack a blazing mass of fire, yet he could not attack Master Gotama with impunity. A man might be such that he could with impunity attack a terrible poisonous serpent, yet he could not attack Master Gotama with impunity. I was bold and forward in conceiving Master Gotama to be attackable by argument. Let the Blessed One, together with the sangha of bhikkhus, accept tomorrow's meal from me."

The Blessed One accepted in silence. . . .

DISCOURSE 146. ADVICE FROM NANDAKA

Thus I heard:

On one occasion the Blessed One was living at Savatthi in Jeta's Grove, Anathapindika's Park.

Then Mahapajapati Gotami went with bhikkhunis[18] to the number of five hundred to the Blessed One and, after paying homage to him, she stood at one side. When she had done so, she said: "Venerable sir, let the Blessed One advise the bhikkunis; let the Blessed One instruct them; let the Blessed One give them a talk on the Dhamma."

Now on that occasion the elder bhikkhus were advising the bhikkhunis in turn, but the venerable Nandaka did not want to advise them in his turn. Then the Blessed One addressed the venerable Ananda thus: "Ananda, whose turn is it today to advise the bhikkhunis?"

"Venerable sir, it is Nandaka's turn to advise the bhikkhunis, but the venerable Nandaka does not want to advise them in his turn."

Then the Blessed One addressed the venerable Nandaka thus: "Advise the bhikkhunis, Nandaka; instruct the bhikkhunis, Nandaka; give a talk divine on the Dhamma to the bhikkhunis."

"Even so, venerable sir," the venerable Nandaka replied. Then, when it was morning, he dressed and taking his bowl and [outer] robe, he went into Savatthi for alms. When he had wandered for alms in Savatthi and had returned from his alms-round after the meal, he went with a companion to the Rajaka Park.

The bhikkhunis saw him coming in the distance, and they prepared a seat and set out water for his feet. The venerable Nandaka sat down on the seat prepared and washed his feet. And the bhikkhunis paid homage to him and stood at one side. When they had done so, the venerable Nandaka said this:

"Sisters, this talk will be in the form of questions. When you know, you should say 'We know'; when you do not know, you should say 'We do not know'; or if any of you have doubt or uncertainty, I too should be questioned thus: 'Venerable sir, what is the meaning of this talk?'"

"Venerable sir, we are satisfied and happy that the venerable Nandaka invites us in this way."

"Sisters, how do you conceive this: Is the eye permanent or impermanent?"

"Impermanent, venerable sir."

"Is what is impermanent, painful or pleasant?"

"Painful, venerable sir."

"Is what is impermanent, painful, and liable to change fit to be seen thus: 'This is mine, this is I, this is my self'?"

"No, venerable sir."

"Sisters, how do you conceive this: Is the ear permanent or impermanent?" . . .

"Is the nose permanent or impermanent?" . . .

"Is the tongue permanent or impermanent?" . . .

"Is the body permanent or impermanent?" . . .

"Is the mind permanent or impermanent?"

"Impermanent, venerable sir."

"Is what is impermanent, painful or pleasant?"

"Painful, venerable sir."

"Is what is impermanent, painful, and liable to change, fit to be seen thus: 'This is mine, this is I, this is my self'?"

"No, venerable sir."

"Why is that?"

"Because, venerable sir, it has already been well seen as it actually is with right understanding by us that these six bases in oneself are impermanent."

"Good, good, sisters. So a noble disciple [thinks] when he sees this as it actually is with right understanding. Sisters, how do you conceive this: Are forms permanent or impermanent?"

"Impermanent, venerable sir."

"Is what is impermanent, painful or pleasant?"

"Painful, venerable sir."

"Is what is impermanent, painful, and liable to change fit to be seen as: 'This is mine, this is I, this is myself'?"

"No, venerable sir."

"Sisters, how do you conceive this: Are sounds permanent or impermanent?" . . .

"Are odors permanent or impermanent?" . . .

"Are flavors permanent or impermanent?" . . .

"Are tangibles permanent or impermanent?" . . .

"Are dhammas permanent or impermanent?"

"Impermanent, venerable sir."

"Is what is impermanent, painful or pleasant?"

"Painful, venerable sir."

"Is what is impermanent, painful, and liable to change fit to be seen as: 'This is mine, this is I, this is my self'?"

"No, venerable sir."

"Why is that?"

"Because, venerable sir, it has already been well seen as it actually is with right understanding by us that these six external bases are impermanent."

"Good, good, sisters. So a noble disciple [thinks] when he sees this as it actually is with right understanding. Sisters, how do you conceive this: Is eye-consciousness permanent?" . . .

"No, venerable sir."

"Is ear-consciousness permanent or impermanent?" . . .

"Is nose-consciousness permanent or impermanent?" . . .

"Is tongue-consciousness permanent or impermanent?" . . .

"Is body-consciousness permanent or impermanent?" . . .

"Is mind-consciousness permanent or impermanent?" . . .

"Impermanent, venerable sir."

"Why is that?"

"Because, venerable sir, it has already been well seen as it actually is with right understanding by us that these six bodies of consciousness are impermanent."

"Good, good, sisters. So a noble disciple [thinks] when he sees this as it actually is with right understanding. Sisters, suppose there were a lamp burning and its oil was impermanent and liable to change, and its wick was impermanent and liable to change, and its flame was impermanent and liable to change, and its radiance was impermanent and liable to change. Would anyone speak rightly who spoke thus: 'When this lamp is burning, its oil is impermanent and liable to change, and so are its wick and its flame, but its radiance is permanent, everlasting, eternal, and not liable to change'?"

"No, venerable sir."

"Why is that?"

"Because, venerable sir, when that lamp is burning, its oil is impermanent and liable to change, and so are its wick and its flame and its radiance."

"So too, sisters, would anyone speak rightly who spoke thus: 'These six bases in oneself are impermanent, but that which is dependent on the six bases in oneself, which I feel as pleasant or painful, or neither painful nor pleasant, is permanent, everlasting, eternal, and not liable to change'?"

"No, venerable sir."

"Why is that?"

"Because, venerable sir, each appropriate feeling arises dependent on the appropriate condition, and with the cessation of the appropriate condition the appropriate feeling ceases."

"Good, good, sisters. So a noble disciple [thinks] when he sees this as it actually is with right understanding. Sisters, suppose there were a great tree standing possessed of heartwood and its root was impermanent and liable to change, and its trunk was impermanent and liable to change, and its branches and foliage were impermanent and liable to change, and its shadow was impermanent and liable to change. Would anyone speak rightly who spoke thus: 'When this great tree stands possessed of heartwood, its root is impermanent and liable to change, and so are its trunk, branches, and foliage, but its shadow is permanent, everlasting, eternal, and not liable to change'?"

"No, venerable sir."

"Why is that?"

"Because, venerable sir, when that great tree stands possessed of heartwood, its root is impermanent and liable to change and so are its trunk, branches, and foliage and its shadow."

"So too, sisters, would anyone speak rightly who spoke thus: 'These six external bases are impermanent and liable to change, but that which is dependent on the six external bases, which I feel as pleasant or painful, or neither painful nor pleasant, is permanent, everlasting, eternal, and not liable to change'?"

"No, venerable sir."

"Why is that?"

"Because, venerable sir, each appropriate feeling arises dependent on the appropriate condition, and with the cessation of the appropriate condition the appropriate feeling ceases."

"Good, good, sisters. So a noble disciple [thinks] when he sees this as it actually is with right understanding." . . .

When the venerable Nandaka had advised the bhikkhunis thus, he dismissed them thus: "Go, sisters, it is time."

Then the bhikkhunis, being satisfied and delighting in the venerable Nandaka's words, rose from their seats, and after paying homage they departed, keeping him on their right. They went to the Blessed One, and after paying homage to him, they stood at one side. When they had done so, the Blessed One said: "Go, sisters, it is time." Then they paid homage to the Blessed One and departed, keeping him on their right. . . .

DISCOURSE 38. LONGER DISCOURSE ON THE DESTRUCTION OF CRAVING

Thus I heard:

On one occasion the Blessed One was living at Savatthi in Jeta's Grove, Anathapindika's Park. . . .

"Bhikkhus, consciousness is reckonable only by the condition dependent on which it arises. When consciousness arises dependent on eye and forms, it is reckoned only as eye-consciousness; when consciousness arises dependent on ear and sounds, it is reckoned only as ear-consciousness; when consciousness arises dependent on nose and odors, it is reckoned only as nose-consciousness; when consciousness arises dependent on tongue and flavors, it is reckoned only as tongue-consciousness; when consciousness arises dependent on body tangibles, it is reckoned only as body-consciousness; and when consciousness arises dependent only on mind and dhammas, it is reckoned only as mind-consciousness.

"A fire is reckoned only by the condition dependent on which it arises. When fire burns dependent on logs, it is reckoned only as a log fire; when fire burns dependent on faggots, it is reckoned only as a faggot fire; when fire burns dependent on grass, it is reckoned only as a grass fire; when fire burns dependent on cow dung, it is reckoned only as a cow-dung fire; when fire burns dependent on chaff, it is reckoned only as a chaff fire; and when fire burns dependent on rubbish, it is reckoned only as a rubbish fire. In the same way, consciousness is reckonable only by the condition dependent on which it arises: When consciousness arises dependent on eye and forms it is reckoned only as eye-consciousness; when . . . consciousness arises dependent on mind and dhammas it is reckoned only as mind-consciousness. . . .

"So, bhikkhus, it is with [1] *ignorance* as condition that [2] *karma-formations*[19] have positive being; with karma-formations as condition, [3] *consciousness*; with consciousness as condition, [4] *name-and-form*;[20] with name-and-form as condition, the [5] *sixfold base*;[21] with the sixfold base as condition, [6] *contact*; with contact as condition, [7] *feeling*; with feeling as condition, [8] *craving*; with craving as condition, [9] *clinging*; with clinging as condition, [10] *being*; with being as condition, [11] *birth*; it is with birth as condition that [12] aging and death have positive being, and also sorrow and lamentation, pain, grief, and despair—that is how there is an origin to this *whole mass of suffering*. . . .[22]

"Good, bhikkhus. So you say thus, and I also say thus: '*That* is, when *this* is; *that* arises with the arising of *this*.' In other words, 'It is with ignorance as condition, that karma-formations arise; with karma-formations as condition, consciousness; with consciousness as condition, name-and-form; with name-and-form as condition, the sixfold base; with the sixfold base as condition, contact; with contact as condition, feeling; with feeling as condition, craving; with craving as condition, clinging; with clinging as condition, being; with being as condition, birth; it is with birth as condition that aging and death have positive being, and also sorrow and lamentation, pain, grief, and despair—that is how there is an origin to this whole mass of suffering.

" 'With the remainderless fading and ceasing of ignorance only, is there cessation of karma-formations; with the cessation of karma-formations, cessation of consciousness; with cessation of consciousness; cessation of name-and-form; with cessation of name-and-form, cessation of the sixfold base; with the cessation of the sixfold base, cessation of contact; with the cessation of contact, cessation of feeling; with the cessation of feeling, cessation of craving; with the cessation of craving, cessation of clinging; with the cessation of clinging, cessation of being; with the cessation of being, cessation of birth; with the cessation of birth, aging and death cease, and also sorrow and lamentation, pain, grief, and despair—that is how there is a cessation to this whole mass of suffering.

"'With cessation of birth, cessation of aging and death'—so it was said. Now is that correct, or not? How does it appear in this case?"

"'With cessation of birth, cessation of aging and death, venerable sir'—so it appears to us in this case. With cessation of birth, cessation of aging and death."

"'With cessation of being, cessation of birth'" . . .

"'With cessation of clinging, cessation of being'" . . .

"'With cessation of craving, cessation of clinging'" . . .

"'With cessation of feeling, cessation of craving'" . . .

"'With cessation of contact, cessation of feeling'" . . .

"'With cessation of the sixfold base, cessation of contact'" . . .

"'With cessation of name-and-form, cessation of sixfold base'" . . .

"'With cessation of consciousness, cessation of name-and-form'" . . .

"'With cessation of karma-formations, cessation of consciousness'" . . .

"'With cessation of ignorance, cessation of karma-formations'—so it was said. Now is that correct, or not, or how does it appear in this case?"

"'With cessation of ignorance, cessation of karma-formations,' venerable sir—so it appears to us in this case. With cessation of ignorance, cessation of karma-formations."

"Good, bhikkhus. So you say thus, and I also say thus: '*That* is not, when *this* is not; *that* ceases with the cessation of *this*. In other words, with cessation of ignorance there is cessation of karma-formations; with the cessation of karma-formations, cessation of consciousness; with the cessation of consciousness, cessation of name-and-form; with the cessation of name-and-form, cessation of the sixfold base; with the cessation of sixfold base, cessation of contact; with the cessation of contact, cessation of feeling; with the cessation of feeling, cessation of craving; with the cessation of craving, cessation of clinging; with the cessation of clinging, cessation of being; with the cessation of being, cessation of birth; with the cessation of birth, aging and death cease, and also sorrow and lamentation, pain, grief, and despair—that is how there is a cessation to this whole mass of suffering.' . . .

"Bhikkhus, knowing and seeing in this way, would you speak thus: 'The teacher is respected by us; we speak as we do out of respect for the teacher'?"

"No, venerable sir."

"Knowing and seeing in this way, would you speak thus: 'A monk told us, and other monks did too; but we do not speak thus'?"

"No, venerable sir."

"Knowing and seeing in this way, would you acknowledge another [teacher]?"

"No, venerable sir."

"Knowing and seeing in this way would you return to the customs of ordinary monks and priests, and to the omens open to the tumult of debate, as having a core of truth?"

"No, venerable sir."

"Do you speak only of what you have yourselves known, seen, and experienced?"

"Yes, venerable sir."

"Good, bhikkhus. So you have been guided by me with a Dhamma with effects visible here and now, not after a lapse of time, inviting inspection, onward-leading, and experienceable by the wise each of himself. For it was with reference to this that it has been said: 'Bhikkhus, this Dhamma has effect visible here and now, not after a lapse of time; it invites inspection, is onward-leading, and is experienceable by the wise each of himself.'"

NOTES

1. Each discourse in the Pali Canon begins with the words "Thus I heard." The narrator is Ananda, who, according to tradition, is the devoted follower of the Buddha who wrote down the discourses from memory shortly after the Buddha died. [D. C. ABEL]
2. *the Blessed One:* the Buddha. [D. C. ABEL]
3. The Nigantha (also known as Mahavira) was a teacher of Jainism, a doctrine that arose in the Buddha's time and, like Buddhism, is still taught today. [D. C. ABEL]
4. *sangha:* community. [D. C. ABEL]
5. *arahant:* perfected one. [D. C. ABEL]
6. *discipline:* literally, "lead away" (from suffering). [D. C. ABEL, AFTER N. THERA, TRANSLATOR]
7. *Aggivessana:* a way of addressing Saccaka; probably the name of his clan. [D. C. ABEL]
8. *Bhikkhus:* monks. [D. C. ABEL]
9. *dhammas:* things (whether conditioned or unconditioned). [D. C. ABEL]
10. *Licchavis:* members of a tribe that helped found the city of Vesali, where this discourse takes place. [D. C. ABEL]
11. *walking up and down:* practicing walking meditation. [N. THERA]
12. *the day's abiding:* abiding in the fruits of the day's meditation. [D. C. ABEL, AFTER N. THERA]
13. *according with Dhamma:* justly. [D. C. ABEL]
14. *the Tathagata:* the perfect one (literally, "one who has thus gone," "one who has thus attained") — an epithet of the Buddha that he uses when speaking of himself. [D. C. ABEL]
15. Since the arguments regarding feeling, perception, and so on are phrased identically to the argument regarding form, the translator does not reproduce them in their entirety. Ellipses in subsequent similar passages likewise indicate the omission of identically phrased arguments. [D. C. ABEL]
16. *the Dhamma:* the law that leads to liberation from suffering. [D. C. ABEL]
17. *nirvana* (this is the Sanskrit form; *nibbana* in Pali): literally, "extinction"; the complete extinction of desire, which produces permanent liberation from suffering. [D C. ABEL]

18. *bhikkhunis:* nuns. [D. C. ABEL]
19. *karma-formations:* the accumulation of *karma* (literally, in Sanskrit, "action, deed"; *kamma* in Pali), the force caused by one's good or bad actions, which causes reincarnation and the nature of that reincarnation. [D. C. ABEL]
20. *name-and-form:* the individual person as composed of mental elements (name) and bodily elements (form). [D. C. ABEL]
21. *sixfold base:* the six internal and external bases of consciousness (described earlier, in Discourse 146). [D. C. ABEL]
22. *whole mass of suffering:* the combination of aging, death, sorrow, lamentation, pain, grief, and despair — the final step in the twelve-step causal sequence. [D. C. ABEL]

A Treatise of Human Nature

David Hume

A biography of David Hume appears on p. 47.

Our reading is from Book I of Hume's *Treatise of Human Nature,* which is entitled "Of the Understanding." In the selection from Part I, Section I, "Of the Origin of Our Ideas," Hume distinguishes between two kinds of perceptions of the mind: *impressions* and *ideas.* Impressions are perceptions that are forceful and lively—namely, "all our sensations, passions and emotions as they make their first appearance in the soul." Ideas are perceptions less forceful and lively than impressions. Hume maintains that all ideas derive from impressions; for example, a faint image I have of a tree comes from my original impression of the tree. When an idea is complex rather than simple, each element can be traced back ultimately to a simple impression.

In Part IV, Section VI, "Of Personal Identity," Hume applies his doctrine of the origin of ideas to the notion of the "self." We may think we have an idea of self as an unchanging entity that underlies all our experiences and makes us the same person from one moment to the next. But if the self is to be a genuine idea, it must derive from an impression. When Hume looks inside what he calls "himself," he finds no impression of a "self"; all he encounters is "a bundle or collection of different perceptions, which succeed each other with an inconceivable rapidity and are in a perpetual flux and movement." Consequently, there is no genuine idea of the self, and therefore no self, no personal identity. Hume then explains how we come to create the fiction of the "self" and rejects the theory that memory produces personal identity.

BOOK I. OF THE UNDERSTANDING

Part I. Of Ideas, Their Origin, Composition, Connection, Abstraction, and so on

Section I. Of the Origin of Our Ideas

All the perceptions of the human mind resolve themselves into two distinct kinds, which I shall call *impressions* and *ideas.* The difference between these consists in the degrees of force and liveliness with which they strike upon the mind and make their way into our thought or consciousness. Those perceptions which enter with most force and violence we may name *impressions;* and under this name I comprehend all our sensations, passions, and emotions as they make their first appearance in the soul. By *ideas* I mean the faint images of these in thinking and reasoning—such as, for instance, are all the perceptions excited by the present discourse, excepting only those which arise from the sight and touch, and excepting the immediate pleasure or uneasiness it may occasion. . . .

There is another division of our perceptions which it will be convenient to observe and which extends itself both to our impressions and ideas. This division is into *simple* and *complex.* Simple perceptions or impressions and ideas are such as admit of no distinction nor separation. The complex are the contrary to these and may be distinguished into parts. Though a particular color, taste, and smell are qualities all united together in this apple, it is easy to perceive they are not the same, but are at least distinguishable from each other.

Having by these divisions given an order and arrangement to our objects, we may now apply ourselves to consider with the more accuracy their qualities and relations. The first circumstance that strikes my eye is the great resemblance between our impressions and ideas in every other particular, except their degree of force and vivacity. The one seems to be in a manner the reflection of the other, so that all the perceptions of the mind are double and appear both as impressions and ideas. When I shut my eyes and think of my chamber, the ideas I form are exact representations of the impressions I felt; nor is there any circumstance of the one, which is not to be found in the other. In running over my other perceptions, I find still the same resemblance and representation. Ideas and impressions appear always to correspond to each other. This circumstance seems to me remarkable and engages my attention for a moment.

Upon a more accurate survey I find I have been carried away too far by the first appearance, and that I must make use of the distinction of perceptions into simple and complex, to limit this general decision[1] that all our ideas and impressions are resembling.[2] I observe that many of our complex ideas never had impressions that corresponded to them, and that many of our complex impressions never are exactly copied in ideas. I can imagine to myself such a city as the New Jerusalem, whose pavement is gold and walls are rubies, though I never saw any such. I have seen Paris; but shall I affirm I can form such an idea of that city, as will perfectly represent all its streets and houses in their real and just[3] proportions?

I perceive therefore, that though there is in general a great resemblance between our *complex* impressions and ideas, yet the rule is not universally true that they are exact copies of each other. We may next consider how the case stands with our *simple* perceptions. After the most accurate examination of which I am capable, I venture to affirm that the rule here holds without any exception, and that every simple idea has a simple impression, which resembles it; and every simple impression a correspondent idea. That idea of red which we form in the dark, and that impression which strikes our eyes in sunshine, differ only in degree, not in nature. That the case is the same with all our simple impressions and ideas, it is impossible to prove by a particular enumeration of them. Everyone may satisfy himself in this point by running over as many as he pleases. But if anyone should deny this universal resemblance, I know no way of convincing him, but by desiring him to show a simple impression that has not a correspondent idea, or a simple idea that has not a correspondent impression. If he does not answer this challenge, as it is certain he cannot, we may from his silence and our own observation establish our conclusion.

Thus we find that all simple ideas and impressions resemble each other; and as the complex are formed from them, we may affirm in general that these two species of perception are exactly correspondent. Having discovered this relation, which requires no farther examination, I am curious to find some other of their qualities. Let us consider how they stand with regard to their existence, and which of the impressions and ideas are causes, and which effects.

The full examination of this question is the subject of the present treatise; and therefore we shall here content ourselves with establishing one general proposition, that all our simple ideas in their first appearance are derived from simple impressions which are correspondent to them and which they exactly represent. . . .

Part IV. Of the Skeptical and Other Systems of Philosophy

Section VI. Of Personal Identity

There are some philosophers who imagine we are every moment intimately conscious of what we call our *self*; that we feel its existence and its continuance in existence; and are certain, beyond the evidence of a demonstration, both of its perfect identity and simplicity. . . .

Unluckily all these positive assertions are contrary to that very experience which is pleaded for them, nor have we any idea of self, after the manner it is here explained. For from what impression could this idea be derived? This question it is impossible to answer without a manifest contradiction and absurdity, and yet it is a question which must necessarily be answered if we would have the idea of self pass for clear and intelligible. It must be some one impression that gives rise to every real idea. But self or person is not any one impression, but that to which our several impressions and ideas are supposed to have a reference. If any impression gives rise to the idea of self, that impression must continue invariably the same through the whole course of our lives, since self is supposed to exist after that manner. But there is no impression constant and invariable. Pain and pleasure, grief and joy, passions and sensations succeed each other and never all exist at the same time. It cannot therefore be from any of these impressions, or from any other, that the idea of self is derived; and consequently there is no such idea.

But farther, what must become of all our particular perceptions upon this hypothesis? All these are different and distinguishable and separable from each other, and may be separately considered, and may exist separately and have no need of anything to support their existence. After what manner therefore do they belong to self, and how are they connected with it? For my part, when I enter most intimately into what I call *myself*, I always stumble on some particular perception or other, of heat or cold, light or shade, love or hatred, pain or pleasure. I never can catch myself at any time without a perception and never can observe anything but the perception. When my perceptions are removed for any time, as by sound sleep, so long am I insensible[4] of myself and may truly be said not to exist. And were all my perceptions removed by death, and could I neither think nor feel nor see nor love nor hate after the dissolution of my body, I should be entirely annihilated, nor do I conceive what is farther requisite to make me a perfect nonentity. If anyone upon serious and unprejudiced reflection thinks he has a different notion of himself, I must confess I can reason no longer with him. All I can allow him is that he may be in the right as well as I, and that we are essentially different in this particular. He may, perhaps, perceive something simple and continued which he calls himself, though I am certain there is no such principle in me.

But setting aside some metaphysicians[5] of this kind, I may venture to affirm of the rest of mankind, that they are nothing but a bundle or collection of different perceptions which succeed each other with an inconceivable rapidity and are in a perpetual flux and movement. Our eyes cannot turn in their sockets without varying our perceptions. Our thought is still more variable than our sight, and all our other senses and faculties contribute to this change; nor is there any single power of the soul which remains unalterably the same, perhaps for one moment. The mind is a kind of theater where several perceptions successively make their appearance—pass, re-pass, glide away, and mingle in an infinite variety of postures and situations. There is properly no *simplicity* in it at one time, nor *identity* in different [times], whatever natural propension[6] we may have to imagine that simplicity and identity. The comparison of the theater must not mislead us. They are the successive perceptions only, that constitute the mind; nor have we the most distant notion of the place where these scenes are represented, or of the materials of which it is composed.

What then gives us so great a propension to ascribe an identity to these successive perceptions and to suppose ourselves possessed of an invariable and uninterrupted existence through the whole course of our lives? . . .

We have a distinct idea of an object that remains invariable and uninterrupted through a supposed variation of time, and this idea we call that of *identity* or *sameness*. We have also a distinct idea of several different objects existing in succession and connected together by a close relation, and this to an accurate view affords as perfect a notion of *diversity* as if there was no manner of relation among the objects. But though these two ideas of identity and [of] a succession of related objects be in themselves perfectly distinct, and even contrary, yet it is certain that in our common way of thinking they are generally confounded with each other. That action of the imagination by which we consider the uninterrupted and invariable object, and that by which we reflect on the succession of related objects, are almost the same to the feeling, nor is there much more effort of thought required in the latter case than in the former. The relation facilitates the transition of the mind from one object to another and renders its passage as smooth as if it contemplated one continued object. This resemblance is the cause of the confusion and mistake and makes us substitute the notion of identity instead of that of related objects. However at one instant we may consider the related succession as variable or interrupted, we are sure the next to ascribe to it a perfect identity and regard it as invariable and uninterrupted. Our propensity to this mistake is so great from the resemblance above-mentioned, that we fall into it before we are aware; and though we incessantly correct ourselves by reflection and return to a more accurate method of thinking, yet we cannot long sustain our philosophy or take off this bias from the imagination. Our last resource is to yield to it and boldly assert that these different related objects are in effect the same, however interrupted and variable. In order to justify to ourselves this absurdity, we often feign some new and unintelligible principle that connects the objects together and prevents their interruption or variation. Thus we feign the continued existence of the perceptions of our senses, to remove the interruption; and run into the notion of a *soul*, and *self*, and *substance*, to disguise the variation. But we may farther observe that where we do not give rise to such a fiction, our propension to confound identity with relation is so great that we are apt to imagine something unknown and mysterious connecting the parts, beside their relation; and this I take to be the case with regard to the identity we ascribe to plants and vegetables. And even when this does not take place, we still feel a propensity to confound these ideas, though we are not able fully to satisfy ourselves in that particular, nor find anything invariable and uninterrupted to justify our notion of identity.

Thus the controversy concerning identity is not merely a dispute of words. For when we attribute identity, in an improper sense, to variable or interrupted objects, our mistake is not confined to the expression, but is commonly attended with a fiction, either of something invariable and uninterrupted, or of something mysterious and inexplicable, or at least with a propensity to such fictions. . . .

The identity which we ascribe to the mind of man is only a fictitious one, and of a like kind with that which we ascribe to vegetables and animal bodies. It cannot, therefore, have a different origin, but must proceed from a like operation of the imagination upon like objects.

But lest this argument should not convince the reader (though in my opinion perfectly decisive), let him weigh the following reasoning, which is still closer and more immediate. It is evident that the identity which we attribute to the human mind, however perfect we may imagine it to be, is not able to run the several different perceptions into one and make them lose their characters of distinction and difference, which are essential to them. It is still true that every distinct perception which enters into the composition of the mind is a distinct existence, and is different and distinguishable and separable from every other perception, either contemporary or successive. But as, notwithstanding this distinction and separability, we suppose the whole train of perceptions to be united by identity, a question naturally arises concerning this relation of identity—whether it be something that really binds our several perceptions together, or only associates their ideas in the imagination. That is, in other words, whether in pronouncing concerning the identity of a person, we observe some real bond among his perceptions, or only feel one among the ideas we form of them. This question we might easily decide, if we would recollect what has been already proved at large—that the understanding never observes any real connection among objects, and that even the union of cause and effect, when strictly examined, resolves itself into a customary association of ideas.[7] For from thence it evidently follows that identity is nothing really belonging to these different perceptions and uniting them together, but is merely a quality which we attribute to them because of the union of their ideas in the imagination, when we reflect upon them. . . .

As memory alone acquaints us with the continuance and extent of this succession of perceptions, it is to be considered upon that account chiefly as the source of personal identity. Had we no memory, we never should have any notion of causation, nor consequently of that chain of causes and effects which constitute our self or person. But having once acquired this notion of causation from the memory, we can extend the same chain of causes—and consequently the identity of our persons—beyond our memory, and can comprehend times and circumstances and actions which we have entirely forgot, but suppose in general to have existed. For how few of our past actions are there of which we have any memory? Who can tell me, for instance, what were his thoughts and actions on the 1st of January 1715, the 11th of March 1719, and the 3rd of August 1733? Or will he affirm, because he has entirely forgot the incidents of these days, that the present self is not the same person with the self of that time; and by that means overturn all the most established notions of personal identity? In this view, therefore, memory does not so much *produce* as *discover* personal identity, by showing us the relation of cause and effect among our different perceptions. It will be incumbent on those who affirm that memory produces entirely our personal identity, to give a reason why we can thus extend our identity beyond our memory.

The whole of this doctrine leads us to a conclusion which is of great importance in the present affair, namely, that all the nice and subtle questions concerning personal identity can never possibly be decided, and are to be regarded rather as grammatical than as philosophical difficulties. Identity depends on the relations of ideas and these relations produce identity, by means of that easy transition they occasion. But as the relations and the easiness of the transition may diminish by insensible[7] degrees, we have no just standard by which we can decide any dispute concerning the time when they acquire or lose a title to the name of identity. All the disputes concerning the identity of connected objects are merely verbal, except so far as the relation of parts gives rise to some fiction or imaginary principle of union, as we have already observed.

NOTES

1. *decision:* conclusion. [D. C. Abel]
2. *resembling:* similar. [D. C. Abel]
3. *just:* proper, fitting. [D. C. Abel]
4. *insensible:* having no sensation. [D. C. Abel]
5. *metaphysicians:* philosophers who speculate about nature and kinds of reality. [D. C. Abel]
6. *propension:* propensity, inclination. [D. C. Abel]
7. Hume's arguments for these claims appear on pp. 167–174 of this book. [D. C. Abel]
8. *insensible:* unable to be sensed. [D. C. Abel]

The Origins of Selves
Daniel C. Dennett

Daniel C. Dennett was born in Boston in 1942. After receiving his bachelor's degree in philosophy from Harvard University in 1963, he went to Oxford University, where he studied
under Gilbert Ryle and completed his doctoral studies in 1965. He then accepted a position at the University of California, Irvine. Dennett began teaching at Tufts University in
1971, where he is now University Professor, Austin B. Fletcher Professor of Philosophy, and
Director of the Center for Cognitive Studies. He has been a visiting professor at Harvard
University, the University of Pittsburgh, Oxford University, and the Ecole Normale
Supérieur in Paris. He has been awarded Guggenheim and Fulbright fellowships and was
elected to the American Academy of Arts and Sciences in 1987.

Dennett's publications include *Content and Consciousness* (1969; 2d ed., 1986),
Brainstorms: Philosophical Essays on Mind and Psychology (1978), *Elbow Room: The Va-
rieties of Free Will Worth Wanting* (1984), *The Intentional Stance* (1987), *Consciousness
Explained* (1991), *Darwin's Dangerous Idea: Evolution and the Meanings of Life* (1995),
Kinds of Minds: Toward an Understanding of Consciousness (1996), *Freedom Evolves*
(2003), and *Breaking the Spell: Religion as a Natural Phenomenon* (2006).

Our reading is Dennett's 1989 article, "The Origins of Selves," which explores the perplexing question of what a "self" is by examining how there came to be creatures that have (or
are) selves. The distinction between self and other began with the evolution of living things,
which seek *self*-preservation from threats arising from the world outside. A primitive self is not
a *thing* inside an organism but an *organization* that "tends to distinguish, control and preserve
portions of the world [and] thereby creates and maintains boundaries." The boundaries are
drawn on the principle "You are what you control and care for." There are no fixed boundaries
that delineate what an organism controls and cares for: The shell that a snail grows becomes
part of its self, and the discarded shell that the hermit crab moves into becomes part of its self.

Human beings have a technique of self-preservation much more sophisticated than
that of snails and crabs: We have language and preserve ourselves by creating and telling
stories about whom we are. Although the human self seems to be the *source* of the narrative we tell, it is in fact not the source but the *product* of this narrative. Using an analogy
from physics, Dennett argues that a human self is a "center of narrative gravity": Just as the
center of gravity of a physical object is an abstraction yet nonetheless real, so the center of
narrative gravity is an abstraction yet quite real. (And this center of narrative gravity would
account for personal identity.) Dennett develops his theory of the narrative self by examining an aberration of the norm from one self per body: multiple personality disorder.

What is a self? Since Descartes[1] in the seventeenth century we have had a vision
of the self as a sort of immaterial ghost that owns and controls a body the way
you own and control your car.

More recently, with the rejection of dualism[2] and the rise of materialism—the
idea that the mind just *is* the brain—we have gravitated to the view that the self must
be a node or module in the brain, the central headquarters responsible for organiz-
ing and directing all the subsidiary bureaucracies that keep life and limb together.

265

Or is the very idea of a self nothing but a compelling fiction, a creed outworn, as some theorists insist, a myth we keep telling ourselves in spite of the advances of science that discredit it?

". . . a myth we keep telling ourselves." A myth we keep telling *whom?* Is a self something else, perhaps even some hard-to-imagine combination of these very different ideas?

On my first trip to London many years ago I found myself looking for the nearest Underground station. I noticed a stairway in the sidewalk labeled "Subway," which in *my* version of English meant subway train, so I confidently descended the stairs and marched forth looking for the trains. After wandering around in various corridors, I found another flight of stairs, leading up, alas, and somewhat dubiously climbed them to find myself on the other side of the intersection from where I had started. I must have missed a turn, I thought, and walked back downstairs to try again. After what seemed to me to be an exhaustive search for hitherto overlooked turnstiles or side entrances, I emerged back on the sidewalk where I had started, feeling somewhat cheated. It finally dawned on me that a subway in London is just a way of crossing the street underground. Searching for the self can be somewhat like that. You enter the brain through the eye, march up the optic nerve, round and round in the cortex, looking behind every neuron, and then, before you know it, you emerge into daylight on the spike of a motor nerve impulse, scratching your head and wondering where the self is.

That is not the way to find the self, or to understand what a self is. (That's a bit like wandering around Manhattan looking for the Big Apple.) Where then might we look? We might look first to origins. As the British biologist D'Arcy Thompson once said, "Everything is what it is because it got that way."[3]

If selves are anything at all, then they exist. *Now* there are selves. There was a time, millions (or billions) of years ago, when there were none—at least none on this planet. So there has to be—as a matter of logic—a true story to be told about how there came to be creatures with selves. This story will have to tell—as a matter of logic—about a process (or a series of processes) involving the activities or behaviors of things that do not yet *have* selves—or *are* not yet selves—but which eventually yield, as a new product, beings that do have selves. That is the true story I would like to tell, but quite obviously it is now—and probably forever—impossible to *know* the details of that story, so we will have to speculate somewhat, guided as firmly as possible by the available facts.

And since this will have to be a brief overview of a rather large and intricate research project, I must resort to simplifications and metaphors to illustrate the outlines without going into the details. That does not mean that I have a different version, right now, for the experts. In fact there are no experts on these topics, and the experts on the details have just as much trouble seeing the overall shape and direction of theory as any novice—perhaps more trouble, since they are so preoccupied with their close-up views of tiny patches of the problem.

BIOLOGY BEGINS IN SELF-PRESERVATION

This story that must be told is analogous to other stories that science is beginning to tell. Compare it, for instance, to the fascinating story of the evolution of sex. There are many organisms today that have no genders and reproduce asexually, and there most certainly was a time when all the organisms that existed did not come in different genders, male and female, and did not engage in *sexual* reproduction. Somehow, by some imaginable series of steps, some of these organisms have to have evolved into organisms that did have genders, and eventually, of course, into us, and the rather exotic—and indeed erotic—transformations and elaborations we have added to the basic biological phenomenon of gender. What sort of conditions were required to foster or necessitate these innovations? Why, in short, did all these changes happen?

There is a nice parallel between the two questions, about the origins of *sex* and the origins of *selves*. There is almost nothing *sexy* (in human terms) about the sex life of insects, oysters, and other simple forms of life, but we can recognize in their mechanical and apparently joyless routines of reproduction the foundations and principles of our much more exciting world of sex. Similarly, there is nothing particularly *selfy* (if I may coin a term) about the primitive precursors of human selves, but they laid the foundations for our particularly human innovations and complications.

The original distinction between self and other is a deep biological principle; one might say it is the deepest principle, for biology begins in self-preservation—in the emergence of entities (the simplest replicators) who resisted destruction and decay, who combated, at least for a short time, the second law of thermodynamics,[4] and passed on their capacity to do this to their descendants.

As soon as something gets into the business of self-preservation, boundaries become important, for if you are setting out to preserve yourself, you don't want to squander effort trying to preserve the whole world; you draw the line. You become, in a word, *selfish*. This primordial form of selfishness (which, as a primordial form, lacks most of the flavors of our brand of human selfishness) is one of the marks of life. Where one bit of granite ends and the next bit begins is a matter of slight moment; the fracture boundary may be real enough, but nothing works to protect the territory, to push back the frontier or retreat. "Me against the world"—this distinction between everything on the *inside* of a closed boundary and everything in the *external world,* is at the heart of all biological processes—not just ingestion and excretion, respiration and transpiration.

Consider, for instance, the immune system, with its millions of different antibodies arrayed in defense of the body against millions of different alien intruders. This army must solve the fundamental problem of recognition: telling one's self (and one's friends) from everything else. And the problem has been solved in much the way human nations and their armies have solved the counterpart problem: by standardized identification-routines. The passports and customs officers in miniature are molecular shapes and shape-detectors. It is important to recognize that this army of antibodies has no generals, no general headquarters with a battle plan, or even a description of the enemy; the antibodies represent their enemies only in the way a million locks represent the keys that open them. Occasionally, misidentifications are made—in autoimmune reactions, for instance, in which a sort of civil war takes place between different factions of what ought to be peacefully co-existing parts of the whole that resides inside the walls.

The distinctions at this level are far from absolute; within the walls of the body are many, many interlopers, ranging from bacteria and viruses through microscopic mites that live like cliff-dwellers in the ecological niche of our skin and scalp, to larger parasites—horrible tapeworms, for instance. These interlopers are all tiny self-protectors in their own right, but some of them, such as the bacteria that populate our digestive systems and without which we would die, are just as essential team members in our quest for self-preservation as the antibodies in our immune systems. Other interlopers are tolerated parasites—not worth the effort to evict, apparently—and still others are indeed the enemy within, deadly if not rooted out and driven out.

This fundamental biological principle of distinguishing self from world, inside from outside, has some remarkable echoes in the highest vaults of our psychology. The psychologist Paul Rozin has shown in a fascinating series of experiments on the nature of *disgust* that there is a powerful and unacknowledged undercurrent of blind resistance to certain acts that, rationally considered, should not trouble us.[5] For example, would you please swallow the saliva in your mouth right now? This act does not fill you with revulsion. But suppose I had handed you a sparkling clean drinking glass and asked you to spit into the glass and then swallow the saliva from the glass. Disgusting! But why? It seems to have to do with our perception that once something is outside of our bodies it is no longer quite part of us anymore; it becomes alien and suspicious; it has renounced its citizenship and becomes something to be rejected.

Border crossings are thus either moments of anxiety or, in a familiar reversal, something to be especially enjoyed: "In addition, they seemed to spend a great deal of time eating and drinking and going to parties, and Frensic, whose appearance tended to limit his sensual pleasure to putting things into himself rather than into other people, was something of a gourmet."[6] Sharpe suggests, in this funny but unsettling passage, that when you get right down to it all pleasure consists in playing around with one's own boundary, or someone else's; and these biological reflections of ours suggest that he is on to something—if not the whole truth, then part of the truth.

In any event, the origin of complex life forms on this planet was also the birth of the most primitive sort of self, whatever sort of self is implied by the self-regard that prevents the lobster, when hungry, from eating itself.

Does a lobster have a self? Or, should we say, are there selves that have lobster bodies? This question is obviously the secular descendant of a question that has troubled theologians for several thousand years: Do animals have immortal souls? Do insects? I must say that I much prefer the secular version to the religious, and will not make any attempt—except by implication, no doubt—to express my opinions about the existence of *souls*. Even the most hard-headed materialist/mechanist/scientist, on the other hand, must face the question of how to describe the distinction between the lobster and the rock behind which the lobster crouches—only one of them is designed around the principle of self-regard. So far as *that* property goes, we can make fairly simple robots or automata that also exhibit it, detecting and retreating from dangers, seeking out shelter and striving to renew their energy resources. This is minimal selfhood, but one must start at the beginning.

So a minimal self is not a *thing* inside a lobster or a lark, and it is not the "whole lobster" or "whole lark" either; it is something abstract which amounts just to the existence of an organization which tends to distinguish, control, and preserve portions of the world, an organization that thereby creates and maintains boundaries. To a first approximation the principle that draws the boundary is this slogan: *You are what you control and care for.*

THE SELF HAS FLEXIBLE BOUNDARIES

Every word in this slogan cries out for further refinement, but I prefer to leave it in its simplest form, since the amendments that will already no doubt have occurred to you illustrate my next point. The boundaries of the minimal self are not only permeable, as we have just seen, but flexible as well. The hermit crab finds the discarded shell of another creature and appropriates it as a portable shelter, but by this appropriation that alien shell is moved inside the boundary—just as much as the shell that a snail grows, utilizing materials it likewise finds in its environment, but ingests and then extrudes.

The beaver's dam, by the same token, is so intimately associated with the beaver's fundamental strategies of survival that it should be included inside the boundary as well, as Richard Dawkins argues—I think conclusively—in *The Extended Phenotype.*[7] One might protest that however loyally the beaver cares for its dam, it doesn't *directly* control the shape of its dam (in the way that it directly controls the posture of its limbs), but one could also go on to point out that it doesn't control its limbs as directly as it controls the motor nerve firings that innervate its limbs—so should we draw the boundary of minimal selfhood inside its limbs? Surely not.

An even more stunning example is the anthill or termite colony, in which there is a boundary not marked by any membrane or even by unbroken proximity of parts. What is particularly striking about the termite colony is that it is an example of a complex system capable of functioning in what seems to be a thoroughly "purposeful and integrated" way simply by having *lots of subsystems doing their own thing* without any central supervision. Indeed most systems on earth that appear to have central controllers (and are usefully described as having them) do not. The colony as a whole builds elaborate mounds, gets to know its territory, organizes foraging expeditions, sends out raiding parties against other colonies, and so on. The group cohesion and coordination is so remarkable that hardheaded observers have been led to postulate the existence of a colony's "group soul."[8] Yet in fact all this group wisdom results from nothing other than myriads of individual termites, specialized as several different castes, going about their individual business—influenced by each other, but quite uninfluenced by any master plan.

In every beehive or termite colony there is, to be sure, a queen bee or queen termite, but these individuals are more patient than agent, more a treasure to be protected than the chief of the protective forces—in fact their name is more fitting today than in earlier ages, for they are much more like Queen Elizabeth II than Queen Elizabeth I. There is no Margaret Thatcher bee, no George Bush termite, no Oval Office in the anthill.[9]

But enough about the bees and the birds. What about us? I know that there will be some among you who will be sure I am leading you on a wild goose chase; the sort of selfhood we have been examining, you think, is *not at all* the sort of selfhood that you have; a human being's self is *entirely different* from the sort of implied self of the lobster or the ant colony. Yes and no. Of course they are different in important ways; the question is, can we build a bridge of evolution or development between them?

First let's look at a similarity, and then a major difference. Do our selves, our non-minimal *selfy* selves, exhibit permeability and flexibility of boundaries? We have noted the hermit crab's shell and the beaver's dam. What of our own clothes, our houses, our automobiles, and the other paraphernalia we strive to control—our "stuff," as George Carlin[10] calls it? Do we expand our personal boundaries—the boundaries of our selves—to enclose any of this? In general, perhaps, no, but there are certainly times when this seems true, psychologically. For instance, some people own cars and drive them, while other people are *motorists*. The inveterate motorist prefers being a four-wheeled gas-consuming agent to being a two-legged food-consuming agent, and his use of the first-person pronoun betrays this identification: "I'm not cornering well on rainy days because my tires are getting bald." So sometimes we enlarge our boundaries; at other times, in response to perceived challenges real or imaginary, we let our boundaries shrink: "I didn't do that! That wasn't the real me talking. Yes, the words came out of my mouth, but I refuse to recognize them as my own." This shrinking tactic has important moral implications. If you make yourself really small, you can externalize virtually everything.[11]

I have reminded you of these familiar speeches to draw out the similarities between our selves and the selves of ants and hermit crabs, but the speeches also draw attention to the most important differences: Ants and hermit crabs don't talk. The hermit crab is designed or organized in such a way as to see to it that it acquires a shell. This organization, we might say, *implies* a shell, and hence, in a *very* weak sense, tacitly *represents the crab as having a shell*. But the crab does not in any stronger sense *represent itself* as having a shell. It doesn't go in for self-representation at all. To whom would it so represent itself and why? It doesn't need to remind it*self* of this aspect of its nature, since its innate design takes care of that problem, and there are no other interested parties in the offing. And the ants, as we have noted, accomplish their communal projects without relying on any explicitly communicated blueprints or edicts.

OUR SELVES ARE THE PRODUCT OF NARRATIVE

We, in contrast, are almost constantly engaged in presenting ourselves to others, and to ourselves, and hence *representing* ourselves—in language and gesture, external and internal. The most obvious difference in our environment that would explain this difference in our behavior is the behavior itself. Our human environment contains not just food and shelter, enemies to fight or flee, and conspecifics[12] with whom to mate, but words, words, words. These words are potent elements of our environment that we readily incorporate, ingesting and extruding them, weaving them like spiderwebs into self-protective strings of *narrative*. Our fundamental tactic of self-protection, self-control, and self-definition is not building dams or spinning webs, but telling stories—and more particularly concocting and controlling the story we tell others, and ourselves, about who we are.

Now we are ready for the strangest idea in my paper, but also, I think, the most important: There is a further similarity between the spiders, the beavers, and us. Spiders don't have to think, consciously and deliberately, about how to spin their webs; that is just something that spider brains are designed to get spiders to do. And even beavers, unlike professional human engineers, do not consciously and deliberately plan the structures they build. And finally, *we* (unlike *professional* human storytellers) do not consciously and deliberately figure out what narratives to tell and how to tell them; like spiderwebs, our tales are *spun by us*; our human consciousness, and our narrative selfhood, is their *product*, not their *source*.

These strings or streams of narrative issue forth *as if* from a single source—not just in the obvious physical sense of flowing from just one mouth, or one pencil or pen, but in a more subtle sense: Their effect on any audience or readers is to encourage them to (try to) posit a unified agent whose words they are, about whom they are—in short, to posit what I call a *center of narrative gravity*.[13] This is yet another abstraction, not a thing in the brain, but still a remarkably robust and almost tangible attractor of properties, the "owner of record" of whatever items and features are lying about unclaimed. Who owns your car? You do. Who owns your clothes? You do. Then who owns your body? You do. When you say "This is my body," you certainly aren't taken as saying "This body owns itself." But what can you be saying, then? If what you say is neither a bizarre and pointless tautology (this body is its own owner, or something like that) nor the metaphysically[14] discredited—or at least highly suspect—claim that you are an immaterial soul or ghost puppeteer who owns and operates this body, what else could you mean? I think we could see more clearly what "This is my body" meant, if we could answer the question: as opposed to what? How about as opposed to this? "No, it isn't; it's mine, and I don't like sharing it!"

If we could see what it would be like for two (or more) selves to vie for control of a single body, we could see better what a single self really is. As scientists of the self, we would like to conduct controlled experiments in which, by varying the initial conditions, we could see just what has to happen, in what order and requiring what resources, for such a talking self to emerge. Are there conditions under which life goes on but no self emerges? Are there conditions under which more than one self emerges? Of course we cannot ethically conduct such experiments, but, as in other scientific investigations of human phenomena, occasionally nature conducts terrible experiments, from which we can cautiously draw conclusions.

ALWAYS ONE SELF TO ONE BODY?

Such an experiment is multiple personality disorder (MPD), in which a single human body *seems* to be shared by several selves—each, typically, with a proper name and an autobiography. Nicholas Humphrey and I have been investigating MPD with an eye to answering these questions about the self.

The idea of multiple personality disorder strikes many people as too outlandish and metaphysically bizarre to believe—a "paranormal" phenomenon to discard along with extrasensory perception, close encounters of the third kind, and witches on broomsticks. I suspect that some of these people have made a simple *arithmetical* mistake: They have failed to notice that two or three or seventeen selves per body is really no more *metaphysically* extravagant than one self per body. One is bad enough!

"I just saw a car drive by with five selves in it."
"What?? The mind reels! What kind of metaphysical nonsense is this?"
"Well, there were also five bodies in the car."
"Oh, well, why didn't you say so? Then everything is OK."
"Oh maybe only four bodies, or three—but definitely five selves."
"What??!!"

The principle of "one to a customer" certainly captures the normal arrangement, but if a body can have one, why not more than one under abnormal conditions?

I don't at all mean to suggest that there is nothing shocking or deeply puzzling about MPD. It is, in fact, a phenomenon of surpassing strangeness—not, I think, because it challenges our presuppositions about what is *metaphysically* possible, but more because it challenges our presuppositions about what is *humanly* possible about the limits of human cruelty and depravity on the one hand, and the limits of human creativity on the other. For the evidence is now voluminous that there are not a handful or a hundred but thousands of cases of MPD in this country, and it almost invariably owes its existence to prolonged early child abuse, usually sexual, and of sickening severity.

These children have often been kept in such extraordinarily terrifying and confusing circumstances that I am more amazed that they survive psychologically at all, than I am that they manage to preserve themselves by a desperate redrawing of their boundaries. What they do, when confronted with overwhelming conflict and pain, is this: They "leave." They create a boundary so that the horror doesn't happen to *them*; it either happens to no one, or to some other self, better able to sustain its organization under such an onslaught—at least this is what they *say* they did, as best they recall.

How can this be? What kind of account could we give, ultimately at the biological level, of such a process of splitting? Does there have to have been a single, whole self that somehow fissioned, amoeba-like? How could that be if a self is not a proper physical part of an organism or a brain, but, as I have suggested, an abstraction? The response to the trauma seems so creative, moreover, that one is inclined at first to suppose that it must be the work of some kind of supervisor in there—a supervisory brain program, a central controller, or whatever. But we should remind ourselves of the termite colony, which also seemed at first, to require a central chief executive to accomplish such clever projects. We can perhaps convince ourselves of the possibility—no more than that—of such a creative process by exploring an extended analogy.

DO I RESEMBLE THE U.S.A.?

Consider the United States of America. At one level of description there is surely nothing wrong with personifying the U.S.A. and talking about it (rather like the termite colony) as if it had an inner self. The U.S.A. has memories, feelings, likes and dislikes, hopes, talents, and so on. It hates Communism, is haunted by the memory of Vietnam, is scientifically creative, socially clumsy, somewhat given to self-righteousness, rather sentimental. But does that mean there is one central agency inside the U.S.A. which embodies all those qualities? Of course not. There is, as it happens, a specific area of the country where much of it comes together. But go to Washington and ask to speak to Mr. American Self, and you'd find there was nobody home; instead you'd find a lot of different agencies (the Defense Department, the Treasury, the courts, the Library of Congress, the National Science Foundation, and so on) operating in relative independence of each other.

To be sure, there is no such thing as Mr. American Self, but as a matter of fact there is in every country on earth a Head of State: a president, queen, chancellor, or some other figurehead. The Head of State may actually be non-executive; certainly he does not himself enact all the subsidiary roles (the U.S. President does not bear arms, sit in the courts, play baseball, or travel to the moon). But nevertheless he is expected at the very least to take an active interest in all these national pursuits. The president is meant to appreciate better than anyone the "state of the Union." He is meant to *represent* different parts of the nation to each other, and to inculcate a common value system. Moreover—and this is most important—he is the "spokesman" when it comes to dealing with other nation states. Other individuals—diplomats and press secretaries—may deliver the actual utterances, but these acts are understood to be relaying his speech acts to the world.

That is not to say that a nation lacking such a figurehead would cease to function day-to-day. But it is to say that in the longer term it may function much better if it does have one. Indeed a good case can be made that nations, unlike termite colonies, require this kind of figurehead as a condition of their political survival—especially given the complexity of international affairs.

The drift of this analogy is obvious. In short, a human being too may need an inner figurehead—especially given the complexities of human social life. If this is accepted (as I think it should be), we can turn to the vexed question of how such a figurehead could be developed or established in the first place. Here the Head of State analogy may seem at first less helpful. For one thing, in the U.S.A. at least, the president is democratically elected by the population. For another, the candidates for the presidency are pre-formed entities, already waiting in the wings.

Yet is this really so? It could equally be argued that the presidential candidates, rather than being pre-formed, are actually brought into being—through a narrative dialectical process—by the very population to which they offer their services as president. Thus the population (or the news media) first try out various fictive versions of what they think their "ideal president" should be, and then the candidates adapt themselves as best they can to fill the bill. To the extent that there is much more than one dominant fiction about "what it means to be American," different candidates mold themselves in different ways. But in the end only one can be elected—and he will of course claim to speak for the whole nation.

In very much a parallel way, Humphrey and I suggest, a human being first creates—unconsciously (the way a spider creates a web)—one or more ideal fictive selves and then elects the best supported of these into office as her Head of Mind. A significant difference in the human case, however, is that there is likely to be considerably more *outside influence.* Parents, friends, and even enemies may all contribute to the image of "what it means to be me" as well as—and maybe over and above—the internal news media. In a multiple personality case, daddy, for example, might lean on the growing child to impose an *invasive* fictive self.

Thus a human being does not start out as single or as multiple—she starts out without any Head of Mind at all. She is poised to fend for herself—just as the lobster or beaver is—but she does not yet have an organization crystallized around one or more centers of narrative gravity. In the normal course of development, she slowly gets acquainted with the various possibilities of selfhood that "make sense"—partly through her own observation, partly through outside influence. In most cases a majority view emerges, strongly favoring one version of "the real me," and it is that version which is installed as her elected Head of Mind. But in some cases the competing fictive selves are so equally balanced, or different constituencies within her are so unwilling to accept the result of the election, that constitutional chaos reigns—and there are snap elections (or coups d'état) all the time.

I think that a model inspired by (underlying, rendering honest) this analogy can account for symptomatology of MPD—the memory black-spots, differences in style, and so forth. Certainly the analogy provides a wealth of detail suggesting so. Once in office, a new Head of State typically downplays certain "unfortunate" aspects of his nation's history (especially those associated with the rival Head of State who immediately preceded him). Moreover he himself, by standing for particular national values, affects the course of future history by encouraging the expression of those values by the population (and so, by a kind of feedback, confirming his own role).

I am still talking in metaphors, however. What translations into the terms of current cognitive science could we formulate? First, what sense can be given to the notion of a "Head of Mind"? The analogy with a spokesman may not be far off the literal truth. The language-producing systems of the brain have to get their instructions from somewhere, and the very demands of pragmatics and grammar would conspire to confer something like Head of Mind authority on whatever subsystem currently controls their input. E. M. Forster[15] once remarked, "How can I tell what I think until I see what I say?" The four "I"s in this sentence are meant to refer to the same thing. But this grammatical tradition may depend—and always has depended—on the fact that the thought expressed in Forster's question is quite literally self-confirming: What "I" (my self) thinks is what "I" (my language apparatus) says.

There can, however, be no guarantee that either the speaker or anyone else who hears him over an extended period will settle on there being just a single "I." Suppose, at different times, different subsystems within the brain produce "clusters" of speech that simply cannot easily be interpreted as the output of a single self. Then—as a Bible scholar may discover when working on the authorship of what is putatively a single-authored text—it may turn out that the clusters make best sense when attributed to different selves.

Another central feature of MPD is selective amnesia, which is the chief difference between the plight of the MPD sufferer and the rest of us (who have our various personae in the various roles we play day to day). MPD sufferers typically have no memory at all for the events that occur during regimes when they are out of power. To those who have even a passing knowledge of computer information processing, the idea of mutually inaccessible "directories" of stored information will already be familiar. In cognitive psychology, new discoveries about state-dependent learning and other evidence of modularization in the brain have led people to recognize that *failure* of access between different subsystems is the norm rather than the exception. Indeed the old Cartesian[16] picture of the mind "transparent to itself" now appears to be rarely if ever achievable (or even desirable) in practice. In this context the out-of-touchness of different selves no longer looks so startling.

The different "alters"[17] of an MPD sufferer almost always have different attitudes towards life and different emotional characters; one will be prudish and reserved, another sexy, a third angry and violent, for instance. What could be the basis for the different "value systems" associated with these rival Heads of Mind? At another level of analysis, psychopharmacological evidence suggests that the characteristic emotional style of different personalities could correspond to the brain-wide activation or inhibition of neural pathways that rely on different neurotransmitter chemicals. Thus the phlegmatic style of one personality could be associated with low norepinephrine levels, the shift to a carnal style with high norepinephrine, and the out-of-control alter could coincide with low dopamine.

Even the idea of an "election" of the current Head of Mind is not implausible. Events very like elections take place in the brain all the time—whenever coherent patterns of activity compete for control of the same network. Consider what happens, for example, when the visual system receives two conflicting images at the two eyes. First there is an attempt at fusion; but if this proves to be unstable, "binocular rivalry" results, with the input from one eye completely taking over while the other is suppressed. Thus we already have, at the level of visual neurophysiology, clear evidence of the mind's general preference for single-mindedness over completeness.

MPD provides a window into alternative possibilities. In the same way that the force of gravity is well-nigh invisible until you have imagined the weightlessness of outer space, so single-selfedness is hard to discern in a body until you have seen, or imagined, multiple-selfedness.

I have not had time to show you the detailed view through this window, but I hope I have succeeded in opening it for you.

NOTES

1. René Descartes (1596–1650) was a French philosopher and mathematician; for a biography, see p. 128. [D. C. ABEL]
2. *dualism:* the theory that a human being consists of two substances—body and mind (soul, self). [D. C. ABEL]
3. D'Arcy Wentworth Thompson, *Growth and Form* (Cambridge, England: Cambridge University Press, 1917). [D. C. DENNETT]
4. *second law of thermodynamics:* the law of physics that states that when a system of heat and energy is left alone, its *entropy* (the amount of disorder) tends to increase. [D. C. ABEL]
5. Paul Rozin and April E. Fallon, "A Perspective on Disgust," *Psychological Review* 94 (January 1987): 23–41. [D. C. DENNETT]
6. Tom Sharpe, *The Great Pursuit* (London, England: Secker & Warburg, 1977), p. 6. [D. C. DENNETT]
7. Richard Dawkins, *The Extended Phenotype: The Gene as the Unit of Selection* (Oxford, England: Oxford University Press, 1982), pp. 195–208. [D. C. ABEL]
8. Eugène N. Marais, *The Soul of the White Ant* (London, England: Methuen, 1937). [D. C. DENNETT]
9. When Dennett wrote this article in 1989, Margaret Thatcher was the British Prime Minister, and George Herbert Walker Bush the U. S. President. [D. C. ABEL]
10. George Carlin (born 1937) is an American comedian. [D. C. ABEL]
11. See the discussion of the moral implications of the "dimensions of the self" in Daniel C. Dennett, *Elbow Room: The Varieties of Free Will Worth Wanting* (Cambridge, Mass.: MIT Press, 1984), especially p. 143. [D. C. DENNETT]
12. *conspecifics:* members of the same species. [D. C. ABEL]
13. See Daniel C. Dennett, "Why Everyone Is a Novelist," *Times Literary Supplement,* September 16–22, 1988, pp. 1016, 1028–1029. [D. C. DENNETT] Reprinted in a slightly revised form as "The Self as a Center of Narrative Gravity," in *Self and Consciousness: Multiple Perspectives,* ed. Frank S. Kessel, Pamela M. Cole, and Dale L. Johnson (Hillsdale, N.J.: Lawrence Erlbaum Associates, 1992), pp. 103–115. [D. C. ABEL]
14. *metaphysically:* relating to *metaphysics,* the study of the nature and kinds of reality. [D. C. ABEL]
15. E. M. Forster (1879–1970) was a British novelist. [D. C. ABEL]
16. *Cartesian:* relating to Descartes. [D. C. ABEL]
17. "*alters*": the various personalities of a person with multiple personality disorder (short for "alter egos"—literally, in Latin, "other I's"). [D. C. ABEL]

CHAPTER 5   # Free Will and Determinism

It seems an obvious fact of our experience that some of the things we do are the result of our own free choice. For example, you probably believe that you freely chose to read this book now, and that you could have chosen to read it earlier or later—or perhaps never! You probably also believe that you could stop reading right now if you decided to. (If you *did* stop, you would probably believe that you could have *not* stopped if you had so chosen.) When we reflect on *why* we choose what we choose, however, we may start to wonder if any of our choices are actually free. You would probably admit that when you choose something, there is some *reason* why you choose it—that your choice has some sort of *cause.* In fact, it seems to be a basic assumption of both common sense and science that *everything* that happens has a cause; it would seem strange if some events (for example, a loud noise right now) "just happened" without having any cause. If a cause is something that necessarily produces a particular effect and if every choice has a cause, then we necessarily choose whatever we choose; our belief that we are free to choose among alternatives is an illusion.

The view that all events are determined by preceding causes and that we can never act otherwise than we do is called *determinism.* Determinists usually locate the causes of human actions in some combination of genetic, environmental, and psychological factors. There are two kinds of determinism, "hard" and "soft." *Hard determinism* accepts determinism and denies the existence of free will and moral responsibility. *Soft determinism* maintains that, although determinism is true, actions with certain kinds of *internal* causes are free, and we are morally responsible for those actions. Since it defends the compatibility of determinism with free will and moral responsibility, soft determinism is also known as *compatibilism.*

Libertarianism is the theory that determinism is false and that human beings can, in some situations, make free choices. Some libertarians are *indeterminists,* making either the general claim that the universe is such that it contains multiple possibilities, or the more specific claim that some events, including some human actions, simply have no cause. Other libertarians (and some soft determinists) are *self-determinists,* agreeing that all our actions have causes but holding that an action is free if it is caused by the *person as a whole* rather than by some preceding set of conditions. (Libertarian self-determinism is sometimes called the *theory of agency* because its proponents define an "agent" precisely as a cause not determined by prior causes.) Like soft determinists, libertarians defend the notion of moral responsibility; unlike them, they deny that an action can be free and determined at the same time.

Our chapter contains two readings that defend hard determinism, two that defend libertarianism, and two that defend soft determinism. Paul-Henri Thiry, Baron d'Holbach, supports hard determinism: We are completely material beings and therefore subject to the causal laws of nature. Holbach contends that, although we do have a will, our will is not free because it necessarily chooses what it thinks will be most advantageous to us. John Hospers contends that our actions are not free and that we are not morally responsible because our actions flow from our character and our character is formed by forces beyond our control. Hospers does not fully accept the determinist thesis that we could not have acted otherwise, since theoretically, if our desires had been different, our actions would have been different.

William James presents an indeterminist defense of libertarianism: Although we can prove neither determinism (hard or soft) nor indeterminism, indeterminism is more plausible because it can better account for "judgments of regret"—judgments that something should have been (or should now be) otherwise than it was (or now is). Richard Taylor proposes a theory of self-determinism: Human actions are free when they are caused by the person as a whole (an agent). He denies the soft determinist claim that an action caused by an internal state of the person (as distinct from the person as a whole) is free.

The final two readings defend soft determinism. W. T. Stace maintains that, although all actions are caused and therefore determined, a particular action is also free if it is caused by an internal psychological state of the agent rather than by an external physical force. Nancy Holmstrom rejects the view that *all* actions proceeding from internal psychological states are free. She seeks to "firm up soft determinism" by showing that an action is free only if the agent has control over the beliefs and desires that cause the action.

A. Hard Determinism

READING 27   ## Of the System of Man's Free Agency

Paul-Henri Thiry, Baron d'Holbach

Paul-Henri Thiry (the French rendering of his original German name, Paul Heinrich Diet-rich), Baron d'Holbach, was born in 1723 in Edesheim, Germany. At the age of twelve, Thiry was taken to Paris to be brought up by his uncle, Franciscus Adam d'Holbach. His uncle, who had made a fortune in Paris and had become a French citizen, carefully directed his ed-ucation. In 1744 Thiry enrolled in the University of Leiden in Holland. He returned to France five years later and became a naturalized citizen. When his uncle died in 1753, Thiry in-herited his fortune and his title, Baron d'Holbach. Holbach's home became a gathering place for many prominent French thinkers, including Jean-Jacques Rousseau, Denis Diderot, and Jean Le Rond d'Alembert. His foreign acquaintances included David Hume, Adam Smith, and Benjamin Franklin. Holbach was an atheist, a materialist, and a severe critic of religion, absolute monarchy, and feudalism. To avoid the personal danger that would result from be-ing known as the proponent of such views, Holbach had his books published in Holland un-der a false name and then had them smuggled back into France. He died in Paris in 1789.

Holbach's major works are *Christianity Unveiled; Being an Examination of the Principles and Effects of Christianity* (1761), *The System of Nature; or, Laws of the Moral and Physical World* (1770), and *Common Sense; or, Natural Ideas Opposed to Supernatural* (1772).

Our selection is from Part I, Chapter 11 of *The System of Nature*, "Of the System of Man's Free Agency." Holbach argues that human beings are completely material and there-fore wholly subject to the laws of nature. We have a will (which Holbach views as a mod-ification of the brain), but our will is not free because it necessarily seeks to preserve or enhance our existence. Forces independent of us create various desires in us. In any situa-tion, we always act in accordance with our strongest desire—namely, the desire for what we think is most advantageous to us. To use one of Holbach's examples, suppose I am ex-tremely thirsty and happen upon a pitcher of water but know that the water is poisoned. If I refrain from drinking, it is because of the strength of my desire to avoid being poisoned; if I drink, it is because my present desire for water overpowers the foreseen harm from the poison. Whether I drink or not, "the two actions will be equally necessary; they will be the effect of that motive which . . . acts in the most coercive manner upon [my] will."

In the latter part of our reading, Holbach responds to several arguments commonly raised by defenders of free will. Some argue that we must be free because we make choices. Holbach responds that although we choose, our choices are never free because we always *necessarily* choose the alternative that exerts the strongest influence on our will. Some pro-ponents of free will try to demonstrate their freedom by performing a simple action such as moving their hand. Holbach replies that the moving of their hand is simply the necessary result of their desire to prove that they are free. Holbach claims that once we understand the causes of our actions, we will see that our actions are never free.

. . . Man is a purely physical being; in whatever manner he is considered, he is connected to universal nature and submitted to the necessary and immutable laws that it imposes on all the beings it contains, according to their peculiar essences or to the respective properties with which, without consulting them, it endows each particular species. Man's life is a line that nature commands him to trace upon the surface of the earth, without his ever being able to swerve from it, even for an instant. He is born without his own consent; his organization in no way depends upon himself; his ideas come to him involuntarily; his habits are in the power of those who cause him to contract them; he is unceasingly modified by causes, whether visible or concealed, over which he has no control, which necessarily regulate his mode of existence, give the hue to his way of thinking, and determine his manner of acting. He is good or bad, happy or miserable, wise or foolish, reasonable or irrational, without his will being for anything in these various states. . . .

It is the actual essence of man to tend to his well-being or to be desirous to conserve his existence. If all the motion of his machine springs as a necessary consequence from this primitive impulse; if pain warns him of that which he ought to avoid; if pleasure announces to him that which he should desire; if it is in his essence to love that which either excites delight or that from which he expects agreeable sensations, and to hate that which either makes him fear contrary impressions or that which afflicts him with uneasinesss—it must necessarily be that he will be attracted by that which he deems advantageous; that his will shall be determined by those objects that he judges useful; that he will be repelled by those beings that he believes detrimental either to his habitual or to his transitory mode of existence. It is only by the aid of experience that man acquires the faculty of understanding what he ought to love or to fear. Are his organs sound? His experience will be true. Are they unsound? It will be false. In the first instance he will have reason, prudence, foresight; he will frequently foresee very remote effects; he will know that what he sometimes contemplates as a good, may possibly become an evil by its necessary or probable consequences; that what must be to him a transient evil, may by its result procure him a solid and durable good. It is experience that enables him to foresee that the amputation of a limb will cause him painful sensation, and he consequently is obliged to fear this operation, and he endeavors to avoid the pain. But if experience has also shown him that the transitory pain this amputation will cause him may be the means of saving his life, the preservation of his existence being of necessity dear to him, he is obliged to submit himself to the momentary pain, with a view to procuring a permanent good by which it will be overbalanced.

The will . . . is a modification of the brain, by which it is disposed to action or prepared to give play to the organs. This will is necessarily determined by the qualities, good or bad, agreeable or painful, of the object or the motive that acts upon his senses, or of which the idea remains with him and is resuscitated by his memory. In consequence, he acts necessarily; his action is the result of the impulse he receives either from the motive, the object, or the idea that has modified his brain or disposed his will. When he does not act according to this impulse, it is because there comes some new cause, some new motive, some new idea, that modifies his brain in a different manner, gives him a new impulse, and determines his will in another way, by which the action of the former impulse is suspended. Thus, the sight of an agreeable object or its idea determines his will to set him in action to procure it. But if a new object or a new idea more powerfully attracts him, it gives a new direction to his will, annihilates the effect of the former, and prevents the action by which it was to be procured. This is the mode in which reflection, experience, or reason necessarily arrests or suspends the action of man's will; without this he would of necessity have followed the earlier impulse that carried him towards a then desirable object. In all this he always acts according to necessary laws, from which he has no means of emancipating himself.

If when tormented with violent thirst, he pictures to himself or really perceives a fountain whose limpid streams might cool his feverish need, is he sufficient master of himself to desire or not to desire the object that can satisfy so lively a need? It will no doubt be conceded that it is impossible that he should not be desirous to satisfy it, but it will be said: If at this moment it is announced to him that the water he so ardently desires is poisoned, he will, notwithstanding his vehement thirst, abstain from drinking it—and it is therefore falsely concluded that he is a free agent. The fact, however, is that the motive in either case is exactly the same: his own conservation. The same necessity that determined him to drink before he knew the water was harmful, upon this new discovery equally determines him not to drink. The desire of conserving himself either annihilates or suspends the former impulse; the second motive becomes stronger than the preceding—that is, the fear of death—or the desire of preserving himself necessarily prevails over the painful sensation caused by his eagerness to drink. But, it will be said, if the thirst is very parching, a thoughtless man, without regarding the danger, will risk swallowing the water. Nothing is gained by this remark. In this case, the earlier impulse only regains the ascendency; he is persuaded that life may possibly be longer preserved, or that he shall derive a greater good by drinking the poisoned water than by enduring the torment that, to his mind, threatens instant dissolution. Thus the first impulse becomes the strongest and necessarily urges him on to action. Nevertheless, in either case, whether he partakes of the water or whether he does not, the two actions will be equally necessary; they will be the effect of that motive which finds itself most powerful, which consequently acts in the most coercive manner upon his will.

This example will serve to explain the whole phenomenon of the human will. This will, or rather the brain, finds itself in the same situation as a ball that, although it has received an impulse that drives it forward in a straight line, is diverted from its course whenever a force superior to the first obliges it to change its direction. The man who drinks the poisoned water appears a madman, but the actions of fools are as necessary as those of the most prudent individuals. The motives that determine the voluptuary and the debauchee to risk their health are as powerful, and their actions are as necessary, as those that cause the wise man to manage his. But, it will be insisted, the debauchee may be prevailed on to change his conduct. This does not imply that he is a free agent, but that motives may be found sufficiently powerful to annihilate the effect of those that previously acted upon him. These new motives determine his will to the new mode of conduct that he adopts, as necessarily as the former motives did to the old mode.

Man is said to *deliberate* when the action of the will is suspended; this happens when two opposite motives act alternately upon him. To deliberate is to hate and to love in succession; it is to be alternately attracted and repelled; it is to be moved sometimes by one motive, sometimes by another. Man only deliberates when he does not distinctly understand the quality of the objects from which he receives impulse, or when experience has not sufficiently apprised him of the effects, more or less remote, that his actions will produce. He would take the air, but the weather is uncertain. He deliberates in consequence; he weighs the various motives that urge his will to go out or to stay at home. He is at length determined by that motive which is most probable. This removes his indecision, which necessarily settles his will, either to remain within or to go out. This motive is always either the immediate or ultimate advantage he finds, or thinks he finds, in the action to which he is persuaded.

Man's will frequently fluctuates between two objects, of which either the presence or the ideas move him alternately. He waits until he has contemplated the objects, or the ideas they have left in his brain, which solicit him to different actions; he then compares these objects or ideas. But even in the time of deliberation, during the comparison, pending these alternatives of love and hatred that succeed each other, sometimes with the utmost rapidity, he is not a free agent for a single instant. The good or the evil that he believes he finds successively in the objects are the necessary motives of these momentary wills, of the rapid motion of desire or fear, that he experiences as long as his uncertainty continues. From this it will be obvious that deliberation is necessary; that uncertainty is necessary; that whatever part he takes, in consequence of this deliberation, it will always necessarily be that which he has judged, whether rightly or wrongly, is most probable to turn to his advantage. . . .

Choice by no means proves the free agency of man: He only deliberates when he does not yet know which to choose of the many objects that move him. He is then in an embarrassment that does not terminate until his will is decided by the greater advantage he believes he shall find in the object he chooses or the action he undertakes. From this it may be seen that choice is necessary, because he would not decide for an object or for an action if he did not believe that he would find in it some direct advantage. That man should have free agency it would be necessary that he should be able to will or choose without motive, or that he could prevent motives from coercing his will. Action always being the effect of his will once determined, and his will being determined by a motive which is not in his own power, it follows that he is never the master of the determination of his own peculiar will—that consequently he never acts as a free agent. It has been believed that man was a free agent because he had a will with the power of choosing, but attention has not been paid to the fact that even his will is moved by causes independent of himself. . . .

It has been believed that man was a free agent because it has been imagined that his soul could at will recall ideas that sometimes suffice to check his most unruly desires. Thus the idea of a remote evil frequently prevents him from enjoying a present and actual good; thus remembrance, which is an almost imperceptible or slight modification of his brain, annihilates at each instant the real objects that act upon his will. But he is not master of recalling to himself his ideas at pleasure. Their association is independent of him; they are arranged in his brain in spite of him and without his own knowledge, where they have made an impression more or less profound. His memory itself depends upon his organization; its fidelity depends upon the habitual or momentary state in which he finds himself. When his will is vigorously determined to some object or idea that excites a very lively passion in him, those objects or ideas that would be able to arrest his action no longer present themselves to his mind. In those moments his eyes are shut to the dangers that menace him, the idea of which ought to make him restrain himself. He marches forward headlong towards the object by whose image he is hurried on; reflection cannot operate upon him in any way; he sees nothing but the object of his desires; the salutary ideas that might be able to arrest his progress disappear, or else display themselves either too faintly or too late to prevent his acting. Such is the case with all those who, blinded by some strong passion, are not in a condition to recall to themselves those motives of which the idea alone, in cooler moments, would be sufficient to deter them from proceeding. The disorder in which they are prevents their judging soundly, renders them incapable of foreseeing the consequence of their actions, and precludes them from benefiting from their experience and from making use of their reason. These are natural operations which suppose a correctness in the manner of associating their ideas, but which their brain is then no more able to perform, in consequence of the momentary delirium it suffers, than their hand is to write while they are taking violent exercise.

Man's mode of thinking is necessarily determined by his manner of being; it must therefore depend on his natural organization and the modification his system receives independently of his will. From this we are obliged to conclude that his thoughts, his reflections, his manner of viewing things, of feeling, of judging, of combining ideas, is neither voluntary nor free—in a word, that his soul is neither mistress of the motion excited in it, nor of representing to itself, when wanted, those images or ideas that are capable of counterbalancing the impulse it receives. This is the reason why man, when in a passion, ceases to reason—at that moment reason is as impossible to be heard, as it is during an ecstasy or in a fit of drunkenness. The wicked are never more than men who are either drunk or mad. If they reason, it is not until tranquility is reestablished in their machine; then, and not till then, the tardy ideas that present themselves to their mind enable them to see the consequence of their actions and give birth to ideas that bring on them that trouble that is designated *shame, regret, remorse.* . . .

In short, the actions of man are never free; they are always the necessary consequence of his temperament; of the received ideas and of the notions, either true or false, that he has formed to himself of happiness; of his opinions, strengthened by example, by education, and by daily experience. So many crimes are witnessed on the earth only because everything conspires to render man vicious and criminal. The religion he has adopted, his government, his education, the examples set before him, irresistibly drive him on to evil. Under these circumstances, morality preaches virtue to him in vain. In those societies where vice is esteemed, where crime is crowned, where venality is constantly recompensed, where the most dreadful disorders are punished only in those who are too weak to enjoy the privilege of committing them with impunity, the practice of virtue is considered nothing more than a painful sacrifice of happiness. Such societies chastise, in the lower orders, those excesses that they respect in the higher ranks. And they frequently have the injustice to condemn those to the penalty of death whom public prejudices, maintained by constant example, have rendered criminal.

Man, then, is not a free agent in any one instant of his life. He is necessarily guided in each step by those advantages, whether real or fictitious, that he attaches to the objects by which his passions are roused. These passions themselves are necessary in a being who unceasingly tends towards his own happiness. Their energy is necessary, since that depends on his temperament. His temperament is necessary, because it depends on the physical elements which enter into his composition. The modification of this temperament is necessary, because it is the infallible and inevitable consequence of the impulse he receives from the incessant action of moral and physical beings.

In spite of these proofs of the lack of free agency in man, so clear to unprejudiced minds, it will perhaps be insisted upon with no small feeling of triumph, that if it be proposed to anyone to move or not to move his hand . . . he evidently appears to be the master of choosing. From this it is concluded that evidence has been offered of his free agency. The reply is that this example is perfectly simple: That a man performs some action which he is *resolved* on doing, does not by any means prove his free agency. The very desire of displaying this quality, excited by the dispute, becomes a necessary motive that decides his will either for the one or the other of these actions. What deludes him in this instance, or that which persuades him he is a free agent at this moment, is that he does not discern the true motive that sets him in action, namely, the desire of convincing his opponent. If in the heat of the dispute he insists and asks, "Am I not the master of throwing myself out of the window?," I shall answer him: No—that while he preserves his reason there is no probability that the desire of proving his free agency will become a motive sufficiently powerful to make him sacrifice his life to the attempt. If, notwithstanding this, to prove he is a free agent he should actually throw himself from the window, it would not be a sufficient warrant to conclude he acted freely, but rather that it was the violence of his temperament that spurred him on to this folly. Madness is a state that depends upon the heat of the blood, not upon the will. A fanatic or a hero braves death as necessarily as a more phlegmatic man or a coward flies from it. . . .

When it is said that man is not a free agent, it is not claimed to compare him to a body moved by a simple impelling cause. He contains within himself causes inherent to his existence; he is moved by an interior organ that has its own peculiar laws and is itself necessarily determined in consequence of ideas formed from perceptions resulting from sensations that it receives from exterior objects. Because the mechanism of these sensations and perceptions, and the manner they engrave ideas on the brain of man, are not known to him because he is unable to unravel all these motions, because he cannot perceive the chain of operations in his soul or the motive principle that acts within him, he supposes himself a free agent. "Motive principle," literally translated, signifies that he moves himself by himself, that he determines himself without cause—when he rather ought to say that he is ignorant how or for why he acts in the manner he does. It is true the soul enjoys an activity peculiar to itself, but it is equally certain that this activity would never be displayed if some motive or some cause did not put it in a condition to exercise itself. At least it will not be claimed that the soul is able either to love or to hate without being moved, without knowing the objects, without having some idea of their qualities. Gunpowder has unquestionably a particular activity, but this activity will never display itself unless fire be applied to it; this, however, immediately sets it in motion.

It is the great complication of motion in man, the variety of his action, and the multiplicity of causes that move him (whether simultaneously or in continual succession) that persuade him that he is a free agent. If all his motions were simple, if the causes that move him did not confound themselves with each other, if they were distinct, and if his machine were less complicated, he would perceive that all his actions were necessary, because he would be enabled to go back instantly to the cause that made him act. . . .

It is, then, for lack of going back to the causes that move him and for lack of being able to analyze into its constituent parts the complicated motion of his machine, that man believes himself a free agent. It is only upon his own ignorance that he bases the profound yet deceitful notion he has of his free agency, and that he builds those opinions that he brings forward as a striking proof of his alleged freedom of action. If, for a short time, each man was willing to examine his own peculiar actions and search out their true motives to discover their concatenation, he would remain convinced that the sentiment he has of his natural free agency is a chimera[1] that must speedily be destroyed by experience.

From all that has been advanced in this chapter, it results that in no one moment of his existence is man a free agent. He is not the architect of his own conformation, which he holds from nature. He has no control over his own ideas or over the modification of his brain; these are due to causes that, in spite of him and without his own knowledge, unceasingly act upon him. He is not the master of not loving or coveting that which he finds amiable or desirable; he is not capable of refusing to deliberate when he is uncertain of the effects certain objects will produce upon him; he cannot avoid choosing that which he believes will be most advantageous to him. In the moment when his will is determined by his choice, he is not able to act otherwise than he does. . . .

In the moral as well as in the physical world, everything that happens is a necessary consequence of causes, either visible or concealed, which are of necessity obliged to act after their peculiar essences. *In man, free agency is nothing more than necessity contained within himself.*

NOTE

1. *chimera:* mental fabrication. [D. C. ABEL]

The Range of Human Freedom

John Hospers

John Hospers was born in 1918 in Pella, Iowa. He attended Central College (now Central University of Iowa), where he received his bachelor's degree in 1939. Two years later he earned a master's degree in English at the University of Iowa. After that, he enrolled in the doctoral program in philosophy at Columbia University, completing his degree in 1944. Hospers then taught at the University of North Carolina, the University of Illinois, and Columbia. In 1948 he accepted a position at the University of Minnesota, where he remained for eight years. From 1956 to 1966 he taught at Brooklyn College of the City University of New York. He then went to the University of Southern California, where he stayed until his retirement in 1988. Hospers was the Libertarian Party candidate for the presidency of the United States in 1972, the year the national party was founded. Since that time he has given many talks in the United States and abroad on the libertarian movement. (Libertarianism as a political movement emphasizing individual rights should not be confused with libertarianism as the philosophical position that free will exists and that determinism is false; Hospers is a political libertarian but not a philosophical libertarian.)

Hospers's principal books are *Meaning and Truth in the Arts* (1946; 2d ed., 1982); *Introduction to Philosophical Analysis* (1953; 3d ed., 1988), *Libertarianism: A Political Philosophy for Tomorrow* (1971), and *Understanding the Arts* (1982). He has also been editor of three philosophical journals—*The Personalist, Pacific Philosophical Quarterly,* and *The Monist.*

Our reading is from "The Range of Human Freedom," a lecture Hospers gave at New York University in 1957. (The lecture was published the following year under the title "What Means This Freedom?") Examining the extent to which we are responsible for our actions, Hospers argues that our actions flow from our character and that our character is formed by forces beyond our control—namely, our genetic inheritance and our environment (especially our early childhood environment). Although it may seem that criminals, for example, are responsible for their crimes, if we understood the deep psychological forces driving them (such as feelings of rejection), we would realize that their actions are the necessary result of those forces. And it is not only people with psychological disturbances who are not responsible; the actions of *every* person derive from character, and no one is responsible for his or her character. Does the fact that some people overcome negative influences of their early environment show that those who fail to overcome negative influences are responsible for not doing so? No, because the ability to overcome these forces is *itself* a result of heredity and environment. Hospers concludes that whether we are "moral" or not is ultimately a matter of luck—the luck of heredity and environment.

Hospers points out that he is not arguing for determinism in the sense of denying that we could have acted otherwise than we did. He observes, however, that when we say that we could have done otherwise, we mean simply that if our *desires* had been different, our *actions* would have been different. But our desires are the product of our character, which is ultimately formed by "conditions occurring outside us, over which we had no control." Hospers distinguishes two levels of moral discourse: actions and the springs of action. "Responsible" and "could have" apply to the first level in the sense that our actions result from our desires, and if we had had different desires, we would have acted differently. But "responsible" and "could have" do not apply to the second, deeper level, since our desires derive from factors beyond our control.

. . . There remains a question in our minds whether we are, in the final analysis, *responsible for any of our actions at all.* The issue may be put this way: How can anyone be responsible for his actions, since they grow out of his character, which is shaped and molded and made what it is by influences—some hereditary, but most of them stemming from early parental environment—that were not of his own making or choosing? . . .

Let us take as an example a criminal who, let us say, strangled several persons and is himself now condemned to die in the electric chair. Jury and public alike hold him fully responsible (at least they utter the words "he is responsible") for the murders were planned down to the minutest detail, and the defendant tells the jury exactly how he planned them. But now we find out how it all came about; we learn of parents who rejected him from babyhood, of the childhood spent in one foster home after another, where it was always plain to him that he was not wanted; of the constantly frustrated early desire for affection, the hard shell of nonchalance and bitterness that he assumed to cover the painful and humiliating fact of being unwanted, and his subsequent attempts to heal these wounds to his shattered ego through defensive aggression. . . . The poor victim is not conscious of the inner forces that exact from him this ghastly toll; he battles, he schemes, he revels in pseudo-aggression, he is miserable, but he does not know what works within him to produce these catastrophic acts of crime. His aggressive actions are the wriggling of a worm on a fisherman's hook. And if this is so, it seems difficult to say any longer, "He is responsible." Rather, we shall put him behind bars for the protection of society, but we shall no longer flatter our feeling of moral superiority by calling him personally responsible for what he did.

Let us suppose it were established that a man commits murder only if, sometime during the previous week, he has eaten a certain combination of foods—say, tuna fish salad at a meal also including peas, mushroom soup, and blueberry pie. What if we were to track down the factors common to all murders committed in this country during the last twenty years and found this factor present in all of them, and only in them? The example is of course empirically absurd; but may it not be that there is *some* combination of factors that regularly leads to homicide, factors such as are described [in the previous paragraph]? When such specific factors are discovered, won't they make it clear that it is foolish and pointless, as well as immoral, to hold human beings responsible for crimes? Or, if one prefers biological to psychological factors, suppose a neurologist is called in to testify at a murder trial and produces X-ray pictures of the brain of the criminal. Anyone can see, he argues, that the *cella turcica* was already calcified at the age of nineteen; it should be a flexible bone, growing, enabling the gland to grow. All the defendant's disorders might have resulted from this early calcification. Now this particular explanation may be empirically false, but who can say that no such factors, far more complex, to be sure, exist?

When we know such things as these, we no longer feel so much tempted to say that the criminal is responsible for his crime; and we tend also (do we not?) to excuse him—not legally (we still confine him to prison) but morally; we no longer call him a monster or hold him personally responsible for what he did. Moreover, we do this in general, not merely in the case of crime: "You must excuse Grandmother for being irritable; she's really quite ill and is suffering some pain all the time." Or: "The dog always bites children after she's had a litter of pups; you can't blame her for it: She's not feeling well, and besides she naturally wants to defend them." Or: "She's nervous and jumpy, but do excuse her: She has a severe glandular disturbance."

Let us note that the more *thoroughly* and *in detail* we know the causal factors leading a person to behave as he does, the more we tend to exempt him from responsibility. When we know nothing of the man except what we see him do, we say he is an ungrateful cad who expects much of other people and does nothing in return, and we are usually indignant. When we learn that his parents were the same way and, having no guilt feelings about this mode of behavior themselves, brought him up to be greedy and avaricious, we see that we could hardly expect him to have developed moral feelings in this direction. When we learn, in addition, that he is not aware of being ungrateful or selfish, but unconsciously represses the memory of events unfavorable to himself, we feel that the situation is unfortunate but "not really his fault." When we know that this behavior of his, which makes others angry, occurs more constantly when he feels tense or insecure, and that he now feels tense and insecure, and that relief from pressure will diminish it, then we tend to "feel sorry for the poor guy" and say he's more to be pitied than censured. We no longer want to say that he is personally responsible; we might rather blame nature or his parents for having given him an unfortunate constitution or temperament.

> In recent years a new form of punishment has been imposed on middle-aged and elderly parents. Their children, now in their twenties, thirties, or even forties, present them with a modern grievance: "My [psycho] analysis proves that *you* are responsible for my neurosis." Overawed by these authoritative statements, the poor tired parents fall easy victims to the newest variations on the scapegoat theory.
>
> In my opinion, this senseless cruelty—which disinters educational sins which had been buried for decades, and uses them as the basis for accusations which the victims cannot answer—is unjustified. Yes, "the truth loves to be centrally located" (Melville),[1] and few parents—since they are human—have been perfect. But granting their mistakes, they acted as *their* neurotic difficulties forced them to act. To turn the tables and declare the children not guilty because of the *impersonal* nature of their own neuroses, while at the same time the parents are *personally* blamed, is worse than illogical; it is profoundly unjust.[2]

And so, it would now appear, neither of the parties is responsible: "They acted as their neurotic difficulties forced them to act." The patients are not responsible for their neurotic manifestations, but then neither are the parents responsible for theirs; and so, of course, for their parents in turn, and theirs before them. It is the twentieth-century version of the family curse, the curse on the House of Atreus.[3]

"But," a critic complains, "it's immoral to exonerate people indiscriminately in this way. I might have thought it fit to excuse somebody because he was born on the other side of the tracks, if I didn't know so many bank presidents who were also born on the other side of the tracks." Now I submit that the most immoral thing in this situation is the critic's caricature of the conditions of the excuse. Nobody is excused merely because he was born on the other side of the tracks. But if he was born on the other side of the tracks *and* was a highly narcissistic infant to begin with *and* was repudiated or neglected by his parents *and* . . . (here we list a finite number of conditions), and if this complex of factors is *regularly* followed by certain behavior traits in adulthood, and moreover *unavoidably* so—that is, they occur no matter what he or anyone else tries to do—then we excuse him morally and say he is not responsible for his deed. If he is not responsible for *A,* a series of events occurring in his babyhood, then neither is he responsible for *B,* a series of things he does in adulthood, provided that *B* inevitably—that is, unavoidably—follows upon the occurrence of *A.* And according to psychiatrists and psychoanalysts, this often happens.

But one may still object that so far we have talked only about neurotic behavior. Isn't nonneurotic or normal or not-unconsciously-motivated (or whatever you want to call it) behavior still within the area of responsibility? There are reasons for answering "No" even here, for the normal person no more than the neurotic one has caused his own character, which makes him what he is. Granted that neurotics are not responsible for their behavior (that part of it which we call neurotic) because it stems from undigested infantile conflicts that they had no part in bringing about, and that are external to them just as surely as if their behavior had been forced on them by a malevolent deity (which is indeed one theory on the subject); but the so-called normal person is equally the product of causes in which his volition took no part. And if, unlike the neurotic's, his behavior is changeable by rational considerations, and if he has the will power to overcome the effects of an unfortunate early environment, this again is no credit to him—he is just lucky. If energy is available to him in a form in which it can be mobilized for constructive purposes, this is no credit to him, for this too is part of his psychic legacy. Those of us who can discipline ourselves and develop habits of concentration of purpose tend to blame those who cannot, and call them lazy and weak-willed. But what we fail to see is that they literally *cannot* do what we expect; if their psyches were structured like ours, they could, but as they are burdened with a tyrannical superego[4] (to use psychoanalytic jargon for the moment) and a weak defenseless ego[5] whose energies are constantly consumed in fighting endless charges of the superego, they simply cannot do it, and it is irrational to expect it of them. We cannot with justification blame them for their inability, any more than we can congratulate ourselves for our ability. This lesson is hard to learn, for we constantly and naively assume that other people are constructed as we ourselves are.

For example: A child raised under slum conditions, whose parents are socially ambitious and envy families with money, but who nevertheless squander the little they have on drink, may simply be unable in later life to mobilize a drive sufficient to overcome these early conditions. Common sense would expect that he would develop the virtue of thrift; he would make quite sure that he would never again endure the grinding poverty he had experienced as a child. But in fact it is not so. The exact conditions are too complex to be specified in detail here, but when certain conditions are fulfilled (concerning the subject's early life), he will always thereafter be a spendthrift, and no rational considerations will be able to change this. He will listen to the rational considerations and see the force of these, but they will not be able to change him, even if he tries; he cannot change his wasteful habits any more than he can lift the Empire State Building with his bare hands. We moralize and plead with him to be thrifty, but we do not see how strong, how utterly overpowering, and how constantly with him, is the opposite drive, which is so easily manageable with us. But he is possessed by the all-consuming, all-encompassing urge to make the world see that he belongs, that he has arrived, that he is just as well off as anyone else, that the awful humiliations were not real, that they never actually occurred, for isn't he now able to spend and spend? The humiliation must be blotted out, and conspicuous, flashy, expensive, and wasteful buying will do this—it shows the world what the world must know! True, it is only for the moment; true, it is in the end self-defeating, for wasteful consumption is the best way to bring poverty back again; but the person with an overpowering drive to mend a lesion to his narcissism cannot resist the avalanche of that drive with this puny rational consideration. A man with his back against the wall and a gun at his throat doesn't think of what may happen ten years hence. (Consciously, of course, he knows nothing of this drive; all that appears to consciousness is its shattering effects. He knows only that he must keep on spending—not why—and that he is unable to resist.) He hasn't in him the psychic capacity, the energy to stem the tide of a drive that at that moment is all-powerful. We, seated comfortably away from this flood, sit in judgment on him and blame him and exhort him and criticize him; but he, carried along by the flood, cannot do otherwise than he does. He may fight with all the strength of which he is capable, but it is not enough. And we, who are rational enough at least to exonerate a man in a situation of "overpowering impulse" when we recognize it to be one, do not even recognize this as an example of it; and so, in addition to being swept away in the flood that childhood conditions rendered inevitable, he must also endure our lectures, our criticisms, and our moral excoriation.

But, one will say, he could have overcome his spendthrift tendencies; some people do. Quite true—some people do. They are lucky. They have it in them to overcome early deficiencies by exerting great effort, and they are capable of exerting the effort. Some of us, luckier still, can overcome them with but little effort; and a few, the luckiest, haven't the deficiencies to overcome. It's all a matter of luck. The least lucky are those who can't overcome them, even with great effort, and those who haven't the ability to exert the effort.

But, one persists, it isn't a matter simply of luck; it *is* a matter of effort. Very well then, it's a matter of effort; without exerting the effort you may not overcome the deficiency. But whether or not you are the kind of person who has it in him to exert the effort is a matter of luck. . . .

The position, then, is this: If we *can* overcome the effects of early environment, the ability to do so is itself a product of the early environment. We did not give ourselves this ability, and if we lack it we cannot be blamed for not having it. Sometimes, to be sure, moral exhortation brings out an ability that is there but not being used, and in this lies its *occasional* utility; but very often its use is pointless, because the ability is not there. The only thing that can overcome a desire, as Spinoza[6] said, is a stronger contrary desire; and many times there simply is no wherewithal for producing a stronger contrary desire. Those of us who do have the wherewithal are lucky.

There is one possible practical advantage in remembering this. It may prevent us (unless we are compulsive blamers) from indulging in righteous indignation and committing the sin of spiritual pride, thanking God that we are not as this publican here.[7] And it will protect from our useless moralizings those who are least equipped by nature for enduring them.

As with responsibility, so with deserts. Someone commits a crime and is punished by the state. "He deserved it," we say self-righteously—as if we were moral and he immoral, when in fact we are lucky and he is unlucky—forgetting that there, but for the grace of God and a fortunate early environment, go we. . . .

I want to make it quite clear that I have not been arguing for determinism. Though I find it difficult to give any sense to the term "indeterminism," because I do not know what it would be like to come across an uncaused event, let us grant indeterminists everything they want, at least in words—influences that suggest but do not constrain, a measure of acausality in an otherwise rigidly causal order, and so on—whatever these phrases may mean. With all this granted, exactly the same situation faces the indeterminist and the determinist; all we have been saying would still hold true. "Are our powers innate or acquired?"

> Suppose the powers are declared innate; then the villain may sensibly ask whether he is responsible for what he was born with. A negative reply is inevitable. Are they then acquired? Then the ability to acquire them—was *that* innate? or acquired? It is innate? Very well then. . . . [8]

The same fact remains—that we did not cause our characters, that the influences that made us what we are are influences over which we had no control and of whose very existence we had no knowledge at the time. This fact remains for "determinism" and "indeterminism" alike. And it is this fact to which I would appeal, not the specific tenets of traditional forms of "determinism," which seem to me, when analyzed, empirically empty.

"But," it may be asked, "isn't it your view that nothing ultimately *could* be other than it is? And isn't this deterministic? And isn't it deterministic if you say that human beings could never act otherwise than they do, and that their desires and temperaments could not, when you consider their antecedent conditions, be other than they are?"

I reply that all these charges rest on confusions.

1. To say that nothing *could* be other than it is, is, taken literally, nonsense; and if taken as a way of saying something else, misleading and confusing. If you say, "I can't do it," this invites the question, "No? Not even if you want to?" "Can" and "could" are power words, used in the context of human action; when applied to nature they are merely anthropomorphic. "Could" has no application to nature—unless, of course, it is uttered in a

theological context: One might say that God *could* have made things different. But with regard to inanimate nature "could" has no meaning. Or perhaps it is intended to mean that the order of nature is in some sense *necessary*. But in that case the sense of "necessary" must be specified. I know what "necessary" means when we are talking about propositions, but not when we are talking about the sequence of events in nature.

2. What of the charge that we could never have acted otherwise than we did? This, I submit, is simply not true. . . . I could have gone to the opera today instead of coming here; that is, if certain conditions had been different, I should have gone. I could have done many other things instead of what I did, if some condition or other had been different, specifically if my desire had been different. I repeat that "could" is a power word, and "I could have done this" means approximately "I *should* have done this *if* I had wanted to." In this sense, all of us could often have done otherwise than we did. I would not want to say that I should have done differently even if *all* the conditions leading up to my action had been the same (this is generally not what we mean by "could" anyway); but to assert that I could have is empty, for if I *did* act differently from the time before, we would automatically say that one or more of the conditions were different, whether we had independent evidence for this or not, thus rendering the assertion immune to empirical refutation. . . .

I conclude, then, with the following suggestion: that we operate on two levels of moral discourse, which we shouldn't confuse. One (let's call it the upper level) is that of actions; the other (the lower, or deeper, level) is that of the springs of action. Most moral talk occurs on the upper level. . . . "Can" and "could" acquire their meaning on this level; so, I suspect, does "freedom." So does the distinction between compulsive and noncompulsive behavior. . . . We are practical beings interested in changing the course of human behavior, so it is natural enough that 99 percent of our moral talk occurs here.

But when we descend to what I have called the lower level of moral discourse, as we occasionally do in thoughtful moments when there is no immediate need for action, then we must admit that we are ultimately the kind of persons we are because of conditions occurring outside us, over which we had no control. But while this is true, we should beware of extending the moral terminology we used on the other level to this one also. "Could" and "can," as we have seen, no longer have meaning here. "Right" and "wrong," which apply only to actions, have no meaning here either. I suspect that the same is true of "responsibility," for now that we have recalled often forgotten facts about our being the product of outside forces, we must ask in all seriousness what would be added by saying that we are not *responsible* for our own characters and temperaments. What would it mean even? Has it a significant opposite? What would it be like to be responsible for one's own character? What possible situation is describable by this phrase? Instead of saying that it is *false* that we are responsible for our own characters, I should prefer to say that the utterance is meaningless—meaningless in the sense that it describes no possible situation, though it *seems* to because the word "responsible" is the same one we used on the upper level, where it marks a real distinction. If this is so, the result is that *moral* terms—at least the terms "could have" and "responsible"—simply drop out on the lower level. What remains, shorn now of moral terminology, is the point [that] whether or not we have personality disturbances, whether or not we have the ability to overcome deficiencies of early environment, is like the answer to the question whether or not we shall be struck down by a dread disease: "It's all a matter of luck." It is important to keep this in mind, for people almost always forget it, with consequences in human intolerance and unnecessary suffering that are incalculable.

NOTES

1. Herman Melville (1819–1891) was an American novelist. [D. C. ABEL]
2. Edmund Bergler, *The Superego* (New York: Grune & Stratton, 1952), p. 320. [J. HOSPERS]
3. In Greek mythology, Atreus was a king of Mycenae. He and his family committed many atrocities against each other. [D. C. ABEL]
4. *superego:* in the psychoanalytic theory of Austrian neurologist Sigmund Freud (1856–1939), the part of the psyche that contains an idealized image of oneself (positive standards) and conscience (negative standards). [D. C. ABEL]
5. *ego:* in psychoanalytic theory, the conscious part of the psyche, by which a person deals with external reality. [D. C. ABEL]
6. Baruch (Benedict de) Spinoza (1632–1677) was a Dutch philosopher. [D. C. ABEL]
7. Hospers alludes to the Gospel story in Luke 18:9–14. [D. C. ABEL]
8. W. I. Matson, "On the Irrelevance of Free-Will to Moral Responsibility, and the Vacuity of the Latter," *Mind*, new series 65 (October 1956), p. 495. [J. HOSPERS]

B. Libertarianism

READING 29 # The Dilemma of Determinism

William James

A biography of William James appears on p. 106.

This reading is from "The Dilemma of Determinism," a lecture James gave in 1884 to students of the Harvard Divinity School. *Determinism,* James explains, is the doctrine that everything happening in the future is already completely predetermined by the way things are now: "Those parts of the universe already laid down absolutely appoint and decree what the other parts shall be." *Indeterminism,* by contrast, allows some "loose play" among the parts of the universe, so that the future holds more than one possibility. According to determinism, the only future that is possible is the one that actually happens; whatever happens, happens by necessity. According to indeterminism, alternative futures are possible; things could have happened differently from the way they did.

James contends that our decision whether to accept determinism or indeterminism will be based on our "postulates of rationality"—whether we think the world is more rational if it is governed by necessity or if it contains multiple possibilities. Determinists are people who think that if chance has a role in the world (that is, if some events are not the product of necessity), the world becomes chaotic and unintelligible. James maintains, however, that an event that happens by chance is just as intelligible as one that happens by necessity. James goes on to argue that the existence of "judgments of regret" (judgments that something should have been or should now be otherwise than it was or now is) makes indeterminism more plausible than determinism. If determinists admit the rationality of judgments of regret, they commit themselves to the pessimistic view that the world, with all its evils, could not be better than it is. If they want to be optimistic, they have to view all judgments of regret as irrational. The only way out of this dilemma is to accept indeterminism.

. . . A common opinion prevails that the juice has ages ago been pressed out of the free will controversy, and that no new champion can do more than warm up stale arguments which everyone has heard. This is a radical mistake. I know of no subject less worn out, or in which inventive genius has a better chance of breaking open new ground—not, perhaps, of forcing a conclusion or of coercing assent, but of deepening our consciousness of *what* the issue between the two parties really is, our sense of what hidden implications the ideas of fate and of free will contain. . . .

To begin, then, I must suppose you acquainted with all the usual arguments on the subject. I cannot stop to take up the arguments from causation, from statistics, from the certainty with which we can foretell each other's conduct, from the fixity of character, and all the rest. But there are two *words* which encumber these classical arguments usually, and which we must immediately dispose of, if we are to make any progress. One is the eulogistic word *freedom,* and the other is the opprobrious word *chance.* The word "chance" I wish to keep, but I wish to get rid of the word "freedom." Its eulogistic associations have so far overshadowed all the rest of its meaning that both parties claim the sole right to use it, and determinists today insist that they alone are freedom's champions. Old-fashioned determinism was what we may call *hard* determinism. It did not shrink from such words as fatality, bondage of the will, necessitation, and the like. Nowadays we have a *soft* determinism[1] which abhors harsh words, and, repudiating fatality, necessity, and even determinism, says that its real name is freedom; for freedom is only necessity understood, and bondage to the highest is identical with true freedom. . . .

Now, this is all a quagmire of evasion under which the real issue of fact has got entirely smothered up. Freedom in all these senses presents simply no problem at all. No matter what the soft determinist means by it—whether he means acting without external constraint, whether he means acting rightly, or whether he means acquiescing in the law of the whole—who cannot answer him that sometimes we are free and sometimes we are not? But there *is* a problem, an issue of fact and not of words, an issue of the most momentous importance, which is often decided without discussion in one sentence, nay, in one clause of a sentence, by those very writers who spin out whole chapters in their efforts to show what "true" freedom is; and that is the question of determinism, about which we are to talk tonight.

Fortunately, no ambiguities hang about this word or about its opposite, indeterminism. Both designate an outward way in which things may happen, and their cold and mathematical sound has no sentimental associations that can bribe our partiality either way in advance. Now, evidence of an external kind to decide between determinism and indeterminism is . . . strictly impossible to find. Let us look at the difference between them and see for ourselves. What does determinism profess?

It professes that those parts of the universe already laid down absolutely appoint and decree what the other parts shall be. The future has no ambiguous possibilities hidden in its womb: The part we call the present is compatible with only one totality. Any other future complement than the one fixed from eternity is impossible. The whole is in each and every part, and welds it with the rest into an absolute unity, an iron block, in which there can be no equivocation or shadow of turning.

> With Earth's first Clay They did the Last Man knead,
> And there of the Last Harvest sow'd the Seed:
>   And the first Morning of Creation wrote
> What the Last Dawn of Reckoning shall read.[2]

Indeterminism, on the contrary, says that the parts have a certain amount of loose play on each other, so that the laying down of one of them does not necessarily determine what the others shall be. It admits that possibilities may be in excess of actualities, and that things not yet revealed to our knowledge may really in themselves be ambiguous. Of two alternative futures we now conceive, both now may be really possible; and the one only become impossible at the very moment when the other excludes it by becoming real itself. Indeterminism thus denies the world to be one unbroken, unbending unit of fact. It says there is a certain ultimate pluralism in it; and, so saying, it corroborates our ordinary unsophisticated view of things. To that view, actualities seem to float in a wider sea of possibilities from out of which they are chosen; and, *somewhere*, indeterminism says such possibilities exist, and form a part of truth.

Determinism, on the contrary, says they exist *nowhere*, and that necessity on the one hand and impossibility on the other are the sole categories of truth. Possibilities that fail to get realized are, for determinism, pure illusions: They never were possibilities at all. There is nothing inchoate, it says, about this universe of ours; all that was or is or shall be actual in it, having been from eternity necessarily and virtually there. The cloud of alternatives our minds escort this mass of actuality withal[3] is a cloud of sheer deceptions, to which "impossibilities" is the only name that rightfully belongs.

The issue, it will be seen, is a perfectly sharp one, which no eulogistic terminology can smear over or wipe out. The truth *must* lie with one side or the other, and its lying with one side makes the other false.

The question relates solely to the existence of possibilities, in the strict sense of the term, as things that *may*, but *need* not, be. Both sides admit that a volition, for instance, has occurred. The indeterminists say another volition might have occurred in its place; the determinists swear that nothing could possibly have occurred in its place. Now can *science* be called in to tell us which of these two point-blank contradictors of each other is right? Science professes to draw no conclusions but such as are based on matters of fact, things that have actually happened. But how can any amount of assurance that any thing actually happened give us the least grain of information as to whether another thing might or might not have happened in its place? Facts can only prove facts. With things that are possibilities and not facts, they have no concern. If we have no other evidence than the evidence of existing facts, the possibility-question must remain a mystery never to be cleared up.

And the truth is that facts practically have hardly anything to do with making us either determinists or indeterminists. Sure enough, we make a flourish of quoting facts this way or that; and, if we are determinists, we talk about the infallibility with which we can predict each other's conduct, while, if we are indeterminists, we lay great stress on the fact that it is just because we cannot foretell each other's conduct, either in war or statecraft or in any of the great and small intrigues and businesses of men, that life is so intensely anxious and hazardous a game. But who does not see the wretched insufficiency of this so-called objective testimony on both sides? What fills up the gaps in our minds is something not objective, not external. What divides us into possibility men and anti-possibility men is different faiths or postulates—postulates of rationality. To this man the world seems more rational with possibilities in it, to that man more rational with possibilities excluded. And talk as we will about having to yield to evidence, what makes us monists or pluralists,[4] determinists or indeterminists, is at bottom always some sentiment like this.

The stronghold of the deterministic sentiment is the antipathy to the idea of chance. As soon as we begin to talk indeterminism to our friends, we find a number of them shaking their heads. This notion of alternative possibility, they say, this admission that any one of several things may come to pass, is, after all, only a roundabout name for *chance;* and chance is something the notion of which no sane mind can for an instant tolerate in the world. What is it, they ask, but barefaced crazy unreason, the negation of intelligibility and law? And, if the slightest particle of it exist anywhere, what is to prevent the whole fabric from falling together, the stars from going out, and chaos from recommencing her topsy-turvy reign?

Remarks of this sort about chance are apt to put an end to discussion about as quickly as anything one can find. I told you a short while ago that "chance" was a word I wished to keep and use. Let us then examine exactly what it means, and see whether it ought to be such a terrible bugbear to us. I fancy that squeezing the thistle boldly will rob it of its sting.

The sting of the word "chance" seems to lie in the assumption that it means something positive, and that, if anything happens by chance, it must needs[5] be something of an intrinsically irrational and preposterous sort. Now, chance means nothing of the kind. It is a purely negative and relative term, giving us no information about that of which it is predicated, except that it happens to be disconnected with something else—not controlled, secured, or necessitated by other things in advance of its own actual presence. As this point is the most subtle point of the whole lecture, and at the same time the point on which all the rest hinges, I want to beg you to pay special attention to it. What I say is that it tells us nothing about what a thing may be in itself to call it chance. It may be a bad thing, it may be a good thing. It may be lucidity, transparency, fitness incarnate, matching the whole system of other things, when it has once befallen, in an unimaginably perfect way. All you mean by calling it chance is that this is not *guaranteed,* that it may also fall out otherwise. For the system of other things has no positive hold on the chance thing. Its origin is in a certain fashion negative: It escapes, and says "Hands off!"—coming, when it comes, as a free gift or not at all. . . .

Nevertheless, many people talk as if the minutest dose of disconnectedness of one part with another, the smallest modicum of independence, the faintest tremor of ambiguity about the future, for example, would ruin everything, and turn this goodly universe into a sort of insane sand-heap or nulliverse, no universe at all. Since future human volitions are as a matter of fact the only ambiguous things we are tempted to believe in, let us stop for a moment to make ourselves sure whether their independent and accidental character need be fraught with such direful consequences to the universe as these.

What is meant by saying that my choice of which way to walk home after the lecture is ambiguous and matter of chance as far as the present moment is concerned? It means that both Divinity Avenue and Oxford Street are called; but that only one, and that one *either* one, shall be chosen.[6] Now, I ask you seriously to suppose that this ambiguity of my choice is real and then to make the impossible hypothesis that the choice is made twice over, and each time falls on a different street. In other words, imagine that I first walk through Divinity Avenue, and then imagine that the powers governing the universe annihilate ten minutes of time with all that it contained, and set me back at the door of this hall just as I was before the choice was made. Imagine then that, everything else being the same, I now make a different choice and traverse Oxford Street. You, as passive spectators, look on and see the two alternative universes—one of them with me walking through Divinity Avenue in it, the other with the same me walking through Oxford Street. Now if you are determinists you believe one of these universes to have been from eternity impossible: You believe it to have been impossible because of the intrinsic irrationality or accidentality somewhere involved in it. But, looking outwardly at these universes, can you say which is the impossible and accidental one, and which the rational and necessary one? I doubt if the most ironclad determinist among you could have the slightest glimmer of light on this point. In other words, either universe *after the fact* and once there would, to our means of observation and understanding, appear just as rational as the other. There would be absolutely no criterion by which we might judge one necessary and the other matter of chance. Suppose now we relieve the gods of their hypothetical task and assume my choice, once made, to be made forever. I go through Divinity Avenue for good and all. If, as good determinists, you now begin to affirm, what all good determinists punctually do affirm, that in the nature of things I *couldn't* have gone through Oxford Street—had I done so it would have been chance, irrationality, insanity, a horrid gap in nature—I simply call your attention to this, that your affirmation is what the Germans call a *Machtspruch*,[7] a mere conception fulminated as a dogma and based on no insight into details. Before my choice, either street seemed as natural to you as to me. Had I happened to take Oxford Street, Divinity Avenue would have figured in your philosophy as the gap in nature, and you would have so proclaimed it with the best of deterministic consciences.

But what a hollow outcry, then, is this against a chance which, if it were present to us, we could by no sensible[8] empirical character whatever distinguish from a rational necessity. . . .

And this at last brings us within sight of our subject. We have seen what determinism means: We have seen that indeterminism is rightly described as meaning chance; and we have seen that chance, the very name of which we are urged to shrink from, as from a metaphysical[9] pestilence, means only the negative fact that no one part of the world can claim to control absolutely the destinies of the whole. But although, in discussing the word "chance," I may at moments have seemed to be arguing for its real existence, I have not meant to do so yet. We have not yet ascertained whether this *is* a world of chance or no. At most, we have agreed that it *seems* so. And I now repeat what I said at the outset, that from any strict theoretical point of view the question is insoluble. To deepen our theoretic sense of the *difference* between a world with chances in it and a deterministic world is the most I can hope to do. And this I may now at last begin upon, after all our tedious clearing of the way.

I wish first of all to show you just what the notion that this is a deterministic world implies. The implications I call your attention to are all bound up with the fact that it is a world in which we constantly have to make what I shall, with your permission, call judgments of regret. Hardly an hour passes in which we do not wish that something might be otherwise; and happy indeed are those of us whose hearts have never echoed the wish of Omar Khayyám,

> That we might clasp ere closed the Book of Fate,
>   And make The Writer on a fairer leaf
> Inscribe our names, or quite obliterate! . . .
>
> Ah Love! could you and I with Fate conspire
> To grasp this sorry Scheme of Things entire,
>   Would we not shatter it to bits—and then
> Remold it nearer to the Heart's Desire![10]

Now it is undeniable that most of these regrets are foolish and quite on a par in point of philosophic value with the criticisms on the universe of that friend of our infancy, the hero of the fable "The Atheist and the Acorn"—

> Fool! had that bough a pumpkin bore,
> Thy whimsies would have worked no more (and so on).[11]

Even from the point of view of our own ends, we should probably make a botch of remodeling the universe. How much more then from the point of view of ends we cannot see! Wise men therefore regret as little as they can. But still some regrets are pretty obstinate and hard to stifle—regrets for acts of wanton cruelty or treachery, for example, whether performed by others or by ourselves. Hardly any one can remain *entirely* optimistic after reading the confession of the murderer at Brockton the other day—how, to get rid of the wife whose continued existence bored him, he inveigled her into a desert[12] spot, shot her four times, and then, as she lay on the ground and said to him "You didn't do it on purpose, did you, dear?," replied "No, I didn't do it on purpose" as he raised a rock and smashed her skull. Such an occurrence, with the mild sentence and self-satisfaction of the prisoner, is a field for a crop of regrets, which one need not take up in detail. We feel that, although a perfect mechanical fit to the rest of the universe, it is a bad *moral* fit, and that something else would *really* have been better in its place.

Now for the deterministic philosophy, the murder, the sentence, and the prisoner's optimism were all necessary from eternity; and nothing else for a moment had a ghost of a chance of being put into their place. To admit such a chance, the determinists tell us, would be to make a suicide of reason, so we must steel our hearts against the thought. And here our plot thickens, for we see the first of those difficult implications of determinism and monism which it is my purpose to make you feel. If this Brockton murder was called for by the rest of the universe, if it had to come at its preappointed hour, and if nothing else would have been consistent with the sense of the whole, what are we to think of the universe? Are we stubbornly to stick to our judgment of regret, and say, though it *couldn't* be, yet it *would* have been a better universe with something different from this Brockton murder in it? That, of course, seems the natural and spontaneous thing for us to do. And yet it is nothing short of deliberately espousing a kind of pessimism. The judgment of regret calls the murder bad. Calling a thing bad means, if it mean anything at all, that the thing ought *not to be,*

that something else ought to be in its stead. Determinism, in denying that anything else *can* be in its stead, virtually defines the universe as a place in which
what ought to be is impossible—in other words, as an organism whose constitution is afflicted with an incurable taint, an irremediable flaw. . . . Regret for the
murder must transform itself, if we are determinists and wise, into a larger regret. It is absurd to regret the murder alone. Other things being what they are,
it could not be different. What we should regret is that whole frame of things of
which the murder is one member. I see no escape whatever from this pessimistic
conclusion, if, being determinists, our judgment of regret is to be allowed to
stand at all.

The only deterministic escape from pessimism is *everywhere* to abandon the
judgment of regret. That this can be done, history shows to be not impossible.
The devil, *quoad existentiam*,[13] may be good. That is, although he be a *principle* of
evil, yet the universe with such a principle in it may practically be a better universe than it could have been without. On every hand, in a small way, we find
that a certain amount of evil is a condition by which a higher form of good is
bought. There is nothing to prevent anybody from generalizing this view, and
trusting that if we could but see things in the largest of all ways, even such matters as this Brockton murder would appear to be paid for by the uses that follow
in their train. An optimism *quand même*,[14] a systematic and infatuated optimism
like that ridiculed by Voltaire[15] in his *Candide,* is one of the possible ideal ways
in which a man may train himself to look on life. Bereft of dogmatic hardness
and lit up with the expression of a tender and pathetic hope, such an optimism
has been the grace of some of the most religious characters that ever lived.

> Throb thine with Nature's throbbing breast,
> And all is clear from east to west.[16]

Even cruelty and treachery may be among the absolutely blessed fruits of
time, and to quarrel with any of their details may be blasphemy. The only real
blasphemy, in short, may be that pessimistic temper of the soul which lets it take
pleasure in such things as regrets, remorse, and grief.

Thus, our deterministic pessimism may become a deterministic optimism at
the price of extinguishing our judgments of regret.

But does not this immediately bring us into a curious logical predicament?
Our determinism leads us to call our judgments of regret wrong, because they
are pessimistic in implying that what is impossible yet ought to be. But how then
about the judgments of regret themselves? If they are wrong, other judgments—
judgments of approval presumably—ought to be in their place. But, as they are
necessitated, nothing else *can* be in their place; and the universe is just what it
was before—namely, a place in which what ought to be appears impossible. We
have got one foot out of the pessimistic bog, but the other one sinks all the
deeper. We have rescued our actions from the bonds of evil, but our judgments
are now held fast. When murders and treacheries cease to be sins, regrets are errors. The theoretic and the active life thus play a kind of see-saw with each other
on the ground of evil. The rise of either sends the other down. Murder and
treachery can't be good without regret being bad; regret can't be good without
treachery and murder being bad. Both, however, are supposed to have been

foredoomed, so *something* must be bad in the world. It must be a place of which either sin or error forms a necessary part. . . .

. . . The only consistent way of representing a world whose parts may affect each other through their conduct being either good or bad is the indeterministic way. What interest, zest, or excitement can there be in achieving the right way, unless we are enabled to feel that the wrong way is also a possible and a natural way—nay, more, a menacing and an imminent way? And what sense can there be in condemning ourselves for taking the wrong way, unless we need have done nothing of the sort, unless the right way was open to us as well? I cannot understand the willingness to act, no matter how we feel, without the belief that acts are really good and bad. I cannot understand the belief that an act is bad, without regret at its happening. I cannot understand regret without the admission of real, genuine possibilities in the world. Only *then* is it other than a mockery to feel, after we have failed to do our best, that an irreparable opportunity is gone from the universe, the loss of which it must forever after mourn. . . .

The world is enigmatical enough in all conscience, whatever theory we may take up toward it. The indeterminism I defend, the free will theory of popular sense based on the judgment of regret, represents that world as vulnerable and liable to be injured by certain of its parts if they act wrong. And it represents their acting wrong as a matter of possibility or accident, neither inevitable nor yet to be infallibly warded off. In all this, it is a theory devoid either of transparency or of stability. It gives us a pluralistic, restless universe, in which no single point of view can ever take in the whole scene; and, to a mind possessed of the love of unity at any cost, it will, no doubt, remain forever inacceptable. A friend with such a mind once told me that the thought of my universe made him sick, like the sight of the horrible motion of a mass of maggots in their carrion bed.

But while I freely admit that the pluralism and the restlessness are repugnant and irrational in a certain way, I find that every alternative to them is irrational in a deeper way. The indeterminism with its maggots, if you please to speak so about it, offends only the native absolutism of my intellect—an absolutism which, after all, perhaps, deserves to be snubbed and kept in check. But the determinism with its necessary carrion, to continue the figure of speech, and with no possible maggots to eat the latter up, violates my sense of moral reality through and through. When, for example, I imagine such carrion as the Brockton murder, I cannot conceive it as an act by which the universe as a Whole logically and necessarily expresses its nature, without shrinking from complicity with such a Whole. And I deliberately refuse to keep on terms of loyalty with the universe by saying blankly that the murder, since it does flow from the nature of the Whole, is *not* carrion. There are *some* instinctive reactions that I, for one, will not tamper with. . . .

Make as great an uproar about chance as you please, I know that chance means pluralism and nothing more. If some of the members of the pluralism are bad, the philosophy of pluralism, whatever broad views it may deny me, permits me, at least, to turn to the other members with a clean breast of affection and an unsophisticated moral sense. And if I still wish to think of the world as a totality, it lets me feel that a world with a *chance* in it of being altogether good, even if the chance never come to pass, is better than a world with no such chance at all. That "chance" whose very notion I am exhorted and conjured to banish from my view of the future as the suicide of reason concerning it, that chance is—what? Just this—the chance that in moral respects the future may be other and better than the past has been. This is the only chance we have any motive for supposing to exist. Shame, rather, on its repudiation and its denial! For its presence is the salt that keeps the world sweet, the air that fills its lungs.

NOTES

1. *soft determinism:* the view that although all actions are determined by preceding causes, actions determined by certain kinds of *internal* causes are free and we are morally responsible for these actions. As James explains, he calls this form of determinism "soft" because it backs away from the harsh implications of determinism as ordinarily understood. The harsh implications of ordinary ("hard") determinism include the denial of free will and moral responsibility. [D. C. ABEL]
2. Omar Khayyám, *Rubáiyát,* trans. Edward Fitzgerald, stanza 79. Omar Khayyám (about 1048–1122) was a Persian poet and astronomer. [D. C. ABEL]
3. *withal:* with. [D. C. ABEL]
4. *Monists* hold that there is just one kind of ultimate reality; *pluralists* hold that there is more than one kind of ultimate reality. [D. C. ABEL]
5. *needs:* necessarily. [D. C. ABEL]
6. James's terms "called" and "chosen" allude to the saying of Jesus, "Many are called, but few are chosen" (Matthew 22:14). [D. C. ABEL]
7. *Machtspruch:* an authoritative decree (literally, in German, "power saying"). [D. C. ABEL]
8. *sensible:* able to be sensed. [D. C. ABEL]
9. *metaphysical:* relating to *metaphysics,* the study of the nature and kinds of reality. [D. C. ABEL]
10. Omar Khayyám, *Rubáiyát,* stanza 106, lines 2–4; stanza 108. [D. C. ABEL]
11. Anne Finch, Countess of Winchilsea, "The Atheist and the Acorn." Finch (1661–1720) was an English poet. [D. C. ABEL]
12. *desert:* desolate. [D. C. ABEL]
13. *quoad existentiam:* (Latin) "as far as existence is concerned." [D. C. ABEL]
14. *quand même:* (French) "despite all this." [D. C. ABEL]
15. Francois-Marie Aroute de Voltaire (1694–1778) was a French writer. [D. C. ABEL]
16. Ralph Waldo Emerson, "Threnody," lines 207–208. Emerson (1803–1882) was an American essayist and poet. [D. C. ABEL]

Freedom and Determinism

Richard Taylor

Richard Taylor was born in 1919 in Charlotte, Michigan. He attended the University of Illinois, receiving his bachelor's degree in 1941. During World War II, when serving in the U.S. Navy, he became interested in philosophy. After the war he began graduate studies in philosophy at Oberlin College. Taylor received his master's degree in 1947 and then enrolled in the doctoral program at Brown University. In 1951 he completed his doctorate and became a member of the faculty at Brown. In 1959 he was appointed William Herbert Perry Faunce Professor of Philosophy. In 1963 Taylor went to Columbia University. Two years later he accepted an appointment at the University of Rochester, where he remained until his retirement in 1985. He has held distinguished visiting professorships at Wells College, Hamilton College, and Hobart and William Smith Colleges. He died in 2003 in Trumansburg, New York.

Taylor's books include *Metaphysics* (1963; 4th ed., 1992), *Action and Purpose* (1966), *Good and Evil: A New Direction* (1970), *With Heart and Mind* (1973), *Freedom, Anarchy, and the Law: An Introduction to Political Philosophy* (1973), *Ethics, Faith, and Reason* (1985), and *Virtue Ethics: An Introduction* (2002).

Our reading is from Chapter 5 of *Metaphysics*, "Freedom and Determinism," which addresses the question of whether any of our actions are free. The theory of determinism states that every event—including every human action—is a necessary result of prior causes. Taylor begins by discussing "soft determinism," the theory that some human actions are both determined and free. Soft determinists define a free action as one not impeded by any obstacle and not coerced by any external force. With this definition, they can claim that an action is both determined and free if it is the necessary result of an *internal* force (a desire, for example). Taylor rejects soft determinism because saying that a person's action was free implies that he or she could have acted otherwise. But if determinism is true (as the soft determinist maintains), the internal state that causes the action is *itself* the necessary result of prior causes, and therefore the person could not have acted otherwise. Taylor also rejects "simple indeterminism" (the theory that some actions are free because they have no causes) because it is at odds with our ordinary notion of responsibility: Actions without causes would occur at random and be wholly beyond a person's control.

Taylor's own solution to the problem of freedom and determinism is a "theory of agency." According to this theory, free actions are those caused by the person (agent) herself or himself. A free action is not caused by something within the person (such as a desire) but by the person as a whole. Whereas every other kind of event in nature is the necessary result of an endless series of prior causes, a free action originates with the person. Taylor is somewhat hesitant to postulate such a striking exception to an otherwise deterministic world, but he believes that his theory of agency is justified because it does more justice to our ordinary experience than alternative theories do.

... We want to learn, if we can, whether determinism is true. ... It can, like all good questions of philosophy, be answered only on the basis of certain data; that is, by seeing whether or not it squares with certain things that everyone knows, or believes himself to know, or with things everyone is at least more sure about than the answer to the question at issue.

Now I could, of course, simply affirm that I am a morally responsible being, in the sense in which my responsibility for my behavior implies that I could have avoided that behavior. But this would take us into the nebulous realm of ethics, and it is, in fact, far from obvious that I am responsible in that sense. Many have doubted that they are responsible in that sense, and it is in any case not difficult to doubt it, however strongly one might feel about it.

There are, however, two things about myself of which I feel quite certain and that have no necessary connection with morals. The first is that I sometimes deliberate, with the view to making a decision—a decision, namely, to do this thing or that. And the second is that whether or not I deliberate about what to do, it is sometimes up to me what I do. This might all be an illusion, of course; but so also might any philosophical theory, such as the theory of determinism, be false. The point remains that it is far more difficult for me to doubt that I sometimes deliberate, and that it is sometimes up to me what to do, than to doubt any philosophical theory whatever, including the theory of determinism. We must, accordingly, if we ever hope to be wiser, adjust our theories to our data and not try to adjust our data to our theories. ...

SOFT DETERMINISM

... The three claims of soft determinism are (1) that the thesis of determinism is true, and that accordingly all human behavior, voluntary or other, like the behavior of all other things, arises from antecedent conditions, given which no other behavior is possible—in short, that all human behavior is caused and determined; (2) that voluntary behavior is nonetheless free to the extent that it is not externally constrained or impeded; and (3) that, in the absence of such obstacles and constraints, the causes of voluntary behavior are certain states, events, or conditions within the agent himself—namely, his own acts of will or volitions, choices, decisions, desires, and so on.

Thus, on this view, I am free, and therefore sometimes responsible for what I do, provided nothing prevents me from acting according to my own choice, desire, or volition, or constrains me to act otherwise. There may, to be sure, be other conditions for my responsibility—such as, for example, an understanding of the probable consequences of my behavior, and that sort of thing—but absence of constraint or impediment is, at least, one such condition. And, it is claimed, it is a condition that is compatible with the supposition that my behavior is caused—for it is, by hypothesis, caused by my own inner choices, desires, and volitions.

THE REFUTATION OF THIS

The theory of soft determinism looks good at first—so good that it has for generations been solemnly taught from innumerable philosophical chairs and implanted in the minds of students as sound philosophy—but no great acumen is needed to discover that far from solving any problem, it only camouflages it.

My free actions are those unimpeded and unconstrained motions that arise from my own inner desires, choices, and volitions; let us grant this provisionally. But now, whence arise those inner states that determine what my body shall do? Are they within my control or not? Having made my choice or decision and acted upon it, could I have chosen otherwise or not?

Here the determinist, hoping to surrender nothing and yet to avoid the problem implied in that question, bids us not to ask it; the question itself, he announces, is without meaning. For to say that I could have done otherwise, he says, means only that I *would* have done otherwise, *if* those inner states that determined my action had been different; if, that is, I had decided or chosen differently. To ask, accordingly, whether I could have chosen or decided differently is only to ask whether, had I decided to decide differently or chosen to choose differently, or willed to will differently, I *would* have decided or chosen or willed differently. And this, of course, *is* unintelligible nonsense.

But it is not nonsense to ask whether the causes of my actions—my own inner choices, decisions, and desires—are themselves caused. And of course they are, if determinism is true, for on that thesis everything is caused and determined. And if they are, then we cannot avoid concluding that, given the causal conditions of those inner states, I could not have decided, willed, chosen, or desired other than I, in fact, did, for this is a logical consequence of the very definition of determinism. Of course we can still say that, *if* the causes of those inner states, whatever they were, had been different, then their effects, those inner states themselves, would have been different, and that in this hypothetical sense I could have decided, chosen, willed, or desired differently—but that only pushes our problem back still another step. For we will then want to know whether the causes of those inner states were within my control, and so on ad infinitum.[1] We are, at each step, permitted to say "could have been otherwise" only in a provisional sense—provided, that is, that something else had been different—but must then retract it and replace it with "could not have been otherwise" as soon as we discover, as we must at each step, that whatever would have to have been different could not have been different.

EXAMPLES

Such is the dialectic of the problem. The easiest way to see the shadowy quality of soft determinism, however, is by means of examples.

Let us suppose that my body is moving in various ways, that these motions are not externally constrained or impeded, and that they are all exactly in accordance with my own desires, choices, or acts of will, and whatnot. When I will that my arm should move in a certain way, I find it moving in that way, unobstructed and unconstrained. When I will to speak, my lips and tongue move, unobstructed and unconstrained, in a manner suitable to the formation of the words I choose to utter. Now, given that this is a correct description of my behavior, namely, that it consists of the unconstrained and unimpeded motions of my body in response to my own volitions, then it follows that my behavior is free, on the soft determinist's definition of "free." It follows further that I am responsible for that behavior; or at least, that if I am not, it is not from any lack of freedom on my part.

But if the fulfillment of these conditions renders my behavior free—that is to say, if my behavior satisfies the conditions of free action set forth in the theory of soft determinism—then my behavior will be no less free if we assume further conditions that are perfectly consistent with those already satisfied.

We suppose further, accordingly, that while my behavior is entirely in accordance with my own volitions, and thus "free" in terms of the conception of freedom we are examining, my volitions themselves are caused. To make this graphic, we can suppose that an ingenious physiologist can induce in me any volition he pleases, simply by pushing various buttons on an instrument to which, let us suppose, I am attached by numerous wires. All the volitions I have in that situation are, accordingly, precisely the ones he gives me. By pushing one button, he evokes in me the volition to raise my hand; and my hand, being unimpeded, rises in response to that volition. By pushing another, he induces the volition in me to kick, and my foot, being unimpeded, kicks in response to that volition. We can even suppose that the physiologist puts a rifle in my hands, aims it at some passerby, and then, by pushing the proper button, evokes in me the volition to squeeze my finger against the trigger, whereupon the passerby falls dead of a bullet wound.

This is the description of a man who is acting in accordance with his inner volitions, a man whose body is unimpeded and unconstrained in its motions, these motions being the effects of those inner states. It is hardly the description of a free and responsible agent. It is the perfect description of a puppet. To render someone your puppet, it is not necessary forcibly to constrain the motions of his limbs, after the fashion in which real puppets are moved. A subtler but no less effective means of making a person your puppet would be to gain complete control of his inner states, and ensuring, as the theory of soft determinism does ensure, that his body will move in accordance with them.

The example is somewhat unusual, but it is no worse for that. It is perfectly intelligible, and it does appear to refute the soft determinist's conception of freedom. . . . The example can, moreover, be modified in perfectly realistic ways, so as to coincide with actual and familiar cases. One can, for instance, be given a compulsive desire for certain drugs, simply by having them administered over a course of time. Suppose, then, that I do, with neither my knowledge nor consent, thus become a victim of such a desire and act upon it. Do I act freely, merely by virtue of the fact that I am unimpeded in my quest for drugs? In a sense I do, surely, but I am hardly free with respect to whether or not I shall use drugs. I never chose to have the desire for them inflicted upon me.

Nor does it, of course, matter whether the inner states that allegedly prompt all my "free" activity are evoked in me by another agent or by perfectly impersonal forces. Whether a desire that causes my body to behave in a certain way is inflicted upon me by another person, for instance, or derived from hereditary factors, or indeed from anything at all, matters not the least. In any case, if it is in fact the cause of my bodily behavior, I cannot help but act in accordance with it. Wherever it came from, whether from personal or impersonal origins, it was entirely caused or determined, and not within my control. Indeed, if determinism is true, as the theory of soft determinism holds it to be, all those inner states that cause my body to behave in whatever ways it behaves must arise from circumstances that existed before I was born; for the chain of causes and effects is infinite, and none could have been the least different, given those that preceded.

SIMPLE INDETERMINISM

We might at first now seem warranted in simply denying determinism, and saying that, insofar as they are free, my actions are not caused; or that, if they are caused by my own inner states—my own desires, impulses, choices, volitions, and whatnot—then these, in any case, are not caused. This is a perfectly clear sense in which a person's action, assuming that it was free, could have been otherwise. If it was uncaused, then, even given the conditions under which it occurred and all that preceded, some other act was nonetheless possible, and he did not have to do what he did. Or if his action was the inevitable consequence of his own inner states, and could not have been otherwise, given these, we can nevertheless say that these inner states, being uncaused, could have been otherwise, and could thereby have produced different actions.

Only the slightest consideration will show, however, that this simple denial of determinism has not the slightest plausibility. For let us suppose it is true, and that some of my bodily motions—namely, those that I regard as my free acts— are not caused at all or, if caused by my own inner states, that these are not caused. We shall thereby avoid picturing a puppet, to be sure—but only by substituting something even less like a human being; for the conception that now emerges is not that of a free person, but of an erratic and jerking phantom, without any rhyme or reason at all.

Suppose that my right arm is free, according to this conception; that is, that its motions are uncaused. It moves this way and that from time to time, but nothing causes these motions. Sometimes it moves forth vigorously, sometimes up, sometimes down, sometimes it just drifts vaguely about—these motions all being wholly free and uncaused. Manifestly I have nothing to do with them at all; they just happen, and neither I nor anyone can ever tell what this arm will be doing next. It might seize a club and lay it on the head of the nearest bystander, no less to my astonishment than his. There will never be any point in asking why these motions occur, or in seeking any explanation of them, for under the conditions assumed there is no explanation. They just happen, from no causes at all.

This is no description of free, voluntary, or responsible behavior. Indeed, so far as the motions of my body or its parts are entirely uncaused, such motions cannot even be ascribed to me as my behavior in the first place, since I have nothing to do with them. The behavior of my arm is just the random motion of a foreign object. Behavior that is mine must be behavior that is within my control, but motions that occur from no causes are beyond the control of anyone. I can have no more to do with, and no more control over, the uncaused motions of my limbs than a gambler has over the motions of an honest roulette wheel. I can only, like him, idly wait to see what happens.

Nor does it improve things to suppose that my bodily motions are caused by my own inner states, so long as we suppose these to be wholly uncaused. The result will be the same as before. My arm, for example, will move this way and that, sometimes up and sometimes down, sometimes vigorously and sometimes just drifting about, always in response to certain inner states, to be sure. But since these are supposed to be wholly uncaused, it follows that I have no control over them and hence none over their effects. If my hand lays a club forcefully on the nearest bystander, we can indeed say that this motion resulted from an inner club-wielding desire of mine; but we must add that I had nothing to do with that desire, and that it arose, to be followed by its inevitable effect, no less to my astonishment than to his. Things like this do, alas, sometimes happen. We are all sometimes seized by compulsive impulses that arise we know not whence, and we do sometimes act upon these. But because they are far from being examples of free, voluntary, and responsible behavior, we need only to learn that the behavior was of this sort to conclude that it was not free, voluntary, or responsible. It was erratic, impulsive, and irresponsible.

DETERMINISM AND SIMPLE INDETERMINISM AS THEORIES

Both determinism and simple indeterminism are loaded with difficulties, and no one who has thought much on them can affirm either of them without some embarrassment. Simple indeterminism has nothing whatever to be said for it, except that it appears to remove the grossest difficulties of determinism, only, however, to imply perfect absurdities of its own. Determinism, on the other hand, is at least initially plausible. People seem to have a natural inclination to believe in it; it is, indeed, almost required for the very exercise of practical intelligence. And beyond this, our experience appears always to confirm it, so long as we are dealing with everyday facts of common experience, as distinguished from the esoteric researches of theoretical physics. But determinism, as applied to human behavior, has implications that few can casually accept, and they appear to be implications that no modification of the theory can efface.

Both theories, moreover, appear logically irreconcilable to the two items of data that we set forth at the outset; namely, (1) that my behavior is sometimes the outcome of my deliberation, and (2) that in these and other cases it is sometimes up to me what I do. Because these were our data, it is important to see, as must already be quite clear, that these theories cannot be reconciled to them.

I can deliberate only about my own future actions, and then only if I do not already know what I am going to do. If a certain nasal tickle warns me that I am about to sneeze, for instance, then I cannot deliberate whether to sneeze or not; I can only prepare for the impending convulsion. But if determinism is true, then there are always conditions existing antecedently to everything I do, sufficient for my doing just that, and such as to render it inevitable. If I can know what those conditions are and what behavior they are sufficient to produce, then I can in every such case know what I am going to do and cannot then deliberate about it.

By itself this only shows, of course, that I can deliberate only in ignorance of the causal conditions of my behavior; it does not show that such conditions cannot exist. It is odd, however, to suppose that deliberation should be a mere substitute for clear knowledge. Ignorance is a condition of speculation, inference, and guesswork, which have nothing whatever to do with deliberation. A prisoner awaiting execution may not know when he is going to die, and he may even entertain the hope of reprieve, but he cannot deliberate about this. He can only speculate, guess—and wait.

Worse yet, however, it now becomes clear that I cannot deliberate about what I am going to do, if it is even *possible* for me to find out in advance, whether I do in fact find out in advance or not. I can deliberate only with the view to deciding what to do, to making up my mind; and this is impossible if I believe that it could be inferred what I am going to do from conditions already existing, even though I have not made that inference myself. If I believe that what I am going to do has been rendered inevitable by conditions already existing, and could be inferred by anyone having the requisite sagacity, then I cannot try to decide whether to do it or not, for there is simply nothing left to decide. I can at best only guess or try to figure it out myself or, all prognostics failing, I can wait and see; but I cannot deliberate. I deliberate in order to *decide* what *to* do, not to *discover* what it is that I am *going* to do. But if determinism is true, then there are always antecedent conditions sufficient for everything that I do, and this can always be inferred by anyone having the requisite sagacity; that is, by anyone having a knowledge of what those conditions are and what behavior they are sufficient to produce.

This suggests what in fact seems quite clear, that determinism cannot be reconciled with our second datum either, to the effect that it is sometimes up to me what I am going to do. For if it is ever really up to me whether to do this thing or that, then, as we have seen, each alternative course of action must be such that I can do it; not that I can do it in some abstruse or hypothetical sense of "can"; not that I could do it if only something were true that is not true; but in the sense that it is then and there within my power to do it. But this is never so, if determinism is true, for on the very formulation of that theory whatever happens at any time is the only thing that can then happen, given all that precedes it. It is simply a logical consequence of this that whatever I do at any time is the only thing I can then do, given the conditions that precede my doing it. Nor does it help in the least to interpose, among the causal antecedents of my behavior, my own inner states, such as my desires, choices, acts of will, and so on. For even supposing these to be always involved in voluntary behavior—which is highly doubtful in itself—it is a consequence of determinism that these, whatever they are at any time, can never be other than what they then are. . . .

It is even more obvious that our data cannot be reconciled to the theory of simple indeterminism. I can deliberate only about my own actions; this is obvious. But the random, uncaused motion of any body whatever, whether it be a part of my body or not, is no action of mine and nothing that is within my power. I might try to guess what these motions will be, just as I might try to guess how a roulette wheel will behave, but I cannot deliberate about them or try to decide what they shall be, simply because these things are not up to me. Whatever is not caused by anything is not caused by me, and nothing could be more plainly inconsistent with saying that it is nevertheless up to me what it shall be.

THE THEORY OF AGENCY

The only conception of action that accords with our data is one according to which people—and perhaps some other things too—are sometimes, but of course not always, self-determining beings; that is, beings that are sometimes the causes of their own behavior. In the case of an action that is free, it must not only be such that it is caused by the agent who performs it, but also such that no antecedent conditions were sufficient for his performing just that action. In the case of an action that is both free and rational, it must be such that the agent who performed it did so for some reason, but this reason cannot have been the cause of it.

Now, this conception fits what people take themselves to be—namely, beings who act, or who are agents, rather than beings that are merely acted upon, and whose behavior is simply the causal consequence of conditions that they have not wrought. When I believe that I have done something, I do believe that it was I who caused it to be done, I who made something happen, and not merely something within me, such as one of my own subjective states, which is not identical with myself. If I believe that something not identical with myself was the cause of my behavior—some event wholly external to myself, for instance, or even one internal to myself, such as a nerve impulse, volition, or whatnot—then I cannot regard that behavior as being an act of mine, unless I further believe that I was the cause of that external or internal event. My pulse, for example, is caused and regulated by certain conditions existing within me, and not by myself. I do not, accordingly, regard this activity of my body as my action, and would be no more tempted to do so if I became suddenly conscious within myself of those conditions or impulses that produce it. This is behavior with which I have nothing to do, behavior that is not within my immediate control, behavior that is not only not free activity, but not even the activity of an agent to begin with; it is nothing but a mechanical reflex. Had I never learned that my very life depends on this pulse beat, I would regard it with complete indifference, as something foreign to me, like the oscillations of a clock pendulum that I idly contemplate.

Now this conception of activity, and of an agent who is the cause of it, involves two rather strange metaphysical[2] notions that are never applied elsewhere in nature. The first is that of a *self* or *person*—for example, a man—who is not merely a collection of things or events, but a self-moving being. For on this view it is a person, and not merely some part of him or something within him, that is the cause of his own activity. Now, we certainly do not know that a human being is anything more than an assemblage of physical things and processes that act in accordance with those laws that describe the behavior of all other physical things and processes. Even though he is a living being, of enormous complexity, there is nothing, apart from the requirements of this theory, to suggest that his behavior is so radically different in its origin from that of other physical objects, or that an understanding of it must be sought in some metaphysical realm wholly different from that appropriate to the understanding of nonliving things.

Second, this conception of activity involves an extraordinary conception of causation according to which an agent, which is a substance and not an event, can nevertheless be the cause of an event. Indeed, if he is a free agent then he can, on this conception, cause an event to occur—namely, some act of his own—without anything else causing him to do so. This means that an agent is sometimes a cause, without being an antecedent sufficient condition; for if I affirm that I am the cause of some act of mine, then I am plainly not saying that my very existence is sufficient for its occurrence, which would be absurd. If I say that my hand causes my pencil to move, then I am saying that the motion of my hand is, under the other conditions then prevailing, sufficient for the motion of the pencil. But if I then say that I cause my hand to move, I am not saying anything remotely like this, and surely not that the motion of my self is sufficient for the motion of my arm and hand, since these are the only things about me that are moving.

This conception of the causation of events by things that are not events is, in fact, so different from the usual philosophical conception of a cause that it should not even bear the same name, for "being a cause" ordinarily just means "being an antecedent sufficient condition or set of conditions." Instead, then, of speaking of agents as *causing* their own acts, it would perhaps be better to use another word entirely, and say, for instance, that they *originate* them, *initiate* them, or simply that they *perform* them.

Now this is, on the face of it, a dubious conception of what a person is. Yet it is consistent with our data, reflecting the presuppositions of deliberation, and appears to be the only conception that is consistent with them, as determinism and simple indeterminism are not. The theory of agency avoids the absurdities of simple indeterminism by conceding that human behavior is caused, while at the same time avoiding the difficulties of determinism by denying that every chain of causes and effects is infinite. Some such causal chains, on this view, have beginnings, and they begin with agents themselves. Moreover, if we are to suppose that it is sometimes up to me what I do, and understand this in a sense that is not consistent with determinism, we must suppose that I am an agent or a being who initiates his own actions, sometimes under conditions that do not determine what action I shall perform. Deliberation becomes, on this view, something that is not only possible but quite rational, for it does make sense to deliberate about activity that is truly my own and that depends in its outcome upon me as its author, and not merely upon something more or less esoteric that is supposed to be intimately associated with me, such as my thoughts, volitions, choices, or whatnot.

One can hardly affirm such a theory of agency with complete comfort, however, and not wholly without embarrassment, for the conception of agents and their powers which is involved in it is strange indeed, if not positively mysterious. In fact, one can hardly be blamed here for simply denying our data outright, rather than embracing this theory to which they do most certainly point. Our data—to the effect that we do sometimes deliberate before acting, and that, when we do, we presuppose among other things that it is up to us what we are going to do—rest upon nothing more than fairly common consent. These data might simply be illusions. It might, in fact, be that no one ever deliberates but only imagines that he does, that from pure conceit he supposes himself to be the master of his behavior and the author of his acts. Spinoza[3] has suggested that if a stone, having been thrown into the air, were suddenly to become conscious, it would suppose itself to be the source of its own motion, being then conscious of what it was doing but not aware of the real cause of its behavior. Certainly we are *sometimes* mistaken in believing that we are behaving as a result of choice deliberately arrived at. A man might, for example, easily imagine that his embarking upon matrimony is the result of the most careful and rational deliberation, when in fact the causes, perfectly sufficient for that behavior, might be of an entirely physiological, unconscious origin. If it is sometimes false that we deliberate and then act as the result of a decision deliberately arrived at, even when we suppose it to be true, it might always be false. . . .

These are, then, dubitable conceptions, despite their being so well implanted in common sense. . . . Perhaps here, as elsewhere in metaphysics, we should be content with discovering difficulties, with seeing what is and what is not consistent with such convictions as we happen to have, and then drawing such satisfaction as we can from the realization that, no matter where we begin, the world is mysterious and that we who try to understand it are even more so. This realization can, with some justification, make one feel wise, even in the full realization of his ignorance.

NOTES

1. *ad infinitum:* (Latin) "to infinity." [D. C. ABEL]
2. *metaphysical:* relating to *metaphysics,* the study of the nature and kinds of reality. [D. C. ABEL]
3. Baruch (Benedict de) Spinoza (1632–1677) was a Dutch philosopher. [D. C. ABEL]

C. Soft Determinism

The Problem of Morals

W. T. Stace

W. T. Stace was born in London in 1886. He received his initial education in England and Scotland and then went to Ireland, where he enrolled in Trinity College in Dublin. He was awarded his bachelor's degree in philosophy from Trinity in 1908. He had planned to become a cleric in the Anglican Church but became skeptical of religion and joined the British Civil Service instead. In 1910 Stace began working for the Civil Service in Ceylon (now Sri Lanka), holding various positions—including those of district judge and mayor of Colombo, the capital city. In 1929 he was awarded an honorary doctor of letters degree by Trinity College. In 1932, after serving twenty-two years in Ceylon, Stace accepted an appointment on the philosophy faculty at Princeton University, where he remained until his retirement in 1955. He died in Cambridge, Massachusetts, in 1967.

Stace's main works are *The Philosophy of Hegel* (1924), *The Theory of Knowledge and Existence* (1932), *The Concept of Morals* (1937), *The Destiny of Western Man* (1942), *Religion and the Modern Mind* (1952), *Time and Eternity* (1952), and *Mysticism and Philosophy* (1960).

Our selection is from the first part of Chapter 11 of *Religion and the Modern Mind,* "The Problem of Morals." Stace explains that since moral rules would be meaningless if we have no freedom to obey or disobey them, a discussion of free will should precede the inquiry into morality. The first part of "The Problem of Morals," consequently, is devoted to the topic of free will. Stace argues here that the longstanding dispute about whether we have free will does not concern a real problem but merely a verbal one—a problem "due to nothing but a confusion about the meanings of words." Philosophers on both sides of the dispute have assumed that "free will" means "indeterminism"—that an action done freely is an action not determined by causes. According to Stace, this definition of free will is incorrect and produces a false dichotomy between freedom and determinism.

Stace holds that the criterion for deciding the correct meaning of a term is common usage. To discover the correct meaning of "free will," Stace presents several examples of ordinary conversations in which people state whether an action they performed was done of their own free will. Some actions are described as free, others as unfree. According to Stace, what distinguishes the two kinds of actions is not *whether* they are determined by a cause, but *what kind* of cause they have. Free actions are caused by the agent's internal psychological states; unfree actions are caused by external physical forces. This ordinary conception of free will is the correct one, and from this conception it is obvious that free will exists and that it is compatible with determinism. Stace goes on to argue that his theory that free actions are determined is compatible with moral responsibility and with the punishment of wrongdoers.

. . . If there is no free will there can be no morality. Morality is concerned with what men ought and ought not to do. But if a man has no freedom to choose what he will do, if whatever he does is done under compulsion, then it does not make sense to tell him that he ought not to have done what he did and that he ought to do something different. All moral precepts would in such case be meaningless. Also, if he acts always under compulsion, how can he be held morally responsible for his actions? How can he, for example, be punished for what he could not help doing?

It is to be observed that those learned professors of philosophy or psychology who deny the existence of free will do so only in their professional moments and in their studies and lecture rooms. For when it comes to doing anything practical, even of the most trivial kind, they invariably behave as if they and others were free. They inquire from you at dinner whether you will choose this dish or that dish. They will ask a child why he told a lie, and will punish him for not having chosen the way of truthfulness. All of which is inconsistent with a disbelief in free will. This should cause us to suspect that the problem is not a real one; and this, I believe, is the case. The dispute is merely verbal, and is due to nothing but a confusion about the meanings of words. It is what is now fashionably called a semantic problem.

How does a verbal dispute arise? Let us consider a case which, although it is absurd in the sense that no one would ever make the mistake which is involved in it, yet illustrates the principle which we shall have to use in the solution of the problem. Suppose that someone believed that the word "man" means a certain sort of five-legged animal—in short, that "five-legged animal" is the correct *definition* of man. He might then look around the world, and rightly observing that there are no five-legged animals in it, he might proceed to deny the existence of men. This preposterous conclusion would have been reached because he was using an incorrect definition of "man." All you would have to do to show him his mistake would be to give him the correct definition, or at least to show him that his definition was wrong. Both the problem and its solution would, of course, be entirely verbal. The problem of free will and its solution, I shall maintain, is verbal in exactly the same way. The problem has been created by the fact that learned men, especially philosophers, have assumed an incorrect definition of free will, and then finding that there is nothing in the world which answers to their definition, have denied its existence. As far as logic is concerned, their conclusion is just as absurd as that of the man who denies the existence of men. The only difference is that the mistake in the latter case is obvious and crude, while the mistake which the deniers of free will have made is rather subtle and difficult to detect.

Throughout the modern period, until quite recently, it was assumed, both by the philosophers who denied free will and by those who defended it, that *determinism is inconsistent with free will*. If a man's actions were wholly determined by chains of causes stretching back into the remote past, so that they could be predicted beforehand by a mind which knew all the causes, it was assumed that they could not in that case be free. This implies that a certain definition of actions done from free will was assumed—namely, that they are actions *not* wholly determined by causes or predictable beforehand. Let us shorten this by saying that free will was defined as meaning indeterminism. This is the incorrect definition which has led to the denial of free will. As soon as we see what the true definition is, we shall find that the question whether the world is deterministic, as Newtonian[1] science implied, or in a measure indeterministic, as current physics teaches, is wholly irrelevant to the problem.

Of course there is a sense in which one can define a word arbitrarily in any way one pleases. But a definition may nevertheless be called correct or incorrect. It is correct if it accords with a *common usage* of the word defined. It is incorrect if it does not. And if you give an incorrect definition, absurd and untrue results are likely to follow. For instance, there is nothing to prevent you from arbitrarily defining a man as a five-legged animal, but this is incorrect in the sense that it does not accord with the ordinary meaning of the word. Also it has the absurd result of leading to a denial of the existence of men. This shows that *common usage is the criterion for deciding whether a definition is correct or not.* And this is the principle which I shall apply to free will. I shall show that indeterminism is not what is meant by the phrase "free will" *as it is commonly used.* And I shall attempt to discover the correct definition by inquiring how the phrase is used in ordinary conversation.

Here are a few samples of how the phrase might be used in ordinary conversation. It will be noticed that they include cases in which the question whether a man acted with free will is asked in order to determine whether he was morally and legally responsible for his acts.

JONES: I once went without food for a week.
SMITH: Did you do that of your own free will?
JONES: No. I did it because I was lost in a desert and could find no food.

But suppose that the man who had fasted was Mahatma Gandhi.[2] The conversation might then have gone:

GANDHI: I once fasted for a week.
SMITH: Did you do that of your own free will?
GANDHI: Yes. I did it because I wanted to compel the British government to give India its independence.

Take another case. Suppose that I had stolen some bread, but that I was as truthful as George Washington. Then, if I were charged with the crime in court, some exchange of the following sort might take place:

JUDGE: Did you steal the bread of your own free will?
STACE: Yes. I stole it because I was hungry.

Or in different circumstances the conversation might run:

JUDGE: Did you steal of your own free will?
STACE: No. I stole because my employer threatened to beat me if I did not.

At a recent murder trial in Trenton some of the accused had signed confessions, but afterwards asserted that they had done so under police duress. The following exchange might have occurred:

JUDGE: Did you sign this confession of your own free will?
PRISONER: No. I signed it because the police beat me up.

Now suppose that a philosopher had been a member of the jury. We could imagine this conversation taking place in the jury room.

FOREMAN OF THE JURY: The prisoner says he signed the confession because he was beaten, and not of his own free will.

PHILOSOPHER: This is quite irrelevant to the case. There is no such thing as free will.

FOREMAN: Do you mean to say that it makes no difference whether he signed because his conscience made him want to tell the truth or because he was beaten?

PHILOSOPHER: None at all. Whether he was caused to sign by a beating or by some desire of his own—the desire to tell the truth, for example—in either case his signing was causally determined, and therefore in neither case did he act of his own free will. Since there is no such thing as free will, the question whether he signed of his own free will ought not to be discussed by us.

The foreman and the rest of the jury would rightly conclude that the philosopher must be making some mistake. What sort of a mistake could it be? There is only one possible answer. The philosopher must be using the phrase "free will" in some peculiar way of his own which is not the way in which men usually use it when they wish to determine a question of moral responsibility. That is, he must be using an incorrect definition of it as implying action not determined by causes.

Suppose a man left his office at noon, and were questioned about it. Then we might hear this:

JONES: Did you go out of your own free will?
SMITH: Yes. I went out to get my lunch.

But we might hear:

JONES: Did you leave your office of your own free will?
SMITH: No. I was forcibly removed by the police.

We have now collected a number of cases of actions which, in the ordinary usage of the English language, would be called cases in which people have acted of their own free will. We should also say in all these cases that they *chose* to act as they did. We should also say that they could have acted otherwise, if they had chosen. For instance, Mahatma Gandhi was not compelled to fast; he chose to do so. He could have eaten if he had wanted to. When Smith went out to get his lunch, he chose to do so. He could have stayed and done some more work, if he had wanted to. We have also collected a number of cases of the opposite kind. They are cases in which men were not able to exercise their free will. They had no choice. They were compelled to do as they did. The man in the desert did not fast of his own free will. He had no choice in the matter. He was compelled to fast because there was nothing for him to eat. And so with the other cases. It ought to be quite easy, by an inspection of these cases, to tell what we ordinarily mean when we say that a man did or did not exercise free will. We ought therefore to be able to extract from them the proper definition of the term. Let us put the cases in a table:

FREE ACTS	UNFREE ACTS
Gandhi fasting because he wanted to free India.	The man fasting in the desert because there was no food.
Stealing bread because one is hungry.	Stealing because one's employer threatened to beat one.
Signing a confession because one wanted to tell the truth.	Signing because the police beat one.
Leaving the office because one wanted one's lunch.	Leaving because forcibly removed.

It is obvious that to find the correct definition of free acts we must discover what characteristic is common to all the acts in the left-hand column and is, at the same time, absent from all the acts in the right-hand column. This characteristic which all free acts have, and which no unfree acts have, will be the defining characteristic of free will.

Is being uncaused, or not being determined by causes, the characteristic of which we are in search? It cannot be, because although it is true that all the acts in the right-hand column have causes, such as the beating by the police or the absence of food in the desert, so also do the acts in the left-hand column. Mr. Gandhi's fasting was caused by his desire to free India, the man leaving his office by his hunger, and so on. Moreover there is no reason to doubt that these causes of the free acts were in turn caused by prior conditions, and that these were again the results of causes, and so on back indefinitely into the past. Any physiologist can tell us the causes of hunger. What caused Mr. Gandhi's tremendously powerful desire to free India is no doubt more difficult to discover. But it must have had causes. Some of them may have lain in peculiarities of his glands or brain, others in his past experiences, others in his heredity, others in his education. Defenders of free will have usually tended to deny such facts. But to do so is plainly a case of special pleading, which is unsupported by any scrap of evidence. The only reasonable view is that all human actions, both those which are freely done and those which are not, are either wholly determined by causes, or at least as much determined as other events in nature. It may be true, as the physicists tell us, that nature is not as deterministic as was once thought. But whatever degree of determinism prevails in the world, human actions appear to be as much determined as anything else. And if this is so, it cannot be the case that what distinguishes actions freely chosen from those which are not free is that the latter are determined by causes while the former are not. Therefore, being uncaused or being undetermined by causes, must be an incorrect definition of free will.

What, then, is the difference between acts which are freely done and those which are not? What is the characteristic which is present to all the acts in the left-hand column and absent from all those in the right-hand column? Is it not obvious that, although both sets of actions have causes, the causes of those in the left-hand column are *of a different kind* from the causes of those in the right-hand column? The free acts are all caused by desires, or motives, or by some sort of internal psychological states of the agent's mind. The unfree acts, on the other hand, are all caused by physical forces or physical conditions outside the agent. Police arrest means physical force exerted from the outside; the absence of food in the desert is a physical condition of the outside world. We may therefore frame the following rough definitions. *Acts freely done are those whose immediate causes are psychological states in the agent. Acts not freely done are those whose immediate causes are states of affairs external to the agent.*

It is plain that if we define free will in this way, then free will certainly exists, and the philosopher's denial of its existence is seen to be what it is—nonsense. For it is obvious that all those actions of men which we should ordinarily attribute to the exercise of their free will, or of which we should say that they freely chose to do them, are in fact actions which have been caused by their own desires, wishes, thoughts, emotions, impulses, or other psychological states.

In applying our definition we shall find that it usually works well, but that there are some puzzling cases which it does not seem exactly to fit. These puzzles can always be solved by paying careful attention to the ways in which words are used, and remembering that they are not always used consistently. I have space for only one example. Suppose that a thug threatens to shoot you unless you give him your wallet, and suppose that you do so. Do you, in giving him your wallet, do so of your own free will or not? If we apply our definition, we find that you acted freely, since the immediate cause of the action was not an actual outside force but the fear of death, which is a psychological cause. Most people, however, would say that you did not act of your own free will but under compulsion. Does this show that our definition is wrong? I do not think so. Aristotle, who gave a solution of the problem of free will substantially the same as ours (though he did not use the term "free will"), admitted that there are what he called "mixed" or borderline cases in which it is difficult to know whether we ought to call the acts free or compelled. In the case under discussion, though no actual force was used, the gun at your forehead so nearly approximated to actual force that we tend to say the case was one of compulsion. It is a borderline case.

Here is what may seem like another kind of puzzle. According to our view an action may be free though it could have been predicted beforehand with certainty. But suppose you told a lie, and it was certain beforehand that you would tell it. How could one then say, "You could have told the truth"? The answer is that it is perfectly true that you could have told the truth *if* you had wanted to. In fact you would have done so, for in that case the causes producing your action, namely your desires, would have been different, and would therefore have produced different effects. It is a delusion that predictability and free will are incompatible. This agrees with common sense. For if, knowing your character, I predict that you will act honorably, no one would say when you do act honorably, that this shows you did not do so of your own free will.

Since free will is a condition of moral responsibility, we must be sure that our theory of free will gives a sufficient basis for it. To be held morally responsible for one's actions means that one may be justly punished or rewarded, blamed or praised, for them. But it is not just to punish a man for what he cannot help doing. How can it be just to punish him for an action which it was certain beforehand that he would do? We have not attempted to decide whether, as a matter of fact, all events, including human actions, are completely determined. For that question is irrelevant to the problem of free will. But if we assume for the purposes of argument that complete determinism is true, but that we are nevertheless free, it may then be asked whether such a deterministic free will is compatible with moral responsibility. For it may seem unjust to punish a man for an action which it could have been predicted with certainty beforehand that he would do.

But that determinism is incompatible with moral responsibility is as much a delusion as that it is incompatible with free will. You do not excuse a man for doing a wrong act because, knowing his character, you felt certain beforehand that he would do it. Nor do you deprive a man of a reward or prize because, knowing his goodness or his capabilities, you felt certain beforehand that he would win it.

Volumes have been written on the justification of punishment. But so far as it affects the question of free will, the essential principles involved are quite simple. The punishment of a man for doing a wrong act is justified, either on the ground that it will correct his own character, or that it will deter other people from doing similar acts. The instrument of punishment has been in the past—and no doubt still is—often unwisely used, so that it may often have done more harm than good. But that is not relevant to our present problem. Punishment, if and when it is justified, is justified only on one or both of the grounds just mentioned. The question then is how, if we assume determinism, punishment can correct character or deter people from evil actions.

Suppose that your child develops a habit of telling lies. You give him a mild beating. Why? Because you believe that his personality is such that the usual motives for telling the truth do not cause him to do so. You therefore supply the missing cause, or motive, in the shape of pain and the fear of future pain if he repeats his untruthful behavior. And you hope that a few treatments of this kind will condition him to the habit of truth-telling, so that he will come to tell the truth without the infliction of pain. You assume that his actions are determined by causes, but that the usual causes of truth-telling do not in him produce their usual effects. You therefore supply him with an artificially injected motive, pain and fear, which you think will in the future cause him to speak truthfully.

The principle is exactly the same where you hope, by punishing one man, to deter others from wrong actions. You believe that the fear of punishment will cause those who might otherwise do evil to do well.

We act on the same principle with nonhuman, and even with inanimate, things, if they do not behave in the way we think they ought to behave. The rose bushes in the garden produce only small and poor blooms, whereas we want large and rich ones. We supply a cause which will produce large blooms, namely fertilizer. Our automobile does not go properly. We supply a cause which will make it go better, namely oil in the works. The punishment for the man, the fertilizer for the plant, and the oil for the car, are all justified by the same principle and in the same way. The only difference is that different kinds of things require different kinds of causes to make them do what they should. Pain may be the appropriate remedy to apply, in certain cases, to human beings, and oil to the machine. It is, of course, of no use to inject motor oil into the boy or to beat the machine.

Thus we see that moral responsibility is not only consistent with determinism, but requires it. The assumption on which punishment is based is that human behavior is causally determined. If pain could not be a cause of truth-telling, there would be no justification at all for punishing lies. If human actions and volitions were uncaused, it would be useless either to punish or reward, or indeed to do anything else to correct people's bad behavior. For nothing that you could do would in any way influence them. Thus moral responsibility would entirely disappear. If there were no determinism of human beings at all, their actions would be completely unpredictable and capricious, and therefore irresponsible. And this is in itself a strong argument against the common view of philosophers that free will means being undetermined by causes.

NOTES

1. *Newtonian:* based on the theories of the English physicist Isaac Newton (1642–1726). [D. C. ABEL]
2. Mohandas (later called Mahatma) Gandhi (1869–1948) was an Indian nationalist leader. He sometimes fasted as a way to help achieve his objectives. [D. C. ABEL]

Firming Up Soft Determinism

Nancy Holmstrom

Nancy Holmstrom was born in 1943 in New York City. She received her bachelor's degree in philosophy from City College of the City University of New York in 1964 and her doctorate in philosophy from the University of Michigan in 1970. She then accepted a position at the University of Wisconsin–Madison. In 1977 she joined the faculty at Rutgers State University in Newark, New Jersey, where she is Associate Professor of Philosophy. Holmstrom has held visiting professorships at the University of Illinois at Chicago (formerly called University of Illinois at Chicago Circle), the University of Hawaii at Hilo, and other schools. Since the 1960s Holmstrom has been active in radical movements and committed to social justice. She was a founding member of the Society for Women in Philosophy and of the Radical Philosophical Association.

Holmstrom's involvement in political activity led to a gradual shift in her philosophical work from topics in the philosophy of mind and metaphysics to issues in political and social philosophy, especially feminist and Marxist theory. In addition to publishing a variety of articles on these topics, Holmstrom is coeditor (with Anatole Anton and Milton Fisk) of *Not for Sale: In Defense of Public Goods* (2000) and editor of *The Socialist Feminist Project: A Contemporary Reader in Theory and Politics* (2002).

In her 1977 article, "Firming Up Soft Determinism," Holmstrom discusses *soft determinism,* the view that determinism is compatible with free will and moral responsibility. (*Hard determinism* denies this compatibility.) This theory (also called *compatibilism*) accepts the determinist thesis that all actions are determined because they result from preceding causes, but it also holds that if a particular action is caused by the agent's beliefs and desires, the action is free and the agent is responsible for performing it. Holmstrom finds this theory inadequate as it stands, since it does not consider the *sources* of the agent's beliefs and desires. For example, an action resulting from desire induced by brainwashing or subliminal advertising is not free.

Holmstrom seeks to remedy this inadequacy in the theory of soft determinism by postulating that an action is free only to the extent that the agent has *control* over the beliefs and desires that cause the performance of the action. Control need not be all or nothing; it is often a matter of degree. Since we have at least some control over many of our beliefs and desires, many of our actions are free to some extent. "There is a continuum between free and unfree, with many or most acts lying somewhere in between." The degree of control depends on the degree to which the source of our desire or belief does not operate on us against our will, and on the degree of our awareness *that* the source is operating on us and *how* and *why* it does so. After developing her views of freedom and control, Holmstrom reflects on how free most people are today.

I

An important position on the question of freedom and determinism holds that determinism and predictability per se constitute no threat to the freedom and responsibility of an agent. What matters, according to this view, called soft determinism, is the basis on which the prediction is made or the nature of the conditions such that, given those conditions, the agent will do what he/she does. When the agent does what he does because of his beliefs and desires[1] to do it, then what the agent does is "up to him"; the causal chain goes through the person or the self, as it were. In such cases the agent can be said to be the cause of the action. Such actions are free. On the other hand, when the causes of an action, or, more generally, of what a person does, are not his/her beliefs and desires to do that action, then what happens is not "up to him" and the action is not free. However, it may not be compelled either. It is where the action is in contradiction to what the agent wants that the act can be said to be compelled. The agent is not responsible for the action because the action occurs in spite of him.

Among the objections that have been raised to this account of the distinction between free and unfree acts is that it provides an insufficient account of what it is for an agent to do an act freely. The problem is the source of the sources of one's allegedly free actions, that is, the sources of one's beliefs and desires. Many philosophers have felt that if an agent's beliefs and desires are themselves determined, then actions proceeding from them must be as unfree as actions that are not caused by the agent's beliefs and desires. For example, Richard Taylor bids us to suppose that

> while my behavior is entirely in accordance with my own volitions, and thus "free" in terms of the conception of freedom we are examining, my volitions themselves are caused. To make this graphic, we can suppose that an ingenious physiologist can induce in me any volition he pleases, simply by pushing various buttons on an instrument to which, let us suppose, I am attached by numerous wires. All the volitions I have in that situation are, accordingly, precisely the ones he gives me. . . .
>
> This is the description of a man who is acting in accordance with his inner volitions, a man whose body is unimpeded and unconstrained in its motions, these motions being the effects of those inner states. It is hardly the description of a free and responsible agent. It is the perfect description of a puppet.[2]

The same point can be made by examples of beliefs and desires acquired by brainwashing, hypnosis, subliminal advertising, and so on. If a person acts because of beliefs and desires acquired in such ways, the action is clearly not free even though the action was done because of the agent's beliefs and desires. This shows that it is not the case that an act is free just because it is caused by the beliefs and desires of the agent to do the act. The standard soft determinist position is inadequate as it stands.

One way of dealing with the objection might be to distinguish freedom of action and freedom of will and to maintain that the act was free but the will was not. However, I think such examples show that these concepts cannot be so easily separated. Because the "will" is unfree in such cases, we would not call the act free. Taylor thinks his point applies much more generally than just to these sorts of examples and concludes that the standard conception of determinism cannot apply to a free act. He introduces, instead, a special notion of "agent causality."[3] I prefer to explore a response to the above objection that remains within the standard compatibilist framework.

I think that the objection I raised to soft determinism shows that soft determinists have too limited a notion of what is required for an agent to be the source of his/her actions. All that they require is that the agent do what he or she pleases. They ignore the question of whether the agent has control over the sources of the actions, his/her desires and beliefs. Taylor inferred that if the desires causing an action are themselves caused then the action is not free. This does not follow. Just because some causes of desires and beliefs, such as brainwashing, make actions resulting from them unfree, it does not follow that any cause of desires and beliefs has the same implications for the freedom of actions resulting from them.

Since the notion of having control is the heart of the notion of freedom for me, let me stop to clarify the concept briefly. If I have control over x then x depends on what I do or do not do. I am an important part of the causal process producing x, such that if I did something different x would be different. Moreover, I must be conscious of x's dependence on me in order for x to be under my control. Whether some insect lives or not depends on whether or not I step on him as I walk down the street. But if I do not know he is there his life is not under my control. So for x to be under my control what I do or do not do must be an important part of the cause of x and I must know this. X therefore must depend on what I want or on my "will" in order for x to be under my control. Now since one can make more or less of a difference, be more or less important a part of the causal process, it therefore follows that one can have more or less control over something. The more control a person has the freer that person is. Clearly, then, a person is not simply free or unfree. Nor is every action simply free or unfree. Rather, there is a continuum between free and unfree, with many or most acts lying somewhere in between. When I say that an act is free what I mean is that the act falls on the free side of the continuum. Or, since there is no line in the middle of a continuum, it might be clearer to say that a free act falls in the direction of the free end of the continuum. Acts are more or less free according to how close they are to the free end of the continuum.

What I want to argue in this paper is that people can have differing amounts of control over what they desire and what they believe. People can be more or less important a part of the causal process leading to their having the desires and beliefs that they do. Our discussion thus far shows that only if they have control over their beliefs and desires do they really have control over their actions. The key question, then, is whether this idea of having control over one's beliefs and desires makes any sense and whether in fact we do have such control. Many people would probably say that while what we do is often up to us, what we believe and desire depends on factors completely beyond our control. Speaking generally, it depends on the way the world is; more specifically, it depends on our biological and psychological natures, the society in which we live, and our particular portion of it (that is, our class, race, ethnic group, and so on). Others would object that it makes no sense to separate the person or self from his/her desires and beliefs, and hence makes no sense to talk of the person having control over his/her desires and beliefs. My major purpose in this paper will be to give substance to the idea that people can have control over the sources of their actions—that is, have control over their desires and beliefs.

If an agent can be said to be the source of his/her beliefs and desires, then it makes sense to say that the agent is a self-determining being. This is a concept that many have taken to be at the heart of freedom, whether they be determinists, indeterminists, or hold to the idea of "agent causality." If we can give substance to this notion of a person having control over his desires and beliefs, we will have given substance to the notion of a self-determining being.

II

Before turning directly to the central task, I wish to raise another sort of counterexample to soft determinism. Some acts that are done because of the agent's desires and beliefs to do them are nevertheless unfree, but for reasons other than the source of those desires and beliefs. However, we will see that these counterexamples do not challenge the fundamental thrust of soft determinism because the examples are all such that we have reason to say that the actions in the examples are not truly self-determined.

A heroin addict steals some money and uses it to buy heroin, which he then takes. It might be said that all three acts (stealing, buying the drug, and taking it) are done because of the addict's desire to achieve a certain state and the belief that these are ways of achieving it. If we imagine that this addict does not want to be an addict, as is the case with most addicts, then these acts of his are crucially different from most acts done because of the agent's beliefs and desires. While the addict wants the heroin he also wants to not take the drug. Moreover, he wants a great number of things which he believes to be incompatible with taking the drug—for example, health, self-respect, an ordinary life, and so on. These contrary desires, values, and beliefs are greater in number and also are part of an integrated whole. The desire to take the drug is not part of such an integrated whole, but nevertheless it outweighs all these contrary desires and beliefs. A kleptomaniac's desire to steal would probably be similar. Most actions done because of the agent's desires are not in conflict with a greater number of his/her integrated desires and beliefs. I think it is this factor which leads compatibilists to reject such cases as not really counterexamples to their analysis of a free act as one resulting from the wants of the agent. An act resulting from such a conflict does not seem to proceed from the self as a free act must: It occurs in spite of the person. Moritz Schlick says, "We consider the man to be more or less unfree, and hold him less accountable, because we rightly view the influence of the drug as 'external,' even though it is found within the body; it prevents him from making decisions in the manner peculiar to his nature."[4] This integrated set of desires, beliefs and values might be said to constitute the person's nature or self as it is at that time. Acts proceeding from desires that are external to this and yet dominant would seem to be unfree. There are certain exceptions to this, however, which we will discover as we progress.

III

I wish at this point to introduce the notion of a second order volition as discussed by Harry Frankfurt in "Freedom of the Will and the Concept of a Person."[5] Someone has a volition of the second order when he wants to have a certain desire[6] and, moreover, wants that desire to be his effective desire—that is, his *will*, in Frankfurt's terminology. The addict in our example may simply suffer from a conflict between the desire to take the drug and a number of contradictory or incompatible desires. However, he may, further, want that the latter desires be his effective desires. If so, then the addict's desire to take the drug is in conflict not only with a greater number of integrated desires and beliefs, but with a second order volition as well. Yet it still determines the addict's actions. By being in conflict with the will he wants to have, it is in conflict with the want with which he has thereby identified himself. Hence, when this desire determines action, the action is in sharp contrast to most acts done because of the agent's beliefs and desires. Instead of being an act that depends on the agent, that is "up to him," it happens against his will. This provides further grounds for saying that the act does not proceed from the self. Quite aside from the nature of the desire that is in conflict with the second order volition in our example (that is, the desire to take heroin), it would seem plausible to take as a sufficient condition for making an act unfree that it proceed from beliefs and desires that are in conflict with a second order volition. A necessary condition, then, of a free act is that it proceed from desires and beliefs that are consistent with second order volitions. This should be seen as a development of the compatibilist account of a free act as one caused by the self, specifically the agent's beliefs and desires.

IV

Consistency with an integrated set of beliefs and desires and with second order volitions is not sufficient for an act to be free. We saw at the outset that the source of the beliefs and desires causing an act is relevant to the freedom of that act. The sorts of examples which first showed us that the soft determinist position was unsatisfactory as thus far presented were examples of acts done because of beliefs and desires that seemed in some way to have been forced upon the agent. Whether the person acquired beliefs and desires (volitions or the reasons for doing what he/she does) by being hooked up to a machine someone else controls, or by being brainwashed or exposed to subliminal advertising, the following is true. The beliefs and desires were acquired by measures taken by others in order to induce them, which measures were taken either explicitly against the person's will (brainwashing), and/or without his/her knowledge (subliminal advertising). (Taylor's case could be either.) Being ignorant of the measures taken to induce the beliefs and desires, the person is as much lacking in control over them as if they were taken explicitly against his/her will. In both cases the person, as an active determining being, is irrelevant to what happens. He/she has no control, and—more importantly—no possibility of control over the beliefs and desires he/she acquires. Actions done because of beliefs and desires acquired under such conditions are not free.

Now is it really necessary that a person's beliefs and desires be caused by other people in order for it to be the case that they were forced upon him/her? Although it was true of our original examples, I do not think it is a necessary condition. While it may sound odd to say they were the result of force or coercion where no persons were the cause, it can certainly be said that the desires were not acquired freely, or even that they were acquired under coercive conditions. The issue about causation of beliefs and desires that is crucial to the freedom of acts resulting from them is whether the person enters into the causal process as an active determinant. If the person does not, then the beliefs and desires were not acquired freely, and acts resulting from them are not free because not self-determined. If, on the contrary, the beliefs and desires are opposed to the person's desires, first or second order, then acts resulting from them are unfree or compelled. All this can be true even though the causes of the beliefs and desires were not measures taken by others to induce them. Suppose that a person lives under conditions of economic scarcity, which entails that not everyone will get what he/she needs and wants. A consequence of a person getting enough for himself and his family is that others will not have enough. A person in these conditions might, partly as a survival mechanism, come to desire that others not have enough—and might act on this desire. If this occurred, it seems to me that such an act would be an unfree one (although perhaps not at the very end of the continuum). If the person did not want to want that others not have enough, if in fact he/she wanted not to want this, then the desire would conflict with a second order volition. Acts resulting from such desires are unfree. However, in the absence of a conflicting or reinforcing second order volition, I would still wish to put the act on the unfree end of the continuum because the desires causing the act were produced under coercive conditions. The conditions were coercive because the person had no control over them, their existence was contrary to his/her desires, and his/her personality and character had little or no effect on their influence. Remove economic scarcity and the desire would be removed (although perhaps not immediately). Similar examples could be given of beliefs and desires caused by particular social systems and particular institutions within a social system.

V

Let us examine in some greater detail the conditions I have given under which desires could be said to have been acquired unfreely or coercively. It might be thought that my conditions apply too widely and would make too many desires turn out to have been unfreely acquired. For example, suppose a person has a strong desire to hear Bach because her parents regularly played Bach records in order to induce that desire. Her desire was acquired because of her parents' efforts to induce the desire. Their efforts consisted of intensively exposing her to the object they wished her to desire. If my conditions apply to such cases then her going to a concert as an adult because she wants to hear Bach played would be unfree—and this is an unattractive conclusion. However, my conditions do not lead to this conclusion, because the conditions I set are not met in the example. The child was not unaware of the causes of her later desire, which is what my condition requires; in fact it was by being aware of the music that was regularly played that she came to desire to hear it. Conceivably, but improbably, she was unaware that hearing the music was the cause of her later desire or that her parents regularly played it in order to produce that desire in her. However, these are different conditions from the one I gave. In general, where the measures taken to induce a desire simply amount to exposing a person to the object of the hoped-for desire, this does not meet my conditions, because the person cannot be unaware of the causes of the desire (although he/she may be unaware that they are the causes).

I am inclined to think that my conditions as they stand thus far are in need of revision in the other direction, that is, to make them apply more widely. Suppose that what was done to induce the desire was not mere exposure to the object, but rather conditioning. If they had conditioned her, the parents would have accompanied the playing of the music with pleasurable stimuli and they would have negatively reinforced any expressions of negative feeling toward the music. If this had been done, the desire would be the result of more than the interrelation of the person and the object of the desire, as is the case when the desire for something comes into being because of exposure to it. A desire that is the result of conditioning is the result of pleasures and pains that accompany the object, but are external to the person, the object, and the relation between them. When a person acquires desires and aversions for things because of pleasures and pains that are intrinsic to those things, such as the pleasures of eating good food, the pains of overeating, then those desires and aversions are freely acquired. Where the pleasures and pains are external, the *person* (that is, his/her personality, reasoning capacities, and so on) is bypassed in the process. This should make the process coercive. However, as my conditions stand they do not give this result. The person could be aware of the elements of the conditioning process (the music, the accompanying pleasures and pains), though unaware of the connections between them, the purposes behind them, and their effect. She was aware of the measures taken and therefore, if it were not explicitly against her will, the conditioning would not be coercive according to what I have said about coercion thus far. I take this to indicate that something more must be said.

In the hopes of working out how conditioning differs from mere exposure, let us go back to the example of the person who acquired a desire to hear the music of Bach because of repeated exposure to his music as a child. Whether the exposure was the deliberate work of others, as in our example, or not, acquisition of a desire through exposure differs from clearly coercive ways of acquiring desires. When people acquire a desire through being acquainted with the object or experience, they have the possibility of coming to have that desire or not. Whether they do or not will depend on facts about them: their aptitudes, beliefs, personality, other desires, and so on. Where this is the case they can be said to have control, or at least the possibility of control, over the desires they acquire. Where, on the other hand, the causes of their beliefs and desires would exist and would effectively operate regardless of the fact that their personality, character, other beliefs and desires are opposed to these causes, then they obviously have no chance of controlling what beliefs and desires they come to have.

We can distinguish, then, between cases where people can have control over their beliefs and desires and those where they cannot. Knowledge is necessary in order that a person have this possibility of control. In the account I gave of when a person could be said to have freely acquired his/her desires, I only required that the person have knowledge of the causes (and also that they not be against the person's will) in order that the causes not be coercive. Oftentimes, however, one needs to have more than simple knowledge of the causes. Conditioning is a case where the person being conditioned might know the causes, that is, might know the elements of the causal process, but might not know their interconnections or the purposes behind them. The person is acquainted with the causes but unaware that they are the causes or how and why they operate. If conditioning would operate regardless of whether a person knew the latter, then it is a causal process that the person cannot have any control over. Hence it is coercive.

Sometimes the efficacy of causal conditions depends on people's ignorance of them, that they are or may be causes, and how and why they operate. In such cases, people's ignorance of these facts would deprive them of whatever control knowledge might give them. People are less free to the extent that they operate on unconscious motives. Successful psychoanalysis can increase the patient's control and therefore freedom, by making conscious things that had hitherto been unconscious. Sometimes just knowing the purposes behind potential causes (for example, that it is designed to convince you, scare you, buy you off, or get you to buy something) can make a difference to whether those purposes are realized. Without the knowledge, one's attitudes towards these purposes cannot come into play and one cannot exercise any control over them. If the efficacy of the causes depends on one's ignorance of such facts about the causes, then the causes are coercive. It is where knowledge about the causes would have made a difference that ignorance makes the causes coercive. Causes of beliefs and desires are coercive where they operate contrary to the person's other beliefs, desires, character, and personality. This is so when the causes are explicitly against the person's will, or unknown to the person, or when they depend for their efficacy on the person's ignorance of certain facts about them. According to these conditions, conditioning would usually be coercive, which, I think, is as it should be.

Suppose one came to know that one was being conditioned and the knowledge made no difference to the efficacy of the causes. Is this a coercive way of acquiring desires? The answer depends on whether the conditioning process was against the person's will. If the causes operate against his/her will then they are coercive. On the other hand, suppose they are not operating against the person's will; in other words, suppose a person voluntarily chooses to be conditioned. A person might deliberately expose himself to conditions which will cause him to have (or not have) certain desires, for example, not to smoke. Once he puts himself into the situation, the causes operate independent of his other beliefs and desires, personality, and so on. His new effective desire not to smoke will be the result of conditioning, and we have said that conditioning is a form of coercion. However, I think that the circumstances of this kind of case make a significant difference. The person's self does enter into the causal process as an active determinant, whereas in most cases of conditioning this is not so. The person in our example who voluntarily has himself conditioned has a second order volition not to smoke, which is in conflict with his or her volition to smoke. If the second order volition were sufficiently strong to outweigh the first order volition by itself, then the new effective desire would be acquired in a completely free manner. However, it is not sufficiently strong to do this by itself. Causes that are independent of the person are necessary to change his desire. However, these other causes come into play only because of his second order volition. He had himself conditioned because he has a desire not to desire to smoke. So I think we can say that the cause of his new effective desire not to smoke is his second order volition. The new desire is not the result of coercion; it does spring from the self. However, it does not only spring from the self. It was not acquired in as free a manner as if the second order volition was sufficient by itself to cause it, but I would still put it towards the free end of the continuum.

What we have come up with is what we started with—and that is, to the extent that the causes of one's actions are themselves caused by things over which people have no control (even with knowledge of them), to that extent one's actions are unfree. What I have tried to do is to make sense of the idea of having control over one's desires. In order to say that one has control over one's desires it is necessary that what we identify as the self determines what one desires and what desires one acts on. To put together the criteria elaborated thus far: In order for actions caused by desires to be free, these desires must first of all not have been coercively acquired. What this means has been explained. Knowledge was seen to be a key factor. Secondly, they must not be contrary to the person's second order volitions. This second condition implies that the person has second order volitions. We will not be able to say that these desires are the desires the person wants to have unless (a) he/she has second order volitions and unless (b) these volitions outweigh first order volitions in the case of a conflict. Thirdly, the desire must be in harmony with an integrated set of desires and beliefs—hence one's self—at that given time. This third requirement must be qualified. A desire causing a free action may be inconsistent with this integrated set if the set does not meet one of the necessary conditions and the desire fulfills both the conditions. If the set was coercively acquired and the conflicting desire was not, or if the conflicting desire is supported by a second order volition and the set is not, then an action caused by the conflicting desire would be free. Any person missing second order volitions is missing an important kind of control over his/her actions, and hence an important dimension of freedom. That is why an action that proceeds from a conflicting desire which is supported by a second order volition is freer than one that proceeded from the integrated set, where there are no effective second order volitions. This sort of situation could lead to a revision of the set—a restructuring of the self. However, lacking an integrated set which is responsible for his/her actions, the person is divided, and it is less possible for that person to be a self-determining being. Therefore, the person is most free when there is an integrated set which is in accordance with his/her second order volitions. Then we can say that this is a self-determining person.

VI

An objection that will almost certainly be raised to what I have said thus far is that I have failed to carry through the logic of my argument. If, in order to have control over one's actions (that is, for one's actions to be free), it is necessary to have control over the causes of one's actions (that is, one's desires), then in order to have control over them, it is also necessary to have control over *their* causes, and in order to have control over them, it is necessary . . . In short, we are led to an infinite regress, or at least to a point where the person cannot possibly have any control—namely, a point before they are born. If it leads back to this point, then we can never have control over what we do. And so it seems we are led back to a choice of hard determinism, indeterminism, or a position like Taylor's.

I do not agree that the logic of my argument has to lead back to this point. In order to take this same analysis further back, one would have to make sense of having control over both (a) the integrated set of beliefs and desires and also over (b) one's second order volitions. Taking the former first, one way of having control over this integrated act would be to have effective second order volitions with respect to it. This is already part of my account. Aside from having effective second order volitions with respect to the integrated set of beliefs, desires, and so on, is there any other way in which one might be said to have or lack control over it? To give any other sense to how one might have control over this integrated set would require that some person or self be found to have control over it. But in the absence of a higher order volition, where and what is this entity that might but does not control this set? Unless some sense can be made of such an entity the idea remains incoherent, and my account thus far has not been shown to lead too far back.

To turn to (b), having control over one's second order volitions, we can make sense of this if we bring in the idea of third order volitions (wanting to want to want), and we could bring in volitions of still higher orders. I am not opposed to this but it is an empirical question just how far back we can go in any given case. Frankfurt deals with the point in the following way:

> There is no *theoretical* [my emphasis] limit to the length of the series of desires of higher and higher orders; nothing but common sense and, perhaps, a saving fatigue. . . . The tendency to generate such a series of acts of forming desires . . . leads to the destruction of a person. . . . It is possible, however, to terminate such a series of acts without cutting it off arbitrarily. When a person identified himself *decisively* with one of his first order desires, this commitment "resounds" throughout the potentially endless array of higher orders. . . . The decisiveness of the commitment he has made means that he has decided that no further question about his second order volition, at any higher order, remains to be asked. It is relatively unimportant whether we explain this by saying that the commitment implicitly generates an endless series of confirming desires of higher orders, or by saying that the commitment is tantamount to a dissolution of the pointedness of all questions concerning higher orders of desire.[7]

A person does not have an indefinite number of orders of volition with respect to a given desire. Once we have reached the point where a person has identified him/herself with a particular volition, the idea of that person having control over his/her desires of that order through volitions of a higher order seems to make no sense, because that person does not go further back. The person, a discriminating being capable of choice among desires, has committed and identified him/herself with a particular volition. To go further back is to leave the person behind. To speak of identifying oneself with a volition requires the possibility of desires of more than one order, but it does not require an indefinite series.

Let us approach the question from a slightly different angle. A second order volition might be the result of a higher order volition, or of coercion, or of neither of these. If a second order volition results from a volition of a higher order, then the person can be said to have control over that [second order] volition. Suppose now that the person's second order volition was not the result of a higher order volition, but neither was it the result of coercion. This would be true where the person had no higher order volitions relevant to the second order volition, but where the causes would not have operated if there had been second order volitions in conflict [with those causes]. (If they would have operated anyway then they would be coercive.) In such cases, it seems to me that the volitions should be said to have been acquired freely. It certainly was not acquired unfreely. The person did not *lack* control, and would have had control if there had been higher order volitions. A person can be said to have acquired a second order volition through coercion if the person has conflicting volitions of a still higher order which are ineffective against these causes. The person then lacks control over his/her second order volitions in an obvious way. Where the person has no volitions of a higher order, or where the person has decisively identified him/herself with the volition, Frankfurt and I have argued that something is wrong with saying that the person lacks control, because the person does not go further back. However, suppose that, if there were a conflicting higher order volition (although there isn't one), it would be ineffective. I am inclined to say that in this case as well, the person lacks control over his/her volitions and the causes are coercive. If this is correct, then a person lacks control over second order volitions if conflicting higher order volitions (whether the person has any or not) would be ineffective against them.

One might argue that because a person lacks control over his/her second order volitions it does not follow that he/she lacks control over his/her first order volitions or over his/her actions. I would want to distinguish between two sorts of cases. Recall that I distinguished two kinds of cases of second order volitions acquired through coercion: (a) ones in which there were conflicting volitions of a higher order, and (b) ones in which there were no volitions of a higher order, but if there had been they would have been ineffective. It seems to me that where the second order volitions result from coercion in the latter sort of case, actions proceeding from them are still free. The sense in which the second order volitions were coerced is a more extended hypothetical sense, and I therefore see little need to infer that the person's first order volitions and actions must also have been coerced. On the other hand, if the person's second order volitions are coerced as described in (a), the person lacked control and was coerced in more obvious and direct ways. Although it does not strictly follow, it seems more consistent with what I have been arguing to conclude that in such cases the person should be said to lack control over his/her first order volitions and his/her actions. I have argued that people have control over their actions when they have control over their causes (beliefs and desires), and that they have control over these when they are caused by second order volitions. If there are higher order volitions which are ineffective against the causes of the second order volitions, then the person has no control over these second order volitions. And it seems closer to the general line of argument I have been using, to conclude that in such cases they also have no control over their first order volitions and actions.

VII

As a prelude to concluding, I wish to consider the implications of my general and abstract analysis to the concrete question of just how free most people are today. We shall see that although my view implies that people can be free, though determined, it is also an implication of my view that most people are quite unfree today. The answer to this question of how free people are is not one that applies to all people just in virtue of their being human, but rather depends on who the people are and where and when they are living. It turns out, then, on my view, that human freedom is closely tied to social and political freedom and is not a distinct metaphysical[8] question. (In considering this part of the philosophical question we are inevitably drawn into empirical issues, including political ones, so my own opinion on these matters will certainly intrude.)

Desires arise in us because of a whole complex set of conditions which affect one another. (Neither they nor their influence can actually be separated, so the following remarks are unavoidably artificial.) These determining conditions include physical and psychological conditions, which to some extent we share with others, but which also differ from person to person. People today are capable of some but not much control over these conditions. Greater knowledge, aided by money, gives a person greater possibilities of control, but there are still very definite limits which no one today is capable of transcending. Greater knowledge will give greater possibilities of human control, but it is probable that there will always be limits that one cannot transcend. What is possible is for a person to exercise some control over the form of the desires these conditions tend to produce, and also over whether and how these desires are acted upon.

How much control a person can exercise over the social and political conditions causing his/her desires depends on the particular social system in which the person lives, and also the place that the person occupies in the system. Some changes are possible in the latter in most societies but usually quite little. In any case, it is only within the framework allowed by that system and it is not possible within the framework of *any* present society for *most* people to change their positions within that framework. As for the framework itself, one cannot change the time in which one lives, and since what social systems are possible depends on the time and place, there is a certain inevitable limitation. However, there are many fewer inevitable limitations on the degree of control one can exercise over social causes than over physical causes—in the future, but also in the present. Given the limitations of time and place, there is great potential today for people to collectively control the social conditions under which they live, and hence the beliefs and desires these conditions tend to produce, even if there are some conditions they still would not be able to control.

However, with some notable exceptions, the ability to control the social conditions in which one lives is only potential today, not actual. This is partially because people do not realize they have this ability. This lack of realization is strongly supported, of course, by the social system in which they live and by those who do control it. There is, again, the possibility of exercising some control over the form of the desires likely to be produced by these conditions, and also over whether and how these desires are acted upon. However, so long as one does not control the social causes of one's beliefs and desires, one does not have much chance of controlling the actual beliefs and desires one comes to have.

Leaving aside the nature of the influence, what is necessary in order to be able to exercise control over the influences acting upon one, is to be a certain kind of person, as well as to have knowledge and the cooperation of others. A person who is critical and discriminating and sees him/herself as actively shaping the world, history, and also him/herself, is capable of doing just that—not alone, but in cooperation with others. There are, of course, varying conditions where people may be more or less aware and/or more or less able not to be passive products. However, it seems that most people today are quite uncritical and undiscriminating and lack this self-conception. Many feel themselves to be more like passive products of history and their own particular environment— and their environment makes them feel that way. However, in the course of struggle against the oppressive aspects of their environment, they can come to realize their potential to bring the world under their conscious collective control. The realization of this is a first step towards changing the framework that keeps them without control. This capacity to change the world and consequently their own nature is unique to human beings. It gives them the potential of being free in the fullest sense that is possible in a deterministic world.

NOTES

1. I intend "beliefs" and "desires" to cover all mental sources of action, whatever exactly these are. [N. HOLMSTROM]
2. Richard Taylor, *Metaphysics* (Englewood Cliffs, N.J.: Prentice-Hall, 1963), p. 45. [N. HOLMSTROM]. This passage from Taylor appears on p. 307 of this book. [D. C. ABEL]
3. Ibid., pp. 50–53; pp. 311–313 of this book. [D. C. ABEL]
4. Moritz Schlick, "When Is a Man Responsible?," in *Free Will and Determinism*, ed. Bernard Berofsky (New York: Harper & Row, 1966), p. 59. [N. HOLMSTROM] Schlick (1882–1936) was a German philosopher. [D. C. ABEL]
5. Harry Frankfurt, "Freedom of the Will and the Concept of a Person," *The Journal of Philosophy* 68 (January 1971), pp. 5–20. [N. HOLMSTROM]
6. In Frankfurt's terminology, the original desire is a *first order* volition; the desire to have this desire is a *second order* volition. [D. C. ABEL]
7. Frankfurt, "Freedom of the Will and the Concept of a Person," pp. 16–17. [N. HOLMSTROM]
8. *metaphysical:* relating to *metaphysics,* the study of the nature and kinds of reality. [D. C. ABEL]

CHAPTER 6

Ethics

All of us could name certain actions that we think are morally right and others that we think are morally wrong. But what is it that makes an action morally right or wrong? Is it the way it affects other people? If so, what kinds of effects are good and what kinds are bad? Is it the intention behind our action? If so, what kinds of intentions are good and what kinds are bad? Is the goodness or evil of an action determined by whether it follows some rule of conduct? If so, how do we know whether the rule itself is good? Even if the rule *is* good, might it be morally better to make an exception to it in a particular situation? Can morality be adequately defined in terms of actions and rules, or does morality depend more on the *kind of person* we are? If so, what kind of qualities make a person good and what kind make a person bad? To ask a more radical question, are all judgments of moral good and evil—whether we are speaking of actions or personal qualities—simply a matter of opinion?

These are some of the questions addressed by the philosophical discipline of ethics. The word "ethics" derives from the Greek *ēthos,* which means "custom" in the singular and "character" in the plural *(ēthē).* The word "morality" has a parallel origin: It derives from the Latin *mos,* which—exactly like the Greek *ēthos*—means "custom" in the singular and "character" in the plural *(mores).* These root meanings indicate that ethics (morality) is concerned with what we do (custom) and with the kind of person we are (character). What we do is of course closely connected with the kind of person we are, since our character is formed largely by the way we habitually act. Using the root meanings as a guide, we can define ethics as the study of how we should live our life and what kind of person we should be. More succinctly, ethics is the study of right conduct and character.

Philosophy is not the only discipline to propose theories about proper conduct and character; theology also sets forth such theories. The principal difference between philosophical ethics and theological ethics is that the former bases its answers on reason and experience, and the latter appeals ultimately to faith and divine revelation. In philosophical ethics, all questions about morality are open to debate—even the question of whether there *is* a correct morality. Theological ethics, by contrast, assumes that the answers given by revelation are true; to call these answers into question is to leave the realm of theological ethics. Although theologians may disagree about the precise *meaning* of revealed moral directives (for example, "Thou shalt not kill"), they do not question their *truth.* The readings in this book, of course, are confined to philosophical ethics.

Our first section of readings, "Classical Ethical Theories," presents selections from four thinkers whose ethical doctrines have become central to the Western philosophical tradition. Aristotle argues that we all ultimately seek happiness and that we should live in a way that leads to happiness. He claims that being happy means living rationally and that living rationally means acting in accordance with excellences (virtues) of intellect and of character. To attain happiness, therefore, we must acquire these excellences. Thomas Aquinas maintains that we should live our lives in a way that conforms to "natural law"—the moral law that derives from the basic inclinations of our human nature. Immanuel Kant contends that being moral means acting out of duty, which in turn means following the "categorical imperative." The categorical imperative states that we may perform an action only if we can consistently will that *everyone* follow the policy upon which our action is based. The final classical theory presented here is that of John Stuart Mill. Mill explains and defends the theory of utilitarianism, the doctrine that we should always act in a way that promotes utility. By "utility" he means the greatest good of the greatest number. Mill defines "good" as pleasure and the absence of pain; he includes in the "greatest number" all creatures capable of feeling pleasure and pain.

The five authors in the second group of readings, "Critiques of Classical Theories," call into question some of the fundamental assumptions of traditional Western ethics. Søren Kierkegaard argues that ethics exalts the universal, subordinating the individual person to universal norms of conduct. Religious faith, however, transports us to a higher sphere of existence, where the individual is superior to the universal. Friedrich Nietzsche characterizes traditional morality as "slave morality" and argues that the qualities that traditional morality classifies as virtues (for example, kindness and selflessness) are actually life-denying vices. He believes that true morality is "master morality," which affirms life by exercising the "will to power." Jean-Paul Sartre rejects the claim that ethics can be based on human nature, because he holds that there *is* no human nature. Our ethical task is to create our nature through our choices. For Sartre, we do not choose something because it is good; it is good because we choose it. James Rachels discusses the challenge to traditional ethics posed by cultural relativism, the doctrine that moral values derive entirely from individual cultural codes and that there are no objective, independently valid moral values. He presents the arguments given to support this doctrine and points out their weaknesses. The final reading is from Rita C. Manning, who approaches ethics from a feminist perspective. She proposes an "ethic of care," arguing that morality consists essentially in having a disposition to care and in expressing this disposition in concrete actions.

A. Classical Ethical Theories

Nicomachean Ethics

Aristotle

Aristotle was born in the town of Stagira in northern Greece in 384 B.C.E. At the age of seventeen, he went to Athens to study at Plato's Academy, where he remained until Plato's death twenty years later. He then spent three years in the city of Assos in Asia Minor and two years in Mytilene on the island of Lesbos. In 343 or 342 he accepted the invitation of King Philip II of Macedon to become the tutor of his thirteen-year-old son, Alexander (later known as Alexander the Great). After a few years at the royal court in Pella, Aristotle returned to Stagira. In 335 he went back to Athens, where he founded a school called the Lyceum. When Alexander died in 323, strong anti-Macedonian sentiment arose in Athens. Because of his connections with Macedon, Aristotle thought it prudent to leave Athens. He went to Chalcis on the island of Euboea, where he died the following year of a stomach ailment.

Aristotle is the author of two very different kinds of philosophical writings: polished works intended for the general reading public, and notes from which he lectured, intended for circulation among his students and associates. The polished works have been entirely lost except for a few fragments; what have survived are the notes from his lectures on a wide variety of topics, including logic, biology, physics, psychology, metaphysics, and ethics.

Our selection is taken from the set of notes known as the *Nicomachean Ethics.* Here Aristotle argues that the ultimate goal everyone seeks is happiness and that being moral is a necessary part of a happy life. Happiness, Aristotle contends, consists in living rationally. Living rationally requires that two parts of a person's soul function well: the part that is rational in the proper sense (the intellectual part, which *has* reason) and the part containing appetites and desires (appetites and desires are not rational in themselves, but they are capable of *listening to and obeying* reason).

These two parts of the soul function well if they possess their respective excellences (virtues, good inner dispositions). *Intellectual excellences* are those that enable reason in the proper sense to carry out its function; *excellences of character* are those qualities that enable appetites and desires to fulfill their functions. Aristotle argues that a person who lives in accordance with intellectual excellences and excellences of character attains happiness and is moral.

Intellectual excellences include such qualities as good sense and wisdom; excellences of character include such traits as courage and moderation. Aristotle defines excellences of character as dispositions to seek the intermediate between the two extremes of excess and deficiency—the intermediate with regard to both affections (emotions) and actions. For example, the excellence of the affection of boldness is *courage,* which lies between rashness and cowardice; the excellence of the action of giving and receiving money is *open-handedness* (generosity), which is intermediate between wastefulness and avarice. Aristotle explains that the way to acquire an excellence of character is to perform the appropriate acts repeatedly. To become a courageous person, for example, one must do courageous things.

338

BOOK I

Chapter 1

Every sort of expert knowledge and every inquiry, and similarly every action and undertaking, seems to seek some good. Because of that, people are right to affirm that the good is "that which all things seek." But there appears to be a certain difference among ends:[1] Some are activities, while others are products of some kind, over and above the activities themselves. Where there are ends over and above the activities, in these cases the products are by their nature better than the activities.

Since there are many sorts of action, and of expertise and knowledge, their ends turn out to be many, too. Thus health is the end of medicine, a ship of shipbuilding, victory of generalship, wealth of household management. But in every case where such activities fall under some single capacity, just as bridle-making falls under horsemanship, along with all the others that produce the equipment for horsemanship, and horsemanship along with every action that has to do with expertise in warfare falls under generalship—so in the same way others fall under a separate one. And in all activities the ends of the controlling ones are more desirable than the ends under them, because it is for the sake of the former that the latter too are pursued. It makes no difference—as in the case of the sorts of knowledge mentioned—whether the ends of the actions are the activities themselves or some other thing over and above these.

Chapter 2

If then there is some end in our practical projects that we wish for because of itself, while wishing for the other things we wish for because of it, and we do not choose everything because of something else (for if *that* is the case, the sequence will go on to infinity, making our desire empty and vain), it is clear that this will be the good, that is, the chief good. So in relation to life, too, knowing it will have great weight. And, like archers with a target, would we not be more successful in hitting the point we need to hit if we had this knowledge?

If so, then one must try to grasp it at least in outline—that is, what it might be and to which sort of expertise or productive capacity it belongs. It would seem to belong to the most sovereign expertise, the most architectonic.[2] Political expertise appears to be like this, for it is this expertise that sets out which of the expertises there needs to be in cities, and what sorts of expertise each group of people should learn, and up to what point. And we see even the most prestigious of the productive capacities falling under it, for example generalship, household management, and rhetoric. Since it makes use of the practical expertises that remain, and furthermore legislates about what one must do and what things one must abstain from doing, the end of this expertise will contain those of the rest; so that this end will be the human good. For even if the good is the same for a single person and for a city, the good of the city is a greater and more complete thing both to achieve and to preserve; for while to do so for one person on his own is satisfactory enough, to do it for a nation or for cities is finer and more godlike. So our inquiry seeks these things, being a political inquiry in a way.

Chapter 3

Our account would be adequate if we achieved a degree of precision appropriate to the underlying material, for precision must not be sought to the same degree in all accounts of things, any more than it is by craftsmen in the things they are producing. Fine things and just things, which are what political expertise inquires about, involve great variation and irregularity, so that they come to seem fine and just by convention alone, and not by nature. Something like this lack of regularity is found also in good things, because of the fact that they turn out to be a source of damage to many people: Some in fact have perished because of wealth, others because of courage. We must be content then, when talking about things of this sort and starting from them, to show what is true about them roughly and in outline, and when talking about things that are for the most part, and starting from these, to reach conclusions too of the same sort. It is in this same way, then, that one must also receive each sort of account, for it is a mark of an educated person to look for precision in each kind of inquiry just to the extent that the nature of the subject allows it. It looks like the same kind of mistake to accept a merely persuasive account from a mathematician and to demand demonstrations from an expert in oratory. . . .

Chapter 4

Let us then resume the argument: Since every sort of knowledge and every undertaking seeks after some good, let us say what it is that we say political expertise seeks, and what the topmost of all achievable goods is. Pretty well most people are agreed about what to call it: Both ordinary people and people of quality say "happiness," and suppose that living well and doing well are the same thing as being happy. But they are in dispute about what happiness actually is, and ordinary people do not give the same answer as intellectuals. The first group identifies it with one of the obvious things that anyone would recognize, like pleasure or wealth or honor, while some pick some other thing and others another (often, too, the same person picks a different thing—when he falls ill, it's health, and if he is poor, it's wealth). But out of consciousness of their own ignorance they are in awe of those who say something impressive and over their heads. Some people used to think that besides these many goods there is another one, existing by itself, which is cause for all of these too of their being good.[3] Now it is presumably rather otiose to examine all these opinions, and enough to examine those that are most widely held, or seem to have some justification. . . .

Chapter 5

. . . To judge from their lives, most people (that is, the most vulgar) seem, not unreasonably, to suppose [happiness] to be pleasure; that is just why they favor the life of consumption. The kinds of lives that stand out here are especially three: the one just mentioned, the political life, and the life of reflection.

Now most of the utterly slavish sort of people obviously decide in favor of a life that belongs to grazing cattle—and not without reason, given that many of those in high places behave like Sardanapallus.[4] People of quality, for their part, those who tend towards a life of action, go for honor, for pretty much this is the end of the political life. But it appears more superficial than what we are looking for, as it seems to be located in those doing the honoring rather than in the person receiving it, and our hunch is that the good is something that belongs to a person and is difficult to take away from him. Again, people seem to pursue honor in order to be convinced that they themselves are good; at any rate they seek to be honored by people of discernment, and among those who know them, and to be honored for excellence. So it is clear, at any rate according to them, that excellence is of greater value. In fact, perhaps one might suppose that this is even more the end of the political life than honor is. But excellence too appears somewhat incomplete, for it seems to be possible actually to be asleep while having one's excellence, or to spend one's life in inactivity, and furthermore to suffer, and to meet with the greatest misfortunes—and no one would call the person who lived this kind of life happy, unless to defend a debating position. . . . Third of the three lives in question, then, is the life of reflection, about which we shall make our investigation in what follows.[5]

The life of the moneymaker is of a sort that is chosen under compulsion of need, and wealth is clearly not the good we are looking for, since it is useful and for the sake of something else. Hence one might be more inclined to take as ends the things mentioned before, because they are valued for themselves. But it appears that they are not what we are looking for either; and yet there are many established arguments that focus on them. Let these things, then, be set aside. . . .

Chapter 7

Let us go back to the good we are looking for—what might it be? For it appears to be one thing in one activity or sphere of expertise, another in another: It is different in medicine and in generalship, and likewise in the rest. What then is the good that belongs to each? Or is it that for which everything else is done? In medicine this is health, in generalship victory, in housebuilding a house, in some other sphere some other thing, but in every activity and undertaking it is the end; for it is for the sake of this that they all do the rest. The consequence is that if there is some one end of all practical undertakings, this will be the practicable[6] good, and if there are more than one, it will be these. Thus as the argument turns in its course, it has arrived at the same point; but we must try even more to achieve precision in this matter.

Since, then, the ends are evidently more than one, and of these we choose some because of something else, as we do wealth, flutes, and instruments in general, it is clear that not all are complete; and the best is evidently something complete. So that if there is some one thing alone that is complete, this will be what we are looking for, and if there are more such things than one, the most complete of these. Now we say that what is worth pursuing for itself is more complete than what is worth pursuing because of something else, and what is never desirable because of something else is more complete than those things that are desirable both for themselves and because of it; while what is complete *without qualification* is what is always desirable in itself and never because of something else. Happiness seems most of all to be like this; for this we do always choose because of itself and never because of something else, while as for honor, pleasure, intelligence, and every excellence, we do choose them because of themselves (since if nothing resulted from them, we would still choose each of them), but we also choose them for the sake of happiness, supposing that we shall be happy through them. But happiness no one chooses for the sake of these things, nor in general because of something else.

The same appears also to follow from considerations of self-sufficiency, for the complete good seems to be self-sufficient. By "self-sufficient" we do not mean sufficient for oneself alone . . . but also for one's parents, children, wife, and generally those one loves, and one's fellow citizens, since man is by nature a civic being. But there must be some limit found here: If the point is extended to ancestors and descendants and loved ones' loved ones, an infinite series will result. But this we must look at on another occasion. The "self-sufficient" we posit [is] what in isolation makes life desirable and lacking in nothing, and we think happiness is like this—and moreover most desirable of all things, it not being counted with other goods. Clearly, if it *were* so counted in with the least of other goods, we would think it more desirable [by the addition of these other goods], for what is added becomes an extra quantity of goods, and the larger total amount of goods is always more desirable. So happiness is clearly something complete and self-sufficient, being the end of our practical undertakings.

But perhaps it appears somewhat uncontroversial to say that happiness is the chief good, and a more distinct statement of what it is is still required. Well, perhaps this would come about if one established the *function* of human beings. For just as for a flute player or a sculptor or any expert, and generally for all those who have some characteristic function or activity, the good—their doing well—seems to reside in their function, so too it would seem to be for the human being, if indeed there is some function that belongs to him. So does a carpenter or a shoemaker have certain functions and activities, while a human being has none, and is by nature a do-nothing? Or just as an eye, a hand, a foot, and generally each and every part of the body appears as having some function, in the same way would one not posit a characteristic function for a human being too, alongside all of these? What, then, should we suppose this to be? Being alive is obviously shared by plants too, and we are looking for what is peculiar to human beings. In that case we must divide off the kind of life that consists in taking in nutriment and growing. Next to consider would be some sort of life of perception, but this too is evidently shared by horses, oxen, and every other animal. There remains a practical sort of life of what possesses reason; and of this, one element "possesses reason" insofar as it is *obedient to* reason, while the other possesses it insofar as it actually *has* it, and itself thinks. Since this life, too, is spoken of in two ways,[7] we must posit the *active* life; for this seems to be called a practical life in the more proper sense.

If the function of a human being is activity of soul in accordance with reason, or not apart from reason, and the function, we say, of a given sort of practitioner and a good practitioner of that sort is generically the same, as for example in the case of a cithara player and a good cithara player, and this is so without qualification in all cases, when a difference in respect of excellence is added to the function (for what belongs to the citharist is to play the cithara, to the good citharist to play it well)—if all this is so, and a human being's function we posit as being a kind of life, and this life [is] activity of soul and actions accompanied by reason, and it belongs to a good man to perform these well and finely, and each thing is completed well when it possesses its proper excellence—if all this is so, the human good turns out to be activity of soul in accordance with excellence (and if there are more excellences than one, in accordance with the best and the most complete). But furthermore it will be this in a complete life. For a single swallow does not make spring, nor does a single day; in the same way, neither does a single day, or a short time, make a man blessed and happy. . . .

Chapter 13

Since happiness is some activity of soul in accordance with complete excellence, we should discuss the subject of excellence; for perhaps in this way we shall get a better view of happiness too. . . .

One aspect of soul is nonrational, while another possesses reason. . . . Of the nonrational, one grade looks likely to be shared, and to have to do with growth—by which I mean what is responsible for the taking in of food and for increase in size; for this sort of capacity of soul one would posit as being in all things that take in food, and in embryos, and this same one too as being in them when they are full-grown, for it is more reasonable to suppose the presence of this one than of any other. Excellence in the exercise of this capacity, then, appears to be something shared and not distinctively human. . . .

But another kind of soul also seems to be nonrational, although participating in a way in reason. Take those with and without self-control: We praise their reason and the aspect of their soul that possesses reason; it gives the right encouragement in the direction of what is best. But there appears to be something else besides reason that is naturally in them, which fights against reason and resists it. . . . But this part too seems to participate in reason, as we have said. At any rate, in the self-controlled person it is obedient to reason—and in the moderate and courageous person it is presumably still readier to listen, for in him it always chimes with reason.

The nonrational, then, too, appears to be double in nature. For the plant-like aspect of soul does not share in reason in any way, while the appetitive and generally desiring part does participate in it in a way, that is, insofar as it is capable of listening to it and obeying it. It is the way one is reasonable when one *takes* account of advice from one's father or loved ones, not when one *has* an account of things, as for example in mathematics. That the nonrational is in a way persuaded by reason is indicated by our practice of admonishing people, and all the different forms in which we reprimand and encourage them. If one should call this too "possessing reason," then the aspect of soul that possesses reason will also be double in nature: One element of it will have it in the proper sense and in itself, another as something capable of listening as if to one's father.

Excellence too is divided according to this difference; for we call some of them intellectual excellences, others excellences of character—intellectual accomplishment, good sense, wisdom on the one hand counting on the side of the intellectual excellences, open-handedness and moderation counting among those of character. For when we talk about character, we do not say that someone is accomplished in a subject or has a good sense of things, but rather that he is mild or moderate. But we do also praise someone accomplished in something for his disposition, and the dispositions we praise are the ones we call excellences.

BOOK II

Chapter 1

Excellence being of two sorts, then, the one intellectual and the other of character, the intellectual sort mostly both comes into existence and increases as a result of teaching (which is why it requires experience and time), whereas excellence of character results from habituation—which is in fact the source of the name it has acquired [*ēthikē*], the word for "character trait" [*ēthos*] being a slight variation of that for "habituation" [*ethos*]. This makes it quite clear that none of the excellences of character come about in us by nature, for no natural way of being is changed through habituation. For example, the stone which by nature moves downwards will not be habituated into moving upwards, even if someone tries to make it so by throwing it upwards ten thousand times, nor will fire move downwards, nor will anything else that is by nature one way be habituated into behaving in another. In that case the excellences develop in us neither by nature nor contrary to nature, but because we are naturally able to receive them and are brought to completion by means of habituation.

Again, in the case of those things that accrue to us by nature, we possess the capacities for them first, and display them in actuality later (something that is evident in the case of the senses: we did not acquire our senses as a result of repeated acts of seeing, or repeated acts of hearing, but rather the other way round—we used them because we had them, rather than acquired them because we used them); whereas we acquire the excellences through having first engaged in the activities. [This] is also the case with the various sorts of expert knowledge—for the way we learn the things we should do, knowing how to do them, is by doing them. For example, people become builders by building, and cithara players by playing the cithara. So too, then, we become just by doing just things, moderate by doing moderate things, and courageous by doing courageous things. What happens in cities testifies to this: Lawgivers make the citizens good through habituation, and this is what every lawgiver aims at, but those who do it badly miss their mark—and this is what makes one constitution different from another, a good one from a bad one.

Again, it is from the same things and through the same things that every excellence is both produced and destroyed, and similarly every expertise; for it is from playing the cithara that both the good and the bad cithara players come about. So too both with builders and the rest: Good building will result in good builders, bad building in bad ones. If it were not like this, there would be no need at all of anyone to teach them, and instead everyone would just become a good builder or a bad one. This, then, is how it is with the excellences too; for it is through acting as we do in our dealings with human beings that some of us become just and others unjust, and through acting as we do in frightening situations, and through becoming habituated to fearing or being confident, that some of us become courageous and some of us cowardly. A similar thing holds too with situations relating to the appetites, and with those relating to temper: Some people become moderate and mild-tempered, others self-indulgent and irascible, the one group as a result of behaving one way in such circumstances, the other as a result of behaving another way.

We may sum up by saying just that dispositions come about from activities of a similar sort. This is why it is necessary to ensure that the activities be of a certain quality, for the varieties of these are reflected in the dispositions. So it does not make a small difference whether people are habituated to behave in one way or in another way from childhood on, but a very great one; or rather, it makes all the difference in the world. . . .

Chapter 4

But someone may raise a problem about how we can say that to become just, people need to do what is just, and to do what is moderate in order to become moderate; for if they are doing what is just and moderate, they are already just and moderate, in the same way in which, if people are behaving literately and musically, they are already expert at reading and writing and in music.

Or does this fail to hold, in fact, even for skills? One can do something literate both by chance and at someone else's prompting. One will only count as literate, then, if one both does something literate and does it in the way a literate person does it; and this is a matter of doing it in accordance with one's own expert knowledge of letters.

Again, neither do the case of the skills and that of the excellences resemble each other: The things that come about through the agency of skills contain in themselves the mark of their being done well, so that it is enough if they turn out in a certain way, whereas the things that come about in accordance with the excellences count as done justly or moderately not merely because they themselves are of a certain kind, but also because of facts about the agent doing them—first if he does them knowingly, secondly if he decides to do them and decides to do them for themselves, and thirdly if he does them from a firm and unchanging disposition. When it is a matter of having skills, these conditions are not relevant, except for knowledge itself; but when it comes to having the excellences, knowledge makes no difference, or a small one, whereas the force of the other conditions is not small but counts for everything, and it is these that result from the repeated performance of just and moderate actions. So things done are called just and moderate whenever they are such that the just person or the moderate person would do them; whereas a person is not just and moderate because he does these things, but also because he does them in the way in which just and moderate people do them. . . .

Chapter 6

. . . Every excellence, whatever it is an excellence of, both gives that thing the finish of a good condition and makes it perform its function well, as for example the eye's excellence makes both it and its functioning excellent; for it is through the excellence of the eye that we see well. Similarly the excellence of a horse both makes it an excellent horse and good at running, carrying its rider, and facing the enemy. If, then, this is so in all cases, the excellence of a human being too will be the disposition whereby he becomes a good human being and from which he will perform his own function well. In what way this will be, we have already said, but it will also be clear in this way too—that is, if we consider what sort of nature excellence has.

Now with everything continuous and divisible it is possible to take a greater and a lesser and an equal amount, and these either with reference to the object itself or relative to us. The equal is a kind of intermediate between what exceeds and what falls short. By intermediate "with reference to the object" I mean what is equidistant from each of its two extremes, which is one and the same for all; whereas by intermediate "relative to us" I mean the sort of thing that neither goes to excess nor is deficient—and this is not one thing, nor is it the same for all. So for example if ten count as many and two as few, six is what people take as intermediate with reference to the object, since it exceeds and is exceeded by the same amount; and this is intermediate in terms of arithmetical proportion. But the intermediate relative to us should not be taken in this way; for if ten minas[8] in weight is a large amount for a particular person to eat and two a small amount, the trainer will not prescribe six minas, because perhaps this too is large for the person who will be taking it, or small—small for Milo,[9] large for the person just beginning his training. Similarly with running and wrestling. It is in this way, then, that every expert tries to avoid excess and deficiency, and looks instead for the intermediate and chooses this—the intermediate, that is, not in the object, but relative to us.

If, then, it is in this way that every kind of expert knowledge completes its function well, by looking to the intermediate and guiding what it produces by reference to this (which is why people are used to saying about products of good quality that nothing can either be taken away from them or added to them, because they suppose that excess and deficiency destroy good quality, while intermediacy preserves it—and skilled experts, as we say, work by looking to this), and if excellence is more precise and better than any expertise, just as nature is, excellence will be effective at hitting upon what is intermediate. I mean excellence of character; for this has to do with affections and actions, and it is in these that there is excess and deficiency, and the intermediate. So, for example, it is possible on occasion to be affected by fear, boldness, appetite, anger, pity, and pleasure and distress in general both too much and too little, and neither is good; but to be affected when one should, at the things one should, in relation to the people one should, for the reasons one should, and in the way one should, is both intermediate and best, which is what belongs to excellence.

In the same way with actions too there is excess, deficiency, and the intermediate. Excellence has to do with affections and actions—things in which excess and deficiency go astray, while what is intermediate is praised and gets it right. . . .

Excellence, then, is a disposition issuing in decisions, depending on intermediacy of the kind relative to us, this being determined by rational prescription and in the way in which the wise person would determine it. And it is intermediacy [because it lies] between two bad states, one involving excess, the other involving deficiency; and also because one set of bad states is deficient, the other excessive, in relation to what is required both in affections and in actions—whereas excellence both finds and chooses the intermediate. Hence excellence, in terms of its essence and the definition that states what it is for excellence to be, is intermediacy; but in terms of what is best, and good practice, it is extremity.

But not every action admits of intermediacy, nor does every affection; for in some cases they have been named in such a way that they are combined with badness from the start, as for example with malice, shamelessness, and grudging ill will; and in the case of actions, fornication, theft, and murder. All these, and others like them, owe their names to the fact that they themselves—not excessive versions of them, or deficient ones—are bad. It is not possible, then, ever to get it right with affections and actions like these, but only to go astray; nor does good practice or the lack of it in relation to such things consist in (for example) fornicating with the woman one should, when one should, and how. Rather, simply doing any one of these things is going astray. . . .

Chapter 7

But we should not simply state this in general terms; we should also show how it fits the particular cases. For with discussions that relate to actions, those of a general sort have a wider application, but those that deal with the subject bit by bit are closer to the truth; for actions have to do with particulars, and the requirement is that we should be in accord on these. So we should take these cases from the chart.[10] Thus with regard to feelings of *fear and boldness,* courage is the intermediate state; while of those people who go to excess, the one who is excessively fearless has no name (many cases are nameless), the one who is excessively bold is rash, and the one who is excessively fearful and deficiently bold is cowardly. With regard to *pleasures and pains*—not all of them, and still less with regard to all pains—the intermediate state is moderation, the excessive state self-indulgence. As for people deficient with regard to pleasures, they hardly occur; which is why people like this, too, have even failed to acquire a name. But let us put them down as "insensate." With regard to the *giving and receiving of money* the intermediate state is open-handedness, while the excessive and deficient states are wastefulness and avariciousness. But in these states excess and deficiency work in opposite ways: The wasteful person is excessive in handing money out and deficient in taking it, while the avaricious person is excessive in taking it and deficient when it comes to giving it out.

NOTES

1. *ends:* goals. [D. C. ABEL]
2. *architectonic:* superior in a hierarchy and directing subordinate members. [D. C. ABEL]
3. Aristotle here refers primarily to Plato, under whom he studied for twenty years. [D. C. ABEL]
4. *Sardanapallus:* the Hellenized name of King Ashurbanipal of Assyria (668–627 B.C.E.), who was famous for his sensual indulgence. [D. C. ABEL]
5. Aristotle discusses this in Book X of the *Nicomachean Ethics* (not included in our reading). [D. C. ABEL]
6. *practicable:* attainable by action. [D. C. ABEL]
7. *in two ways:* The practical life of reason can be spoken of in a *passive* sense, as merely possessing the ability to reason, or in an *active* sense, as actually exercising this ability. [D. C. ABEL]
8. *minas:* units of weight equivalent to approximately 1 pound. [D. C. ABEL]
9. Milo of Croton was a famous Greek wrestler of the sixth century B.C.E. [D. C. ABEL]
10. Aristotle evidently refers to a chart that he used when presenting this material to his students. [D. C. ABEL]

Treatise on Law

Thomas Aquinas

A biography of Thomas Aquinas appears on p. 32.

This reading is from Aquinas's "Treatise on Law," a section of the First Part of Part Two of the *Summa Theologiae*. Aquinas argues that to be moral means to follow the "natural law." By "natural law" he does not mean the laws of nature, such as the law of gravity, but the moral law that follows from the nature of human beings. Natural law is a subset of eternal law—the law by which God governs the entire universe. According to Aquinas, God directs all creatures by instilling in them natural inclinations. But human beings are subject to eternal law in a special way: Unlike other material creatures, they have reason and free will, which enable them to decide whether and how to fulfill their natural tendencies.

The first precept (command) of the natural law is that "we should do and seek good, and shun evil." To specify what the good is for human beings, Aquinas distinguishes among three levels of natural human inclination. As a substance (thing), we are inclined to preserve our own existence; as an animal, to preserve the existence of our species; as a *rational* animal, to know the truth and live harmoniously with others. Consequently, the natural law dictates that we should (1) preserve our own lives, (2) preserve our species, and (3) seek the truth and live peacefully in society. To be moral is to follow these commands. As Aquinas explains elsewhere, if the commands come into conflict in some situation, we must use the virtue of prudence to decide which one to follow. Aquinas maintains that these precepts are written in the hearts of all human beings, but that strong emotions, evil customs, or corrupt habits can prevent a person from knowing the conclusions properly drawn from them.

QUESTION 91. ON DIFFERENT KINDS OF LAW

First Article. Is There an Eternal Law?

. . . Law is simply a dictate of practical reason[1] by a ruler who governs a [complete] community. But supposing that God's providence rules the world . . . , his reason evidently governs the entire community of the universe. And so the plan of governance of the world existing in God as the ruler of the universe has the nature of law. And since God's reason conceives eternally, as Proverbs 8:23 says, not temporally, we need to say that such law is eternal. . . .

Second Article. Is There a Natural Law in Us?

. . . Law, since it is a rule or measure, can belong to things in two ways: in one way to those who rule and measure; in a second way to those ruled and measured, since things are ruled or measured insofar as they partake of the rule or measure. But the eternal law rules and measures everything subject to God's providence. . . . And so everything evidently shares in some way in the eternal law, namely, insofar as all things have inclinations to their own acts and ends[2] from its imprint on them. But the rational creature is subject to God's providence in a more excellent way than other things, since such a creature also shares in God's providence in providing for itself and others. And so it shares in the eternal plan whereby it has its natural inclination to its requisite activity and end. And we call such participation in the eternal law by rational creatures the natural law. And so Psalm 4:6, after saying "Offer just sacrifices," asks "Who shows us just things?" and replies: "The light of your countenance, O Lord, has been inscribed on us." The Psalmist thus signifies that the light of natural reason whereby we discern good and evil is simply the imprint of God's light in us. And so it is clear that the natural law is simply rational creatures' participation in the eternal law. . . .

QUESTION 94. ON THE NATURAL LAW

Second Article. Does the Natural Law Include Several Precepts or Only One?

. . . There is a priority regarding the things that fall within the understanding of all persons. For what first falls within our understanding is *being,* the understanding of which is included in everything that one understands. And so the first indemonstrable principle[3] is that one cannot at the same time affirm and deny the same thing. And this principle is based on the nature of being and nonbeing, and all other principles are based on it, as the *Metaphysics* says.[4] And as being is the first thing that without qualification falls within our understanding, so *good* is the first thing that falls within the understanding of practical reason. And practical reason is ordered to action, since every efficient cause[5] acts for the sake of an end, which has the nature of good. And so the first principle in practical reason is one based on the nature of good, namely, that good is what all things seek.[6] Therefore, the first precept of the natural law is that we should do and seek good, and shun evil. And all the other precepts of the natural law are based on that precept, so that all the things that practical reason by nature understands to be human goods or evils belong to precepts of the natural law as things to be done or shunned.

And since good has the nature of end, and evil the nature of the contrary, reason by nature understands to be good all the things for which human beings have a natural inclination, and so to be things to be actively sought, and understands contrary things as evil and to be shunned. Therefore, the ordination of our natural inclinations ordains the precepts of the natural law.

First, for example, human beings have an inclination for good by the nature they share with all substances, namely, as every substance by nature seeks to preserve itself. And regarding this inclination, means that to preserve our human life and to prevent the contrary belong to the natural law.

Second, human beings have more particular inclinations by the nature they share with other animals. And so the *Digest* says that things "that nature has taught all animals"[7]—such as the sexual union of male and female, and the upbringing of children, and the like—belong to the natural law.

Third, human beings have inclinations for good by their rational nature, which is proper to them. For example, human beings by nature have inclinations to know truths about God and to live in society with other human beings. And so things that relate to such inclinations belong to the natural law—for example, that human beings shun ignorance, that they not offend those with whom they ought to live sociably, and other such things regarding those inclinations.

Fourth Article. Is the Natural Law the Same for All Human Beings?

. . . Things to which nature inclines human beings belong to the natural law, as I have said before, and one of the things proper to human beings is that their nature inclines them to act in accord with reason. And it belongs to reason to advance from the general to the particular, as the *Physics* makes clear.[8] And regarding that process, theoretical reason proceeds in one way, and practical reason in another way. For inasmuch as theoretical reason is especially concerned about necessary things, which cannot be otherwise disposed, its particular conclusions, just like its general principles, are true without exception. But practical reason is concerned about contingent[9] things, which include human actions. And so the more reason goes from the general to the particular, the more exceptions we find, although there is some necessity in the general principles. Therefore, truth in theoretical matters, both first principles and conclusions, is the same for all human beings, although some know only the truth of the principles, which we call universal propositions, and not the truth of the conclusions. But truth in practical matters, or practical rectitude, is the same for all human beings only regarding the general principles, not regarding the particular conclusions. And not all of those with practical rectitude regarding particulars know the truth in equal measure.

Therefore, the truth or rectitude regarding the general principles of both theoretical and practical reason is the same for all persons and known in equal measure by all of them. And the truth regarding the particular conclusions of theoretical reason is the same for all persons, but some know such truth less than others. For example, it is true for all persons that triangles have three angles equal to two right angles, although not everybody knows this.

But the truth or rectitude regarding particular conclusions of practical reason is neither the same for all persons nor known in equal measure even by those for whom it is the same. For example, it is correct and true for all persons that they should act in accord with reason. And it follows as a particular conclusion from this principle that those holding goods in trust should return the goods to the goods' owners. And this is indeed true for the most part, but it might in particular cases be injurious, and so contrary to reason, to return the goods (for example, if the owner should be seeking to attack one's country). And the more the particular conclusion goes into particulars, the more exceptions there are (for example, if one should declare that entrusted goods should be returned to their owners with such and such safeguards or in such and such ways). For the more particular conditions are added to the particular conclusion, the more ways there may be exceptions, so that the conclusion about returning or not returning entrusted goods is erroneous.

Therefore we should say that the natural law regarding general first principles is the same for all persons both as to their rectitude and as to knowledge of them. And the natural law regarding particulars, which are, as it were, conclusions from the general principles, is for the most part the same for all persons both as to its rectitude and as to knowledge of it. Nonetheless, it can be wanting in rather few cases both as to its rectitude and as to knowledge of it. As to rectitude, the natural law can be wanting because of particular obstacles, just as natures that come to be and pass away are wanting in rather few cases because of obstacles. And also as to knowledge of the natural law, the law can be wanting because emotions or evil habituation or evil natural disposition has perverted the reason of some. For example, the Germans of old did not consider robbery wicked, as Caesar's *Gallic Wars* relates,[10] although robbery is expressly contrary to the natural law.

Fifth Article. Can the Natural Law Vary?

. . . We can understand the mutability of the natural law in two ways. We can understand it in one way by things being added to it. And then nothing prevents the natural law changing, since both divine law and human laws add to natural law many things beneficial to human life.

We can understand the mutability of the natural law in a second way by way of substraction, namely, that things previously subject to the law cease to be so. And then the natural law is altogether immutable as to its first principles. And as to its secondary precepts, which we said are proper proximate conclusions, as it were, from the first principles, the natural law is not so changed that what it prescribes is not for the most part completely correct. But it can be changed regarding particulars and in rather few cases, due to special causes that prevent observance of such precepts, as I have said before.

Sixth Article. Can the Natural Law Be Excised from the Hearts of Human Beings?

. . . As I have said before, there belong to the natural law, indeed primarily, very general precepts, precepts that everyone knows; and more particular, secondary precepts, which are like proximate conclusions from first principles. Therefore, regarding the general principles, the natural law in general can in no way be excised from the hearts of human beings. But the natural law is wiped out regarding particular actions insofar as desires or other emotions prevent reason from applying the general principles to particular actions, as I have said before.

And the natural law can be excised from the hearts of human beings regarding the other, secondary precepts, either because of wicked opinions, just as errors in theoretical matters happen regarding necessary conclusions, or because of evil customs or corrupt habits. For example, some did not think robbery a sin, or even sins against nature to be sinful, as the Apostle [Paul] also says in Romans 1:24–28.

NOTES

1. *practical reason:* reason as used to direct practical activity. Practical reason is contrasted with *theoretical reason,* which is reason as directed toward knowing the truth for its own sake. As Aquinas explains later on, the first thing that falls within the understanding of practical reason is the *good* (the goal of every practical action), whereas the first thing that falls within the understanding of theoretical reason is *being* (the goal of our desire to know reality). [D. C. ABEL]

2. *ends:* goals. [D. C. ABEL]

3. *indemonstrable principle:* a principle that cannot be proved (demonstrated) because there is nothing more fundamental on which to base a proof. [D. C. ABEL]

4. Aristotle, *Metaphysics,* Book III, Chapter 3. [RICHARD J. REGAN, TRANSLATOR]

5. *efficient cause:* an agent that brings something into being or imparts change. [D. C. ABEL]

6. This definition of *good* is given by Aristotle in *Nicomachean Ethics,* Book I, Chapter 1. The text appears on p. 339 of this book. [D. C. ABEL]

7. *Digest,* Book I, Title 1, no. 1. The *Digest* is a codification of the works of classical jurists published by the Roman emperor Justinian in 533. The quotation cited here is attributed to the Roman jurist Ulpian (died 228 C.E.). [D. C. ABEL]

8. Aristotle, *Physics,* Book I, Chapter 1. [RICHARD J. REGAN]

9. *contingent:* capable of being otherwise. [D. C. ABEL]

10. Gaius Julius Caesar, *Gallic Wars,* Book VI, Chapter 23. [RICHARD J. REGAN]. Caesar (100–44 B.C.E.) was a Roman general, politician, and author. [D. C. ABEL]

Groundwork of the Metaphysics of Morals

Immanuel Kant

A biography of Immanuel Kant appears on p. 175.

This reading is taken from Kant's *Groundwork of the Metaphysics of Morals,* a work whose aim, Kant explains in his preface, is "to seek out and establish the supreme principle of morality." According to Kant, the moral worth of an action is determined by one's motive, not by the consequences of the action. And the proper motive (what makes a will a *good* will) is to do one's duty simply because it is one's duty. To act out of duty means to act out of respect for the law, and to act out of respect for the law means to follow the "categorical imperative." This imperative states that our action should be "universalizable," which means that the personal policy (maxim) on which our action is based must be one that we could consistently will that all persons follow. If our maxim cannot be universalized, the action is immoral. For example, the maxim of making a false promise to escape a difficulty cannot consistently be universalized because, if everyone followed it, promises would no longer be able to function as promises because no one would believe them. The categorical imperative is, for Kant, the ultimate criterion for determining the morality of any action.

   According to Kant, the categorical imperative can be expressed in various equivalent ways, including the injunction that we should always treat persons (including ourselves) as ends in themselves, and never simply as means to an end. Returning to his example of making a false promise, he explains that such a promise is immoral because it uses the person lied to merely as means to obtain one's end.

Section I. Transition from Common Rational to Philosophic Moral Cognition

It is impossible to think of anything at all in the world, or indeed even beyond it, that could be considered good without limitation except a *good will.* Understanding, wit, judgment and the like, whatever such talents of mind may be called, or courage, resolution, and perseverance in one's plans, as qualities of temperament, are undoubtedly good and desirable for many purposes, but they can also be extremely evil and harmful if the will which is to make use of these gifts of nature, and whose distinctive constitution is therefore called *character,* is not good. It is the same with gifts of fortune. Power, riches, honor, even health and that complete well-being and satisfaction with one's condition called *happiness,* produce boldness and thereby often arrogance as well unless a good will is present which corrects the influence of these on the mind and, in so doing, also corrects the whole principle of action and brings it into conformity with universal ends[1]—not to mention that an impartial rational spectator can take no delight in seeing the uninterrupted prosperity of a being graced with no feature of a pure and good will, so that a good will seems to constitute the indispensable condition even of worthiness to be happy.

Some qualities are even conducive to this good will itself and can make its work much easier. Despite this, however, they have no inner unconditional worth but always presuppose a good will, which limits the esteem one otherwise rightly has for them and does not permit their being taken as absolutely good. Moderation in affects and passions, self-control, and calm reflection are not only good for all sorts of purposes but even seem to constitute a part of the inner worth of persons. But they lack much that would be required to declare them good without limitation (however unconditionally they were praised by the ancients), for without the basic principles of a good will they can become extremely evil, and the coolness of a scoundrel makes him not only far more dangerous but also immediately more abominable in our eyes than we would have taken him to be without it.

A good will is not good because of what it effects or accomplishes, because of its fitness to attain some proposed end, but only because of its volition—that is, it is good in itself and, regarded for itself, is to be valued incomparably higher than all that could merely be brought about by it in favor of some inclination and indeed, if you will, of the sum of all inclinations. Even if, by a special disfavor of fortune or by the [stingy] provision of a stepmotherly nature, this will should wholly lack the capacity to carry out its purpose—if with its greatest efforts it should yet achieve nothing and only the good will were left (not, of course, as a mere wish but as the summoning of all means insofar as they are in our control)—then, like a jewel, it would still shine by itself, as something that has its full worth in itself. Usefulness or fruitlessness can neither add anything to this worth nor take anything away from it. Its usefulness would be, as it were, only the setting to enable us to handle it more conveniently in ordinary commerce or to attract to it the attention of those who are not yet expert enough, but not to recommend it to experts or to determine its worth. . . .

We have, then, to explicate the concept of a will that is to be esteemed in itself and that is good apart from any further purpose, as it already dwells in natural sound understanding and needs not so much to be taught as only to be clarified—this concept that always takes first place in estimating the total worth of our actions and constitutes the condition of all the rest. In order to do so, we shall set before ourselves the concept of *duty*, which contains that of a good will though under certain subjective limitations and hindrances—which, however, far from concealing it and making it unrecognizable, rather bring it out by contrast and make it shine forth all the more brightly.

I here pass over all actions that are already recognized as contrary to duty, even though they may be useful for this or that purpose; for in their case the question whether they might have been done *from duty* never arises, since they even conflict with it. I also set aside actions that are really in conformity with duty but to which human beings have *no inclination immediately* and which they still perform because they are impelled to do so through another inclination. For in this case it is easy to distinguish whether an action in conformity with duty is done from duty or from a self-seeking purpose. It is much more difficult to note this distinction when an action conforms with duty and the subject has, besides, an *immediate inclination* to it. For example, it certainly conforms with duty that a shopkeeper not overcharge an inexperienced customer, and where there is a good deal of trade a prudent merchant does not overcharge but keeps a fixed general price for everyone, so that a child can buy from him as well as everyone else. People are thus served honestly, but this is not nearly enough for us to believe that the merchant acted in this way from duty and basic principles of honesty. His advantage required it; it cannot be assumed here that he had, besides, an immediate inclination toward his customers, so as from love, as it were, to give no one preference over another in the matter of price. Thus the action was done neither from duty nor from immediate inclination but merely for purposes of self-interest.

On the other hand, to preserve one's life is a duty, and besides everyone has an immediate inclination to do so. But on this account the often anxious care that most people take of it still has no inner worth and their maxim[2] has no moral content. They look after their lives *in conformity with duty* but not *from duty.* On the other hand, if adversity and hopeless grief have quite taken away the taste for life; if an unfortunate man, strong of soul and more indignant about his fate than despondent or dejected, wishes for death and yet preserves his life without loving it, not from inclination or fear but from duty, then his maxim has moral content.

To be beneficent where one can is a duty, and besides there are many souls so sympathetically attuned that, without any other motive of vanity or self-interest they find an inner satisfaction in spreading joy around them and can take delight in the satisfaction of others so far as it is their own work. But I assert that in such a case an action of this kind, however it may conform with duty and however amiable it may be, has nevertheless no true moral worth but is on the same footing with other inclinations, for example, the inclination to honor, which, if it fortunately lights upon what is in fact in the common interest and in conformity with duty and hence honorable, deserves praise and encouragement but not esteem—for the maxim lacks moral content, namely, that of doing such actions not from inclination but from duty. Suppose, then, that the mind of this philanthropist were overclouded by his own grief, which extinguished all sympathy with the fate of others, and that while he still had the means to benefit others in distress their troubles did not move him because he had enough to do with his own; and suppose that now, when no longer incited to it by any inclination, he nevertheless tears himself out of this deadly insensibility and does the action without any inclination, simply from duty; then the action first has its genuine moral worth. Still further: If nature had put little sympathy in the heart of this or that man; if (in other respects an honest man) he is by temperament cold and indifferent to the sufferings of others, perhaps because he himself is provided with the special gift of patience and endurance toward his own sufferings and presupposes the same in every other or even requires it; if nature had not properly fashioned such a man (who would in truth not be its worst product) for a philanthropist, would he not still find within himself a source from which to give himself a far higher worth than what a mere good-natured temperament might have? By all means! It is just then that the worth of character comes out, which is moral and incomparably the highest, namely, that he is beneficent not from inclination but from duty. . . .

The second proposition[3] is this: An action from duty has its moral worth not in the purpose to be attained by it but in the maxim in accordance with which it is decided upon, and therefore does not depend upon the realization of the object of the action but merely upon the *principle of volition* in accordance with which the action is done, without regard for any object of the faculty of desire. That the purposes we may have for our actions, and their effects as ends and incentives of the will, can give actions no unconditional and moral worth is clear from what has gone before. In what, then, can this worth lie, if it is not to be in the will in relation to the hoped for effect of the action? It can lie nowhere else than in the principle of the will, without regard for the ends that can be brought about by such an action. For the will stands between its a priori principle, which is formal, and its a posteriori incentive, which is material,[4] as at a crossroads; and since it must still be determined by something, it must be determined by the formal principle of volition as such when an action is done from duty, where every material principle has been withdrawn from it.

The third proposition, which is a consequence of the two preceding, I would express as follows: Duty is the necessity of an action from respect for law. For an object as the effect of my proposed action I can indeed have *inclination* but never *respect*, just because it is merely an effect and not an activity of a will. In the same way, I cannot have respect for inclination as such, whether it is mine or that of another; I can at most in the first case approve it and in the second sometimes even love it, that is, regard it as favorable to my own advantage. Only what is connected with my will merely as ground and never as effect, what does not serve my inclination but outweighs it or at least excludes it altogether from calculations in making a choice—hence the mere law for itself—can be an object of respect and so a command. Now an action from duty [must] put aside entirely the influence of inclination and with it every object of the will; hence there is left for the will nothing that could determine it except objectively the law and subjectively pure respect for this practical law, and [consequently] the maxim of complying with such a law even if it infringes upon all my inclinations.

Thus the moral worth of an action does not lie in the effect expected from it and so too does not lie in any principle of action that needs to borrow its motive from this expected effect. For all these effects (agreeableness of one's condition, indeed even promotion of others' happiness) could have been also brought about by other causes, so that there would have been no need, for this, of the will of a rational being—in which, however, the highest and unconditional good alone can be found. Hence nothing other than the *representation of the law* in itself, which can of course occur only in a rational being, insofar as it and not the hoped-for effect is the determining ground of the will, can constitute the preeminent good we call moral, which is already present in the person himself who acts in accordance with this representation and need not wait upon the effect of his action.

But what kind of law can that be, the representation of which must determine the will, even without regard for the effect expected from it, in order for the will to be called good absolutely and without limitation? Since I have deprived the will of every impulse that could arise for it from obeying some law, nothing is left but the conformity of actions as such with universal law, which alone is to serve the will as its principle, that is, *I ought never to act except in such a way that I could also will that my maxim should become a universal law.* Here mere conformity to law as such, without having as its basis some law determined for certain actions, is what serves the will as its principle, and must so serve it, if duty is not to be everywhere an empty delusion and a chimerical[5] concept. Common human reason also agrees completely with this in its practical appraisals and always has this principle before its eyes. Let the question be, for example: May I, when hard pressed, make a promise with the intention not to keep it? Here I easily distinguish two significations the question can have: whether it is *prudent,* or whether it is in *conformity with duty,* to make a false promise. The first can undoubtedly often be the case. I see very well that it is not enough to get out of a present difficulty by means of this subterfuge, but that I must reflect carefully whether this lie may later give rise to much greater inconvenience for me than that from which I now extricate myself. And since, with all my supposed cunning, the results cannot be so easily foreseen, but once confidence in me is lost this could be far more prejudicial to me than all the troubles I now think to avoid, I must reflect whether the matter might be handled more prudently by proceeding on a general maxim and making it a habit to promise nothing except with the intention of keeping it. But it is soon clear to me that such a maxim will still be based only on results feared. To be truthful from duty, however, is something entirely different from being truthful from anxiety about detrimental results, since in the first case the concept of the action in itself already contains a law for me, while in the second I must first look about elsewhere to see what effects on me might be combined with it. For if I deviate from the principle of duty this is quite certainly evil; but if I am unfaithful to my maxim of prudence this can sometimes be very advantageous to me, although it is certainly safer to abide by it. However, to inform myself in the shortest and yet infallible way about the answer to this problem, whether a lying promise is in conformity with duty, I ask myself: Would I indeed be content that my maxim (to get myself out of difficulties by a false promise) should hold as a universal law (for myself as well as for others)? And could I indeed say to myself that everyone may make a false promise when he finds himself in a difficulty he can get out of in no other way? Then I soon become aware that I could indeed will the lie, but by no means a universal law to lie; for in accordance with such a law there would properly be no promises at all, since it would be futile to avow my will with regard to my future actions to others who would not believe this avowal or, if they rashly did so, would pay me back in like coin; and thus my maxim, as soon as it were made a universal law, would have to destroy itself.

I do not therefore need any penetrating acuteness to see what I have to do in order that my volition be morally good. Inexperienced in the course of the world, incapable of being prepared for whatever might come to pass in it, I ask myself only: Can you also will that your maxim become a universal law? If not, then it is to be repudiated, and that not because of a disadvantage to you or even to others forthcoming from it but because it cannot fit as a principle into a possible giving of universal law. Reason, however, forces from me immediate respect for such lawgiving. Although I do not yet see what this respect is based upon (this the philosopher may investigate), I at least understand this much: that it is an estimation of a worth that far outweighs any worth of what is recommended by inclination, and that the necessity of my action from pure respect for the practical law is what constitutes duty, to which every other motive must give way because it is the condition of a will good in itself, the worth of which surpasses all else. . . .

Section II. Transition from Popular Moral Philosophy to the Metaphysics of Morals

. . . In order to advance by natural steps in this study—not merely from common moral appraisal (which is here very worthy of respect) to philosophic, as has already been done, but from a popular philosophy, which goes no further than it can by groping with the help of examples, to metaphysics (which no longer lets itself be held back by anything empirical and, since it must measure out the whole sum of rational cognition of this kind, goes if need be all the way to ideas, where examples themselves fail us)—we must follow and present distinctly the practical faculty of reason, from its general rules of determination to the point where the concept of duty arises from it.

Everything in nature works in accordance with laws. Only a rational being has the capacity to act in accordance with the *representation of laws*—that is, in accordance with principles—or has a *will*. Since reason is required for the derivation of actions from laws, the will is nothing other than practical reason. If reason infallibly determines the will, the actions of such a being that are cognized as objectively necessary are also subjectively necessary—that is, the will is a capacity to choose only that which reason independently of inclination cognizes as practically necessary, that is, as good. However, if reason solely by itself does not adequately determine the will; if the will is exposed also to subjective conditions (certain incentives) that are not always in accord with the objective ones; in a word, if the will is not in itself completely in conformity with reason (as is actually the case with human beings), then actions that are cognized as objectively necessary are subjectively contingent,[6] and the determination of such a will in conformity with objective laws is *necessitation*—that is to say, the relation of objective laws to a will that is not thoroughly good is represented as the determination of the will of a rational being through grounds of reason, indeed, but grounds to which this will is not by its nature necessarily obedient.

The representation of an objective principle, insofar as it is necessitating for a will, is called a *command* (of reason), and the formula of the command is called an *imperative*. . . .

All imperatives command either *hypothetically* or *categorically*. The former represent the practical necessity of a possible action as a means to achieving something else that one wills (or that it is at least possible for one to will). The categorical imperative would be that which represented an action as objectively necessary of itself, without reference to another end.

Since every practical law represents a possible action as good and thus as necessary for a subject practically determinable by reason, all imperatives are formulas for the determination of action that is necessary in accordance with the principle of a will which is good in some way. Now if the action would be good merely as a means *to something else*, the imperative is *hypothetical*; if the action is represented as *in itself* good, hence as necessary in a will in itself conforming to reason as its principle, then it is *categorical*. . . .

When I think of a hypothetical imperative in general, I do not know beforehand what it will contain; I do not know this until I am given the condition. But when I think of a categorical imperative, I know at once what it contains. For, since the imperative contains, beyond the law, only the necessity that the maxim be in conformity with this law, while the law contains no condition to which it would be limited, nothing is left with which the maxim of action is to conform but the universality of a law as such; and this conformity alone is what the imperative properly represents as necessary.

There is, therefore, only a single categorical imperative and it is this: *Act only in accordance with that maxim through which you can at the same time will that it become a universal law.*

Now if all imperatives of duty can be derived from this single imperative as from their principle, then, even though we leave it undecided whether what is called duty is not as such an empty concept, we shall at least be able to show what we think by it and what the concept wants to say.

Since the universality of law in accordance with which effects take place constitutes what is properly called *nature* in the most general sense (as regards its form)—that is, the existence of things insofar as it is determined in accordance with universal laws—the universal imperative of duty can also go as follows: *Act as if the maxim of your action were to become by your will a universal law of nature.*

We shall now enumerate a few duties in accordance with the usual division of them into duties to ourselves and to other human beings and into perfect and imperfect duties.[7]

1. Someone feels sick of life because of a series of troubles that has grown to the point of despair, but is still so far in possession of his reason that he can ask himself whether it would not be contrary to his duty to himself to take his own life. Now he inquires whether the maxim of his action could indeed become a universal law of nature. His maxim, however, is: From self-love I make it my principle to shorten my life when its longer duration threatens more troubles than it promises agreeableness. The only further question is whether this principle of self-love could become a universal law of nature. It is then seen at once that a nature whose law it would be to destroy life itself by means of the same feeling whose destination is to impel toward the furtherance of life would contradict itself and would therefore not subsist as nature. Thus that maxim could not possibly be a law of nature and, accordingly, altogether opposes the supreme principle of all duty.

2. Another finds himself urged by need to borrow money. He well knows that he will not be able to repay it but sees also that nothing will be lent him unless he promises firmly to repay it within a determinate time. He would like to make such a promise, but he still has enough conscience to ask himself:

Is it not forbidden and contrary to duty to help oneself out of need in such a way? Supposing that he still decided to do so, his maxim of action would go as follows: When I believe myself to be in need of money I shall borrow money and promise to repay it, even though I know that this will never happen. Now this principle of self-love or personal advantage is perhaps quite consistent with my whole future welfare, but the question now is whether it is right. I therefore turn the demand of self-love into a universal law and put the question as follows: How would it be if my maxim became a universal law? I then see at once that it could never hold as a universal law of nature and be consistent with itself, but must necessarily contradict itself. For the universality of a law that everyone, when he believes himself to be in need, could promise whatever he pleases with the intention of not keeping it, would make the promise and the end one might have in it itself impossible, since no one would believe what was promised him but would laugh at all such expressions as vain pretenses.

3. A third finds in himself a talent that by means of some cultivation could make him a human being useful for all sorts of purposes. However, he finds himself in comfortable circumstances and prefers to give himself up to pleasure than to trouble himself with enlarging and improving his fortunate natural predispositions. But he still asks himself whether his maxim of neglecting his natural gifts, besides being consistent with his propensity to amusement, is also consistent with what one calls duty. He now sees that a nature could indeed always subsist with such a universal law, although (as with the South Sea Islanders) the human being should let his talents rust and be concerned with devoting his life merely to idleness, amusement, procreation—in a word, to enjoyment. Only he cannot possibly *will* that this become a universal law or be put in us as such by means of natural instinct, for as a rational being he necessarily wills that all the capacities in him be developed, since they serve him and are given to him for all sorts of possible purposes.

4. Yet a fourth, for whom things are going well while he sees that others (whom he could very well help) have to contend with great hardships, thinks: "What is it to me? Let each be as happy as heaven wills or as he can make himself; I shall take nothing from him nor even envy him. Only I do not care to contribute anything to his welfare or to his assistance in need." Now if such a way of thinking were to become a universal law, the human race could admittedly very well subsist, no doubt even better than when everyone prates about sympathy and benevolence and even exerts himself to practice them occasionally, but on the other hand also cheats where he can, sells the rights of human beings, or otherwise infringes upon them. But although it is possible that a universal law of nature could very well subsist in accordance with such a maxim, it is still impossible to *will* that such a principle hold everywhere as a law of nature, for a will that decided this would conflict with itself, since many cases could occur in which one would need the love and sympathy of others and in which, by such a law of nature arisen from his own will, he would rob himself of all hope of the assistance he wishes for himself.

These are a few of the many actual duties, or at least of what we take to be such, whose derivation from the one principle cited above is clear. We must be able to will that a maxim of our action become a universal law; this is the canon of moral appraisal of action in general. Some actions are so constituted that their maxim cannot even be *thought* without contradiction as a universal law of nature, far less could one *will* that it should become such. In the case of others that inner impossibility is indeed not to be found, but it is still impossible to will that their maxim be raised to the universality of a law of nature because such a will would contradict itself. It is easy to see that the first is opposed to strict or narrower (unremitting) duty, the second only to wide (meritorious) duty;[8] and so all duties, as far as the kind of obligation (not the object of their action) is concerned, have by these examples been set out completely in their dependence upon the one principle. . . .

The human being and in general every rational being exists as an end in itself, not merely as a means to be used by this or that will at its discretion; instead he must in all his actions, whether directed to himself or also to other rational beings, always be regarded at the same time as an end. All objects of the inclinations have only a conditional worth, for if there were not inclinations and the needs based on them, their object would be without worth. But the inclinations themselves, as sources of needs, are so far from having an absolute worth [that] makes one wish to have them, that it must instead be the universal wish of every rational being to be altogether free from them. Thus the worth of any object to be acquired by our action is always conditional. Beings the existence of which rests not on our will but on nature, if they are beings without reason, still have only a relative worth, as means, and are therefore called *things*, whereas rational beings are called *persons* because their nature already marks them out as ends in themselves—that is, as something that may not be used merely as a means—and hence so far limits all choice (and is an object of respect). These therefore are not merely subjective ends, the existence of which as an effect of our action has a worth *for us*, but rather *objective ends*—that is, beings the existence of which is in itself an end, and indeed one such that no other end, to which they would serve merely as means, can be put in its place, since without it nothing of absolute worth would be found anywhere. But if all worth were conditional and therefore contingent, then no supreme practical principle for reason could be found anywhere.

If, then, there is to be a supreme practical principle and, with respect to the human will,[9] a categorical imperative, it must be one such that, from the representation of what is necessarily an end for everyone because it is an end in itself, it constitutes an objective principle of the will and thus can serve as a universal practical law. The ground of this principle is: *Rational nature exists as an end in itself.* The human being necessarily represents his own existence in this way; so far it is thus a *subjective* principle of human actions. But every other rational being also represents his existence in this way consequent on just the same rational ground that also holds for me; thus it is at the same time an *objective* principle from which, as a supreme practical ground, it must be possible to derive all laws of the will. The practical imperative will therefore be the following: *So act that you use humanity, whether in your own person or in the person of any other, always at the same time as an end, never merely as a means.* We shall see whether this can be carried out.

To keep to the preceding examples:

First, as regards the concept of necessary duty to oneself, someone who has suicide in mind will ask himself whether his action can be consistent with the idea of humanity as an end in itself. If he destroys himself in order to escape from a trying condition, he makes use of a person merely as a means to maintain a tolerable condition up to the end of life. A human being, however, is not a thing and hence not something that can be used merely as a means, but must in all his actions always be regarded as an end in itself. I cannot, therefore, dispose of a human being in my own person by maiming, damaging, or killing him. (I must here pass over a closer determination of this principle that would prevent any misinterpretation, for example, as to having limbs amputated in order to preserve myself, or putting my life in danger in order to preserve my life, and so forth; that belongs to morals proper.)

Second, as regards necessary duty to others, or duty owed them, he who has it in mind to make a false promise to others sees at once that he wants to make use of another human being merely as a means, without the other at the same time containing in himself the end; for he whom I want to use for my purposes by such a promise cannot possibly agree to my way of behaving toward him, and so himself contain the end of this action. This conflict with the principle of other human beings is seen more distinctly if examples of assaults on the freedom and property of others are brought forward. For then it is obvious that he who transgresses the rights of human beings intends to make use of the person of others merely as means, without taking into consideration that, as rational beings, they are always to be valued at the same time as ends, that is, only as beings who must also be able to contain in themselves the end of the very same action.

Third, with respect to contingent (meritorious) duty to oneself, it is not enough that the action does not conflict with humanity in our person as an end in itself; it must also *harmonize* with it. Now there are in humanity predispositions to greater perfection, which belong to the end of nature with respect to humanity in our subject. To neglect these might admittedly be consistent with the *preservation* of humanity as an end in itself, but not with the *furtherance* of this end.

Fourth, concerning meritorious duty to others, the natural end that all human beings have is their own happiness. Now humanity might indeed subsist if no one contributed to the happiness of others but yet did not intentionally withdraw anything from it; but there is still only a negative and not a positive agreement with humanity as an end in itself unless everyone also tries, as far as he can, to further the ends of others. For the ends of a subject who is an end in itself must as far as possible be also *my* ends, if that representation is to have its full effect in me.

NOTES

1. *ends:* goals. [D. C. Abel]
2. *maxim:* the personal policy that motivates one's action. In the case described here, the maxim would be to follow one's inclination to preserve one's life.

Kant later contrasts a maxim with a *universal law*, which binds all rational creatures. [D. C. ABEL]

3. Kant did not label the first proposition, but it is implicit in the preceding paragraphs: An action must be done from duty in order to have moral worth. [D. C. ABEL]

4. *A priori* means "independent of experience" (literally, in Latin, "from what comes earlier"); *a posteriori* means "dependent on experience" ("from what comes later"). Duty is an a priori principle of the will because it binds prior to any experience; the incentive of an action is a posteriori because it depends on the person's experience. Kant here draws a further contrast between duty and incentive: Duty is a *formal* principle because it refers to the general form any action should take; incentive is *material* because it involves the situation ("matter") of a particular action. [D. C. ABEL]

5. *chimerical:* produced by mental fabrication. [D. C. ABEL]

6. *contingent:* capable of being otherwise. [D. C. ABEL]

7. In Kant's terminology, a *perfect duty* is one that prohibits a specific kind of action, without exception; an *imperfect duty* commands us to achieve some general goal without specifying what means we are to use. Kant's following four examples illustrate, respectively: (1) a perfect duty to ourselves (not to commit suicide), (2) a perfect duty to others (not to make false promises), (3) an imperfect duty to ourselves (to develop our talents), and (4) an imperfect duty to others (to help those in need). [D. C. ABEL]

8. An *unremitting* duty is a perfect duty and is *necessary*; a *meritorious* duty is an imperfect duty and is *contingent* (see notes 6 and 7). [D. C. ABEL]

9. The categorical imperative applies only to a will that is not perfectly good, such as the human will. A "holy will," such as the divine will, does not need an imperative because it automatically wills the good. [D. C. ABEL]

Utilitarianism

John Stuart Mill

John Stuart Mill was born in London in 1806. He was educated personally by his father, the Scottish economist and philosopher James Mill, who put him through a rigorous program of study from his earliest years. Mill was reading Greek at age three and Latin at age eight. As a boy he read works of many classical authors in the original language, including works by Plato and Aristotle. When he was thirteen, he began studying the economic theories of Adam Smith and David Ricardo. The following year he traveled to France and spent a year with the family of Samuel Bentham (brother of English jurist and philosopher Jeremy Bentham). After returning to England, he began to study Roman law, with a view to possibly becoming a lawyer. But in 1823, when he was seventeen, he took a job at the British East India Company, where he was employed for the next thirty-five years. Mill was elected to Parliament in 1865, but failed to gain reelection in 1868. After his defeat he retired to Avignon, France, where he died in 1873.

Mill's major writings include *A System of Logic* (1843), *Principles of Political Economy* (1848), *On Liberty* (1859), *Utilitarianism* (published serially in *Fraser's Magazine* in 1861, separately in 1863), and *The Subjection of Women* (written in 1861, published in 1869).

Our reading is from *Utilitarianism*, the work that has become the most popular and influential treatment of utilitarianism. Utilitarianism is the moral theory that was first set forth by Jeremy Bentham. It claims that the morality of an action is determined by how well it promotes "utility," which is defined as the greatest good for the greatest number. Utilitarians differ, however, on how to define "good" and whom to include in the "greatest number."

According to Mill, "good" means happiness, and happiness means pleasure and the absence of pain; the "greatest number" includes not only human beings but all creatures capable of feeling pleasure and pain. Mill's version of utilitarianism, therefore, claims that the moral thing to do in any situation is the action that causes the greatest sum total of pleasure for all the sentient beings involved. Mill typically says that utility is to be determined wholly on the basis of the *individual action,* but at times he seems to endorse the view that one should always follow the *rule* (for example, "Don't kill innocent people") that, when universally followed, would promote the greatest utility—even if, in a particular situation, following the rule would not do so. Philosophers have come to call these two versions of utilitarianism, respectively, *act utilitarianism* and *rule utilitarianism.*

In our selection from Chapter II, "What Utilitarianism Is," Mill briefly describes his theory and then defends it against several objections. In the selection from Chapter IV, "Of What Sort of Proof the Principle of Utility Is Susceptible," he explains in what sense one can prove that the happiness (pleasure) of the individual and the group are desirable and are the only things desirable.

CHAPTER II. WHAT UTILITARIANISM IS

. . . The creed which accepts as the foundation of morals, utility, or the greatest happiness principle, holds that actions are right in proportion as they tend to promote happiness, wrong as they tend to produce the reverse of happiness. By happiness is intended pleasure and the absence of pain; by unhappiness, pain and the privation of pleasure. To give a clear view of the moral standard set up by the theory, much more requires to be said—in particular, what things it includes in the ideas of pain and pleasure, and to what extent this is left an open question. But these supplementary explanations do not affect the theory of life on which this theory of morality is grounded—namely, that pleasure and freedom from pain are the only things desirable as ends;[1] and that all desirable things (which are as numerous in the utilitarian as in any other scheme) are desirable either for the pleasure inherent in themselves, or as means to the promotion of pleasure and the prevention of pain.

Now such a theory of life excites in many minds, and among them in some of the most estimable in feeling and purpose, inveterate dislike. To suppose that life has (as they express it) no higher end than pleasure—no better and nobler object of desire and pursuit—they designate as utterly mean and grovelling; as a doctrine worthy only of swine, to whom the followers of Epicurus[2] were, at a very early period, contemptuously likened; and modern holders of the doctrine are occasionally made the subject of equally polite comparisons by its German, French, and English assailants.

When thus attacked, the Epicureans have always answered that it is not they, but their accusers, who represent human nature in a degrading light, since the accusation supposes human beings to be capable of no pleasures except those of which swine are capable. If this supposition were true, the charge could not be gainsaid, but would then be no longer an imputation; for if the sources of pleasure were precisely the same to human beings and to swine, the rule of life which is good enough for the one would be good enough for the other. The comparison of the Epicurean life to that of beasts is felt as degrading, precisely because a beast's pleasures do not satisfy a human being's conceptions of happiness. Human beings have faculties more elevated than the animal appetites, and when once made conscious of them, do not regard anything as happiness which does not include their gratification. I do not, indeed, consider the Epicureans to have been by any means faultless in drawing out their scheme of consequences from the utilitarian principle. To do this in any sufficient manner, many Stoic,[3] as well as Christian elements require to be included. But there is no known Epicurean theory of life which does not assign to the pleasures of the intellect, of the feelings and imagination, and of the moral sentiments, a much higher value as pleasures than to those of mere sensation. It must be admitted, however, that utilitarian writers in general have placed the superiority of mental over bodily pleasures chiefly in the greater permanency, safety, uncostliness, and so on, of the former—that is, in their circumstantial advantages rather than in their intrinsic nature.[4] And on all these points utilitarians have fully proved their case; but they might have taken the other, and, as it may be called, higher ground, with entire consistency. It is quite compatible with the principle of utility to recognize the fact that some *kinds* of pleasure are more desirable and more valuable than others. It would be absurd that while in estimating all other things, quality is considered as well as quantity, the estimation of pleasures should be supposed to depend on quantity alone.

If I am asked what I mean by difference of quality in pleasures, or what makes one pleasure more valuable than another, merely as a pleasure, except its being greater in amount, there is but one possible answer. Of two pleasures, if there be one to which all or almost all who have experience of both give a decided preference, irrespective of any feeling of moral obligation to prefer it, that is the more desirable pleasure. If one of the two is, by those who are competently acquainted with both, placed so far above the other that they prefer it, even though knowing it to be attended with a greater amount of discontent, and would not resign it for any quantity of the other pleasure which their nature is capable of, we are justified in ascribing to the preferred enjoyment a superiority in quality, so far outweighing quantity as to render it, in comparison, of small account.

Now it is an unquestionable fact that those who are equally acquainted with and equally capable of appreciating and enjoying both, do give a most marked preference to the manner of existence which employs their higher faculties. Few human creatures would consent to be changed into any of the lower animals for a promise of the fullest allowance of a beast's pleasures. No intelligent human being would consent to be a fool, no instructed person would be an ignoramus, no person of feeling and conscience would be selfish and base, even though they should be persuaded that the fool, the dunce, or the rascal is better satisfied with his lot than they are with theirs. They would not resign what they possess more than he for the most complete satisfaction of all the desires which they have in common with him. If they ever fancy they would, it is only in cases of unhappiness so extreme that to escape from it they would exchange their lot for almost any other, however undesirable in their own eyes. A being of higher faculties requires more to make him happy, is capable probably of more acute suffering, and is certainly accessible to it at more points, than one of an inferior type. But in spite of these liabilities, he can never really wish to sink into what he feels to be a lower grade of existence. We may give what explanation we please of this unwillingness; we may attribute it to pride, a name which is given indiscriminately to some of the most and to some of the least estimable feelings of which mankind are capable; we may refer it to the love of liberty and personal independence, an appeal to which was with the Stoics one of the most effective means for the inculcation of it; to the love of power, or to the love of excitement, both of which do really enter into and contribute to it. But its most appropriate appellation is a sense of dignity, which all human beings possess in one form or other and in some, though by no means in exact, proportion to their higher faculties; and which is so essential a part of the happiness of those in whom it is strong, that nothing which conflicts with it could be, otherwise than momentarily, an object of desire to them. Whoever supposes that this preference takes place at a sacrifice of happiness—that the superior being, in anything like equal circumstances, is not happier than the inferior—confounds the two very different ideas of happiness and content. It is indisputable that the being whose capacities of enjoyment are low has the greatest chance of having them fully satisfied; and a highly-endowed being will always feel that any happiness which he can look for, as the world is constituted, is imperfect. But he can learn to bear its imperfections, if they are at all bearable; and they will not make him envy the being who is indeed unconscious of the imperfections, but only because he feels not at all the good which those imperfections qualify. It is better to be a human being dissatisfied than a pig satisfied; better to be Socrates dissatisfied than a fool satisfied. And if the fool or the pig is of a different opinion, it is because they only know their own side of the question. The other party to the comparison knows both sides. . . .

I have dwelt on this point, as being a necessary part of a perfectly just conception of utility or happiness, considered as the directive rule of human conduct. But it is by no means an indispensable condition to the acceptance of the utilitarian standard—for that standard is not the agent's own greatest happiness, but the greatest amount of happiness altogether. And if it may possibly be doubted whether a noble character is always the happier for its nobleness, there can be no doubt that it makes other people happier and that the world in general is immensely a gainer by it. Utilitarianism, therefore, could only attain its end by the general cultivation of nobleness of character, even if each individual were only benefited by the nobleness of others, and his own, so far as happiness is concerned, were a sheer deduction from the benefit. But the bare enunciation of such an absurdity as this last, renders refutation superfluous.

According to the greatest happiness principle, as above explained, the ultimate end, with reference to and for the sake of which all other things are desirable (whether we are considering our own good or that of other people), is an existence exempt as far as possible from pain, and as rich as possible in enjoyments, both in point of quantity and quality—the test of quality, and the rule for measuring it against quantity, being the preference felt by those who, in their opportunities of experience, to which must be added their habits of self-consciousness and self-observation, are best furnished with the means of comparison. This, being according to the utilitarian opinion the end of human action, is necessarily also the standard of morality, which may accordingly be defined [as] the rules and precepts for human conduct, by the observance of which an existence such as has been described might be, to the greatest extent possible, secured to all mankind; and not to them only, but, so far as the nature of things admits, to the whole sentient creation. . . .

I must again repeat what the assailants of utilitarianism seldom have the justice to acknowledge, that the happiness which forms the utilitarian standard of what is right in conduct is not the agent's own happiness, but that of all concerned. As between his own happiness and that of others, utilitarianism requires him to be as strictly impartial as a disinterested and benevolent spectator. In the golden rule of Jesus of Nazareth, we read the complete spirit of the ethics of utility. To do as one would be done by,[5] and to love one's neighbor as oneself,[6] constitute the ideal perfection of utilitarian morality. As the means of making the nearest approach to this ideal, utility would enjoin, first, that laws and social arrangements should place the happiness, or (as speaking practically it may be called) the interest, of every individual, as nearly as possible in harmony with the interest of the whole; and secondly, that education and opinion, which have so vast a power over human character, should so use that power as to establish in the mind of every individual an indissoluble association between his own happiness and the good of the whole—especially between his own happiness and the practice of such modes of conduct, negative and positive, as regard for the universal happiness prescribes, so that not only he may be unable to conceive the possibility of happiness to himself consistently with conduct opposed to the general good, but also that a direct impulse to promote the general good may be in every individual one of the habitual motives of action, and the sentiments connected therewith may fill a large and prominent place in every human being's sentient existence. If the impugners of the utilitarian morality represented it to their own minds in this its true character, I know not what recommendation possessed by any other morality they could possibly affirm to be wanting to it; what more beautiful or more exalted developments of human nature any other ethical system can be supposed to foster or what springs of action, not accessible to the utilitarian, such systems rely on for giving effect to their mandates.

The objectors to utilitarianism cannot always be charged with representing it in a discreditable light. On the contrary, those among them who entertain anything like a just idea of its disinterested character sometimes find fault with its standard as being too high for humanity. They say it is exacting too much to require that people shall always act from the inducement of promoting the general interests of society. But this is to mistake the very meaning of a standard of morals and to confound the rule of action with the motive of it. It is the business of ethics to tell us what are our duties, or by what test we may know them; but no system of ethics requires that the sole motive of all we do shall be a feeling of duty. On the contrary, ninety-nine hundredths of all our actions are done from other motives, and rightly so done, if the rule of duty does not condemn them. It is the more unjust to utilitarianism that this particular misapprehension should be made a ground of objection to it, inasmuch as utilitarian moralists have gone beyond almost all others in affirming that the motive has nothing to do with the morality of the action, though much with the worth of the agent. He who saves a fellow creature from drowning does what is morally right, whether his motive be duty or the hope of being paid for his trouble; he who betrays the friend that trusts him is guilty of a crime, even if his object be to serve another friend to whom he is under greater obligations. But to speak only of actions done from the motive of duty and in direct obedience to principle: It is a misapprehension of the utilitarian mode of thought, to conceive it as implying that people should fix their minds upon so wide a generality as the world, or society at large. The great majority of good actions are intended not for the benefit of the world, but for that of individuals, of which the good of the world is made up. And the thoughts of the most virtuous man need not on these occasions travel beyond the particular persons concerned, except so far as is necessary to assure himself that in benefiting them he is not violating the rights—that is, the legitimate and authorized expectations—of anyone else. The multiplication of happiness is, according to the utilitarian ethics, the object of virtue. The occasions on which any person (except one in a thousand) has it in his power to do this on an extended scale, in other words, to be a public benefactor, are but exceptional; and on these occasions alone is he called on to consider public utility. In every other case, private utility, the interest or happiness of some few persons, is all he has to attend to. Those alone the influence of whose actions extends to society in general, need concern themselves habitually about so large an object. In the case of abstinences indeed—of things which people forbear to do, from moral considerations, though the consequences in the particular case might be beneficial—it would be unworthy of an intelligent agent not to be consciously aware that the action is of a class which, if practiced generally, would be generally injurious, and that this is the ground of the obligation to abstain from it. The amount of regard for the public interest implied in this recognition is no greater than is demanded by every system of morals, for they all enjoin to abstain from whatever is manifestly pernicious to society. . . .

We not uncommonly hear the doctrine of utility inveighed against as a *godless* doctrine. If it be necessary to say anything at all against so mere an assumption, we may say that the question depends upon what idea we have formed of the moral character of the Deity. If it be a true belief that God desires, above all things, the happiness of his creatures, and that this was his purpose in their creation, utility is not only not a godless doctrine, but more profoundly religious than any other. If it be meant that utilitarianism does not recognize the revealed will of God as the supreme law of morals, I answer that a utilitarian who believes in the perfect goodness and wisdom of God necessarily believes that whatever God has thought fit to reveal on the subject of morals, must fulfill the requirements of utility in a supreme degree. . . .

Again, defenders of utility often find themselves called upon to reply to such objections as this—that there is not time, previous to action, for calculating and weighing the effects of any line of conduct on the general happiness. This is exactly as if anyone were to say that it is impossible to guide our conduct by Christianity because there is not time, on every occasion on which anything has to be done, to read through the Old and New Testaments. The answer to the objection is that there has been ample time, namely the whole past duration of the human species. During all that time mankind have been learning by experience the tendencies of actions, on which experience all the prudence, as well as all the morality of life, is dependent. People talk as if the commencement of this course of experience had hitherto been put off, and as if, at the moment when some man feels tempted to meddle with the property or life of another, he had to begin considering for the first time whether murder and theft are injurious to human happiness. Even then I do not think that he would find the question very puzzling; but, at all events, the matter is now done to his hand.[7] It is truly a whimsical supposition that if mankind were agreed to considering utility to be the test of morality, they would remain without any agreement as to what *is* useful, and would take no measures for having their notions on the subject taught to the young and enforced by law and opinion. There is no difficulty in proving any ethical standard whatever to work ill, if we suppose universal idiocy to be conjoined with it. But on any hypothesis short of that, mankind must by this time have acquired positive beliefs as to the effects of some actions on their happiness; and [the] beliefs which have thus come down are the rules of morality for the multitude, and for the philosopher until he has succeeded in finding better. . . .

CHAPTER IV. OF WHAT SORT OF PROOF THE PRINCIPLE OF UTILITY IS SUSCEPTIBLE

. . . Questions of ultimate ends do not admit of proof, in the ordinary acceptation of the term. To be incapable of proof by reasoning is common to all first principles—to the first premises of our knowledge, as well as to those of our conduct. But the former, being matters of fact, may be the subject of a direct appeal to the faculties which judge of fact, namely our senses and our internal consciousness. Can an appeal be made to the same faculties on questions of practical ends? Or by what other faculty is cognizance taken of them?

Questions about ends are, in other words, questions about what things are desirable. The utilitarian doctrine is that happiness is desirable, and the only thing desirable, as an end; all other things being only desirable as means to that end. What ought to be required of this doctrine—what conditions is it requisite that the doctrine should fulfill—to make good its claim to be believed?

The only proof capable of being given that an object is visible, is that people actually see it. The only proof that a sound is audible, is that people hear it—and so of the other sources of our experience. In like manner, I apprehend, the sole evidence it is possible to produce that anything is desirable, is that people do actually desire it. If the end which the utilitarian doctrine proposes to itself were not, in theory and in practice, acknowledged to be an end, nothing could ever convince any person that it was so. No reason can be given why the general happiness is desirable, except that each person, so far as he believes it to be attainable, desires his own happiness. This, however, being a fact, we have not only all the proof which the case admits of, but all which it is possible to require, that happiness is a good: that each person's happiness is a good to that person, and the general happiness, therefore, a good to the aggregate of all persons. Happiness has made out its title as *one* of the ends of conduct, and consequently one of the criteria of morality.

But it has not, by this alone, proved itself to be the sole criterion. To do that, it would seem, by the same rule, necessary to show not only that people desire happiness, but that they never desire anything else. Now it is palpable that they do desire things which, in common language, are decidedly distinguished from happiness. They desire, for example, virtue and the absence of vice, no less really than pleasure and the absence of pain. The desire of virtue is not as universal, but it is as authentic a fact, as the desire of happiness. And hence the opponents of the utilitarian standard deem that they have a right to infer that there are other ends of human action besides happiness, and that happiness is not the standard of approbation and disapprobation.

But does the utilitarian doctrine deny that people desire virtue, or maintain that virtue is not a thing to be desired? The very reverse. It maintains not only that virtue is to be desired, but that it is to be desired disinterestedly, for itself. Whatever may be the opinion of utilitarian moralists as to the original conditions by which virtue is made virtue; however they may believe (as they do) that actions and dispositions are only virtuous because they promote another end than virtue; yet this being granted, and it having been decided, from considerations of this description, what *is* virtuous, they not only place virtue at the very head of the things which are good as means to the ultimate end, but they also recognize as a psychological fact the possibility of its being, to the individual, a good in itself, without looking to any end beyond it; and hold that the mind is not in a right state, not in a state conformable to utility, not in the state most conducive to the general happiness, unless it does love virtue in this manner—as a thing desirable in itself, even although, in the individual instance, it should not produce those other desirable consequences which it tends to produce, and on account of which it is held to be virtue. This opinion is not, in the smallest degree, a departure from the happiness principle. The ingredients of happiness are very various and each of them is desirable in itself, and not merely when considered as swelling an aggregate. The principle of utility does not mean that any given pleasure, as music, for instance, or any given exemption from pain, as for example health, are to be looked upon as means to a collective something termed happiness, and to be desired on that account. They are desired and desirable in and for themselves; besides being means, they are a part of the end. Virtue, according to the utilitarian doctrine, is not naturally and originally part of the end, but it is capable of becoming so; and in those who love it disinterestedly it has become so, and is desired and cherished, not as a means to happiness, but as a part of their happiness. . . .

We have now, then, an answer to the question, of what sort of proof the principle of utility is susceptible. If the opinion which I have now stated is psychologically true—if human nature is so constituted as to desire nothing which is not either a part of happiness or a means of happiness—we can have no other proof, and we require no other, that these are the only things desirable. If so, happiness is the sole end of human action, and the promotion of it the test by which to judge of all human conduct—from whence it necessarily follows that it must be the criterion of morality, since a part is included in the whole.

And now to decide whether this is really so, whether mankind do desire nothing for itself but that which is a pleasure to them, or of which the absence is a pain—we have evidently arrived at a question of fact and experience, dependent, like all similar questions, upon evidence. It can only be determined by practiced self-consciousness and self-observation, assisted by observation of others. I believe that these sources of evidence, impartially consulted, will declare that desiring a thing and finding it pleasant, aversion to it and thinking of it as painful, are phenomena entirely inseparable, or rather two parts of the same phenomenon; in strictness of language, two different modes of naming the same psychological fact; that to think of an object as desirable (unless for the sake of its consequences) and to think of it as pleasant are one and the same thing; and that to desire anything, except in proportion as the idea of it is pleasant, is a physical and metaphysical[8] impossibility.

NOTES

1. *ends:* goals. [D. C. ABEL]
2. Epicurus (341–270 B.C.E.) was a Greek philosopher. [D. C. ABEL]

3. *Stoic:* relating to Stoicism, the school of philosophy founded by the Greek philosopher Zeno of Citium (about 335–263 B.C.E.). [D. C. ABEL]
4. Mill refers here primarily to Jeremy Bentham (1748–1832), and English jurist and philosopher, who first proposed the theory of utilitarianism. [D. C. ABEL]
5. Matthew 7:21; Luke 6:31. [D. C. ABEL]
6. Matthew 22:39. [D. C. ABEL]
7. *done to his hand:* done for him. [D. C. ABEL]
8. *metaphysical:* relating to *metaphysics,* the study of the nature and kinds of reality. [D. C. ABEL]

B. Critiques of Classical Theories

READING 37

Is There a Teleological Suspension of the Ethical?

Søren Kierkegaard

Søren Kierkegaard was born in 1813 in Copenhagen, Denmark. His father was plagued by a sense of guilt for having cursed God, and Kierkegaard inherited his father's anxiety-filled piety. He enrolled in the University of Copenhagen in 1830, first taking a wide variety of courses in the liberal arts and then concentrating on theology and philosophy. His father died in 1838, leaving him a fortune large enough to support the continuation of his studies at the University of Copenhagen and, after that, a life devoted to reflection and writing. Kierkegaard completed his degree in theology in 1840. Later that year he proposed marriage to a young woman named Regine Olsen. But he came to believe that his unique philosophical and religious vocation would be incompatible with marriage, and in 1841 he made the anguished decision to break the engagement. Kierkegaard then retreated to Berlin. Six months later he returned to Copenhagen, where he spent his remaining years reflecting on his Christian faith and exploring philosophical questions. He died in Copenhagen in 1855 at the age of forty-two.

Kierkegaard's major works include *Either/Or* (1843), *Fear and Trembling* (1843), *Philosophical Fragments* (1844), *Stages on Life's Way* (1845), *Concluding Unscientific Postscript* (1846), *Works of Love* (1847), and *The Sickness unto Death* (1849).

Our selection is from *Fear and Trembling,* a book whose title is taken from the passage in which Paul tells the Philippians to work out their salvation "in fear and trembling" (Philippians 1:12). The book presents Kierkegaard's reflection on the biblical story of Abraham being commanded by God to sacrifice Isaac, his only son (Genesis 22:1–18). Even though Abraham did not end up slaying Isaac (because, as he was about to do so, God intervened and told him to sacrifice a ram instead), Abraham's willingness to obey the terrible divine command made him "the father of faith." Since the killing of one's son violates a fundamental ethical precept, Abraham's obedience to God raises, for Kierkegaard, the question "Is there a teleological suspension of the ethical?"—which is the title of Problem 1 of *Fear and Trembling,* which constitutes our reading.

By "the ethical," Kierkegaard means universal norms of conduct, derived from reason. In ethics, the universal is higher than the particular individual, and has its telos (end, goal) in itself: The individual is to follow ethical rules because they are ethical. A "teleological suspension" of the ethical would be the subordination of the ethical to a higher telos, one that places the individual higher than the universal. Kierkegaard argues that Abraham's personal relation with God, which places him in "an absolute relation to the absolute," suspends and transcends the ethical realm. Abraham is not a tragic hero, because the actions of a tragic hero can be explained ethically and rationally. Abraham "acts by virtue of the absurd, for it is precisely the absurd that he as the single individual is higher than the universal." Abraham is a "knight of faith" who has crossed over from the ethical sphere of human existence to the higher, religious sphere.

The ethical as such is the universal, and as the universal it applies to everyone, which from another angle means that it applies at all times. It rests immanent in itself, has nothing outside itself that is its telos,[1] but is itself the telos for everything outside itself, and when the ethical has absorbed this into itself, it goes not further. The single individual, sensately[2] and psychically qualified in immediacy, is the individual who has his telos in the universal, and it is his ethical task continually to express himself in this, to annul his singularity in order to become the universal. As soon as the single individual asserts himself in his singularity before the universal, he sins, and only by acknowledging this can he be reconciled again with the universal. Every time the single individual, after having entered the universal, feels an impulse to assert himself as the single individual, he is in a spiritual trial from which he can work himself only by repentantly surrendering as the single individual in the universal. If this is the highest that can be said of man and his existence, then the ethical is of the same nature as a person's eternal salvation, which is his telos forevermore and at all times, since it would be a contradiction for this to be capable of being surrendered (that is, teleologically suspended), because as soon as this is suspended it is relinquished, whereas that which is suspended is not relinquished but is preserved in the higher, which is its telos.

If this is the case, then Hegel is right in "The Good and Conscience,"[3] where he qualifies man only as the individual and considers this qualification as a "moral form of evil" that must be annulled in the teleology of the moral in such a way that the single individual who remains in that stage either sins or is immersed in spiritual trial. But Hegel is wrong in speaking about faith; he is wrong in not protesting loudly and clearly against Abraham's enjoying honor and glory as a father of faith when he ought to be sent back to a lower court and shown up as a murderer.

Faith is namely this paradox, that the single individual is higher than the universal—yet, please note, in such a way that the movement repeats itself, so that after having been in the universal he as the single individual isolates himself as higher than the universal. If this is not faith, then Abraham is lost, then faith has never existed in the world precisely because it has always existed. For if the ethical—that is, social morality—is the highest and if there is in a person no residual incommensurability in some way such that this incommensurability is not evil (that is, the single individual, who is to be expressed in the universal), then no categories are needed other than what Greek philosophy had or what can be deduced from them by consistent thought. Hegel should not have concealed this, for, after all, he had studied Greek philosophy.

People who are profoundly lacking in learning and are given to clichés are frequently heard to say that a light shines over the Christian world, whereas darkness enshrouds paganism. This kind of talk has always struck me as strange, inasmuch as every more thorough thinker, every more earnest artist still regenerates himself in the eternal youth of the Greeks. The explanation for such a statement is that one does not know what one should say but only that one must say something. It is quite right to say that paganism did not have faith, but if something is supposed to have been said thereby, then one must have a clearer understanding of what faith is, for otherwise one falls into such clichés. It is easy to explain all existence, faith along with it, without having a conception of what faith is, and the one who counts on being admired for such an explanation is not such a bad calculator; for it is as Boileau says, *"Un sot trouve toujours un plus sot, qui l'admire."*[4] Faith is precisely the paradox that the single individual as the single individual is higher than the universal, is justified before it, not as inferior to it but as superior—yet in such a way, please note, that it is the single individual who, after being subordinate as the single individual to the universal, now by means of the universal becomes the single individual who as the single individual is superior, that the single individual as the single individual stands in an absolute relation to the absolute. This position cannot be mediated, for all mediation takes place only by virtue of the universal; it is and remains for all eternity a paradox, impervious to thought. And yet faith is this paradox, or else (and I ask the reader to bear these consequences *in mente*[5] even though it would be too prolix for me to write them all down) or else faith has never existed simply because it has always existed, or else Abraham is lost.

It is certainly true that the single individual can easily confuse this paradox with spiritual trial, but it ought not to be concealed for that reason. It is certainly true that many persons may be so constituted that they are repulsed by it, but faith ought not therefore to be made into something else to enable one to have it, but one ought rather to admit to not having it, while those who have faith ought to be prepared to set forth some characteristics whereby the paradox can be distinguished from a spiritual trial.

The story of Abraham contains just such a teleological suspension of the ethical. There is no dearth of keen minds and careful scholars who have found analogies to it. What their wisdom amounts to is the beautiful proposition that basically everything is the same. If one looks more closely, I doubt very much that anyone in the whole wide world will find one single analogy, except for a later one, which proves nothing if it is certain that Abraham represents faith and that it is manifested normatively in him, whose life not only is the most paradoxical that can be thought but is also so paradoxical that it simply cannot be thought. He acts by virtue of the absurd, for it is precisely the absurd that he as the single individual is higher than the universal. This paradox cannot be mediated, for as soon as Abraham begins to do so, he has to confess that he was in a spiritual trial, and if that is the case, he will never sacrifice Isaac, or if he did sacrifice Isaac, then in repentance he must come back to the universal. He gets Isaac back again by virtue of the absurd. Therefore, Abraham is at no time a tragic hero but is something entirely different, either a murderer or a man of faith. Abraham does not have the middle term[6] that saves the tragic hero. This is why I can understand a tragic hero but cannot understand Abraham, even though in a certain demented sense I admire him more than all others.

In ethical terms, Abraham's relation to Isaac is quite simply this: The father shall love the son more than himself. But within its own confines the ethical has various gradations. We shall see whether this story contains any higher expression for the ethical that can ethically explain his behavior, can ethically justify his suspending the ethical obligation to the son, but without moving beyond the teleology of the ethical.

When an enterprise of concern to a whole nation[7] is impeded, when such a project is halted by divine displeasure, when the angry deity sends a dead calm that mocks every effort, when the soothsayer carries out his sad task and announces that the deity demands a young girl as sacrifice—then the father must heroically bring this sacrifice.[8] He must nobly conceal his agony, even though he could wish he were "the lowly man who dares to weep"[9] and not the king who must behave in a kingly manner. Although the lonely agony penetrates his breast and there are only three persons in the whole nation who know his agony, soon the whole nation will be initiated into his agony and also into his deed, that for the welfare of all he will sacrifice her, his daughter, this lovely young girl. "O bosom! O fair cheeks, flaxen hair."[10] And the daughter's tears will agitate him, and the father will turn away his face, but the hero must raise the knife. And when the news of it reaches the father's house, the beautiful Greek maidens will blush with enthusiasm, and if the daughter was engaged, her betrothed will not be angry but will be proud to share in the father's deed, for the girl belonged more tenderly to him than to the father.

When the valiant judge[11] who in the hour of need saved Israel binds God and himself in one breath by the same promise, he will heroically transform the young maiden's jubilation, the beloved daughter's joy to sorrow, and all Israel will sorrow with her over her virginal youth. But every freeborn man will understand, every resolute woman will admire Jephthah, and every virgin in Israel will wish to behave as his daughter did, because what good would it be for Jephthah to win the victory by means of a promise if he did not keep it—would not the victory be taken away from the people again?

When a son forgets his duty,[12] when the state entrusts the sword of judgment to the father, when the laws demand punishment from the father's hand, then the father must heroically forget that the guilty one is his son, he must nobly hide his agony. But no one in the nation, not even the son, will fail to admire the father, and every time the Roman laws are interpreted, it will be remembered that many interpreted them more learnedly but no one more magnificently than Brutus.

But if Agamemnon, while a favorable wind was taking the fleet under full sail to its destination, had dispatched that messenger who fetched Iphigenia to be sacrificed; if Jephthah, without being bound by any promise that decided the fate of the nation, had said to his daughter: Grieve now for two months over your brief youth, and then I will sacrifice you; if Brutus had had a righteous son and yet had summoned the lictors[13] to put him to death—who would have understood them? If, on being asked why they did this, these three men had answered: It is an ordeal in which we are being tried—would they have been better understood?

When in the crucial moment Agamemnon, Jephthah, and Brutus heroically have overcome the agony, heroically have lost the beloved, and have only to complete the task externally, there will never be a noble soul in the world without tears of compassion for their agony, of admiration for their deed. But if in the crucial moment these three men were to append to the heroic courage with which they bore the agony the little phrase, "But it will not happen anyway"— who then would understand them? If they went on to explain, "This we believe by virtue of the absurd"—who would understand them any better? For who would not readily understand that it was absurd, but who would understand that one could then believe it?

The difference between the tragic hero and Abraham is very obvious. The tragic hero is still within the ethical. He allows an expression of the ethical to have its telos in a higher expression of the ethical; he scales down the ethical relation between father and son or daughter and father to a feeling that has its dialectic in its relation to the idea of moral conduct. Here there can be no question of an ideological suspension of the ethical itself.

Abraham's situation is different. By his act he transgressed the ethical altogether and had a higher telos outside it, in relation to which he suspended it. For I certainly would like to know how Abraham's act can be related to the universal, whether any point of contact between what Abraham did and the universal can be found other than that Abraham transgressed it. It is not to save a nation, not to uphold the idea of the state that Abraham does it; it is not to appease the angry gods. If it were a matter of the deity's being angry, then he was, after all, angry only with Abraham, and Abraham's act is totally unrelated to the universal, is a purely private endeavor. Therefore, while the tragic hero is great because of his moral virtue, Abraham is great because of a purely personal virtue. There is no higher expression for the ethical in Abraham's life than that the father shall love the son. The ethical in the sense of the moral is entirely beside the point. Insofar as the universal was present, it was cryptically in Isaac, hidden, so to speak, in Isaac's loins, and must cry out with Isaac's mouth, "Do not do this! You are destroying everything."

Why, then, does Abraham do it? For God's sake and—the two are wholly identical—for his own sake. He does it for God's sake because God demands this proof of his faith; he does it for his own sake so that he can prove it. The unity of the two is altogether correctly expressed in the word already used to describe this relationship: It is an ordeal, a temptation. A temptation—but what does that mean? As a rule, what tempts a person is something that will hold him back from doing his duty, but here the temptation is the ethical itself, which would hold him back from doing God's will. But what is duty? Duty is simply the expression for God's will.

Here the necessity of a new category for the understanding of Abraham becomes apparent. Paganism does not know such a relationship to the divine. The tragic hero does not enter into any private relationship to the divine, but the ethical is the divine, and thus the paradox therein can be mediated in the universal.

Abraham cannot be mediated; in other words, he cannot speak. As soon as I speak, I express the universal, and if I do not do so, no one can understand me. As soon as Abraham wants to express himself in the universal, he must declare that his situation is a spiritual trial, for he has no higher expression of the universal that ranks above the universal he violates.

Therefore, although Abraham arouses my admiration, he also appalls me. The person who denies himself and sacrifices himself because of duty gives up the finite in order to grasp the infinite and is adequately assured; the tragic hero gives up the certain for the even more certain, and the observer's eye views him with confidence. But the person who gives up the universal in order to grasp something even higher that is not the universal—what does he do? Is it possible that this can be anything other than a spiritual trial? And if it is possible, but the individual makes a mistake, what salvation is there for him? He suffers all the agony of the tragic hero, he shatters his joy in the world, he renounces everything, and perhaps at the same time he barricades himself from the sublime joy that was so precious to him that he would buy it at any price. The observer cannot understand him at all; neither can his eye rest upon him with confidence. Perhaps the believer's intention cannot be carried out at all, because it is inconceivable. Or if it could be done but the individual has misunderstood the deity—what salvation would there be for him? The tragic hero needs and demands tears, and where is the envious eye so arid that it could not weep with Agamemnon? But where is the soul so gone astray that it has the audacity to weep for Abraham? The tragic hero finishes his task at a specific moment in time, but as time passes he does what is no less significant: He visits the person encompassed by sorrow, who cannot breathe because of his anguished sighs, whose thoughts oppress him, heavy with tears. He appears to him, breaks the witchcraft of sorrow, loosens the bonds, evokes the tears, and the sufferer forgets his own sufferings in those of the tragic hero. One cannot weep over Abraham. One approaches him with a *horror religiosus*,[14] as Israel approached Mount Sinai.[15] What if he himself is distraught, what if he had made a mistake, this lonely man who climbs Mount Moriah,[16] whose peak towers sky-high over the flatlands of Aulis;[17] what if he is not a sleepwalker safely crossing the abyss while the one standing at the foot of the mountain looks up, shakes with anxiety, and then in his deference and horror does not even dare to call to him? Thanks, and once again thanks, to a man who, to a person overwhelmed by life's sorrows and left behind naked, reaches out the words, the leafage of language by which he can conceal his misery. Thanks to you, great Shakespeare, you who can say everything, everything, everything just as it is. And yet, why did you never articulate this torment? Did you perhaps reserve it for yourself, like the beloved's name that one cannot bear to have the world utter, for with his little secret that he cannot divulge the poet buys this power of the word to tell everybody else's dark secrets. A poet is not an apostle; he drives out devils only by the power of the devil.

But if the ethical is ideologically suspended in this manner, how does the single individual in whom it is suspended exist? He exists as the single individual in contrast to the universal. Does he sin, then? For from the point of view of the idea, this is the form of sin. Thus, even though the child does not sin, because it is not conscious of its existence as such, its existence, from the point of view of the idea, is nevertheless sin, and the ethical makes its claim upon it at all times. If it is denied that this form can be repeated in such a way that it is not sin, then judgment has fallen upon Abraham. How did Abraham exist? He had faith. This is the paradox by which he remains at the apex, the paradox that he cannot explain to anyone else, for the paradox is that he as the single individual places himself in an absolute relation to the absolute. Is he justified? Again, his justification is the paradoxical, for if he is, then he is justified not by virtue of being something universal but by virtue of being the single individual.

How does the single individual reassure himself that he is legitimate? It is a simple matter to level all existence to the idea of the state or the idea of a society. If this is done, it is also simple to mediate, for one never comes to the paradox that the single individual as the single individual is higher than the universal— something I can also express symbolically in a statement by Pythagoras[18] to the effect that the odd number is more perfect than the even number. If occasionally there is any response at all these days with regard to the paradox, it is likely to be: One judges it by the result. Aware that he is a paradox who cannot be understood, a hero who has become a *skandalon*[19] to his age will shout confidently to his contemporaries, "The result will indeed prove that I was justified." This cry is rarely heard in our age, inasmuch as it does not produce heroes—this is its defect—and it likewise has the advantage that it produces few caricatures. When in our age we hear the words "It will be judged by the result," then we know at once with whom we have the honor of speaking. Those who talk this way are a numerous type whom I shall designate under the common name of assistant professors. With security in life, they live in their thoughts; they have a *permanent* position and a *secure* future in a well-organized state. They have hundreds—yes, even thousands—of years between them and the earthquakes of existence. They are not afraid that such things can be repeated, for then what would the police and the newspapers say? Their life task is to judge the great men, judge them according to the result. Such behavior toward greatness betrays a strange mixture of arrogance and wretchedness—arrogance because they feel called to pass judgment, wretchedness because they feel that their lives are in no way allied with the lives of the great. Anyone with even a smattering *erectioris ingenii*[20] never becomes an utterly cold and clammy worm, and when he approaches greatness, he is never devoid of the thought that since the creation of the world it has been customary for the result to come last, and that if one is truly going to learn something from greatness one must be particularly aware of the beginning. If the one who is to act wants to judge himself by the result, he will never begin. Although the result may give joy to the entire world, it cannot help the hero, for he would not know the result until the whole thing was over, and he would not become a hero but by making a beginning.

Moreover, in its dialectic the result (insofar as it is finitude's response to the infinite question) is altogether incongruous with the hero's existence. Or should Abraham's receiving Isaac by a *marvel*[21] be able to prove that Abraham was justified in relating himself as the single individual to the universal? If Abraham actually had sacrificed Isaac, would he therefore have been less justified?

But we are curious about the result, just as we are curious the way a book turns out. We do not want to know anything about the anxiety, the distress, the paradox. We carry on an aesthetic flirtation with the result. It arrives just as unexpectedly but also just as effortlessly as a prize in a lottery; and when we have heard the result, we have built ourselves up. And yet no manacled robber of churches is so despicable a criminal as the one who plunders holiness in this way. And not even Judas, who sold his Lord for thirty pieces of silver, is more contemptible than someone who peddles greatness in this way.

It is against my very being to speak inhumanly about greatness, to make it a dim and nebulous far-distant shape or to let it be great but devoid of the emergence of the humanness without which it ceases to be great. For it is not what happens to me that makes me great, but what I do; and certainly there is no one who believes that someone became great by winning the big lottery prize. A person might have been born in lowly circumstances, but I would still require him not to be so inhuman toward himself that he could imagine the king's castle only at a distance and ambiguously dream of its greatness, and destroy it at the same time he elevates it because he elevated it so basely. I require him to be man enough to tread confidently and with dignity there as well. He must not be so inhuman that he insolently violates everything by barging right off the street into the king's hall—he loses more thereby than the king. On the contrary, he should find a joy in observing every bidding of propriety with a happy and confident enthusiasm, which is precisely what makes him a free spirit. This is merely a metaphor, for that distinction is only a very imperfect expression of the distance of spirit. I require every person not to think so inhumanly of himself that he does not dare to enter those palaces where the memory of the chosen ones lives, or even those where they themselves live. He is not to enter rudely and foist his affinity upon them. He is to be happy for every time he bows before them, but he is to be confident, free of spirit, and always more than a charwoman, for if he wants to be no more than that, he will never get in. And the very thing that is going to help him is the anxiety and distress in which the great were tried; for otherwise, if he has any backbone, they will only arouse his righteous envy. And anything that can be great only at a distance, that someone wants to make great with empty and hollow phrases—is destroyed by that very person.

Who was as great in the world as that favored woman, the mother of God, the Virgin Mary? And yet how do we speak of her? That she was the favored one among women does not make her great, and if it would not be so very odd for those who listen to be able to think just as inhumanly as those who speak, then every young girl might ask, "Why am I not so favored?" And if I had nothing else to say, I certainly would not dismiss such a question as stupid—because, viewed abstractly, vis-à-vis a favor, every person is just as entitled to it as the other. We leave out the distress, the anxiety, the paradox. My thoughts are as pure as anybody's, and he who can think this way surely has pure thoughts, and, if not, he can expect something horrible—for anyone who has once experienced these images cannot get rid of them again, and if he sins against them, they take a terrible revenge in a silent rage, which is more terrifying than the stridency of ten ravenous critics. To be sure, Mary bore the child wondrously, but she nevertheless did it "after the manner of women,"[22] and such a time is one of anxiety, distress, and paradox. The angel was indeed a ministering spirit, but he was not a meddlesome spirit who went to the other young maidens in Israel and said, "Do not scorn Mary; the extraordinary is happening to her." The angel went only to Mary, and no one could understand her. Has any woman been as infringed upon as was Mary, and is it not true here also that the one whom God blesses he curses in the same breath? This is the spirit's view of Mary, and she is by no means—it is revolting to me to say it but even more so that people have inanely and unctuously made her out to be thus—she is by no means a lady idling in her finery and playing with a divine child. When, despite this, she said. "Behold, I am the handmaid of the Lord"[23]—then she is great, and I believe it should not be difficult to explain why she became the mother of God. She needs worldly admiration as little as Abraham needs tears, for she was no heroine and he was no hero, but both of them became greater than these, not by being exempted in any way from the distress and the agony and the paradox, but became greater by means of these.

It is great when the poet in presenting his tragic hero for public admiration dares to say, "Weep for him, for he deserves it." It is great to deserve the tears of those who deserve to shed tears. It is great that the poet dares to keep the crowd under restraint, dares to discipline men to examine themselves individually to see if they are worthy to weep for the hero—for the slop water of the snivelers is a debasement of the sacred. But even greater than all this is the knight of faith's daring to say to the noble one who wants to weep for him, "Do not weep for me, but weep for yourself."[24]

We are touched, we look back to those beautiful times. Sweet sentimental longing leads us to the goal of our desire, to see Christ walking about in the promised land. We forget the anxiety, the distress, the paradox. Was it such a simple matter not to make a mistake? Was it not terrifying that this man walking around among the others was God? Was it not terrifying to sit down to eat with him? Was it such an easy matter to become an apostle? But the result, the eighteen centuries [since the time of Christ]—that helps, that contributes to this mean deception whereby we deceive ourselves and others. I do not feel brave enough to wish to be contemporary with events like that, but I do not for that reason severely condemn those who made a mistake, nor do I depreciate those who saw what was right.

But I come back to Abraham. During the time before the result, either Abraham was a murderer every minute, or we stand before a paradox that is higher than all mediations.

The story of Abraham contains, then, an ideological suspension of the ethical. As the single individual he became higher than the universal. This is the paradox, which cannot be mediated. How he entered into it is just as inexplicable as how he remains in it. If this is not Abraham's situation, then Abraham is not even a tragic hero but a murderer. It is thoughtless to want to go on calling him the father of faith, to speak of it to men who have an interest only in words. A person can become a tragic hero through his own strength—but not a knight of faith. When a person walks what is in one sense the hard road of the tragic hero, there are many who can give him advice, but he who walks the narrow road of faith has no one to advise him—no one understands him. Faith is a marvel, and yet no human being is excluded from it; for that which unites all human life is passion, and faith is a passion.

NOTES

1. *telos* (Greek): end, goal. [D. C. ABEL]
2. *sensately:* in a manner relating to the senses. [D. C. ABEL]
3. Georg Wilhelm Friedrich Hegel, *Philosophy of Right,* Part Two, Section 3 (paragraphs 129–41). Hegel (1770–1831) was a German philosopher. [D. C. ABEL]
4. "A fool always finds a greater fool to admire him." Nicolas Boileau-Despréaux, *L'Art poétique,* Canto I, line 232. Boileau (1636–1711) was a French critic. [D. C. ABEL]
5. *in mente:* (Latin) in mind. [D. C. ABEL]
6. *middle term:* in logic, that which connects two elements and allows one to make an inference about the relation of those elements. [D. C. ABEL]
7. *whole nation:* the Greeks, who were fighting the Trojans. [D. C. ABEL]
8. When adverse winds prevented the Greek fleet from sailing for Troy, the soothsayer Calchas announced that favorable winds would blow only if King Agamemnon sacrificed his daughter Iphigenia as a sacrifice to the goddess Artemis. [D. C. ABEL]
9. A paraphrase of Euripides, *Iphigenia at Aulis,* line 448. Euripides (484–406 B.C.E.) was a Greek dramatist. [D. C. ABEL]
10. Euripides, *Iphigenia at Aulis,* line 681. [D. C. ABEL]
11. Jephtha; see Judges 11:30–40. [H. V. HONG AND E. H. HONG, TRANSLATORS]
12. When Marcus Junius Brutus (85–42 B.C.E.) was consul of Rome, his sons took part in a conspiracy to restore the king whom he had expelled. Brutus ordered the execution of his sons. [D. C. ABEL]
13. *lictors:* Roman officials who attended chief magistrates and administered punishments. [D. C. ABEL]
14. *horror religiousus:* (Latin) religious dread, awe. [D. C. ABEL]
15. See Exodus 19:12. [H. V. HONG AND E. H. HONG]
16. *Mount Moriah:* the place where Abraham was to sacrifice Isaac. [D. C. ABEL]
17. *Aulis:* the place in Greece where Agamemnon nearly sacrificed his daughter. [D. C. ABEL]
18. Pythagoras (about 580–500 B.C.E.) was a Greek philosopher and mathematician. [D. C. ABEL]
19. *skandalon:* (Greek) stumbling block, offense. [D. C. ABEL]
20. *erectioris ingenii:* (Latin) of a nobler nature. [D. C. ABEL]
21. God enabled Abraham's wife Sarah to conceive Isaac when Abraham was 99 years old and Sarah was 90 (Genesis 17). [D. C. ABEL]
22. Genesis 18:11. [H. V. HONG AND E. H. HONG]
23. Luke 1:38. [H. V. HONG AND E. H. HONG]
24. On his way to his crucifixion, Jesus tells the women following him, "Do not weep for me; weep for yourselves and for your children" (Luke 23:28). [D. C. ABEL]

Beyond Good and Evil
Friedrich Nietzsche

Friedrich Nietzsche was born in Röcken, Prussia, in 1844. After graduating from the Lutheran boarding school at Pforta in 1864, he enrolled in the University of Bonn to study theology. There he began to doubt his Christian faith (he eventually became an atheist and harsh critic of Christianity) and in 1865 transferred to the University of Leipzig to study classical philology (Greek and Latin language and literature) and music. He was recognized as a brilliant student of philology, and at the age of twenty-four, before he had even finished his doctorate, he was offered the chair of classical philology at the University of Basel in Switzerland. The University of Leipzig quickly granted his degree, and Nietzsche assumed the professorship at Basel in 1869. Ten years later, because of his increasingly bad health, Nietzsche resigned his position. For the next ten years, half blind and in unremitting pain, he wandered through Switzerland, Germany, and Italy in search of a cure. His mental health began to deteriorate as well; in 1889 he collapsed on the streets of Turin, Italy, completely insane. He died in Weimar in 1900.

Nietzsche's principal works are *The Birth of Tragedy out of the Spirit of Music* (1872), *Human, All Too Human* (1878), *The Gay Science* (1882), *Thus Spoke Zarathustra* (1883–1885), *Beyond Good and Evil* (1886), and *On the Genealogy of Morals* (1887).

Our selection is from *Beyond Good and Evil,* a book consisting of about three hundred aphorisms on various subjects. The topic of Part 9, from which our reading comes, is "What Is Noble?" According to Nietzsche, to be noble means to see oneself as the center and origin of all value. In fact, the terms "good" and "bad" originally designated simply what the aristocracy did and did not value. For Nietzsche, "life *is* precisely will to power," and historically members of the aristocracy exercised their will to power by exploiting common people and using them as they saw fit. Nietzsche calls the morality of the ruling aristocracy a "master morality." He contrasts this kind of morality with "slave morality," which arose when common people tried to make their inferior and despicable lives more bearable by exalting as virtues such qualities as kindness, sympathy, selflessness, patience, and humility (the cornerstones of Christian morality). Slave morality gave rise to the pair of terms "good" and "evil," which Nietzsche contrasts with the "good" and "bad" of master morality. In slave morality, "good" refers to the slaves' (false) values, and "evil" to the (legitimate and noble) values of the rulers. Since rulers are not in the inferior position of slaves, they need not subscribe to slave values and are "beyond good and evil."

Nietzsche bemoans the fact that modern civilization, with its democratic and egalitarian tendencies, is replacing life-affirming master morality with life-denying slave morality. Yet there are still elements of master morality in some souls, and it is to these souls that Nietzsche's praise of "what is noble" is addressed.

PART 9. WHAT IS NOBLE?

257

Every enhancement so far in the type "man" has been the work of an aristocratic society—and that is how it will be, again and again, since this sort of society believes in a long ladder of rank order and value distinctions between men, and in some sense needs slavery. Without the *pathos of distance* as it grows out of the in-grained differences between stations, out of the way the ruling caste maintains an overview and keeps looking down on subservient types and tools, and out of this caste's equally continuous exercise in obeying and commanding, in keeping away and below—without *this* pathos, that *other,* more mysterious pathos could not have grown at all, that demand for new expansions of distance within the soul itself, the development of states that are increasingly high, rare, distant, tautly drawn and comprehensive, and in short, the enhancement of the type "man," the constant "self-overcoming of man" (to use a moral formula in a supramoral sense). Of course, you cannot entertain any humanitarian illusions about how an aristocratic society originates (and any elevation of the type "man" will presuppose an aristocratic society): The truth is harsh. Let us not be deceived about how every higher culture on earth has *begun!* Men whose nature was still natural, barbarians in every terrible sense of the word, predatory people who still possessed an unbroken strength of will and lust for power, threw themselves on weaker, more civilized, more peaceful races of tradesmen perhaps, or cattle breeders; or on old and mellow cultures in which the very last life-force was flaring up in brilliant fireworks of spirit and corruption. The noble caste always started out as the barbarian caste. Their supremacy was in psychic, not physical strength—they were *more complete* people (which at any level amounts to saying "more complete beasts").

258

Corruption, as an expression of the fact that anarchy threatens inside the in-stincts and that the foundation of the affects, which we call "life," has been shaken—corruption means fundamentally different things, depending on the life-form in which it manifests itself. When, for instance, an aristocracy like that in France at the beginning of the Revolution[1] throws away its privileges with a sublime disgust and sacrifices itself to an excess of its moral feeling, then this is corruption. It was really just the final act of that centuries-long corruption in which the aristocracy gradually relinquished its dominant authority and was reduced to a mere *function* of the kingdom (and, in the end, to its trinket and showpiece). But the essential feature of a good, healthy aristocracy is that it does *not* feel that it is a function (whether of the kingdom or of the community) but instead feels itself to be the *meaning* and highest justification (of the kingdom or community)—and, consequently, that it accepts in good conscience the sacrifice of countless people who have to be pushed down and shrunk into incomplete human beings, into slaves, into tools, all *for the sake of the aristocracy.* Its fun-damental belief must always be that society *cannot* exist for the sake of society, but only as the substructure and framework for raising an exceptional type of being up to its higher duty and to a higher state of *being.* In the same way, the sun-seeking, Javanese climbing plant called the *Sipo matador* will wrap its arms around an oak tree so often and for such a long time that finally, high above the oak, although still supported by it, the plant will be able to unfold its highest crown of foliage and show its happiness in the full, clear light.

259

Mutually refraining from injury, violence, and exploitation, placing your will on par with the other's—in a certain, crude sense, these practices can become good manners between individuals when the right conditions are present (namely, that the individuals have genuinely similar quantities of force and measures of value, and belong together within a single body). But as soon as this principle is taken any further, and maybe even held to be the *fundamental principle of society,* it immediately shows itself for what it is: the will to *negate* life, the principle of disintegration and decay. Here we must think things through thoroughly and ward off any sentimental weakness: Life itself is *essentially* a process of appropriating, injuring, overpowering the alien and the weaker, oppressing, being harsh, imposing your own form, incorporating, and at least, the very least, exploiting. But what is the point of always using words that have been stamped with slanderous intentions from time immemorial? Even a body within which (as we presupposed earlier) particular individuals treat each other as equal (which happens in every healthy aristocracy)—if this body is living and not dying, it will have to treat other bodies in just those ways that the individuals it contains *refrain* from treating each other. It will have to be the embodiment of will to power, it will want to grow, spread, grab, win dominance—not out of any morality or immorality, but because it is *alive,* and because life *is* precisely will to power.

But there is no issue on which the base European consciousness is less willing to be instructed than this. These days, people everywhere are lost in rapturous enthusiasms, even in scientific disguise, about a future state of society where "the exploitative character" will fall away. To my ears, that sounds as if someone is promising to invent a life that dispenses with all organic functions. "Exploitation" does not belong to a corrupted or imperfect, primitive society: It belongs to the *essence* of being alive as a fundamental organic function; it is a result of genuine will to power, which is just the will of life. Although this is an innovation at the level of *theory,* at the level of *reality,* it is the *primal fact* of all history. Let us be honest with ourselves to this extent at least!

260

As I was wandering through the many subtle and crude moralities that have been dominant or that still dominate over the face of the earth, I found certain traits regularly recurring together and linked to each other. In the end, two basic types became apparent to me and a fundamental distinction leaped out. There is a *master morality* and a *slave morality.* I will immediately add that in all higher and more mixed cultures, attempts to negotiate between these moralities also appear, although more frequently the two are confused and there are mutual misunderstandings. In fact, you sometimes find them sharply juxtaposed—inside the same person even, within a single soul.

Moral value distinctions have arisen within either a dominating type that, with a feeling of well-being, was conscious of the difference between itself and those who were dominated—or alternatively, these distinctions arose among the dominated people themselves, the slaves and dependents of every rank. In the first case, when dominating people determine the concept of "good," it is the elevated, proud states of soul that are perceived as distinctive and as determining rank order. The noble person separates himself off from creatures in which the opposite of such elevated, proud states is expressed: He despises them. It is immediately apparent that, in this first type of morality, the contrast between "good" and "bad" amounts to one between "noble" and "despicable" (the contrast between "good" and "*evil*" has a different lineage). People who were cowardly, apprehensive, and petty; people who thought narrowly in terms of utility—these were the ones despised. But the same can be said about distrustful people with their uneasy glances, about grovelers, about dog-like types of people who let themselves be mistreated, about begging flatterers and, above all, about liars—it is a basic belief of aristocrats that base peoples are liars. "We who are truthful"—that is what the nobility of ancient Greece called themselves.

It is obvious that moral expressions everywhere were first applied to *people* and then, only later and derivatively, to *actions* (which is why it is a tremendous mistake when historians of morality take their point of departure from questions such as "Why do acts of pity get praised?"). The noble type of person feels that *he* determines value, he does not need anyone's approval, he judges that "what is harmful to me is harmful in itself," he knows that he is the one who gives honor to things in the first place, he *creates values*. He honors everything he sees in himself: This sort of morality is self-glorifying. In the foreground, there is the feeling of fullness, of power that wants to overflow, the happiness associated with a high state of tension, the consciousness of a wealth that wants to make gifts and give away. The noble person helps the unfortunate too, although not (or hardly ever) out of pity, but rather more out of an impulse generated by the overabundance of power.

In honoring himself, the noble man honors the powerful as well as those who have power over themselves, who know how to speak and be silent, who joyfully exercise severity and harshness over themselves, and have respect for all forms of severity and harshness. "Wotan[2] has put a hard heart in my breast," reads a line from an old Scandinavian saga; this rightly comes from the soul of a proud Viking. This sort of a man is even proud of *not* being made for pity, which is why the hero of the saga adds, by way of warning, "If your heart is not hard when you are young, it will never be hard." The noble and brave types of people who think this way are the furthest removed from a morality that sees precisely pity, actions for others, and *désintéressement*[3] as emblematic of morality. A faith in yourself, pride in yourself, and a fundamental hostility and irony with respect to "selflessness" belong to a noble morality just as certainly as does a slight disdain and caution towards sympathetic feelings and "warm hearts."

The powerful are the ones who *know* how to honor; it is their art, their realm of invention. A profound reverence for age and origins—the whole notion of justice is based on this double reverence—a faith and a prejudice in favor of forefathers and against future generations is typical of the morality of the powerful. And when, conversely, people with "modern ideas" believe almost instinctively in "progress" and "the future" and show a decreasing respect for age, this gives sufficient evidence of the ignoble origin of these "ideas." But, most of all, the morality of dominating types is foreign and painful to contemporary taste due to its stern axiom that people have duties only towards their own kind; that when it comes to creatures of a lower rank, to everything alien, people are allowed to act as they see fit or "from the heart," and in any event, "beyond good and evil." Things like pity might have a place here. The capacity and duty to experience extended gratitude and vengefulness (both only among your own kind), subtlety in retaliation, refinement in concepts of friendship, a certain need to have enemies (as flue holes, as it were, for the affects of jealousy, irascibility, arrogance—basically in order to be a good *friend*)—all these are characteristic features of noble morality which, as I have suggested, is not the morality of "modern ideas," and this makes it difficult for us to relate to, and also difficult for us to dig it up and lay it open.

It is different with the second type of morality, *slave morality*. What if people who were violated, oppressed, suffering, unfree, exhausted, and unsure of themselves were to moralize—what type of moral valuations would they have? A pessimistic suspicion of the whole condition of humanity would probably find expression, perhaps a condemnation of humanity would probably find expression, perhaps a condemnation of humanity along with its condition. The slave's gaze resents the virtues of the powerful. It is skeptical and distrustful, it has a *subtle* mistrust of all the "good" that is honored there—it wants to convince itself that even happiness is not genuine there. Conversely, qualities that serve to alleviate existence for suffering people are pulled out and flooded with light: pity, the obliging, helpful hand, the warm heart, patience, industriousness, humility, and friendliness receive full honors here, since these are the most useful qualities and practically the only way of holding up under the pressure of existence. Slave morality is essentially a morality of utility.

Here we have the point of origin for that famous opposition between "good" and "*evil*." Evil is perceived as something powerful and dangerous; it is felt to contain a certain awesome quality, a subtlety and strength that block any incipient contempt. According to the slave morality then, "evil" inspires fear; but according to the master morality, it is "*good*" that inspires and wants to inspire fear, while the "bad" man is seen as contemptible. The opposition comes to a head when, following the logic of slave morality, a hint of contempt (however slight and well disposed) finally comes to be associated with even its idea of "good," because within the terms of slave morality, the good man must always be *unthreatening:* He is good-natured, easy to deceive, maybe a bit stupid, *un bonhomme.*[4] Wherever slave morality holds sway, language shows a tendency for the words "good" and "stupid" to come closer together.

A final fundamental distinction: The desire for *freedom*, the instinct for happiness, and subtleties in the feeling of freedom necessarily belong to slave morals and morality, just as an artistry and enthusiasm in respect and devotion are invariant symptoms of an aristocratic mode of thinking and valuing. This clearly shows why love *as passion* (our European specialty) must have had a purely noble descent: It is known to have been invented in the knightly poetry of Provence, by those magnificent, inventive men of the "*gai saber.*"[5] Europe is indebted to these men for so many things, almost for itself.

261

Vanity is perhaps one of the most difficult things for a noble person to comprehend: He will be tempted to keep denying it when a different type of man will
almost be able to feel it in his hands. He has difficulty imagining creatures who
would try to inspire good opinions about themselves that they themselves do
not hold—and consequently do not "deserve" either—and who would then
end up *believing* these good opinions. For one thing, this strikes the noble as being so tasteless and showing such a lack of self-respect, and, for another thing,
it seems so baroque and unreasonable to him, that he would gladly see vanity
as an exception and stay skeptical in most of the cases where it is brought up.
For example, he will say: "I can be wrong about my own worth and still insist
that other people acknowledge it to be what I say it is—but that is not vanity (instead, it is arrogance or, more frequently, it is what they call 'humility' or 'modesty')." Or alternatively: "There are many reasons why I can enjoy other people's
good opinions, perhaps because I love and honor them and rejoice in each of
their joys, and perhaps also because their good opinions confirm and reinforce
my faith in my own good opinion of myself, perhaps because other people's
good opinions are useful or look as though they could be useful to me, even
when I don't agree with them—but none of that is vanity."

It is only when forced (namely with the help of history) that the noble person realizes that from time immemorial, in all strata of people who are in some
way dependent, base people *were* only what they were *considered to be:* Not being at all accustomed to positing values, the only value the base person attributes to himself is the one his masters have attributed to him (creating values is
the true *right of masters*). We can see it as the result of a tremendous atavism[6]
that, to this day, ordinary people still *wait* for an opinion to be pronounced about
themselves before instinctively deferring to it. And this is by no means only the
case with "good" opinions—they defer to bad and unfair ones as well (for instance, just think about most of the self-estimations and self-underestimations
that devout women accept from their father confessors and, in general, that devout Christians accept from their church).

As a matter of fact, in keeping with the slow approach of a democratic order of things (and its cause, the mixing of blood between masters and slaves),
the originally rare and noble urge to ascribe to yourself a value that comes *from*
yourself, and to "think well" of yourself is now increasingly widespread and encouraged. But in every age it is opposed by an older, broader, and more thoroughly ingrained tendency—and in the phenomenon of "vanity," this older
tendency gains mastery over the younger. The vain take pleasure in *every* good
opinion they hear about themselves (abstracted entirely from the point of view
of utility, and just as much removed from truth or falsity), just as they suffer
from every bad opinion. This is because they submit—they *feel* submissive—to
both good and bad opinions out of that oldest instinct of submissiveness which
erupts within them. This is "the slave" in the blood of the vain, a remnant of the
mischief of the slave. And how much "slave" is still left over in women, for instance!—they try to *seduce* people into having good opinions of them. By the same
token, it is the slave who submits to these opinions immediately afterwards, as if

he were not the one who had just called for them. And to say it again: Vanity is an atavism. . . .

265

At the risk of annoying innocent ears I will propose this: Egoism belongs to the essence of the noble soul. I mean that firm belief that other beings will, by nature, have to be subordinate to a being "like us" and will have to sacrifice themselves. The noble soul accepts this fact of its egoism without any question mark, and also without feeling any harshness, compulsion, or caprice in it, but rather as something that may well be grounded in the primordial law of things. If the noble soul were to try to name this phenomenon, it would call it "justice itself." It admits to itself, under certain circumstances (that at first give it pause), that there are others with rights equal to its own. As soon as it is clear about this question of rank, it will move among these equals and "equally righted" ones with an assured modesty and a gentle reverence equal to how it treats itself, in accordance with an inborn, celestial mechanics that all stars know so well. This is just *another* piece of its egoism, this finesse and self-limitation in dealing with equals—every star is an egoist of this sort. And the noble soul honors *itself* in them and in the rights that it gives them; it has no doubt that the exchange of rights and honors belongs to the natural state of things too, as the *essence* of all interaction. The noble soul gives as it takes, out of the passionate and sensitive instinct of retribution that is so fundamental to it. The concept of "mercy" is senseless and noisome *inter pares.*[7] There might be a sublime way of letting gifts fall down on you from above, as it were, and lapping them up like raindrops; but the noble soul has no talent for this art and conduct. Its egoism gets in the way: It does not generally like looking "upwards," but rather *ahead*, horizontally and slowly, or downwards; *it knows that it is high up.* . . .

272

Signs of nobility: never thinking about debasing our duties into duties for everyone; not wanting to relinquish, not wanting to share your own responsibility; considering privileges and the exercise of these privileges as a *duty*. . . .

287

What is noble? What does the word "noble" still mean to us today? How do noble people reveal who they are, how can they be recognized under this heavy, overcast sky of incipient mob rule that makes everything leaden and opaque? There are no actions that prove who they are—actions are always ambiguous, always unfathomable—and there are no "works" either. Among artists and scholars these days, you will find plenty of people whose works reveal them to be driven by a deep desire for nobility. But this very need *for* nobility is fundamentally different from the needs *of* the noble soul itself, and almost serves as an eloquent and dangerous testimony to the absence of such needs. It is not works, it is *faith* that is decisive here, faith that establishes rank order (this old, religious formula now acquires a new and deeper meaning): some fundamental certainty that a noble soul has about itself, something that cannot be looked for, cannot be found, and perhaps cannot be lost either. *The noble soul has reverence for itself.*

NOTES

1. The French Revolution began in 1789 and ended in 1799. [D. C. ABEL]
2. Wotan (Woden, Odin) is the supreme god of Norse mythology. [D. C. ABEL]
3. *désintéssement:* (French) "unselfishness." [D. C. ABEL]
4. *un bonhomme:* (French) a simpleminded person; literally, "a good person." [D. C. ABEL]
5. *gai saber:* the art of the troubadours (a fourteenth-century French term that means, literally, "the merry science"). [D. C. ABEL]
6. *atavism:* the recurrence of a trait that appeared in one's remote ancestors. [D. C. ABEL]
7. *inter pares:* (Latin) "among equals." [D. C. ABEL]

Existentialism Is a Humanism

Jean-Paul Sartre

Jean-Paul Sartre was born in Paris in 1905. At the age of nineteen he began studying philosophy at the Ecole Normale Supérieure in Paris. After receiving his graduate degree in 1929, he served in the military for a little over a year. He then began teaching philosophy at Le Havre. Sartre spent the 1933–1934 academic year doing research at the Institut Français in Berlin. Upon returning to France, he taught at Le Havre and other French schools until 1939, when he was drafted by the army to fight in World War II. He was captured by the Germans in 1940, but escaped the following year. Sartre then went to Paris, where he resumed teaching and participated in the resistance movement against the Nazi occupation of France. During the occupation he wrote his main philosophical work, *Being and Nothingness: An Essay in Phenomenological Ontology.* When the war ended, he gave up teaching to devote himself entirely to writing. He was sympathetic to Marxism, and he traveled to a number of communist countries, often meeting with heads of state. Sartre died in Paris in 1980; his funeral was attended by 25,000 people.

Sartre's major works, in addition to *Being and Nothingness* (1943), include *Nausea* (a novel, 1938), *The Psychology of Imagination* (1940), *Existentialism Is a Humanism* (1946), *The Ways of Freedom* (a three-volume novel, 1945–1949), *Critique of Dialectical Reason* (1960; only the first volume of a projected longer work was completed), *The Words* (his autobiography, 1964), and *The Family Idiot* (a three-volume biography of Gustave Flaubert, 1971–1972).

Our reading is from *Existentialism Is a Humanism,* which was delivered as a public lecture in Paris in 1945 and published the following year. By 1945 Sartre had become known as an "existentialist" thinker, and the purpose of his lecture was to explain, in an accessible way, some basic tenets of his version of existentialism. He makes clear that the basic concept in his existentialist philosophy is human freedom. We are radically free, and through our choices we create our own "essence," making ourselves into the kind of person we are. There is no preexistent pattern of human nature to guide us in making choices and no God with a plan for us to follow (Sartre is an atheist); each of us is free to fashion our essence in any way we wish. This freedom brings with it burdensome responsibility: We alone are responsible for who we are—not our genetic inheritance, our psychological makeup, or environmental influences.

What should we choose? We would all like to know the "right" thing to choose, but unfortunately there is no objective basis for determining what is "right": We cannot base our choices either on human nature or on God's will, for there is no human nature and there is no God. Ironically things receive value simply from the fact that we choose them. The only ethical guideline Sartre offers is that we should value freedom above all else. He argues that to value our own freedom requires that we also value the freedom of others.

. . . What is this that we call existentialism?

Most of those who are making use of this word would be highly confused if required to explain its meaning. For since it has become fashionable, people cheerfully declare that this musician or that painter is "existentialist." A columnist in

Clartés signs himself "The Existentialist," and indeed the word is now so loosely applied to so many things that it no longer means anything at all. It would appear that, for the lack of any novel doctrine such as that of surrealism, all those who are eager to join in the latest scandal or movement now seize upon this philosophy—in which, however, they can find nothing to their purpose. For in truth this is of all teachings the least scandalous and the most austere: It is intended strictly for technicians and philosophers. All the same, it can easily be defined.

The question is complicated only because there are two kinds of existentialists. There are, on the one hand, the Christians, among whom I shall name Jaspers and Gabriel Marcel,[1] both professed Catholics; and, on the other, the existential atheists, among whom we must place Heidegger[2] as well as the French existentialists and myself. What they have in common is simply the fact that they believe that *existence* comes before *essence*—or, if you will, that we must begin from the subjective. What exactly do we mean by that?

If one considers an article of manufacture—as, for example, a book or a paper-knife[3]—one sees that it has been made by an artisan who had a conception of it; and he has paid attention, equally, to the conception of a paper-knife and to the preexistent technique of production that is a part of that conception and is, at bottom, a formula. Thus the paper-knife is at the same time an article producible in a certain manner and one which, on the other hand, serves a definite purpose, for one cannot suppose that a man would produce a paper-knife without knowing what it was for. Let us say, then, of the paper-knife that its essence—that is to say, the sum of the formulas and the qualities that made its production and its definition possible—precedes its existence. The presence of such-and-such a paper-knife or book is thus determined before my eyes. Here, then, we are viewing the world from a technical standpoint, and we can say that production precedes existence.

When we think of God as the creator, we are thinking of him, most of the time, as a supernal artisan. Whatever doctrine we may be considering, whether it be a doctrine like that of Descartes, or of Leibniz himself,[4] we always imply that the will follows, more or less, from the understanding or at least accompanies it, so that when God creates he knows precisely what he is creating. Thus, the conception of man in the mind of God is comparable to that of the paper-knife in the mind of the artisan: God makes man according to a procedure and a conception, exactly as the artisan manufactures a paper-knife, following a definition and a formula. Thus each individual man is the realization of a certain conception that dwells in the divine understanding. . . .

Atheistic existentialism, of which I am a representative, declares with greater consistency that if God does not exist, there is at least one being whose existence comes before its essence—a being that exists before it can be defined by any conception of it. That being is man or, as Heidegger has it, the human reality. What do we mean by saying that existence precedes essence? We mean that man first of all exists, encounters himself, surges up in the world—and defines himself afterwards. If man as the existentialist sees himself is not definable, it is because to begin with he is nothing. He will not be anything until later, and then he will be what he makes of himself. Thus, there is no human nature, because there is no God to have a conception of it. Man simply is. Not that he is simply what he conceives himself to be, but he is what he wills, and as he conceives himself after already existing—as he wills to be after that leap towards existence.

Man is nothing else but that which he makes of himself. That is the first principle of existentialism. And this is what people call its "subjectivity," using the word as a reproach against us. But what do we mean to say by this, but that man is of a greater dignity than a stone or a table? For we mean to say that man primarily exists—that man is, before all else, something that propels itself towards a future and is aware that it is doing so. Man is indeed a project that possesses a subjective life, instead of being a kind of moss or a fungus or a cauliflower. Before that projection of the self, nothing exists, not even in the heaven of intelligence. Man will only attain existence when he is what he purposes to be—not, however, what he may *will* to be, for what we usually understand by willing is a conscious decision taken, much more often than not, after we have made ourselves what we are. I may will to join a party, to write a book, or to marry—but in such a case what is usually called my will is probably a manifestation of a prior and more spontaneous decision. If, however, it is true that existence is prior to essence, man is responsible for what he is. Thus, the first effect of existentialism is that it puts every man in possession of himself as he is and places the entire responsibility for his existence squarely upon his own shoulders. And when we say that man is responsible for himself, we do not mean that he is responsible only for his own individuality, but that he is responsible for *all* men.

The word "subjectivism" is to be understood in two senses, and our adversaries play upon only one of them. Subjectivism means, on the one hand, the freedom of the individual subject; and, on the other, that man cannot pass beyond human subjectivity. It is the latter that is the deeper meaning of existentialism. When we say that man chooses himself, we do mean that every one of us must choose himself; but by that we also mean that in choosing for himself he chooses for all men. For in effect, of all the actions a man may take in order to create himself as he wills to be, there is not one that is not creative, at the same time, of an image of man such as he believes he ought to be. To choose between this or that is at the same time to affirm the value of that which is chosen, for we are unable ever to choose the worse. What we choose is always the better; and nothing can be better for *us* unless it is better for *all*. If, moreover, existence precedes essence and we will to exist at the same time as we fashion our image, that image is valid for all and for the entire epoch in which we find ourselves.

Our responsibility is thus much greater than we had supposed, for it concerns mankind as a whole. If I am a worker, for instance, I may choose to join a Christian rather than a Communist trade union. And if, by that membership, I choose to signify that resignation is, after all, the attitude that best becomes a man, that man's kingdom is not upon this earth, I do not commit myself alone to that view. Resignation is my will for everyone, and my action is, in consequence, a commitment on behalf of all mankind. Or if, to take a more personal case, I decide to marry and to have children, even though this decision proceeds simply from my situation, from my passion or my desire, I am thereby committing not only myself, but humanity as a whole, to the practice of monogamy. I am thus responsible for myself and for all men, and I am creating a certain image of man as I would have him to be. In fashioning myself, I fashion man.

This may enable us to understand what is meant by such terms—perhaps a little grandiloquent—as anguish, abandonment, and despair. As you will soon see, it is very simple.

First, what do we mean by "anguish"? The existentialist frankly states that man is in anguish. His meaning is as follows: When a man commits himself to anything, fully realizing that he is not only choosing what he will be, but is thereby at the same time a legislator deciding for the whole of mankind—in such a moment a man cannot escape from the sense of complete and profound responsibility. There are many, indeed, who show no such anxiety. But we affirm that they are merely disguising their anguish or are in flight from it. Certainly, many people think that in what they are doing they commit no one but themselves to anything. And if you ask them "What would happen if everyone did so?," they shrug their shoulders and reply "Everyone does not do so." But in truth, one ought always to ask oneself what would happen if everyone did as one is doing; nor can one escape from that disturbing thought except by a kind of self-deception.[5] The man who lies in self-excuse by saying "Everyone will not do it" must be ill at ease in his conscience, for the act of lying implies the universal value that it denies. By its very disguise his anguish reveals itself. . . .

When we speak of "abandonment" (a favorite word of Heidegger) we only mean to say that God does not exist and that it is necessary to draw the consequences of his absence right to the end. The existentialist is strongly opposed to a certain type of secular moralism that seeks to suppress God at the least possible expense. Towards 1880, when the French professors endeavored to formulate a secular morality, they said something like this: God is a useless and costly hypothesis, so we will do without it. However, if we are to have morality, a society, and a law-abiding world, it is essential that certain values should be taken seriously; they must have an a priori[6] existence ascribed to them. It must be considered obligatory a priori to be honest, not to lie, not to beat one's wife, to bring up children, and so forth. So we are going to do a little work on this subject, which will enable us to show that these values exist all the same, inscribed in an intelligible heaven—although, of course, there is no God. In other words—and this is, I believe, the purport of all that we in France call radicalism—nothing will be changed if God does not exist; we shall rediscover the same norms of honesty, progress, and humanity, and we shall have disposed of God as an out-of-date hypothesis that will die away quietly of itself.

The existentialist, on the contrary, finds it extremely embarrassing that God does not exist, for there disappears with him all possibility of finding values in an intelligible heaven. There can no longer be an a priori Good, since there is no infinite and perfect consciousness to think it. It is nowhere written that the Good exists, that one must be honest or must not lie, since we are now upon the plane where there are only men. Dostoyevsky[7] once wrote, "If God did not exist, everything would be permitted"—and that, for existentialism, is the starting point. Everything is indeed permitted if God does not exist, and man is in consequence [abandoned], for he cannot find anything to depend upon either within or outside himself. He discovers forthwith that he is without excuse. For if indeed existence precedes essence, one will never be able to explain one's action by reference to a given and specific human nature; in other words, there is no determinism[8]—man is free, man *is* freedom. Nor, on the other hand, if God does not exist, are we provided with any values or commands that could legitimize our behavior. Thus we have neither behind us nor before us in a luminous realm of values, any means of justification or excuse. We are left alone, without excuse. That is what I mean when I say that man is condemned to be free: condemned, because he did not create himself; yet nevertheless [he is free because] from the moment that he is thrown into this world he is responsible for everything he does. The existentialist does not believe in the power of passion. He will never regard a grand passion as a destructive torrent upon which a man is swept into certain actions as by fate, and which, therefore, is an excuse for them. He thinks that man is responsible for his passion. Neither will an existentialist think that a man can find help through some sign [given] upon earth for his orientation, for he thinks that the man himself interprets the sign as he chooses. He thinks that every man, without any support or help whatever, is condemned at every instant to invent man. As Ponge[9] has written in a very fine article, "Man is the future of man." That is exactly true. Only, if one took this to mean that the future is laid up in heaven, that God knows what it is, it would be false, for then it would no longer even be a future. If, however, it means that, whatever man may now appear to be, there is a future to be fashioned, a virgin future that awaits him—then it is a true saying. But in the present, one is [abandoned].

As an example by which you may the better understand this state of abandonment, I will refer to the case of a pupil of mine who sought me out in the following circumstances. His father was quarrelling with his mother and was also inclined to be a "collaborator";[10] his elder brother had been killed in the German offensive of 1940 and this young man, with a sentiment somewhat primitive but generous, burned to avenge him. His mother was living alone with him, deeply afflicted by the semi-treason of his father and by the death of her eldest son, and her one consolation was in this young man. But he, at this moment, had the choice between going to England to join the Free French Forces or of staying near his mother and helping her to live. He fully realized that this woman lived only for him and that his disappearance—or perhaps his death—would plunge her into despair. He also realized that, concretely and in fact, every action he performed on his mother's behalf would be sure of effect in the sense of aiding her to live, whereas anything he did in order to go and fight would be an ambiguous action that might vanish like water into sand and serve no purpose. For instance, to set out for England he would have to wait indefinitely in a Spanish camp on the way through Spain; or, on arriving in England or in Algiers, he might be put into an office to fill out forms. Consequently, he found himself confronted by two very different modes of action: the one concrete, immediate, but directed towards only one individual; and the other an action addressed to an end infinitely greater, a national collectivity, but for that very reason ambiguous—and it might be frustrated on the way. At the same time, he was hesitating between two kinds of morality: on the one side, the morality of sympathy, of personal devotion; and on the other side, a morality of wider scope but of more debatable validity. He had to choose between those two. What could help him to choose? Could the Christian doctrine? No. Christian doctrine says: Act with charity, love your neighbor, deny yourself for others, choose the way that is hardest, and so forth. But which is the harder road? To whom does one owe the more brotherly love, the patriot or the mother? Which is the more useful aim, the general one of fighting in and for the whole community, or the precise aim of helping one particular person to live? Who can give an answer to that a priori? No one. Nor is it given in any ethical scripture. The Kantian ethic says: "Never regard another as a means, but always as an end."[11] Very well; if I remain with my mother, I shall be regarding her as the end and not as a means. But by the same token I am in danger of treating as means those who are fighting on my behalf. And the converse is also true, that if I go to the aid of the combatants I shall be treating them as the end, at the risk of treating my mother as a means.

If values are uncertain, if they are still too abstract to determine the particular, concrete case under consideration, nothing remains but to trust in our instincts. That is what this young man tried to do, and when I saw him he said: "In the end, it is feeling that counts; the direction in which it is really pushing me is the one I ought to choose. If I feel that I love my mother enough to sacrifice everything else for her—my will to be avenged, all my longings for action and adventure—then I stay with her. If, on the contrary, I feel that my love for her is not enough, I go." But how does one estimate the strength of a feeling? The value of his feeling for his mother was determined precisely by the fact that he was standing by her. I may say that I love a certain friend enough to sacrifice such and such a sum of money for him, but I cannot prove that unless I have done it. I may say, "I love my mother enough to remain with her," if actually I have remained with her. I can only estimate the strength of this affection if I have performed an action by which it is defined and ratified. But if I then appeal to this affection to justify my action, I find myself drawn into a vicious circle.

Moreover, as Gide[12] has very well said, a sentiment that is play-acting and one that is vital are two things that are hardly distinguishable one from another. To decide that I love my mother by staying beside her, and to play a comedy the upshot of which is that I do so—these are nearly the same thing. In other words, feeling is formed by the deeds that one does; therefore I cannot consult it as a guide to action. And that is to say that I can neither seek within myself for an authentic impulse to action, nor can I expect, from some ethic, formulas that will enable me to act. You may say that the youth did, at least, go to a professor to ask for advice. But if you seek counsel—from a priest, for example—you have selected that priest; and at bottom you already knew, more or less, what he would advise. In other words, to choose an adviser is nevertheless to commit oneself by that choice. If you are a Christian, you will say, "Consult a priest." But there are collaborators, priests who are resisters,[13] and priests who wait for the tide to turn: Which will you choose? Had this young man chosen a priest of the resistance, or one of the collaboration, he would have decided beforehand the kind of advice he was to receive. Similarly, in coming to me he knew what advice I should give him, and I had but one reply to make: "You are free, therefore choose—that is to say, invent. No rule of general morality can show you what you ought to do: No signs are [given] in this world." The Catholics will reply, "Oh, but they are!" Very well; still, it is I myself, in every case, who have to interpret the signs.

While I was imprisoned, I made the acquaintance of a somewhat remarkable man, a Jesuit,[14] who had become a member of that order in the following manner. In his life he had suffered a succession of rather severe setbacks. His father had died when he was a child, leaving him in poverty, and he had been awarded a free scholarship in a religious institution where he had been made continually to feel that he was accepted for charity's sake, and, in consequence, he had been denied several of those distinctions and honors that gratify children. Later, about the age of eighteen, he came to grief in a [love] affair. And finally, at twenty-two—this was a trifle in itself, but it was the last drop that overflowed his cup—he failed in his military examination. This young man, then, could regard himself as a total failure: It was a sign—but a sign of what? He might have taken refuge in bitterness or despair. But he took it (very cleverly for him) as a sign that he was not intended for secular successes, and that only the attainments of religion, those of sanctity and of faith, were accessible to him. He interpreted his record as a message from God, and became a member of the order. Who can doubt but that this decision as to the meaning of the sign was his, and his alone? One could have drawn quite different conclusions from such a series of reverses—as, for example, that he had better become a carpenter or a revolutionary. For the decipherment of the sign, however, he bears the entire responsibility. That is what "abandonment" implies, that we ourselves decide our being. And with this abandonment goes anguish.

As for "despair," the meaning of this expression is extremely simple. It merely means that we limit ourselves to a reliance upon that which is within our wills, or within the sum of the probabilities that render our action feasible. Whenever one wills anything, there are always these elements of probability. If I am counting upon a visit from a friend, who may be coming by train or by tram, I presuppose that the train will arrive at the appointed time, or that the tram will not be derailed. I remain in the realm of possibilities, but one does not rely upon any possibilities beyond those that are strictly concerned in one's action. Beyond the point at which the possibilities under consideration cease to affect my action, I ought to disinterest myself. For there is no God and no [antecedent] design that can adapt the world and all its possibilities to my will. When Descartes said "Conquer yourself rather than the world," what he meant was, at bottom, the same—that we should act without hope.

Marxists[15] to whom I have said this have answered: "Your action is limited, obviously, by your death; but you can rely upon the help of others. That is, you can count both upon what the others are doing to help you elsewhere, as in China and in Russia, and upon what they will do later, after your death, to take up your action and carry it forward to its final accomplishment, which will be the revolution. Moreover, you *must* rely upon this; not to do so is immoral." To this I rejoin, first, that I shall always count upon my comrades-in-arms in the struggle insofar as they are committed, as I am, to a definite, common cause, in the unity of a party or a group that I can more or less control—that is, in which

I am enrolled as a militant and whose movements at every moment are known to me. In that respect, to rely upon the unity and the will of the party is exactly like my reckoning that the train will run on time or that the tram will not be derailed. But I cannot count upon men whom I do not know; I cannot base my confidence upon human goodness or upon man's interest in the good of society, seeing that man is free and that there is no human nature that I can take as foundational. I do know not where the Russian revolution will lead. I can admire it and take it as an example insofar as it is evident today that the proletariat[16] plays a part in Russia that it has attained in no other nation. But I cannot affirm that this will necessarily lead to the triumph of the proletariat; I must confine myself to what I can see. Nor can I be sure that comrades-in-arms will take up my work after my death and carry it to the maximum perfection, seeing that those men are free agents and will freely decide tomorrow what man is then to be. Tomorrow, after my death, some men may decide to establish Fascism, and the others may be so cowardly or so slack as to let them do so. If so, Fascism will then be the truth of man, and so much the worse for us. In reality, things will be such as men have decided they shall be. Does that mean that I should abandon myself to quietism?[17] No. First I ought to commit myself and then act my commitment, according to the time-honored formula that "one need not hope in order to undertake one's work." Nor does this mean that I should not belong to a party, but only that I should be without illusion and that I should do what I can. For instance, if I ask myself "Will the social ideal, as such, ever become a reality?," I cannot tell. I only know that whatever may be in my power to make it so, I shall do. Beyond that, I can count upon nothing.

Quietism is the attitude of people who say, "Let others do what I cannot do." The doctrine I am presenting before you is precisely the opposite of this, since it declares that there is no reality except in action. It goes further, indeed, and adds: "Man is nothing else but what he purposes; he exists only in so far as he realizes himself. He is therefore nothing else but the sum of his actions, nothing else but what his life is." Hence we can well understand why some people are horrified by our teaching. For many have but one resource to sustain them in their misery, and that is to think: "Circumstances have been against me. I was worthy to be something much better than I have been. I admit I have never had a great love or a great friendship, but that is because I never met a man or a woman who was worthy of it. If I have not written any very good books, it is because I had not the leisure to do so. If I have had no children to whom I could devote myself, it is because I did not find the man I could have lived with. So there remains within me a wide range of abilities, inclinations, and potentialities, unused but perfectly viable, that endow me with a worthiness that could never be inferred from the mere history of my actions." But in reality and for the existentialist, there is no love apart from the deeds of love; there is no potentiality of love other than that which is manifested in loving; there is no genius other than that which is expressed in works of art. The genius of Proust[18] is the totality of the works of Proust; the genius of Racine[19] is the series of his tragedies, outside of which there is nothing. Why should we attribute to Racine the capacity to write yet another tragedy when that is precisely what he did not write? In life, a man commits himself, draws his own portrait, and there is nothing but that portrait. No doubt this thought may seem comfortless to one who has not made a success of his life. On the other hand, it puts everyone in a position to understand that reality alone is reliable; that dreams, expectations, and hopes serve to define a man only as deceptive dreams, abortive hopes, unfulfilled expectations—that is to say, they define him negatively, not positively. Nevertheless, when one says "You are nothing else but what you live," it does not imply that an artist is to be judged solely by his works of art, for a thousand other things contribute no less to his definition as a man. What we mean to say is that a man is no other than a series of undertakings, that he is the sum, the organization, the set of relations that constitute these undertakings.

In the light of all this, what people reproach us with is not, after all, our pessimism, but the sternness of our optimism. If people condemn our works of fiction, in which we describe characters that are base, weak, cowardly, and sometimes even frankly evil, it is not only because those characters are base, weak, cowardly, or evil. For suppose that, like Zola,[20] we showed that the behavior of these characters was caused by their heredity, or by the action of their environment upon them, or by determining factors, psychic or organic. People would be reassured; they would say, "You see, that is what we are like, no one can do anything about it." But the existentialist, when he portrays a coward, shows him as responsible for his cowardice. He is not like that on account of a cowardly heart or lungs or cerebrum; he has not become like that through his physiological organism. He is like that because he has made himself into a coward by his actions. There is no such thing as a cowardly temperament. There are nervous temperaments, there is what is called impoverished blood, and there are also rich temperaments. But the man whose blood is poor is not a coward for all that, for what produces cowardice is the act of giving up or giving way—and a temperament is not an action. A coward is defined by the deed that he has done. What people feel obscurely, and with horror, is that the coward as we present him is guilty of being a coward. What people would prefer would be to be born either a coward or a hero. . . .

I declare that freedom, in respect of concrete circumstances, can have no other end and aim but itself; and when once a man has seen that values depend upon himself, in that state of [abandonment] he can will only one thing, and that is freedom as the foundation of all values. That does not mean that he wills it in the abstract; it simply means that the actions of men of good faith have, as their ultimate significance, the quest of freedom itself as such. A man who belongs to some communist or revolutionary society wills certain concrete ends that imply the will to freedom, but that freedom is willed in community. We will freedom for freedom's sake, and in and through particular circumstances. And in thus willing freedom, we discover that it depends entirely upon the freedom of others and that the freedom of others depends upon our own. Obviously, freedom as the definition of a man does not depend upon others, but as soon as there is a commitment, I am obliged to will the liberty of others at the same time as mine. I cannot make liberty my aim unless I make that of others equally my aim. Consequently, when I recognize . . . that man is a being whose existence precedes his essence and that he is a free being who cannot, in any circumstances, but will his freedom; at the same time I realize that I cannot *not* will the freedom of others.

Thus, in the name of that will to freedom that is implied in freedom itself, I can form judgments upon those who seek to hide from themselves the wholly voluntary nature of their existence and its complete freedom. Those who hide from this total freedom, in a guise of solemnity or with deterministic excuses, I shall call cowards.

NOTES

1. Karl Jaspers (1883–1968) was a German philosopher; Marcel (1889–1973) was a French philosopher. [D. C. ABEL]
2. Martin Heidegger (1889–1976) was a German philosopher. [D. C. ABEL]
3. *paper-knife:* a flat knife used mainly to cut apart pages of books (pages of some French books are folded together but not precut). [D. C. ABEL]
4. René Descartes (1596–1650) was a French philosopher and mathematician; for a biography, see p. 128. Gottfried Wilhelm Leibniz (1646–1716) was a German philosopher and mathematician. [D. C. ABEL]
5. *self-deception:* literally, "bad faith" *(mauvaise foi).* [D. C. ABEL]
6. *a priori:* independent of personal experience or judgment (literally, in Latin, "from what comes earlier"). [D. C. ABEL]
7. Fyodor Dostoyevsky (1821–1881) was a Russian novelist. [D. C. ABEL]
8. *determinism:* the doctrine that all human actions are determined by preceding causes and that we can never act otherwise than we do. [D. C. ABEL]
9. Francis Ponge (1889–1988) was a French poet and essayist. [D. C. ABEL]
10. *collaborator:* one who collaborated with the Nazis during their occupation of France during World War II. [D. C. ABEL]
11. This ethical doctrine of the German philosopher Immanuel Kant (1724–1804) appears in this book, pp. 354–364. For a biography of Kant, see p. 175. [D. C. ABEL]
12. André Gide (1859–1951) was a French novelist, essayist, and critic. [D. C. ABEL]
13. *resisters:* members of an underground movement that resisted the Nazi occupation of France during World War II. [D. C. ABEL]
14. *Jesuit:* a member of the Society of Jesus, a Roman Catholic religious order. [D. C. ABEL]
15. *Marxists:* followers of the socialist doctrine of the German philosopher Karl Marx. For a biography of Marx, see p. 470. [D. C. ABEL]
16. *proletariat:* wage-laborers; contrasted in Marxism with the *bourgeoisie* (capitalists, who own the means of production). For Marx's discussion of these classes, see pp. 471–477. [D. C. ABEL]
17. *quietism:* the attitude of being passive, of not getting involved. [D. C. ABEL]
18. Marcel Proust (1871–1922) was a French novelist. [D. C. ABEL]
19. Jean Racine (1639–1699) was a French dramatist. [D. C. ABEL]
20. Emile Zola (1849–1902) was a French novelist. [D. C. ABEL]

The Challenge of Cultural Relativism

James Rachels, revised by Stuart Rachels

James Rachels was born in Columbus, Georgia, in 1941. He attended Mercer University in Macon and received his bachelor's degree in 1962. He then began doctoral studies in philosophy at the University of North Carolina at Chapel Hill, completing his Ph.D. in 1967. Rachels held appointments at the University of Richmond (1966–1968), New York University (1968–1972), and the University of Miami (1972–1977). In 1977 he accepted an appointment at the University of Alabama at Birmingham, and the following year began a five-year term as Dean of the School of Arts and Humanities. After serving as acting Academic Vice President from 1983 to 1984, he was named University Professor of Philosophy, a position he held until his death in Birmingham in 2003.

James Rachels's publications include *Understanding Philosophy* (1976), *The End of Life: Euthanasia and Morality* (1986), *The Elements of Moral Philosophy* (1976; 4th ed., 2003), *The Right Thing to Do: Readings in Moral Philosophy* (editor, 1989; 3d ed., 2003), and *Created from Animals: The Moral Implications of Darwinism* (1990).

Stuart Rachels, son of James Rachels, was born in New York City in 1969. After completing his undergraduate degree in philosophy at Emory University in 1991, he enrolled in Oxford University, where he earned a bachelor's degree in philosophy and politics in 1993. He then entered the graduate program in philosophy at Syracuse University, completing his doctorate in 1998. After teaching for a year at the University of Colorado at Boulder, he accepted an appointment as Assistant Professor of Philosophy at the University of Alabama at Tuscaloosa. He was promoted to Associated Professor in 2004.

Stuart Rachels has published articles on ethical theory in such journals as *The Australian Journal of Philosophy, Bioethics, Nous*, and *Philosophical Studies*. After his father's death, he produced revised editions of *The Elements of Moral Philosophy* (5th ed., 2007) and *The Right Thing to Do* (4th ed., 2007).

Our reading is from Chapter 2 of *The Elements of Moral Philosophy,* "The Challenge of Cultural Relativism." Cultural relativism is the doctrine that all moral values derive entirely from individual cultural codes, and that there are no objective, independently correct moral values. In other words, there are no *absolute* truths about what is right and wrong because judgments of right and wrong are all *relative* to a given culture. The authors explain that many thinkers conclude that because different cultures have different moral codes, cultural relativism must be true. They point out, however, that the existence of cultural differences of opinion does not prove that there are no objectively correct answers about what is right and wrong. They show that if we accept cultural relativism, we are committed to several implausible consequences. They then argue that differences in cultural values are less drastic than they at first appear to be, and that certain basic values are common to all cultures.

HOW DIFFERENT CULTURES HAVE DIFFERENT MORAL CODES

Darius, a king of ancient Persia, was intrigued by the variety of cultures he encountered in his travels. He had found, for example, that the Callatians (a tribe of Indians) customarily ate the bodies of their dead fathers. The Greeks, of course, did not do that—the Greeks practiced cremation and regarded the funeral pyre as the natural and fitting way to dispose of the dead. Darius thought that a sophisticated understanding of the world must include an appreciation of such differences between cultures. One day, to teach this lesson, he summoned some Greeks who happened to be present at his court and asked them what they would take to eat the bodies of their dead fathers. They were shocked, as Darius knew they would be, and replied that no amount of money could persuade them to do such a thing. Then Darius called in some Callatians, and while the Greeks listened asked them what they would take to burn their dead fathers' bodies. The Callatians were horrified and told Darius not even to mention such an awful thing.

This story, recounted by Herodotus in his *Histories*,[1] illustrates a recurring theme in the literature of social science: Different cultures have different moral codes. What is thought right within one group may be utterly abhorrent to the members of another group, and vice versa. Should we eat the bodies of the dead or burn them? If you were a Greek, one answer would seem obviously correct; but if you were a Callatian, the opposite would seem equally certain.

It is easy to give additional examples of the same kind. Consider the Eskimos. The Eskimos are the indigenous peoples of northern Canada, Greenland, and northeastern Siberia. (Today, none of these peoples call themselves "Eskimos"; however, I'll use that term because it's the only one that refers to this scattered Arctic population.) Traditionally Eskimos have lived in small settlements, separated by great distances. Prior to the twentieth century, the outside world knew little about them. Then explorers began to bring back strange tales.

Eskimo customs turned out to be very different from our own. The men often had more than one wife, and they would share their wives with guests, lending them for the night as a sign of hospitality. Moreover, within a community a dominant male might demand—and get—regular sexual access to other men's wives. The women however, were free to break these arrangements simply by leaving their husbands and taking up with new partners—free, that is, so long as their former husbands chose not to make trouble. All in all, the Eskimo practice was a volatile scheme that bore little resemblance to what we call marriage.

But it was not only their marriage and sexual practices that were different. The Eskimos also seemed to have less regard for human life. Infanticide, for example, was common. Knud Rasmussen, one of the most famous early explorers, reported that he met one woman who had borne twenty children but had killed ten of them at birth. Female babies, he found, were especially liable to be destroyed, and this was permitted simply at the parents' discretion, with no social stigma attached to it. Old people also, when they became too feeble to contribute to the family, were left out in the snow to die. So there seemed to be, in this society, remarkably little respect for life.

To most Americans, these were disturbing revelations. Our own way of living seems so natural and right that for many of us it is hard to conceive of others living so differently. And when we do hear of such things, we tend immediately to categorize the other peoples as "backward" or "primitive." But to anthropologists, there was nothing particularly surprising about the Eskimos. Since the time of Herodotus, enlightened observers have been accustomed to the idea that conceptions of right and wrong differ from culture to culture. If we assume that our ethical ideas will be shared by all peoples at all times, we are merely naive.

CULTURAL RELATIVISM

To many thinkers, this observation—"different cultures have different moral codes"—has seemed to be the key to understanding morality. The idea of universal truth in ethics, they say, is a myth. The customs of different societies are all that exist. These customs cannot be said to be "correct" or "incorrect," for that implies we have an independent standard of right and wrong by which they may be judged. But there is no such independent standard; every standard is culture-bound. The great pioneering sociologist William Graham Sumner, writing in 1906, put it like this:

> The "right" way is the way which the ancestors used and which has been handed down. The tradition is its own warrant. It is not held subject to verification by experience. The notion of right is in the folkways. It is not outside of them, of independent origin, and brought to test them. In the folkways, whatever is, is right. This is because they are traditional and therefore contain in themselves the authority of the ancestral ghosts. When we come to the folkways we are at the end of our analysis.[2]

This line of thought has probably persuaded more people to be skeptical about ethics than any other single thing. *Cultural relativism*, as it has been called, challenges our ordinary belief in the objectivity and universality of moral truth. It says, in effect, that there is no such thing as universal truth in ethics; there are only the various cultural codes, and nothing more. Moreover, our own code has no special status; it is merely one among many. As we shall see, this basic idea is really a compound of several different thoughts.

It is important to distinguish the various elements of cultural relativism because, on analysis, some parts turn out to be correct, while others seem to be mistaken. The following claims have all been made by cultural relativists:

1. Different societies have different moral codes.
2. The moral code of a society determines what is right within that society; that is, if the moral code of a society says that a certain action is right, then that action *is* right, at least within that society.
3. There is no objective standard that can be used to judge one society's codes better than another's. In other words, there is no "universal truth" in ethics; there are no moral truths that hold for all people at all times.

4. The moral code of our own society has no special status; it is merely one among many.
5. It is mere arrogance for us to try to judge the conduct of other peoples. We should adopt an attitude of tolerance toward the practices of other cultures.

These five propositions may seem to go together, but they are independent of one another, in the sense that some of them might be false even if others are true. Indeed, two of them appear to be inconsistent with each other. The second proposition says that right and wrong are determined by the norms of a society; the fifth proposition says that we should always be tolerant of other cultures. But what if the norms of a society favor intolerance? For example, when the Nazi army marched into Poland on September 1, 1939, thus beginning World War II, this was an intolerant action of the first order. But what if it was in line with Nazi ideals? A cultural relativist, it seems, cannot criticize the Nazis for being intolerant, if all they're doing is following their own moral code.

Given that cultural relativists take pride in their tolerance, it would be ironic if their theory actually supported people in intolerant cultures being intolerant of other cultures. However, it need not have that implication. Properly understood, cultural relativism holds that the norms of a culture reign supreme *within the bounds of the culture itself*. Thus, once the German soldiers entered Poland, they became bound by the norms of Polish society — norms that obviously excluded the mass slaughter of innocent Poles. "When in Rome," the old saying goes, "do as the Romans do." Cultural relativists agree.

THE CULTURAL DIFFERENCES ARGUMENT

Cultural relativism is a theory about the nature of morality. At first blush it seems quite plausible. However, like all such theories, it may be evaluated by subjecting it to rational analysis; and when we analyze cultural relativism, we find that it is not so plausible as it first appears to be.

The first thing to notice is that at the heart of cultural relativism there is a certain *form of argument*. Cultural relativists argue from facts about the differences between cultural outlooks to a conclusion about the status of morality. Thus, we are invited to accept this reasoning:

(1) The Greeks believed it was wrong to eat the dead, whereas the Callatians believed it was right to eat the dead.
(2) Therefore, eating the dead is neither objectively right nor objectively wrong. It is merely a matter of opinion, which varies from culture to culture.

Or, alternatively:

(1) The Eskimos see nothing wrong with infanticide, whereas Americans believe infanticide is immoral.
(2) Therefore, infanticide is neither objectively right nor objectively wrong. It is merely a matter of opinion, which varies from culture to culture.

Clearly, these arguments are variations of one fundamental idea. They are both special cases of a more general argument, which says:

(1) Different cultures have different moral codes.
(2) Therefore, there is no objective "truth" in morality. Right and wrong are only matters of opinion, and opinions vary from culture to culture.

We may call this the *cultural differences argument*. To many people, it is persuasive. But from a logical point of view, is it sound?

It is not sound. The trouble is that the conclusion does not follow from the premise—that is, even if the premise is true, the conclusion still might be false. The premise concerns what people *believe*—in some societies, people believe one thing; in other societies, people believe differently. The conclusion, however, concerns what *really is the case:* The trouble is that this sort of conclusion does not follow logically from this sort of premise.

Consider again the example of the Greeks and Callatians. The Greeks believed it was wrong to eat the dead; the Callatians believed it was right. Does it follow, *from the mere fact that they disagreed,* that there is no objective truth in the matter? No, it does not follow; it could be that the practice was objectively right (or wrong) and that one of them was simply mistaken.

To make the point clearer, consider a different matter. In some societies, people believe the earth is flat. In other societies, such as our own, people believe the earth is (roughly) spherical. Does it follow, from the mere fact that people disagree, that there is no "objective truth" in geography? Of course not; we would never draw such a conclusion because we realize that, in their beliefs about the world, the members of some societies might simply be wrong. There is no reason to think that if the world is round everyone must know it. Similarly, there is no reason to think that if there is moral truth everyone must know it. The fundamental mistake in the cultural differences argument is that it attempts to derive a substantive conclusion about a subject from the mere fact that people disagree about it.

This is a simple point of logic, and it is important not to misunderstand it. We are not saying that the conclusion of the argument is false. That is still an open question. The logical point is merely that the conclusion does not follow from the premise. This is important, because in order to determine whether the conclusion is true, we need arguments in its support. Cultural relativism proposes this argument, but it is fallacious. So it proves nothing.

THE CONSEQUENCES OF TAKING CULTURAL RELATIVISM SERIOUSLY

Even if the cultural differences argument is unsound, cultural relativism might still be true. What would it be like if it were true?

In the passage quoted above, William Graham Sumner summarizes the essence of cultural relativism. He says that there is no measure of right and wrong other than the standards of one's society: "The notion of right is in the folkways. It is not outside of them, of independent origin, and brought to test them. In the folkways, whatever is, is right." Suppose we took this seriously. What would be some of the consequences?

1. *We could no longer say that the customs of other societies are morally inferior to our own.* This, of course, is one of the main points stressed by cultural relativism. We would have to stop condemning other societies merely because they are "different." So long as we concentrate on certain examples, such as the funerary practices of the Greeks and Callatians, this may seem to be a sophisticated, enlightened attitude.

However, we would also be stopped from criticizing other, less benign practices. For example, the Chinese government has a long tradition of suppressing political dissent within its own borders. At any given time, thousands of political prisoners in China are doing hard labor, and in the Tiananmen Square episode of 1989, Chinese troops slaughtered hundreds, if not thousands, of peaceful protesters. Cultural relativism would preclude us from saying that the Chinese government's policies of oppression are wrong. (We could not even say that a society that respects free speech is *better* than Chinese society, for that would imply a universal standard of comparison.) The failure to condemn *these* practices does not seem enlightened; on the contrary, political oppression seems wrong wherever it occurs. Nevertheless, if we accept cultural relativism, we have to regard such political practices as immune from criticism.

2. *We could decide whether actions are right or wrong just by consulting the standards of our society.* Cultural relativism suggests a simple test for determining what is right and what is wrong: All we need do is ask whether the action is in accordance with the code of the society in question. Suppose a resident of India wonders if her society's caste system—a system of rigid social hierarchy—is morally correct. All she has to do is ask whether this policy conforms to her society's moral code. If it does, there is nothing to worry about, at least from a moral point of view.

This implication of cultural relativism is disturbing because few of us think that our society's code is perfect—we can think of all sorts of ways in which it might be improved. Yet cultural relativism not only forbids us from criticizing the codes of *other* societies; it also stops us from criticizing our own. After all, if right and wrong are relative to culture, this must be true for our own culture just as much as for other cultures.

3. *The idea of moral progress is called into doubt.* We think that at least some social changes are for the better. Throughout most of Western history the place of women in society was narrowly circumscribed. They could not own property; they could not vote or hold political office; and generally they were under the almost absolute control of their husbands. Recently much of this has changed, and most people think of it as progress.

But if cultural relativism is correct, can we legitimately view this as progress? Progress means replacing a way of doing things with a better way. But by what standard do we judge the new ways as better? If the old ways were in accordance with the social standards of their time, then cultural relativism would say it is a mistake to judge them by the standards of a different time. Eighteenth-century society was a different society from the one we have now. To say that we have made progress implies a judgment that present-day society is better—just the sort of transcultural judgment that, according to cultural relativism, is unacceptable.

Our ideas about social *reform* will also have to be reconsidered. Reformers such as Martin Luther King, Jr., have sought to change their societies for the better. Within the constraints imposed by cultural relativism, there is one way this might be done. If a society is not living up to its own ideals, the reformer may be regarded as acting for the best in promoting those ideals. After all, those ideals are the standards by which we judge his or her proposals. But no one may challenge the ideals themselves, for those ideals are by definition correct. According to cultural relativism, then, the idea of social reform makes sense only in this limited way.

These three consequences of cultural relativism have led many thinkers to reject it as implausible on its face. It does make sense, they say, to condemn some practices, such as slavery and anti-Semitism, wherever they occur. It makes sense to think that our own society has made some moral progress, while admitting that it is still imperfect and in need of reform. Because cultural relativism implies that these judgments make no sense, the argument goes, it cannot be right.

WHY THERE IS LESS DISAGREEMENT THAN IT SEEMS

The original impetus for cultural relativism comes from the observation that cultures differ dramatically in their views of right and wrong. But just how much do they differ? It is true that there are differences. However, it is easy to overestimate the extent of those differences. Often, when we examine what seems to be a dramatic difference, we find that the cultures do not differ nearly as much as it appears.

Consider a culture in which people believe it is wrong to eat cows. This may even be a poor culture, in which there is not enough food; still, the cows are not to be touched. Such a society would appear to have values very different from our own. But does it? We have not yet asked *why* these people will not eat cows. Suppose it is because they believe that after death the souls of humans inhabit the bodies of animals, especially cows, so that a cow may be someone's grandmother. Now shall we say that their values are different from ours? No; the difference lies elsewhere. The difference is in our belief systems, not in our values. We agree that we shouldn't eat Grandma; we simply disagree about whether the cow is (or could be) Grandma.

The point is that many factors work together to produce the customs of a society. The society's values are only one of them. Other matters, such as the religious and factual beliefs held by its members, and the physical circumstances in which they must live, are also important. We cannot conclude, then, merely because customs differ, that there is a disagreement about values. The difference in customs may be attributable to some other aspect of social life. Thus there may be less disagreement about values than there appears to be.

Consider again the Eskimos, who often kill perfectly normal infants, especially girls. We do not approve of such things; in our society, a parent who killed a baby would be locked up. Thus there appears to be a great difference in the values of our two cultures. But suppose we ask why the Eskimos do this. The explanation is not that they have less affection for their children or less respect for human life. An Eskimo family will always protect its babies if conditions permit. But they live in a harsh environment, where food is in short supply. A fundamental postulate of Eskimo thought is: "Life is hard, and the margin of safety small." A family may want to nourish its babies but be unable to do so.

As in many traditional societies, Eskimo mothers would nurse their infants over a much longer period than mothers in our culture — for four years, and perhaps even longer. So, even in the best of times, there were limits to the number of infants one mother could sustain. Moreover, Eskimos were nomadic; unable to farm, they had to move about in search of food. Infants had to be carried, and a mother could carry only one baby in her parka as she traveled and went about her outdoor work.

Infant girls were more readily disposed of for two reasons. First, in Eskimo society the males were the primary food providers — they were the hunters — and it is obviously important to maintain a sufficient number of food providers. But there was an important second reason as well. Because the hunters suffered a large casualty rate, the adult men who died prematurely far outnumbered the women who died early. If male and female infants had survived in equal numbers, the female adult population would have greatly outnumbered the adult male population. Examining the available statistics, one writer concluded that "were it not for female infanticide . . . there would be approximately one-and-a-half times as many females in the average Eskimo local group as there are food-producing males."[3]

So among the Eskimos, infanticide did not signal a fundamentally different attitude toward children. Instead, it arose from the recognition that drastic measures are sometimes needed to ensure the family's survival. Even then, however, killing the baby was not the first option considered. Adoption was common; childless couples were especially happy to take a more fertile couple's "surplus." Killing was the last resort. I emphasize this in order to show that the raw data of the anthropologists can be misleading; it can make the differences in values between cultures appear greater than they are. The Eskimos' values were not all that different from our own. It is only that life forces upon them choices that we do not have to make.

HOW ALL CULTURES HAVE SOME VALUES IN COMMON

It should not be surprising that, despite appearances, the Eskimos were protective of their children. How could it be otherwise? How could a group survive that did not value its young? It is easy to see that, in fact, all cultural groups must protect their infants. Babies are helpless and cannot survive if they are not given extensive care for a period of years. Therefore, if a group did not care for its young, the young would not survive, and the older members of the group would not be replaced. After a while, the group would die out. This means that any cultural group that continues to exist must care for its young. Infants that are not cared for must be the exception rather than the rule.

Similar reasoning shows that other values must be more or less universal. Imagine what it would be like for a society to place no value at all on truth telling. When one person spoke to another, there would be no presumption that she was telling the truth, for she could just as easily be speaking falsely. Within that society, there would be no reason to pay attention to what anyone says. (I ask you what time it is, and you say "Four o'clock." But there is no presumption that you are speaking truly; you could just as easily have said the first thing that came into your head. So I have no reason to pay attention to your answer. In fact, there was no point in my asking you in the first place.) Communication would then be extremely difficult, if not impossible. And because complex societies cannot exist without communication among their members, society would become impossible. It follows that in any complex society there must be a presumption in favor of truthfulness. There may of course be exceptions to this rule: There may be situations in which it is thought to be permissible to lie. Nevertheless, these will be exceptions to a rule that *is* in force in the society.

Here is one more example of the same type. Could a society exist in which there was no prohibition on murder? What would this be like? Suppose people were free to kill other people at will, and no one thought there was anything wrong with it. In such a "society," no one could feel safe. Everyone would have to be constantly on guard, and to survive they would have to avoid other people as much as possible. This would inevitably result in individuals trying to become as self-sufficient as possible—after all, associating with others would be dangerous. Society on any large scale would collapse. Of course, people might band together in smaller groups with others that they could trust not to harm them. But notice what this means: They would be forming smaller societies that did acknowledge a rule against murder. The prohibition of murder, then, is a necessary feature of all societies.

There is a general theoretical point here, namely, that *there are some moral rules that all societies must have in common, because those rules are necessary for society to exist.* The rules against lying and murder are two examples. And in fact, we do find these rules in force in all viable cultures. Cultures may differ in what they regard as legitimate exceptions to the rules, but this disagreement exists against a broad background of agreement. Therefore, it is a mistake to overestimate the amount of difference between cultures. Not every moral rule can vary from society to society.

JUDGING A CULTURAL PRACTICE TO BE UNDESIRABLE

In 1996, a seventeen-year-old girl named Fauziya Kassindja arrived at Newark International Airport and asked for asylum. She had fled her native country of Togo, a small west African nation, to escape what people there call "excision." Excision is a permanently disfiguring procedure that is sometimes called "female circumcision," although it bears little resemblance to the Jewish practice. More commonly, at least in Western newspapers, it is referred to as "female genital mutilation."

According to the World Health Organization, the practice is widespread in twenty-six African nations, and two million girls each year are "excised." In some instances, excision is part of an elaborate tribal ritual, performed in small traditional villages, and girls look forward to it because it signals their acceptance into the adult world. In other instances, the practice is carried out by families living in cities on young women who desperately resist.

Fauziya Kassindja was the youngest of five daughters in a devoutly Muslim family. Her father, who owned a successful trucking business, was opposed to excision, and he was able to defy the tradition because of his wealth. His first four daughters were married without being mutilated. But when Fauziya was sixteen, he suddenly died. Fauziya then came under the authority of her aunt, who arranged a marriage for her and prepared to have her excised. Fauziya was terrified, and her mother and oldest sister helped her escape.

In America, Fauziya was imprisoned for nearly eighteen months while the authorities decided what to do with her. During this time, she was subjected to humiliating strip searches, denied medical treatment for her asthma, and generally treated like a dangerous criminal. Finally, she was granted asylum, but not before she became the center of a controversy about how we should regard the cultural practices of other peoples. A series of articles in *The New York Times*[4] encouraged the idea that excision is a barbaric practice that should be condemned. Other observers were reluctant to be so judgmental. Live and let live, they said; after all, our culture probably seems just as strange to them.

Suppose we are inclined to say that excision is bad. Would we merely be imposing the standards of our own culture? If cultural relativism is correct, that is all we can do, for there is no culture-neutral moral standard to which we may appeal. But is that true?

Is There a Culture-Neutral Standard of Right and Wrong?

There is much that can be said against excision. Excision is painful and it results in the permanent loss of sexual pleasure. Its short-term effects include hemorrhage, tetanus, and septicemia. Sometimes the woman dies. Long-term effects include chronic infection, scars that hinder walking, and continuing pain.

Why, then, has it become a widespread social practice? It is not easy to say. Excision has no apparent social benefits. Unlike Eskimo infanticide, it is not necessary for the group's survival. Nor is it a matter of religion. Excision is practiced by groups with various religions, including Islam and Christianity, neither of which commends it.

Nevertheless, a number of reasons are given in its defense. Women who are incapable of sexual pleasure are said to be less likely to be promiscuous; thus there will be fewer unwanted pregnancies in unmarried women. Moreover, wives for whom sex is only a duty are less likely to be unfaithful to their husbands; and because they will not be thinking about sex, they will be more attentive to the needs of their husbands and children. Husbands, for their part, are said to enjoy sex more with wives who have been excised. (The women's own lack of enjoyment is said to be unimportant.) Men will not want unexcised women, as they are unclean and immature. And above all, it has been done since antiquity, and we may not change the ancient ways.

It would be easy, and perhaps a bit arrogant, to ridicule these arguments. But we may notice an important feature of this whole line of reasoning: It attempts to justify excision by showing that excision is beneficial—men, women, and their families are said to be better off when women are excised. Thus we might approach this reasoning, and excision itself, by asking whether this is true: Is excision, on the whole, helpful or harmful?

In fact, this is a standard that might reasonably be used in thinking about any social practice whatever: We may ask *whether the practice promotes or hinders the welfare of the people whose lives are affected by it.* And, as a corollary, we may ask if there is an alternative set of social arrangements that would do a better job of promoting their welfare. If so, we may conclude that the existing practice is deficient.

But this looks like just the sort of independent moral standard that cultural relativism says cannot exist. It is a single standard that may be brought to bear in judging the practices of any culture, at any time, including our own. Of course, people will not usually see this principle as being "brought in from the outside" to judge them, because viable cultures value human happiness.

Why, Despite All This, Thoughtful People May Be Reluctant to Criticize Other Cultures

Although they are personally horrified by excision, many thoughtful people are reluctant to say it is wrong, for at least three reasons. First, there is an understandable nervousness about "interfering in the social customs of other peoples." Europeans and their cultural descendants in America have a shabby history of destroying native cultures in the name of Christianity and enlightenment. Recoiling from this record, some people refuse to make any negative judgments about other cultures, especially cultures that resemble those that have been wronged in the past. We should notice, however, that there is a difference between (a) judging a cultural practice to be deficient, and (b) thinking that we should announce the fact, conduct a campaign, apply diplomatic pressure, or send in the troops. The first is just a matter of trying to see the world clearly, from a moral point of view. The second is another matter altogether. Sometimes it may be right to "do something about it," but often it will not be.

Second, people also feel, rightly enough, that they should be tolerant of other cultures. Tolerance is, no doubt, a virtue—a tolerant person is willing to live in peaceful cooperation with those who see things differently. But there is nothing in the nature of tolerance that requires us to say that all beliefs, all religions, and all social practices are equally admirable. On the contrary, if we did not think that some were better than others, there would be nothing for us to tolerate.

Finally, people may be reluctant to judge because they do not want to express contempt for the society being criticized. But again, this is misguided: To condemn a particular practice is not to say that the culture is on the whole contemptible or that it is generally inferior to any other culture, including one's own. It could have many admirable features. In fact, we should expect this to be true of most human societies—they are mixes of good and bad practices. Excision happens to be one of the bad ones.

WHAT CAN BE LEARNED FROM CULTURAL RELATIVISM

So far, in discussing cultural relativism, I have dwelled on its mistakes. I have said that it rests on an unsound argument, that it has implausible consequences, and that the extent of moral disagreement is far less than it suggests. This all adds up to a rather thorough repudiation of the theory. Nevertheless, it is still an appealing idea, and you may have the feeling that all this is a little unfair. The theory must have something going for it — why else has it been so influential? In fact, I think there is something right about cultural relativism, and there are two lessons we should learn from the theory, even if we ultimately reject it.

First, cultural relativism warns us, quite rightly, about the danger of assuming that all our preferences are based on some absolute rational standard. They are not. Many (but not all) of our practices are merely peculiar to our society, and it is easy to lose sight of that fact. In reminding us of it, the theory does a service.

Funerary practices are one example. The Callatians, according to Herodotus, were "men who eat their fathers"—a shocking idea, to us at least. But eating the flesh of the dead could be understood as a sign of respect. It could be taken as a symbolic act that says: We wish this person's spirit to dwell within us. Perhaps this was the understanding of the Callatians. On such a way of thinking, burying the dead could be seen as an act of rejection, and burning the corpse as positively scornful. If this is hard to imagine, then we may need to have our imaginations stretched. Of course we may feel a visceral repugnance at the idea of eating human flesh in any circumstances. But what of it? This repugnance may be, as the relativists say, only a matter of what is customary in our particular society.

There are many other matters that we tend to think of in terms of objective right and wrong that are really nothing more than social conventions. During the 2004 Super Bowl halftime show, Justin Timberlake ripped off part of Janet Jackson's costume, thus exposing one of her breasts to the audience. CBS quickly cut to an aerial view of the stadium, but as far as the country was concerned, the damage had been done. Half a million viewers complained, and the federal government fined CBS $550,000. In America, a publicly exposed breast is scandalous. In other cultures, however, such displays are common. Objectively speaking, the display of a woman's breast is neither right nor wrong. Cultural relativism begins with the valuable insight that many of our practices are like this; they are only cultural products. Then it goes wrong by inferring that, because some practices are like this, all must be.

The second lesson has to do with keeping an open mind. In the course of growing up, each of us has acquired some strong feelings: We have learned to think of some types of conduct as acceptable, and we have learned to reject others. Occasionally, we may find those feelings challenged. For example, we may have been taught that homosexuality is immoral, and we may feel quite uncomfortable around gay people and see them as alien and perverted. But then someone suggests that this may be a mere prejudice; that there is nothing evil about homosexuality; that gay people are just people, like anyone else, who happen, through no choice of their own, to be attracted to others of the same sex. Because we feel so strongly about the matter, we may find it hard to take this seriously. Even after we listen to the arguments, we may still have the unshakable feeling that homosexuals must be unsavory.

Cultural relativism provides an antidote for this kind of dogmatism. When he tells the story of the Greeks and Callatians, Herodotus adds:

> For if anyone, no matter who, were given the opportunity of choosing from among all the nations of the world the set of beliefs that he thought best, he would inevitably, after careful consideration of their relative merits, choose that of his own country. Everyone without exception believes his own native customs, and the religion he was brought up in, to be the best.[5]

Realizing this can help us broaden our minds. We can see that our feelings are not necessarily perceptions of the truth—they may be nothing more than the result of cultural conditioning. Thus, when we hear it suggested that some element of our social code is *not* really the best, and we find ourselves instinctively resisting the suggestion, we might stop and remember this. Then we may be more open to discovering the truth, whatever that might be.

We can understand the appeal of cultural relativism, then, even though the theory has serious shortcomings. It is an attractive theory because it is based on a genuine insight: that many of the practices and attitudes we think so natural are really only cultural products. Moreover, keeping this thought firmly in view is important if we want to avoid arrogance and keep an open mind. These are important points, not to be taken lightly. But we can accept them without accepting the whole theory.

NOTES

1. Herodotus, *The Histories,* trans. Aubrey de Sélincourt, rev. A. R. Burn (Harmondsworth, England: Penguin, 1972), pp. 219–220. [J. RACHELS] Herodotus (about 484–425 B.C.E.) was a Greek historian. [D. C. ABEL]
2. William Graham Summer, *Folkways* (Boston: Ginn, 1906), p. 28. [J. RACHELS]
3. E. Adamson Hoebel, *The Law of Primitive Man: A Study in Comparative Legal Dynamics* (Cambridge, Mass.: Harvard University Press, 1954), p. 76. [J. RACHELS]
4. *The New York Times,* April 15, 25; May 2, 3; July 8; September 11, October 5, 12; December 28, 1996; articles written mainly by Celia W. Dugger. [J. RACHELS]
5. Herodotus, *The Histories,* p. 219. [J. RACHELS]

Just Caring

Rita C. Manning

Rita C. Manning received her bachelor's degree in philosophy from the University of Massachusetts, Boston, in 1977. She then enrolled in the graduate program in philosophy at the University of California at Riverside, completing her master's degree in 1979 and her doctorate in 1982. She taught at California State University, San Bernardino, from 1979 to 1984 and at California State University, Hayward, during the 1984–1985 academic year. Manning then was appointed Professor of Philosophy at San José State University. In 1994–1995 she was Visiting Professor at the United States Military Academy in West Point, New York. Since 2003 she has served as Department Chair at San José State.

Manning has published articles on various topics in ethical theory and applied ethics, and two books: *Speaking from the Heart: A Feminist Perspective on Ethics* (1992) and *Social Justice in a Diverse Society* (coeditor with René Trujillo, 1996).

Our reading is from Chapter 4 of *Speaking from the Heart,* entitled "Just Caring." Manning proposes and defends an "ethic of caring." This ethic has two components: a disposition to care (a willingness to be open to others and give lucid attention to their needs) and an obligation to "care for" (to express our caring disposition in concrete actions). The objects of care include not only persons and animals, but also values, institutions, and all entities that cannot meet a need without help. How one carries out an ethic of caring with regard to these objects "depends upon one's ability to care for, one's obligation to care for oneself, and one's sense of the appropriateness of the need and the best way to meet it."

Manning explains that caring rests on our natural human capacity for empathy: When we see someone suffering, we feel the suffering almost as our own and want to do something to alleviate it. But since the range of our natural empathy is limited, our caring must be expanded by considerations of justice, by rules and rights (hence the title of Manning's chapter, "Just Caring").

Manning presents arguments to show that we have a general obligation to care and then discusses limitations on this obligation, such as the need to avoid "caring burnout," which limits our ability to care in the future. She concludes by examining how the ethic of caring is related to other ethical theories.

. . . An ethic of caring, as I shall defend it, includes two elements. First is a disposition to care. This is a willingness to receive others, a willingness to give the lucid attention required to appropriately fill the needs of others. In this sense, an ethic of care is contextual; my actions must be guided by this lucid attention. I see this disposition to care as nourished by a spiritual awareness similar to the awareness argued for by proponents of the women's spirituality movement. As Starhawk describes this awareness: "Immanent justice rests on the first principle of magic: All things are interconnected. All is relationship. Perhaps the ultimate ethic of immanence is to choose to make that relationship one of love . . . ; love for all the eternally self-creating world, love of the light and the mysterious darkness, and raging love against all that would diminish the unspeakable beauty of the world."[1]

This disposition to care assumes a commitment to an ideal of caring; the ethically preferred world is one in which creatures are caring and cared for. Its institutions support and sustain caring while simultaneously reducing the need for care by eliminating the poverty, despair, and indifference that create a need for care.

Second, in addition to being sensitive to one's place in the world and to one's general obligation to be a caring person, one is also obligated to care for. (I am following Noddings[2] in using "care for" to indicate caring as expressed in action.) In the paradigm case, caring for involves acting in some appropriate way to respond to the needs of persons and animals, but can also be extended to responding to the needs of communities, values, or objects.

We are obligated to adopt this model of caring, insofar as we can, in our moral deliberations. This qualification refers not only to physical, emotional, and psychological incapacity, but to the larger inability to simply adopt a moral life that is radically different from the way of life we have participated in all our lives. This is a kind of incapacity that we all share. We simply cannot choose to have another's moral sensibilities, even if we are convinced that they are finer in some sense than our own. It doesn't follow that we have no obligations to become more morally sensitive; the point here is that we cannot simply will ourselves to begin to see the moral universe in some radically new way. But even where we can adopt a model of caring, we are morally permitted and sometimes morally obliged to appeal to rules and rights. In Gilligan's idiom,[3] we are required to listen to the voices of both care and justice.

In what follows, I shall first fill in some of the details of this model. Specifically, I shall discuss what it is to care for someone or something and when we are obligated to care for. Next, I shall say something about the role of rules and rights in this model.

I. CARING

I have often wondered if taking a class in moral philosophy was the best way for students to become sensitive to moral concerns. It seemed to me that a better way would be to have students work in soup kitchens or shelters for the homeless. Taking care of my children has made me more open to moral concerns. In taking care of the hungry, homeless, and helpless, we are engaged in caring for. In the standard case, caring for is immediate; it admits of no surrogates. When we directly care for some creature, we are in physical contact. Our eyes meet, our hands touch. However, not every need can be met in this immediate way, and sometimes we must accept surrogates. Not every need can be met by individual action; in such cases, we must seek collective action. But when we can do the caring for directly, we ought to do so, at least some of the time. The need of the other may sometimes require that a particular person do the caring for. If my child needs my attention, I cannot meet this need by sending her to a therapist. Even when the needs of the other do not require our personal attention, we must provide some of the caring for directly in order to develop and sustain our ability to care.

Day-to-day interactions with other persons create a web of reciprocal caring. In these interactions, one is obliged to be a caring person. One is free, to a certain extent, to choose when and how to care for these others. One's choice is limited by one's relationships with these others and by their needs. A pressing need calls up an immediate obligation to care for; roles and responsibilities call up an obligation to respond in a caring manner. In the first case, one is obligated (though this obligation can be limited by a principle of supererogation)[4] to respond; in the second, one can choose, within limits, when and how to care.

A creature in need who is unable to meet this need without help calls for a caring response on my part. This response need not always be direct. Sometimes it is better to organize a political response. (Many, for example, who are confronted on the street by homeless people are unsure about how to respond, convinced that their immediate response will not be enough, and might even be counterproductive.) Certain relationships obligate us to provide direct caring for. When my daughter falls and asks me to "kiss it and make it better," I can't send her to my neighbor for the kiss.

Our roles (for example, as mother, as teacher, as volunteer) put us in particular relationships to others. These roles require and sustain caring. Obligations to infant children and animals involve meeting their basic needs for physical sustenance (food, shelter, clothing, health care) and for companionship and love. Obligations to students are grounded upon roles of teacher and philosopher and the students' psychological needs to discover who they are and how they can live with integrity. Here, one ought to feel a connection with the students but also with teaching and philosophy. But if a student needs another kind of care, we may be obligated to provide it, though not single-handedly. The response depends upon one's ability to care for, one's obligation to care for oneself, and one's sense of the appropriateness of the need and the best way to meet it.

In discharging obligations to care for, which are based on role responsibility, one should be conscious of the need to fill those roles conscientiously. The role of teacher, for example, requires a certain impartiality; the role of mother requires a fierce devotion to each particular child. But one is free, to a certain extent, to choose roles. In adopting or reshaping roles, one should be sensitive to the need to be cared for as well as the capacity to care. In critiquing socially designed and assigned roles, we should aim for roles and divisions of roles that make caring more likely to occur.

Caring for can involve a measure of self-sacrifice. The rescuers of Jessica McClure, the little girl who fell into a well,[5] who went without sleep for days, and the parents of an infant who go without uninterrupted sleep for months, are involved in caring for.

Caring for involves an openness to the one cared for; it requires seeing the real need and satisfying it insofar as we are able. In satisfying it, we should be sensitive not just to the need but to the feelings of those in need.

Caring for does not require feeling any particular emotion toward the one cared for, but an openness to the possibility that some emotional attachment may form in the process of caring for. Nor does it require an ongoing relationship with the one cared for. One may meet the one cared for as stranger, though the caring for will change that.

Obviously, a model of caring along the lines I am defending must include an account of needs. An account of needs must recognize that needs are in some sense social, so identifying needs requires an understanding of biology, psychology, and other relevant social sciences.

Such an account would draw a distinction between subsistence needs and psychological needs. Subsistence needs will usually be needs that must be filled if physical existence is to continue, while psychological needs are needs that must be filled if human flourishing is to occur. Filling subsistence needs does not automatically benefit both the carer and the cared for. Rather, the carer is likely to feel burdened by filling such needs, though the recognition that one has filled such needs often creates a sense of virtue in the carer. Filling psychological needs can often be more fulfilling. It is more likely to be done in a reciprocal relationship, and in such a relationship filling psychological needs requires that both parties share the roles of carer and cared for.

Finally, one need not respond to every need. In choosing how and when to respond, one should consider the seriousness of the need, the benefit to the one needing care of filling this particular need, one's own capacity to fill the need, and the competing needs of others, including oneself, that will be affected by filling this particular need.

II. OBJECTS OF CARE

One can care for persons, animals, ideas, values, institutions, and objects. Later, I will discuss caring for persons and animals in some detail, but here I want to make some brief remarks about caring for ideas, values, institutions, and objects. In caring for ideas, values, and institutions, one devotes oneself to their survival, growth, and flourishing in much the same way as we devote ourselves to the growth and flourishing of a child. In doing so, we are caring for ourselves (insofar as these are our ideas and values) and persons and animals (insofar as these ideas and values support a network of care that embraces persons and animals). In caring for objects, one is devoted primarily to their survival (although some objects, trees, for example, can be said to grow and flourish). The choice of objects of care should reflect our own need to be cared for and our capacity to care. But decisions about what to care for should not depend exclusively upon our own needs and capacities. We should also be sensitive to the needs that summon the obligation to care for. If we understand our obligation to care for as following from the existence of need and helplessness, we should care for ideas, institutions, values, objects, and practices that would diminish such needs. One might argue that we could virtually eliminate the need to care for by creating appropriate institutions, values, and practices and hence undermine our capacity to care. But even in a perfectly just world, children would need care, and people and animals would get sick. Furthermore, human needs include more than needs for physical sustenance. Human needs for companionship and intimacy would exist even in a world free from the horrors of war, homelessness, sickness, and disease. . . .

IV. KNOWING HOW AND WHEN TO CARE

It is not unreasonable to expect an ethic to give us some guidance about how to act, though, as I have argued [earlier in this book], it is unreasonable to expect a calculus. An ethic of care, then, ought to give us some guidance about how and when to care.

Noddings explicitly acknowledges her great debt to Hume,[6] as do I. It seems reasonable then to begin by looking at Hume's answer to this question. Hume saw morality as resting upon a human capacity for sympathetic identification with others.[7] When we see someone suffering, for example, we feel the suffering almost as if it were our own. Our desire to do something to relieve the suffering springs naturally from this empathic response. This natural sentiment is supplanted by an appeal to justice when the sentiment is lacking. Suppose, for example, that the suffering is taking place in a distant place and we are merely aware of it. Our awareness does not excite in us the same empathic response that the immediate perception of the suffering would. What we must do in this case is remind ourselves that although we do not know the sufferer, we can assume that the sufferer shares essential characteristics with someone who is close to us. Since we cannot find any reason to reject the appeal of the one while desiring to respond to the other, we recognize the demands made on us by the absent sufferer. Here what we see is sentiment, colored by reflection. This reflection results in rather general principles, though the principles are seen as derivative of our experience and our sentiments.

Noddings makes a similar move when she distinguishes natural from ethical caring.[8] Natural caring is the caring that one is inclined to do, that springs from ties of affection to others. In the absence of such inclination, one must summon up ethical caring. Both Hume and Noddings are vague about precisely what caring demands in any particular situation. Hume suggests that, at least with respect to general principles, we let experience be our guide; we look for those principles that will make the world more comfortable for the social creatures we are. Noddings rejects an appeal to general principles, but offers instead a strategy for deciding what to do. When natural caring is absent, one should ask oneself what the ideal caring self would do in this situation. She is not suggesting that we appeal to an impartial observer here. Instead, she asks us to remember a situation in which we were ideally caring; we appeal here to our own ideal of caring.

What is implied in both Hume and Noddings is that when sentiment and natural caring do motivate us, we freely follow their dictates. Both of them admit that this capacity can stagnate and die or it can flourish, and, accordingly, we have an obligation to support this capacity in ourselves. Noddings argues that we can only learn to care if we have been cared for as children, and if we have been given opportunities to care. If we have been, then, as adults, we sustain and enrich this capacity by continuing to seek opportunities to care actively for others.

Assuming we are caring persons, both Hume and Noddings suggest that we can trust our impulses; our instincts will guide us toward proper caring, at least when we are caring in the context of a fully present other. There is, of course, an additional requirement that Noddings in particular pays attention to: that we know how the other feels and what the other wants and how the other is likely to be affected by our actions.

Martha Nussbaum combines both sentiment and awareness in her notion of moral imagination. She describes moral imagination as the ability to see "a complex concrete reality in a highly lucid and richly responsive way; . . . taking in what is there, with imagination and feeling."[9]

I agree with Hume, Noddings, and Nussbaum that our interactions with others can and should be guided by our moral imaginations, by our sentiments balanced by our rich understanding of the context. Obviously our responses to strangers will not be guided by the same degree of understanding and sentiment as our responses to those close to us. However, Hume and Noddings are right to suggest that we imagine ourselves in contact with them, that we try to become as aware as we can be of their situations, that we allow this awareness to occasion an emotional response, and that we act, in the full knowledge that our actions, based as they are on insufficient understanding and often less than vibrant sentiment, might not be the right ones. I also agree with Nussbaum and Hume that general principles have a role to play. We appeal to our experiences with intimate others to generate a set of general principles, though we keep in mind that these are merely rules of thumb, based on past experience. But in the absence of understanding and rich emotional response, this might be the only way to guide our actions toward strangers.

V. DEFENSE OF A GENERAL OBLIGATION TO CARE

I am inclined to see the obligation to care as moral bedrock. If it can be said to rest on anything, it rests on our human capacity for caring interaction. Rather than offer a defense of care in terms of appeals to general principles, I would offer a defense of something like general principles in terms of care. Still, for those who find the appeal to general principles more compelling than the obligation to care, I offer a defense of care in terms of such suitably general principles.

The obligation to respond as carer when appropriate can be defended on three grounds. The first is the need. Here one might appeal to Peter Singer's principle, "If it is in our power to prevent something very bad happening without thereby sacrificing anything of comparable moral significance, we ought to do it."[10]

The second is the recognition that human relationships require a continuous kind of caring. This caring involves three components: being receptive to the other, being accepting of the other, and being on call for the other when he/she is in need.[11] Unless we want to do away with human relationships, we must be open to the demands of caring that such relationships require. But caring in human relationships is, as human relationships are, reciprocal.

The third defense is that we cannot develop and sustain the ability to care unless we do some active caring. This is an empirical claim, and we must look both to social science and to our own experience in evaluating it, but there is an obvious way in which caring for enhances our ability to care. When we make the real attempt to care for, we must understand the needs of the one cared for. We must also see how that one wants the needs to be addressed. This ability to notice needs and wants and to empathize as well as sympathize is developed through caring. Of course, one might ask here why one should want to develop this capacity to care. It seems to me that the right response is to point out that human lives devoid of caring impulses and responses would be nasty, brutish, short, and lonely.[12]

Nel Noddings offers a different defense of the general obligation to care, one which seems to offer some problematic consequences. Noddings's theory is that morality essentially involves one obligation: the obligation to care. Caring involves two elements, natural caring and ethical caring. Natural caring requires engrossment in the other, "seeing the other's reality as possible for me,"[13] and the motivation to act "based on recognition of the other's wants and desires and ... the objective elements of his problematic situation."[14] Ethical caring involves summoning natural caring by remembering "our most caring and tender moments" and recognizing that these moments represent our best self. Ethical caring can only be achieved in situations where dynamic, mutual relationships are possible.

This analysis provides, according to Noddings, an analysis of obligation.

> I can be obligated to P if: (1) there exists or is potential a relation between P and me; (2) there exists the dynamic potential for growth in relation, including the potential for increased reciprocity and mutuality.

We are only obligated when these conditions obtain because, in her view, it is only under these conditions that caring can occur. Noddings denies that "universal caring" is a possibility and admits to the following three consequences of her analysis. First, "I am not obligated to starving children in Africa." Her argument for this is not exactly clear, but it appears that she would want to say that my ongoing relationships confer obligations that are primary. She says that fulfilling obligations to the starving children in Africa would require me to "abandon my obligations" to those to whom I am already related. Second, we have no obligations to animals because there is no possibility for genuine mutuality from animals. Third, the life of one caring (the ethically preferred life for all according to Noddings) must, in some sense, be a private life. "Her public life is limited by her insistence upon meeting the other as one caring. . . . When . . . reaching out destroys or drastically reduces her actual caring, she retreats and renews her contact with those who address her."

I want to take issue with each of these consequences, but I don't think that by doing so I am rejecting Noddings's account. Indeed, I am puzzled about why Noddings thought she was committed to them. It seems to me that a sympathetic reading of her could justify the exactly opposite conclusions.

Noddings needn't grant that helping the starving in Africa requires abandoning obligations to those to whom one is related. However, I suspect that she would still want to insist that I am not obligated to the starving in Africa. There is no present relationship between me and the starving children in Africa, nor is it likely that such a relationship will begin in the future. She gives us the example of a missionary who decides to go to Africa to help the starving. She says that this person might well have such obligations because this person will begin to have such relationships.

I don't agree that we have no obligations to the starving in Africa, in part because I don't accept Noddings's assumption about the primacy of current obligations. It seems to me that we have self-interested reasons for wanting to meet the obligations to those with whom we share a relationship. First, the possibility and hence the expectation of reciprocity gives us a self-interested reason for meeting these obligations first. Second, if we are truly "engrossed" by the persons for whom we care, we will receive some pleasure in meeting these obligations. I don't want to argue that no moral reasons can be offered where reasons of self-interest naturally obtain, but I do think that we should be suspicious of ethical theories that restrict our obligations to those duties that we have a self-interested reason to perform.

Noddings might have argued that we can have mutually reciprocal relationships with animals, or she might have taken the same stance with regard to animals that she takes with regard to abortion. In the latter case, she argues that the prospective mother can grant "sanctity" to the first-trimester fetus by viewing it as a "product of love between a man deeply cared for and me," and, as such, "joined to others through formal chains of caring." Because the caring exists for this mother, abortion would be immoral. If the mother chooses not to sanctify the fetus, no such relationship exists in the first trimester, and hence abortion would not be immoral. As the fetus begins to develop, it becomes "more nearly capable of response as cared for." At this point the relationship begins to exist and grow, and abortion is again immoral. It sounds like she is saying that if I choose to view myself as involved in a relationship with a fetus, then I have obligations toward it, even if it is not now capable of having a mutually reciprocal relationship with me. Why can't I then choose to see myself as involved in a relationship with animals, or at least with some animals? If I choose to see the animal this way, then I do have an obligation toward the animal. But this is not a very satisfactory consequence for a defender of animal rights; according to this view, if I don't choose to view myself as in a relationship with animals, I am free to treat them any way I want. I would be inclined to say that if we do have obligations toward animals—and I think we do—it is in virtue of qualities that the animals possess, for example the ability to suffer, and not in virtue of our willingness to recognize such qualities.

The claim that one must withdraw from the public sphere and retreat to the private when neglecting those to whom one is already related strikes me as a classic defense of the stereotypical role of the housewife. It tends to reinforce both self-interest and moral cowardice in the face of injustice, inequality, and suffering outside our own little worlds.

What is objectionable about all these consequences is the implication that one can choose all one's obligations. While obligations are created through voluntary commitments, this does not exhaust the possibilities. Further, Noddings's desire to thus limit our obligations is incompatible with the distinction she makes between natural and ethical caring. If one is obligated to do some ethical caring, and this involves calling upon one's ideal caring self, won't this ideal caring self feel some obligation toward animals and starving children in Africa? I'm convinced that it would, for much the same reasons that Hume thinks that the demands of justice will assert themselves after some reflection. We can come to recognize that the starving children in Africa share crucial characteristics with the children we know and love; we can see that animals share important characteristics as well. Surely, our ideal caring selves will not ignore this.

VI. LIMITATIONS ON OBLIGATIONS TO CARE

I don't think that we are obligated to be like Mother Teresa,[15] who cares for continuously. But how are we to limit our obligation to care? One strategy for limiting our obligation to care for focuses on the defenses of this obligation. First, we have a prima facie obligation[16] to care for when we come across a creature in need who is unable to meet that need without help, when our caring is called upon as a part of a reciprocal relationship, or when caring is indicated as part of our role responsibility. Actual obligations rest upon the seriousness of the need, the assessment of the appropriateness of filling the need, and the ability to do something about filling it. But we must also recognize that we are persons who must be cared for and who deserve such care. The continuous caring for required to respond to needs for physical sustenance is, for most of us, incompatible with caring for ourselves. But not all caring for involves responding to physical needs. The caring for required to sustain relationships, which is usually reciprocal, can be a source of great strength to the person doing the caring for. And finally, allowing ourselves to suffer caring burnout also diminishes our ability to care for others in the future. I don't mean to argue that caring for requires no sacrifice. Indeed, where the need is great and the ability to meet it sufficient, we are required to sacrifice. But one is not required to adopt this as a form of life.

The obligation to care for is not an all-or-nothing thing. Being unable to care for now does not eliminate the possibility that one may be obligated to meet this need later. This is a general point about obligations. I might owe someone money and be unable to pay it back now, through no fault of my own. If I later come into a windfall, I am obligated to pay the money back then. In addition, there is no one right way to care for. Our assessment of the appropriateness of the need, our ability to meet the need, and our sense of the most successful way of doing so provide some guidance here. Perhaps immediate caring for is the best way to meet a need in one case, and cooperative political activity the most successful way of meeting other needs. I would want to leave these kinds of choices up to the agent. . . .

VIII. CARING AND OTHER ETHICAL THEORIES

As I argued in [an earlier chapter of this book], caring as I describe it is not an ethical theory in any full-blown sense. I have just now argued that it is not an ethical theory in the sense of a set of rules to be rigidly applied. Still, one might wonder if it could be compared to virtue theory,[17] or to what I call perspectivism.

Hume's influence is broad and obvious. I have adopted both his picture of what a moral philosophy should be (the art of suggesting and testing moral strategies in light of our real world experience) and his conviction that humans have a capacity for care and that this capacity explains the force morality has for humans (and perhaps other animals).

One might think that I am simply defending virtue ethics, but I don't believe so. Virtue ethics requires that the virtue not enter into the deliberations of the virtuous person: The brave person does not do an act because it is the act that would be chosen by a brave person; she does it because she thinks it is the right thing to do and because she is more interested in the rightness of the act than the personal consequences of doing so. In Noddings's and my view, caring does and must enter into the deliberation of the caring person. The caring person must sometimes ask herself what her ideal caring self would do in the situation. Still, an ethic of care has much in common with virtue theory. They both emphasize the importance of habit and inclination. Neither pretends to provide a calculus for moral decision making; rather they insist that the context coupled with the character of the actor and some general rules of thumb will provide all the cues.

Nietzsche[18] offers a model that is similar in some respects to an ethic of care. Both Nietzsche and an ethic of care suggest that we answer questions about how to live our lives by taking a particular perspective. He advocates taking an "eternal recurrence" perspective. He invites us to imagine living our lives over and over again, eternally. We can then ask ourselves, "If I were to live this moment over, eternally, what would I have wanted to do?" An ethic of care invites us to take the perspective of our ideal caring selves. Both views share with the virtue tradition the belief that the ideal moral agent should internalize this perspective to a certain extent so that one's actions flow naturally from a settled disposition. Nietzsche's view is broader than an ethic of care because he is concerned with how we live our lives and not just how we make moral decisions.

The next ethic I wish to consider is the land ethic, first described by Aldo Leopold and recently elaborated and defended by J. Baird Callicott.[19] As Leopold puts it: "A thing is right when it tends to preserve the integrity, stability, and beauty of the biotic community. It is wrong when it tends otherwise."[20] An ethic of care is similar to a land ethic in two ways. First, they are both holistic ethics; second, they share a commitment to the sacredness of the natural world.

A land ethic is holistic in the following sense: The good of any part is defined in terms of the good of the whole. Callicott draws many implications from this view, one being that right now humans are a blight upon the earth because they are squeezing out other species. The land ethic's commitment to the sacredness of the natural world is shown by this definition of the good in terms of what is good for the whole, the whole being the natural world.

An ethic of care is holistic in two ways. First, it recognizes that we are embedded in connections of care and that our self-identity is, in large part, a function of our role in these complex interconnections. In this sense, we see ourselves as part of a larger whole, and inseparable from this whole. An ethic of care, as I conceive it, is holistic in a larger sense as well. It assumes an underlying picture of the earth as one body, and of ourselves as part of this body. It sees an attitude of awe as the appropriate response to the recognition that we are part of this sacred body. Not every version of an ethic of care need be holistic in this second sense. Noddings, for example, is not committed to this. But I think it allows us to escape from the parochialism of an ethic of care that is grounded only in human attachments.

So, while both ethics are holistic, they are holistic in different ways. There is a second way in which they differ. A land ethic, as Callicott describes it, is indifferent to the value that humans put on other humans and certain animals.

Both a land ethic and an ethic of care are ethics for and from the perspective of humans. In this sense, neither can escape from human psychology. If an ethic is seen as providing guidance for living a good human life, then we must recognize important features of human psychology—the attachments of humans to other humans and certain animals, for example. While Callicott tries to ignore this, an ethic of care takes it as central.

IX. CONCLUSION

An ethic of care has many advantages. It allows us to reconceptualize, and thereby better understand, many moral quandaries, such as that of the porcupine and the moles.[21] It strikes many, and women in particular, as a truer picture of their own moral intuitions. It assumes a theory of human nature that is an improvement upon abstract individualism. It generates a theory of moral education that focuses on the enhancement of the capacity to care. Finally, and most importantly, it might, if widely adopted, make the world a better place.

NOTES

1. Starhawk, *Dreaming the Dark: Magic, Sex and Politics* (Boston: Beacon Press, 1982), p. 44. [R. C. MANNING]
2. Nel Noddings, *Caring: A Feminine Approach to Ethics and Moral Education* (Berkeley: University of California Press, 1984). [R. C. MANNING]
3. Carol Gilligan, *In a Different Voice: Psychological Theory and Women's Development* (Cambridge, Mass.: Harvard University Press, 1982). [R. C. MANNING]
4. *supererogation:* doing more than required by duty or obligation. [D. C. ABEL]
5. In 1987 the baby Jessica McClure was rescued after being trapped for nearly sixty hours in a 22-foot well into which she had fallen in Midland, Texas. [D. C. ABEL]
6. David Hume (1711–1776) was a Scottish philosopher and historian; for a biography, see p. 47. [D. C. ABEL]
7. David Hume, *An Enquiry Concerning the Principles of Morals,* ed. L. A. Selby-Bigge, 2nd ed. (Oxford, England: Clarendon Press, 1962), Section 3; *A Treatise of Human Nature,* ed. L. A. Selby-Bigge (Oxford, England: Oxford University Press, 1964), Part III, Section 1. [R. C. MANNING]
8. Nel Noddings, *Caring,* Chapter 4. [R. C. MANNING]

9. Martha Nussbaum, "'Finely Aware and Richly Responsible': Literature and the Moral Imagination," *The Journal of Philosophy* 82 (October 1985): 521. [R. C. MANNING]

10. Peter Singer, *Practical Ethics* (Cambridge, England: Cambridge University Press, 1979), p. 168. [R. C. MANNING]

11. This analysis is from Milton Mayeroff, *On Caring* (New York: Harper & Row, 1971). [R. C. MANNING]

12. Manning refers here to the famous remark by the English philosopher Thomas Hobbes (1588–1679) that before the formation of society and government, human life was "solitary, poor, nasty, brutish, and short" (*Leviathan*, Part I, Chapter XIII). For a biography of Hobbes, see p. 441 of this book; the quotation is on p. 443. [D. C. ABEL]

13. Noddings, *Caring*, p. 14. [R. C. MANNING]

14. Ibid., p. 24. The remaining passages from *Caring* cited in Section V are taken from pp. 86–89. [R. C. MANNING]

15. Mother Teresa (1910–1997) was an Albanian-born Roman Catholic nun who devoted her life to caring for the poor and dying in India. [D. C. ABEL]

16. *prima facie obligation:* an obligation that holds unless it is overridden by another, stronger obligation. [D. C. ABEL]

17. *virtue theory:* ethical theory in which the virtue of the agent is the primary factor in morality, rather than the consequences of actions or an intrinsic quality of actions (also called *virtue ethics*). [D. C. ABEL]

18. Friedrich Nietzsche (1844–1900) was a German philosopher; for a biography, see p. 384. [D. C. ABEL]

19. J. Baird Callicott, *In Defense of the Land Ethic* (Albany: State University of New York Press, 1989). [R. C. MANNING]

20. Aldo Leopold, *A Sand County Almanac* (New York: Oxford University Press, 1949), pp. 224–25. [R. C. MANNING]

21. In the story of the porcupine and the moles, a family of moles allows a porcupine to move into their cave for the winter. But the cave is small, and when the porcupine moves around, his quills scratch the moles. The moles ask the porcupine to leave, but he refuses. [D. C. ABEL]

CHAPTER 7

Political and Social Philosophy

Most of us would agree that we have a certain obligation to obey the laws passed by our government. But what gives government the authority to tell us what to do? And what is the extent of its authority? Most of us would assert that individuals have certain fundamental rights that no government has the authority to violate. But what are these rights and where do they come from? Does *society* have rights also? Does it have the right to demand that I sacrifice my self-interest for the good of society as a whole? If I live in a society, am I obliged to obey *all* its laws, or only those that I consider just? What standard can I use to determine whether a law—or a society—is just or not? These are some of the questions explored by political and social philosophy.

Political philosophy and social philosophy are so closely related that they are sometimes considered a single field. Strictly speaking, however, political philosophy is a part of social philosophy. Social philosophy deals with any group of "associates" (*socii* in Latin, the root of the word "social"), whereas political philosophy deals with one specific kind of association, namely the state (*polis* in Greek, the root of the word "political"). Social and political matters are, of course, studied by sociologists and political scientists as well as by philosophers. The main difference is that sociologists and political scientists focus on the actual structure and workings of social and political institutions; social and political philosophers theorize about the way social and political institutions *should* be structured and about the nature and grounds of authority, justice, and rights.

This chapter contains nine readings, organized chronologically. In the first reading, Plato (expressing his views in a dialogue between Socrates and Crito) maintains that by living in a society and accepting its benefits we enter into a tacit agreement to obey its laws, and that we are obligated to keep our agreement. In the next reading, Thomas Hobbes argues that human beings originally lived in a "state of nature" in which there was no society and no government. Because life in the state of nature was filled with fear and insecurity, human beings formed a "social contract" by which they transferred their rights to a common power and gave this "leviathan" (Hobbes's reference is to a biblical sea monster) absolute power to enforce the terms of the contract. John Locke, like Hobbes, maintains that political society began when human beings left the state of nature by initiating a social contract. However, the state of nature he depicts is less bleak than Hobbes's, and the government established by the social contract has limited rather than absolute authority.

Mary Wollstonecraft argues that society treats women unjustly by denying their rationality and failing to provide them with the same kind of education that men receive— an education that develops one's rational abilities and thereby enables one to reach one's full human potential. Karl Marx and Friedrich Engels contend that eventually there will be no need for government. The class struggle between capitalists (owners of the means of production) and workers will result in the victory of the workers. After capitalism has been destroyed and power has shifted temporarily from the capitalists to the workers, the equality of all people will be achieved, human fulfillment will be possible, and political power will be unnecessary. John Stuart Mill argues that the only legitimate reason for government to exercise power over an individual is to prevent that person from harming others; individuals should have the liberty to do anything they wish, provided others are not harmed.

Martin Luther King, Jr., defends his use of nonviolent protest as a way to help African-Americans gain the civil rights that American society for centuries refused to extend to them. He argues that nonviolent protest can be justified even when it is illegal: There is no obligation to obey an unjust law, and even a *just* law may be violated if it is used for unjust purposes. John Rawls presents a general theory of social justice: A society will be just if each person has the greatest liberty compatible with a similar liberty for others, and if social and economic inequalities are arranged in a way likely to work to everyone's advantage. In the final reading, Joseph Raz explores the nature and necessity of multiculturalism in the contemporary world. He suggests several political policies that would promote the plurality of cultural groups.

Crito

Plato

A biography of Plato appears on p. 4.

Our reading is the *Crito,* a conversation between Socrates and his longtime friend Crito. The scene is Socrates' prison cell: He has been sentenced to death and will be executed as soon as the Athenian ship returns from its religious expedition to the island of Delos. Crito, who has been regularly visiting Socrates in prison, brings the news that the ship has been sighted and will soon arrive. Crito urges Socrates, one last time, to escape and save his life; all the arrangements have been made. Since Socrates seems unwilling to escape, despite his innocence of the charges for which he was condemned, Crito gives Socrates several reasons for escaping. Socrates replies that he will escape only if it would be moral to do so. He then states two moral principles that he and Crito have long agreed are valid: One should never willingly wrong or mistreat others, even if wronged or mistreated by them, and one should fulfill one's just agreements.

To determine whether his escape would violate these moral principles, Socrates imagines the laws of Athens addressing him. Their speech convinces Socrates that to escape would be wrong because Socrates would be breaking both principles. First, Socrates would be mistreating another, namely the laws. The laws, moreover, had benefited Socrates and had never mistreated him (at his trial, it was the *jurors* who were unjust, not the laws). Second, Socrates would be breaking a just agreement—his agreement to abide by the laws of Athens. Socrates argues that when we live in a society and accept its benefits, we enter into a tacit agreement to obey its laws and are obligated to keep our agreement.

Socrates' conversation with Crito not only sets forth his theory of political obligation; it also illustrates his conviction that philosophy requires one to act in accordance with one's principles, no matter what the cost. To violate a moral principle is to harm one's soul, and no bodily benefit gained by an unjust action can outweigh the damage that injustice does to one's soul.

SOCRATES: Why have you come so early, Crito? Or is it not still early?
CRITO: It certainly is.
SOCRATES: How early?
CRITO: Early dawn.
SOCRATES: I am surprised that the warder was willing to listen to you.
CRITO: He is quite friendly to me by now, Socrates. I have been here often and I have given him something.
SOCRATES: Have you just come, or have you been here for some time?
CRITO: A fair time.
SOCRATES: Then why did you not wake me right away but sit there in silence?
CRITO: By Zeus no, Socrates. I wish I myself were not in distress and awake so long. I have been surprised to see you so peacefully asleep. It was on purpose that I did not wake you, so that you should spend your time most agreeably. Often in the past throughout my life, I have considered the way you live happily, and especially so now that you bear your present misfortune so easily and lightly.

SOCRATES: It would not be fitting at my age to resent the fact that I must die now.

CRITO: Other men of your age are caught in such misfortunes, but their age does not prevent them resenting their fate.

SOCRATES: That is so. Why have you come so early?

CRITO: I bring bad news, Socrates—not for you, apparently, but for me and all your friends the news is bad and hard to bear. Indeed, I would count it among the hardest.

SOCRATES: What is it? Or has the ship arrived from Delos, at the arrival of which I must die?[1]

CRITO: It has not arrived yet, but it will, I believe, arrive today, according to a message some men brought from Sunium,[2] where they left the ship. This makes it obvious that it will come today, and that your life must end tomorrow.

SOCRATES: May it be for the best. If it so please the gods, so be it. However, I do not think it will arrive today.

CRITO: What indication have you of this?

SOCRATES: I will tell you. I must die the day after the ship arrives.

CRITO: That is what those in authority say.

SOCRATES: Then I do not think it will arrive on this coming day, but on the next. I take as witness of this a dream I had a little earlier during this night. It looks as if it was the right time for you not to wake me.

CRITO: What was your dream?

SOCRATES: I thought that a beautiful and comely woman dressed in white approached me. She called me and said: "Socrates, may you arrive at fertile Phthia on the third day."[3]

CRITO: A strange dream, Socrates.

SOCRATES: But it seems clear enough to me, Crito.

CRITO: Too clear it seems, my dear Socrates, but listen to me even now and be saved. If you die, it will not be a single misfortune for me. Not only will I be deprived of a friend, the like of whom I shall never find again, but many people who do not know you or me very well will think that I could have saved you if I were willing to spend money, but that I did not care to do so. Surely there can be no worse reputation than to be thought to value money more highly than one's friends, for the majority will not believe that you yourself were not willing to leave prison while we were eager for you to do so.

SOCRATES: My good Crito, why should we care so much for what the majority think? The most reasonable people, to whom one should pay more attention, will believe that things were done as they were done.

CRITO: You see, Socrates, that one must also pay attention to the opinion of the majority. Your present situation makes clear that the majority can inflict not the least but pretty well the greatest evils if one is slandered among them.

SOCRATES: [I wish] that the majority could inflict the greatest evils, for they would then be capable of the greatest good, and that would be fine, but now they cannot do either. They cannot make a man either wise or foolish, but they inflict things haphazardly.

CRITO: That may be so. But tell me this, Socrates, are you anticipating that I and your other friends would have trouble with the informers if you escape from here, as having stolen you away, and that we should be compelled to lose all our property or pay heavy fines and suffer other punishment besides? If you have any such fear, forget it. We would be justified in running this risk to save you, and worse, if necessary. Do follow my advice, and do not act differently.

SOCRATES: I do have these things in mind, Crito, and also many others.

CRITO: Have no such fear. It is not much money that some people require to save you and get you out of here. Further, do you not see that those informers are cheap, and that not much money would be needed to deal with them? My money is available and is, I think, sufficient. If, because of your affection for me, you feel you should not spend any of mine, there are those strangers here ready to spend money. One of them, Simmias the Theban, has brought enough for this very purpose—Cebes, too, and a good many others. So, as I say, do not let this fear make you hesitate to save yourself, nor let what you said in court trouble you, that you would not know what to do with yourself if you left Athens, for you would be welcomed in many places to which you might go. If you want to go to Thessaly, I have friends there who will greatly appreciate you and keep you safe, so that no one in Thessaly will harm you.

Besides, Socrates, I do not think that what you are doing is just, to give up your life when you can save it, and to hasten your fate as your enemies would hasten it, and indeed have hastened it in their wish to destroy you. Moreover, I think you are betraying your sons by going away and leaving them, when you could bring them up and educate them. You thus show no concern for what their fate may be. They will probably have the usual fate of orphans. Either one should not have children, or one should share with them to the end the toil of upbringing and education. You seem to me to choose the easiest path, whereas one should choose the path that a good and courageous man would choose, particularly when one claims throughout one's life to care for virtue.

I feel ashamed on your behalf and on behalf of us, your friends, lest all that has happened to you be thought due to cowardice on our part: the fact that your trial came to court when it need not have done so, the handling of the trial itself, and now this absurd ending which will be thought to have got beyond our control through some cowardice and unmanliness on our part, since we did not save you, or you save yourself, when it was possible and could be done if we had been of the slightest use. Consider, Socrates, whether this is not only evil but shameful, both for you and for us. Take counsel with yourself, or rather the time for counsel is past and the decision should have been taken, and there is no further opportunity, for this whole business must be ended tonight. If we delay now, then it will no longer be possible—it will be too late. Let me persuade you on every count, Socrates, and do not act otherwise.

SOCRATES: My dear Crito, your eagerness is worth much if it should have some right aim; if not, then the greater your keenness the more difficult it is to deal with. We must therefore examine whether we *should* act in this way or not, as not only now but at all times I am the kind of man who listens to nothing within me but the argument that on reflection seems best to me. I cannot, now that this fate has come upon me, discard the arguments I used; they seem to me much the same. I value and respect the same principles as before, and if we have no better arguments to bring up at this moment, be sure that I shall not agree with you, not even if the power of the majority were to frighten us with more bogeys, as if we were children, with threats of incarcerations and executions and confiscation of property. How should we examine this matter most reasonably? Would it be by taking up first your argument about the opinions of men, whether it is sound in every case that one should pay attention to some opinions, but not to others? Or was that well-spoken *before* the necessity to die came upon me, but *now* it is clear that this was said in vain for the sake of argument—that it was in truth play and nonsense? I am eager to examine together with you, Crito, whether this argument will appear in any way different to me in my present circumstances, or whether it remains the same, whether we are to abandon it or believe it. It was said on every occasion by those who thought they were speaking sensibly, as I have just now been speaking, that one should greatly value some people's opinions, but not others. Does that seem to you a sound statement?

You, as far as a human being can tell, are exempt from the likelihood of dying tomorrow, so the present misfortune is not likely to lead you astray. Consider then, do you not think it a sound statement that one must not value all the opinions of men, but some and not others, nor the opinions of all men, but those of some and not of others? What do you say? Is this not well said?

CRITO: It is.

SOCRATES: One should value the good opinions, and not the bad ones?

CRITO: Yes.

SOCRATES: The good opinions are those of wise men, the bad ones those of foolish men?

CRITO: Of course.

SOCRATES: Come then, what of statements such as this: Should a man professionally engaged in physical training pay attention to the praise and blame and opinion of any man, or to those of one man only, namely a doctor or trainer?

CRITO: To those of one only.

SOCRATES: He should therefore fear the blame and welcome the praise of that one man, and not those of the many?

CRITO: Obviously.

SOCRATES: He must then act and exercise, eat and drink in the way the one, the trainer and the one who knows, thinks right, not all the others?

CRITO: That is so.

SOCRATES: Very well. And if he disobeys the one and disregards his opinion and his praises, while valuing those of the many who have no knowledge, will he not suffer harm?

CRITO: Of course.

SOCRATES: What is that harm, where does it tend, and what part of the man who disobeys does it affect?

CRITO: Obviously the harm is to his body, which it ruins.

SOCRATES: Well said. So with other matters, not to enumerate them all, and certainly with actions just and unjust, shameful and beautiful, good and bad, about which we are now deliberating, should we follow the opinion of the many and fear it, or that of the one, if there is one who has knowledge of these things and before whom we feel fear and shame more than before all the others? If we do not follow his directions, we shall harm and corrupt that part of ourselves that is improved by just actions and destroyed by unjust actions. Or is there nothing in this?

CRITO: I think there certainly is, Socrates.

SOCRATES: Come now, if we ruin that which is improved by health and corrupted by disease by not following the opinions of those who know, is life worth living for us when that is ruined? And that is the body, is it not?

CRITO: Yes.

SOCRATES: And is life worth living with a body that is corrupted and in bad condition?

CRITO: In no way.

SOCRATES: And is life worth living for us with that part of us corrupted that unjust action harms and just action benefits? Or do we think that part of us, whatever it is, that is concerned with justice and injustice, is inferior to the body?

CRITO: Not at all.

SOCRATES: It is more valuable?

CRITO: Much more.

SOCRATES: We should not then think so much of what the majority will say about us, but what he will say who understands justice and injustice (the one, that is), and what the truth itself will say. So that, in the first place, you were wrong to believe that we should care for the opinion of the many about what is just, beautiful, good, and their opposites. "But," someone might say, "the many are able to put us to death."

CRITO: That too is obvious, Socrates, and someone might well say so.

SOCRATES: And, my admirable friend, that argument that we have gone through remains, I think, as before. Examine the following statement in turn as to whether it stays the same or not, that the most important thing is not life, but the good life.

CRITO: It stays the same.

SOCRATES: And that the good life, the beautiful life, and the just life are the same—does that still hold, or not?

CRITO: It does hold.

SOCRATES: As we have agreed so far, we must examine next whether it is just for me to try to get out of here when the Athenians have not acquitted me. If it is seen to be just, we will try to do so; if it is not, we will abandon the idea. As for those questions you raise about money, reputation, and the upbringing of children, Crito, those considerations in truth belong to those people who easily put men to death and would bring them to life again if they could, without thinking—I mean the majority of men. For us, however, since our argument leads to this, the only valid consideration, as we were saying just now, is whether we should be acting rightly in giving money and gratitude to those who will lead me out of here, and acting rightly ourselves in helping with the escape, or whether in truth we shall do wrong in doing all this. If it appears that we shall be acting unjustly, then we have no need at all to take into account whether we shall have to die if we stay here and keep quiet, or suffer in another way, rather than do wrong.

CRITO: I think you put that beautifully, Socrates, but see what we should do.

SOCRATES: Let us examine the question together, my dear friend, and if you can make any objection while I am speaking, make it and I will listen to you, but if you have no objection to make, my dear Crito, then stop now from saying the same thing so often, that I must leave here against the will of the Athenians. I think it important to persuade you before I act, and not to act against your wishes. See whether the start of our inquiry is adequately stated, and try to answer what I ask you in the way you think best.

CRITO: I shall try.

SOCRATES: Do we say that one must never in any way do wrong willingly, or must one do wrong in one way and not in another? Is to do wrong never good or admirable, as we have agreed in the past, or have all these former agreements been washed out during the last few days? Have we at our age failed to notice for some time that in our serious discussions we were no different from children? Above all, is the truth such as we used to say it was, whether the majority agree or not, and whether we must still suffer worse things than we do now or will be treated more gently, that nonetheless, wrongdoing or injustice is in every way harmful and shameful to the wrongdoer? Do we say so or not?

CRITO: We do.

SOCRATES: So one must never do wrong.

CRITO: Certainly not.

SOCRATES: Nor must one, when wronged, inflict wrong in return, as the majority believe, since one must never do wrong.

CRITO: That seems to be the case.

SOCRATES: Come now, should one mistreat anyone or not, Crito?

CRITO: One must never do so.

SOCRATES: Well then, if one is oneself mistreated, is it right, as the majority say, to mistreat in return, or is it not?

CRITO: It is never right.

SOCRATES: Mistreating people is no different from wrongdoing.

CRITO: That is true.

SOCRATES: One should never do wrong in return, nor mistreat any man, no matter how one has been mistreated by him. And Crito, see that you do not agree to this, contrary to your belief. For I know that only a few people hold this view or will hold it, and there is no common ground between those who hold this view and those who do not, but they inevitably despise each other's views. So then consider very carefully whether we have this view in common, and whether you agree, and let this be the basis of our deliberation: that neither to do wrong nor to return a wrong is ever right, nor is bad treatment in return for bad treatment. Or do you disagree and do not share this view as a basis for discussion? I have held it for a long time and still hold it now, but if you think otherwise, tell me now. If, however, you stick to our former opinion, then listen to the next point.

CRITO: I stick to it and agree with you. So say on.

SOCRATES: Then I state the next point, or rather I ask you: When one has come to an agreement that is just with someone, should one fulfill it or cheat on it?

CRITO: One should fulfill it.

SOCRATES: See what follows from this: If we leave here without the city's permission, are we mistreating people whom we should least mistreat? And are we sticking to a just agreement, or not?

CRITO: I cannot answer your question, Socrates. I do not know.

SOCRATES: Look at it this way. If, as we were planning to run away from here, or whatever one should call it, the laws and the state came and confronted us and asked: "Tell me, Socrates, what are you intending to do? Do you not by this action you are attempting intend to destroy us, the laws, and indeed the whole city, as far as you are concerned? Or do you think it possible for a city not to be destroyed if the verdicts of its courts have no force but are nullified and set at naught by private individuals?" What shall we answer to this and other such arguments? For many things could be said, especially by an orator on behalf of this law we are destroying, which orders that the judgments of the courts shall be carried out. Shall we say in answer, "The city wronged me, and its decision was not right." Shall we say that, or what?

CRITO: Yes, by Zeus, Socrates, that is our answer.

SOCRATES: Then what if the laws said: "Was that the agreement between us, Socrates, or was it to respect the judgments that the city came to?" And if we wondered at their words, they would perhaps add: "Socrates, do not wonder at what we say but answer, since you are accustomed to proceed by question and answer. Come now, what accusation do you bring against us and the city, that you should try to destroy us? Did we not, first, bring you to birth, and was it not through us that your father married your mother and begot you? Tell us, do you find anything to criticize in those of us who are concerned with marriage?" And I would say that I do not criticize them. "Or in those of us concerned with the nurture of babies and the education that you too received? Were those assigned to that subject not right to instruct your father to educate you in the arts and in physical culture?" And I would say that they were right. "Very well," they would continue, "and after you were born and nurtured and educated, could you, in the first place, deny that you are our offspring and servant, both you and your forefathers? If that is so, do you think that we are on an equal footing as regards the right, and that whatever we do to you it is right for you to do to us? You were not on an equal footing with your father as regards the right, nor with your master if you had one, so as to retaliate for anything they did to you, to revile them if they reviled you, to beat them if they beat you, and so with many other things. Do you think you have this right to retaliation against your country and its laws? That if we undertake to destroy you and think it right to do so, you can undertake to destroy us, as far as you can, in return? And will you say that you are right to do so, you who truly care for virtue? Is your wisdom such as not to realize that your country is to be honored more than your mother, your father and all your ancestors, that it is more to be revered and more sacred, and that it counts for more among the gods and sensible men, that you must worship it, yield to it, and placate its anger more than your father's? You must either persuade it or obey its orders, and endure in silence whatever it instructs you to endure, whether blows or bonds; and if it leads you into war to be wounded or killed, you must obey. To do so is right, and one must not give way or retreat or leave one's post, but both in war and in courts and everywhere else, one must obey the commands of one's city and country, or persuade it as to the nature of justice. It is impious to bring violence to bear against your mother or father; it is much more so to use it against your country." What shall we say in reply, Crito, that the laws speak the truth, or not?

CRITO: I think they do.

SOCRATES: "Reflect now, Socrates" the laws might say, "that if what we say is true, you are not treating us rightly by planning to do what you are planning. We have given you birth, nurtured you, educated you, we have given you and all other citizens a share of all the good things we could. Even so, we give every Athenian the opportunity, once arrived at voting age and having observed the affairs of the city and us the laws, that if we do not please him, he can take his possessions and go wherever he pleases. Not one of our laws raises any obstacle or forbids it, if you are not satisfied with us or the city, if one of you wants to go and live in a colony or wants to go anywhere else and keep his property. We say, however, that whoever of you remains, when he sees how we conduct our trials and manage the city in other ways, has in fact come to an agreement with us to obey our instructions. We say that the one who disobeys does wrong in three ways, because in us he disobeys his parents, also those who brought him up, and because, in spite of his agreement, he neither obeys us nor, if we do something wrong, does he try to persuade us to do better. Yet we only propose things; we do not issue savage commands to do whatever we order. We give two alternatives, either to persuade us or to do what we say. He [who disobeys] does neither. We do say that you too, Socrates, are open to those charges if you do what you have in mind. You would be among, not the least, but the most guilty of the Athenians."

If I should say "Why so?," they might well be right to upbraid me and say that I am among the Athenians who most definitely came to that agreement with them. They might well say: "Socrates, we have convincing proofs that we and the city were congenial to you. You would not have dwelled here most consistently of all the Athenians if the city had not been exceedingly pleasing to you. You have never left the city, even to see a festival, nor for any other reason except military service; you have never gone to stay in any other city, as people do; you have had no desire to know another city or other laws. We and our city satisfied you. So decisively did you choose us and agree to be a citizen under us. Also, you have had children in this city, thus showing that it was congenial to you. Then at your trial you could have assessed your penalty at exile if you wished, and you are now attempting to do against the city's wishes what you could then have done with her consent. Then you prided yourself that you did not resent death, but you chose, as you said, death in preference to exile. Now, however, those words do not make you ashamed, and you pay no heed to us, the laws, as you plan to destroy us, and you act like the meanest type of slave by trying to run away, contrary to your commitments and your agreement to live as a citizen under us. First then, answer us on this very point, whether we speak the truth when we say that you agreed, not only in words but by your deeds, to live in accordance with us." What are we to say to that, Crito? Must we not agree?

CRITO: We must, Socrates.

SOCRATES: "Surely," they might say, "you are breaking the commitments and agreements that you made with us without compulsion or deceit, and under no pressure of time for deliberation. You have had seventy years during which you could have gone away if you did not like us, and if you thought our agreements unjust. You did not choose to go to Sparta or to Crete, which you are always saying are well governed, nor to any other city, Greek or foreign. You have been away from Athens less than the lame or the blind or other handicapped people. It is clear that the city has been outstandingly more congenial to you than to other Athenians, and so have we, the laws—for what city can please without laws? Will you then not now stick to our agreements? You will, Socrates, if we can persuade you, and not make yourself a laughingstock by leaving the city.

"For consider what good you will do yourself or your friends by breaking our agreements and committing such a wrong. It is pretty obvious that your friends will themselves be in danger of exile, disfranchisement, and loss of property. As for yourself, if you go to one of the nearby cities—Thebes or Megara, both are well governed—you will arrive as an enemy to their government; all who care for their city will look on you with suspicion, as a destroyer of the laws. You will also strengthen the conviction of the jury that they passed the right sentence on you, for anyone who destroys the laws could easily be thought to corrupt the young and the ignorant. Or will you avoid cities that are well governed and men who are civilized? If you do this, will your life be worth living? Will you have social intercourse with them and not be ashamed to talk to them? And what will you say? The same as you did here, that virtue and justice are man's most precious possessions, along with lawful behavior and the laws? Do you not think that Socrates would appear to be an unseemly kind of person? One must think so. Or will you leave those places and go to Crito's friends in Thessaly? There you will find the greatest license and disorder, and they may enjoy hearing from you how absurdly you escaped from prison in some disguise, in a leather jerkin or some other things in which escapees wrap themselves, thus altering your appearance. Will there be no one to say that you, likely to live but a short time more, were so greedy for life that you transgressed the most important laws? Possibly not, Socrates, if you do not annoy anyone; but if you do, many disgraceful things will be said about you.

"You will spend your time ingratiating yourself with all men, and be at their beck and call. What will you do in Thessaly but feast, as if you had gone to Thessaly to attend a banquet? As for those conversations of yours about justice and the rest of virtue, where will they be? You say you want to live for the sake of your children, that you may bring them up and educate them. How so? Will you bring them up and educate them by taking them to Thessaly and making strangers of them, that they may enjoy that too? Or not so, but they will be better brought up and educated here, while you are alive, though absent? Yes, your friends will look after them. Will they look after them if you go and live in Thessaly, but not if you go away to the underworld? If those who profess themselves your friends are any good at all, one must assume that they will.

"Be persuaded by us who have brought you up, Socrates. Do not value either your children or your life or anything else more than goodness, in order that when you arrive in Hades you may have all this as your defense before the rulers there. If you do this deed, it will not be better or more just or more pious for you here, nor for any one of your friends; nor will it be better for you when you arrive yonder. As it is, you depart, if you depart, after being wronged not by us, the laws, but by men. But if you depart after shamefully returning wrong for wrong and mistreatment for mistreatment, after breaking your agreements and commitments with us, after mistreating those you should mistreat least—yourself, your friends, your country, and us— we shall be angry with you while you are still alive; and our brothers, the laws of the underworld, will not receive you kindly, knowing that you tried to destroy us as far as you could. Do not let Crito persuade you, rather than us, to do what he says."

Crito, my dear friend, be assured that these are the words I seem to hear, as the Corybants[4] seem to hear the music of their flutes, and the echo of these words resounds in me and makes it impossible for me to hear anything else. As far as my present beliefs go, if you speak in opposition to them, you will speak in vain. However, if you think you can accomplish anything, speak.

CRITO: I have nothing to say, Socrates.

SOCRATES: Let it be then, Crito, and let us act in this way, since this is the way the god is leading us.

NOTES

1. Delos is an island in the Aegean Sea, about 85 miles from Athens. It was sacred to the god Apollo, and every year the Athenians sent a ship there in thanksgiving to him. Socrates' execution had been delayed because ritual purity required that no one be executed during the religious expedition. [D. C. ABEL]
2. *Sunium:* a promontory overlooking the Saronic Gulf of the Aegean Sea, about 30 miles from Athens. [D. C. ABEL]
3. This verse parallels the words of the Greek hero Achilles in Homer's *Iliad*, "I shall reach fertile Phthia on the third day" (Book III, line 363). Phthia is Achilles' homeland; hence Socrates interprets his dream to mean that he will die (his soul will arrive in the next world, its true home) in two days. ("On the third day" means "in two days," since the Greeks, when counting a series, began with the present member of the series.) [D. C. ABEL]
4. *Corybants:* priests of the fertility and nature goddess Cybele, whose worship involved frenzied dances. [D. C. ABEL]

Leviathan

Thomas Hobbes

Thomas Hobbes was born in Malmesbury, England, in 1588. He began his schooling at age four and enrolled in Oxford University when he was fourteen. Upon receiving his bachelor's degree in 1608, Hobbes began working as a private tutor, which remained his occupation for most of his life. After a trip to France and Italy in 1610, he studied classical Greek and Roman culture to gain a greater understanding of life. On a second journey to the Continent in 1629, Hobbes became convinced that all reality consists of matter in motion, and wondered if the powerful deductive method of geometry could be used to explain human nature and human society in terms of matter and motion. During a third trip to the Continent (1634–1637), his interest in philosophy and natural science was fueled by conversations with leading thinkers of the day, including Marin Mersenne, Pierre Gassendi, and Galileo. The England to which Hobbes returned was in political turmoil, and Hobbes, fearing that his political views might cost him his life, fled to France in 1640. During his eleven-year exile in France, he worked on his project of explaining human social and political behavior as instances of matter in motion. After returning to England, Hobbes continued to write and publish. He died in 1679 in Derbyshire, England, at the age of ninety-one.

Hobbes's main works are *De Cive* (in Latin, 1642; literally, "On the Citizen," but entitled *Philosophical Rudiments Concerning Government and Society* by Hobbes in his English translation, 1651), *De Corpore Politico* ("On the Body Politic," 1650), *Leviathan; or, The Matter, Form, and Power of a Commonwealth, Ecclesiastical and Civil* (1651), and *The Questions Concerning Liberty, Necessity, and Chance* (1656).

Our reading is from *Leviathan,* Hobbes's masterpiece of political philosophy. Hobbes begins by describing the "state of nature," the condition of human life before the formation of society and government. Each person tries to further his or her own interests by whatever means possible; there is a constant war of "every man against every man." Since there are no laws, there is no such thing as "justice" or "injustice." Life in the state of nature is "solitary, poor, nasty, brutish, and short." Hobbes goes on to explain that the "law of nature" dictates that people do whatever best preserves their lives. Since people in the state of nature would be more secure if they transferred (most of) their rights to a common power, the law of nature requires that they do so. This transferring of rights constitutes a "social contract" and is the foundation of society and government.

With the social contract, justice and injustice are born: To be just is to observe the contract, and to be unjust is to violate it. And justice will be assured only if the common power is a "leviathan"—a "mortal god" with absolute authority to force observance of the contract. According to Hobbes, "Covenants without the sword are but words." Only the terror of punishment by a power with absolute sovereignty will ensure justice and make life secure.

PART I. OF MAN

Chapter XIII. Of the Natural Condition of Mankind as Concerning Their Felicity and Misery

Nature has made men so equal in the faculties of the body and mind, as that though there be found one man sometimes manifestly stronger in body or of quicker mind than another, yet when all is reckoned together, the difference between man and man is not so considerable, as that one man can thereupon claim to himself any benefit to which another may not pretend,[1] as well as he. For as to the strength of body, the weakest has strength enough to kill the strongest, either by secret machination or by confederacy with others that are in the same danger with himself.

And as to the faculties of the mind, setting aside the arts grounded upon words—and especially that skill of proceeding upon general and infallible rules, called science, which very few have, and but in few things, as being not a native faculty born with us; nor attained, as prudence, while we look after somewhat[2] else—I find yet a greater equality among men than that of strength. For prudence is but experience, which equal time equally bestows on all men in those things they equally apply themselves unto. That which may perhaps make such equality incredible is but a vain conceit of one's own wisdom, which almost all men think they have in a greater degree than the vulgar—that is, than all men but themselves and a few others, whom by fame, or for concurring with themselves, they approve. For such is the nature of men, that howsoever they may acknowledge many others to be more witty or more eloquent or more learned, yet they will hardly believe there be many so wise as themselves; for they see their own wit at hand, and other men's at a distance. But this proves rather that men are in that point more equal than unequal. For there is not ordinarily a greater sign of the equal distribution of anything, than that every man is contented with his share.

From this equality of ability arises equality of hope in the attaining of our ends.[3] And therefore if any two men desire the same thing, which nevertheless they cannot both enjoy, they become enemies; and in the way to their end, which is principally their own conservation, and sometimes their delectation only, endeavor to destroy or subdue one another. And from hence it comes to pass that where an invader has no more to fear than another man's single power, if one plant, sow, build, or possess a convenient seat, others may probably be expected to come prepared with forces united to dispossess and deprive him, not only of the fruit of his labor, but also of his life or liberty. And the invader again is in the like danger of another.

And from this diffidence of one another, there is no way for any man to secure himself, so reasonable as anticipation—that is, by force or wiles to master the persons of all men he can, so long, till he see no other power great enough to endanger him. And this is no more than his own conservation requires, and is generally allowed. Also because there be some, that taking pleasure in contemplating their own power in the acts of conquest, which they pursue farther than their security requires; if others, that otherwise would be glad to be at ease within modest bounds, should not by invasion increase their power, they would not be able, [for a] long time, by standing only on their defense, to subsist. And by consequence, such augmentation of dominion over men being necessary to a man's conservation, it ought to be allowed him.

Again, men have no pleasure, but on the contrary a great deal of grief, in keeping company where there is no power able to overawe them all. For every man looks that his companion should value him at the same rate he sets upon himself, and upon all signs of contempt or undervaluing naturally endeavors, as far as he dares (which among them that have no common power to keep them in quiet, is far enough to make them destroy each other), to extort a greater value from his contemners, by damage; and from others, by the example.

So that in the nature of man we find three principal causes of quarrel: first, competition; secondly, diffidence; thirdly, glory.

The first makes men invade for gain; the second, for safety; and the third, for reputation. The first use violence to make themselves masters of other men's persons, wives, children, and cattle; the second, to defend them; the third, for trifles, as a word, a smile, a different opinion, and any other sign of undervalue, either direct in their persons or by reflection in their kindred, their friends, their nation, their profession, or their name.

Hereby it is manifest that during the time men live without a common power to keep them all in awe, they are in that condition which is called *war*; and such a war, as is of every man against every man. For war consists not in battle only, or the act of fighting; but in a tract of time where the will to contend by battle is sufficiently known; and therefore the notion of *time* is to be considered in the nature of war, as it is in the nature of weather. For as the nature of foul weather lies not in a shower or two of rain, but in an inclination thereto of many days together; so the nature of war consists not in actual fighting, but in the known disposition thereto, during all the time there is no assurance to the contrary. All other time is *peace.*

Whatsoever therefore is consequent to a time of war, where every man is enemy to every man; the same is consequent to the time wherein men live without other security than what their own strength and their own invention shall furnish them withal.[4] In such condition, there is no place for industry,[5] because the fruit thereof is uncertain, and consequently no culture[6] of the earth; no navigation nor use of the commodities that may be imported by sea; no commodious building; no instruments of moving and removing such things as require much force; no knowledge of the face of the earth; no account of time; no arts; no letters; no society; and, which is worst of all, continual fear and danger of violent death; and the life of man, solitary, poor, nasty, brutish, and short.

It may seem strange to some man that has not well weighed these things, that nature should thus dissociate and render men apt to invade and destroy one another; and he may therefore, not trusting to this inference made from the passions, desire perhaps to have the same confirmed by experience. Let him therefore consider with himself, when taking a journey, he arms himself and seeks to go well accompanied; when going to sleep, he locks his doors; when even in his house he locks his chests; and this when he knows there be laws and public officers, armed, to revenge all injuries shall be done him; what opinion he has of his fellow-subjects, when he rides armed; of his fellow citizens, when he locks his doors; and of his children and servants, when he locks his chests. Does he not there as much accuse mankind by his actions, as I do by my words? But neither of us accuse man's nature in it. The desires and other passions of man are in themselves no sin. No more are the actions that proceed from those passions, till they know a law that forbids them; which, till laws be made, they cannot know; nor can any law be made, till they have agreed upon the person that shall make it.

It may peradventure[7] be thought, there was never such a time nor condition of war as this; and I believe it was never generally so, over all the world. But there are many places where they live so now. For the savage people in many places of America, except the government of small families, the concord whereof depends on natural lust, have no government at all and live at this day in that brutish manner. . . . It may be perceived what manner of life there would be, where there were no common power to fear, by the manner of life which men that have formerly lived under a peaceful government use[8] to degenerate into in a civil war.

But though there had never been any time wherein particular men were in a condition of war one against another; yet in all times, kings and persons of sovereign authority, because of their independency, are in continual jealousies and in the state and posture of gladiators, having their weapons pointing and their eyes fixed on one another; that is, their forts, garrisons, and guns upon the frontiers of their kingdoms, and continual spies upon their neighbors—which is a posture of war. But because they uphold thereby the industry of their subjects, there does not follow from it that misery which accompanies the liberty of particular men.

To this war of every man against every man, this also is consequent, that nothing can be unjust. The notions of right and wrong, justice and injustice, have there no place. Where there is no common power, there is no law; where no law, no injustice. Force and fraud are in war the two cardinal virtues. Justice and injustice are none of the faculties neither of the body nor mind. If they were, they might be in a man that were alone in the world, as well as his senses and passions. They are qualities that relate to men in society, not in solitude. It is consequent also to the same condition that there be no propriety, no dominion, no *mine* and *yours* distinct, but only that to be every man's, that he can get, and for so long as he can keep it. And thus much for the ill condition which man by mere nature is actually placed in—though with a possibility to come out of it, consisting partly in the passions, partly in his reason.

The passions that incline men to peace are fear of death, desire of such things as are necessary to commodious living, and a hope by their industry to obtain them. And reason suggests convenient articles of peace, upon which men may be drawn to agreement. These articles are they which otherwise are called the laws of nature, whereof I shall speak more particularly in the two following chapters.

Chapter XIV. Of the First and Second Natural Laws, and of Contracts

The *right of nature*, which writers commonly call *jus naturale*,[9] is the liberty each man has to use his own power as he will himself, for the preservation of his own nature, that is to say, of his own life; and consequently of doing anything which, in his own judgment and reason, he shall conceive to be the aptest means thereunto.

By *liberty* is understood, according to the proper signification of the word, the absence of external impediments, which impediments may often take away part of a man's power to do what he would, but cannot hinder him from using the power left him, according as his judgment and reason shall dictate to him.

A *law of nature, lex naturalis*,[10] is a precept or general rule found out by reason, by which a man is forbidden to do that which is destructive of his life or [to] take away the means of preserving the same, and to omit that by which he thinks it may be best preserved. For though they that speak of this subject use to confound *jus* and *lex, right* and *law,* yet they ought to be distinguished because *right* consists in liberty to do or to forbear, whereas *law* determines and binds to one of them—so that law and right differ as much as obligation and liberty, which in one and the same matter are inconsistent.

And because the condition of man, as has been declared in the precedent chapter, is a condition of war of everyone against everyone, in which case everyone is governed by his own reason; and there is nothing he can make use of, that may not be a help unto him, in preserving his life against his enemies; it follows that in such a condition every man has a right to every thing, even to one another's body. And therefore, as long as this natural right of every man to everything endures, there can be no security to any man, how strong or wise soever he be, of living out the time which nature ordinarily allows men to live. And consequently it is a precept, or general rule of reason, *that every man ought to endeavor peace, as far as he has hope of obtaining it; and when he cannot obtain it, that he may seek and use all helps, and advantages of war.* The first branch of which rule contains the first and fundamental law of nature, which is *to seek peace and follow it.* The second, the sum of the right of nature, which is *by all means we can, to defend ourselves.*

From this fundamental law of nature, by which men are commanded to endeavor peace, is derived this second law: *that a man be willing, when others are so too, as far forth as for peace and defense of himself he shall think it necessary, to lay down this right to all things; and be contented with so much liberty against other men, as he would allow other men against himself.* For as long as every man holds this right of doing anything he likes, so long are all men in the condition of war. But if other men will not lay down their right, as well as he, then there is no reason for anyone to divest himself of his; for that were to expose himself to prey, which no man is bound to, rather than to dispose himself to peace. . . .

To lay down a man's right to anything is to divest himself of the liberty of hindering another of the benefit of his own right to the same. For he that renounces or passes away his right, gives not to any other man a right which he had not before, because there is nothing to which every man had not right by nature: but only stands out of his way, that he may enjoy his own original right without hindrance from him; not without hindrance from another. So that the effect which redounds to one man by another man's defect of right, is but so much diminution of impediments to the use of his own right original.

Right is laid aside, either by simply renouncing it or by transferring it to another—by simply *renouncing,* when he cares not to whom the benefit thereof redounds; by *transferring*, when he intends the benefit thereof to some certain person or persons. . . .

Whensoever a man transfers his right or renounces it, it is either in consideration of some right reciprocally transferred to himself, or for some other good he hopes for thereby. For it is a voluntary act; and of the voluntary acts of every man, the object is some good to himself. And therefore there be some rights which no man can be understood by any words or other signs to have abandoned or transferred. As first a man cannot lay down the right of resisting them that assault him by force to take away his life, because he cannot be understood to aim thereby at any good to himself. The same may be said of wounds and chains and imprisonment; both because there is no benefit consequent to such patience,[11] as there is to the patience of suffering[12] another to be wounded or imprisoned; as also because a man cannot tell, when he sees men proceed against him by violence, whether they intend his death or not. And lastly, the motive and end for which this renouncing and transferring of right is introduced, is nothing else but the security of a man's person in his life and in the means of so preserving life, as not to be weary of it. And therefore if a man by words or other signs seem to despoil himself of the end for which those signs were intended, he is not to be understood as if he meant it or that it was his will, but that he was ignorant of how such words and actions were to be interpreted.

The mutual transferring of right is that which men call *contract*.

There is difference between transferring of right to the thing and transferring, or tradition, that is delivery of the thing itself. For the thing may be delivered together with the translation[13] of the right, as in buying and selling with ready money, or exchange of goods or lands; and it may be delivered sometime after.

Again, one of the contractors may deliver the thing contracted for on his part and leave the other to perform his part at some determinate time after, and in the meantime be trusted; and then the contract on his part is called *pact* or *covenant*; or both parts may contract now, to perform hereafter—in which cases, he that is to perform in time to come, being trusted, his performance is called *keeping of promise* or *faith*; and the failing of performance, if it be voluntary, *violation of faith*. . . .

If a covenant be made wherein neither of the parties perform presently, but trust one another; in the condition of mere nature, which is a condition of war of every man against every man, upon any reasonable suspicion, it is void. But if there be a common power set over them both, with right and force sufficient to compel performance, it is not void. For he that performs first has no assurance the other will perform after, because the bonds of words are too weak to bridle men's ambition, avarice, anger, and other passions, without the fear of some coercive power; which in the condition of mere nature, where all men are equal and judges of the justness[14] of their own fears, cannot possibly be supposed. And therefore he which performs first, does but betray himself to his enemy—contrary to the right, [which] he can never abandon, of defending his life and means of living.

But in a civil estate, where there is a power set up to constrain those that would otherwise violate their faith, that fear is no more reasonable; and for that cause, he which by the covenant is to perform first, is obliged so to do.

The cause of fear, which makes such a covenant invalid, must be always something arising after the covenant made, as some new fact or other sign of the will not to perform; else it cannot make the covenant void. For that which could not hinder a man from promising, ought not to be admitted as a hindrance of performing. . . .

Chapter XV. Of Other Laws of Nature

From that law of nature by which we are obliged to transfer to another such rights, as being retained, hinder the peace of mankind, there follows a third, which is this, *that men perform their covenants made*—without which, covenants are in vain and but empty words; and the right of all men to all things remaining, we are still in the condition of war.

And in this law of nature consists the fountain and original[15] of *justice.* For where no covenant has preceded, there has no right been transferred, and every man has right to every thing; and consequently no action can be unjust. But when a covenant is made, then to break it is *unjust;* and the definition of *injustice* is no other than *the nonperformance of covenant.* And whatsoever is not unjust, is *just.*

But because covenants of mutual trust, where there is a fear of nonperformance on either part, as has been said in the former chapter, are invalid, though the original of justice be the making of covenants; yet injustice actually there can be none, till the cause of such fear be taken away—which, while men are in the natural condition of war, cannot be done. Therefore before the names of *just* and *unjust* can have place, there must be some coercive power to compel men equally to the performance of their covenants, by the terror of some punishment greater than the benefit they expect by the breach of their covenant; and to make good that propriety[16] which by mutual contract men acquire in recompense of the universal right they abandon—and such power there is none before the erection of a commonwealth. And this is also to be gathered out of the ordinary definition of justice in the schools, for they say that *justice is the constant will of giving to every man his own.* And therefore where there is no *own,* that is, no propriety, there is no injustice; and where there is no coercive power erected, that is, where there is no commonwealth, there is no propriety, all men having right to all things. Therefore where there is no commonwealth, there nothing is unjust—so that the nature of justice consists in keeping of valid covenants. But the validity of covenants begins not but with the constitution of a civil power, sufficient to compel men to keep them; and then it is also that propriety begins. . . .

And though this may seem too subtle a deduction of the laws of nature to be taken notice of by all men (whereof the most part are too busy in getting food, and the rest too negligent to understand), yet to leave all men inexcusable, they have been contracted into one easy sum, intelligible even to the meanest capacity, and that is: *Do not that to another, which you would not have done to yourself*—which shows him that he has no more to do in learning the laws of nature but, when weighing the actions of other men with his own, [and] they seem too heavy, to put them into the other part of the balance, and his own into their place, that his own passions and self-love may add nothing to the weight. And then there is none of these laws of nature that will not appear unto him very reasonable. . . .

PART II. OF COMMONWEALTH

Chapter XVII. Of the Causes, Generation, and Definition of a Commonwealth

The final cause,[17] end, or design of men, who naturally love liberty and dominion over others, in the introduction of that restraint upon themselves, in which we see them live in commonwealths, is the foresight of their own preservation and of a more contented life thereby—that is to say, of getting themselves out from that miserable condition of war, which is necessarily consequent, as has been shown in Chapter XIII, to the natural passions of men, when there is no visible power to keep them in awe and tie them by fear of punishment to the performance of their covenants and observation of those laws of nature set down in the fourteenth and fifteenth chapters.

For the laws of nature, as *justice, equity, modesty, mercy,* and, in sum, *doing to others as we would be done to,* of themselves, without the terror of some power to cause them to be observed, are contrary to our natural passions that carry us to partiality, pride, revenge, and the like. And covenants without the sword are but words, and of no strength to secure a man at all. Therefore notwithstanding the laws of nature, which everyone has then kept, when he has the will to keep them, when he can do it safely, if there be no power erected, or not great enough for our security; every man will, and may lawfully, rely on his own strength and art for caution against all other men. And in all places where men have lived by small families, to rob and spoil one another has been a trade, and [one that was] so far from being reputed against the law of nature, that the greater spoils they gained, the greater was their honor; and men observed no other laws therein but the laws of honor—that is, to abstain from cruelty, leaving to men their lives and instruments of husbandry.[18] And as small families did then, so now do cities and kingdoms (which are but greater families), for their own security, enlarge their dominions upon all pretenses of danger and fear of invasion, or assistance that may be given to invaders, and endeavor, as much as they can, to subdue or weaken their neighbors by open force and secret arts, for want of other caution, justly—and are remembered for it in after ages with honor. . . .

The only way to erect . . . a common power as may be able to defend [human beings] from the invasion of foreigners and the injuries of one another, and thereby to secure them in such sort, as that by their own industry and by the fruits of the earth they may nourish themselves and live contentedly, is to confer all their power and strength upon one man, or upon one assembly of men, that may reduce all their wills, by plurality of voices, unto one will—which is as much as to say, to appoint one man, or assembly of men, to bear their person;

and everyone to own[19] and acknowledge himself to be author of whatsoever he that so bears their person shall act, or cause to be acted, in those things which concern the common peace and safety; and therein to submit their wills, everyone to his will, and their judgments to his judgment. This is more than consent or concord; it is a real unity of them all in one and the same person, made by covenant of every man with every man, in such manner as if every man should say to every man, *I authorize and give up my right of governing myself to this man, or to this assembly of men, on this condition, that you give up your right to him and authorize all his actions in like manner.* This done, the multitude so united in one person is called a *commonwealth,* in Latin *civitas.* This is the generation of that great *leviathan* or rather, to speak more reverently, of that *mortal god,* to which we owe under the *immortal God* our peace and defense. For by this authority, given him by every particular man in the commonwealth, he has the use of so much power and strength conferred on him, that by terror thereof he is enabled to perform the wills of them all, to peace at home and mutual aid against their enemies abroad. And in him consists the essence of the commonwealth, which, to define it, is *one person, of whose acts a great multitude, by mutual covenants one with another, have made themselves every one the author, to the end he may use the strength and means of them all, as he shall think expedient, for their peace and common defense.*

And he that carries this person is called *sovereign* and [is] said to have *sovereign power;* and everyone besides, his *subject.*

NOTES

1. *pretend:* lay claim (to). [D. C. ABEL]
2. *somewhat:* something. [D. C. ABEL]
3. *ends:* goals. [D. C. ABEL]
4. *withal:* with. [D. C. ABEL]
5. *industry:* systematic labor. [D. C. ABEL]
6. *culture:* cultivation. [D. C. ABEL]
7. *peradventure:* perhaps. [D. C. ABEL]
8. *use:* are accustomed. [D. C. ABEL]
9. *jus naturale:* (Latin) "natural right." [D. C. ABEL]
10. *lex naturalis:* (Latin) "natural law." [D. C. ABEL]
11. *patience:* the enduring of something. [D. C. ABEL]
12. *suffering:* allowing. [D. C. ABEL]
13. *translation:* transferring. [D. C. ABEL]
14. *justness:* reasonableness. [D. C. ABEL]
15. *original:* origin. [D. C. ABEL]
16. *propriety:* private ownership; proprietorship. [D. C. ABEL]
17. *final cause:* the purpose (end, goal) for which something is done. [D. C. ABEL]
18. *husbandry:* agriculture. [D. C. ABEL]
19. *own:* accept. [D. C. ABEL]

The Second Treatise of Government

John Locke

A biography of John Locke appears on p. 139.

This reading is from Locke's *Second Treatise of Government,* the treatise following the one in which he criticizes Robert Filmer's defense of the divine right of kings. Locke begins the *Second Treatise* by describing the "state of nature"—the condition that human beings are in before there is any government. People are free to do whatever they wish, provided their actions do not violate the "law of nature." The law of nature forbids harming others or taking their property, except as a way of punishing those who have broken the law of nature. (According to Locke, any transgressor of the law of nature may be punished by anyone.) Positively, the law of nature requires that a person preserve his or her own life and (except when doing so conflicts with self-preservation) the lives of others. People remain in this state of nature "till by their own consents they make themselves members of some politic society."

Political society arises when, through a "social contract," individuals transfer to the community their power to punish transgressors of the law of nature. Members of the community agree to abide by the decisions of the majority. The primary motive for people forming a political society, Locke explains, is to establish a fairer and more reliable way of preserving their property. Anticipating the objection that most people are born into a political society and do not formally enter into a social contract, Locke explains that consent can be tacit as well as explicit. In the final section, he shows how a social contract can be dissolved from without, by foreign conquest, or from within, when the rulers alter the legislature or abuse "the lives, liberties, or fortunes of the people."

CHAPTER II. OF THE STATE OF NATURE

To understand political power aright and derive it from its original,[1] we must consider what state all men are naturally in, and that is a state of perfect freedom to order their actions and dispose of their possessions and persons as they think fit, within the bounds of the law of nature, without asking leave or depending upon the will of any other man.

A state also of equality, wherein all the power and jurisdiction is reciprocal, no one having more than another—there being nothing more evident than that creatures of the same species and rank, promiscuously[2] born to all the same advantages of nature and the use of the same faculties, should also be equal one among another without subordination or subjection, unless the lord and master of them all should, by any manifest declaration of his will, set one above another and confer on him, by an evident and clear appointment, an undoubted right to dominion and sovereignty. . . .

But though this be a state of *liberty,* yet it is not a state of *license.* Though man in that state have an uncontrollable liberty to dispose of his person or possessions, yet he has not liberty to destroy himself, or so much as any creature in his possession, but where some nobler use than its bare preservation calls for it. The *state of nature* has a law of nature to govern it, which obliges everyone. And reason, which is that law, teaches all mankind, who will but consult it, that being all equal and independent, no one ought to harm another in his life, health, liberty, or possessions. For men, being all the workmanship of one omnipotent and infinitely wise maker, all the servants of one sovereign master, sent into the world by his order, and about his business—they are his property, whose workmanship they are, made to last during his, not one another's pleasure. And being furnished with like faculties, sharing all in one community of nature, there cannot be supposed any such subordination among us that may authorize us to destroy one another, as if we were made for one another's uses, as the inferior ranks of creatures are for ours. Everyone, as he is bound to preserve himself and not to quit[3] his station willfully, so by the like reason, when his own preservation comes not in competition, ought he, as much as he can, to preserve the rest of mankind and may not, unless it be to do justice on an offender, take away or impair the life, or what tends to the preservation of the life, the liberty, health, limb, or goods of another.

And that all men may be restrained from invading others' rights and from doing hurt to one another, and the law of nature be observed, which wills the peace and preservation of all mankind, the execution of the law of nature is, in that state, put into every man's hands, whereby everyone has a right to punish the transgressors of that law to such a degree as may hinder its violation. For the law of nature would, as all other laws that concern men in this world, be in vain if there were nobody that in the state of nature had a power to execute that law and thereby preserve the innocent and restrain offenders. And if *anyone* in the state of nature may punish another for any evil he has done, *everyone* may do so. For in that state of perfect equality where naturally there is no superiority or jurisdiction of one over another, what any may do in prosecution of that law, everyone must needs[4] have a right to do.

And thus, in the state of nature one man comes by a power over another, but yet no absolute or arbitrary power to use[5] a criminal, when he has got him in his hands, according to the passionate heats or boundless extravagancy of his own will; but only to retribute to him, so far as calm reason and conscience dictate, what is proportionate to his transgression, which is so much as may serve for reparation and restrain—for these two are the only reasons why one man may lawfully do harm to another, which is that we call *punishment*. In transgressing the law of nature, the offender declares himself to live by another rule than that of reason and common equity, which is that measure God has set to the actions of men for their mutual security. And so he becomes dangerous to mankind—the tie which is to secure them from injury and violence being slighted and broken by him: which being a trespass against the whole species and the peace and safety of it, provided for by the law of nature, every man upon this score, by the right he has to preserve mankind in general, may restrain—or where it is necessary, destroy—things noxious to them, and so may bring such evil on anyone who has transgressed that law, as may make him repent the doing of it and thereby deter him, and by his example others, from doing the like mischief. And in this case and upon this ground, every man has a right to punish the offender and be executioner of the law of nature. . . .

Besides the crime which consists in violating the law and varying from the right rule of reason, whereby a man so far becomes degenerate and declares himself to quit the principles of human nature and to be a noxious creature, there is commonly injury done to some person or other, and some other man receives damage by his transgression; in which case he who has received any damage, has, besides the right of punishment common to him with other men, a particular right to seek reparation from him that has done it. And any other person who finds it just may also join with him that is injured and assist him in recovering from the offender so much as may make satisfaction for the harm he has suffered.

From these two distinct rights, the one of *punishing* the crime for restraint and preventing the like offense, which right of punishing is in everybody, the other of *taking reparation,* which belongs only to the injured party, comes it to pass that the magistrate, who by being magistrate has the common right of punishing put into his hands, can often, where the public good demands not the execution of the law, remit the punishment of criminal offenses by his own authority, but yet cannot remit the satisfaction due to any private man for the damage he has received. That [satisfaction], he who has suffered the damage has a right to demand in his own name, and he alone can remit. The damnified[6] person has this power of appropriating to himself the goods or service of the offender by right of self-preservation, as every man has a power to punish the crime, to prevent its being committed again, by the right he has of preserving all mankind and doing all reasonable things he can in order to that end. And thus it is, that every man in the state of nature has a power to kill a murderer, both to deter others from doing the like injury, which no reparation can compensate, by the example of the punishment that attends it from everybody; and also to secure men from the attempts of a criminal, who having renounced reason (the common rule and measure God has given to mankind), has, by the unjust violence and slaughter he has committed upon one, declared war against all mankind and therefore may be destroyed as a lion or a tiger, one of those wild savage beasts with whom men can have no society nor security. And upon this is grounded that great law of nature, "Whoso sheds man's blood, by man shall his blood be shed." And Cain was so fully convinced that everyone had a right to destroy such a criminal, that after the murder of his brother, he cries out, "Everyone that finds me shall slay me"[7]—so plain was it writ in the hearts of all mankind.

By the same reason may a man in the state of nature *punish the lesser breaches* of that law. It will perhaps be demanded,[8] with death? I answer, each transgression may be punished to that degree, and with so much severity, as will suffice to make it an ill bargain to the offender, give him cause to repent, and terrify others from doing the like. . . .

It is often asked as a mighty objection, "Where are, or ever were there, any men in such a state of nature?" To which it may suffice as an answer at present, that since all princes and rulers of independent governments all through the world are in a state of nature, it is plain the world never was, nor ever will be, without numbers of men in that state. I have named all governors of independent communities, whether they are or are not in league with others—for it is not every compact that puts an end to the state of nature between men, but only this one of agreeing together mutually to enter into one community and make one body politic. Other promises and compacts men may make one with another, and yet still be in the state of nature. The promises and bargains for truck,[9] and so on, between the two men in the desert[10] island, mentioned by Garcilaso de la Vega[11] in his history of Peru, or between a Swiss and an Indian in the woods of America, are binding to them, though they are perfectly in a state of nature, in reference to one another—for truth and keeping of faith belongs to men as men, and not as members of society.

To those that say, there were never any men in the state of nature, I . . . affirm that all men are naturally in that state and remain so, till by their own consents they make themselves members of some politic society. . . .

CHAPTER V. OF PROPERTY

Whether we consider natural *reason*, which tells us that men, being once born, have a right to their preservation, and consequently to meat and drink and such other things as nature affords for their subsistence; or *revelation*, which gives us an account of those grants God made of the world to Adam and to Noah and his sons, it is very clear that God, as King David says (Psalms 115:16), "has given the earth to the children of men"—given it to mankind in common. . . .

God, who has given the world to men in common, has also given them reason to make use of it to the best advantage of life, and convenience. The earth and all that is therein is given to men for the support and comfort of their being. And though all the fruits it naturally produces and beasts it feeds belong to mankind in common, as they are produced by the spontaneous hand of nature; and nobody has originally a private dominion, exclusive of the rest of mankind, in any of them, as they are thus in their natural state: yet being given for the use of men, there must of necessity be a means to appropriate them some way or other, before they can be of any use or at all beneficial to any particular man. The fruit or venison which nourishes the wild Indian, who knows no enclosure and is still a tenant in common, must be his, and so his (that is, a part of him) that another can no longer have any right to it, before it can do him any good for the support of his life.

Though the earth and all inferior creatures be common to all men, yet every man has a property in his own person—this nobody has any right to but himself. The labor of his body and the work of his hands, we may say, are properly his. Whatsoever then he removes out of the state that nature has provided and left it in, he has mixed his labor with, and joined to it something that is his own, and thereby makes it his property. It being by him removed from the common state nature has placed it in, it has by this labor something annexed to it that excludes the common right of other men. For this labor being the unquestionable property of the laborer, no man but he can have a right to what that is once joined to, at least where there is enough, and as good, left in common for others.

He that is nourished by the acorns he picked up under an oak, or the apples he gathered from the trees in the wood, has certainly appropriated them to himself. Nobody can deny but the nourishment is his. I ask then, when did they begin to be his? When he digested? or when he ate? or when he boiled? or when he brought them home? or when he picked them up? And it is plain, if the first gathering made them not his, nothing else could. That labor put a distinction between them and common; that added something to them more than nature, the common mother of all, had done—and so they became his private right. And will anyone say he had no right to those acorns or apples he thus appropriated because he had not the consent of all mankind to make them his? Was it a robbery thus to assume to himself what belonged to all in common? If such a consent as that was necessary, man had starved, notwithstanding the plenty God had given him. We see in commons, which remain so by compact, that it is the taking any part of what is common and removing it out of the state nature leaves it in, which begins the property; without which the common is of no use. And the taking of this or that part does not depend on the express consent of all the commoners. Thus the grass my horse has bit, the turfs my servant has cut, and the ore I have dug in any place, where I have a right to them in common with others, become my property, without the assignation or consent of anybody. The labor that was mine, removing them out of that common state they were in, has fixed my property in them. . . .

CHAPTER VII. OF POLITICAL OR CIVIL SOCIETY

. . . Man being born (as has been proved) with a title to perfect freedom and an uncontrolled enjoyment of all the rights and privileges of the law of nature, equally with any other man or number of men in the world, has by nature a power not only to preserve his property—that is, his life, liberty, and estate—against the injuries and attempts of other men, but [also] to judge of and punish the breaches of that law in others, as he is persuaded the offense deserves, even with death itself, in crimes where the heinousness of the fact, in his opinion, requires it. But because no political society can be nor subsist without having in itself the power to preserve the property, and in order thereunto, punish the offenses of all those of that society—there, and there only, is political society, where every one of the members has quitted[12] this natural power, resigned it up into the hand of the community in all cases that exclude him not from appealing for protection to the law established by it. And thus all private judgment of every particular member being excluded, the community comes to be umpire by settled standing rules, indifferent and the same to all parties; and by men having authority from the community for the execution of those rules, decides all the differences that may happen between any members of that society concerning any matter of right; and punishes those offenses which any member has committed against the society, with such penalties as the law has established. Whereby it is easy to discern who are, and who are not, in political society together. Those who are united into one body and have a common established law and judicature to appeal to, with authority to decide controversies between them and punish offenders, are in civil society one with another. But those who have no such common people (I mean on earth) are still in the state of nature, each being, where there is no other, judge for himself and executioner—which is, as I have before showed it, the perfect state of nature.

And thus the commonwealth comes by a power to set down what punishment shall belong to the several transgressions which they think worthy of it, committed among the members of that society (which is the *power of making laws*), as well as it has the power to punish any injury done unto any of its members by anyone that is not of it (which is the *power of war and peace*), and all this for the preservation of the property of all the members of that society, as far as it is possible. But though every man who has entered into civil society and is become a member of any commonwealth, has thereby quitted his power to punish offenses against the law of nature in prosecution of his own private judgment; yet with the judgment of offenses, which he has given up to the legislative[13] in all cases where he can appeal to the magistrate, he has given a right to the commonwealth to employ his force for the execution of the judgments of the commonwealth, whenever he shall be called to it—which indeed are his own judgments, they being made by himself or his representative. And herein we have the original of the legislative and executive power of civil society, which is to judge by standing laws how far offenses are to be punished when committed within the commonwealth; and also to determine, by occasional judgments founded on the present circumstances of the fact, how far injuries from without are to be vindicated; and in both these to employ all the force of all the members when there shall be need.

Wherever, therefore, any number of men are so united into one society as to quit everyone his executive power of the law of nature and to resign it to the public, there and there only is a political, or civil, society. And this is done wherever any number of men in the state of nature enter into society to make one people, one body politic, under one supreme government; or else when anyone joins himself to, and incorporates with, any government already made. For hereby he authorizes the society or (which is all one) the legislative thereof to make laws for him, as the public good of the society shall require—to the execution whereof, his own assistance (as to his own decrees) is due. And this puts men out of the state of nature into that of a *commonwealth,* by setting up a judge on earth with authority to determine all the controversies and redress the injuries that may happen to any member of the commonwealth; which judge is the legislative, or magistrates appointed by it. And wherever there are any number of men, however associated, that have no such decisive power to appeal to, there they are still in the state of nature. . . .

CHAPTER VIII. OF THE BEGINNING OF POLITICAL SOCIETIES

Men being, as has been said, by nature all free, equal, and independent, no one can be put out of this estate and subjected to the political power of another without his own consent. The only way whereby anyone divests himself of his natural liberty and puts on the bonds of civil society is by agreeing with other men to join and unite into a community, for their comfortable, safe, and peaceable living one among another in a secure enjoyment of their properties and a greater security against any that are not of it. This any number of men may do, because it injures not the freedom of the rest; they are left as they were in the liberty of the state of nature. When any number of men have so consented to make one community or government, they are thereby presently incorporated and make *one body politic*, wherein the majority have a right to act and conclude[14] the rest.

For when any number of men have, by the consent of every individual, made a community, they have thereby made that community one body, with a power to act as one body, which is only by the will and determination of the majority. For that which acts[15] any community, being only the consent of the individuals of it, and it being necessary to that which is one body to move one way, it is necessary the body should move that way whither the greater force carries it, which is the *consent of the majority*—or else it is impossible it should act or continue one body, one community, which the consent of every individual that united into it agreed that it should. And so everyone is bound by that consent to be concluded by the majority. And therefore we see that in assemblies empowered to act by positive laws, where no number is set by that positive law which empowers them, the act of the majority passes for the act of the whole and of course determines, as having by the law of nature and reason, the power of the whole.

And thus every man, by consenting with others to make one body politic under one government, puts himself under an obligation to everyone of that society to submit to the determination of the majority and to be concluded by it; or else this original compact, whereby he with others incorporates into one society, would signify nothing and be no compact, if he be left free and under no other ties than he was in before in the state of nature. For what appearance would there be of any compact? What new engagement if he were no farther tied by any decrees of the society than he himself thought fit and did actually consent to? This would be still as great a liberty as he himself had before his compact, or anyone else in the state of nature has, who may submit himself and consent to any acts of it if he thinks fit. . . .

Every man being, as has been showed, naturally free, and nothing being able to put him into subjection to any earthly power but only his own *consent*; it is to be considered what shall be understood to be a sufficient declaration of a man's consent, to make him subject to the laws of any government. There is a common distinction of an *express* and *tacit* consent, which will concern our present case. Nobody doubts but an express consent of any man entering into any society makes him a perfect member of that society, a subject of that government. The difficulty is what ought to be looked upon as a tacit consent and how far it binds—that is, how far anyone shall be looked on to have consented and thereby submitted to any government, where he has made no expressions of it at all. And to this I say that every man that has any possessions or enjoyment of any part of the dominions of any government, does thereby give his tacit consent and is as far forth obliged to obedience to the laws of that government, during such enjoyment, as anyone under it—whether this his possession be of land to him and his heirs forever, or a lodging only for a week, or whether it be barely traveling freely on the highway. And in effect, [this consent] reaches as far as the very being of anyone within the territories of that government. . . .

CHAPTER IX. OF THE ENDS[16] OF POLITICAL SOCIETY AND GOVERNMENT

If man in the state of nature be so free, as has been said; if he be absolute lord of his own person and possessions, equal to the greatest, and subject to nobody, why will he part with his freedom? Why will he give up this empire and subject himself to the dominion and control of any other power? To which it is obvious to answer that though in the state of nature he has such a right, yet the enjoyment of it is very uncertain and constantly exposed to the invasion of others. For all being kings as much as he, every man his equal, and the greater part no strict observers of equity and justice, the enjoyment of the property he has in this state is very unsafe, very unsecure. This makes him willing to quit a condition which, however free, is full of fears and continual dangers—and it is not without reason that he seeks out and is willing to join in society with others who are already united, or have a mind to unite, for the mutual preservation of their lives, liberties, and estates, which I call by the general name *property*.

The great and chief end, therefore, of men's uniting into commonwealths and putting themselves under government is the preservation of their property. To which in the state of nature there are many things wanting:

First, there wants[17] an established, settled, known law, received and allowed by common consent to be the standard of right and wrong, and the common measure to decide all controversies between them. For though the law of nature be plain and intelligible to all rational creatures, yet men being biased by their interest, as well as ignorant for want of study of it, are not apt to allow of it as a law binding to them in the application of it to their particular cases.

Secondly, in the state of nature there wants a known and indifferent judge with authority to determine all differences according to the established law. For everyone in that state being both judge and executioner of the law of nature, men being partial to themselves, passion and revenge is very apt to carry them too far, and with too much heat, in their *own* cases—as well as negligence and unconcernedness, to make them too remiss in *other men's*.

Thirdly, in the state of nature there often wants power to back and support the sentence when right, and to give it due execution. They who by any injustice offended, will seldom fail, where they are able, by force to make good their injustice. Such resistance many times makes the punishment dangerous, and frequently destructive, to those who attempt it.

Thus mankind, notwithstanding all the privileges of the state of nature, being but in an ill condition while they remain in it, are quickly driven into society. Hence it comes to pass that we seldom find any number of men live any time together in this state. The inconveniences that they are therein exposed to by the irregular and uncertain exercise of the power every man has of punishing the transgressions of others, make them take sanctuary under the established laws of government and therein seek the preservation of their property. It is this makes them so willingly give up every one his single power of punishing, to be exercised by such alone, as shall be appointed to it among them; and by such rules as the community, or those authorized by them to that purpose, shall agree on. And in this we have the original right and rise of both the legislative and executive power as well as of the governments and societies themselves.

For in the state of nature (to omit[18] the liberty he has of innocent delights) a man has two powers:

The first is to do whatsoever he thinks fit for the preservation of himself and others within the permission of the law of nature—by which law, common to them all, he and all the rest of mankind are one community, make up one society, distinct from all other creatures. And were it not for the corruption and viciousness of degenerate men, there would be no need of any other—no necessity that men should separate from this great and natural community, and by positive agreements combine into smaller and divided associations.

The other power a man has in the state of nature is the power to punish the crimes committed against that law. Both these he gives up when he joins in a private (if I may so call it) or particular politic society and incorporates into any commonwealth, separate from the rest of mankind.

The first power—namely, of doing whatsoever he thought for the preservation of himself and the rest of mankind—he gives up to be regulated by laws made by the society, so far forth as the preservation of himself and the rest of that society shall require, which laws of the society in many things confine the liberty he had by the law of nature.

Secondly, the power of punishing he wholly gives up and engages his natural force (which he might before employ in the execution of the law of nature, by his own single authority, as he thought fit) to assist the executive power of the society, as the law thereof shall require. For being now in a new state, wherein he is to enjoy many conveniences from the labor, assistance, and society of others in the same community, as well as protection from its whole strength, he is to part also with as much of his natural liberty in providing for himself as the good prosperity and safety of the society shall require—which is not only necessary but just, since the other members of the society do the like.

But though men when they enter into society give up the equality, liberty, and executive power they had in the state of nature into the hands of the society, to be so far disposed of by the legislative as the good of the society shall require; yet it being only with an intention in everyone the better to preserve himself, his liberty, and property (for no rational creature can be supposed to change his condition with an intention to be worse), the power of the society, or legislative constituted by them, can never be supposed to extend farther than the common good, but is obliged to secure everyone's property by providing against those three defects above mentioned, that made the state of nature so unsafe and uneasy. And so whoever has the legislative or supreme power of any commonwealth is bound to govern by established standing laws, promulgated and known to the people, and not by extemporary decrees; by indifferent and upright judges, who are to decide controversies by those laws; and to employ the force of the community at home only in the execution of such laws, or abroad to prevent or redress foreign injuries and secure the community from inroads and invasion. And all this [is] to be directed to no other end but the peace, safety, and public good of the people.

CHAPTER XX. OF THE DISSOLUTION OF GOVERNMENT

He that will with any clearness speak of the dissolution of government ought in the first place to distinguish between the dissolution of the *society* and the dissolution of the *government*. That which makes the community and brings men out of the loose state of nature into one politic society is the agreement which everyone has with the rest to incorporate and act as one body, and so be one distinct commonwealth. The usual and almost only way whereby this union is dissolved is the inroad of foreign force making a conquest upon them. For in that case (not being able to maintain and support themselves as one entire and independent body), the union belonging to that body which consisted therein must necessarily cease, and so everyone return to the state he was in before, with a liberty to shift for himself and provide for his own safety, as he thinks fit, in some other society. Whenever the society is dissolved, it is certain the government of that society cannot remain. . . .

Besides this overturning from *without,* governments are dissolved from *within.*

First, when the legislative is altered. Civil society being a state of peace amongst those who are of it, from whom the state of war is excluded by the umpirage[19] which they have provided in their legislative for the ending all differences that may arise amongst any of them, it is in their legislative that the members of a commonwealth are united and combined together into one coherent, living body. This is the soul that gives form, life, and unity to the commonwealth; from hence the several members have their mutual influence, sympathy, and connection. And therefore when the legislative is broken or dissolved, dissolution and death follows. . . .

There is . . . , secondly, another way whereby governments are dissolved, and that is when the legislative or the prince (either of them) acts contrary to their trust. . . .

The legislative acts against the trust reposed in them when they endeavor to invade the property of the subject and to make themselves, or any part of the community, masters or arbitrary disposers of the lives, liberties, or fortunes of the people.

The reason why men enter into society is the preservation of their property, and the end why they choose and authorize a legislative is that there may be laws made and rules set as guards and fences to the properties of all the members of the society, to limit the power and moderate the dominion of every part and member of the society. For since it can never be supposed to be the will of the society that the legislative should have a power to destroy that which everyone designs to secure by entering into society, and for which the people submitted themselves to legislators of their own making, whenever the legislators endeavor to take away and destroy the property of the people, or to reduce them to slavery under arbitrary power, they put themselves into a state of war with the people, who are thereupon absolved from any farther obedience and are left to the common refuge which God has provided for all men against force and violence. Whensoever therefore the legislative shall transgress this fundamental rule of society and, either by ambition, fear, folly or corruption, endeavor to grasp themselves, or put into the hands of any other, an absolute power over the lives, liberties, and estates of the people, by this breach of trust they forfeit the power the people had put into their hands for quite contrary ends, and it devolves to the people, who have a right to resume their original liberty and, by the establishment of a new legislative (such as they shall think fit), provide for their own safety and security, which is the end for which they are in society. . . .

In both the forementioned cases, when either the legislative is changed or the legislators act contrary to the end for which they were constituted, those who are guilty are guilty of rebellion. For if anyone by force takes away the established legislative of any society and the laws by them made, pursuant to their trust, he thereby takes away the umpirage which everyone had consented to for a peaceable decision of all their controversies and a bar to the state of war amongst them. They who remove or change the legislative take away this decisive power, which nobody can have but by the appointment and consent of the people; and so destroying the authority which the people did, and nobody else can, set up, and introducing a power which the people has not authorized, they actually introduce a state of war, which is that of force without authority. And thus, by removing the legislative established by the society (in whose decisions the people acquiesced and united, as to that of their own will), they untie the knot and expose the people anew to the state of war. And if those who by force take away the legislative are rebels, the legislators themselves, as has been shown, can be no less esteemed[20] so—when they, who were set up for the protection and preservation of the people, their liberties and properties, shall by force invade and endeavor to take them away.

NOTES

1. *original:* origin. [D. C. ABEL]
2. *promiscuously:* diversely. [D. C. ABEL]
3. *quit:* depart from. [D. C. ABEL]
4. *needs:* necessarily. [D. C. ABEL]
5. *use:* treat. [D. C. ABEL]
6. *damnified:* having suffered damage. [D. C. ABEL]
7. Genesis 4:14. [D. C. ABEL]
8. *demanded:* asked. [D. C. ABEL]
9. *truck:* barter. [D. C. ABEL]
10. *desert:* desolate. [D. C. ABEL]
11. Garcilaso de la Vega (1539–1616) was a Spanish (Peruvian-born) historian. [D. C. ABEL]
12. *quitted:* relinquished. [D. C. ABEL]
13. *legislative:* legislature. [D. C. ABEL]
14. *conclude:* bind, oblige. [D. C. ABEL]

15. *acts:* actuates; moves to action. [D. C. ABEL]
16. *ends:* purposes, goals. [D. C. ABEL]
17. *wants:* is lacking. [D. C. ABEL]
18. *omit:* disregard. [D. C. ABEL]
19. *umpirage:* authority to make a final decision. [D. C. ABEL]
20. *esteemed:* considered. [D. C. ABEL]

A Vindication of the Rights of Woman

Mary Wollstonecraft

Mary Wollstonecraft was born in London, England, in 1759. When she was nineteen, she took a job as a companion to an elderly widow in Bath. Two years later she returned to London to care for her dying mother. In 1783 Wollstonecraft helped establish two schools, one in Islington and the other in Newington Green. In 1786 she began working as a governess in County Cork, Ireland, and in the following year published her first book, *Thoughts on the Education of Daughters*. Deciding to make her living as a writer, Wollstonecraft moved back to London. In 1788 she published *Mary: A Fiction* (a largely autobiographical novel), *Original Stories from Real Life* (a children's book), and a translation from the French of Jacques Necker's *Of the Importance of Religious Opinions*. That year she also began working as a translator and reviewer for the journal *The Analytic Review*. Two years later she wrote *A Vindication of the Rights of Men*—a response to the British politician Edmund Burke's *Reflections on the Revolution in France*. In 1792 Wollstonecraft published her best-known work, *A Vindication of the Rights of Woman*. That same year she went to France to write a short history of the French Revolution, which was published in 1794. Returning to London, she resumed her job at *The Analytic Review* and also became an active member of the group of radical thinkers that met regularly in the home of Joseph Johnson, the publisher of her books and of *The Analytic Review*. Members of the group included William Blake, William Wordsworth, Thomas Paine, and William Godwin. Wollstonecraft died in London in 1797. (Since Wollstonecraft married Godwin several months before her death, she is also known as Mary Wollstonecraft Godwin.)

Our reading is from the Introduction and Chapter IV of *A Vindication of the Rights of Woman*. In the Introduction, Wollstonecraft states the thesis of her book: The misery of women is due primarily to the faulty education they receive—an education designed by men to turn women into "alluring mistresses." In Chapter IV, "Observations on the State of Degradation to Which Woman Is Reduced by Various Causes," Wollstonecraft argues that reason is the distinctively human trait and that the degradation of women is due primarily to the suppression of their rationality and an overemphasis on their feelings and emotions. By denying that women are rational and by maintaining an educational system that develops the rational potential of men only, society prevents women from attaining human perfection. Reason, not pleasure, is the foundation of virtue; by training women to value pleasure and to delight in the trivial attentions and courtesies bestowed by men, society stunts the human development of women. Ironically, by turning women into "creatures of sensation" rather than into fully human beings, men make women less fit to carry out their domestic duties.

INTRODUCTION

After considering the historic page and viewing the living world with anxious solicitude, the most melancholy emotions of sorrowful indignation have depressed my spirits, and I have sighed when obliged to confess that either nature has made a great difference between man and man, or that the civilization which has hitherto taken place in the world has been very partial. I have turned over various books written on the subject of education and patiently observed the conduct of parents and the management of schools. But what has been the result? A profound conviction that the neglected education of my fellow creatures is the grand source of the misery I deplore; and that women, in particular, are rendered weak and wretched by a variety of concurring causes originating from one hasty conclusion. The conduct and manners of women, in fact, evidently prove that their minds are not in a healthy state. For, like the flowers which are planted in too rich a soil, strength and usefulness are sacrificed to beauty; and the flaunting leaves, after having pleased a fastidious eye, fade, disregarded on the stalk, long before the season when they ought to have arrived at maturity. One cause of this barren blooming I attribute to a false system of education, gathered from the books written on this subject by men who, considering females rather as women than human creatures, have been more anxious to make them alluring mistresses than affectionate wives and rational mothers. And the understanding of the sex has been so bubbled[1] by this specious homage that the civilized women of the present century, with a few exceptions, are only anxious to inspire love, when they ought to cherish a nobler ambition, and by their abilities and virtues exact respect. . . .

My own sex, I hope, will excuse me if I treat them like rational creatures instead of flattering their *fascinating* graces and viewing them as if they were in a state of perpetual childhood, unable to stand alone. I earnestly wish to point out in what true dignity and human happiness consists—I wish to persuade women to endeavor to acquire strength, both of mind and body, and to convince them that the soft phrases, susceptibility of heart, delicacy of sentiment, and refinement of taste, are almost synonymous with epithets of weakness, and that those beings who are only the objects of pity and that kind of love which has been termed its sister, will soon become objects of contempt.

Dismissing, then, those pretty feminine phrases which the men condescendingly use to soften our slavish dependence, and despising that weak elegancy of mind, exquisite sensibility, and sweet docility of manners supposed to be the sexual characteristics of the weaker vessel, I wish to show that elegance is inferior to virtue; that the first object of laudable ambition is to obtain a character as a human being, regardless of the distinction of sex; and that secondary views should be brought to this simple touchstone. . . .

CHAPTER IV. OBSERVATIONS ON THE STATE OF DEGRADATION TO WHICH WOMAN IS REDUCED BY VARIOUS CAUSES

. . . Reason is . . . the simple power of improvement, or (more properly speaking) of discerning truth. Every individual is in this respect a world in itself. More or less may be conspicuous in one being than another, but the nature of reason must be the same in all, if it be an emanation of divinity, the tie that connects the creature with the Creator. For can that soul be stamped with the heavenly image, that is not perfected by the exercise of its own reason? Yet outwardly ornamented with elaborate care and so adorned to delight man, "that with honor he may love,"[2] the soul of woman is not allowed to have this distinction. And man, ever placed between her and reason, she is always represented as only created to see through a gross medium, and to take things on trust. But dismissing these fanciful theories and considering woman as a whole (let it be what it will) instead of a part of man, the inquiry is whether she have reason or not. If she have—which, for a moment, I will take for granted—she was not created merely to be the solace of man, and the sexual should not destroy the human character.

Into this error men have probably been led by viewing education in a false light—not considering it as the first step to form a being advancing gradually towards perfection, but only as a preparation for life. On this sensual error (for I must call it so) has the false system of female manners been reared, which robs the whole sex of its dignity and classes the brown and fair with the smiling flowers that only adorn the land. This has ever been the language of men, and the fear of departing from a supposed sexual character has made even women of superior sense adopt the same sentiments. Thus understanding, strictly speaking, has been denied to woman; and instinct, sublimated into wit and cunning for the purposes of life, has been substituted in its stead.

The power of generalizing ideas, of drawing comprehensive conclusions from individual observations, is the only acquirement . . . that really deserves the name of knowledge. Merely to observe, without endeavoring to account for anything, may (in a very incomplete manner) serve as the common sense of life. But where is the store laid up that is to clothe the soul when it leaves the body?

This power has not only been denied to women, but writers have insisted that it is inconsistent, with a few exceptions, with their sexual character. Let men prove this, and I shall grant that woman only exists for man. I must, however, previously remark that the power of generalizing ideas, to any great extent, is not very common amongst men or women. But this exercise is the true cultivation of the understanding, and everything conspires to render the cultivation of the understanding more difficult in the female than the male world.

I am naturally led by this assertion to the main subject of the present chapter, and shall now attempt to point out some of the causes that degrade the sex and prevent women from generalizing their observations.

I shall not go back to the remote annals of antiquity to trace the history of woman; it is sufficient to allow that she has always been either a slave or a despot, and to remark that each of these situations equally retards the progress of reason. The grand source of female folly and vice has ever appeared to me to arise from narrowness of mind, and the very constitution of civil governments has put almost insuperable obstacles in the way to prevent the cultivation of the female understanding. Yet virtue can be built on no other foundation! The same obstacles are thrown in the way of the rich, and the same consequences ensue.

Necessity has been proverbially termed the mother of invention. The aphorism may be extended to virtue. It is an acquirement—and an acquirement to which pleasure must be sacrificed. And who sacrifices pleasure when it is within the grasp, whose mind has not been opened and strengthened by adversity or the pursuit of knowledge goaded on by necessity? Happy is it when people have the cares of life to struggle with, for these struggles prevent their becoming a prey to enervating vices, merely from idleness! But if from their birth men and women be placed in a torrid zone, with the meridian sun of pleasure darting directly upon them, how can they sufficiently brace their minds to discharge the duties of life, or even to relish the affections that carry them out of themselves?

Pleasure is the business of woman's life, according to the present modification[3] of society; and while it continues to be so, little can be expected from such weak beings. Inheriting, in a lineal descent from the first fair defect in nature,[4] the sovereignty of beauty, they have, to maintain their power, resigned the natural rights which the exercise of reason might have procured them, and chosen rather to be short-lived queens than labor to obtain the sober pleasures that arise from equality. Exalted by their inferiority (this sounds like a contradiction), they constantly demand homage as women, though experience should teach them that the men who pride themselves upon paying this arbitrary insolent respect to the sex, with the most scrupulous exactness, are most inclined to tyrannize over, and despise, the very weakness they cherish. . . .

Ah! Why do women (I write with affectionate solicitude) condescend to receive a degree of attention and respect from strangers, different from that reciprocation of civility which the dictates of humanity and the politeness of civilization authorize between man and man? And why do they not discover, when "in the noon of beauty's power,"[5] that they are treated like queens only to be deluded by hollow respect, till they are led to resign, or not assume, their natural prerogatives? Confined then in cages like the feathered race, they have nothing to do but to plume themselves and stalk with mock majesty from perch to perch. It is true they are provided with food and raiment, for which they neither toil nor spin;[6] but health, liberty, and virtue are given in exchange. But where amongst mankind has been found sufficient strength of mind to enable a being to resign these adventitious prerogatives—one who, rising with the calm dignity of reason above opinion, dared to be proud of the privileges inherent in man? And it is vain to expect it while hereditary power chokes the affections and nips reason in the bud.

The passions of men have thus placed women on thrones and, till mankind become more reasonable, it is to be feared that women will avail themselves of the power which they attain with the least exertion and which is the most indisputable. They will smile—yes, they will smile—though told that:

> In beauty's empire is no mean,
> And woman, either slave or queen,
> Is quickly scorn'd when not ador'd.[7]

But the adoration comes first, and the scorn is not anticipated. . . .

I lament that women are systematically degraded by receiving the trivial attentions which men think it manly to pay to the sex, when in fact they are insultingly supporting their own superiority. It is not condescension to bow to an inferior. So ludicrous, in fact, do these ceremonies appear to me, that I scarcely am able to govern my muscles when I see a man start with eager and serious solicitude to lift a handkerchief or shut a door, when the *lady* could have done it herself, had she only moved a pace or two.

A wild wish has just flown from my heart to my head, and I will not stifle it though it may excite a horselaugh. I do earnestly wish to see the distinction of sex confounded in society, unless where love animates the behavior. For this distinction is, I am firmly persuaded, the foundation of the weakness of character ascribed to woman; is the cause why the understanding is neglected, while accomplishments are acquired with sedulous care. And the same cause accounts for their preferring the graceful before the heroic virtues.

Mankind, including every description, wish to be loved and respected by *something;* and the common herd will always take the nearest road to the completion of their wishes. The respect paid to wealth and beauty is the most certain, and unequivocal—and, of course, will always attract the vulgar eye of common minds. Abilities and virtues are absolutely necessary to raise men from the middle rank of life into notice. And the natural consequence is notorious: The middle rank contains most virtue and abilities. Men have thus, in one station, at least an opportunity of exerting themselves with dignity and of rising by the exertions which really improve a rational creature. But the whole female sex are, till their character is formed, in the same condition as the rich—for they are born (I now speak of a state of civilization) with certain sexual privileges, and while they are gratuitously granted them, few will ever think of works of supererogation[8] to obtain the esteem of a small number of superior people.

When do we hear of women who, starting out of obscurity, boldly claim respect on account of their great abilities or daring virtues? Where are they to be found? "To be observed, to be attended to, to be taken notice of with sympathy, complacency, and approbation, are all the advantages which they seek."[9] "True!" my male readers will probably exclaim. But let them, before they draw any conclusion, recollect that this was not written originally as descriptive of women, but of the rich. In Dr. Smith's *Theory of Moral Sentiments* I have found a general character of people of rank and fortune that, in my opinion, might with the greatest propriety be applied to the female sex.[10] . . . For if, excepting warriors, no great men of any denomination have ever appeared amongst the nobility, may it not be fairly inferred that their local situation swallowed up the man and produced a character similar to that of women, who are *localized* (if I may be allowed the word) by the rank they are placed in, by *courtesy?* Women, commonly called ladies, are not to be contradicted in company, are not allowed to exert any manual strength. And from them the negative virtues only are expected, when any virtues are expected: patience, docility, good humor, and flexibility—virtues incompatible with any vigorous exertion of intellect. Besides, by living more with each other and being seldom absolutely alone, they are more under the influence of sentiments than passions. Solitude and reflection are necessary to give to wishes the force of passions, and to enable the imagination to enlarge the object and make it the most desirable. The same may be said of the rich; they do not sufficiently deal in general ideas, collected by impassioned thinking or calm investigation, to acquire that strength of character on which great resolves are built. . . .

In the middle rank of life, to continue the comparison, men in their youth are prepared for professions, and marriage is not considered as the grand feature in their lives; while women, on the contrary, have no other scheme to sharpen their faculties. It is not business, extensive plans, or any of the excursive flights of ambition that engross their attention—no, their thoughts are not employed in rearing such noble structures. To rise in the world and have the liberty of running from pleasure to pleasure, they must marry advantageously, and to this object their time is sacrificed and their persons often legally prostituted. A man when he enters any profession has his eye steadily fixed on some future advantage (and the mind gains great strength by having all its efforts directed to one point), and, full of his business, pleasure is considered as mere relaxation; while women seek for pleasure as the main purpose of existence. In fact, from the education which they receive from society, the love of pleasure may be said to govern them all. But does this prove that there is a sex in souls? It would be just as rational to declare that the courtiers in France, when a destructive system of despotism had formed their character, were not men because liberty, virtue, and humanity were sacrificed to pleasure and vanity—fatal passions, which have ever domineered over the *whole* race!

The same love of pleasure, fostered by the whole tendency of their education, gives a trifling turn to the conduct of women in most circumstances. For instance, they are ever anxious about secondary things, and on the watch for adventures instead of being occupied by duties.

A man, when he undertakes a journey, has, in general, the end[11] in view. A woman thinks more of the incidental occurrences, the strange things that may possibly occur on the road, the impression that she may make on her fellow-travellers. And above all, she is anxiously intent on the care of the finery that she carries with her, which is more than ever a part of herself, when going to figure on a new scene—when, to use an apt French turn of expression, she is going to produce a sensation. Can dignity of mind exist with such trivial cares?

In short, women in general, as well as the rich of both sexes, have acquired all the follies and vices of civilization and missed the useful fruit. It is not necessary for me always to premise that I speak of the condition of the whole sex, leaving exceptions out of the question. Their senses are inflamed and their understandings neglected; consequently they become the prey of their senses (delicately termed *sensibility*) and are blown about by every momentary gust of feeling. Civilized women are, therefore, so weakened by false refinement that, respecting morals, their condition is much below what it would be were they left in a state nearer to nature. Ever restless and anxious, their overexercised sensibility not only renders them uncomfortable themselves, but troublesome (to use a soft phrase) to others. All their thoughts turn on things calculated to excite emotion. And feeling when they should reason [instead], their conduct is unstable and their opinions are wavering—not the wavering produced by deliberation or progressive views, but by contradictory emotions. By fits and starts they are warm in many pursuits. Yet this warmth, never concentrated into perseverance, soon exhausts itself. Exhaled by its own heat, or meeting with some other fleeting passion to which reason has never given any specific gravity, neutrality ensues. Miserable indeed must be that being whose cultivation of mind has only tended to inflame its passions! A distinction should be made between inflaming and strengthening them. The passions thus pampered, while the judgment is left unformed, what can be expected to ensue? Undoubtedly, a mixture of madness and folly!

This observation should not be confined to the *fair* sex. However, at present I only mean to apply it to them.

Novels, music, poetry, and gallantry all tend to make women the creatures of sensation, and their character is thus formed in the mold of folly during the time they are acquiring accomplishments—the only improvement they are excited, by their station in society, to acquire. This overstretched sensibility naturally relaxes the other powers of the mind and prevents intellect from attaining that sovereignty which it ought to attain to render a rational creature useful to others and content with its own station; for the exercise of the understanding, as life advances, is the only method pointed out by nature to calm the passions.

Satiety has a very different effect, and I have often been forcibly struck by an emphatic description of damnation: when the spirit is represented as continually hovering with abortive eagerness round the defiled body, unable to enjoy anything without the organs of sense. Yet, to their senses are women made slaves, because it is by their sensibility that they obtain present power.

And will moralists pretend to assert that this is the condition in which one half of the human race should be encouraged to remain with listless inactivity and stupid acquiescence? Kind instructors! What were we created for? To remain, it may be said, innocent—they mean in a state of childhood. We might as well never have been born, unless it were necessary that we should be created to enable man to acquire the noble privilege of reason, the power of discerning good from evil, while we lie down in the dust from whence we were taken, never to rise again.

It would be an endless task to trace the variety of meannesses, cares, and sorrows into which women are plunged by the prevailing opinion that they were created rather to feel than reason, and that all the power they obtain must be obtained by their charms and weakness:

Fine by defect, and amiably weak![12]

And made by this amiable weakness entirely dependent—excepting what they gain by illicit sway—on man, not only for protection but advice, is it surprising that, neglecting the duties that reason alone points out and shrinking from trials calculated to strengthen their minds, they only exert themselves to give their defects a graceful covering, which may serve to heighten their charms in the eye of the voluptuary, though it sink them below the scale of moral excellence?

Fragile in every sense of the word, they are obliged to look up to man for every comfort. In the most trifling dangers they cling to their support with parasitical tenacity, piteously demanding succor; and their *natural* protector extends his arm or lifts up his voice to guard the lovely trembler—from what? Perhaps the frown of an old cow or the jump of a mouse; a rat would be a serious danger. In the name of reason, and even common sense, what can save such beings from contempt, even though they be soft and fair? . . .

In the regulation of a family, in the education of children, understanding in an unsophisticated sense is particularly required—strength both of body and mind. Yet the men who, by their writings, have most earnestly labored to domesticate women, have endeavored, by arguments dictated by a gross appetite which satiety had rendered fastidious, to weaken their bodies and cramp their minds. But if even by these sinister methods they really *persuaded* women, by working on their feelings, to stay at home and fulfill the duties of a mother and mistress of a family, I should cautiously oppose opinions that led women to right conduct by prevailing on them to make the discharge of such important duties the main business of life, though reason were insulted. Yet—and I appeal to experience—if by neglecting the understanding they be as much, nay, *more* detached from these domestic employments than they could be by the most serious intellectual pursuit (though it may be observed that the mass of mankind will never vigorously pursue an intellectual object), I may be allowed to infer that reason is absolutely necessary to enable a woman to perform any duty properly. And I must again repeat that sensibility is not reason.

The comparison with the rich still occurs to me. For when men neglect the duties of humanity, women will follow their example; a common stream hurries them both along with thoughtless celerity. Riches and honors prevent a man from enlarging his understanding and enervate all his powers by reversing the order of nature, which has ever made true pleasure the reward of labor. Pleasure—enervating pleasure—is, likewise, within women's reach without earning it. But till hereditary possessions are spread abroad, how can we expect men to be proud of virtue? And till they are, women will govern them by the most direct means, neglecting their dull domestic duties to catch the pleasure that sits lightly on the wing of time.

NOTES

1. *bubbled:* duped. [D. C. ABEL]
2. Apparently a reference to John Milton, *Paradise Lost*, Book VIII, lines 57–58: "O when meet now / Such pairs, in love and mutual Honour join'd?" Milton (1608–1678) was an English poet. [D. C. ABEL]
3. *modification:* restriction. [D. C. ABEL]
4. A reference to Milton, who calls woman "this fair defect / Of nature" (*Paradise Lost*, Book X, lines 891–892). [D. C. ABEL]
5. Apparently Wollstonecraft's paraphrase of a passage in Adam Beuvius, *Henrietta of Gerstenfeld: A German Story*, vol. 2 (London, England: William Lane, 1788), p. 24. Beuvius (flourished 1775–1783) was a German writer. [D. C. ABEL]
6. An allusion to Jesus' statement, "Consider the lilies of the field, how they grow; they neither toil nor spin, yet I tell you, even Solomon in all his glory was not arrayed like one of these" (Matthew 6:28). [D. C. ABEL]
7. Anna Letitia Barbauld, "Song V," lines 16–18. Barbauld (1743–1825) was a British writer and poet. [D. C. ABEL]
8. *supererogation:* doing more than required by duty or obligation. [D. C. ABEL]
9. Adam Smith, *The Theory of Moral Sentiments* (London, England: A. Millar, 1759), Part I, Section III, Chapter II, pp. 109–10. Smith (1723–1790) was a Scottish economist. [D. C. ABEL]
10. Ibid., pp. 117–20. [D. C. ABEL]
11. *end:* purpose, goal. [D. C. ABEL]
12. A nearly verbatim quotation of Alexander Pope, *Moral Essays*, Epistle II, "To a Lady: Of the Characters of Women," line 44 (Pope has "delicately" instead of "amiably"). [D. C. ABEL]

Manifesto of the Communist Party

Karl Marx and Friedrich Engels

Karl Marx was born in 1818 in Trier, Prussia. He began studying law at the University of Bonn at the age of seventeen, but soon transferred to the University of Berlin, where he became interested in philosophy. In 1841 he received his doctorate in philosophy from the University of Jena. Unable to get a teaching position because of his association with the politically radical Young Hegelians, Marx in 1842 became editor of the *Rhenish Gazette,* a liberal newspaper in the Rhineland. He then moved to Paris to take a job as coeditor of a new socialist publication, the *German-French Annals.* The *Annals* was soon shut down by the authorities, and Marx was expelled from Paris in 1844. He moved to Brussels, Belgium, where he worked to promote communism. In 1849 he settled in London, where he lived for the rest of his life. In 1867 he published the first volume of *Capital,* his comprehensive work on economics; the drafts of the second and third volumes were still uncompleted when Marx died in 1883.

Friedrich Engels was born in Barmen, Prussia, in 1820. He attended secondary school but dropped out before graduating. In 1838 he went to Bremen to work in the office of his father's textile company to prepare for a career in business. He soon developed an interest in politics and associated with the Young Hegelians, becoming a communist in 1842. He then went to Manchester, England, to work as a clerk in a cotton mill owned by his father. In 1844 he went to Paris to visit with Marx, and the two became friends and lifelong collaborators. Engels followed Marx to Brussels when Marx was exiled in 1845; there they coauthored *The German Ideology* (written in 1845, not published in full until 1932) and the *Manifesto of the Communist Party* (1848). Engels later moved back to Manchester and worked again for his father's company. He shared his salary with Marx, who was living in London. After Marx's death, Engels edited and published the second and third volumes of *Capital* (1885, 1894). Engels died in London in 1895.

Our reading is from the *Manifesto of the Communist Party,* a document Marx and Engels wrote as the platform of the Communist League, an international association of workers. Marx and Engels explain that communism interprets the history of society as the history of class struggles. Although the classes vary with the historical epoch, they are always the result of the prevailing economic system. The two classes produced by the industrial revolution are the bourgeoisie (capitalists, who own the means of production) and the proletariat (wage-laborers employed by the bourgeoisie). Under capitalism, workers become just one more commodity, bought and sold at market prices. To earn enough money simply to survive, they must work long hours under increasingly inhumane conditions.

Marx and Engels argue that capitalism, ironically, contains the seeds of its own destruction: On the one hand, its very success leads to overproduction and thus to economic ruin; on the other hand, it drives the oppressed workers to unite to overthrow the entire capitalist system. The fall of capitalism and the victory of the proletariat are therefore inevitable. Marx and Engels explain that the goal of the Communist Party is to hasten the end of capitalism by uniting the workers of all countries and encouraging them to revolt. The revolution will abolish private property (private ownership of the means of production)

470

and shift political power from the bourgeoisie to the proletariat. Eventually the distinction between bourgeoisie and proletariat will disappear, and with it the need for political power.

I. BOURGEOIS AND PROLETARIANS[1]

The history of all hitherto existing society is the history of class struggles.

Freeman and slave, patrician and plebeian, lord and serf, guild master[2] and journeyman, in a word, oppressor and oppressed, stood in constant opposition to one another, carried on an uninterrupted, now hidden, now open fight—a fight that each time ended either in a revolutionary reconstitution of society at large or in the common ruin of the contending classes.

In the earlier epochs of history, we find almost everywhere a complicated arrangement of society into various orders, a manifold gradation of social rank. In ancient Rome we have patricians, knights, plebeians, slaves; in the Middle Ages, feudal lords, vassals, guild masters, journeymen, apprentices, serfs; in almost all of these classes, again, subordinate gradations.

The modern bourgeois society that has sprouted from the ruins of feudal society has not done away with class antagonisms. It has but established new classes, new conditions of oppression, new forms of struggle in place of the old ones.

Our epoch, the epoch of the bourgeoisie, possesses, however, this distinctive feature: It has simplified the class antagonisms. Society as a whole is more and more splitting up into two great hostile camps, into two great classes directly facing each other: bourgeoisie and proletariat.

From the serfs of the Middle Ages sprang the chartered burghers[3] of the earliest towns. From these [burghers] the first elements of the bourgeoisie were developed.

The discovery of America, the rounding of the Cape,[4] opened up fresh ground for the rising bourgeoisie. The East Indian and Chinese markets, the colonization of America, trade with the colonies, the increase in the means of exchange and in commodities generally, gave to commerce, to navigation, to industry, an impulse never before known, and thereby to the revolutionary element in the tottering feudal society a rapid development.

The feudal system of industry, under which industrial production was monopolized by closed guilds, now no longer sufficed for the growing wants of the new markets. The manufacturing system took its place. The guild masters were pushed on one side by the manufacturing middle class. Division of labor between the different corporate guilds vanished in the face of division of labor in each single workshop.

Meantime the markets kept ever growing, the demand ever rising. Even manufacture no longer sufficed. Thereupon, steam and machinery revolutionized industrial production. The place of manufacture was taken by the giant, modern industry; the place of the industrial middle class, by industrial millionaires, the leaders of whole industrial armies, the modern bourgeois.

Modern industry has established the world market, for which the discovery of America paved the way. This market has given an immense development to commerce, to navigation, to communication by land. This development has, in its turn, reacted on the extension of industry. And in proportion as industry, commerce, navigation, railways extended, in the same proportion the bourgeoisie developed, increased its capital, and pushed into the background every class handed down from the Middle Ages.

We see, therefore, how the modern bourgeoisie is itself the product of a long course of development, of a series of revolutions in the modes of production and of exchange. . . .

The bourgeoisie historically has played a most revolutionary part.

The bourgeoisie, wherever it has got the upper hand, has put an end to all feudal, patriarchal, idyllic relations. It has pitilessly torn asunder the motley feudal ties that bound man to his "natural superiors" and has left remaining no other nexus between man and man than naked self-interest, than callous "cash payment." It has drowned the most heavenly ecstasies of religious fervor, of chivalrous enthusiasm, of philistine sentimentalism, in the icy water of egotistical calculation. It has resolved personal worth into exchange value, and in place of the numberless indefeasible[5] chartered freedoms has set up that single, unconscionable freedom—free trade. In one word, for exploitation veiled by religious and political illusions, it has substituted naked, shameless, direct, brutal exploitation.

The bourgeoisie has stripped of its halo every occupation hitherto honored and looked up to with reverent awe. It has converted the physician, the lawyer, the priest, the poet, the man of science, into its paid wage-laborers.

The bourgeoisie has torn away from the family its sentimental veil and has reduced the family relation to a mere money relation. . . .

The bourgeoisie cannot exist without constantly revolutionizing the instruments of production, and thereby the relations of production, and with them the whole relations of society. Conservation of the old modes of production in unaltered form was, on the contrary, the first condition of existence for all earlier industrial classes. Constant revolutionizing of production, uninterrupted disturbance of all social conditions, everlasting uncertainty and agitation, distinguish the bourgeois epoch from all earlier ones. All fixed, fast-frozen relations, with their train of ancient and venerable prejudices and opinions, are swept away; all new-formed ones become antiquated before they can ossify. All that is solid melts into air, all that is holy is profaned, and man is at last compelled to face with sober senses his real conditions of life and his relations with his kind.

The need of a constantly expanding market for its products chases the bourgeoisie over the whole surface of the globe. It must nestle everywhere, settle everywhere, establish connections everywhere.

The bourgeoisie has through its exploitation of the world market given a cosmopolitan character to production and consumption in every country. To the great chagrin of reactionists, it has drawn from under the feet of industry the national ground on which it stood. All old-established national industries have been destroyed or are daily being destroyed. They are dislodged by new industries whose introduction becomes a life and death question for all civilized nations, by industries that no longer work up indigenous raw material but raw material drawn from the remotest zones—industries whose products are consumed not only at home, but in every quarter of the globe. In place of the old wants, satisfied by the productions of the country, we find new wants, requiring for their satisfaction the products of distant lands and [climates]. In place of the old local and national seclusion and self-sufficiency, we have intercourse in every direction, universal interdependence of nations. And as in material, so also in intellectual production. The intellectual creations of individual nations become common property. National one-sidedness and narrow-mindedness become more and more impossible, and from the numerous national and local literatures there arises a world literature.

The bourgeoisie, by the rapid improvement of all instruments of production, by the immensely facilitated means of communication, draws all, even the most barbarian, nations into civilization. The cheap prices of its commodities are the heavy artillery with which it batters down all Chinese walls, with which it forces the barbarians' intensely obstinate hatred of foreigners to capitulate. It compels all nations, on pain of extinction, to adopt the bourgeois mode of production; it compels them to introduce what it calls civilization into their midst—that is, to become bourgeois themselves. In one word, it creates a world after its own image. . . .

Modern bourgeois society with its relations of production, of exchange, and of property, a society that has conjured up such gigantic means of production and of exchange, is like the sorcerer who is no longer able to control the powers of the nether world whom he has called up by his spells. For many a decade past, the history of industry and commerce is but the history of the revolt of modern productive forces against modern conditions of production, against the property relations that are the conditions for the existence of the bourgeoisie and of its rule. It is enough to mention the commercial crises that by their periodical return put on its trial, each time more threateningly, the existence of the entire bourgeois society. In these crises a great part not only of the existing products, but also of the previously created productive forces, are periodically destroyed. In these crises there breaks out an epidemic that in all earlier epochs would have seemed an absurdity—the epidemic of overproduction. Society suddenly finds itself put back into a state of momentary barbarism; it appears as if a famine, a universal war of devastation, had cut off the supply of every means of subsistence; industry and commerce seem to be destroyed. And why? Because there is too much civilization, too much means of subsistence, too much industry, too much commerce. The productive forces at the disposal of society no longer tend to further the development of the conditions of bourgeois property. On the contrary, they have become too powerful for these conditions by which they are fettered, and so soon as they overcome these fetters, they bring disorder into the whole of bourgeois society, endanger the existence of bourgeois property. The conditions of bourgeois society are too narrow to comprise the wealth created by them. And how does the bourgeoisie get over these crises? On the one hand, by enforced destruction of a mass of productive forces; on the other, by the conquest of new markets and by the more thorough exploitation of the old ones—that is to say, by paving the way for more extensive and more destructive crises and by diminishing the means whereby crises are prevented.

The weapons with which the bourgeoisie felled feudalism to the ground are now turned against the bourgeoisie itself.

But not only has the bourgeoisie forged the weapons that bring death to itself; it has also called into existence the men who are to wield those weapons—the modern working class, the proletarians.

In proportion as the bourgeoisie, that is, capital, is developed, in the same proportion is the proletariat, the modern working class, developed—a class of laborers who live only so long as they find work and who find work only so long as their labor increases capital. These laborers, who must sell themselves piecemeal, are a commodity like every other article of commerce and are consequently exposed to all the vicissitudes of competition, to all the fluctuations of the market.

Owing to the extensive use of machinery and to division of labor, the work of the proletarians has lost all individual character and consequently all charm for the workman. He becomes an appendage of the machine, and it is only the most simple, most monotonous, and most easily acquired knack that is required of him. Hence, the cost of production of a workman is restricted, almost entirely, to the means of subsistence that he requires for his maintenance and for the propagation of his race. But the price of a commodity, and therefore also of labor, is equal to its cost of production. In proportion, therefore, as the repulsiveness of the work increases, the wage decreases. Nay more, in proportion as the use of machinery and division of labor increases, in the same proportion the burden of toil also increases, whether by prolongation of the working hours, by increase of the work exacted in a given time, or by increased speed of the machinery, and so on.

Modern industry has converted the little workshop of the patriarchal master into the great factory of the industrial capitalist. Masses of laborers, crowded into the factory, are organized like soldiers. As privates of the industrial army they are placed under the command of a perfect hierarchy of officers and sergeants. Not only are they slaves of the bourgeois class and of the bourgeois state; they are daily and hourly enslaved by the machine, by the overlooker, and, above all, by the individual bourgeois manufacturer himself. The more openly this despotism proclaims gain to be its end and aim, the more petty, the more hateful, and the more embittering it is.

The less the skill and exertion of strength implied in manual labor—in other words, the more modern industry becomes developed—the more is the labor of men superseded by that of women. Differences of age and sex have no longer any distinctive social validity for the working class. All are instruments of labor, more or less expensive to use, according to their age and sex.

No sooner is the exploitation of the laborer by the manufacturer, so far, at an end and he receives his wages in cash, than he is set upon by the other portions of the bourgeoisie: the landlord, the shopkeeper, the pawnbroker, and so on.

The lower strata of the middle class—the small tradespeople, shopkeepers, and retired tradesmen generally, the handicraftsmen and peasants—all these sink gradually into the proletariat, partly because their diminutive capital does not suffice for the scale on which modern industry is carried on and is swamped in the competition with the large capitalists, partly because their specialized skill is rendered worthless by new methods of production. Thus the proletariat is recruited from all classes of the population.

The proletariat goes through various stages of development. With its birth begins its struggle with the bourgeoisie. At first the contest is carried on by individual laborers, then by the workpeople of a factory, then by the operatives of one trade, in one locality, against the individual bourgeois who directly exploits them. They direct their attacks not against the bourgeois conditions of production, but against the instruments of production themselves. They destroy imported wares that compete with their labor, they smash to pieces machinery, they set factories ablaze, they seek to restore by force the vanished status of the workman of the Middle Ages.

At this stage the laborers still form an incoherent mass scattered over the whole country and broken up by their mutual competition. If anywhere they unite to form more compact bodies, this is not yet the consequence of their own active union but of the union of the bourgeoisie—which class, in order to attain its own political ends, is compelled to set the whole proletariat in motion and is moreover yet, for a time, able to do so. At this stage, therefore, the proletarians do not fight their enemies but the enemies of their enemies: the remnants of absolute monarchy, the landowners, the nonindustrial bourgeois, the petty bourgeoisie.[6] Thus the whole historical movement is concentrated in the hands of the bourgeoisie; every victory so obtained is a victory for the bourgeoisie.

But with the development of industry the proletariat not only increases in number; it becomes concentrated in greater masses, its strength grows, and it feels that strength more. The various interests and conditions of life within the ranks of the proletariat are more and more equalized, in proportion as machinery obliterates all distinctions of labor and nearly everywhere reduces wages to the same low level. The growing competition among the bourgeois and the resulting commercial crises make the wages of the workers ever more fluctuating. The unceasing improvement of machinery, ever more rapidly developing, makes their livelihood more and more precarious; the collisions between individual workmen and individual bourgeois take more and more the character of collisions between two classes. Thereupon the workers begin to form combinations (trade unions) against the bourgeois; they club together in order to keep up the rate of wages; they found permanent associations in order to make provision beforehand for these occasional revolts. Here and there the contest breaks out into riots.

Now and then the workers are victorious, but only for a time. The real fruit of their battles lies not in the immediate result, but in the ever-expanding union of the workers. This union is helped on by the improved means of communication that are created by modern industry and that place the workers of different localities in contact with one another. It was just this contact that was needed to centralize the numerous local struggles, all of the same character, into one national struggle between classes. But every class struggle is a political struggle. And that union, to attain which the burghers of the Middle Ages, with their miserable highways, required centuries, the modern proletarians, thanks to railways, achieve in a few years.

This organization of the proletarians into a class, and consequently into a political party, is continually being upset again by the competition between the workers themselves. But it ever rises up again, stronger, firmer, mightier. It compels legislative recognition of particular interests of the workers by taking advantage of the divisions among the bourgeoisie itself. Thus the Ten Hours bill in England was carried.[7]

Altogether collisions between the classes of the old society further, in many ways, the course of development of the proletariat. The bourgeoisie finds itself involved in a constant battle—at first with the aristocracy; later on, with those portions of the bourgeoisie itself, whose interests have become antagonistic to the progress of industry; at all times, with the bourgeoisie of foreign countries. In all these battles it sees itself compelled to appeal to the proletariat, to ask for its help, and thus to drag it into the political arena. The bourgeoisie itself, therefore, supplies the proletariat with its own elements of political and general education. In other words, it furnishes the proletariat with weapons for fighting the bourgeoisie.

Further, as we have already seen, entire sections of the ruling classes are, by the advance of industry, precipitated into the proletariat, or are at least threatened in their conditions of existence. These also supply the proletariat with fresh elements of enlightenment and progress.

Finally, in times when the class struggle nears the decisive hour, the process of dissolution going on within the ruling class—in fact within the whole range of old society—assumes such a violent, glaring character, that a small section of the ruling class cuts itself adrift and joins the revolutionary class, the class that holds the future in its hands. Just as, therefore, at an earlier period, a section of the nobility went over to the bourgeoisie, so now a portion of the bourgeoisie goes over to the proletariat, and in particular, a portion of the bourgeois ideologists who have raised themselves to the level of comprehending theoretically the historical movement as a whole.

Of all the classes that stand face to face with the bourgeoisie today, the proletariat alone is a really revolutionary class. The other classes decay and finally disappear in the face of modern industry; the proletariat is its special and essential product. . . .

All the preceding classes that got the upper hand sought to fortify their already acquired status by subjecting society at large to their conditions of appropriation. The proletarians cannot become masters of the productive forces of society, except by abolishing their own previous mode of appropriation and thereby also every other previous mode of appropriation. They have nothing of their own to secure and to fortify; their mission is to destroy all previous securities for, and insurances of, individual property.

All previous historical movements were movements of minorities or in the interest of minorities. The proletarian movement is the self-conscious, independent movement of the immense majority, in the interest of the immense majority. The proletariat, the lowest stratum of our present society, cannot stir, cannot raise itself up, without the whole superincumbent strata of official society being sprung into the air.

Though not in substance, yet in form, the struggle of the proletariat with the bourgeoisie is at first a national struggle. The proletariat of each country must, of course, first of all settle matters with its own bourgeoisie.

In depicting the most general phases of the development of the proletariat, we traced the more or less veiled civil war raging within existing society, up to the point where that war breaks out into open revolution and where the violent overthrow of the bourgeoisie lays the foundation for the sway of the proletariat.

Hitherto every form of society has been based, as we have already seen, on the antagonism of oppressing and oppressed classes. But in order to oppress a class, certain conditions must be assured to it under which it can at least continue its slavish existence. The serf, in the period of serfdom, raised himself to membership in the commune, just as the petty bourgeois, under the yoke of feudal absolutism, managed to develop into a bourgeois. The modern laborer, on the contrary, instead of rising with the progress of industry, sinks deeper and deeper below the conditions of existence of his own class. He becomes a pauper, and pauperism develops more rapidly than population and wealth. And here it becomes evident that the bourgeoisie is unfit any longer to be the ruling class in society and to impose its conditions of existence upon society as an overriding law. It is unfit to rule because it is incompetent to assure an existence to its slave within his slavery, because it cannot help letting him sink into such a state that it has to feed him, instead of being fed by him. Society can no longer live under this bourgeoisie. In other words, its existence is no longer compatible with society.

The essential condition for the existence and for the sway of the bourgeois class is the formation and augmentation of capital; the condition for capital is wage-labor. Wage-labor rests exclusively on competition between the laborers. The advance of industry, whose involuntary promoter is the bourgeoisie, replaces the isolation of the laborers, due to competition, by their revolutionary combination, due to association. The development of modern industry, therefore, cuts from under its feet the very foundation on which the bourgeoisie produces and appropriates products. What the bourgeoisie, therefore, produces above all is its own gravediggers. Its fall and the victory of the proletariat are equally inevitable.

II. PROLETARIANS AND COMMUNISTS

In what relation do the Communists stand to the proletarians as a whole?

The Communists do not form a separate party opposed to other working-class parties.

They have no interests separate and apart from those of the proletariat as a whole.

They do not set up any sectarian principles of their own, by which to shape and mold the proletarian movement.

The Communists are distinguished from the other working-class parties by this only: (1) In the national struggles of the proletarians of the different countries, they point out and bring to the front the common interests of the entire proletariat, independently of all nationality. (2) In the various stages of development which the struggle of the working class against the bourgeoisie has to pass through, they always and everywhere represent the interests of the movement as a whole.

The Communists therefore are on the one hand, *practically*, the most advanced and resolute section of the working-class parties of every country, that section which pushes forward all others. On the other hand, *theoretically,* they have over the great mass of the proletariat the advantage of clearly understanding the line of march, the conditions, and the ultimate general results of the proletarian movement.

The immediate aim of the Communists is the same as that of all the other proletarian parties: formation of the proletariat into a class, overthrow of the bourgeois supremacy, conquest of political power by the proletariat.

The theoretical conclusions of the Communists are in no way based on ideas or principles that have been invented, or discovered by this or that would-be universal reformer.

They merely express, in general terms, actual relations springing from an existing class struggle, from a historical movement going on under our very eyes. The abolition of existing property relations is not at all a distinctive feature of Communism.

All property relations in the past have continually been subject to historical change consequent upon the change in historical conditions.

The French Revolution, for example, abolished feudal property in favor of bourgeois property.

The distinguishing feature of Communism is not the abolition of property generally, but the abolition of bourgeois property. But modern bourgeois private property[8] is the final and most complete expression of the system of producing and appropriating products that is based on class antagonisms, on the exploitation of the many by the few.

In this sense, the theory of the Communists may be summed up in the single [phrase]: Abolition of private property. . . .

The first step in the revolution by the working class is to raise the proletariat to the position of ruling class, to win the battle of democracy.

The proletariat will use its political supremacy to wrest, by degrees, all capital from the bourgeoisie, to centralize all instruments of production in the hands of the state, that is, of the proletariat organized as the ruling class; and to increase the total of productive forces as rapidly as possible.

Of course, in the beginning this cannot be effected except by means of despotic inroads on the rights of property, and on the conditions of bourgeois production— by means of measures, therefore, which appear economically insufficient and untenable but which, in the course of the movement, outstrip themselves, necessitate further inroads upon the old social order, and are unavoidable as a means of entirely revolutionizing the mode of production.

These measures will, of course, be different in different countries.

Nevertheless, in the most advanced countries the following will be pretty generally applicable:

1. Abolition of property in land and application of all rents of land to public purposes.
2. A heavy progressive or graduated income tax.
3. Abolition of all right of inheritance.
4. Confiscation of the property of all emigrants and rebels.

5. Centralization of credit in the hands of the state, by means of a national bank with state capital and an exclusive monopoly.
6. Centralization of the means of communication and transport in the hands of the state.
7. Extension of factories and instruments of production owned by the state. The bringing into cultivation of wastelands, and the improvement of the soil generally in accordance with a common plan.
8. Equal liability of all to labor. Establishment of industrial armies, especially for agriculture.
9. Combination of agriculture with manufacturing industries. Gradual abolition of the distinction between town and country, by a more equable distribution of the population over the country.
10. Free education for all children in public schools. Abolition of children's factory labor in its present form. Combination of education with industrial production, and so on, and so on.

When, in the course of development, class distinctions have disappeared and all production has been concentrated in the hands of a vast association of the whole nation, the public power will lose its political character. Political power, properly so called, is merely the organized power of one class for oppressing another. If the proletariat during its contest with the bourgeoisie is compelled by the force of circumstances to organize itself as a class; if, by means of a revolution, it makes itself the ruling class and, as such, sweeps away by force the old conditions of production—then it will, along with these conditions, have swept away the conditions for the existence of class antagonisms and of classes generally, and will thereby have abolished its own supremacy as a class.

In place of the old bourgeois society, with its classes and class antagonisms, we shall have an association in which the free development of each is the condition for the free development of all.

IV. POSITION OF THE COMMUNISTS IN RELATION TO THE VARIOUS EXISTING OPPOSITION PARTIES

. . . The Communists everywhere support every revolutionary movement against the existing social and political order of things.

In all these movements they bring to the front, as the leading question in each, the property question, no matter what its degree of development at the time.

Finally, they labor everywhere for the union and agreement of the democratic parties of all countries.

The Communists disdain to conceal their views and aims. They openly declare that their ends can be attained only by the forcible overthrow of all existing social conditions. Let the ruling classes tremble at a Communist revolution. The proletarians have nothing to lose but their chains. They have a world to win.

WORKING MEN OF ALL COUNTRIES, UNITE!

NOTES

1. By *bourgeoisie* [the class of bourgeois people] is meant the class of modern capitalists, owners of the means of social production and employers of wage labor; by *proletariat*, the class of modern wage-laborers who, having no means of production of their own, are reduced to selling their labor power in order to live. [F. ENGELS]

2. *guild master:* a full member of a guild—not a master within, not a head of a guild. [F. ENGELS]

3. *chartered burghers:* inhabitants of a chartered town who have full municipal rights; citizens. [D. C. ABEL]

4. *the Cape:* the Cape of Good Hope, at the southern tip of Africa. [D. C. ABEL]

5. *indefeasible:* incapable of being annulled or forfeited. [D. C. ABEL]

6. *petty bourgeoisie:* less wealthy members of the bourgeoisie, especially shop-keepers and artisans. [D. C. ABEL]

7. The Ten Hours Act, passed in 1847, limited the labor in industry of women and children to ten hours a day. [D. C. ABEL]

8. *private property:* private ownership of the means of production. [D. C. ABEL]

On Liberty

John Stuart Mill

A biography of John Stuart Mill appears on p. 365.

Our reading is from *On Liberty,* Mill's classic defense of the freedom of the individual to do whatever does not harm other people. Mill's thesis is that "the only purpose for which power can be rightfully exercised over any member of a civilized community, against his will, is to prevent harm to others." We may not force people to do or refrain from doing something because we think (rightly or wrongly) that it is for their own good; individuals are sovereign in matters that concern only themselves. (Anticipating an objection, Mill explains that his principle of liberty applies only to rational, mature adults; children, for example, may be prevented from doing things that injure themselves.) A just society, consequently, must preserve freedom of consciousness (thought, opinion, feeling, conscience), freedom of tastes and pursuits, and freedom of association. The exercise of the latter two freedoms is subject to the condition that the actions of the individuals or the group do not harm others.

Mill goes on to give a detailed defense of two liberties he considers especially important: the freedom to express one's opinion and the freedom to live in a way that expresses one's individuality. With regard to the latter, he contends that the free development of individuality is something desirable for its own sake, as an essential part of human well-being. People who cultivate their unique traits live richer and more vibrant lives than those who submerge themselves in uniformity. To the degree that people develop their individuality, they become more valuable to themselves. Society benefits, too, because the more valuable people are to themselves, the more valuable they can be to others.

CHAPTER I. INTRODUCTORY

. . . The object of this essay is to assert one very simple principle, as entitled to govern absolutely the dealings of society with the individual in the way of compulsion and control, whether the means used be physical force in the form of legal penalties, or the moral coercion of public opinion. That principle is that the sole end[1] for which mankind are warranted, individually or collectively, in interfering with the liberty of action of any of their number is self-protection; that the only purpose for which power can be rightfully exercised over any member of a civilized community, against his will, is to prevent harm to others. His own good, either physical or moral, is not a sufficient warrant. He cannot rightfully be compelled to do or forbear because it will be better for him to do so, because it will make him happier, [or] because, in the opinions of others, to do so would be wise, or even right. These are good reasons for remonstrating with him, or reasoning with him, [or] persuading him, or entreating him, but not for compelling him or visiting him with any evil in case he do otherwise. To justify that, the conduct from which it is desired to deter him must be calculated to produce evil to someone else. The only part of the conduct of anyone for which he is amenable to society is that which concerns others. In the part which merely concerns himself, his independence is, of right, absolute. Over himself, over his own body and mind, the individual is sovereign.

It is perhaps hardly necessary to say that this doctrine is meant to apply only to human beings in the maturity of their faculties. We are not speaking of children or of young persons below the age which the law may fix as that of manhood or womanhood. Those who are still in a state to require being taken care of by others must be protected against their own actions as well as against external injury. For the same reason, we may leave out of consideration those backward states of society in which the race itself may be considered as in its nonage.[2] The early difficulties in the way of spontaneous progress are so great that there is seldom any choice of means for overcoming them; and a ruler full of the spirit of improvement is warranted in the use of any expedients that will attain an end, perhaps otherwise unattainable. Despotism is a legitimate mode of government in dealing with barbarians, provided the end be their improvement, and the means justified by actually effecting that end. Liberty, as a principle, has no application to any state of things anterior to the time when mankind have become capable of being improved by free and equal discussion. Until then, there is nothing for them but implicit obedience to an Akbar or a Charlemagne,[3] if they are so fortunate as to find one. But as soon as mankind have attained the capacity of being guided to their own improvement by conviction or persuasion (a period long since reached in all nations with whom we need here concern ourselves), compulsion, either in the direct form or in that of pains and penalties for noncompliance, is no longer admissible as a means to their own good, and justifiable only for the security of others.

It is proper to state that I forgo any advantage which could be derived to my argument from the idea of abstract right, as a thing independent of utility.[4] I regard utility as the ultimate appeal on all ethical questions—but it must be utility in the largest sense, grounded on the permanent interests of man as a progressive being. Those interests, I contend, authorize the subjection of individual spontaneity to external control only in respect to those actions of each which concern the interest of other people. If anyone does an act hurtful to others, there is a prima facie[5] case for punishing him by law or, where legal penalties are not safely applicable, by general disapprobation. There are also many positive acts for the benefit of others which he may rightfully be compelled to perform, such as: to give evidence in a court of justice; to bear his fair share in the common defense or in any other joint work necessary to the interest of the society of which he enjoys the protection; and to perform certain acts of individual beneficence, such as saving a fellow-creature's life or interposing to protect the defenseless against ill-usage—things which whenever it is obviously a man's duty to do, he may rightfully be made responsible to society for not doing. A person may cause evil to others not only by his actions but by his inaction, and in either case he is justly accountable to them for the injury. The latter case, it is true, requires a much more cautious exercise of compulsion than the former. To make anyone answerable for doing evil to others is the rule; to make him answerable for not preventing evil is, comparatively speaking, the exception. . . .

This, then, is the appropriate region of human liberty. It comprises, first, the inward domain of consciousness, demanding liberty of conscience in the most comprehensive sense; liberty of thought and feeling; absolute freedom of opinion and sentiment on all subjects, practical or speculative, scientific, moral, or theological. The liberty of expressing and publishing opinions may seem to fall under a different principle, since it belongs to that part of the conduct of an individual which concerns other people; but, being almost of as much importance as the liberty of thought itself and resting in great part on the same reasons, is practically inseparable from it. Secondly, the principle requires liberty of tastes and pursuits; of framing the plan of our life to suit our own character; of doing as we like, subject to such consequences as may follow—without impediment from our fellow creatures, so long as what we do does not harm them, even though they should think our conduct foolish, perverse, or wrong. Thirdly, from this liberty of each individual follows the liberty, within the same limits, of combination among individuals; freedom to unite for any purpose not involving harm to others—the persons combining being supposed to be of full age and not forced or deceived.

No society in which these liberties are not, on the whole, respected is free, whatever may be its form of government; and none is completely free in which they do not exist absolute and unqualified. The only freedom which deserves the name is that of pursuing our own good in our own way, so long as we do not attempt to deprive others of theirs or impede their efforts to obtain it. Each is the proper guardian of his own health, whether bodily, or mental and spiritual. Mankind are greater gainers by suffering[6] each other to live as seems good to themselves, than by compelling each to live as seems good to the rest. . . .

It will be convenient for the argument if, instead of at once entering upon the general thesis, we confine ourselves in the first instance to a single branch of it, on which the principle here stated is, if not fully, yet to a certain point, recognized by the current opinions. This one branch is the liberty of thought, from which it is impossible to separate the cognate liberty of speaking and of writing. Although these liberties, to some considerable amount, form part of the political morality of all countries which profess religious toleration and free institutions, the grounds, both philosophical and practical, on which they rest are perhaps not so familiar to the general mind, nor so thoroughly appreciated by many even of the leaders of opinion, as might have been expected. . . .

CHAPTER II. OF THE LIBERTY OF THOUGHT AND DISCUSSION

The time, it is to be hoped, is gone by, when any defense would be necessary of the "liberty of the press" as one of the securities against corrupt or tyrannical government. No argument, we may suppose, can now be needed against permitting a legislature or an executive, not identified in interest with the people, to prescribe opinions to them and determine what doctrines or what arguments they shall be allowed to hear. This aspect of the question, besides, has been so often and so triumphantly enforced by preceding writers that it needs not be specially insisted on in this place. Though the law of England on the subject of the press is as servile to this day as it was in the time of the Tudors,[7] there is little danger of its being actually put in force against political discussion, except during some temporary panic, when fear of insurrection drives ministers and judges from their propriety. And speaking generally, it is not, in constitutional countries, to be apprehended that the government, whether completely responsible to the people or not, will often attempt to control the expression of opinion, except when in doing so it makes itself the organ of the general intolerance of the public. Let us suppose therefore that the government is entirely at one with the people and never thinks of exerting any power of coercion unless in agreement with what it conceives to be their voice. But I deny the right of the people to exercise such coercion, either by themselves or by their government. The power itself is illegitimate. The best government has no more title to it than the worst. It is as noxious, or more noxious, when exerted in accordance with public opinion than when in opposition to it. If all mankind minus one were of one opinion, and only one person were of the contrary opinion, mankind would be no more justified in silencing that one person, than he, if he had the power, would be justified in silencing mankind. Were an opinion a personal possession of no value except to the owner, if to be obstructed in the enjoyment of it were simply a private injury, it would make some difference whether the injury was inflicted only on a few persons or on many. But the peculiar evil of silencing the expression of an opinion is that it is robbing the human race; posterity as well as the existing generation; those who dissent from the opinion, still more than those who hold it. If the opinion is right, they are deprived of the opportunity of exchanging error for truth; if wrong, they lose what is almost as great a benefit, the clearer perception and livelier impression of truth, produced by its collision with error. . . .

The necessity to the mental well-being of mankind (on which all their other well-being depends) of freedom of opinion, and freedom of the expression of opinion, [rests] on four distinct grounds. . . .

First, if any opinion is compelled to silence, that opinion may, for aught we can certainly know, be true. To deny this is to assume our own infallibility.

Secondly, though the silenced opinion be an error, it may, and very commonly does, contain a portion of truth; and since the general or prevailing opinion on any subject is rarely or never the whole truth, it is only by the collision of adverse opinions that the remainder of the truth has any chance of being supplied.

Thirdly, even if the received opinion be not only true but the whole truth, unless it is suffered to be, and actually is, vigorously and earnestly contested, it will, by most of those who receive it, be held in the manner of a prejudice, with little comprehension or feeling of its rational grounds. And not only this, but, fourthly, the meaning of the doctrine itself will be in danger of being lost or enfeebled and deprived of its vital effect on the character and conduct—the dogma becoming a mere formal profession, inefficacious for good, but cumbering the ground and preventing the growth of any real and heartfelt conviction from reason or personal experience. . . .

CHAPTER III. OF INDIVIDUALITY, AS ONE OF THE ELEMENTS OF WELL-BEING

Such being the reasons which make it imperative that human beings should be free to form opinions and to express their opinions without reserve; and such the baneful consequences to the intellectual, and through that to the moral nature of man, unless this liberty is either conceded or asserted in spite of prohibition; let us next examine whether the same reasons do not require that men should be free to act upon their opinions—to carry these out in their lives, without hindrance, either physical or moral, from their fellow men, so long as it is at their own risk and peril. This last proviso is of course indispensable. No one pretends that actions should be as free as opinions. On the contrary, even opinions lose their immunity when the circumstances in which they are expressed are such as to constitute their expression a positive instigation to some mischievous act. An opinion that corn dealers are starvers of the poor, or that private property is robbery, ought to be unmolested when simply circulated through the press, but may justly incur punishment when delivered orally to an excited mob assembled before the house of a corn dealer, or when handed about among the same mob in the form of a placard. Acts of whatever kind which without justifiable cause do harm to others may be, and in the more important cases absolutely require to be, controlled by the unfavorable sentiments and, when needful, by the active interference of mankind. The liberty of the individual must be thus far limited; he must not make himself a nuisance to other people. But if he refrains from molesting others in what concerns them and merely acts according to his own inclination and judgment in things which concern himself, the same reasons which show that opinion should be free, prove also that he should be allowed, without molestation, to carry his opinions into practice at his own cost. That mankind are not infallible; that their truths for the most part are only half-truths; that unity of opinion, unless resulting from the fullest and freest comparison of opposite opinions, is not desirable, and diversity not an evil but a good, until mankind are much more capable than at present of recognizing all sides of the truth, are principles applicable to men's modes of action, not less than to their opinions. As it is useful that while mankind are imperfect there should be different opinions, so is it that there should be different experiments of living; that free scope should be given to varieties of character, short of injury to others; and that the worth of different modes of life should be proved practically, when anyone thinks fit to try them. It is desirable, in short, that in things which do not primarily concern others, individuality should assert itself. Where not the person's own character, but the traditions or customs of other people are the rule of conduct, there is wanting one of the principal ingredients of human happiness, and quite the chief ingredient of individual and social progress.

In maintaining this principle, the greatest difficulty to be encountered does not lie in the appreciation of means towards an acknowledged end, but in the indifference of persons in general to the end itself. If it were felt that the free development of individuality is one of the leading essentials of well-being; that it is not only a coordinate element with all that is designated by the terms civilization, instruction, education, culture, but is itself a necessary part and condition of all those things—[then] there would be no danger that liberty should be undervalued, and the adjustment of the boundaries between it and social control would present no extraordinary difficulty. But the evil is that individual spontaneity is hardly recognized by the common modes of thinking as having any intrinsic worth or deserving any regard on its own account. . . .

It is not by wearing down into uniformity all that is individual in themselves, but by cultivating it and calling it forth, within the limits imposed by the rights and interests of others, that human beings become a noble and beautiful object of contemplation. And as the works partake the character of those who do them, by the same process human life also becomes rich, diversified, and animating, furnishing more abundant aliment to high thoughts and elevating feelings, and strengthening the tie which binds every individual to the race, by making the race infinitely better worth belonging to. In proportion to the development of his individuality, each person becomes more valuable to himself and is therefore capable of being more valuable to others. There is a greater fullness of life about his own existence, and when there is more life in the units there is more in the mass which is composed of them. . . .

CHAPTER IV. OF THE LIMITS TO THE AUTHORITY OF SOCIETY OVER THE INDIVIDUAL

What, then, is the rightful limit to the sovereignty of the individual over himself? Where does the authority of society begin? How much of human life should be assigned to individuality, and how much to society?

Each will receive its proper share if each has that which more particularly concerns it. To individuality should belong the part of life in which it is chiefly the individual that is interested; to society, the part which chiefly interests society.

Though society is not founded on a contract and though no good purpose is answered by inventing a contract in order to deduce social obligations from it, everyone who receives the protection of society owes a return for the benefit, and the fact of living in society renders it indispensable that each should be bound to observe a certain line of conduct towards the rest. This conduct consists, first, in not injuring the interests of one another—or rather certain interests which, either by express legal provision or by tacit understanding, ought to be considered as rights; and secondly, in each person's bearing his share (to be fixed on some equitable principle) of the labors and sacrifices incurred for defending the society or its members from injury and molestation. These conditions society is justified in enforcing at all costs to those who endeavor to withhold fulfillment. Nor is this all that society may do. The acts of an individual may be hurtful to others, or wanting in due consideration for their welfare, without going the length of violating any of their constituted rights. The offender may then be justly punished by opinion, though not by law. As soon as any part of a person's conduct affects prejudicially the interests of others, society has jurisdiction over it and the question whether the general welfare will or will not be promoted by interfering with it becomes open to discussion. But there is no room for entertaining any such question when a person's conduct affects the interests of no persons besides himself, or needs not affect them unless they like (all the persons concerned being of full age and the ordinary amount of understanding). In all such cases there should be perfect freedom, legal and social, to do the action and stand the consequences. . . .

Neither one person nor any number of persons is warranted in saying to another human creature of ripe years that he shall not do with his life for his own benefit what he chooses to do with it. He is the person most interested in his own well-being; the interest which any other person, except in cases of strong personal attachment, can have in it is trifling compared with that which he himself has. The interest which society has in him individually (except as to his conduct to others) is fractional and altogether indirect; while, with respect to his own feelings and circumstances, the most ordinary man or woman has means of knowledge immeasurably surpassing those that can be possessed by anyone else. The interference of society to overrule his judgment and purposes in what only regards himself, must be grounded on general presumptions which may be altogether wrong—and even if right, are as likely as not to be misapplied to individual cases by persons no better acquainted with the circumstances of such cases than those are who look at them merely from without. In this department, therefore, of human affairs, individuality has its proper field of action. In the conduct of human beings towards one another, it is necessary that general rules should for the most part be observed, in order that people may know what they have to expect; but in each person's own concerns, his individual spontaneity is entitled to free exercise. Considerations to aid his judgment, exhortations to strengthen his will, may be offered to him, even obtruded on him, by others; but he himself is the final judge. All errors which he is likely to commit against advice and warning are far outweighed by the evil of allowing others to constrain him to what they deem his good.

NOTES

1. *end:* purpose, goal. [D. C. ABEL]
2. *nonage:* the state of being a minor. [D. C. ABEL]
3. Akbar (1542–1605) was a Mogul emperor of a territory comprising most of what is now India; Charlemagne (742–814) was king of the Franks and then emperor of the West. [D. C. ABEL]
4. *utility:* usefulness in promoting good. Mill holds that the good is pleasure and that the ultimate criterion of morality is the promotion of the greatest pleasure of the greatest number of sentient creatures; see pp. 365–373 of this book. [D. C. ABEL]
5. *prima facie:* on first appearance (literally, in Latin, "at first glance"). [D. C. ABEL]
6. *suffering:* allowing. [D. C. ABEL]
7. *Tudors:* the English royal house that ruled from 1485 to 1603. [D. C. ABEL]

Letter from Birmingham Jail

Martin Luther King, Jr.

Martin Luther King, Jr., was born in 1929 in Atlanta, Georgia. He attended Morehouse College and during his senior year decided to follow in his father's footsteps and become a Baptist minister. Upon graduating in 1948, he entered Crozer Theological Seminary in Chester, Pennsylvania. There he was deeply influenced by Mohandas Gandhi's philosophy of nonviolence and became convinced that black Americans should use this strategy to attain their civil rights. King received his bachelor of divinity degree in 1951. He then began doctoral studies in theology at Boston University, completing his degree in 1955. While still working on his doctorate, King became pastor at the Dexter Avenue Baptist Church in Montgomery, Alabama. In 1954 he led a boycott of the city transit company to protest segregated seating on buses. Within a year the buses were desegregated. Encouraged by this success, King began to work for civil rights on a national basis by forming the Southern Christian Leadership Conference. In 1960 he moved to Atlanta, where he directed the Conference and served as copastor (with his father) at Ebenezer Baptist Church. In 1963 he and many others were arrested and jailed for participating in a demonstration in Birmingham. Later that year King helped organize a massive demonstration in Washington, D.C., for civil rights legislation. King addressed the crowd, proclaiming "I have a dream"—a dream of interracial equality and harmony. The following year King received the Nobel Peace Prize. In 1968, while in Memphis to support a strike by sanitation workers, he was killed by a sniper's bullet.

King's works include *Stride toward Freedom: The Montgomery Story* (1958), *Why We Can't Wait* (1964), and *Where Do We Go from Here: Chaos or Community?* (1967).

Our reading is King's "Letter from Birmingham Jail" (published in *Why We Can't Wait),* an essay King wrote in 1963 when in jail for protesting segregation at lunch counters and discrimination in hiring practices. King's essay is a response to eight members of the clergy who had published a statement criticizing his civil rights activities as "unwise and untimely." King explains that blacks in America have waited for more than three centuries to gain their basic human rights—and that they should wait no longer. In answer to the objection that his nonviolent activities sometimes violate laws, King distinguishes just and unjust laws. Just laws should be obeyed, but unjust laws are not binding because they contradict moral laws and degrade human beings. There are some situations in which even just laws are not binding, however. For example, a law requiring a permit for a parade is just, but it need not be obeyed when it is used for the unjust purpose of denying citizens the right of peaceful assembly and protest. King explains that a person who breaks a just law as a form of protest must do so openly and with a willingness to accept the penalty. Responding to the charge that he is an extremist, King points out that nonviolent protest is certainly less extreme than violence. He admits, however, that in a certain way he is an extremist—an extremist for love and justice. In the final section of his letter, King expresses his disappointment at the white church and its leadership.

April 16, 1963

My Dear Fellow Clergymen:

While confined here in the Birmingham city jail, I came across your recent statement calling my present activities "unwise and untimely." Seldom do I pause to answer criticism of my work and ideas. If I sought to answer all the criticisms that cross my desk, my secretaries would have little time for anything other than such correspondence in the course of the day, and I would have no time for constructive work. But since I feel that you are men of genuine good will and that your criticisms are sincerely set forth, I want to try to answer your statement in what I hope will be patient and reasonable terms.

I think I should indicate why I am here in Birmingham, since you have been influenced by the view which argues against "outsiders coming in." I have the honor of serving as president of the Southern Christian Leadership Conference, an organization operating in every southern state, with headquarters in Atlanta, Georgia. We have some eighty-five affiliated organizations across the South, and one of them is the Alabama Christian Movement for Human Rights. Frequently we share staff, educational and financial resources with our affiliates. Several months ago the affiliate here in Birmingham asked us to be on call to engage in a nonviolent direct-action program if such were deemed necessary. We readily consented, and when the hour came we lived up to our promise. So I, along with several members of my staff, am here because I was invited here. I am here because I have organizational ties here.

But more basically, I am in Birmingham because injustice is here. Just as the prophets of the eighth century B.C. left their villages and carried their "thus saith the Lord" far beyond the boundaries of their home towns, and just as the Apostle Paul left his village of Tarsus and carried the gospel of Jesus Christ to the far corners of the Greco-Roman world, so am I compelled to carry the gospel of freedom beyond my own home town. Like Paul, I must constantly respond to the Macedonian call for aid.

Moreover, I am cognizant of the interrelatedness of all communities and states. I cannot sit idly by in Atlanta and not be concerned about what happens to Birmingham. Injustice anywhere is a threat to justice everywhere. We are caught in an inescapable network of mutuality, tied in a single garment of destiny. Whatever affects one directly, affects all indirectly. Never again can we afford to live with the narrow, provincial "outside agitator" idea. Anyone who lives inside the United States can never be considered an outsider anywhere within its bounds.

You deplore the demonstrations taking place in Birmingham. But your statement, I am sorry to say, fails to express a similar concern for the conditions that brought about the demonstrations. I am sure that none of you would want to rest content with the superficial kind of social analysis that deals merely with effects and does not grapple with underlying causes. It is unfortunate that demonstrations are taking place in Birmingham, but it is even more unfortunate that the city's white power structure left the Negro community with no alternative.

In any nonviolent campaign there are four steps: collection of the facts to determine whether injustices exist, negotiation, self-purification, and direct action. We have gone through all these steps in Birmingham. There can be no gainsaying the fact that racial injustice engulfs this community. Birmingham is probably the most thoroughly segregated city in the United States. Its ugly record of brutality is widely known. Negroes have experienced grossly unjust treatment in the courts. There have been more unsolved bombings of Negro homes and churches in Birmingham than in any other city in the nation. These are the hard brutal facts of the case. On the basis of these conditions, Negro leaders sought to negotiate with the city fathers. But the latter consistently refused to engage in good-faith negotiation.

Then, last September, came the opportunity to talk with leaders of Birmingham's economic community. In the course of negotiations, certain promises were made by the merchants—for example, to remove the stores' humiliating racial signs. On the basis of these promises, the Reverend Fred Shuttlesworth and the leaders of the Alabama Christian Movement for Human Rights agreed to a moratorium on all demonstrations. As the weeks and months went by, we realized that we were the victims of a broken promise. A few signs, briefly removed, returned; the others remained.

As in so many past experiences, our hopes had been blasted, and the shadow of deep disappointment settled upon us. We had no alternative except to prepare for direct action, whereby we would present our very bodies as a means of laying our case before the conscience of the local and the national community. Mindful of the difficulties involved, we decided to undertake a process of self-purification. We began a series of workshops on nonviolence, and we repeatedly asked ourselves: "Are you able to accept blows without retaliating?" "Are you able to endure the ordeal of jail?" We decided to schedule our direct-action program for the Easter season, realizing that except for Christmas, this is the main shopping period of the year. Knowing that a strong economic-withdrawal program would be the by-product of direct action, we felt that this would be the best time to bring pressure to bear on the merchants for the needed change.

Then it occurred to us that Birmingham's mayoralty election was coming up in March, and we speedily decided to postpone action until after election day. When we discovered that the Commissioner of Public Safety, Eugene "Bull" Connor, had piled up enough votes to be in the run-off, we decided again to postpone action until the day after the run-off so that the demonstrations could not be used to cloud the issues. Like many others, we waited to see Mr. Connor defeated, and to this end we endured postponement after postponement. Having aided in this community need, we felt that our direct-action program could be delayed no longer.

You may well ask: "Why direct action? Why sit-ins, marches and so forth? Isn't negotiation a better path?" You are quite right in calling for negotiation. Indeed, this is the very purpose of direct action. Nonviolent direct action seeks to create such a crisis and foster such a tension that a community which has constantly refused to negotiate is forced to confront the issue. It seeks so to dramatize the issue that it can no longer be ignored. My citing the creation of tension as part of the work of the nonviolent resister may sound rather shocking. But I must confess that I am not afraid of the word "tension." I have earnestly opposed violent tension, but there is a type of constructive nonviolent tension which is necessary for growth. Just as Socrates felt that it was necessary to create a tension in the mind so that individuals could rise from the bondage of myths and half-truths to the unfettered realm of creative analysis and objective appraisal, so must we see the need for nonviolent gadflies[1] to create the kind of tension in society that will help men rise from the dark depths of prejudice and racism to the majestic heights of understanding and brotherhood.

The purpose of our direct-action program is to create a situation so crisis-packed that it will inevitably open the door to negotiation. I therefore concur with you in your call for negotiation. Too long has our beloved Southland been bogged down in a tragic effort to live in monologue rather than dialogue.

One of the basic points in your statement is that the action that I and my associates have taken in Birmingham is untimely. Some have asked: "Why didn't you give the new city administration time to act?" The only answer that I can give to this query is that the new Birmingham administration must be prodded about as much as the outgoing one, before it will act. We are sadly mistaken if we feel that the election of Albert Boutwell as mayor will bring the millennium to Birmingham. While Mr. Boutwell is a much more gentle person than Mr. Connor, they are both segregationists, dedicated to maintenance of the status quo. I have hope that Mr. Boutwell will be reasonable enough to see the futility of massive resistance to desegregation. But he will not see this without pressure from devotees of civil rights. My friends, I must say to you that we have not made a single gain in civil rights without determined legal and nonviolent pressure. Lamentably, it is an historical fact that privileged groups seldom give up their privileges voluntarily. Individuals may see the moral light and voluntarily give up their unjust posture; but, as Reinhold Niebuhr[2] has reminded us, groups tend to be more immoral than individuals.

We know through painful experience that freedom is never voluntarily given by the oppressor; it must be demanded by the oppressed. Frankly, I have yet to engage in a direct-action campaign that was "well timed" in the view of those who have not suffered unduly from the disease of segregation. For years now I have heard the word "Wait!" It rings in the ear of every Negro with piercing familiarity. This "Wait" has almost always meant "Never." We must come to see, with one of our distinguished jurists, that "justice too long delayed is justice denied."[3]

We have waited for more than 340 years for our constitutional and God-given rights. The nations of Asia and Africa are moving with jetlike speed toward gaining political independence, but we still creep at horse-and-buggy pace toward gaining a cup of coffee at a lunch counter. Perhaps it is easy for those who have never felt the stinging darts of segregation to say "Wait." But when you have seen vicious mobs lynch your mothers and fathers at will and drown your sisters and brothers at whim; when you have seen hate-filled policemen curse, kick, and even kill your black brothers and sisters; when you see the vast majority of your twenty million Negro brothers smothering in an air-tight cage of poverty in the midst of an affluent society; when you suddenly find your tongue twisted and your speech stammering as you seek to explain to your six-year-old daughter why she can't go to the public amusement park that has just been advertised on television, and see tears welling up in her eyes when she is told that Funtown is closed to colored children, and see ominous clouds of inferiority beginning to form in her little mental sky, and see her beginning to distort her personality by developing an unconscious bitterness toward white people; when you have to concoct an answer for a five-year-old son who is asking, "Daddy, why do white people treat colored people so mean?"; when you take a cross-country drive and find it necessary to sleep night after night in the uncomfortable corners of your automobile because no motel will accept you; when you are humiliated day in and day out by nagging signs reading "white" and "colored"; when your first name becomes "nigger," your middle name becomes "boy" (however old you are), and your last name becomes "John," and your wife and mother are never given the respected title "Mrs."; when you are harried by day and haunted by night by the fact that you are a Negro, living constantly at tiptoe stance, never quite knowing what to expect next, and are plagued with inner fears and outer resentments; when you are forever fighting a degenerating sense of "nobodiness"—then you will understand why we find it difficult to wait. There comes a time when the cup of endurance runs over, and men are no longer willing to be plunged into the abyss of despair. I hope, sirs, you can understand our legitimate and unavoidable impatience.

You express a great deal of anxiety over our willingness to break laws. This is certainly a legitimate concern. Since we so diligently urge people to obey the Supreme Court's decision of 1954 outlawing segregation in the public schools, at first glance it may seem rather paradoxical for us consciously to break laws. One may well ask, "How can you advocate breaking some laws and obeying others?" The answer lies in the fact that there are two types of laws: just and unjust. I would be the first to advocate obeying just laws. One has not only a legal but a moral responsibility to obey just laws. Conversely, one has a moral responsibility to disobey unjust laws. I would agree with St. Augustine that "an unjust law is no law at all."[4]

Now, what is the difference between the two? How does one determine whether a law is just or unjust? A just law is a man-made code that squares with the moral law or the law of God. An unjust law is a code that is out of harmony with the moral law. To put it in the terms of St. Thomas Aquinas: An unjust law is a human law that is not rooted in eternal law and natural law.[5] Any law that uplifts human personality is just. Any law that degrades human personality is unjust. All segregation statutes are unjust because segregation distorts the soul and damages the personality. It gives the segregator a false sense of superiority and the segregated a false sense of inferiority. Segregation, to use the terminology of the Jewish philosopher Martin Buber, substitutes an "I–it" relationship for an "I–thou" relationship and ends up relegating persons to the status of things.[6] Hence segregation is not only politically, economically, and sociologically unsound; it is morally wrong and sinful. Paul Tillich has said that sin is separation.[7] Is not segregation an existential expression of man's tragic separation, his awful estrangement, his terrible sinfulness? Thus it is that I can urge men to obey the 1954 decision of the Supreme Court, for it is morally right; and I can urge them to disobey segregation ordinances, for they are morally wrong.

Let us consider a more concrete example of just and unjust laws. An unjust law is a code that a numerical or power majority group compels a minority group to obey but does not make binding on itself. This is *difference* made legal. By the same token, a just law is a code that a majority compels a minority to follow and that it is willing to follow itself. This is *sameness* made legal.

Let me give another explanation. A law is unjust if it is inflicted on a minority that, as a result of being denied the right to vote, had no part in enacting or devising the law. Who can say that the legislature of Alabama which set up that state's segregation laws was democratically elected? Throughout Alabama all sorts of devious methods are used to prevent Negroes from becoming registered voters, and there are some counties in which, even though Negroes constitute a majority of the population, not a single Negro is registered. Can any law enacted under such circumstances be considered democratically structured?

Sometimes a law is just on its face and unjust in its application. For instance, I have been arrested on a charge of parading without a permit. Now, there is nothing wrong in having an ordinance which requires a permit for a parade. But such an ordinance becomes unjust when it is used to maintain segregation and to deny citizens the First Amendment privilege of peaceful assembly and protest.

I hope you are able to see the distinction I am trying to point out. In no sense do I advocate evading or defying the law, as would the rabid segregationist. That would lead to anarchy. One who breaks an unjust law must do so openly, lovingly, and with a willingness to accept the penalty. I submit that an individual who breaks a law that conscience tells him is unjust, and who willingly accepts the penalty of imprisonment in order to arouse the conscience of the community over its injustice, is in reality expressing the highest respect for law.

Of course, there is nothing new about this kind of civil disobedience. It was evidenced sublimely in the refusal of Shadrach, Meshach, and Abednego to obey the laws of Nebuchadnezzar, on the ground that a higher moral law was at stake.[8] It was practiced superbly by the early Christians, who were willing to face hungry lions and the excruciating pain of chopping blocks rather than submit to certain unjust laws of the Roman Empire. To a degree, academic freedom is a reality today because Socrates practiced civil disobedience. In our own nation, the Boston Tea Party represented a massive act of civil disobedience.

We should never forget that everything Adolf Hitler did in Germany was "legal" and everything the Hungarian freedom fighters did in Hungary was "illegal." It was "illegal" to aid and comfort a Jew in Hitler's Germany. Even so, I am sure that, had I lived in Germany at the time, I would have aided and comforted my Jewish brothers. If today I lived in a Communist country where certain principles dear to the Christian faith are suppressed, I would openly advocate disobeying that country's antireligious laws.

I must make two honest confessions to you, my Christian and Jewish brothers. First, I must confess that over the past few years I have been gravely disappointed with the white moderate. I have almost reached the regrettable conclusion that the Negro's great stumbling block in his stride toward freedom is not the White Citizen's Counciler or the Ku Klux Klanner, but the white moderate, who is more devoted to "order" than to justice; who prefers a negative peace, which is the absence of tension, to a positive peace, which is the presence of justice; who constantly says, "I agree with you in the goal you seek, but I cannot agree with your methods of direct action"; who paternalistically believes he can set the timetable for another man's freedom; who lives by a mythical concept of time and who constantly advises the Negro to wait for a "more convenient season." Shallow understanding from people of good will is more frustrating than absolute misunderstanding from people of ill will. Lukewarm acceptance is much more bewildering than outright rejection.

I had hoped that the white moderate would understand that law and order exist for the purpose of establishing justice and that when they fail in this purpose they become the dangerously structured dams that block the flow of social progress. I had hoped that the white moderate would understand that the present tension in the South is a necessary phase of the transition from an obnoxious negative peace, in which the Negro passively accepted his unjust plight, to a substantive and positive peace, in which all men will respect the dignity and worth of human personality. Actually, we who engage in nonviolent direct action are not the creators of tension. We merely bring to the surface the hidden tension that is already alive. We bring it out in the open, where it can be seen and dealt with. Like a boil that can never be cured so long as it is covered up but must be opened with all its ugliness to the natural medicines of air and light, injustice must be exposed, with all the tension its exposure creates, to the light of human conscience and the air of national opinion before it can be cured.

In your statement you assert that our actions, even though peaceful, must be condemned because they precipitate violence. But is this a logical assertion? Isn't this like condemning a robbed man because his possession of money precipitated the evil act of robbery? Isn't this like condemning Socrates because his unswerving commitment to truth and his philosophical inquiries precipitated the act by the misguided populace in which they made him drink hemlock?[9] Isn't this like condemning Jesus because his unique God-consciousness and never-ceasing devotion to God's will precipitated the evil act of crucifixion? We must come to see that, as the federal courts have consistently affirmed, it is wrong to urge an individual to cease his efforts to gain his basic constitutional rights because the quest may precipitate violence. Society must protect the robbed and punish the robber.

I had also hoped that the white moderate would reject the myth concerning time in relation to the struggle for freedom. I have just received a letter from a white brother in Texas. He writes: "All Christians know that the colored people will receive equal rights eventually, but it is possible that you are in too great a religious hurry. It has taken Christianity almost two thousand years to accomplish what it has. The teachings of Christ take time to come to earth." Such an attitude stems from a tragic misconception of time, from the strangely irrational notion that there is something in the very flow of time that will inevitably cure all ills. Actually, time itself is neutral; it can be used either destructively or constructively. More and more I feel that the people of ill will have used time much more effectively than have the people of good will. We will have to repent in this generation not merely for the hateful words and actions of the bad people but for the appalling silence of the good people. Human progress never rolls in on wheels of inevitability; it comes through the tireless efforts of men willing to be coworkers with God, and without this hard work, time itself becomes an ally of the forces of social stagnation. We must use time creatively, in the knowledge that the time is always ripe to do right. Now is the time to make real the promise of democracy and transform our pending national elegy into a creative psalm of brotherhood. Now is the time to lift our national policy from the quicksand of racial injustice to the solid rock of human dignity.

You speak of our activity in Birmingham as extreme. At first I was rather disappointed that fellow clergymen would see my nonviolent efforts as those of an extremist. I began thinking about the fact that I stand in the middle of two opposing forces in the Negro community. One is a force of complacency, made up in part of Negroes who, as a result of long years of oppression, are so drained of self-respect and a sense of "somebodiness" that they have adjusted to segregation; and in part of a few middle-class Negroes who, because of a degree of academic and economic security and because in some ways they profit by segregation, have become insensitive to the problems of the masses. The other force is one of bitterness and hatred, and it comes perilously close to advocating violence. It is expressed in the various black nationalist groups that are springing up across the nation, the largest and best-known being Elijah Muhammad's Muslim movement.[10] Nourished by the Negro's frustration over the continued existence of racial discrimination, this movement is made up of people who have lost faith in America, who have absolutely repudiated Christianity, and who have concluded that the white man is an incorrigible "devil."

I have tried to stand between these two forces, saying that we need emulate neither the "do-nothingism" of the complacent nor the hatred and despair of the black nationalist. For there is the more excellent way of love and nonviolent protest. I am grateful to God that, through the influence of the Negro church, the way of nonviolence became an integral part of our struggle.

If this philosophy had not emerged, by now many streets of the South would, I am convinced, be flowing with blood. And I am further convinced that if our white brothers dismiss as "rabble-rousers" and "outside agitators" those of us who employ nonviolent direct action, and if they refuse to support our nonviolent efforts, millions of Negroes will, out of frustration and despair, seek solace and security in black-nationalist ideologies—a development that would inevitably lead to a frightening racial nightmare.

Oppressed people cannot remain oppressed forever. The yearning for freedom eventually manifests itself, and that is what has happened to the American Negro. Something within has reminded him of his birthright of freedom, and something without has reminded him that it can be gained. Consciously or unconsciously, he has been caught up by the zeitgeist,[11] and with his black brothers of Africa and his brown and yellow brothers of Asia, South America, and the Caribbean, the United States Negro is moving with a sense of great urgency toward the promised land of racial justice. If one recognizes this vital urge that has engulfed the Negro community, one should readily understand why public demonstrations are taking place. The Negro has many pent-up resentments and latent frustrations, and he must release them. So let him march; let him make prayer pilgrimages to the city hall; let him go on freedom rides—and try to understand why he must do so. If his repressed emotions are not released in nonviolent ways, they will seek expression through violence; this is not a threat but a fact of history. So I have not said to my people, "Get rid of your discontent." Rather, I have tried to say that this normal and healthy discontent can be channeled into the creative outlet of nonviolent direct action. And now this approach is being termed extremist.

But though I was initially disappointed at being categorized as an extremist, as I continued to think about the matter I gradually gained a measure of satisfaction from the label. Was not Jesus an extremist for love: "Love your enemies, bless them that curse you, do good to them that hate you, and pray for them which despitefully use you, and persecute you." Was not Amos an extremist for justice: "Let justice roll down like waters and righteousness like an ever-flowing stream." Was not Paul an extremist for the Christian gospel: "I bear in my body the marks of the Lord Jesus." Was not Martin Luther an extremist: "Here I stand; I cannot do otherwise, so help me God." And John Bunyan:[12] "I will stay in jail to the end of my days before I make a butchery of my conscience." And Abraham Lincoln: "This nation cannot survive half slave and half free." And Thomas Jefferson: "We hold these truths to be self-evident, that all men are created equal . . . " So the question is not whether we will be extremists, but what kind of extremists we will be. Will we be extremists for hate or for love? Will we be extremists for the preservation of injustice or for the extension of justice? In that dramatic scene on Calvary's hill three men were crucified. We must never forget that all three were crucified for the same crime—the crime of extremism. Two were extremists for immorality, and thus fell below their environment. The other, Jesus Christ, was an extremist for love, truth, and goodness, and thereby rose above his environment. Perhaps the South, the nation, and the world are in dire need of creative extremists.

I had hoped that the white moderate would see this need. Perhaps I was too optimistic; perhaps I expected too much. I suppose I should have realized that few members of the oppressor race can understand the deep groans and passionate yearnings of the oppressed race, and still fewer have the vision to see that injustice must be rooted out by strong, persistent, and determined action. I am thankful, however, that some of our white brothers in the South have grasped the meaning of this social revolution and committed themselves to it. They are still all too few in quantity, but they are big in quality. Some—such as Ralph McGill, Lillian Smith, Harry Golden, James McBride Dabbs, Ann Braden, and Sarah Patton Boyle—have written about our struggle in eloquent and prophetic terms. Others have marched with us down nameless streets of the South. They have languished in filthy, roach-infested jails, suffering the abuse and brutality of policemen who view them as "dirty nigger-lovers." Unlike so many of their moderate brothers and sisters, they have recognized the urgency of the moment and sensed the need for powerful "action" antidotes to combat the disease of segregation.

Let me take note of my other major disappointment. I have been so greatly disappointed with the white church and its leadership. Of course, there are some notable exceptions. I am not unmindful of the fact that each of you has taken some significant stands on this issue. I commend you, Reverend Stallings, for your Christian stand on this past Sunday, in welcoming Negroes to your worship service on a nonsegregated basis. I commend the Catholic leaders of this state for integrating Spring Hill College several years ago.

But despite these notable exceptions, I must honestly reiterate that I have been disappointed with the church. I do not say this as one of those negative critics who can always find something wrong with the church. I say this as a minister of the gospel who loves the church, who was nurtured in its bosom, who has been sustained by its spiritual blessings, and who will remain true to it as long as the cord of life shall lengthen.

When I was suddenly catapulted into the leadership of the bus protest in Montgomery, Alabama, a few years ago, I felt we would be supported by the white church. I felt that the white ministers, priests, and rabbis of the South would be among our strongest allies. Instead, some have been outright opponents, refusing to understand the freedom movement and misrepresenting its leaders; all too many others have been more cautious than courageous and have remained silent behind the anesthetizing security of stained-glass windows.

In spite of my shattered dreams, I came to Birmingham with the hope that the white religious leadership of this community would see the justice of our cause and, with deep moral concern, would serve as the channel through which our just grievances could reach the power structure. I had hoped that each of you would understand. But again I have been disappointed.

I have heard numerous southern religious leaders admonish their worshipers to comply with a desegregation decision because it is the law, but I have longed to hear white ministers declare: "Follow this decree because integration is morally right and because the Negro is your brother." In the midst of blatant injustices inflicted upon the Negro, I have watched white churchmen stand on the sideline and mouth pious irrelevancies and sanctimonious trivialities. In the midst of a mighty struggle to rid our nation of racial and economic injustice, I have heard many ministers say: "Those are social issues, with which the gospel has no real concern." And I have watched many churches commit themselves to a completely otherworldly religion which makes a strange, unbiblical distinction between body and soul, between the sacred and the secular.

I have traveled the length and breadth of Alabama, Mississippi, and all the other southern states. On sweltering summer days and crisp autumn mornings I have looked at the South's beautiful churches with their lofty spires pointing heavenward. I have beheld the impressive outlines of her massive religious-education buildings. Over and over I have found myself asking: "What kind of people worship here? Who is their God? Where were their voices when the lips of Governor Barnett[13] dripped with words of interposition and nullification? Where were they when Governor Wallace[14] gave a clarion call for defiance and hatred? Where were their voices of support when bruised and weary Negro men and women decided to rise from the dark dungeons of complacency to the bright hills of creative protest?"

Yes, these questions are still in my mind. In deep disappointment I have wept over the laxity of the church. But be assured that my tears have been tears of love. There can be no deep disappointment where there is not deep love. Yes, I love the church. How could I do otherwise? I am in the rather unique position of being the son, the grandson, and the great-grandson of preachers. Yes, I see the church as the body of Christ. But, oh! How we have blemished and scarred that body through social neglect and through fear of being nonconformists.

There was a time when the church was very powerful—in the time when the early Christians rejoiced at being deemed worthy to suffer for what they believed. In those days the church was not merely a thermometer that recorded the ideas and principles of popular opinion; it was a thermostat that transformed the mores of society. Whenever the early Christians entered a town, the people in power became disturbed and immediately sought to convict the Christians for being "disturbers of the peace" and "outside agitators." But the Christians pressed on, in the conviction that they were "a colony of heaven," called to obey God rather than man. Small in number, they were big in commitment. They were too God-intoxicated to be "astronomically intimidated." By their effort and example they brought an end to such ancient evils as infanticide and gladiatorial contests.

Things are different now. So often the contemporary church is a weak, ineffectual voice with an uncertain sound. So often it is an archdefender of the status quo. Far from being disturbed by the presence of the church, the power structure of the average community is consoled by the church's silent—and often even vocal—sanction of things as they are.

But the judgment of God is upon the church as never before. If today's church does not recapture the sacrificial spirit of the early church, it will lose its authenticity, forfeit the loyalty of millions, and be dismissed as an irrelevant social club with no meaning for the twentieth century. Every day I meet young people whose disappointment with the church has turned into outright disgust.

Perhaps I have once again been too optimistic. Is organized religion too inextricably bound to the status quo to save our nation and the world? Perhaps I must turn my faith to the inner spiritual church, the church within the church, as the true *ekklēsia*[15] and the hope of the world. But again I am thankful to God that some noble souls from the ranks of organized religion have broken loose from the paralyzing chains of conformity and joined us as active partners in the struggle for freedom. They have left their secure congregations and walked the streets of Albany, Georgia, with us. They have gone down the highways of the South on tortuous rides for freedom. Yes, they have gone to jail with us. Some have been dismissed from their churches, have lost the support of their bishops and fellow ministers. But they have acted in the faith that right defeated is stronger than evil triumphant. Their witness has been the spiritual salt that has preserved the true meaning of the gospel in these troubled times. They have carved a tunnel of hope through the dark mountain of disappointment.

I hope the church as a whole will meet the challenge of this decisive hour. But even if the church does not come to the aid of justice, I have no despair about the future. I have no fear about the outcome of our struggle in Birmingham, even if our motives are at present misunderstood. We will reach the goal of freedom in Birmingham and all over the nation, because the goal of America is freedom. Abused and scorned though we may be, our destiny is tied up with America's destiny. Before the pilgrims landed at Plymouth, we were here. Before the pen of Jefferson etched the majestic words of the Declaration of Independence across the pages of history, we were here. For more than two centuries our forebears labored in this country without wages; they made cotton king; they built the homes of their masters while suffering gross injustice and shameful humiliation—and yet out of a bottomless vitality they continued to thrive and develop. If the inexpressible cruelties of slavery could not stop us, the opposition we now face will surely fail. We will win our freedom because the sacred heritage of our nation and the eternal will of God are embodied in our echoing demands.

Before closing I feel impelled to mention one other point in your statement that has troubled me profoundly. You warmly commended the Birmingham police force for keeping "order" and "preventing violence." I doubt that you would have so warmly commended the police force if you had seen its dogs sinking their teeth into unarmed, nonviolent Negroes. I doubt that you would so quickly commend the policemen if you were to observe their ugly and inhumane treatment of Negroes here in the city jail; if you were to watch them push and curse old Negro women and young Negro girls; if you were to see them slap and kick old Negro men and young boys; if you were to observe them, as they did on two occasions, refuse to give us food because we wanted to sing our grace together. I cannot join you in your praise of the Birmingham police department.

It is true that the police have exercised a degree of discipline in handling the demonstrators. In this sense they have conducted themselves rather "nonviolently" in public. But for what purpose? To preserve the evil system of segregation. Over the past few years I have consistently preached that nonviolence demands that the means we use must be as pure as the ends we seek. I have tried to make clear that it is wrong to use immoral means to attain moral ends. But now I must affirm that it is just as wrong, or perhaps even more so, to use moral means to preserve immoral ends. Perhaps Mr. Connor and his policemen have been rather nonviolent in public, as was Chief Pritchett in Albany, Georgia, but they have used the moral means of nonviolence to maintain the immoral end of racial injustice. As T. S. Eliot has said, "The last temptation is the greatest treason: To do the right deed for the wrong reason."[16]

I wish you had commended the Negro sit-inners and demonstrators of Birmingham for their sublime courage, their willingness to suffer, and their amazing discipline in the midst of great provocation. One day the South will recognize its real heroes. They will be the James Merediths,[17] with the noble sense of purpose that enables them to face jeering and hostile mobs, and with the agonizing loneliness that characterizes the life of the pioneer. They will be old, oppressed, battered Negro women, symbolized in a seventy-two-year-old woman in Montgomery, Alabama, who rose up with a sense of dignity and with her people decided not to ride segregated buses, and who responded with ungrammatical profundity to one who inquired about her weariness: "My feet is tired, but my soul is at rest." They will be the young high school and college students, the young ministers of the gospel and a host of their elders, courageously and nonviolently sitting in at lunch counters and willingly going to jail for conscience' sake. One day the South will know that when these disinherited children of God sat down at lunch counters, they were in reality standing up for what is best in the American dream and for the most sacred values in our Judeo-Christian heritage, thereby bringing our nation back to those great wells of democracy which were dug deep by the founding fathers in their formulation of the Constitution and the Declaration of Independence.

Never before have I written so long a letter. I'm afraid it is much too long to take your precious time. I can assure you that it would have been much shorter if I had been writing from a comfortable desk, but what else can one do when he is alone in a narrow jail cell, other than write long letters, think long thoughts, and pray long prayers?

If I have said anything in this letter that overstates the truth and indicates an unreasonable impatience, I beg you to forgive me. If I have said anything that understates the truth and indicates my having a patience that allows me to settle for anything less than brotherhood, I beg God to forgive me.

I hope this letter finds you strong in the faith. I also hope that circumstances will soon make it possible for me to meet each of you, not as an integrationist or a civil rights leader but as a fellow clergyman and a Christian brother. Let us all hope that the dark clouds of racial prejudice will soon pass away and the deep fog of misunderstanding will be lifted from our fear-drenched communities, and in some not-too-distant tomorrow the radiant stars of love and brotherhood will shine over our great nation with all their scintillating beauty.

Yours for the cause of Peace and Brotherhood,
MARTIN LUTHER KING, JR.

NOTES

1. Socrates (about 470–399 B.C.E.) compared himself to a gadfly (a fly that stings cattle) and Athens to a lazy horse: He believed that he had a divine mission to arouse complacent Athenians, through his probing questions, to care about their souls and to seek virtue. [D. C. ABEL]
2. Niebuhr (1892–1971) was an American theologian. [D. C. ABEL]
3. This quotation is attributed to the British politician William Ewart Gladstone (1809–1898). [D. C. ABEL]
4. Augustine, *On Free Choice of the Will,* Book I, Chapter 5. Augustine (345–430) was a North African theologian and philosopher; for a biography, see p. 67. [D. C. ABEL]
5. Thomas Aquinas, *Summa Theologiae,* Part Two, First Part, Question 95, Second Article. Aquinas (about 1224–1274) was an Italian theologian and philosopher; for a biography, see p. 32. [D. C. ABEL]
6. Martin Buber, *I and Thou,* 2d ed., trans. Ronald Gregor Smith (New York: Scribner, 1958). Buber (1878–1965) was an Israeli (Austrian-born) philosopher. [D. C. ABEL]
7. Paul Tillich, *Systematic Theology,* vol. 2 (Chicago: University of Chicago Press, 1957), pp. 59–66. Tillich (1886–1965) was an American (German-born) theologian. [D. C. ABEL]
8. Daniel 3:1–30. [D. C. ABEL]

9. Socrates was convicted by the Athenians of impiety and the corruption of youth and was executed by being given hemlock (a poison) to drink. [D. C. ABEL]

10. Elijah Muhammad (1897–1975) was an American religious leader who directed the Black Muslim movement. [D. C. ABEL]

11. *zeitgeist:* the cultural and moral climate of an era (literally, in German, "spirit of the time"). [D. C. ABEL]

12. Bunyan (1628–1688) was an English preacher and author. [D. C. ABEL]

13. Ross Barnett (1898–1987) was governor of Mississippi from 1960 to 1964. [D. C. ABEL]

14. George Wallace (1919–1998) was governor of Alabama from 1963 to 1967, 1971 to 1979, and 1983 to 1987. [D. C. ABEL]

15. *ekklēsia:* (Greek) "assembly of citizens," "church." [D. C. ABEL]

16. T. S. Eliot, *Murder in the Cathedral,* Part I (lines spoken by the character Thomas Becket). Eliot (1888–1965) was a British (American-born) poet and critic. [D. C. ABEL]

17. James Meredith (born 1933) in 1962 became the first African-American student to attend the University of Mississippi. His enrollment sparked riots on campus. [D. C. ABEL]

A Theory of Justice

John Rawls

John Rawls was born in 1921 in Baltimore, Maryland. He received his undergraduate education at Cornell University and then served in the U.S. Army during World War II. After the war he enrolled in the doctoral program in philosophy at Princeton University, receiving his degree in 1950. He then taught at Princeton for two years. During the following academic year, Rawls was a Fulbright Fellow at Oxford University. In 1953 he accepted a position at Cornell, where he taught for six years. Rawls taught at Harvard University from 1959 to 1960 and at the Massachusetts Institute of Technology for the following two years. In 1962 he returned to Harvard. He was named James Bryan Conant University Professor at Harvard in 1979—a position he held until his retirement in 1997. He died in 2002 in Lexington, Massachusetts.

Rawls's principal works are *A Theory of Justice* (1971), *Political Liberalism* (1993), *The Law of Peoples; with, The Idea of Public Reason Revisited* (1999), *Collected Papers* (1999), and *Lectures on the History of Moral Philosophy* (2000).

Our selection is from *A Theory of Justice,* the work in which Rawls sets forth his theory about how to assign basic rights and duties to members of a society and how to distribute benefits. Rawls contends that the specific laws and practices in a society will be just if they result from basic principles that are themselves just. To determine which basic principles are just, Rawls uses the device of a hypothetical "original position." In the original position, individuals who are prevented by a "veil of ignorance" from knowing their personal status in their society (for example, whether they are rich or poor, talented or untalented) rationally deliberate about what principles of justice should govern the society in which they will live. Rawls argues that the impartiality and objectivity of the people in the original position would lead them to adopt two basic principles of justice.

The first principle states that each person is to have the maximum basic liberty compatible with a similar liberty for others. (Basic liberties includes such things as the freedom of speech, the right to vote, and freedom from arbitrary arrest.) The second principle is that social and economic inequalities be arranged in a way likely to work to everyone's advantage and that there be equality of opportunity to attain the higher social and economic positions. (An example of a social inequality would be some people having authority and others being subject to them.) Rawls stipulates, however, that this second principle cannot be employed if it violates the first. In other words, social or economic advantages do not justify the violation of anyone's basic liberties, even if the very people whose liberties are curtailed would share in those advantages. A society whose subsequent laws and practices conformed to these two basic principles would, according to Rawls, be a just society.

CHAPTER I. JUSTICE AS FAIRNESS

1. The Role of Justice

Justice is the first virtue of social institutions, as truth is of systems of thought. A theory however elegant and economical must be rejected or revised if it is untrue; likewise laws and institutions no matter how efficient and well-arranged must be reformed or abolished if they are unjust. Each person possesses an inviolability founded on justice that even the welfare of society as a whole cannot override. For this reason justice denies that the loss of freedom for some is made right by a greater good shared by others. It does not allow that the sacrifices imposed on a few are outweighed by the larger sum of advantages enjoyed by many. Therefore in a just society the liberties of equal citizenship are taken as settled; the rights secured by justice are not subject to political bargaining or to the calculus of social interests. The only thing that permits us to acquiesce in an erroneous theory is the lack of a better one; analogously, an injustice is tolerable only when it is necessary to avoid an even greater injustice. Being first virtues of human activities, truth and justice are uncompromising.

These propositions seem to express our intuitive conviction of the primacy of justice. No doubt they are expressed too strongly. In any event I wish to inquire whether these contentions or others similar to them are sound, and if so how they can be accounted for. To this end it is necessary to work out a theory of justice in the light of which these assertions can be interpreted and assessed. I shall begin by considering the role of the principles of justice. Let us assume, to fix ideas, that a society is a more or less self-sufficient association of persons who in their relations to one another recognize certain rules of conduct as binding and who for the most part act in accordance with them. Suppose further that these rules specify a system of cooperation designed to advance the good of those taking part in it. Then, although a society is a cooperative venture for mutual advantage, it is typically marked by a conflict as well as by an identity of interests. There is an identity of interests since social cooperation makes possible a better life for all than any would have if each were to live solely by his own efforts. There is a conflict of interests since persons are not indifferent as to how the greater benefits produced by their collaboration are distributed, for in order to pursue their ends[1] they each prefer a larger to a lesser share. A set of principles is required for choosing among the various social arrangements which determine this division of advantages and for underwriting an agreement on the proper distributive shares. These principles are the principles of social justice: They provide a way of assigning rights and duties in the basic institutions of society and they define the appropriate distribution of the benefits and burdens of social cooperation.

Now let us say that a society is well-ordered when it is not only designed to advance the good of its members but when it is also effectively regulated by a public conception of justice. That is, it is a society in which (1) everyone accepts and knows that the others accept the same principles of justice, and (2) the basic social institutions generally satisfy and are generally known to satisfy these principles. In this case, while men may put forth excessive demands on one another, they nevertheless acknowledge a common point of view from which their claims may be adjudicated. If men's inclination to self-interest makes their vigilance against one another necessary, their public sense of justice makes their secure association together possible. Among individuals with disparate aims and purposes, a shared conception of justice establishes the bonds of civic friendship; the general desire for justice limits the pursuit of other ends. One may think of a public conception of justice as constituting the fundamental charter of a well-ordered human association.

Existing societies are of course seldom well-ordered in this sense, for what is just and unjust is usually in dispute. Men disagree about which principles should define the basic terms of their association. Yet we may still say, despite this disagreement, that they each have a conception of justice. That is, they understand the need for, and they are prepared to affirm, a characteristic set of principles for assigning basic rights and duties and for determining what they take to be the proper distribution of the benefits and burdens of social cooperation. Thus it seems natural to think of the concept of justice as distinct from the various conceptions of justice and as being specified by the role which these different sets of principles, these different conceptions, have in common. Those who hold different conceptions of justice can, then, still agree that institutions are just when no arbitrary distinctions are made between persons in the assigning of basic rights and duties and when the rules determine a proper balance between competing claims to the advantages of social life. Men can agree to this description of just institutions since the notions of an arbitrary distinction and of a proper balance, which are included in the concept of justice, are left open for each to interpret according to the principles of justice that he accepts. These principles single out which similarities and differences among persons are relevant in determining rights and duties, and they specify which division of advantages is appropriate. Clearly this distinction between the concept and the various conceptions of justice settles no important questions. It simply helps to identify the role of the principles of social justice. . . .

2. The Subject of Justice

Many different kinds of things are said to be just and unjust—not only laws, institutions, and social systems, but also particular actions of many kinds, including decisions, judgments, and imputations. We also call the attitudes and dispositions of persons, and persons themselves, just and unjust. Our topic, however, is that of social justice. For us the primary subject of justice is the basic structure of society, or more exactly, the way in which the major social institutions distribute fundamental rights and duties and determine the division of advantages from social cooperation. By major institutions I understand the political constitution and the principal economic and social arrangements. Thus the legal protection of freedom of thought and liberty of conscience, competitive markets, private property in the means of production, and the monogamous family are examples of major social institutions. Taken together as one scheme, the major institutions define men's rights and duties and influence their life prospects, what they can expect to be, and how well they can hope to do. The basic structure is the primary subject of justice because its effects are so profound and present from the start. The intuitive notion here is that this structure contains various social positions and that men born into different positions have different expectations of life determined, in part, by the political system as well as by economic and social circumstances. In this way the institutions of society favor certain starting places over others. These are especially deep inequalities. Not only are they pervasive, but they affect men's initial chances in life; yet they cannot possibly be justified by an appeal to the notions of merit or desert. It is these inequalities, presumably inevitable in the basic structure of any society, to which the principles of social justice must in the first instance apply. These principles, then, regulate the choice of a political constitution and the main elements of the economic and social system. The justice of a social scheme depends essentially on how fundamental rights and duties are assigned and on the economic opportunities and social conditions in the various sectors of society. . . .

3. The Main Idea of the Theory of Justice

My aim is to present a conception of justice which generalizes and carries to a higher level of abstraction the familiar theory of the social contract as found, say, in Locke, Rousseau, and Kant.[2] In order to do this, we are not to think of the original contract as one to enter a particular society or to set up a particular form of government. Rather, the guiding idea is that the principles of justice for the basic structure of society are the object of the original agreement. They are the principles that free and rational persons concerned to further their own interests would accept in an initial position of equality as defining the fundamental terms of their association. These principles are to regulate all further agreements; they specify the kinds of social cooperation that can be entered into and the forms of government that can be established. This way of regarding the principles of justice I shall call justice as fairness.

Thus we are to imagine that those who engage in social cooperation choose together, in one joint act, the principles which are to assign basic rights and duties and to determine the division of social benefits. Men are to decide in advance how they are to regulate their claims against one another and what is to be the foundation charter of their society. Just as each person must decide by rational reflection what constitutes his good—that is, the system of ends which it is rational for him to pursue—so a group of persons must decide once and for all what is to count among them as just and unjust. The choice which rational men would make in this hypothetical situation of equal liberty, assuming for the present that this choice problem has a solution, determines the principles of justice.

In justice as fairness the original position of equality corresponds to the state of nature in the traditional theory of the social contract. This original position is not, of course, thought of as an actual historical state of affairs, much less as a primitive condition of culture. It is understood as a purely hypothetical situation characterized so as to lead to a certain conception of justice. Among the essential features of this situation is that no one knows his place in society, his class position or social status; nor does anyone know his fortune in the distribution of natural assets and abilities, his intelligence, strength, and the like. I shall even assume that the parties do not know their conceptions of the good or their special psychological propensities. The principles of justice are chosen behind a veil of ignorance. This ensures that no one is advantaged or disadvantaged in the choice of principles by the outcome of natural chance or the contingency of social circumstances. Since all are similarly situated and no one is able to design principles to favor his particular condition, the principles of justice are the result of a fair agreement or bargain. For given the circumstances of the original position, the symmetry of everyone's relations to each other, this initial situation is fair between individuals as moral persons, that is, as rational beings with their own ends and capable, I shall assume, of a sense of justice. The original position is, one might say, the appropriate initial status quo, and thus the fundamental agreements reached in it are fair. This explains the propriety of the name "justice as fairness": It conveys the idea that the principles of justice are agreed to in an initial situation that is fair. The name does not mean that the concepts of justice and fairness are the same, any more than the phrase "poetry as metaphor" means that the concepts of poetry and metaphor are the same.

Justice as fairness begins, as I have said, with one of the most general of all choices which persons might make together, namely, with the choice of the first principles of a conception of justice which is to regulate all subsequent criticism and reform of institutions. Then, having chosen a conception of justice, we can suppose that they are to choose a constitution and a legislature to enact laws, and so on, all in accordance with the principles of justice initially agreed upon. Our social situation is just if it is such that by this sequence of hypothetical agreements we would have contracted into the general system of rules which defines it. Moreover, assuming that the original position does determine a set of principles (that is, that a particular conception of justice would be chosen), it will then be true that whenever social institutions satisfy these principles those engaged in them can say to one another that they are cooperating on terms to which they would agree if they were free and equal persons whose relations with respect to one another were fair. They could all view their arrangements as meeting the stipulations which they would acknowledge in an initial situation that embodies widely accepted and reasonable constraints on the choice of principles. The general recognition of this fact would provide the basis for a public acceptance of the corresponding principles of justice. No society can, of course, be a scheme of cooperation which men enter voluntarily in a literal sense; each person finds himself placed at birth in some particular position in some particular society, and the nature of this position materially affects his life prospects. Yet a society satisfying the principles of justice as fairness comes as close as a society can to being a voluntary scheme, for it meets the principles which free and equal persons would assent to under circumstances that are fair. In this sense its members are autonomous and the obligations they recognize self-imposed.

One feature of justice as fairness is to think of the parties in the initial situation as rational and mutually disinterested. This does not mean that the parties are egoists—that is, individuals with only certain kinds of interests, say in wealth, prestige, and domination. But they are conceived as not taking an interest in one another's interests. They are to presume that even their spiritual aims may be opposed, in the way that the aims of those of different religions may be opposed. Moreover, the concept of rationality must be interpreted as far as possible in the narrow sense, standard in economic theory, of taking the most effective means to given ends. . . .

I shall maintain . . . that the persons in the initial situation would choose two rather different principles: The first requires equality in the assignment of basic rights and duties, while the second holds that social and economic inequalities, for example, inequalities of wealth and authority, are just only if they result in compensating benefits for everyone, and in particular for the least advantaged members of society. These principles rule out justifying institutions on the grounds that the hardships of some are offset by a greater good in the aggregate. It may be expedient but it is not just that some should have less in order that others may prosper. But there is no injustice in the greater benefits earned by a few provided that the situation of persons not so fortunate is thereby improved. The intuitive idea is that since everyone's well-being depends upon a scheme of cooperation without which no one could have a satisfactory life, the division of advantages should be such as to draw forth the willing cooperation of everyone taking part in it, including those less well situated. Yet this can be expected only if reasonable terms are proposed. The two principles mentioned seem to be a fair agreement on the basis of which those better endowed, or more fortunate in their social position, neither of which we can be said to deserve, could expect the willing cooperation of others when some workable scheme is a necessary condition of the welfare of all. Once we decide to look for a conception of justice that nullifies the accidents of natural endowment and the contingencies of social circumstance as counters in quest for political and economic advantage, we are led to these principles. They express the result of leaving aside those aspects of the social world that seem arbitrary from a moral point of view. . . .

4. The Original Position and Justification

I have said that the original position is the appropriate initial status quo which ensures that the fundamental agreements reached in it are fair. This fact yields the name "justice as fairness." It is clear, then, that I want to say that one conception of justice is more reasonable than another, or justifiable with respect to it, if rational persons in the initial situation would choose its principles over those of the other for the role of justice. Conceptions of justice are to be ranked by their acceptability to persons so circumstanced. Understood in this way, the question of justification is settled by working out a problem of deliberation: We have to ascertain which principles it would be rational to adopt given the contractual situation. This connects the theory of justice with the theory of rational choice.

If this view of the problem of justification is to succeed, we must, of course, describe in some detail the nature of this choice problem. A problem of rational decision has a definite answer only if we know the beliefs and interests of the parties, their relations with respect to one another, the alternatives between which they are to choose, the procedure whereby they make up their minds, and so on. As the circumstances are presented in different ways, correspondingly different principles are accepted. The concept of the original position, as I shall refer to it, is that of the most philosophically favored interpretation of this initial choice situation for the purposes of a theory of justice. . . .

One should not be misled, then, by the somewhat unusual conditions which characterize the original position. The idea here is simply to make vivid to ourselves the restrictions that it seems reasonable to impose on arguments for principles of justice, and therefore on these principles themselves. Thus it seems reasonable and generally acceptable that no one should be advantaged or disadvantaged by natural fortune or social circumstances in the choice of principles. It also seems widely agreed that it should be impossible to tailor principles to the circumstances of one's own case. We should ensure further that particular inclinations and aspirations, and persons' conceptions of their good do not affect the principles adopted. The aim is to rule out those principles that it would be rational to propose for acceptance, however little the chance of success, only if one knew certain things that are irrelevant from the standpoint of justice. For example, if a man knew that he was wealthy, he might find it rational to advance the principle that various taxes for welfare measures be counted unjust; if he knew that he was poor, he would most likely propose the contrary principle. To represent the desired restrictions, one imagines a situation in which everyone is deprived of this sort of information. One excludes the knowledge of those contingencies which sets men at odds and allows them to be guided by their prejudices. In this manner the veil of ignorance is arrived at in a natural way. This concept should cause no difficulty if we keep in mind the constraints on arguments that it is meant to express. At any time we can enter the original position, so to speak, simply by following a certain procedure—namely, by arguing for principles of justice in accordance with these restrictions.

It seems reasonable to suppose that the parties in the original position are equal. That is, all have the same rights in the procedure for choosing principles; each can make proposals, submit reasons for their acceptance, and so on. Obviously the purpose of these conditions is to represent equality between human beings as moral persons, as creatures having a conception of their good and capable of a sense of justice. The basis of equality is taken to be similarity in these two respects. Systems of ends are not ranked in value; and each man is presumed to have the requisite ability to understand and to act upon whatever principles are adopted. Together with the veil of ignorance, these conditions define the principles of justice as those which rational persons concerned to advance their interests would consent to as equals when none are known to be advantaged or disadvantaged by social and natural contingencies.

There is, however, another side to justifying a particular description of the original position. This is to see if the principles which would be chosen match our considered convictions of justice or extend them in an acceptable way. We can note whether applying these principles would lead us to make the same judgments about the basic structure of society which we now make intuitively and in which we have the greatest confidence; or whether, in cases where our present judgments are in doubt and given with hesitation, these principles offer a resolution which we can affirm on reflection. There are questions which we feel sure must be answered in a certain way. For example, we are confident that religious intolerance and racial discrimination are unjust. We think that we have examined these things with care and have reached what we believe is an impartial judgment not likely to be distorted by an excessive attention to our own interests. These convictions are provisional fixed points which we presume any conception of justice must fit. But we have much less assurance as to what is the correct distribution of wealth and authority. Here we may be looking for a way to remove our doubts. We can check an interpretation of the initial situation, then, by the capacity of its principles to accommodate our firmest convictions and to provide guidance where guidance is needed.

In searching for the most favored description of this situation we work from both ends. We begin by describing it so that it represents generally shared and preferably weak conditions. We then see if these conditions are strong enough to yield a significant set of principles. If not, we look for further premises equally reasonable. But if so, and these principles match our considered convictions of justice, then so far well and good. But presumably there will be discrepancies. In this case we have a choice. We can either modify the account of the initial situation or we can revise our existing judgments, for even the judgments we take provisionally as fixed points are liable to revision. By going back and forth, sometimes altering the conditions of the contractual circumstances, at others withdrawing our judgments and conforming them to principle, I assume that eventually we shall find a description of the initial situation that both expresses reasonable conditions and yields principles which match our considered judgments duly pruned and adjusted. This state of affairs I refer to as reflective equilibrium. It is an equilibrium because at last our principles and judgments coincide; and it is reflective since we know to what principles our judgments conform and the premises of their derivation. At the moment everything is in order. But this equilibrium is not necessarily stable. It is liable to be upset by further examination of the conditions which should be imposed on the contractual situation and by particular cases which may lead us to revise our judgments. Yet, for the time being, we have done what we can to render coherent and to justify our convictions of social justice. We have reached a conception of the original position. . . .

CHAPTER II. THE PRINCIPLES OF JUSTICE

11. Two Principles of Justice

I shall now state in a provisional form the two principles of justice that I believe would be chosen in the original position. . . .

> First, each person is to have an equal right to the most extensive basic liberty compatible with a similar liberty for others.

> Second, social and economic inequalities are to be arranged so that they are both (a) reasonably expected to be to everyone's advantage, and (b) attached to positions and offices open to all. . . .

By way of general comment, these principles primarily apply, as I have said, to the basic structure of society. They are to govern the assignment of rights and duties and to regulate the distribution of social and economic advantages. As their formulation suggests, these principles presuppose that the social structure can be divided into two more or less distinct parts, the first principle applying to the one, the second to the other. They distinguish between those aspects of the social system that define and secure the equal liberties of citizenship and those that specify and establish social and economic inequalities. The basic liberties of citizens are, roughly speaking, political liberty (the right to vote and to be eligible for public office) together with freedom of speech and assembly; liberty of conscience and freedom of thought; freedom of the person along with the right to hold (personal) property; and freedom from arbitrary arrest and seizure as defined by the concept of the rule of law. These liberties are all required to be equal by the first principle, since citizens of a just society are to have the same basic rights.

The second principle applies, in the first approximation, to the distribution of income and wealth and to the design of organizations that make use of differences in authority and responsibility, or chains of command. While the distribution of wealth and income need not be equal, it must be to everyone's advantage, and at the same time, positions of authority and offices of command must be accessible to all. One applies the second principle by holding positions open, and then, subject to this constraint, arranges social and economic inequalities so that everyone benefits.

These principles are to be arranged in a serial order with the first principle prior to the second. This ordering means that a departure from the institutions of equal liberty required by the first principle cannot be justified by, or compensated for, by greater social and economic advantages. The distribution of wealth and income, and the hierarchies of authority, must be consistent with both the liberties of equal citizenship and equality of opportunity. . . .

The two principles . . . are a special case of a more general conception of justice that can be expressed as follows:

> All social values—liberty and opportunity, income and wealth, and the bases of self-respect—are to be distributed equally unless an unequal distribution of any, or all, of these values is to everyone's advantage.

Injustice, then, is simply inequalities that are not to the benefit of all. Of course, this conception is extremely vague and requires interpretation.

As a first step, suppose that the basic structure of society distributes certain primary goods, that is, things that every rational man is presumed to want. These goods normally have a use whatever a person's rational plan of life. For simplicity, assume that the chief primary goods at the disposition of society are rights and liberties, powers and opportunities, income and wealth. . . . These are the social primary goods. Other primary goods such as health and vigor, intelligence and imagination, are natural goods; although their possession is influenced by the basic structure, they are not so directly under its control. Imagine, then, a hypothetical initial arrangement in which all the social primary goods are equally distributed: Everyone has similar rights and duties, and income and wealth are evenly shared. This state of affairs provides a benchmark for judging improvements. If certain inequalities of wealth and organizational powers would make everyone better off than in this hypothetical starting situation, then they accord with the general conception.

Now it is possible, at least theoretically, that by giving up some of their fundamental liberties men are sufficiently compensated by the resulting social and economic gains. The general conception of justice imposes no restrictions on what sort of inequalities are permissible; it only requires that everyone's position be improved. We need not suppose anything so drastic as consenting to a condition of slavery. Imagine instead that men forgo certain political rights when the economic returns are significant and their capacity to influence the course of policy by the exercise of these rights would be marginal in any case. It is this kind of exchange which the two principles as stated rule out; being arranged in serial order, they do not permit exchanges between basic liberties and economic and social gains. The serial ordering of principles expresses an underlying preference among primary social goods. When this preference is rational, so likewise is the choice of these principles in this order.

NOTES

1. *ends:* goals. [D. C. ABEL]
2. Social contract theories explain the origin of organized society in terms of an agreement (actual or hypothetical) among individuals. Social contract theorists include the English philosopher John Locke (1632–1704), the French (Swiss-born) philosopher Jean-Jacques Rousseau (1712–1778), and the German philosopher Immanuel Kant (1724–1804). Locke's and Kant's biographies appear, respectively, on p. 139 and p. 175. [D. C. ABEL]

Multiculturalism

Joseph Raz

Joseph Raz was born in 1939 in Haifa, Palestine (now Israel). After completing his Master of Law degree at Hebrew University of Jerusalem in 1963, he enrolled in the graduate program in philosophy at Oxford University, where he received his doctorate in 1967. He then accepted an appointment as Lecturer in Law in Philosophy at Hebrew University. In 1970 he returned to Oxford, where he was a research fellow at Nuffield College (1970–1972) and a tutorial fellow at Balliol College (1972–1985). Raz has been Professor of the Philosophy of Law at Oxford since 1985 and Professor at Columbia Law School since 1995. He has held visiting appointments at numerous institutions, including the Australian National University, the University of Toronto, the University of California–Berkeley, Yale University, and the University of Michigan. His book *The Morality of Freedom* received the W. J. M. Mackenzie Book Prize from the Political Studies Association and the Elaine and David Spitz Book Prize from the Conference for the Study of Political Thought. Raz was awarded an honorary doctorate by Catholic University in Brussels, Belgium (1993), and was the first recipient of the International Prize for Legal Research from the National Autonomous University of Mexico (2005).

Raz has published over one hundred scholarly articles and eight books, including *The Concept of a Legal System* (1970; 2d ed., 1980), *Practical Reason and Norms* (1975; 2d ed., 1990), *The Authority of Law* (1979), *Engaging Reason: On the Theory of Value and Action* 1999), *Value, Respect, and Attachment* (2001), and *The Practice of Value* (2003).

Our reading is Raz's 1998 article "Multiculturalism," which was originally presented as a lecture at the University of Bremen, Germany, in 1997. Raz discusses some of the theoretical, political, and practical challenges to multiculturalism. On the theoretical level, how can the universality of multiculturalism be combined with the particularity of human relationships? Politically, can multiculturalism emerge as a political bond that supplements or replaces nationalism? Morally—and perhaps most fundamentally—why is multiculturalism necessary?

Raz contends that we should think of multiculturalism not primarily as an ethical or political theory, but as "a way of marking a renewed sensitivity, a heightened awareness of certain issues and certain needs people encounter in today's political reality." Nonetheless, multiculturalism includes the ethical and political precept that we respect the identity of groups and foster their material and cultural prosperity. To follow this precept, we must conceive of our societies as consisting not of a majority and minorities, but as a plurality of cultural groups. Raz suggests several political policies that would promote this plurality. He argues that multiculturalism is necessary, even in societies in which individuals already have the right to nondiscrimination and other civil and political rights, because these rights do not guarantee the change in sensitivity and awareness that is essential to multiculturalism. For a multicultural society to be unified, members of diverse cultural groups need to be able to identify with the political society, and for this to occur the political society must respect all its diverse groups. We must recognize that universal human values are realized in different ways in different cultures.

1

You will remember the dark and haunting music introducing us to the dungeon where Florestan is languishing.[1] When Leonore first sees him, she is unnerved by her inability to recognize him. Her doubt persists, but after a couple of minutes it no longer troubles her:

> Whoever you are, I will save you.
> By God, you shall not be a victim!
> For sure, I'll loosen your chains.
> I'll free you, poor man![2]

In those few minutes, Leonore turned from a devoted wife struggling to save her husband to a moral volunteer sharing in the struggle of the oppressed wherever they are, and the opera has completed its transformation from the romantic comedy of the opening scene into the political drama that it is.

This journey from love for an individual to sympathy for human beings is a powerful modern narrative. We are often told that morality emerged in this way, as a universalized understanding and universalized sympathy: We come to understand that others have the feelings, hopes, and aches that we and our loved ones have, and we extend our sympathies from our loved ones to all those who, as we now see, are like them.

This Enlightenment[3] narrative provides ammunition to some modern critics of the so-called "Enlightenment project." The Enlightenment, they say, has thrown out the baby with the bath water. In recognizing that morality overcomes people's partiality to themselves, the Enlightenment has—those critics claim—created a monster: a universalized individual who is stripped of everything that makes people human, and is reduced to a sheer abstraction. The Enlightenment project is the morality of this abstract individual, and, like abstract individuals, it is barren of any content.

As a challenge to the universality of morality, such criticism is totally misguided and confused. The universality of morality is rooted in the nature of moral thought—in the fact that generality is of the essence of all conceptual thought, that morality is necessarily knowable, and that moral principles are essentially intelligible, rather than arbitrary givens. But the confused criticism of the universality of morals arises out of comprehensible, even laudable, motives and concerns. It reflects the realization that, in respecting humans as humans, we are in danger of understanding them and their needs as if they were our own clones, as if what is good for us is good for them. From childhood on we are saturated with words of wisdom that emphasize the universality of morality: "Love thy neighbor as thyself," we are told. "Do unto others as you would be done by." These are, of course, when properly understood, perfectly true words of wisdom. But they are also very dangerous. They are liable to encourage the tendency to understand others by direct reference to oneself: "When I was young I did not have a television. I do not understand why the young today must have television." "I never went to a mosque, why should we give those newcomers mosques just because they want them?"

One of the *theoretical*—rather than merely political—*challenges* multicultur-alism gives rise to is how to combine the truth of universalism with the truth in particularism. Multiculturalism is a new word. *The Oxford English Dictionary* traces it back to the late 1950s and early 1960s. But does it designate a new eth-ical idea? Does it respond to a new social and political reality? The answer to these questions is far from clear. After all, people have lived in societies that were, for much of their history, multicultural. So what is distinctive about the idea? The coexistence of cultural, ethnic, and religious communities within one political society, within one state, has been the condition of European countries long before they knew of themselves as European. Large-scale immigration from one country to another is a more fitful aspect of history, but it is certainly not new. The nineteenth century in particular saw massive movement of people in Europe, and predominantly out of Europe to Argentina, Canada, the United States, South Africa, and so on. To be sure, many aspects of immigration during the second half of the twentieth century are without precedent. But that does not explain why multiculturalism arose in the late twentieth century and not before.

You may say that apart from the word there is nothing new in it, that it is sim-ply a return to how we were before the triumph of nationalism and its ideology some hundred and fifty years ago. For I believe that it was not until the triumph of nationalism that the thought that seems so natural as to be almost inescapable to us—that is, the thought that only common ethnicity, a common language, and a common culture can constitute the cement that bonds a political community—became the commonplace that it is today. Some of us were brought up to think of nationalism as liable to lead to regrettable extremes, but as essentially a liberating, and therefore an essentially just movement. The ideology of one nation one state was, however, responsible for many of the acts of oppression that Europe has known over the last two centuries, and for much of the misery that parts of Eu-rope experience today. In a way multiculturalism is one of the strands in modern political thought that is trying to undo some of the harm done by nationalism.

I say that it is but one of several political and theoretical moves sharing this aim. The dominant one is of course that of the European Union itself, namely the movement towards political integration of the countries of the Common Mar-ket, and others, which will pull aspects of their sovereignty together to create a Federal Europe. Developments in the Union are a product of political fears and economic hopes. Neither are particularly good foundations for a political com-munity. Their theoretical underpinnings are clearer, I suspect, to historians than to philosophers, but the reaction against nationalism is no less evident there than it is in multiculturalism. Both multiculturalism and its big brother, the Eu-ropean Union, reject the thesis that a common nationality is necessary for the vi-ability of a political community. So does another European movement familiar to all of us: the movement whose slogan is "Europe of the Regions." I think that it is a mistake to regard it simply as a revival of the national movements that lost in the battle for nationalist supremacy during the nineteenth century. Some of the advocates of the ideas of Europe of the Regions did not participate in that struggle. The Scots are an example of such a people. The eighteenth century was in many ways the golden age of Scotland, and the country did not share in the nationalist fervor of the nineteenth century. Besides, while Europe of the

Regions is advocated by supporters of various nationalist movements, for the most part they do not wish to secede from their countries, and they do not uphold the traditional nationalist ideal of the nation-state. Rather they support devolution of powers to the regions within larger political units, both national and European. Europe of the Regions, along with the movement for a European Union and for multiculturalism, reject common nationality as the common bond on which political units must be based.

All three have to face the same hard challenge: What can replace common nationality as the cementing bond of a political unit? For it cannot be denied that nationalism has proven a very effective political cement for people in the grip of nationalist fervor or anxiety. Those who wish to displace it are inevitably suspected of political naïveté. This is the *political challenge,* as against the theoretical challenge, that multiculturalism—along with the European movement and the ideal of Europe of the Regions—has to face: How do they conceive of the political bond? What will replace nationalism, according to them?

But perhaps the most basic challenge to multiculturalism, the challenge that has to be addressed before any of the others is the *moral challenge:* Why multiculturalism? What is the moral reason for trying to go down this road in the first place? Our countries are, no doubt, far from ideal. But we uphold—I will be assuming—certain ideals, which I will call the ideals of Western liberalism, or, if you prefer, the ideals of Western social democracy. These combine an endorsement of democratic government, individual liberties, a welfare state, and a market-driven economy. These headlines allow for considerable disagreement both about the implementation of these ideals, their precise nature, and their justification. But for my purpose today there is no need to explore those. The basic point is that these ideals give the lie to the charge that anything here is blinkered by a devotion to an abstract and barren conception of a universal Man. Rather, liberal politics arise out of the application of a universal humanistic morality to the conditions of the Western capitalist societies in their post-industrial stage. Within the political frameworks that these principles sanction, and that to a lesser or greater degree do in fact prevail in the Western democracies, cultural institutions can and sometimes do flourish, various churches can and do operate, diversity is unhindered, and no legitimate human interests are ignored. So what is the moral need for a new ideal, that of multiculturalism?

2

In a way, multiculturalism is not a new doctrine. Morality is after all universal, and therefore immutable. Moreover, the fundamentals of morality, inasmuch as they apply to us, are not a mystery. In one way or another they are known. Rather, multiculturalism brings with it a new way of conceiving an old truth, putting it center stage, not letting us forget about it. It reflects a new sensitivity to the facts that establish this moral truth. And in particular it warns us against the dangers of each one of us understanding the universal in terms of him- or herself, a danger that is particularly great when the other is an alien in our country—when we are at home, and he is not.

I am suggesting that we should not think of multiculturalism *primarily* as an ethical or political theory, but as a way of marking a renewed sensitivity, a heightened awareness of certain issues and certain needs people encounter in today's political reality. The term was used first in, and applied to, Canada. Multiculturalism means—among other things—the coexistence within the same political society of a number of sizable cultural groups wishing, and in principle able, to maintain their distinct identity. Multiculturalism is with us to stay. Insofar as one can discern the trend of historical events, it is likely to grow in size and importance. In its birthplace, Canada, three forms of multiculturalism exist: first, the coexistence of indigenous people—Inuits and various American Indian nations alongside the "old immigrants" of European stock; second, the coexistence of anglophone and francophone communities[4] of "old immigrants"; and third, the coexistence of the immigrants of west European stock, who are mostly "old immigrants," with the mostly new immigrants from Asia and southern Europe. In Britain the situation is very different. We have predominantly two forms of multiculturalism: the coexistence of the four peoples—Scots, Welsh, Irish, and English—whose union created the United Kingdom; and their coexistence with new immigrant communities, mainly Afro-Caribbean, Hindu-Indian, and a variety of Muslim communities—Pakistani, Bangladeshi, Indian, and others.

It is the diverse forms that multiculturalism takes in different countries that makes it difficult to think of multiculturalism as more than a new moral sensitivity. The multicultural policies appropriate in different countries vary greatly, and any useful generalizations one can think of allow for many exceptions. Nevertheless multiculturalism is more than just a new moral sensitivity. I have suggested elsewhere[5] that what we may call *liberal multiculturalism* is a normative precept motivated by concern for the dignity and well-being of all human beings. It is a precept that affirms that, in the circumstances of contemporary Western societies, a political attitude of fostering and encouraging the prosperity, cultural and material, of cultural groups, and respecting their identity, is justified.

This precept has far-reaching ramifications. It calls on us radically to reconceive society, changing its self-image. We should learn to think of our societies as consisting not of a majority and minorities, but as constituted by a plurality of cultural groups. Naturally such developments take a long period to come to fruition, and they cannot be secured through government action alone, as they require a widespread change in attitude. The current attitude of the population at large, and the speed with which it accepts the precepts of multiculturalism, set limits on the practicability and good sense of proceeding with various concrete policies to advance and implement liberal multiculturalism. But we must think long-term to set short-term policies within a sensible context. The size of cultural groups and their viability is another variable affecting the way various concrete measures should be pursued. Where publicly funded programs are called for, relative size is inevitably a consideration. So is viability. There is no point in trying to prop up by public action cultures that have lost their vitality, that have become moribund, and whose communities—usually their young members—drift away from them. Of course multiculturalism changes the prospects of survival for cultures it supports. That is its aim. But it recognizes that deliberate public policies can serve a useful purpose only if they find response in the population they are meant to serve. They can serve to facilitate development desired by the population, but not to force cultural activities down the throats of an indifferent population.

The more concrete policies, which become appropriate gradually, as developments justify, will be varied and highly dependent on local conditions. They will include measures like the following:

(1) The young of all cultural groups of significant size should be educated, if their parents so desire, in the culture of their groups. But all of them should also be educated to be familiar with the history and traditions of all the main cultures in the country and an attitude of respect for them should be cultivated.

(2) The different customs and practices of the different groups should, within the limits of permissible toleration, be recognized in law and by all public bodies in society, as well as by private companies and organizations that serve the public, be it as large employers, providers of services, and in other ways. At the moment petty intolerance is rife in many countries. In Britain people still have to fight to be allowed to wear traditional dress to school or to work, to give one example.

(3) It is crucial to break the link between poverty, undereducation, and ethnicity. So long as certain ethnic groups are so overwhelmingly overrepresented among the poor, ill-educated, unskilled, and semiskilled workers, the possibilities of cultivating respect for their cultural identity, even the possibility of members of the group being able to have self-respect and to feel pride in their cultures, are greatly undermined.

(4) There should be a generous policy of public support for autonomous cultural institutions, such as communal charities, voluntary organizations, libraries, museums, theater, dance, musical, or other artistic groups. Here (as in education) the policy calls for allocation of public resources. In the competition for them, the size of the groups concerned is an important factor. It works in two ways. By and large it favors the larger groups with a more committed membership. But it also calls for disproportionate support for small groups that are strong enough to pass the viability test. Given that the overheads are significant, the per capita cost of support for small viable cultural groups is greater than for large ones.

(5) Public space, streets, squares, parks, shopping arcades, and so on (as well as air space on television) should accommodate all the cultural groups. Where they differ in their aesthetic sense, in their preferences for colors, patterns, smells, music, noise, and speed, the way to do so may involve dividing some public spaces between them (as often happens without direction in ethnic neighborhoods), while preserving others as common to all.

Of course all such measures are designed to lead to relatively harmonious coexistence of nonoppressive and tolerant communities. They therefore have their limits. But it is important not to use false standards as tests of the limits of toleration. The fact that the Turkish government does not tolerate certain practices of the Kurds, let us say, in Turkey, is no reason why the Kurds from Turkey should not be allowed to continue with the practices when they settle in Europe.

Similarly, the fact that tolerating certain practices of immigrant communities will lead to a change in the character of some neighborhoods or public spaces in one's country is no reason for suppressing them. It is natural that we should wish to preserve the character of neighborhoods and public spaces. Our lives, and the quality of our lives, are bound up with them. But so are the lives of others, and many of them—be they the younger generation (that is, our children) or members of other cultural groups—may find uncongenial what we find congenial. We owe them what we owe ourselves, that is, the ability to feel at home in their own home, for once they emigrated to a country it has become their home.

Nevertheless there are significant limits to toleration. I will mention four. First, all cultural communities should be denied the right to repress their own members. This applies as much to homophobia among native Germans, as to female circumcision among Somali immigrants. Second, no community has a right to be intolerant of those who do not belong to it. All forms of racism or other manifestations of lack of respect should be discouraged by public policy, though not necessarily outlawed or criminalized. Third, the opportunity to leave one's community must be a viable option for its members. There should be a public recognition of a right of exit from one's community. Finally, liberal multiculturalism will require all groups to allow their members access to adequate opportunities for self-expression and for participation in the economic life of the country, and the cultivation of the attitudes and skills required for effective participation in the political culture of the state.

3

I have mentioned some concrete multicultural policies, not in order to recommend them to any government for immediate implementation; as I mentioned, we have to assess such policies carefully against local conditions and available alternatives. I mentioned them to illustrate the sort of policy consequences I have in mind when discussing multiculturalism. I will say no more of its practical consequences. I hope, however, that what I said begins to address the third challenge, which I called the *moral challenge.* "Why multiculturalism," it asked, "given that we have civil and political rights, including a right to nondiscrimination?" One way in which the challenge can be understood is this: Can all the policies and political attitudes that multiculturalism advocates be encompassed by and derived from doctrines of basic rights and nondiscrimination? The preceding remarks show that the answer is No. Policies such as teaching everyone in a country the language and culture of minority groups cannot be derived from doctrines of nondiscrimination. Moreover, I want to emphasize again that multiculturalism involves more than specific policies. It involves a change in attitudes, and in the ways we understand our societies and think of them. To repeat the point: It involves primarily thinking of our societies as consisting not of a majority and minorities, but as constituted by a plurality of cultural groups. Nothing like this follows from rights against discrimination, or of freedom of religion, or any of the other basic rights.

Not everyone will take the fact that the precepts of multiculturalism cannot be derived from traditional liberal rights as a point in their favor. On the contrary, many will say that this shows that multiculturalism cannot be justified. But that would be a mistake. Those who take this stand are really guilty of a charge leveled by some antiliberal writers: They disregard the fact that people's prosperity and dignity derive their concrete forms from the shared social meanings in the societies in which they live.

People's well-being consists in their success in valuable relationships and activities. Their social and other skills to engage in activities and pursue relationships derive from their own cultures, and their sense of their own dignity is bound up with their sense of themselves as members of certain cultures. Up to a point people can retrain and acquire the skills needed to make a life in another culture. In a multicultural society, it is important to give people the opportunity to do so. This is what I called the right to exit. But not all could do so, and not all would want to do so. The case for letting people have the chance to carry on with their own cultures and ways of life derives in part from the fact that people's ability to retrain and adapt are limited. But it depends on something even more important: on the fact that such demands—that is, *the demand for a forced retraining and adaptation*—is liable to undermine people's dignity and self-respect. It shows that the state, their state, has no respect for their culture, finds it inferior, and plots its elimination.

It is tempting to reply to this that the problem is one of transition. The considerations I mentioned—the difficulty and pain of adapting to a new culture and abandoning one's own, and people's limited capacity for successful adaptation to a new culture—are all factors that affect people who are already conscious of belonging to one culture rather than another. Newborn babies have no such problems. They may just as easily be brought up to be Chinese, as Indonesian, as French or German, or Turks. This is true. But it is not really relevant unless one is willing to contemplate the monstrosity of tearing children away from their parents and bringing them up as prescribed by the state. Given the fact that parents are the most formative influence on children, if the problem is one of transition, then the transition is stretched out over many generations.

So the *moral challenge* "Why multiculturalism?" is answered by our concern for the well-being and dignity of people. Unfortunately, this answer only serves to emphasize the seriousness of the *political challenge*: What, according to multiculturalist views, is the bond that unites a political society, since they reject common nationality as a common bond?

4

I think that we have to admit that this is a serious challenge. It also harbors serious dangers. The truth is that our understanding of the bonds that keep a political society together is very tenuous. There are serious dangers of acting immorally out of exaggerated fears and anxieties. Let me reflect first on the dangers.

One of the most familiar bonds that holds countries together is a common enemy. As we know, most commonly though not exclusively the enemy is a foreign country that represents a threat to one's existence or to one's vital interests.

Sometimes it is an ideological enemy: an alien religion or ideology. Sometimes it is an enemy within.

If I may deviate for a moment: The thesis about the advantages of having a common enemy was the first theoretical political thesis I was ever struck by. I was a teenager at an Israeli high school when we had a lecture in a series in which successful people talked about ideas from various aspects of the economy and society. That time the lecturer was a leading Israeli politician, and he explained that the absence of peace between Israel and its neighbors should not be regarded, as official Israeli propaganda and public media presented it, as a tragedy. On the contrary, it was a blessing—a factor that galvanized the national energies. It led Israelis to high achievements in science and technology. It created an educated and alert people, and stopped the assimilation of the country into the Middle East with its Levantine[6] culture of sloth, slovenliness, and sleaze.

I expect you do not need me to argue against the proposition that we should strive for a state of perpetual cold or hot war in order to foster unity. The point I am making is that we reject that proposition not because we believe that the threat of a common enemy cannot bring people together. Everyone I know believes that it can. We reject it as a means of forging unity in spite of the fact that it is an effective means, because it is an immoral means.

So we should be careful in invoking the clarion call of national unity, and of the need for a common bond. We should not let it lead us to policies of oppression against groups living in our countries. Having said that I should immediately add that the question of a political bond is very important. We are all struggling with it at several levels: The enterprise of European unity depends on our ability to forge or to strengthen a sense of European identity as the backbone of the Union. Often the political leaders of Europe seem to be but little aware of this fact. Too often they give the impression that they think that unity depends on institutional ties, and on common economic interests alone. This mistake is even more unforgivable today than it was when it was made by the leaders of the communist movement, if only because we have their mistake to learn from.

As I said before, in various aspects of politics and political theory we are struggling to replace the ideology of nationalism that has dominated Europe for a hundred and fifty years. European unity and multiculturalism both raise the same political challenge, for both aim to replace nationalism as the common bond of political society. The need for such a bond cannot be doubted. Political societies are characterized by the fact that they claim authority over individuals, and in the name of that authority they not infrequently require individuals to make sacrifices for the benefit of other members of the same political society. Redistributive taxation, regional policies, and all the institutions of the welfare state are examples of state institutions imposing sacrifices on some for the sake of others. The willingness to share is not purchased easily. Without it a political society soon disintegrates, or has to rely on extensive use of force and coercion. How is the willingness to share maintained?

Some of the things that can be safely said about this question are true but do not take us far enough. Members of a modern political society need to share a common culture. This is true, but it is easy to read exaggerated conclusions from this harmless observation. We know that a common culture does not mean a common religion, and it does not mean membership of a common ethnic or racial group. It does not even mean a common language, though the absence of a common language can be a nuisance. When I say that none of these is *necessary* for a willingness to share in a common political society I do not mean that they do not help. They certainly do help where they are present. But they are not necessary, and this is just as well, for the thought that political societies must be based on common religion or race is not much more appealing than the suggestion that they must be based on a common enemy.

So what is the truth in the talk of the importance of a common culture? It is not easy to summarize. There are many diverse factors to consider. Here are a few: First, for a country's economy to function well there must be a general knowledge of the basic skills required for it—a more general sharing of the more general skills, and a smattering of understanding and more specialized training in the more specialized skills. Second, a democratic political system depends on literacy, access to information, a certain understanding of political issues and of political processes. Third, willingness to share depends on capacity for empathy: It depends on the ability of people to feel for others and that depends on their ability to understand and empathize with other people's experiences, aspirations, and anxieties.

A variety of factors contribute to the realization of these conditions. Sharing in the same economic system leads to acquisition of similar skills and to a shared understanding of the relatively technical aspect of how things work, and what people's fortunes depend on. The existence of democratic institutions and of free mass media spreads a shared understanding of the nature of political processes, and of the constraints that political action must meet. It also familiarizes people with the lifestyles prevalent in the society, and with other people's points of view and aspirations. The existence of a common education, and of a multicultural syllabus that makes the cultures of all cultural groups familiar to all members of a society, are essential to the spread of mutual understanding and respect.

I have listed some factors that show the truth in the thesis that a common culture is necessary for a political society. But let me repeat again my caution on the matter. For one thing, a common culture is not enough. In some sense all European countries share a common culture, so do all those countries that once belonged to the French Empire or to the British Empire. But this does not make them ready to participate in one political society. Other factors are important as well: Restricting inequalities of income and wealth helps to limit gaps in life expectancy, in health, and in general expectations—gaps that often make people on the opposite sides of the social and economic divide incapable of understanding and empathizing with each other.

But none of this gets to the heart of the matter. And it is our limited understanding of what lies at the heart of the matter that accounts for our uncertainties. Ultimately political unity depends on people's free and willing identification with the political society they belong to—for example, on the fact that they feel

German, that their sense of their own identity as German is totally instinctive and unproblematic; and it depends on the fact that they are proud to be German.

Among the things that our very imperfect understanding of the condition of identification teaches us are the following few: First, identification involves a sense of belonging, of being a part of a larger whole. Second, people identify with a variety of groupings and institutions: They belong to a family, to a workplace, to a party, to a sports club, to a religious group, and so on. We know that multiple identifications do not generally conflict with each other. On the contrary, they are often mutually supportive. Third, it is particularly important that identification with a political society does not replace, but incorporates identification with other groups in that society. It is generally agreed that the communist attempt to suppress all other groups has been disastrous, and many studies nowadays emphasize the importance of the coexistence of a multiplicity of foci of identification.

Coming now to points more directly relevant to multiculturalism: It is of vital importance for the ability of one group to be able to identify with the political society that their membership of the smaller group is respected by the political society. This applies to all aspects of identity. A political society that does not respect gays, or Christians, or black people, cannot expect that those it fails to respect will identify with it, and it does not deserve their allegiance. So an important condition of identification with a political society is that that society respects its members. To respect them it has to respect their cultures, their religions, and so on. To that extent multiculturalism, far from being a threat to the common bond that unites a political society, is one of the factors contributing to it.

5

I will say nothing about the *theoretical challenge* that liberal multiculturalism encounters. What I have said so far is sufficient to show how I see the universal and the particular to be complementary rather than antagonistic, and the point has always been clear in the best philosophical tradition—that is, the one descending from Aristotle: The universal must find expression in the particular, and the particular can only get its meaning from the fact that it is subsumed under the universal. In placing multiculturalism in that tradition I am placing it firmly beyond what mere toleration will vindicate.

The thought is not that we must excuse members of other cultures their cultures, for they know no better. That is true too, but it is only part of the truth. Nor is it the thought that one must tolerate cultural minorities or they will destabilize the state. That is true too, but it is not the core concern. At the heart of multiculturalism lies the recognition that universal values are realized in a variety of different ways in different cultures, and that they are all worthy of respect. This, I should emphasize, is not to endorse all aspects of any culture. My culture no less than others is flawed. Many cultures are flawed in similar ways: The suppression of sexuality, at least in some of its forms, is common to many, to give but one example. We should fight superstition, repression, and error wherever we find them, in our culture and in others. When we do so we are of course constrained by principles of toleration and of respect for people. But we should not confuse the fight against error and repression with the condemnation of cultures other than our own. We should recognize that they realize important values, and that they provide a home and a focus of identity that are entirely positive to their members, just as our culture realizes important values and provides a home and a focus of identity for us.

This is why multiculturalism transcends what any principles of toleration can provide. Principles of toleration restrain us regarding what we may do in the elimination of error. Multiculturalism denies that the variety of cultures it enjoins us to protect and support are in error. They are seen essentially as different ways in which universal values are realized.

These comments bring me—at the conclusion of my talk—to the point I started from: the thought that multiculturalism is primarily a matter of a new moral sensibility. I said there that it is a sensibility that takes more seriously the otherness of the other, a sensibility that stops us from forcing our own ways on the other, just because he follows a different style of life, because he comes from a different culture. Think of the point I just made a minute ago: We tend to condemn alien cultures when we find them riddled with error. But we do not condemn our own culture when we find it riddled with error. The idea is not even conceivable for most people. For each person his own culture covers the horizon.

This is well and good, but then nor should we condemn other cultures for their failings; rather we should—as we do with our own—reject the failings but not the culture as a whole. The ability to do so requires more than theoretical knowledge of the right moral principle. It requires understanding and sensitivity. To acquire it we must do more than understand others and the role their own culture plays in their life. We must understand ourselves better, we must acquire the ability not to take our culture for granted, to regard it not as the epitome of human achievement but as no more than one necessarily imperfect manifestation of the human spirit. As I said, there is nothing theoretically new in that. But there is a long way from knowing it, to being able to live by it.

NOTES

1. In the opera *Fidelio* by German composer Ludwig van Beethoven (1770–1827), Leonore rescues her husband Florestan from death in a political prison. The lyrics are by German librettist Josef Sonnleithner (1776–1835), who based them on the play *Leonore; or, Conjugal Love*, by French dramatist Jean-Nicolas Bouilly (1763–1842). [D. C. ABEL]
2. Beethoven, *Fidelio*, Act II, no. 12. [D. C. ABEL]
3. *Enlightenment:* an eighteenth-century philosophical movement that had great confidence in the power of reason to understand the universe and improve the human condition. [D. C. ABEL]

4. *Anglophone* communities are English-speaking; *francophone* communities are French-speaking. [D. C. ABEL]
5. Joseph Raz, "Liberal Multiculturalism," in *Ethics in the Public Domain: Essays in the Morality of Law and Politics*, 2d ed. (Oxford, England: Clarendon Press, 1995), pp. 170–91. [D. C. ABEL]
6. *Levantine:* relating to the Levant, the region bordering on the eastern Mediterranean Sea. [D. C. ABEL]

Sources and Credits

Reading 11: From Blaise Pascal, *Pensées,* trans. A. J. Krailsheimer, rev. ed., pp. 115, 121–25, 127–30, 133–34, 196–97, 230, 246. London, England: Penguin Books, 1995. Copyright © A. J. Krailsheimer, 1966, 1995. Reproduced by permission of Penguin Books Ltd.

Reading 12: From William James, "The Will to Believe." *New World* 5 (June 1896).

Reading 13: From Plato, *Republic,* trans. G. M. A. Grube, 2d ed., rev. C. D. C. Reeve. Copyright © 1992 by Hackett Publishing Company, Inc. Reprinted by permission of Hackett Publishing Company, Inc. All rights reserved.

Reading 14: From René Descartes, *Meditations on First Philosophy,* revised ed., ed. and trans. John Cottingham. Copyright © 1996 by Cambridge University Press. Reprinted with the permission of Cambridge University Press.

Reading 15: From John Locke, *An Essay Concerning Human Understanding,* ed. Alexander Campbell Fraser, vol. 1. Oxford, England: Clarendon Press, 1894 (updated stylistically).

Reading 16: From George Berkeley, *The Works of George Berkeley, D.D.,* ed. Alexander Campbell Fraser, vol. 1. Oxford, England: Clarendon Press, 1901 (updated stylistically).

Reading 17: From David Hume, *Enquiries Concerning the Human Understanding and Concerning the Principles of Morals,* ed. L. A. Selby-Bigge. 2d ed. Oxford, England: Clarendon Press, 1902 (updated stylistically).

Reading 18: From Immanuel Kant, *Critique of Pure Reason,* ed. and trans. Paul Guyer and Allen W. Wood. Copyright © 1998 by Cambridge University Press. Reprinted with the permission of Cambridge University Press.

Reading 19: From Alison M. Jaggar, "Love and Knowledge: Emotion in Feminist Epistemololgy," in *Inquiry,* Vol. 32 (July 1989). Used by permission of Scandinavian University Press.

Reading 20: From René Descartes, *Meditations on First Philosophy,* revised ed., ed. and trans. John Cottingham. Copyright © 1996 by Cambridge University Press. Reprinted with the permission of Cambridge University Press.

Reading 21: From D. M. Armstrong, *The Nature of Mind and Other Essays.* © University of Queensland Press, St. Lucia, Queensland, 1980. Reprinted by permission of University of Queensland Press.

Reading 22: Thomas Nagel, "What Is It Like to Be a Bat?" *Philosophical Review* 83 (October 1974).

Reading 23: From "Facing Up to the Problem of Consciousness" by David J. Chalmers from *Journal of Consciousness Studies* 2, No. 3, 1995, pp. 200–219. Reprinted by permission of David Chalmers.

Reading 24: From *A Treasury of the Buddha's Discourses From the Majjhima-Nikaya (Middle Collection),* ed. Phra Khantipalo, trans. Nyanamoli Thera, vols. 2 and 3. Bangkok, Thailand: Mahumakut Rajavidyalays Press, [1977].

Reading 25: From David Hume, *A Treatise of Human Nature,* ed. L. A. Selby-Bigge. Oxford, England: Clarendon Press, 1888 (updated stylistically).

Reading 26: Daniel C. Dennett, "The Origins of Selves," *Cogito,* vol. 3 (1989), pp. 163–73. Reprinted by permission of Taylor & Francis. The Taylor & Francis journals website address is http://www.tandf.co.uk/journals.

Reading 27: From Paul-Henri Thiry, Baron d'Holbach, *The System of Nature; or, Laws of the Moral and Physical World,* trans. H. D. Robinson, vol. 1. Boston: J. P. Mendum, 1889 (updated stylistically).

Reading 44: From John Locke, *Two Treatises on Government*. London, England: R. Butler, 1821 (updated stylistically).

Reading 45: From Mary Wollstonecraft, *A Vindication of the Rights of Woman*. London, England: Walter Scott, 1891 (updated stylistically).

Reading 46: From Karl Marx and Friedrich Engels, *Manifesto of the Communist Party*, trans. Samuel Moore. Chicago: Charles H. Kerr, 1888.

Reading 47: From John Stuart Mill, *On Liberty*, 4th ed. London: Longmans, Green, Reader & Dyer, 1869.

Reading 48: Reprinted by arrangement with the Estate of Martin Luther King, Jr., c/o Writers House as agent for the proprietor, New York, N.Y. Copyright 1963 Dr. Martin Luther King, Jr., copyright renewed 1991 Coretta Scott King.

Reading 49: Reprinted by permission of the publisher from *A Theory of Justice* by John Rawls, pp. 3–7, 11–15, 17–21, 54, 60–63, Cambridge, Mass.: The Belknap Press of Harvard University Press, Copyright © 1971, 1999 by the President and Fellows of Harvard College.

Reading 50: "Multiculturalism" by Joseph Raz from *Ratio Juris*, Vol. 11, No. 3, September 1998, pp. 193–205. Reprinted by permission of Blackwell Publishers.

Diagram on p. 124: From *The Great Dialogues of Plato* by Plato, translated by W. H. D. Rouse, copyright © 1956, renewed © 1984 by J. C. G. Rouse. Used by permission of Dutton Signet, a division of Penguin Putnam, Inc.

Diagram on p. 121: From Samuel Enoch Stumpf and Donald C. Abel, *Elements of Philosophy: An Introduction*, 4th ed. © 2002, 1993, 1986, 1979 by The McGraw-Hill Companies. Reproduced with permission of The McGraw-Hill Companies.

Headnotes for Readings 8, 11, 21, 26, 37, 40, 41, 42, and 45 from *Discourses—Primis Philosophy Database*, by Donald C. Abel. Copyright by The McGraw-Hill Companies. Reproduced with permission of The McGraw-Hill Companies.

Index

a posteriori argument, 47–49
a posteriori cognition, 177
a priori argument, 47–48
a priori cognition, 175–178, 182
Abraham, 374–380, 382
The Academy, 4
act utilitarianism, 365
action
    causes of, 277–279, 284, 306
    continuum from unfree
        to free, 322, 324
    control and, 331–332
    direct, 490
    external causes of, 284
    free, 306, 307, 308,
        317–319, 331–332
    imperatives and, 359–360
    individual, 365
    internal causes of, 277–279
    morality of, 357, 365
    unfree, 322, 323, 324
    universalizable, 354
    wrong, 435–436
Action and Purpose (Taylor), 304
actualities, 297
"Advice from Nandaka" (Pali
    Canon), 245, 251–254
aesthetic, transcendental,
    183–184
Agamemnon, 377–379
Agassiz, Louis, 106
agency
    causation and, 312, 323–324
    intelligence and, 47
    law and, 41
    theory of, 278, 304,
        311–313
agent causality, 323
Aggivessana. See Saccaka
Ajasattu Vedehiputta of Magadha
    (King), 247–248
Akbar, 482

Alabama Christian Movement
    for Human Rights, 489–490
Albert the Great, 32
Alciphron (Berkeley), 150
Alexander the Great, 338
Ambrose, 67
amnesia, selective, 275
analytic judgements, 179
analytic of concepts, 185–186
Ananda, 252
The Ancestor's Tale (Dawkins), 56
Anselm, 25, 27
Anton, Anatole, 322
Apologie de la religion chrétienne
    (Pascal), 100
Apology (Plato), 4
Aquinas, Thomas, 25, 32, 336,
    349, 492
Archimedes, 132, 201
arguments for the existence of God
    from design, 25, 57
    from experience, 52
    ontological, 25, 27
    a posteriori, 47–49
    a priori, 47–48
    rational, 24
Arguments for the Existence of
    God (Hick), 89
aristocracy, 384–385
Aristotle, 336, 338, 365, 522
Armstrong, D. M., 199–200, 209
Asimov, Isaac, 60
Assaji, 244–246
astronomy, 20
atheism, 58, 280, 392
    existentialism and, 393–394
"The Atheist and the Acorn"
    (Finch), 300
Augustine, 25, 37, 67–77, 89,
    91–92, 492
Augustinian theodicy, 90,
    91–92, 93

The Authority of Law (Raz), 512
automatism, 217–218
awareness, 238

Barnett, Ross, 497
basic liberties, 502, 509–510
Bateson, Gregory, 241
behavior
    neurotic, 289–290
    normal, 290
    selective, 217–218
behaviorism, 209
    definitions of mind and,
        212–216
Being and Nothingness (Sartre),
    392
Belief, Truth, and Knowledge
    (Armstrong), 209
Bentham, Jeremy, 365
Bentham, Samuel, 365
Berkeley, George, 116, 150
Beyond Good and Evil
    (Nietzsche), 384–391
The Birth of Tragedy out of the
    Spirit of Music (Nietzsche),
    384
Blake, William, 462
Blanshard, Brand, 3
The Blind Watchmaker (Dawkins),
    56–66
body politic, 456
Boethius, 33
Boileau-Despréaux, Nicolas, 376
Book of Exodus, 36
Boston Tea Party, 493
bourgeoise, 470–479
    conflicts of, 476
    revolutionary role of,
        472–474
Boutwell, Albert, 491
Boyle, Sarah Patton, 496
Braden, Ann, 496

Brainstorms: Philosophical Essays on Mind and Psychology (Dennett), 265
Breaking the Spell (Dennett), 265
Brutus, Marcus Junius, 378
Buddha, 200, 244–245. *See also* Gotama, Siddhatta
Buddhism. *See also* Gotama, Siddhatta
    Theravada, 24
    12-step causal sequence in, 255
Bunyan, John, 496
Burke, Edmund, 462

Caesar, Julius, 352
Callicott, J. Baird, 424–425
Candide (Voltaire), 301
Cantor, Georg, 224
capital, 474
Capital (Marx and Engels), 470
capitalism, 470
caring
    disposition to, 415–416
    ethic of, 337, 415, 419, 423–425
    how and when to, 419–420
    limitations on, 423
    nature of, 416–418
    needs and, 418
    objects of, 418
    obligation to, 415–416, 417, 420–423
    openness and, 417
    other ethical theories and, 423–425
    self-sacrifice and, 417
Carlin, George, 270
categorical imperative, 336, 354, 359–360, 362
categories, 186
causality, 109, 117, 165, 295
    agency and, 312, 323–324
    agent, 323
    Buddhism and, 255
    custom and, 173–174
    determinism and, 289, 292, 306
    experience and discovering, 168–170
    memory and, 263–264
    synthetic propositions and, 182
causes
    of action, 277–279, 284, 306
    of beliefs/desires, 323–324, 326–329
    of evil, 67–68, 77
    external, 284
    ignorance of, 286
    internal, 277–279
    of quarrels, 443

The Cave (Republic), 123–126, 124f
Cebes, 432
The Cement of the Universe (Mackie), 78
center of narrative gravity, 265, 271
"The Challenge of Cultural Relativism" (Rachels, J. and Rachels, S.), 402–414
Chalmers, David J., 200, 230–231
    theory of consciousness by, 231, 237–242
chance, 296, 303
    determinism and, 298–299
    indeterminism and, 299
character, 354
    excellences of, 338, 344
Charlemagne, 482
choice, 283
Christianity Unveiled (Holbach), 280
Christina (Queen), 128
Cicero, Marcus Tullius, 3
The City of God (Augustine), 67
civil disobedience, 492–494. *See also* nonviolent protest
civil society. *See* political society
class struggle, 428, 470–471, 476
Clifford, William Kingdon, 106, 108
coercion, 328–329, 481, 484
    volitions and, 332
cognition
    abilities of, 233
    empirical, 177, 178
    experience and, 176, 177, 239
    function of, 233–234
    objects and, 175, 176
    a posteriori, 177
    a priori, 175–178, 182
    pure, 177, 178
    science and, 176
Collected Papers (Rawls), 502
command, 359
common culture, 521
Common Sense; or, Natural Ideas Opposed to Supernatural (Holbach), 280
commonwealth, 448–449
    powers of, 455
    will and, 449
communism, 470, 493
Communist Party, 470
    policies of, 478–479
    proletariats and, 477–479
A Companion to Feminist Philosophy (Jaggar and Young), 188
compatibilism, 278, 322, 325. *See also* soft determinism
complex systems, self and, 269–270

Concealment and Exposure and Other Essays (Nagel), 220
The Concept of a Legal System (Raz), 512
The Concept of Mind (Ryle), 212
The Concept of Morals (Stace), 314
conceptions of justice, 503–504, 507, 510
Concluding Unscientific Postscript (Kierkegaard), 374
Connor, Eugene, 490–491
The Conquest of Happiness (Russell), 19
conscious design, 47, 64
The Conscious Mind: In Search of a Fundamental Theory (Chalmers), 230–231, 238
consciousness, 21, 109, 199–200, 291
    Chalmers' theory of, 231, 237–242
    easy problems of, 230, 231–232
    experience and, 230, 232–233, 236–237
    fundamental entities and, 236–237
    hard problem of, 230, 231–233
    information and, 241
    mind-body problem and, 221
    narrative and, 271
    naturalistic account of, 231
    nature of, 200, 220, 245, 247, 249–251
    nonreductive explanation of, 236–237, 238
    objectivity and, 237
    as perception of state of mind, 218
    phenomenal, 233
    problem of, 216–219, 230–231
    reductionism and, 220, 234
    self and, 249–251
    states of, 252–254
    structure of, 238
    subjective nature of, 200, 220
    theory of, 237–242
Consciousness Explained (Dennett), 265
contemplation, philosophic, 22–23
Content and Consciousness (Dennett), 265
contract, 446
    social, 428, 441, 450, 505
    society and, 486
contrivance, indication of, 41–44, 50

control
    determinism and, 322
    free action and, 331–332
    freedom and, 324–325
    individual exercise of,
        333–334
    knowledge and, 329–330,
        333
    of second order volitions,
        331–332
    self, 343, 355
Cooper, Anthony Ashley (Earl
    of Shaftesbury), 139
Copernicus, Nicolaus, 176, 210
corruption, 385
counterfactual hypothesis, 94
*Created from Animals: The Moral
    Implications of Darwinism*
    (Rachels, J.), 402
Creator, 25
Critique of Dialectical Reason
    (Sartre), 392
Critique of Judgement (Kant), 175
Critique of Practical Reason
    (Kant), 175
Critique of Pure Reason (Kant),
    175–186
Crito, 428, 430–440
Crito (Plato), 4, 430–440
cultural codes, 402
cultural conditioning, 414
cultural differences argument,
    405–406
cultural identity, 521–522
cultural relativism, 337,
    402–414
    argument for, 405–406
    consequences of, 406–408
    culture-neutral standards
        and, 411–412
    definition of, 404–405
    lessons of, 413–414
    values in common and,
        409–410
cumulative selection, 25, 56, 59,
    61–65
cupidity, 71–74
custom, 173–174

Dabbs, James McBride, 496
Daedalus, 13, 17
d'Alembert, Jean Le Rond, 280
Damascene, 33, 34
Darius (King), 403
Darwin, Charles, 57–59
Darwinian world-view, 66
Darwin's Dangerous Idea
    (Dennett), 265
Davidson, Donald, 228
Dawkins, Richard, 25, 56, 269
De Cive (Hobbes), 441
De Corpore Politico (Hobbes), 441

De Hebdomatibus (Boethius), 33
definition(s)
    arbitrary, 316
    from common usage, 316
    of cultural relativism,
        404–405
    of determinism, 277–278, 295
    of ethics, 335–336, 374–375
    of evil, 79–80
    of existentialism, 392–393
    of free will, 314–319
    of indeterminism, 278, 295
    of justice, 447
    of mental process, 211–216
    of mind, 212–216
    of morality, 335–336
    of outlaw emotions, 194
    of philosophy, 1–3, 118–119
    verbal disputes and, 315
deliberation, 283, 305, 309–310,
    313, 507
Dennett, Daniel C., 200, 265
Descartes, René, 116, 128, 139,
    199, 201, 212, 214, 393, 398
design, argument from, 25, 57
designer, evidence of, 41, 43, 44,
    47, 50, 56
desire
    causes of, 323–324, 326–329
    induced, 328
    inordinate, 71, 73–74
despotism, 482
The Destiny of Western Man
    (Stace), 314
determinism, 87, 292, 318
    causality and, 289, 292, 306
    chance and, 298–299
    claims of, 305
    control and, 322
    definition of, 277–278, 295
    free will and, 315, 322
    freedom and, 307–308, 322
    hard, 277–278, 296, 322, 331
    implications of, 300–301
    judgements and, 295
    morality and, 320–322
    possibility and, 297
    self, 278, 311
    soft, 277–279, 296, 304–306,
        322–334
    as theory, 309–311
deterministic free will, 320
Dhamma, 248, 251–252, 255, 257
d'Holbach, Franciscus Adam,
    280
dialectical method, 2, 122. *See
    also* Socratic method
*Dialogues Concerning Natural
    Religion* (Hume), 47–54
Diderot, Denis, 280
Dietrich, Paul Heinrich. *See*
    Thiry, Paul-Henri

"The Dilemma of Determinism"
    (James), 295–303
Dionysius the Younger, 4
direct action, 490. *See also* non-
    violent protest
discord, 97
Discourse on Method (Descartes),
    128
discovery, 191
dispassionate investigation, 188,
    190–191, 195
    ideological function of,
        192–193
disposition to behave, 209,
    212–215
Disputed Questions (Aquinas), 32
The Divided Line, 121–123, 121f
divine right of kings, 450
division of labor, 471, 474
dopamine, 275
Dostoyevsky, Fyodor, 395
double-aspect theory of infor-
    mation, 231, 241–242
doubt, method of, 128–132
dualism, 199, 265
Dummukkha, 250
duty, 354–363, 360–363

ego, 290
egoism, 390
Either/Or (Kierkegaard), 374
*Elbow Room: The Varieties of Free
    Will Worth Wanting*
    (Dennett), 265
The Elements of Moral Philosophy
    (Rachels, J.), 402
Eliot, T. S., 499
emotion(s)
    appropriateness on, 195
    epistemic potential of,
        196–197
    expression of, 192
    feminist theory and,
        194–195
    hypothesis and, 191
    knowledge and, 117, 188,
        189, 191, 196
    outlaw, 189, 194–195, 197
    philosophy and, 189–190
    reason and, 188–190
    science and, 188, 189
    societal groups and, 192
    uses of, 190
    Western philosophy and,
        189–190
emotional constitution, 193, 196
emotional hegemony, 193–194
empirical universality, 178
empiricism, 108, 116–117, 177
    cognition and, 177–178
    inference and, 190
Enchiridion (Augustine), 37

*The End of Life: Euthanasia and
    Morality* (Rachels, J.), 402
*Engaging Reason: On the Theory
    of Value and Action* (Raz),
    512
Engels, Friedrich, 428, 470
The Enlightenment, 513
*An Enquiry Concerning Human
    Understanding* (Hume), 47,
    165–174
*An Enquiry Concerning the Prin-
    ciples of Morals* (Hume), 47
Epictetus, 3
Epicureans, 366
epistemology, 115
    emotion and, 196–197
    reason and, 189–190
equal liberty, 505
equality, 428. *See also* social
    inequality
    state of nature and, 442
Equality and Partiality (Nagel), 220
*An Essay Concerning Human
    Understanding* (Locke),
    139–148
*An Essay towards a New Theory of
    Vision* (Berkeley), 150
eternal law, 349–350
ethics, 305
    of care, 337, 415, 419,
        423–425
    definition of, 335–336,
        374–375
    gradations within, 377
    holistic, 424–425
    ideological suspension of,
        379, 382
    land, 424–425
    morality and, 375
    multiculturalism and, 519
    philosophical, 336
    teleological suspension of,
        374, 378
    theological, 336
    universal truth in, 404
    virtue, 423–424
Ethics, Faith, and Reason (Taylor),
    304
Ethics: Inventing Right and Wrong
    (Mackie), 78
"The Ethics of Belief" (Clifford),
    106
Euclid, 167
Europe of the Regions, 514–515
European Common Market, 514
European Union, 514, 520
Euthyphro, 4–18
Euthyphro (Plato), 4–18
evil, 24–26, 89–98, 335, 388
    adequate solutions to, 78,
        79–80
    avoiding, 79

cause of, 67–68, 77
    as counterpoint to good,
        78, 81–82
    definition of, 79–80
    of discord, 97
    existence of God and, 78–79
    fallacious solutions to, 78,
        80–88
    fear and, 71–72, 74
    free will and, 25, 85–88,
        90–91
    as illusion, 80, 90
    justice and, 68
    as means to good, 78, 82–85
    as necessity, 78, 81–85
    of needless triviality, 97
    neglect of eternal and, 77
    omnipotence and, 78–88
    orders of, 83–86
    partial, 80
    possible solutions to, 90
    as privation of good, 80
    process theology and, 97
    source of, 70–71
    theism and, 90
"Evil and Omnipotence"
    (Mackie), 78–88
Evil and the God of Love (Hick), 89
Evodius, 67–77
evolution, 56
    cumulative selection and,
        64–65
    guided, 65
excellences, 336, 341. *See also*
    virtue(s)
    of character, 338, 344
    development of, 344–345
    happiness and, 343
    intellectual, 338, 344
    intermediacy and, 346–347
excision, 410–412
existentialism, 392–401
    abandonment and, 395–398
    anguish and, 395
    atheistic, 393–394
    definition of, 392–393
    despair and, 398
    freedom and, 392, 400–401
    God and, 395–396
    optimism of, 400
Existentialism is a Humanism
    (Sartre), 392–401
experience. *See also* intuition;
    sense experience
    arguments from, 52
    causality understood from,
        168–170
    cognition and, 176, 177, 239
    conclusions from, 170–172
    consciousness and, 230,
        232–233, 236–237
    as fundamental, 236–237

imagination and, 223
    inference and, 171–172
    judgement and, 179–180
    knowledge and, 115,
        168–174, 178
    mind-body problem and, 225
    non-observability of, 237
    objectivity and, 226, 228
    objects and, 175, 176
    physical explanation and,
        235
    reductionism and, 226–227
    senses and, 173
    as source of knowledge, 142
    subjective nature of, 221,
        232–233
    synthetic judgements and,
        179–180
experimental reasoning, 50
*Explaining Consciousness: The
    "Hard Problem"* (Shear), 230
exploitation, 386, 474
The Extended Phenotype
    (Dawkins), 56, 269
external causes, 284

"Facing Up to the Problem of
    Consciousness"
    (Chalmers), 230–242
faith
    individual v. universal
        and, 375–376
    nature of, 375–376
    reason and, 24–26
Faith and Knowledge (Hick), 89
The Family Idiot (Sartre), 392
fear, evil and, 71–72, 74
Fear and Trembling
    (Kierkegaard), 374
feminism, 192, 196–197, 322, 337
Feminist Frameworks (Jaggar),
    188
*Feminist Politics and Human
    Nature* (Jaggar and
    Rothenberg), 188
The Fifth Dimension (Hick), 89
Filmer, Robert, 450
final causes, economy of, 49
"Firming Up Soft Determinism"
    (Holmstrom), 322–334
first efficient cause, 32, 36
first mover, 25, 32, 36
Fisk, Milton, 322
Flaubert, Gustave, 392
Forster, E. M., 274–275
Frankfurt, Harry, 326, 331–332
Franklin, Benjamin, 280
free action, 306, 307, 308, 317–319
    continuum from unfree
        action to, 322, 324
    control and, 331–332
    unfree action v., 323

free speech, 407
free will, 37, 67, 78, 277–279, 280
    definition of, 314–319
    determinism and, 315, 322
    deterministic, 320
    evil and, 25, 85–88, 90–91
    existence of, 2, 282–285
    God and, 86
    as ignorance of cause, 286
    indeterminism and, 302,
        314–315
    morality and, 314–315,
        317, 319–320
    omnipotence and, 86
freedom, 296, 388
    control and, 324–325
    determinism and, 307–308,
        322
    existentialism and, 392,
        400–401
    liberties and, 483
    in modern society, 333–334
    of opinion, 484
    types of, 333, 481, 483
    of will, 323
Freedom, Anarchy, and the Law
    (Taylor), 304
"Freedom and Determinism"
    (Taylor), 304–313
Freedom Evolves (Dennett), 265
French Revolution, 385, 462, 478
functional states, 222
fundamental entities, 236

Galileo, 441
Gandhi, Mohandas, 316–318,
    488
Gassendi, Pierre, 139, 441
Gaunilo, 27, 30
Gautama, Siddharta. *See* Gotama,
    Siddhatta
The Gay Science (Nietzsche), 384
Gender/Body/Knowledge (Jaggar
    and Bordo), 188
The German Ideology (Marx and
    Engels), 470
Gide, André, 397
Gilligan, Carol, 416
Glaucon, 118
God(s). *See also* Creator
    as Creator, 25
    existence of, 2, 24–25, 28–31,
        32–38, 48, 49, 100, 128,
        130–131, 135–138,
        163–164, 201, 206
    existentialism and, 395–396
    free will and, 86
    Greek, 10
    guided evolution theory
        and, 65
    justice and, 9
    natural theology and, 39

nature of, 68, 78
    omnipotence of, 78–88
    piety and, 8, 10–13, 16–17
    problem of evil and exis-
        tence of, 78–79
    as proof of material things,
        206–208
    religion and, 24
    sin and, 69
    unknowability of, 100, 101
    will and, 86
The God Delusion (Dawkins), 56
*God, Power, and Evil: A Process
    Theodicy* (Griffin), 96
Godwin, Mary Wollstonecraft.
    See Wollstonecraft, Mary
Godwin, William, 462
Golden, Harry, 496
good, 335, 388
    evil as counterpoint to, 78,
        81–82
    evil as means to, 78, 82–85
    evil as privation of, 80
    happiness as highest, 340,
        342
    highest, 29, 340, 342
    natural law and, 349–351
    orders of, 83–86
    primary, 510
    process theology and, 98
    rationality and, 349, 351
    utilitarianism and, 365
    volition and, 355
    will, 354–355, 359
"The Good and Conscience"
    (Hegel), 375
Good and Evil: A New Direction
    (Taylor), 304
Goodall, Jane, 195
Gotama, Siddhatta, 244–257
Gotami, Mahapajapati, 251
government
    authority of, 427
    consent of governed to, 456
    dissolution of, 459–460
    goals of, 457–459
    obligation of governed to,
        456
    social contract and, 428
greatest happiness principle,
    365, 368
greatness, 380–381
Griffin, David, 96, 98
*Groundwork of the Metaphysics of
    Morals* (Kant), 175, 354–363
guided evolution, 65

habituation, 344
happiness, 336, 338, 354, 368,
    371, 388
    excellence and, 343
    as highest good, 340, 342

will and, 76
hard determinism, 277–278, 296,
    322, 331
Harvey, William, 210
Hegel, Georg Wilhelm
    Friedrich, 215, 375
Hegelian dialectic, 215
Heidegger, Martin, 393, 395
hemoglobin number, 60–61
Herodotus, 403–404, 413–414
Hick, John, 25, 89
Hiero, 52
Histories (Herodotus), 403
History of England (Hume), 47
Hitler, Adolf, 493
Hobbes, Thomas, 210–211, 428,
    441
Holbach, Baron d'. *See* Thiry,
    Paul-Henri
Holmstrom, Nancy, 279, 322
Hospers, John, 278, 287
Human, All Too Human (Nietzsche),
    384
human rights, 488
Hume, David, 25, 47, 58–59, 83,
    116, 165, 178, 182, 200, 259,
    280, 419–420, 423–424
Hume's Moral Theory (Mackie), 78
Humphrey, Nicholas, 272, 274
hypothesis, 106–107, 122
    counterfactual, 94
    emotion and, 191
    live, 106–107, 110
    religious, 26
    religious belief and,
        106–107, 112–113
hypothetical imperative,
    359–369

ideas
    complex, 144
    impressions and, 165,
        259–261
    knowledge and, 145
    origin of, 142–144, 259–261
    perception and, 166
    relations of, 167
    simple, 144–148
identity
    cultural, 521–522
    personal, 200, 261–264
ignorance, 40
    of cause, 40
    veil of, 502, 508
illusion, evil as, 80, 90
imagination, 207
    experience and, 223
immortality of soul, 100, 103–104
imperative(s)
    action and, 359–360
    categorical, 336, 354, 359–360
    hypothetical, 359–360

impressions
changing nature of, 261
ideas and, 165, 259–261
perception and, 166
self and, 261
senses and, 165
indeterminism, 278, 292,
296–297, 331
chance and, 299
definition of, 278, 295
free will and, 302,
314–315
possibility and, 297
simple, 304, 308–311
as theory, 309–311
individual action, 365
individuality
action and, 365
control and, 333–334
faith and, 375–376
sovereignty of, 481
universality and, 375–376
well-being and, 484–486
inference, 50, 52, 189
chain of reasoning for,
171–172
empiricism and, 190
of existence, 207
experience and, 171–172
of whole from part, 51
information
consciousness and, 241
double-aspect theory of,
231, 241–242
nature of, 241–242
inordinate desire, 71, 73–74. *See
also* cupidity
mind and, 73–74
*An Inquiry into Meaning and
Truth* (Russell), 19
instantaneous creation, 65
intelligent designer, 25, 56
The Intentional Stance (Dennett),
265
intentional states, 222
intermediacy, 346–347
internal causes, 277–279
internal sense, 143
An Interpretation of Religion
(Hick), 89
*Introduction to Philosophical
Analysis* (Hospers), 287
intuition, 175, 183–184
objects and, 176
Iphigenia, 377
Irenaean theodicy, 90, 92, 93–96
Irenaeus (Saint), 25, 89, 93–94
"Is There a Teleological Suspen-
sion of the Ethical?"
(Kierkegaard), 374–382
Isaac, 374, 376, 378, 380
Jackson, Janet, 413

Jaggar, Alison, 117, 188
James, William, 3, 26, 106, 278, 295
Jansenism, 100
Jaspers, Karl, 393
Jefferson, Thomas, 496
Jephthah, 377–378
Johnson, Joseph, 462
Judas, 381
judgement(s)
analytic, 179
determinism and, 295
experience and, 179–180
logical function of understanding in, 185
mathematics and, 180–181
metaphysics and, 182
pure, 178
pure reason and, 182–183
reason and, 180–182
of regret, 295, 301–302
science and, 181
synthetic, 175, 179–183
understanding in, 185
"Just Caring" (Manning), 415–425
*Just Methodologies: An Interdisci-
plinary Feminist Reader*
(Jaggar), 188
justice, 434
conceptions of, 503–504,
507, 510
definition of, 447
evil and, 68
as fairness, 502–509
God and, 9
injustice as threat to, 489
law and, 428, 488, 492–493
liberty and, 503
main idea of, 505–507
original position and,
507–509
piety and, 9–10, 14
primacy of, 503
principles of, 503–504,
509–511
rights and, 503
role of, 502–504
social, 2, 428, 502–504
spirit and, 73
in state of nature, 441
subject of, 504–505
war and, 444
justification, 191, 507–509

Kant, Immanuel, 27, 117, 175,
218, 336, 354, 397, 505
Kassindja, Fauziya, 410–411
Keller, Evelyn Fox, 195
Khayyám, Omar, 300
Kierkegaard, Søren, 337, 374
Kinds of Minds (Dennett), 265
King, Martin Luther, Jr., 408,
428, 488, 500

knowledge. *See also* cognition;
epistemology
acquisition of, 22
control and, 329–330, 333
custom and, 173–174
discovered, 136
emotion and, 117, 188, 189,
191, 196
experience and, 115, 142,
168–174, 178
ideas and, 145
impossible, 19
innate, 136, 139, 140–142
of matters of fact, 165,
167–168
nature of, 2, 22, 108, 115,
339, 340
objects and, 175
origin of, 142–144
philosophy and, 20
a priori, 175
sight and, 115
simple ideas and, 145
theories of, 115–117, 118–120
women and, 464

land ethic, 424–425
The Last Word (Nagel), 220
law. *See also* natural law
agency and, 41
eternal, 349–350
just, 428, 488, 492
political society and, 454–455
rationality and, 359
responsibility to, 492
rule of, 510
segregation and, 492
source of, 444
universal, 357–358, 360–361
unjust, 428, 493
The Law of Peoples (Rawls), 502
*Lectures on the History of Moral
Philosophy* (Rawls), 502
legislature, 459–460
Leibniz, Gottfried Wilhelm, 393
Leopold, Aldo, 424
A Letter Concerning Toleration
(Locke), 139
"Letter from Birmingham Jail"
(King), 488–501
Letter to the Hebrews (Paul), 34
Letter to the Romans (Paul), 35
Leviathan (Hobbes), 441–449
liberal multiculturalism, 516,
518, 522
libertarianism (philosophical),
278, 287
libertarianism (political), 287
*Libertarianism: A Political Philosophy
for Tomorrow* (Hospers), 287
liberty, 445, 448
basic, 502, 509–510

of discussion, 483–484
equal, 505
freedom and, 483
just society and, 503
limits on, 485
as principle, 482
respect for, 483
state of nature and, 450–451
of thought, 483–484
types of, 481–483
life
statistical improbability of, 65
as will to power, 386
Lincoln, Abraham, 496
Locke, John, 78, 116, 139, 150, 218, 428, 450, 505
logic
of cultural relativism, 405–406
justification and, 191
transcendental, 184
of understanding in judgements, 185
"Longer Discourse on the Destruction of Craving" (Pali Canon), 245, 254–257
Lost Island (Proslogion), 27, 30–31
"Love and Knowledge: Emotion in Feminist Epistemology" (Jaggar), 188–198
Luther, Martin, 496

Mackie, J. L., 25–26, 78, 92
Manichaeism, 67
Manifesto of the Communist Party (Marx and Engels), 470–479
Manning, Rita C., 337, 415
Marcel, Gabriel, 393
Marx, Karl, 428, 470
Marxism, 198, 322, 392, 398. *See also* communism; Communist Party
Mary (Virgin), 381–382
Mary: A Fiction (Wollstonecraft), 462
master morality, 337, 384, 386, 387–388
materialism, 209, 211–212, 221, 227–228, 265, 268, 280
A Materialist Theory of the Mind (Armstrong), 209
mathematics, 210
judgements in, 180–181
philosophy and, 20
pure, 181, 182
matter, existence of, 151–152, 206–208
Maurice of Nassau, 128
Maxwell, James Clerk, 236
McClintock, Barbara, 195

McClure, Jessica, 417
McGill, Ralph, 496
McGinn, Colin, 236
Meaning and Truth in the Arts (Hospers), 287
Meditations on First Philosophy (Descartes), 128–138, 201–208
Meletus, 4, 5, 7, 14, 17
Melville, Herman, 289
memory, 165, 173, 284
causality and, 263–264
self and, 263–264
Meno (Plato), 4
mental process, defining, 211–216
mental states, 209
reportability of, 231, 233
Meredith, James, 499
Mersenne, Marin, 441
The Metaphor of God Incarnate (Hick), 89
metaphysics, 176
judgements in, 182
morality and, 359–363
science and, 183
Metaphysics (Aristotle), 33, 37, 350
Metaphysics (Taylor), 304
method of doubt, 128–132
middle term, 376
The Middle-Length Discourses of the Budda (Pali Canon), 244–257
Mill, James, 365
Mill, John Stuart, 336, 365, 428, 481
Milo of Croton, 346
mind, 150
behaviorism and, 209, 212–216
body and, 2
consciousness as perception of state of, 218
definitions of, 212–216
inordinate desire and, 73–74
materialist theory of, 209, 211–212, 222
nature of, 199–200, 201–205, 209–210, 262–263
original state of, 139, 141–142
self and, 205
structure of, 175
will and, 76
mind-body problem, 199, 220
consciousness and, 221
experience and, 225
The Mind-Body Problem: An Opinionated Introduction (Armstrong), 209
minimal self, 268–269
The Miracle of Theism (Mackie), 78
monism, 297, 300

Monologion (Anselm), 27
moral balance, principle of, 92
moral questions, 110, 211
morality, 2
of action, 357, 365
codes of, 403–404
common values and, 409–410
culture-neutral standards for, 411–412
definition of, 335–336
determinism and, 320–322
development of, 93
directives for, 336
ethics and, 375
free will and, 314–315, 317, 319–320
groups v. individuals and, 491
hard determinism and, 287
individuality and, 491
levels of discourse on, 287–288, 293–294
master, 337, 384, 386, 387–388
metaphysics and, 359–363
nature of, 405
nobility and, 387
progress in, 407
responsibility and, 277–278, 288, 293–294, 304, 305
slave, 337, 384, 386, 388
societal standards and, 407
universality of, 513, 515
value distinctions in, 386–388
worth of action and, 357
The Morality of Freedom (Raz), 512
Mortal Questions (Nagel), 220
motive principle, 285
Muhammad, Elijah, 495
multiculturalism, 429, 512
ethical challenge of, 519
liberal, 516, 518, 522
moral challenge of, 515, 518–519
nature of, 514, 516
policies for, 516–517
political challenge of, 515, 519
theoretical challenges of, 514, 522
toleration and, 523
"Multiculturalism" (Raz), 512–523
multiple personality disorder (MPD), 272, 274–275
Mysticism and Philosophy (Stace), 314

Nagel, Thomas, 3, 200, 220, 232
Nandaka, 245, 251–254
Nansen, Fridtjof, 107

narrative
consciousness and, 271
self and, 265, 270–271
nationalism, 514
natural law, 42, 95, 336, 441,
444–448, 450–452
good and, 349–351
mutability of, 352
nature of, 349–350
permanence of, 352
precepts of, 350–351
universality of, 351–352
natural religion, 47
natural right, 444
natural selection, 56, 58, 191
cumulative, 25, 56, 59, 61–65
evolution and, 64–65
single-step, 61–62, 64–65
natural theology, 39
Natural Theology (Paley), 39–45,
56, 57–58
naturalistic fallacy, 80
nature
of caring, 416–418
of consciousness, 200, 220,
245, 247, 249–251
of experience, 221, 232–233
of faith, 375–376
of God, 68, 78
of human beings, 210
of impressions, 261
of information, 241–242
of knowledge, 2, 22, 108,
115, 339, 340
of mind, 199–200, 201–205,
209–210, 262–263
of morality, 405
of multiculturalism, 514,
516
of natural law, 349–350
of nobility, 390–391
of perception, 249, 259–260
of philosophy, 2–3
of piety, 4, 7–8, 10–13, 69
of self, 244, 259
of space, 184
state of, 428, 441, 442–444,
450–453, 457–458
of thought, 166–167, 223
of time, 185
of truth, 22
of will, 74–75, 280–282
nature of human beings, 210
"The Nature of Mind"
(Armstrong), 209–219
*The Nature of Mind and Other
Essays* (Armstrong), 209
nature, state of, 428, 441,
442–444, 457–458
Nausea (Sartre), 392
necessary being, 32
Necker, Jacques, 462

needless triviality, 97
needs
psychological, 418
subsistence, 418
neobehaviorism, 227
neurotic behavior, 289–290
Nicomachean Ethics (Aristotle),
338–348
Niebuhr, Reinhold, 491
Nietzsche, Friedrich, 337, 384, 424
nobility
egoism and, 390
morality and, 387
nature of, 390–391
vanity and, 389–390
Noddings, Nel, 416, 419–422,
424–425
nonrandom survival, 59–60, 65
nonviolent protest, 428, 488,
489–490, 494
norepinephrine, 275
normal behavior, 290
*Not for Sale: In Defense of Public
Goods* (Holmstrom, Anton,
and Fisk), 322
Nussbaum, Martha, 420

"Observations on the State of De-
gradation to Which Woman
Is Reduced by Various
Causes" (Wollstonecraft),
462, 463–469
"Of Personal Identity" (Hume),
261–264
*Of the Importance of Religious
Opinions* (Necker), 462
"Of the Origin of Our Ideas"
(Hume), 259–261
"Of the System of Man's Free
Agency" (Holbach),
280–286
"Of the Understanding"
(Hume), 259–264
Olsen, Regine, 374
omnipotence
evil and, 78–88
free will and, 86
God and, 78–88
paradox of, 86, 88
On Behalf of the Fool (Gaunilo),
27, 29–30
On Free Choice of the Will
(Augustine), 67–77
On Liberty (Mill, J. S.), 365,
481–487
On the Existence of God
(Aquinas), 32–38
On the Geneology of Morals
(Nietzsche), 384
ontological argument, 25, 27
option, 106–107, 109–110
religion and, 111

organizational invariance, 231,
240–241
organized complexity, 58, 65
Origin of Species (Darwin), 58
original position, 502, 507–509
Original Stories from Real Life
(Wollstonecraft), 462
"The Origins of Selves"
(Dennett), 265–276
*Our Knowledge of the External
World* (Russell), 19
outlaw emotions, 189, 197
definition of, 194
feminist theory and, 194–195

Paine, Thomas, 462
Paley, William, 25, 39, 56, 57–59
Pali Canon, 244
paradox of omnipotence, 86, 88
partial evil, 80
Pascal, Blaise, 26, 100, 110
Pascal's wager, 26, 100, 101–103
Pasenadi of Kosala (King), 247–248
passional nature, religious belief
and, 106–109
The Passions of the Soul (Descartes), 128
pathos of distance, 385
Paul (Apostle), 34–35, 374, 489,
496
peace, 443
negative, 493
positive, 493–494
Pensées (Pascal), 100–105
perception, 148, 151–158, 159,
165–166, 223, 224
ideas and, 166
impressions and, 166
nature of, 249, 259–260
of qualities, 148, 159
self and, 248, 261
sense, 217–218
of state of mind, 218
thought and, 166
Perception and the Physical World
(Armstrong), 209
personal identity, 200, 261–264
perspectivism, 423–424
Phaedo (Plato), 4
Phaedrus (Plato), 189
phenomenal consciousness, 233
Philip II of Macedon (King), 338
philosophic contemplation, 22–23
*Philosophic Rudiments Concerning
Government and Society*
(Hobbes), 441
Philosophical Fragments
(Kierkegaard), 374
philosophical inquiry, 2
philosophy
definition of, 1–3, 118–119
emotion and, 189–190

Greek conception of, 1
knowledge and, 20
mathematics and, 20
nature of, 2–3
political, 427
religion and, 211
science and, 20
social, 427
uncertainty of, 20–21
value of, 2–3, 19–23
The Philosophy of Hegel (Stace), 314
Philosophy of Mind (Chalmers), 230
Philosophy of Religion (Hick), 89
physicalism, 281. *See also* materialism
experience and, 235
reductionism and, 235
Pieper, Josef, 3
piety
gods and, 8, 10–13, 16–17
justice and, 9–10, 14
nature of, 4, 7–8, 10–13, 69
Plato, 2–3, 4, 67, 116, 118, 189, 198, 365, 427, 430
Plotinus, 67
pluralism, 297, 302
A Pluralistic Universe (James), 106
plurality, 512
political authority, 2
limits to, 486–487
origin of, 450
political body, 456
Political Liberalism (Rawls), 502
political obligation, 430, 436–440
political philosophy, 427
political society, 450
beginning of, 455–457
goals of, 457–459
law and, 454–455
powers of, 454–455
Ponge, Francis, 396
positivism, 190, 191, 193, 197
The Possibility of Altruism (Nagel), 220
Posterior Analytics (Aristotle), 33
postulates of rationality, 295
Practical Reason and Norms (Raz), 512
The Practice of Value (Raz), 512
Pragmatism: A New Name for Old Ways of Thinking (James), 106
precision, 340
primary goods, 510
Principia Mathematica (Russell and Whitehead), 19
principle(s)
causes of quarrel, 443
of greatest happiness, 365, 368
of justice, 503–504, 509–511
liberty as, 482

of moral balance, 92
motive, 285
of social justice, 503–504
of volition, 357
The Principles of Mathematics (Russell), 19
The Principles of Moral and Political Philosophy (Paley), 39
Principles of Philosophy (Descartes), 128
Principles of Political Economy (Mill, J. S.), 365
Principles of Psychology (James), 106
private utility, 369
problem of consciousness, 216–219, 230–233
problem of evil, 24–26, 67–77, 89–98
adequate solutions to, 78, 79–80
avoiding, 79
existence of God and, 78–79
fallacious solutions to, 78, 80–88
free will and, 25, 85–88, 90–91
omnipotence and, 78–88
possible solutions to, 90
theism and, 90
The Problem of Evil (Hick), 89–98
"The Problem of Morals" (Stace), 314–321
Problems from Locke (Mackie), 78
The Problems of Philosophy (Russell), 19. *See also The Value of Philosophy*
process theodicy, 90, 96–98
process theology, 89, 90, 96–98
evil and, 97
Prolegomena to Any Future Metaphysics (Kant), 175
proletariat(s), 470–479
Communists and, 477–479
development of, 475–476
revolutionary nature of, 476–477
property, 453–454, 457
private, 470
propositions, 178
of existence, 202
synthetic, 175, 182
Proslogion and Exchange with Gaunilo (Anselm), 27–29
Proteus, 17
Proust, Marcel, 399
Provincial Letters (Pascal), 100
Psalms, 27, 33
psychological needs, 418
psychology, 20
The Psychology of Imagination (Sartre), 392
Pythagoras, 380

qualia, 233
qualities, 162
perception of, 148, 159
primary, 139, 146–148, 150, 159
secondary, 139, 147–148, 150, 159
sensible, 159
quarrels, principle causes of, 443
The Questions Concerning Liberty, Necessity, and Chance (Hobbes), 441
quietism, 399

Rachels, James, 337, 402
Rachels, Stuart, 402
Racine, Jean, 399
"The Range of Human Freedom" (Hospers), 287–294
Rasmussen, Knud, 403
rationalism, 116–117, 202
rationality, 190
choice and, 507
good and, 349, 351
law and, 359
postulates of, 295
religious belief and, 2, 24
will and, 359
Rawls, John, 428, 502
Raz, Joseph, 429, 512
reason, 463
emotion and, 188–190
epistemology and, 189–190
experimental, 50
faith and, 24–26
inference and, 171–172
possessing, 343–344
societal groups and, 192
synthetic judgements and, 180–182
virtue and, 462
women and, 465
The Reasonableness of Christianity (Locke), 139
reductionism, 220–221, 225
consciousness and, 220, 234
experience and, 226–227
physical explanation and, 235
reflection, 143, 355. *See also* internal sense
Reflections on the Revolution in France (Burke), 462
regret, judgements of, 295, 301–302
religion
God and, 24
natural, 47
options and, 111
philosophy and, 211
role of, 24
Religion and the Modern Mind (Stace), 314

religious belief, 337
    hypothesis and, 106–107,
       112–113
    options and, 111
    passional nature and,
       106–109
    proof and, 24
    rational argumentation
       and, 24
    rationality of, 2
    skepticism and, 109, 111
religious hypothesis, 26
Reply to Gaunilo (Anselm), 27,
    30–31
Republic (Plato), 4, 116, 118–126
revealed religion, 47
revealed theology, 39
Ricardo, David, 365
right(s)
    to assembly, 493
    divine, of kings, 450
    human, 488
    justice and, 503
    of punishment, 452
    of reparation, 452
    transfer of, 445–446
    will and, 75–76
The Right Thing to Do: Readings in
    Moral Philosophy (Rachels,
    J. and Rachels, S.), 402
River Out of Eden (Dawkins), 56
Rose, Hilary, 195
Rothenberg, Paula, 188
Rousseau, Jean-Jacques, 280, 505
Royce, Josiah, 3
Rozin, Paul, 268
Rufus, William, 27
rule of law, 510
rule utilitarianism, 365
Rules for the Direction of the Mind
    (Descartes), 128
Russell, Bertrand, 2–3, 19
Ryle, Gilbert, 212–213

Saccaka, 244–251
Sardanapallus, 341
Sartre, Jean-Paul, 337, 392
Schleiermacher, Friedrich, 92
Schlick, Moritz, 325
science. *See also* mathematics
    authority of, 210–211
    cognition and, 176
    dispassionate investigation
      and, 188
    emotion and, 188, 189
    judgements in, 181
    metaphysics and, 183
    natural, 181, 182, 209
    nature of human beings
      and, 210
    philosophy and, 20
    physical, 20

second order volition, 326, 330
    control of, 331–332
The Second Treatise of Government
    (Locke), 450–460
Segner, Johann Andreas, 181
segregation statutes, 492
selection, 58
    cumulative, 25, 56, 59, 61–65
    evolution and, 64–65
    single-step, 61–62, 64–65
selective behavior, 217–218
self, 311
    boundaries of, 267–270, 272
    complex systems and,
      269–270
    consciousness and,
      249–251
    control of, 343, 355
    existence of, 2, 128, 132–134,
      200, 201
    as figurehead, 273–275
    impression and, 261
    memory and, 263–264
    mind and, 205
    minimal, 268–269
    narrative and, 265, 270–271
    nature of, 244, 259
    origin of, 265–276
    origin of ideas to, 259
    perceptions and, 248, 261
    preservation of, 265,
      266–269, 282
    primitive, 265
    projection of, 394
    as reference, 261
    sacrifice of, 417
    thought and, 203
self-assertion, 22
self-determination, 278, 311
The Selfish Gene (Dawkins), 56
self-sufficiency, 342
sense experience, 207
sense perception, 217–218
senses, 151–154, 156
    experience and, 173
    impressions and, 165
    perception and, 217–218
Shakespeare, William, 62
Shannon, C. E., 241
Sharpe, Tom, 268
"Shorter Discourse to Saccaka"
    (Pali Canon), 244, 245–251
Shuttlesworth, Fred, 490
The Sickness unto Death
    (Kierkegaard), 374
sieving, 60–61
sight, knowledge and, 115
Simias the Theban, 432
Simonides, 52
simple indeterminism, 304,
    308–309
    as theory, 309–311

sin
    Augustinian theodicy and,
      92
    God and, 69
    source of, 68–69, 77
Singer, Peter, 420
single-step selection, 61–62, 64–65
skepticism, 1, 67, 94, 109, 172
    religious belief and, 109, 111
slave morality, 337, 384, 386
    utility and, 388
Smith, Adam, 280, 365, 466
Smith, Lillian, 496
social contract, 428, 441, 450, 505
social democracy, 515
social inequality, 502, 504
social institutions, 504
social justice, 2, 428, 502
    principles of, 503–504
Social Justice in a Diverse Society
    (Manning and Trujillo), 415
social philosophy, 427
social reform, 408
The Socialist Feminist Project
    (Holmstrom), 322
society. *See also* political society
    common bonds and,
      519–520
    contract and, 486
    emotion and, 192
    freedom in, 333–334
    liberty and, 503
    limits to authority of,
      486–487
    morality standards of, 407
    rights of, 427
Socrates, 1, 2, 4–18, 198, 368,
    428, 430–440, 491, 493
Socratic method, 2, 4
soft determinism, 277–279, 296,
    304, 305, 322–334
    freedom and, 307–308
    inadequacy of, 323–325
    refutation of, 306
Some Thoughts Concerning
    Education (Locke), 19
sophism, 48, 206
soul, immortality of, 100, 103–104
Southern Christian Leadership
    Conference, 488, 489
sovereignty, 87, 449
    of individuals, 481
space, nature of, 184
Speaking from the Heart: A Femi-
    nist Perspective on Ethics
    (Manning), 415
Spinoza, Baruch, 292, 313
spiritual trial, 376, 379
Stace, W. T., 279, 314
Stages on Life's Way
    (Kierkegaard), 374
Starhawk, 415

state of nature, 428, 441, 442–444, 450–453, 457–458
Stoics, 366–367
Stride toward Freedom: The Montgomery Story (King), 488
structural coherence, 231, 238–240
The Subjection of Women (Mill, J. S.), 365
subjectivism, 394
subjectivity, 393–394
subsistence needs, 418
Summa Contra Gentiles (Aquinas), 32
Summa Theologiae (Aquinas), 32, 349. *See also* "Treatise on God" "Treatise on Law"
Sumner, William Graham, 404, 406
superego, 290
surrealism, 393
survival, nonrandom, 59–60, 65
Symposium (Plato), 4, 198
synthetic judgements, 175, 179–183
synthetic proposition, 175, 182
A System of Logic (Mill, J. S.), 365
The System of Nature (Holbach), 280

Tantalus, 13
Taylor, Richard, 278, 304, 323–324, 326, 331
Ten Hours bill, 476
Thalberg, Irving, 193
theodices, 90
    Augustinian, 90, 91–92, 93
    Iranean, 90, 92, 93–96
    process, 90, 96–98
theology
    ethics of, 336
    natural, 39
    process, 89, 90, 96–98
    revealed, 39
theory of agency, 278, 304, 311–313
A Theory of Justice (Rawls), 502–511
The Theory of Knowledge and Existence (Stace), 314
Theory of Moral Sentiments (Smith, A.), 466
Theravada Buddhism, 24
Thirty Tyrants, 4
Thiry, Paul-Henri (Baron d'Holbach), 278, 280
Thompson, D'Arcy, 266
thought, 51, 123, 184
    bounded nature of, 166–167, 223
    experience synthesized and, 175
    liberty of, 483–484
    perception and, 166

self and, 203
state of being and, 284
Thoughts on the Education of Daughters (Wollstonecraft), 462
Three Dialogues Between Hylas and Philonous (Berkeley), 150–164
Thus Spoke Zarathustra (Nietzsche), 384
Timberlake, Justin, 413
Time and Eternity (Stace), 314
time, nature of, 185
Tinbergen, Niko, 56
tolerance, 412
toleration, 517–518, 523
Toward a Science of Consciousness III (Chalmers, Hameroff, and Kaszniak), 230
tragic hero, 376, 378–379
transcendental aesthetic, 183–184
transcendental doctrine of elements, 183–185
transcendental logic, 184. *See also* analytic of concepts
A Treatise Concerning the Principles of Human Knowledge (Berkeley), 150
A Treatise of Human Nature (Hume), 47, 259–264
Treatise on God (Aquinas), 32–38
Treatise on Law (Aquinas), 349–352
On the Trinity (Augustine), 67
triviality, needless, 97
Trujillo, René, 415
truth
    absolute, 402
    nature of, 22
    objective, 406
    relative, 402
    self-evidence of, 33–34
    universal, 404, 410
Truth and Truthmakers (Armstrong), 209
Truth, Probability, and Paradox (Mackie), 78
Turing machine, 221
Two Treatises of Government (Locke), 139

uncertainty, philosophy and, 20–21
understanding, 69, 123, 126
    categories and, 186
    cultivation of, 464
    in judgements, 185
    observation as source of, 142–143
    operations of, 167–172
    will and, 393

Understanding Philosophy (Rachels, J.), 402
unfree action, 317–319
    continuum from free action to, 322, 324
    free action v., 323
universal law, 357–358, 361
    categorical imperative and, 360
universality
    empirical, 178
    faith and, 375–376
    individuality and, 375–376
    of morality, 513, 515
    of natural law, 351–352
universalization, 354
Universals and Scientific Realism (Armstrong), 209
Unweaving the Rainbow (Dawkins), 56
utilitarianism, 336, 365–372
    act, 365
    rule, 365
    virtue and, 369, 371–372
Utilitarianism (Mill, J. S.), 365–372
utility, 336, 365, 368, 482
    of end, 42
    private, 369
    slave morality and, 388

"The Value of Philosophy" (Russell), 19–23
Value, Respect, and Attachment (Raz), 512
vanity, 389–390
The Varieties of Religious Experience (James), 106
de la Vega, Garcilaso, 453
veil of ignorance, 502, 508
verbal dispute, 315
verification, 115
The View from Nowhere (Nagel), 220
A View of the Evidence of Christianity (Paley), 39
A Vindication of the Rights of Men (Wollstonecraft), 462
A Vindication of the Rights of Woman (Wollstonecraft), 462
virtue(s), 336, 337, 338, 432, 463
    ethics of, 423–424
    reason and, 462
    utilitarianism and, 369, 371–372
Virtue Ethics: An Introduction (Taylor), 304
volition
    coercion and, 332
    good will and, 355
    principle of, 357
    second order, 326, 330–332
Voltaire, 301

Wallace, George, 497
war, state of, 443–445
Washington, George, 316
The Ways of Freedom (Sartre), 392
Weil, Simone, 3
*What Does It All Mean? A Very
    Short Introduction to
    Philosophy* (Nagel), 220
"What Is It Like to Be a Bat?"
    (Nagel), 220–229
"What Is Noble?" (Nietzsche),
    384–391
"What Means This Freedom?"
    (Hospers). *See* "The Range
    of Human Freedom"
"Of What Sort of Proof the Prin-
    ciple of Utility is Suscepti-
    ble" (Mill, J. S.), 365, 371–372
"What Utilitarianism Is" (Mill,
    J. S.), 365–370
*Where Do We Go from Here: Chaos
    or Community?* (King), 488

Whitehead, Alfred North, 19,
    89, 96–97
Why We Can't Wait (King), 488
will. *See also* free will
    commonwealth and, 449
    evil and, 25, 85–88, 90–91
    freedom of, 323
    God and, 86
    good, 354–355, 359
    happiness and, 76
    as ignorance of cause, 286
    indeterminism and, 302,
        314–315
    living rightly and, 75–76
    mind and, 76
    nature of, 74–75, 280–282
    to power, 337, 384, 386
    rationality and, 359
    understanding and, 393
"The Will to Believe" (James),
    106–113
William the Conqueror, 27

wisdom, 3
With Heart and Mind (Taylor), 304
Wittgenstein, Ludwig, 3
Wollstonecraft, Mary, 428, 462
women
    education and, 462–463
    knowledge and, 464
    reason and, 465
The Words (Sartre), 392
Wordsworth, William, 462
Works of Love (Kierkegaard), 374
World Health Organization, 411
world markets, 472
A World of States of Affairs
    (Armstrong), 209
wrong action, 435–436

Young Hegelians, 470
Young, Iris, 188

Zola, Emile, 400